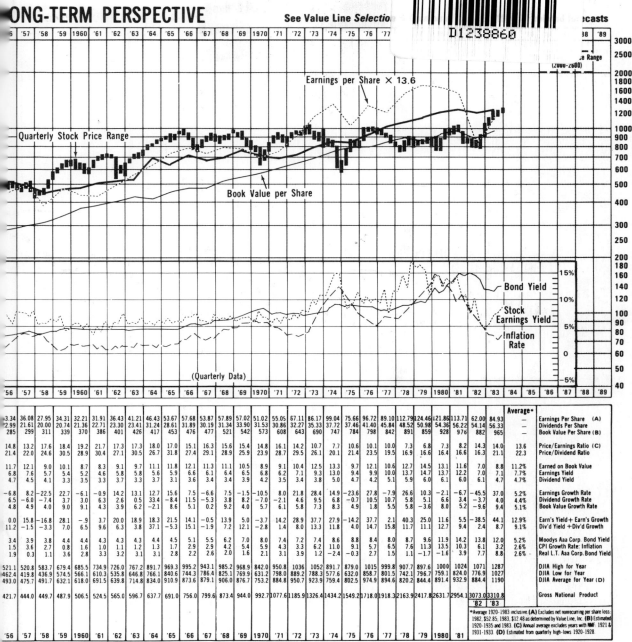

Earnings per Share × 13.6

Quarterly Stock Price Range

Book Value per Share

Bond Yield

Stock Earnings Yield

Inflation Rate

(Quarterly Data)

	'56	'57	'58	'59	1960	'61	'62	'63	'64	'65	'66	'67	'68	'69	1970	'71	'72	'73	'74	'75	'76	'77	'78	'79	1980	'81	'82	'83	Average*	
	3.34	36.08	27.95	34.31	32.21	31.91	36.43	41.21	46.43	53.67	57.68	53.87	57.89	57.02	51.02	55.05	67.11	86.17	99.04	75.66	96.72	89.10	112.79	124.46	121.86	113.71	62.00	84.93	—	Earnings Per Share (A)
	2.99	21.61	20.00	20.74	21.36	22.71	23.30	23.41	31.24	28.61	31.89	30.19	31.34	33.90	31.53	30.86	32.27	35.33	37.72	37.46	41.40	45.84	48.52	50.98	54.36	56.22	54.14	56.33	—	Dividends Per Share
	285	299	311	339	370	386	401	426	417	453	476	477	521	542	573	608	643	690	747	784	798	842	891	859	928	976	882	965	—	Book Value Per Share (B)
	14.8	13.2	17.6	18.4	19.2	21.7	17.3	17.3	18.0	17.0	15.1	16.3	15.6	15.4	14.8	16.1	14.2	10.7	7.7	10.6	10.1	10.0	7.3	6.8	7.3	8.2	14.3	14.0	13.6	Price/Earnings Ratio (C)
	21.4	22.0	24.6	30.5	28.9	30.4	27.1	30.5	26.7	31.8	27.4	29.1	28.9	25.9	23.9	28.7	29.5	26.1	20.1	21.4	23.5	19.5	16.9	16.6	16.4	16.6	16.3	21.1	22.3	Price/Dividend Ratio
	11.7	12.1	9.0	10.1	8.7	8.3	9.1	9.7	11.1	11.8	12.1	11.3	11.1	10.5	8.9	9.1	10.4	12.5	13.3	9.7	12.1	10.6	12.7	14.5	13.1	11.6	7.0	8.8	11.2	Earned on Book Value
	6.8	7.6	5.7	5.4	5.2	4.6	5.8	5.8	5.6	5.9	6.6	6.1	6.4	6.5	6.8	6.2	7.1	9.3	13.0	9.4	9.9	10.0	13.7	14.8	13.7	12.2	7.0	7.1	7.7	Earnings Yield
	4.7	4.5	4.1	3.3	3.5	3.3	3.7	3.3	3.7	3.1	3.6	3.4	3.4	3.9	4.2	3.5	3.4	3.8	5.0	4.7	4.2	5.1	5.9	6.0	6.1	6.0	6.1	4.7	4.7	Dividend Yield
	−6.8	8.2	−22.5	22.7	−6.1	−0.9	14.2	13.1	12.7	15.6	7.5	−6.6	7.5	−1.5	−10.5	8.0	21.8	28.4	14.9	−23.6	27.8	−7.9	26.6	10.3	−2.1	−6.7	−45.5	37.0	5.2	Earnings Growth Rate
	6.5	−1.5	−7.4	3.7	3.0	6.3	2.6	0.5	33.4	−8.4	11.5	−5.3	3.8	8.2	−7.0	−2.1	4.6	9.5	6.8	−0.7	10.5	5.8	5.1	6.6	3.4	−3.7	4.0	4.4	5.2	Dividend Growth Rate
	4.8	4.9	4.0	9.0	9.1	4.3	3.9	6.2	−2.1	8.6	5.1	0.2	9.2	4.0	5.7	6.1	5.8	7.3	8.3	4.9	1.8	5.5	5.8	−3.6	8.0	5.2	−9.6	9.4	5.1	Book Value Growth Rate
	0.0	15.8	−16.8	28.1	−.9	3.7	20.0	18.9	18.3	21.5	14.1	−0.5	13.9	5.0	−3.7	14.2	28.9	37.7	27.9	−14.2	37.7	2.1	40.3	25.0	11.6	5.5	−38.5	44.1	12.9	Earn's Yield + Earn's Growth
	11.2	−1.5	−3.3	7.0	6.5	9.6	6.3	3.8	37.1	−5.3	15.1	−1.9	7.2	12.1	−2.8	1.4	8.0	13.3	11.8	4.0	14.7	15.8	11.7	11.1	12.7	9.4	2.4	8.7	9.1	Div'd Yield + Div'd Growth
	3.4	3.9	3.8	4.4	4.4	4.3	4.3	4.4	4.5	5.1	5.5	6.2	7.0	8.0	7.4	7.2	7.4	8.6	8.8	8.4	8.0	8.7	9.6	11.9	14.2	13.8	13.8	12.0	5.2	Moodys Aaa Corp. Bond Yield
	1.5	3.6	2.7	0.8	1.6	1.0	1.1	1.2	1.3	1.7	2.9	2.9	4.2	5.4	5.9	4.3	3.3	6.2	11.0	9.1	5.7	6.5	7.6	11.3	13.5	10.3	6.1	3.2	2.6	CPI Growth Rate: Inflation
	1.9	0.3	1.1	3.6	2.8	3.3	3.2	3.1	3.1	2.8	2.6	2.2	2.6	2.0	1.6	2.1	3.1	3.9	1.2	−2.4	−0.3	2.7	1.5	1.1	−1.7	−1.6	3.9	7.7	2.6	Real L.T. Aaa Corp. Bond Yield
	521.1	520.8	583.7	679.4	685.5	734.9	726.0	767.2	891.7	969.3	995.2	943.1	985.2	968.9	842.0	950.8	1036	1052	891.7	879.0	1015	999.8	907.7	897.6	1000	1024	1071	1287		DJIA High for Year
	462.4	419.8	436.9	574.5	566.1	610.3	535.8	646.8	766.1	840.6	744.3	786.4	825.1	769.9	631.2	798.0	889.2	788.3	577.6	632.0	858.7	801.5	742.1	796.7	759.1	824.0	776.9	1027		DJIA Low for Year
	493.0	475.7	491.7	632.1	618.0	691.5	639.8	714.8	834.0	910.9	873.6	879.1	906.0	876.7	753.2	884.8	950.7	923.9	759.4	802.5	974.9	894.6	820.2	844.4	891.4	932.9	884.4	1190		DJIA Average for Year (D)
	421.7	444.0	449.7	487.9	506.5	524.5	565.0	596.7	637.7	691.0	756.0	799.6	873.4	944.0	992.7	1077.6	1185.9	1326.4	1434.2	1549.2	1718.0	1918.3	2163.9	2417.8	2631.7	2954.1	3073.0	3310.8		Gross National Product

'82 '83

*Average 1920-1983 inclusive. (A) Excludes net nonrecurring per share loss: 1982, $52.85; 1983, $12.48 as determined by Value Line, Inc. (B) Estimated 1920-1935 and 1983. (C) Annual average excludes years with NMF: 1921 & 1931-1933 (D) Estimated from quarterly high-lows 1920-1928.

D1238860

MODERN INVESTMENTS AND SECURITY ANALYSIS

McGraw-Hill Finance Guide Series

CONSULTING EDITOR

Charles A. D'Ambrosio, *University of Washington*

Bowlin, Martin, and Scott: Guide to Financial Analysis
Farrell: Guide to Portfolio Management
Gup: Guide to Strategic Planning
Riley and Montgomery: Guide to Computer-Assisted Investment Analysis
Smith: Guide to Working Capital Management
Weston and Sorge: Guide to International Finance

McGraw-Hill Series in Finance

CONSULTING EDITOR

Charles A. D'Ambrosio, *University of Washington*

Brealey and Myers: Principles of Corporate Finance
Campbell: Financial Institutions, Markets, and Economic Activity
Christy and Clendenin: Introduction to Investments
Coates: Investment Strategy
Doherty: Corporate Risk Management: A Financial Exposition
Edmister: Financial Institutions: Markets and Management
Francis: Investments: Analysis and Management
Francis: Management of Investments
Fuller and Farrell: Modern Investments and Security Analysis
Garbade: Securities Markets
Haley and Schall: The Theory of Financial Decisions
Hastings and Mietus: Personal Finance
Henning, Pigott, and Scott: International Financial Management
Jensen and Smith: The Modern Theory of Corporate Finance
Lang and Gillespie: Strategy for Personal Finance
Levi: International Finance: Financial Management and the International Economy
Martin, Petty, and Klock: Personal Financial Management
Robinson and Wrightsman: Financial Markets: The Accumulation and Allocation of Wealth
Schall and Haley: Introduction to Financial Management
Sharpe: Portfolio Theory and Capital Markets
Stevenson: Fundamentals of Finance
Troelstrup and Hall: The Consumer in American Society: Personal and Family Finance

MODERN INVESTMENTS AND SECURITY ANALYSIS

Russell J. Fuller

Professor of Finance
Washington State University, Pullman

James L. Farrell, Jr.

M.P.T. Associates, Inc.

McGRAW-HILL BOOK COMPANY

New York St. Louis San Francisco Auckland Bogotá
Hamburg Johannesburg London Madrid Mexico Milan Montreal
New Delhi Panama Paris São Paulo Singapore Sydney Tokyo Toronto

1 2 3 4 5 6 7 8 9 0 DOCDOC 8 9 4 3 2 1 0 9 8 7

ISBN 0-07-022621-0

Library of Congress Cataloging-in-Publication Data

Fuller, Russell.
    Modern investments and security analysis.

    Includes bibliographies and index.
    1. Investments.   2. Securities.   I. Farrell, James L.
II. Title.
HG4521.F87   1987   332.6   86-20903
ISBN 0-07-022621-0

This book was set in Times Roman by Harper Graphics, Inc.
The editor was Paul V. Short;
the production supervisors were Phil Galea and Fred Schulte;
the cover was designed by Joseph Gillians.
Project supervision was done by The Total Book.
R. R. Donnelley & Sons Company was printer and binder.

ABOUT THE AUTHORS

RUSSELL J. FULLER is Professor of Finance at Washington State University and President of Northwest Investment Advisors. Professor Fuller began his investment career as a security analyst with a regional brokerage firm and subsequently was a portfolio manager and Director of Research for an investment counseling firm. Dr. Fuller has had articles published in the *Journal of Finance, Journal of Financial and Quantitative Analysis, Journal of Portfolio Management* and the *Financial Analysts Journal*, as well a monograph for the Financial Analysts Research Foundation. He currently is on the editorial board of the *Journal of Portfolio Management*. A Chartered Financial Analyst (CFA), Professor Fuller lives in Pullman, Washington and is an avid pheasant hunter.

JAMES L. FARRELL, Jr., is currently chairman of a New York based investment counseling subsidiary. He has broad experience in portfolio management, quantitative research and product development, and security analysis, and is a Chartered Financial Analyst, CFA. Mr. Farrell has also written extensively and lectured frequently on applied financial research and portfolio management. He is chairman of the "Q" Group, a cooperative group of institutional investors, brokerage firms, pension and endowment fund sponsors concerned with innovative applications of financial research. He is author of *Guide to Portfolio Management*, McGraw-Hill, 1983, and is Adjunct Professor of Finance at New York University. Mr. Farrell holds a Ph.D. from New York University, an M.B.A. from the Wharton School of Finance, and a B.S. from the University of Notre Dame.

To Our Parents

George B. and Lois A. Fuller

James L. and Barbara Farrell

CONTENTS

PREFACE

To our way of thinking, there is no subject that is more exciting, more interesting and more useful than investments. When teaching investments one sees the topic literally come alive during the course of the semester as students observe prices of stocks and bonds changing in the real-world and ask the question "why?" To an educator, there is nothing more rewarding than having students who can answer their own questions. One of the primary objectives of this book is that by the end of a semester readers will be able to explain changes in security prices.

In addition, readers should have a better understanding of the economic environment influencing the securities markets, be able to manage their personal investments better and have the requisite background to begin a career as an investment professional. However, we should caution that a text book can provide only the basic knowledge for investment success. No text book can supply the most important ingredients for success—common sense and good judgment. Common sense is probably innate and good judgment can only be gained by experience in the real-world class room. Thus, future successful investors will come from one of two groups: (1) those who are well schooled in the principles underlying investments and security analysis, are endowed with common sense, and are experienced enough to have gained good judgment; and (2) those who, by random chance, are lucky. Since good luck has a tendency to be offset by bad luck, over the longer term successful investors are almost exclusively members of the first group.

MARKET CYCLES AND TEACHING CYCLES

Like the stock market, the teaching of investments seems to go in cycles. For many years investment courses emphasized the analysis of individual securities, and the text book market was dominated by Graham and Dodd's classic *Security Analysis*. Starting in the 1950s the theory of finance literally began an intellectual revolution, precipitated by Markowitz's *Portfolio Theory*. New theories on how assets are priced and how to form optimal portfolios proliferated and began to dominate the teaching of investments, almost to the exclusion of teaching fundamental security analysis.

We sense that the pendulum is now beginning to swing back toward the teaching of security analysis, and the orientation of this book is security analysis. This is not to say we treat financial theory lightly—we do not. In fact, one of the purposes of this book is to show the linkage between the modern theories of finance and the analytical techniques used by investors in evaluating security prices.

AFTER READING THIS BOOK, YOU SHOULD:

To aid the learning process, each chapter begins with a note indicating what you are about to read, and dispersed through out the chapters are little reminders concerning the important points of the material you have just read. In a like vein, it is appropriate to indicate here what we believe you will learn after reading the entire text.

> After reading this text, you should:
> 1 Be able to personally analyze individual bonds and stocks
> 2 Be able to make intelligent decisions regarding the allocation of assets and the formation of optimal portfolios
> 3 Be able to ask penetrating questions of those who offer investment advise

ACKNOWLEDGMENTS

There is a story that Albert Einstein was asked how he reached intellectual heights never before achieved by humankind and he replied that he was "standing on big shoulders." Einstein was, of course, acknowledging the contributions of those who came before him and thus made it possible for him to extend our knowledge.

A textbook primarily assimilates and organizes the contributions of others. We would like to acknowledge some of those who have contributed to the theory and application of investments: John B. Williams on the theory of value, Benjamin Graham and David Dodd on security analysis, Harry Markowitz on portfolio theory, Franco Modigliani and Merton Miller on the theory of the firm, Jack Treynor, William Sharpe and John Lintner on capital asset pricing theory, and Eugene Fama on market efficiency. Others have built upon the work of these pioneers and certainly Fisher Black, Michael Jensen, Richard Roll, Steve Ross and Myron Scholes must be mentioned. There are many others who have contributed to our understanding of finance and the securities markets and we would like to extend a general acknowledgment to them as well.

We also must acknowledge those who helped in the preparation of this book. Albert Frakes of Washington State University was particularly helpful in the preparation of the chapter on financial statements (Chapter 6), as was Robert Rogowski, also of Washington State University, for the chapters on bonds (Chapters 14–16). John Settle, formerly at WSU and now at Portland State University read the original drafts of the entire manuscript and his insights were particularly valuable. In addition, the following read various parts of the manuscript and provided many helpful suggestions: Hartman L. Butler, Jr., The Institute of Chartered Financial Analysts; J. Kimball Dietrich, University of California at Los Angeles; Samuel Eisenstadt, The Value Line Survey; E. Bruce Fredrikson, Syracuse University; John D. Markese, DePaul University; Richard McEnally, University of North Carolina; Dennis T. Officer, University of Kentucky; Fredrick Puritz, State University of New York at Oneonta; Gary G. Schlarbaum, First Chicago Investment Advisors; Andrew J. Senchack, University of Texas at Austin;

J. Clay Singleton, University of Nebraska; Tina Umer, Schiller International University, West Germany; Robert Vandell, University of Virginia; Theo Vermaelon, Leuven University, Belgium.

Russell Fuller
James L. Farrell, Jr.

intended to give the reader some of the necessary background material. Chapter 1

AN OVERVIEW

Before beginning to study the topics of investments and security analysis, it is essential that one have an understanding and appreciation of the markets within which investments are made. Part One of this text, which consists of Chapters 1 through 5, is designed to give the reader some of the necessary background material. Chapter 1 defines the concept of investment and briefly introduces the major factors which determine investment rates of return. In addition, the first chapter discusses the impact that modern portfolio theory has had on the investment profession.

Chapter 2 provides a description of the securities markets and how they operate. Details of the exchanges and over-the-counter markets are presented in addition to a discussion of the "mechanics" of executing trades.

The third and fourth chapters deal with the problem of quantifying risk and return. Chapter 3 illustrates how to calculate mean returns and variances of returns for both ex post (historical) and ex ante (expected) returns of individual securities. The procedures for measuring the mean and variance of returns for portfolios are also presented. In addition, empirical data on the historical returns generated by stocks and bonds are presented in Chapter 3. Chapter 4 discusses some of the more recent innovations in the theory of investments, such as the market model, betas, alphas, and security market lines.

It is important that investors understand the market environment in which they will be competing for profits. Chapter 5 covers the topic of market efficiency and its implications for investors. While this chapter is longer than other chapters, it is essentially a review of a number of studies of market efficiency. Thus, it should not be particularly difficult reading. Chapter 5 attempts to highlight the results of these studies so that the reader will know which areas of endeavor may produce above-normal profits and which areas are not likely to do so.

CHAPTER 1

INTRODUCTION

After reading this chapter, you should:

1 Understand the concept of investment
2 Know the major factors which determine the returns required for investing in securities
3 Understand the role of security analysis and its limitations
4 Be aware of the impact modern portfolio theory has had on the investment profession

In early 1973 the stock of Polaroid Corporation sold for $143 per share, which was more than 100 times its latest earnings per share. Less than 18 months later the same stock sold for under 20 times earnings and a price of $14 per share.

In late 1980 Apple Computer, at that time a relatively small firm, offered its common stock to the public for the first time at $22 per share and the stock promptly rose to over $30 in the next few days of trading. Based on 52 million shares outstanding, the market was valuing the common stock of Apple Computer at over *$1.5 billion*! At the same time, the market value of Greyhound Corporation, operator of the world's largest bus system and one of the world's largest meatpackers, was only $600 million, or approximately one-third the value of Apple Computer. At this time Greyhound had revenues of $4.7 billion and profits of $121 million, while Apple Computer had revenues of $118 million and profits of $12 million.

Why did Polaroid sell for over 100 times earnings in one year and for less than 20 times earnings 18 months later? Why did the market place three times the value on Apple Computer as on Greyhound when Apple's current earnings were only one-tenth the earnings of Greyhound? These are the types of questions one considers when studying investments and, in particular, security analysis.

Students tend to find such a course of study interesting, even exciting. This is true whether the classroom is on a university campus or in the "real world" of the practicing investment professional. Most practitioners find that they may spend their lifetimes studying the security markets, progressively discerning better how prices are determined, but never fully understanding the process. *Investments is a fascinating subject*.

1-1 THE INVESTMENT PROCESS

The examples of Polaroid, Apple Computer, and Greyhound illustrated security analysis problems, and a good part of the emphasis of this book will be on security analysis. However, the reader should be aware that there is much more to the total investment process than security analysis. This process can be divided into five steps:

THE INVESTMENT PROCESS

1 Setting goals and objectives
2 Determining the appropriate risk level
3 Estimating the risk and return characteristics of individual securities
4 Forming optimal portfolios
5 Performance review

With any problem, the first step is to identify one's goals and objectives. The parents of three small children may, for their investment plan, set a goal of being able to send all three children to college. To achieve this goal, they might set an objective of accumulating $75,000 over the next 10 years. Similarly the board of directors for a large corporation will, in conjunction with representatives of the firm's employees, set goals and objectives for the corporation's pension plan.

Determining the amount of risk one is willing to assume to achieve investment objectives is one of the most critical and difficult aspects of the investment process. This decision will largely determine the mix of assets to be held in the investment portfolio. As a simple example, those investors with less tolerance for risk might hold a higher percentage of bonds in their portfolios, while those willing to assume more risk would hold a higher percentage of stocks. Substantial progress has been made over the past 2 decades in quantifying and measuring risk. But, as will become apparent as the reader progresses through this book, more work remains to be done in this area.

Security analysis represents the third step in the investment process. Individual securities must be carefully analyzed to determine their risk and return characteristics. These characteristics are then used as the "inputs" for the fourth step, which is the construction of optimal portfolios. Given estimates of risk and return for individual securities and the relationships between securities, portfolios can be formed which attempt to provide the maximum return for a given level of risk.

Finally, investors should monitor the results of their portfolios in order to determine whether the goals and objectives are being met. In addition, reviewing their portfolio's performance may provide some insights which will improve their security analysis and portfolio selection techniques.

1-2 INVESTMENT DEFINED

Investment has many meanings. A portfolio manager purchasing 10,000 shares of IBM for a pension fund is obviously investing the fund's assets. When your grandmother buys $5000 of municipal bonds, she is also investing. However, when a young couple makes a down payment on their first house, are they investing?

In this book we will use a broad and simple definition of investment. We define investment as *postponed consumption*:

Investment = postponed consumption

Pensions are a classic example of postponed consumption. When employees do not take all their wages as current income, but rather have part of their wages held back until they are ready for retirement, they postpone consumption. Similarly, when individuals buy bonds, stocks, or other financial assets, they are postponing consumption and therefore investing.

Even the purchase of a house can be viewed at least partly as postponed consumption. For example, suppose that a young couple purchases a small house for $50,000 by making a 10% down payment of $5000 and assuming a mortgage which requires $500 monthly payments, or $6000 per year. Admittedly, they bought the house because they want to live in it, which is a form of consumption. However, a great deal of their total use (consumption) of the house will occur over a number of years, not just the *current* time period. To see this, contrast purchasing the house by making a down payment with leasing a house. It is possible that the couple could combine the $6000 per year of mortgage payments with the $5000 down payment and instead use the total of $11,000 to lease a much larger house for 1 year. This strategy would increase their current consumption, but probably at the expense of their future consumption.

We can illustrate the trade-off between present and future consumption graphically, as is done in Figure 1-1. In Figure 1-1 it is assumed that an individual has $100 of wealth which he can either spend on current consumption or invest at a 3% interest rate for 1 year at the end of which he will consume his wealth. Thus, this person's current consumption (C_0) can range anywhere from zero (he invests the entire $100) to as high as $100 (he consumes all his wealth now). His future consumption (C_1) can be as high as $103 to as low as zero. Most likely this person will choose to consume part of his wealth initially and invest the difference. For example, he might choose to spend $60 initially ($C_0 = $60) and invest $40. The $40 invested at 3% will be worth $41.20 at the end of 1 year.

1-3 DETERMINANTS OF RATES OF RETURN

The fact that this person's wealth will be $103 at the end of 1 year if he invests the full $100 (or $41.20 if he invests $40) illustrates the important concept of the *time*

FIGURE 1-1   The trade-off between present and future consumption.

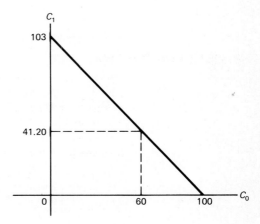

preference for money. Everything else held constant (*ceteris paribus*), individuals generally prefer current consumption to future consumption. In order to entice individuals to invest (to postpone consumption), a potential investment must offer a positive rate of return. This will result in the investor having greater future wealth and therefore greater future consumption opportunities than her current consumption opportunities, thus providing an incentive for the investor to postpone consumption.

So far our example has not considered the effects of inflation or risk. Now suppose that inflation is expected to be 3% over the next year. If this is the case, it will take $103 one year from now to purchase the *same* amount of goods that $100 will purchase today. The future consumption opportunities provided by an investment which offers a 3% nominal return will be no greater than the investor's current consumption opportunities when the inflation rate is 3%. That is to say, the *real rate of return* on the investment is zero. Therefore, as a general rule, investors will add[1] the rate of inflation to the real rate of return which they require.

> Nominal rate = stated market rate
> Real rate = nominal rate minus inflation rate

In our simple example, the required nominal rate of return would be increased to 6% (a 3% real rate plus 3% for inflation.)

So far we haven't considered risk. We typically think of U.S. government securities as being risk-free since the chance of not being paid the promised interest and principal is essentially zero. Thus, the term *risk-free rate* usually refers to the rate of return for U.S. Treasury obligations.

For other securities, a major factor which individuals must consider in their investment/consumption decisions is the issue of risk. If the future benefits from an investment are not known with certainty (i.e., the investment is risky), then individuals will require an even higher expected return on the investment. For example, if investors demand a 6% nominal rate of return on a risk-free investment, they might require an additional 1% *risk premium* for investing in corporate bonds, making the required nominal rate of return on such bonds 7%; for common stocks they might demand a 4% risk premium, resulting in a required nominal rate of return of 10%; etc.

In very general terms, we can identify three major factors which determine the return investors require in order to forgo current consumption and therefore invest:

1 The time preference for consumption as measured by the risk-free real rate of return

2 The expected rate of inflation

3 The risk associated with the investment

---

[1]Actually, the process of adjusting for inflation should be multiplicative, rather than additive. That is, if an investor requires a 3% *real* rate of return for postponing $100 of consumption, he would want to have $103 of real purchasing power at the end of 1 year. If inflation is 3%, he would require, in nominal dollars, 1.03 *times* this amount, i.e., 1.03 × 103 real dollars = 106.09 nominal dollars. Thus, he would require a 6.09% nominal return, instead of just 6.00%. However, since in most cases simply adding the rate of inflation to the real rate is "close enough," this is the procedure that will be used in this text.

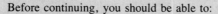

Required return = risk-free real rate + expected inflation + risk premium

Note that the first two factors (the risk-free real rate of return and inflation) will affect the rate of return required on *all* potential investments. Only the third factor (the risk associated with an investment) is *unique to each investment opportunity*.

Before continuing, you should be able to:

1 Define investment
2 Identify three major determinants of the required return for investment
3 Identify which of these three factors affect all investments in the same way and which factor is unique to each investment

1-4 RISK AND RETURN

The preceding section postulated that the returns required by investors are at least partially a function of the risk associated with investments. Rather than take such statements at face value, the critical reader will want to see some evidence to support this argument. Although risk will not be defined in quantitative terms until Chapters 3 and 4, Figure 1-2 suggests on an intuitive level that common stocks have clearly been riskier investments than government bonds and treasury bills over the past 50 years or so. In Figure 1-2 the top chart represents the annual returns generated by the Standard & Poor's Composite Index, a portfolio consisting of the stocks of 500 large U.S. corporations. The second and third charts represent the annual returns generated by a portfolio of long-term U.S. government bonds and treasury bills, respectively. It is obvious that the returns generated by common stocks varied considerably more than either the bond or treasury bill returns, and consequently most observers would agree that stocks were the riskier investment. Over this same period, stocks provided an average return of 9.8%, which was considerably more than the average return of 4.1% and 3.4% generated by government bonds and treasury bills respectively. This provides some evidence that riskier investments, on average, do provide higher returns.

It should also be obvious from Figure 1-2 that the variability of returns can be substantial. To take the extreme example, in 1931 holders of common stocks suffered an average loss on their investment of 43%; just 2 years later stockholders enjoyed a positive return of 54% on their investment!

1-5 PRICES AND RATES OF RETURN

There is a direct linkage between rates of return and prices. We will argue in later chapters that the price of any asset is equal to the sum of the discounted cash payments which the owners of the asset will receive. For example, the current price of a share of common stock (P_0) can be written mathematically as

$$P_0 = \sum_{t=1}^{n} \frac{E(D_t)}{(1 + r)^t} \tag{1-1}$$

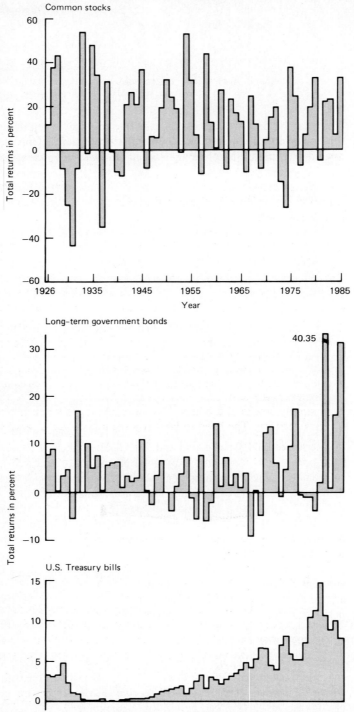

FIGURE 1-2   Year-by-year total return on common stocks, government bonds, and treasury bills. (*Source: Stocks, Bonds, Bills, and Inflation: 1986 Yearbook,* Ibbotson Associates, Chicago, 1986, exhibits 2A and 2C.*

where $E(D_t)$ = dividend expected to be received in year t, including any liquidating
dividend or future sale price

r = rate of return investors expect, given the stock's risk, in order to
postpone consumption and buy the stock

Thus, it is the rate of return r which investors require in order to invest in a particular
asset that is used *to discount the expected future cash flows* associated with the asset.
And, since the price of an asset is simply the present value of its future cash flows,
the linkage between rates of return and prices is completed. One can easily see from
Equation (1-1) that if the required rate of return is increased, asset prices will fall,
and vice versa.

1-6 SECURITIES

Broadly defined, a security represents evidence of a property right. That is, a security
represents a claim on an asset and any future cash flows the asset may generate. The
security itself is usually a document which identifies the investor's rights or claims.
When studying investments, we typically think of securities as stocks or bonds. A
bond indicates that the investor is to receive certain interest and principal payments
at specified times. A stock certificate indicates that the investor owns a certain number
of shares of a corporation and therefore has a claim to a certain percentage of the cash
dividends and other distributions made to the firm's shareholders.

However, the term *securities* covers a much broader spectrum of claims on assets
than simply stocks and bonds. The note one signs when borrowing money to buy a
car is a security. The deed to land is a security. Even a pawn ticket can be classified
as a security. Thus, the study of investments and security analysis is applicable to
much more than the world of stocks and bonds. Basic valuation principles can be
applied to real estate as well as to major corporations. Security analysis techniques
can be used by bank lending officers, credit analysts, and others, as well as the typical
Wall Street analyst. While we will concentrate on stocks and bonds, many parts of
this book are applicable to the general problem of how to value any asset, or security.

1-7 SECURITY ANALYSIS

Security analysis involves the process of estimating the future cash flows which will
accrue to the owners of a particular security, and the risk associated with these prospective cash flows. Generally the analyst's job also includes the task of estimating,
either explicitly or implicitly, the future price of the security. Before these estimates
can be made, a great deal of preparatory work must be done. This includes the gathering
of a variety of data regarding the industries the firm competes in, as well as data
unique to the firm. These data must then be carefully analyzed before projections can
be made.

For example, an analyst following the stock of Ford Motor Company would be
interested in the prospects for the auto industry, both in the United States and abroad.
Ford also manufactures trucks, tractors, farm implements, and electronic equipment—
thus, the analyst would have to be knowledgeable of these industries also. Since these

industries are very sensitive to the level of overall economic activity, macroeconomic forecasts (probably received from economists employed by the same firm as the analyst) would be a crucial input. In order to estimate Ford's market share, the analyst should have an estimate of the capital spending plans and marketing strategies of Ford's competitors, including the Japanese and European auto manufacturers. Finally, the analyst would examine the data unique to Ford, such as Ford's manufacturing capacity and capital spending plans, the firm's dealer network, its marketing strategy, and the company's financial structure and capacity for additional financing.

This example of the analyst's job with respect to Ford is by no means complete. There are many other factors the analyst would have to consider before making any projections about Ford's ability to pay future dividends or interest, the future price of Ford's securities, and the risk associated with ownership of Ford's common stock or bonds. Thus, the analyst's job is not an easy task and should be approached with a sense of humility. Stock market participants, as well as economists, demographers, political analysts, even the CIA, can all testify that forecasting is a hazardous profession.[2]

1-8 GRAHAM AND DODD AND MODERN PORTFOLIO THEORY

For many years the process of security analysis was almost synonymous with what is now the generic term "Graham and Dodd." Graham and Dodd, as used in this text, will refer to two things: (1) the book, *Security Analysis*, by Graham, Dodd, and Cottle,[3] which described in great detail the techniques used by security analysts and for many years was considered the bible of the profession; (2) the approach so strongly advocated by Benjamin Graham, of bringing both careful analysis *and* common sense to bear on the investment decision-making process.

A great deal has been learned in the field of finance since the last edition of *Security Analysis* was written in 1962. This new knowledge has been popularized under the title of modern portfolio theory, or MPT. Although there is no clear consensus of what MPT entails, MPT is probably best described as encompassing the *efficient markets* literature and modern *capital asset pricing theories*.

1-8-1 The Efficient Market Hypothesis   While there is no universally accepted definition of the efficient market hypothesis (EMH), in general the EMH suggests that all publicly available information will be reflected so quickly in the prices of securities that no investor will be able to consistently earn above-normal profits. The driving force behind market efficiency is simply competition—as long as there exist many investors with similar objectives, they will "compete away" abnormal profits so that

---

[2]Some of the better-known forecasting gaffes are: government officials, beginning as early as the 1920s, repeatedly predicted that the United States would run out of oil in 10 years. Demographers warned in the late 1960s that there would not be enough elementary schools available for the coming bulge in the 5- to 10-year age group—in fact, many elementary schools had to close for lack of students. In the late 1970s the CIA indicated that Iran would continue to be a *stabilizing* force in the Middle East. Of course, the lack of forecasting ability on the part of economists and stock market participants is well known.

[3]B. Graham, D. Dodd, and S. Cottle, *Security Analysis*, 4th ed., McGraw-Hill, New York, 1962. The first edition of this classic book was published in 1934

securities will be priced to yield a normal return, commensurate with their risk. Most studies of market efficiency have been conducted since the last edition of Graham, Dodd, and Cottle was written.

1-8-2 Capital Market Theories   In addition to the efficient markets literature, beginning in the mid-1960s new theories of asset pricing were developed. The most important of these is the capital asset pricing model (CAPM) of Sharpe and Lintner,[4] which has had a tremendous impact on the field of investments from the viewpoint of both the investment practitioner and the academic researcher. The CAPM provided a new definition of risk which was quickly accepted by the academic community but was initially viewed with a great deal of skepticism by many investment professionals. While some aspects of the CAPM remain controversial, the model continues to be one of the most important theories in finance.

According to the CAPM, the correct measure of risk is termed *systematic risk*, which is measured by the security's *beta*. We will spend considerable space in the ensuing chapters discussing systematic risk. For now, suffice it to say that *beta measures the covariability of the security's returns with the returns of a large portfolio* such as the S&P 500 index. The more a particular security's price covaries (varies together) with general changes in the prices of all securities, the greater its market-related risk.

Since systematic risk is concerned only with *market-related risk*, it does not consider any of the more traditional concepts of risk such as business risk, financial risk, and liquidity risk.

Systematic risk = market-related risk

It may be, however, that systematic risk is a function of these traditional measures of risk. While the CAPM does not address this issue, the empirical evidence does show that there is at least a correlation between betas (systematic risk) and such traditional risk measures as financial leverage and variability of earnings.

The impact of the efficient market hypothesis and the CAPM on the investment profession has been substantial. For example, the performances of portfolio managers and security analysts are now frequently measured in the framework of the CAPM. The idea of market efficiency has also been the genesis for *index funds*, which now constitute a large and growing proportion of professionally managed money. An index fund operates under the premise that securities are generally correctly priced. The fund, therefore, does not attempt to outguess the market by trying to identify under-

---

[4]The development of the CAPM is usually credited to the following two papers: W. Sharpe, "Capital Asset Prices: A Theory of Market Equilibrium under Conditions of Risk," *Journal of Finance* (September 1964); J. Lintner, "The Valuation of Risk Assets and the Selection of Risky Investments in Stock Portfolios and Capital Budgets," *Review of Economics and Statistics* (December 1965). Others frequently acknowledged for the development of the model are: J. Treynor, "Toward a Theory of the Market Value of Risky Assets," unpublished manuscript (1961); J. Mossin, "Equilibrium in a Capital Asset Market," *Econometrica* (October 1966); and F. Black, "Capital Market Equilibrium with Restricted Borrowing," *Journal of Business* (July 1972).

priced securities. Rather, the index fund aims to match the performance of some agreed-upon index by carefully diversifying and minimizing transaction costs, such as commissions. The growth of such funds has been dramatic in recent years, as the amount of money being indexed has increased from a base of nearly zero in 1973 to over $50 billion in 1985.[5] This growth has been particularly prominent for large institutional portfolios. For example, over half of the pension funds with assets over $500 million indexed at least part of their assets in 1979.[6]

However, as will be discussed in Chapter 5, some of the early enthusiasm for MPT may have been overdone. The security markets are probably not as efficient as may have been originally thought to be the case when much of the initial EMH literature was produced. And, while systematic risk is certainly a valid concept, the original Sharpe-Lintner version of the CAPM may be misspecified. Nevertheless, it would appear that the security analyst has much to be gained by studying these concepts in addition to the more traditional Graham and Dodd material. Thus, one of the primary purposes of this book is to bring together traditional Graham and Dodd security analysis and MPT. Interestingly, the two concepts, when properly understood, tend to be mutually consistent. In fact, when MPT is utilized as a framework for making investment decisions, security analysis has been called "the first, and cornerstone, step in the MPT decision process."[7]

1-9 ORGANIZATION OF THE TEXT

The text is organized into six parts with each part covering a major topical area. The following is a brief description of each of these parts of the book:

• Part One, "An Overview," presents descriptive material on the securities markets, an introduction to risk and return, and a discussion of market efficiency.

• Part Two, "Analytical Tools and Valuation Concepts," discusses some of the problems involved in analyzing financial statements and presents a number of tools used by analysts in formulating projections, as well as the time value of money concept and general valuation principles.

• Part Three, "Analyzing Equity Securities," covers many of the techniques and problems associated with estimating earnings, dividends, and the risk of common stocks.

• Part Four, "Analyzing Fixed-Income Securities," covers many of the fascinating problems in analyzing bonds and constructing fixed-income portfolios.

• Part Five, "Asset Pricing Theories," explores in more detail such topics as the CAPM, arbitrage pricing theory, and option pricing.

• Part Six, "Portfolio Management," discusses some of the broader issues involved in forming portfolios, as well as the topics of mutual funds, performance measurement, and international investments.

---

[5]J. Rohrer, "Ferment in Academia," *Institutional Investor* (July 1985).
[6]"An Indexing Update," *Institutional Investor* (November 1980).
[7]R. L. Hagin, "Modern Portfolio Theory, Topics and Applications," published by the research department of Kidder, Peabody & Co., New York, May 1980. Mr. Hagin has also expressed this idea in *Modern Portfolio Theory*, Dow Jones–Irwin, Homewood, Ill., 1979.

Each part of the text consists of a number of related chapters. As a general rule, the chapters within a part should be read in sequence. The appendices at the end of several chapters may be skipped without loss of continuity. They are provided for the student who wants to delve into some specialized areas in greater detail.

At the beginning of each chapter there is a summary of the key concepts in the chapter. This is done to alert the reader, in advance, as to what the most important topics are so that the student will recognize them as he or she progresses through the chapter. In addition ''reminders'' are interspersed throughout the chapters to notify the reader of basic concepts he or she should master before proceeding. (See, for example, the reminder at the end of Section 1-3.) Hopefully these reminders will make the learning process a little easier.

Now, having dispensed with the introduction, let's proceed to Chapter 2, which presents a description of the markets in which securities are traded.

CHAPTER 2

SECURITIES MARKETS

After reading this chapter, you should:

1 Understand the basic characteristics of the major classes of securities
2 Understand the difference between primary and secondary markets
3 Develop some knowledge concerning the major exchanges and the over-the-counter markets
4 Be aware of the major types of trading arrangements, such as different kinds of orders, margin accounts, short selling, and the cost of trading
5 Have an awareness of recent innovations in the U.S. securities markets, such as the third and fourth markets and the proposed central market

A securities market is a mechanism for bringing together buyers and sellers of a particular type of security or financial asset. Thus, the New York Stock Exchange enables investors to buy and sell certain stocks (and some bonds). Many other stocks and most bonds are bought and sold in the over-the-counter market. As another example, the Chicago Board of Options Exchange represents a market for buying and selling options on common stocks.

Some markets have a central location, such as the New York Stock Exchange, which is located at 11 Wall Street in New York City. However, such a central location is not necessary to today's world of modern communications. The over-the-counter market has no central location—it consists of many broker-dealer firms located throughout the country. All securities markets, however, do provide the service of bringing together buyers and sellers so that a transaction can take place.

These buyers and sellers set prices of financial assets, which in turn will ultimately influence the allocation of resources throughout the economy. If the price of a firm's stock and bonds is high, the firm will be able to raise more capital than if the prices are low. New capital, of course, is a major source of funds used by the firm for purchasing physical assets. These physical assets, combined with labor, produce the goods and services we consume in a modern economy. Thus, by setting the price of capital, the securities markets have an impact on the well-being of everyone in an economy, whether or not any particular person directly participates in the investment process.

2-1 CLASSES OF SECURITIES

The first step in studying securities markets is to develop an understanding of the different classes of securities. Securities can be categorized into *four broad groups: bonds, common stocks, preferred stocks, and derived securities*. The following is a brief discussion of the characteristics of these classes of securities.

There are many different types of bonds, such as mortgage bonds, debentures, and senior and subordinated notes. A discussion of the unique characteristics of these different types of bonds is deferred until later chapters. For now, one needs to be aware that bonds have a *fixed maturity*—that is, there is a specified date at which time the firm must pay all liabilities it owes to the owners of a particular bond issue. Bondholders generally have what is termed a *fixed claim on the income of the firm*. That is, bondholders are entitled to a fixed interest payment each year (or semiannual period), regardless of what the income of the firm may be during the period. Bondholders also have the right to receive their interest payment before any dividends may be distributed to the equity owners. In addition, bondholders have what is termed a *fixed claim on the assets of the firm*. This means that when the bonds mature, or in the event of the liquidation of the firm, the bondholders are entitled to receive a stated amount (the principal), and this claim has priority over any of the claims of the equity owners. Finally, the claims of bondholders are legally binding. If the company defaults on either interest or principal payments, it can be forced into bankruptcy.

Common stocks lie at the other end of the securities spectrum. Common stocks, or equity shares, are said to be *perpetual*. That is, there is no maturity for common stocks since the equity shares exist as long as the corporation exists. In addition, holders of common stock have what is termed a *residual claim against the income and assets of the firm*. That is, holders of common stock have the *last claim* to the firm's income, or the assets of the firm in the event of liquidation. But the equity owners can claim *everything that remains* after all other claims have been satisfied, i.e., the residual.[1] Thus, the potential for gain is greater for holders of common stock than for debt holders whose gain is fixed. On the other hand, the risk is correspondingly greater for the equity owners since they have the last claim to the firm's income and assets. Finally, there is no legal requirement to pay dividends. Rather, dividends are paid at the discretion of the company's board of directors.

Preferred stock is occasionally referred to as a *hybrid security* since its characteristics lie somewhere between those of common stock and bonds. Similar to bonds, the claims of holders of preferred stock on the firm's income are *limited* since preferred stock pays a fixed dividend; and the holders' claims on the assets of the firm in the event of liquidation are also fixed at a stated amount (usually the par value). On the other hand, like common stock, preferred stock is a *perpetual* liability of the firm, although many preferred-stock issues now have sinking-fund provisions through which the company gradually retires the issue by buying back the preferred stock. Also, like common stock, the decision to pay preferred-stock dividends is at the discretion of the board of directors, whereas interest payments are mandatory. Finally, preferred-stock dividends are treated the same as common-stock dividends for tax purposes. From the viewpoint of the investor, preferred dividends are treated as dividend income, subject to the same dividend-exclusion provisions as are common dividends. From the viewpoint of the firm, preferred dividends, like common dividends, are *not* a tax-deductible expense, whereas interest payments on bonds are a deductible expense.

---

[1]The reader should bear in mind that this is a greatly simplified presentation. In reality, when a firm is in default or in the process of forced liquidation, the claims on the firm's income and assets will be determined by the courts. There have been many times when all the claims of the bondholders have not been satisfied and the equity shareholders have still been awarded some part of the firm's assets.

Thus preferred stock has some characteristics which are similar to bonds and some which are similar to common stock. These general characteristics of bonds, preferred stocks, and common stocks are summarized in Table 2-1.

The securities we term *derived securities* include such financial assets as warrants, options, convertible bonds, and *futures*. They are classified as derived securities because part, if not all, of their value is derived from the value of another security. For example, the value of a call option is derived from the value of the common stock against which the call option is written; the value of a commodity futures contract is derived from the value of the commodity which must be delivered in the future.

2-2 PRIMARY MARKETS

Before one begins to study specific securities markets, the general distinction between *primary* and *secondary* markets should be understood. Primary markets are those in which the seller of the securities is also the issuer of the securities—that is, the firm is the seller of the securities. For example, if General Motors should issue some additional common stock, this would be sold in what is called the *primary market*, and *General Motors would receive the proceeds from the sale*.

Primary issues of securities occur relatively infrequently. More often, when an investor buys a security, the seller is another investor. Such trades occur in what are termed the *secondary markets*. An example might be the purchase of 100 shares of IBM on the New York Stock Exchange. In this case, the proceeds go to the seller of the stock, who would be an investor. The issuer of the stock (IBM) is not involved, other than that there has been a change in its shareholders.

2-2-1 Brokers and Dealers The vast majority of trades made by investors are executed by a securities firm acting as either a broker or a dealer. A firm acting in a brokerage capacity serves as an agent for investors by finding another person to take the other side of the trade. For example, if the broker's customer is a buyer, the broker finds a seller of the security being traded. For its services, the broker is compensated by a commission.

TABLE 2-1 CHARACTERISTICS OF BONDS, PREFERRED STOCK, AND COMMON STOCK

	Bonds	Preferred stock	Common stock
Claim on income:			
Priority	First	Second	Last
Amount	Fixed	Fixed	Residual
Claim on assets:			
Priority	First	Second	Last
Amount	Fixed	Fixed	Residual
Mandatory or discretionary claim	Mandatory	Discretionary	Discretionary
Maturity	Fixed	Perpetual	Perpetual

A dealer, on the other hand, may *take positions* in various securities—that is, the dealer may buy and sell securities for its own account. While the dealer may have positions in the securities it trades for only a short time, it nevertheless assumes the usual risks of ownership. If the dealer has a *long position* in the stock (owns the stock) and the stock goes down in price, the dealer loses money. Conversely, if the dealer has a *short position* in a stock, the dealer has temporarily sold more stock than it owns. In this case, if the stock increases in price, the dealer will lose money when it covers its short position by buying stock in the market at prices higher than the dealer originally sold the stock for. Dealers are compensated by the difference between the *bid price* (the price at which they will buy a security from an investor) and the *ask price* (the price at which they will sell a security to a customer). Since dealers will buy or sell securities for their own account in order to balance customers' orders, dealers are also frequently called *market makers*. Many securities firms act as both brokers and dealers.

2-2-2 Investment Bankers and Public Offerings   Most primary issues of securities are sold by the firm to the public through investment bankers. The investment banker is a broker-dealer firm which provides a number of services, depending upon the type of offering, to the issuing firm and the investing public. In a typical public offering, investment bankers will provide three services: (1) the managing, or advisory, function; (2) the underwriting, or risk-bearing, function; and (3) the selling, or distribution, function.

In a *negotiated underwriting* the *managing underwriter* (the lead investment banker) typically has been involved with the offering almost from the day the firm issuing the securities originally decided to raise new capital. The managing underwriter traditionally advises the issuing firm as to what type of securities the market will be most receptive to, when to issue the securities, and most importantly, at what price. In addition, the lead underwriter is responsible for ensuring that all the legal reporting requirements are met.

Another important function of the managing underwriter is the formation of an *underwriting syndicate*. The members of the underwriting syndicate literally buy the securities from the issuing firm on the day of the offering. Thus, the issuing firm is assured that it will receive the proceeds from the issue without having to worry about whether or not the investing public will eventually buy the securities. Because the underwriters are the owners of the securities (at least until they are resold to the public), the underwriters bear the risk that the securities are properly priced. As a rule, however, the underwriters presell the issue. That is, the salespeople for the underwriting firms know that the issue is to be offered on a particular date, and prior to this day they talk to their customers (the investing public) to see if their customers are interested in buying the issue and at what price. As a result of this preselling process, the managing underwriter generally has a very good idea of the price at which the public will be willing to buy the securities.

When the securities are actually sold to the public, they are sold either by members of the underwriting syndicate or by members of the *selling group*. The members of the selling group are broker-dealer firms that buy the securities from the underwriters and in turn resell the securities to their customers. Figure 2-1 helps illustrate the overall underwriting process.

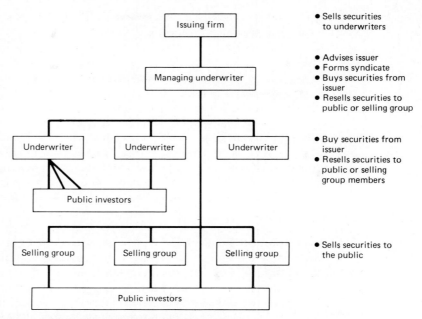

FIGURE 2-1   An illustration of the underwriting process.

Information concerning a public offering of securities is available in the *prospectus*. The prospectus is a document which, by law, must be furnished to each investor who buys the securities on the offering. In addition to information regarding the offering itself, the prospectus provides detailed data on the operations and financial condition of the firm issuing the securities. If a firm has made a recent public offering of securities, the prospectus is required reading for the serious investor interested in the company.

2-2-3 Initial Public Offerings   The securities involved in a public offering can be classified into two groups, seasoned and unseasoned securities. An offering of *seasoned securities* would, for example, involve the issuance of *additional* shares of General Motors common stock. The securities are said to be seasoned because there already are shares of GM trading in the marketplace and therefore investors have an excellent idea as to the price the new shares should trade at—obviously the new shares will be priced at or very close to the price of the existing shares.

In contrast, *initial public offerings* are involved with *unseasoned* issues—that is, the securities are being offered to the public for the first time and, thus, there is no established market price for them. In this case, the offering price is negotiated between the investment bankers and the issuing firm.

Since the underwriters want to have the offering sell out quickly, there is an incentive to *underprice* the new securities,[2] and apparently this is the case. A study by Ibbotson[3]

[2]It is sometimes argued that the issuing firm may also have an incentive for underpricing the initial public offering of its common stock. The positive price action of its stock after the offering may create a

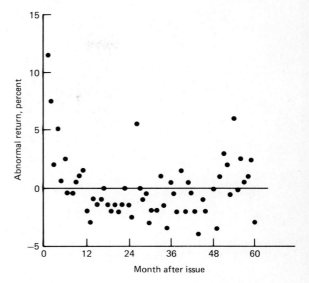

FIGURE 2-2   Abnormal returns from initial common-stock offerings. [*Source: R. Ibbotson, "Price Performance of Common Stock New Issues,"* Journal of Financial Economics *(September 1975), p. 252.*]

found that by the end of the month in which the initial public offering of common stock was made, investors who bought the stock at the offering price enjoyed a profit, on average, of 11.4%. This profit was after adjusting for changes in the overall level of stock prices and the risk involved and is referred to as an "abnormal" return. After the first month, the new issues tended to be correctly priced, as they no longer generated abnormal returns. This can be seen from Figure 2-2, where the abnormal returns are plotted on the vertical axis and the number of months after the offering date are plotted on the horizontal axis. Note that for the first month, the average abnormal return was very high. However, after the first month, the abnormal returns are scattered about the horizontal axis and would average very close to zero.

Thus, while it appears that new issues of unseasoned securities are underpriced on the offering, the market adjusts the price to its normal level within the first month of trading. While it might also appear that a good investment strategy would be to buy all new issues and reap the first month's windfall, one should bear in mind two factors. First, the 11.4% abnormal profit in the first month represents an *average*. As Ibbotson reported, the first month return for any *individual* new issue varied substantially, from an abnormal loss of minus 59% to abnormal profits greater than 70%. The other fact to bear in mind is that this performance of new issues is not unknown to the investing public. Thus, the demand by investors for these new issues tends to exceed the supply of stock to be offered. As a result, the underwriters ration these issues among their best customers. Since costs may be incurred in becoming a "best customer" (such as being willing to buy slow-moving seasoned issues underwritten by the investment

---

favorable impression of the firm in the minds of investors and thereby make it easier for the firm to raise additional equity capital in the future.

[3]R. Ibbotson, "Price Performance of Common Stock New Issues," *Journal of Financial Economics* (September 1975).

banker), it is not clear that these investors will experience positive abnormal returns on their total portfolios.

Before continuing, be sure you understand:
1 The general characteristics of the three broad classes of securities
2 The difference between primary and secondary markets
3 The difference between seasoned issues and new issues
4 The function of investment bankers

2-3 ORGANIZED EXCHANGES

In the *secondary markets* one investor sells to another investor and the firm that issued the securities is not involved. Most trading in the secondary markets takes place on organized exchanges such as the New York Stock Exchange (NYSE) and the American Stock Exchange (ASE).

To illustrate how trading takes place on the organized exchanges, consider the following example. Mrs. Jones wants to buy 200 shares of Merck, which is listed on the NYSE. She calls her broker, who works for a NYSE member firm and places an order to buy 200 shares "at the market," which means Mrs. Jones is willing to pay whatever price sellers of the stock demand. (This isn't as risky as it may seem, since market orders on listed stocks are almost always executed at or very near the previous price, unless the market order is for an unusually large number of shares.) Mrs. Jones' broker immediately informs his firm's trading department, which in turn wires the information to the firm's *floor brokers* at the NYSE. The floor brokers walk out onto the floor of the exchange to the desk of the *specialist* who is responsible for trading in Merck. When the broker arrives at the specialist's desk, he finds that there is another broker who has a customer that is willing to sell 100 shares of Merck at the market, but that there are no other sellers at the moment. In this case, Mrs. Jones' broker would buy the 100 shares from the other broker, and most likely the specialist would agree to sell to Mrs. Jones' broker the second 100 shares at, or slightly above, the most recent price for Merck. (Specialists are members of the exchange who have the responsibility of "maintaining an orderly market" by taking the opposite side of unbalanced orders—in the above example, the specialist sold Mrs. Jones the second 100 shares.) The floor broker then reports the trade to his firm's trading department which in turn notifies Mrs. Jones' broker who quickly calls Mrs. Jones and reports the results of the trade.

Thus, a number of people are involved in the execution of a single trade. Yet, under normal conditions it takes only a few minutes for the transaction to be completed and the customer notified. When one considers how long it takes to buy and sell other types of assets (for example, real estate), the securities markets are marvelously fast.

There are a number of organized securities exchanges, among which the NYSE is by far the most important. Table 2-2 lists statistics on exchange trading volume. Note that in 1983 the NYSE accounted for 80% of the number of shares traded and 85% of the trading based on dollar volume. The next largest exchange, in terms of trading volume, is the American Stock Exchange, which in 1983 accounted for approximately

7% of the total number of shares traded on the exchanges, but only 3% of the dollar volume. As one can see, the other exchanges[4] *combined* accounted for about 12% of the exchange volume. Thus, we will concentrate on the New York (NYSE) and American (ASE) stock exchanges.

Table 2-3 indicates the number of companies whose common stock was listed on the NYSE and the ASE over time, in addition to the total number of shares and their market value. Notice that while the number of companies listed on the NYSE is not quite double the number listed on the ASE (1543 versus 819 in 1984), the number of shares outstanding and the market value of the shares are substantially greater. This is because companies whose common stock is listed on the NYSE tend to be much larger than those listed on the ASE.

Table 2-4 presents the requirements for listing a stock on the NYSE and the ASE. Again, one can see from its listing requirements that the NYSE is oriented toward larger companies than is the ASE. In fact, some view the ASE as a steppingstone to listing on the NYSE. In many cases, small companies have first listed their shares on the ASE, waited until they met the NYSE requirements, and then listed on the big board.

2-4 OVER-THE-COUNTER MARKETS

The term over-the-counter was originally used to describe the manner in which securities were traded many years ago when investors literally bought stocks and bonds "over the counter" at their local bank. Today the term over-the-counter (OTC) continues to be used as a designation for the unlisted securities trading market, even though the OTC market is one of the most modern and efficient securities markets in the world.

The OTC market is not physically located in any one place. Rather, it consists of a number of broker-dealers throughout the country who are linked together through an electronic communications network. For any individual security traded in the OTC market there will typically be a number of broker-dealer firms which make a market in the security by setting competitive *bid* quotes to buy, and *ask* quotes to sell the security.

It is safe to say that more individual securities are traded OTC than are listed on the exchanges, although exact data on OTC trading are hard to find since it is not a centralized market. The vast majority of bonds are bought and sold in the OTC market. Many bank and finance company stocks are also traded OTC, as are mutual funds. In addition, the common stocks of many smaller companies are traded in this market.

2-4-1 NASDAQ   In 1971, the National Association of Securities Dealers (NASD), which includes almost all broker-dealers, put into operation a nationwide communications network known as the NASD Automated Quotation System (NASDAQ). This system allows any broker to know, almost instantaneously, the most recent bid-ask quotes of each dealer firm making a market in any security carried on the NASDAQ

---

[4]The abbreviations in Table 2-2 stand for New York, American, Midwest, Pacific, Philadelphia, Boston, and Cincinnati stock exchanges, respectively.

TABLE 2-2 PERCENTAGE OF TRADING VOLUME BY EXCHANGES

Year	Total share or dollar volume (thousands)	NYSE	AMEX	MSE	PSE	PHLX	BSE	CSE	Other*
			Share volume†						
1935	681,971	73.13	12.42	1.91	2.69	1.10	0.96	0.03	7.76
1940	377,897	75.44	13.20	2.11	2.78	1.33	1.19	0.08	3.87
1945	769,018	65.87	21.31	1.77	2.98	1.06	0.66	0.05	6.30
1950	893,320	76.32	13.54	2.16	3.11	0.97	0.65	0.09	3.16
1955	1,321,401	68.85	19.19	2.09	3.08	0.85	0.48	0.05	5.41
1960	1,441,120	68.47	22.27	2.20	3.11	0.88	0.38	0.04	2.65
1961	2,142,523	64.99	25.58	2.22	3.41	0.79	0.30	0.04	2.67
1962	1,711,945	71.31	20.11	2.34	2.95	0.87	0.31	0.04	2.07
1963	1,880,793	72.93	18.83	2.32	2.82	0.83	0.29	0.04	1.94
1964	2,118,326	72.81	19.42	2.43	2.65	0.93	0.29	0.03	1.44
1965	2,671,012	69.90	22.53	2.63	2.33	0.81	0.26	0.05	1.49
1966	3,313,899	69.38	22.84	2.56	2.68	0.86	0.40	0.05	1.23
1967	4,646,553	64.40	28.41	2.35	2.46	0.87	0.43	0.02	1.06
1968	5,407,923	61.98	29.74	2.63	2.64	0.89	0.78	0.01	1.33
1969	5,134,856	63.16	27.61	2.84	3.47	1.22	0.51	0.00	1.19
1970	4,834,887	71.28	19.03	3.16	3.68	1.63	0.51	0.02	0.69
1971	6,172,668	71.34	18.42	3.52	3.72	1.91	0.43	0.03	0.63
1972	6,518,132	70.47	18.22	3.71	4.13	2.21	0.59	0.03	0.64
1973	5,899,678	74.92	13.75	4.09	3.68	2.19	0.71	0.04	0.62
1974	4,950,833	78.47	10.27	4.39	3.48	1.82	0.86	0.04	0.67
1975	6,381,669	80.92	8.96	4.05	3.25	1.54	0.84	0.13	0.31
1976	7,125,201	80.03	9.35	3.87	3.93	1.41	0.78	0.44	0.19
1977	7,134,946	79.54	9.73	3.95	3.71	1.49	0.66	0.64	0.28
1978	9,564,663	80.08	10.75	3.58	3.14	1.50	0.60	0.15	0.21
1979	10,977,775	79.78	10.82	3.29	3.38	1.64	0.54	0.27	0.28
1980	15,584,209	79.95	10.79	3.83	2.80	1.51	0.56	0.32	0.24
1981	15,969,398	80.68	9.32	4.60	2.87	1.55	0.51	0.37	0.10
1982	22,500,576	81.19	6.96	5.08	3.62	2.18	0.48	0.42	0.08
1983	30,316,014	80.00	7.29	5.48	3.53	2.20	0.65	0.01	0.85

*Other includes all exchanges not listed above.
†Share volume for exchanges includes stocks, rights, and warrants.

system. The market makers, using a system known as Level III of NASDAQ, enter their bid-ask quotes through a terminal. These quotes are placed in a central computer file and update the dealer's previous quotes. Level II of NASDAQ allows the trading departments of brokerage firms to see all the bid-ask quotes and the names of the dealers making the quotes. The trading department can then identify the market maker with the most favorable quote for their customer, call that dealer, and arrange the trade. The market makers are required to execute trades at their bid and ask prices for at least one "normal unit of trading," which in the case of common stocks is 100 shares. Individual account executives (stockbrokers) generally have quotation terminals which are tied into Level I of NASDAQ. This allows the stockbroker to see median bid-ask quotes for any security listed on NASDAQ.

To be included on NASDAQ, a security must meet certain minimum requirements. For example, there must be two market makers for the security and a minimum number

TABLE 2-2   PERCENTAGE OF TRADING VOLUME BY EXCHANGES (*Continued*)

Year	Total share or dollar volume (thousands)	NYSE	AMEX	MSE	PSE	PHLX	BSE	CSE	Other*
		Dollar volume‡							
1935	$15,396,139	86.64	7.83	1.32	1.39	0.88	1.34	0.04	0.56
1940	8,419,772	85.17	7.68	2.07	1.52	1.11	1.91	0.09	0.45
1945	16,284,552	82.75	10.81	2.00	1.78	0.96	1.16	0.06	0.48
1950	21,808,284	85.91	6.85	2.35	2.19	1.03	1.12	0.11	0.44
1955	38,039,107	86.31	6.98	2.44	1.90	1.03	0.78	0.09	0.47
1960	45,309,825	83.80	9.35	2.72	1.94	1.03	0.60	0.07	0.49
1961	64,071,623	82.43	10.71	2.75	1.99	1.03	0.49	0.07	0.53
1962	54,855,293	86.32	6.81	2.75	2.00	1.05	0.46	0.07	0.54
1963	64,437,900	85.19	7.51	2.72	2.39	1.06	0.41	0.06	0.66
1964	72,461,584	83.49	8.45	3.15	2.48	1.14	0.42	0.06	0.81
1965	89,549,093	81.78	9.91	3.44	2.43	1.12	0.42	0.08	0.82
1966	123,697,737	79.77	11.84	3.14	2.84	1.10	0.56	0.07	0.68
1967	162,189,211	77.29	14.48	3.08	2.79	1.13	0.66	0.03	0.54
1968	197,116,367	73.55	17.99	3.12	2.65	1.13	1.04	0.01	0.51
1969	176,389,759	73.48	17.59	3.39	3.12	1.43	0.67	0.01	0.31
1970	131,707,946	78.44	11.11	3.76	3.81	1.99	0.67	0.03	0.19
1971	186,375,130	79.07	9.98	4.00	3.79	2.29	0.58	0.05	0.24
1972	205,956,263	77.77	10.37	4.29	3.94	2.56	0.75	0.05	0.27
1973	178,863,622	82.07	6.06	4.54	3.55	2.45	1.00	0.06	0.27
1974	118,828,272	83.62	4.39	4.89	3.50	2.02	1.23	0.06	0.29
1975	157,555,469	85.04	3.66	4.82	3.25	1.72	1.18	0.17	0.16
1976	195,244,815	84.35	3.87	4.75	3.82	1.68	0.93	0.53	0.07
1977	187,393,082	83.96	4.60	4.79	3.53	1.62	0.73	0.74	0.03
1978	249,603,319	84.35	6.17	4.19	2.84	1.63	0.61	0.17	0.04
1979	300,728,389	83.65	6.93	3.82	2.85	1.80	0.56	0.35	0.04
1980	476,416,379	83.54	7.32	4.32	2.27	1.59	0.51	0.40	0.05
1981	491,017,044	84.74	5.41	5.04	2.32	1.60	0.50	0.40	0.00
1982	603,361,387	85.28	3.27	5.83	3.05	1.59	0.51	0.47	0.00
1983	958,304,168	85.06	3.29	6.29	2.87	1.56	0.66	0.16	0.13

‡Dollar volume for exchanges includes stocks, rights, and warrants.
Source: U.S. Securities and Exchange Commission, *Annual Report*, 1984, p. 109.

of publicly held shares, and the issuing firm must meet certain requirements with respect to the amount of capital and total assets. As of the end of 1983 approximately 4500 issues were included in the NASDAQ system.[5] Trading volume for 1983 was almost 16 billion shares, which compares with the 30.3 billion shares traded on the exchanges for the same year. (See Table 2-2.) However, the NASDAQ volume figures are overstated as they reflect the number of shares bought and sold by market makers plus their net inventory changes.

2-5 TRADING ARRANGEMENTS

When an investor places an order with a broker-dealer, a number of different trading arrangements can be used. These arrangements include the type of order placed, the

[5]U.S. Securities and Exchange Commission, *Annual Report*, 1984.

TABLE 2-3   SHARES LISTED ON THE NYSE AND ASE

Year	NYSE			ASE		
	Number of companies	Number of shares (millions)	Market value (millions of dollars)	Number of companies	Number of shares (millions)	Market value (millions of dollars)
1935	800	1,318	46,946	N.A.	N.A.	N.A.
1938	N.A.	N.A.	N.A.	786	693	10,801
1945	912	1,592	73,765	646	631	14,360
1950	1,057	2,353	93,807	621	574	12,312
1960	1,143	6,458	306,967	828	1,584	24,171
1961	1,163	7,088	387,841	891	1,799	33,011
1962	1,186	7,659	345,846	910	1,803	24,365
1963	1,214	8,108	411,318	908	1,742	26,130
1964	1,247	9,229	474,322	930	1,762	28,220
1965	1,273	10,058	537,481	939	1,726	30,987
1966	1,286	10,939	482,541	947	1,828	27,859
1967	1,274	11,622	605,817	968	1,864	42,965
1968	1,273	13,196	692,337	994	2,192	61,213
1969	1,311	15,082	629,453	1,079	2,631	47,716
1970	1,351	16,045	636,380	1,151	2,807	38,442
1971	1,426	17,500	741,827	1,234	3,117	47,752
1972	1,505	19,159	871,540	1,315	3,300	54,114
1973	1,506	20,967	721,012	1,279	3,323	37,376
1974	1,567	21,737	511,055	1,222	3,228	22,011
1975	1,557	22,478	685,110	1,181	3,110	27,937
1976	1,576	24,500	858,299	1,118	3,081	34,226
1977	1,575	26,093	796,639	1,048	3,055	35,559
1978	1,581	27,573	822,736	964	2,972	37,086
1979	1,565	30,033	960,606	904	2,996	55,835
1980	1,570	33,709	1,242,803	869	4,074	80,943
1981	1,565	38,298	1,143,794	860	4,332	63,020
1982	1,526	39,516	1,305,355	840	4,496	59,495
1983	1,550	45,118	1,584,155	839	5,243	78,524
1984	1,543	49,092	1,586,098	819	5,402	67,520

Data for number of shares and market value of shares include both common and preferred shares.
Source: *1985 Fact Book*, New York Stock Exchange, p. 79; *1984 Amex Fact Book*, American Stock Exchange, p. 7.

TABLE 2-4   NYSE AND ASE LISTING REQUIREMENTS

	NYSE	ASE
Pretax income, most recent year	$ 2,500,000	$ 750,000
Pretax income, previous 2 years	$ 2,000,000	. . . . .
Net income, most recent year	. . . . .	$ 400,000
Tangible net worth	. . . . .	$4,000,000
Net tangible assets	$16,000,000	. . . . .
Market value of publicly held shares	$18,000,000	$3,000,000
Number of publicly held shares	1,100,000	500,000
Number of round-lot holders	2,000	800

Sources: *1985 Fact Book*, New York Stock Exchange, and *1984 Amex Fact Book*, American Stock Exchange.

cost of executing the trade, and the method of paying for the transaction. The following is a brief summary of some of the more frequently encountered trading arrangements.

2-5-1 Market Orders   The type of order most frequently used is a ''market order.'' A market order indicates that the investor is willing to buy or sell at the best price currently prevailing. For example, a market buy order indicates that the investor is willing to pay the lowest offer price available; a market sell order indicates the investor is willing to sell at the highest bid price currently available. Thus, market orders are used when investors want to buy or sell quickly and are trading in small enough quantities that they will not change the current market price substantially.

2-5-2 Limit Orders   The second most frequently used order is a limit order. A limit order means that the investor has specified the price at which he will buy or sell a security. For example, suppose that an investor wants to buy 3000 shares of XYZ stock, which represents a relatively large order for this particular security. XYZ is currently 25 bid, 25½ offered. That is, at least 100 shares of stock can be bought at the offering price of 25½ or sold at the bid price of 25. Since a market order to buy 3000 shares could cause the price to increase significantly, the investor might place a limit order to buy 3000 shares at 25¼. In this case, the investor will buy any number of shares that are offered at 25¼, up to 3000 shares. If fewer than 3000 shares are offered at or below the limit price, the investor will simply have to wait until more shares are offered at his limit. Obviously, with limit orders investors run the risk that they may not be able to buy or sell the desired number of shares.

Limit orders are placed as either *day orders* or *open orders*. A limit day order is good until the end of the current trading day. For example, if our investor placed a limit day order to buy 3,000 shares of XYZ at 25¼ and by the end of the trading day only 1000 shares had been purchased, the remainder of his order would be canceled. On the other hand, open orders are generally *good until canceled*, or GTC, although sometimes a specific time limit such as one week will be placed on the order. If our investor had placed an open limit order to buy 3000 XYZ and had bought only 1000 shares at the end of the day, the remainder of his order would continue to be carried on the specialist's books the following day and as long thereafter as necessary to fill the order or until the investor canceled it.

2-5-3 Margin Accounts   There are two basic types of accounts which an investor may use to buy and sell securities. One type is known as a *cash account* because the investor must pay the brokerage firm for the full amount of the securities purchased. The second most common type of account is the *margin account*. When stocks are bought in margin accounts the investor may borrow, from the brokerage firm, part of the purchase price of the securities and is charged interest on the amount borrowed. Thus, like any form of borrowing, buying on margin creates financial leverage. If the purchased securities increase in value at a rate which exceeds the rate of interest being charged on the unpaid balance, then the investor's profits will be leveraged upward. Conversely, if the securities purchased on margin do not increase in value at a rate greater than the interest rate, then the investor suffers a lower rate of return than if she had fully paid for the securities. Of course, if securities purchased on margin should decline in value, the investor suffers a double whammy—a loss on the securities and interest expenses.

A simple example will help to illustrate the concept of financial leverage. Assume that you purchase 200 shares of a stock at a price of $25 per share. Thus, the total value of the purchase is $5000. Further, assume that you put up $2500 in equity and borrow $2500 from your broker in a margin account at a 10% interest rate and hold the stock for 1 year. If the stock increases in price by 20%, from $25 to $30, the return on your equity would be 30%; however, if the stock decreases in price by 20% to $20, you would have a negative return on your equity of 50%, as shown below:

	Stock price = $30 (20% increase)	Stock price = $20 (20% decrease)
Value of stock	$6000	$4000
Minus cost	(5000)	(5000)
Minus interest	(250)	(250)
Profit (loss)	750	(1250)
Return on $2500 equity	+30%	−50%

Thus, while buying on margin may increase the potential for gain, it also increases the risk.

2-5-4 Short Selling   Short selling mystifies many people, especially the first time they are exposed to it. But it is important to understand short selling. Therefore, let's take the mystery out of short selling.

Basically, short selling is the opposite of the normal investment procedure—you sell the security *first* and then buy back the security at a later date. Generally, a short-selling strategy is based on the expectation that a security is going to *decline* in price. An example will help illustrate the concept. Suppose an investor believes that ABC stock, which sells at $15 per share, is overvalued and will fall in price within a reasonable time period. This investor sells short 100 shares at $15, and fortunately her judgment is right, as 1 week later the stock price drops to $12. At that time the investor closes out (covers) her short position by buying back 100 shares in the market-place for a $300 profit. The following summarizes these transactions:

Today: sell short 100 shares at $15, proceeds =	$1500
1 week later: buy 100 shares at $12, cost =	$1200
Profit =	$ 300

Short selling raises the question of how investors can sell a security before they buy it. How can one sell something she does not own? The answer is that the short seller's brokerage firm borrows the stock from another investor who owns the stock. This borrowed stock is then delivered to the person who bought the stock from the short seller. When the short seller covers or closes out her short position by buying stock in the marketplace, the stock she purchases is used to replace the stock which was originally borrowed to start the short-selling process.

The fact that one has to borrow stock in order to sell short raises two important points. First, the person from whom the stock was borrowed will obviously want to continue receiving the dividends associated with the stock, as will the person who bought the stock from the short seller. Thus, there are *two* claims to the same stock and the stock's dividends. The person who bought the stock from the short seller will be issued a stock certificate and will receive dividends from the issuing firm. Therefore, the short seller is obligated to *pay dividends to the person from whom the stock was borrowed*. Second, the person from whom the stock was borrowed may want to sell the stock before the short seller has completed the transaction by buying back the stock in the marketplace. If the short seller's brokerage firm is not able to borrow additional stock from a different investor, the short seller may be "bought in"—that is, the short seller may be *forced* to buy back the stock in the marketplace in order to replace the borrowed stock. This may occur when the stock price is high, resulting in a loss for the short seller.

The risk associated with short selling is clearly greater than owning, or being "long" the stock. First, the short seller makes money if the stock price declines and loses money if the price rises. Since, over long periods of time stock prices on balance have risen, not fallen, the short seller is working against the law of averages. Second, the short seller pays dividends while the owner of stock receives dividends. Third, the maximum possible gain from short selling is equal to the price of the stock, since the price can only fall to zero. Conversely, the potential loss from a short position is nearly unlimited, as there is no limit to how high the stock price can go. Again, this is the opposite of being long the stock, in which case the potential loss is limited to the price paid and the potential for gains is theoretically unlimited.

2-5-5 Insurance The bull market which ended in 1969 was accompanied by a significant increase in trading volume. Because of the "back-office crunch" some investors found that their brokerage firms were not able to deliver stock or bond certificates by the required settlement date—this is known as a *fail to deliver*. Even worse, some of the brokerage firms were on the verge of bankruptcy, including the second largest firm in the industry at that time. As a result of these problems, Congress passed the Securities Investor Protection Act of 1970 which established the *Securities Investor Protection Corporation (SIPC)*. The SIPC insures investors' accounts at all broker-dealer firms which are members of exchanges registered with the Securities and Exchange Commission. These accounts are currently insured for up to $100,000 by the SIPC against loss due to the broker-dealer's failing. In addition many broker-dealers have arranged for additional insurance from private insurance companies that, together with SIPC coverage, insure accounts for $1 million or more.

Before continuing, you should:

1 Understand how trades are executed on exchanges and in the OTC market
2 Have an appreciation for the relative importance of the various secondary markets
3 Know the difference between market orders and limit orders
4 Understand the concepts of buying on margin and short selling

2-6 THE COST OF TRADING

A number of costs are associated with trading securities. The obvious costs are commissions charged on each trade. However, two other costs associated with trading are even more important than commissions—these are the market makers' spread (the difference between the bid and ask price) and the price concession one must make to trade large blocks of a security. However, let's examine commission costs first.

2-6-1 Commissions   Certainly one of the major costs of investing is the commission paid on each trade. On May 1, 1975, the Securities and Exchange Commission forced the brokerage community to drop their long-standing practice of using a fixed commission schedule and to begin employing competitive, negotiated rates. Since this time, referred to as "Mayday" in the trade, the commissions an investor may pay can vary considerably, depending upon the size of the trade, the frequency with which the investor makes trades with a particular broker, and the type of services provided by the broker. In general, the more business an investor does with a broker, the lower the commission rate. Thus, large institutional investors are able to negotiate substantially lower commission rates than small, individual investors. However, if the small investor is not interested in many of the services provided by the traditional, full-line brokerage firms (such as research reports or individual advice from a stockbroker) then the small investor may be better served by dealing with one of the *discount houses* which only provide services related to the execution of the trade and do not provide any of the frills. These discount houses will execute trades for small investors based on a commission rate that is substantially less than that of the full-line brokerage firms.

Table 2-5 lists the NYSE commission schedule which existed prior to May 1, 1975. This schedule continues to serve as a guide for negotiating commissions, as many institutional investors will negotiate a discount from this outdated but industrywide standard, since the current commission schedules of brokerage firms will vary from firm to firm. From the viewpoint of the small investor, the pre-Mayday schedule is, unfortunately, lower than that which prevails today. Figure 2-3 lists the results of a study by Schreiner and Smith[6] which indicates that for small trades, the commission rate has increased since 1975, while for large trades the rate has decreased. For example, the commission rate on 200 shares of a $5 stock ($1000 total value) was approximately 3.6% in 1975 versus approximately 4.8% in 1978 (see the top line of the left graph in Figure 2-3). In general, the commission rate has increased for trades

---

[6]J. Schreiner and K. Smith, "The Impact of Mayday on Diversification Cost," *Journal of Portfolio Management* (summer 1980).

TABLE 2-5   NYSE FIXED-COMMISSION SCHEDULE
(Prior to May 1, 1975)

100-share orders and odd-lot* orders		Multiple round-lot* orders	
Money involved	Minimum commission	Money involved	Minimum commission
Under $ 100	Negotiated	$ 100–$ 2,499	1.3% + $ 12.00
$ 100–$ 799	2.0% + $ 6.40	$ 2,500–$ 19,999	0.9% + $ 22.00
$ 800–$2,499	1.3% + $12.00	$20,000–$ 29,999	0.6% + $ 82.00
$2,500 and above	0.9% + $22.00	$30,000–$300,000	0.4% + $142.00
		Over $300,000	Negotiated

Plus, on multiple round lots:
First to tenth round lot . . . . $6 per round lot
Eleventh round lot and above . . . . $4 per round lot
Plus, on any order involving money of less than $5000, the commission computed according to the above shall be increased by 10%; on any order involving money more than $5000, the commission computed according to the above shall be increased by 24.2%.

*A round lot consists of 100 shares. An odd lot consists of less than 100 shares.

of $1000 to $10,000 in value since 1975. However, for larger trades ($100,000 or more), rates have come down with the advent of negotiated commissions. The dashed lines in Figure 2-3 assume the investor is able to negotiate a 40% reduction in commissions from the 1975 rate on trades involving $100,000 or more, which is not an

FIGURE 2-3   Percentage brokerage commissions for four dollar transaction sizes. [*Source: J. Schreiner and K. Smith, "The Impact of Mayday on Diversification Costs," Journal of Portfolio Management (summer 1980). Reprinted by permission.*]

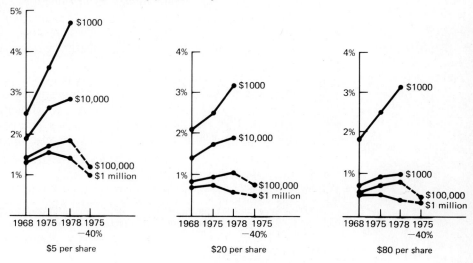

unreasonable assumption. In these cases, the commission rate is less, and in some cases substantially less, than 1%.

Unfortunately, the small investor generally is not able to negotiate any substantial reduction in commissions, and, as Schreiner and Smith note, his commission rate has risen on average since 1975. However, if one is willing to forgo the services of a full-line brokerage firm and utilize a discount broker, commission costs can be substantially reduced. For example, listed below is a comparison of commission charges as advertised by one discount brokerage firm in 1982.

	Commission		
	On 200 shares at $15	On 500 shares at $30	On 300 shares at $60
Full-service firm	$88.00	$265.00	$275.00
Discount firm	$49.00	$109.25	$ 80.00
% savings	44%	59%	71%

While this is not a complete commission schedule, it is probably representative of the difference in commission costs between full-service firms and discount houses. The easiest way to learn more about discount brokers is to read their advertisements in the *Wall Street Journal* and other financial publications.

Given the many different commission schedules available today and the variety of services provided by brokerage firms, it certainly will pay for the investor to shop around. For those who do not want the many services provided by full-line brokerage firms, discount houses may be the best choice. Conversely, those who want the advice of a stockbroker may be better off paying the higher commissions typically associated with the full-line broker. However, as Schreiner and Smith point out, the latter group of investors may do better by putting their money into a no-load mutual fund.[7] The mutual fund, by trading in much larger dollar amounts, will be able to negotiate substantially lower commissions than can individual investors. The mutual funds' lower commission rates may more than offset the management fee charged by the managers of the fund.[8]

In addition to commissions, other direct costs are associated with investing. However, these costs tend to be small relative to commissions. The state of New York levies a tax on security sales that occur in the state, which is generally the case since both the NYSE and the ASE are located in New York. The tax rate is 1¼ cents per share for stock selling at less than $5, 2½ cents per share for stock selling between

---

[7]A no-load mutual fund does not charge the investor a commission for purchasing the fund. A load fund does charge a commission. See Chapter 21 for a discussion of mutual funds.

[8]Actually the commission burden on small investors is even greater than indicated by Schreiner and Smith. See R. A. Strong, ''The Impact of Mayday on Diversification Cost: Comment,'' *Journal of Portfolio Management* (spring 1981).

$5 and $9.99, 3¾ cents per share for stock selling between $10 and $19.99, and 5 cents per share for stock selling at $20 or more. In addition, the SEC charges a fee of 1 cent per $500 of securities sold. The New York state tax and the SEC fee are charged only to the seller of the security and are relatively small compared with brokerage commissions. An example will help to illustrate. Suppose an investor sells 200 shares of a $25 stock at the rate prevailing before May 1, 1975 (see Table 2-5). The total cost of executing the transaction would be as follows:

Total value of transaction	= 200 × $25	= $5,000
Commission: 0.009 × $5,000	= $45.00	
Plus	22.00	
Plus 2 × $6	= 12.00	
	$79.00	
Plus 10%	7.90	
Total commission		$86.90
New York state tax (5¢ per share)		10.00
SEC fee (1¢ per $500)		0.10
Total cost of executing transaction		$97.00

The total transaction cost of $97 represents 1.9% of the $5000 value of the trade. Many analysts use 2% as a ball park estimate of the typical commission costs for a small trade.

2-6-2 Total Trading Costs As noted earlier, trading costs consist not only of commissions but also of the bid-ask spread and any price concessions one must make in order to trade large blocks of a security. Figure 2-4 illustrates the total cost of trading. Using the midpoint between the bid and ask price (the midprice) as a starting point, buyers must add one-half of the market maker's spread to arrive at the ask price. To the ask price, buyers must add price concessions they may be forced to make for trading in any quantity which exceeds the quantity the market maker is willing to trade at his posted ask price. On top of these two costs, the buyer must also pay commissions. Conversely, a seller must subtract from the bid price any price concessions and commissions.

FIGURE 2-4 Components of trading costs.

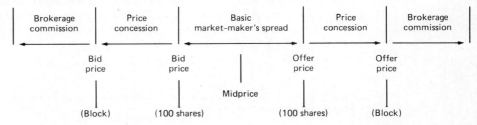

One study attempted to measure the total cost of trading.[9] The top half of Table 2-6 reports the size of the bid-ask spread as a percentage of the midprice. The sample was divided into various groups based on the market value of the firm's stock. Note that the spread for stocks in the smallest market values group was 6.55% of the price, whereas for the largest market value group the spread/cost ratio was only 0.52%. Clearly, the bid-ask spread is a more important factor for small capitalization stocks.

The bottom half of Table 2-6 reports the findings concerning the total cost of trading—market maker's spread, price concessions, and commissions. These findings are based on a large number of actual trades and are on a *round-trip* basis—that is, they measure the cost of both buying and selling a block of stock. Again, the sample was divided into groups based on market value. However, this time the sample was also divided into groups based on the size of the trade, i.e., for block sizes ranging from $5000 to $20,000,000. Note that as one reads down the columns, the total cost of trading decreases for a given block size. Thus, as one deals with larger market capitalization stocks, the total cost of trading decreases. As one reads across the rows, the cost of trading increases because one is forced to accept larger price concessions when trading larger blocks of a particular stock. Thus, the largest trading cost is associated with large blocks of small market capitalization stocks and the smallest trading cost is associated with small blocks of large capitalization costs. For the small capitalization stocks, the total trading cost is quite high, regardless of the size of the block. Investors buying and selling small capitalization stocks should be aware that the total trading cost of these securities can be as high as 30%, or more, which far exceeds just the commission cost. Even in the largest capitalization stocks, the round-trip trading cost can be as much as 8% if one is trading large blocks. This presents a serious problem for large institutional investors who, simply because of the amount of money under management, must deal in large blocks.

2-7 THE MARKET FOR DEBT SECURITIES

While the majority of equity securities, in terms of both volume and value, are traded on the exchanges, the opposite holds for debt securities. Although hard data are difficult to obtain with respect to bond trading, it is safe to say that most long-term bond trading takes place in the OTC market, while all the trading in short-term government securities takes place in the OTC market.

Debt securities can be categorized by the issuer of the securities. For our purposes, we will consider three types of issuers—corporations, the federal government and its agencies, and municipal governments. Corporate bonds are traded both on the exchanges and over-the-counter, although most of the trading takes place OTC. While OTC trading data are difficult to obtain, we do have data concerning the exchanges. As of the end of 1984, 3751 bond issues which had a combined market value of $1.02 trillion were listed on the NYSE.[10] However, the average trading volume for corporate bonds on the NYSE is relatively small. For example, in 1984 daily trading in bonds averaged $28 million per day compared with $3 billion per day in common stocks.

---

[9]T. F. Loeb, "Trading Cost: The Critical Link between Investment Information and Results," *Financial Analysts Journal* (May–June 1983).
[10]*1985 Fact Book*, New York Stock Exchange, New York, p. 79.

TABLE 2-6   TRADING COSTS

Market capitalization and market maker's spread

Capitalization sector, millions of dollars	No. of issues	Percentage of U.S. market	Average price	Average spread	Spread/ midprice,* %
0– 10	1009	0.36	$ 4.58	$0.30	6.55
10– 25	754	0.89	10.30	0.42	4.07
25– 50	613	1.59	15.16	0.46	3.03
50– 75	362	1.60	18.27	0.34	1.86
75– 100	202	1.27	21.85	0.32	1.46
100– 500	956	15.65	28.31	0.32	1.13
500–1000	238	12.29	35.43	0.27	0.76
1000–1500	102	8.87	44.34	0.29	0.65
Over 1500	180	57.48	52.40	0.27	0.52

Market capitalization, block size, and total spread/price cost, %†

Capitalization sector, millions of dollars	Block size, thousands of dollars								
	5	25	250	500	1000	2500	5,000	10,000	20,000
0–10 ($4.58)‡	17.3	27.3	43.8						
10–25 ($10.30)	8.9	12.0	23.8	33.4					
25–50 ($15.16)	5.0	7.6	18.8	25.9	30.0				
50–75 ($18.27)	4.3	5.8	9.6	16.9	25.4	31.5			
75–100 ($21.85)	2.8	3.9	5.9	8.1	11.5	15.7	25.7		
100–500 ($28.31)	1.8	2.1	3.2	4.4	5.6	7.9	11.0	16.2	
500–1000 ($35.43)	1.9	2.0	3.1	4.0	5.6	7.7	10.4	14.3	20.0
1000–1500 ($44.34)	1.9	1.95	2.7	3.3	4.6	6.2	8.9	13.6	18.1
Over 1500 ($57.48)	1.1	1.2	1.3	1.7	2.1	2.8	4.1	5.9	8.0

*Round-trip trading cost for 100 shares *excluding* commission costs.
†Round-trip trading cost *including* commission costs.
‡Average price of issues in capitalization sector.
Source: T. F. Loeb, "Trading Cost, the Critical Link between Investment Information and Results," *Financial Analysts Journal* (May–June 1983).

All federal and municipal government debt issues are traded in the OTC market by dealer firms which tend to specialize in certain types of issues. For example, some dealers are very active in the federal government treasury bill market but may not deal at all in the municipal bond market. In addition to the larger investment banking firms, many large commercial banks act as dealers in the government securities markets.

2-8 THE THIRD AND FOURTH MARKETS

Since the late 1960s there have been a number of changes in the operation of the securities markets. These changes have been the result of competition within the securities industry and the result of external pressure from the Securities and Exchange Commission and Congress. The broad classification of secondary securities markets is occasionally divided into four categories of secondary markets. The *first market* represents the exchanges, while the *second market* represents over-the-counter trading. The *third market* represents over-the-counter trading of shares which are listed on an exchange, and the *fourth market* represents direct trading between two investors (typically large institutional investors) without a brokerage firm acting as an intermediary.

2-8-1 The Third Market   The third market was created during the era of fixed commissions. During this period, the commission schedule did not adequately allow for the economies of scale associated with executing large orders—the incremental cost associated with executing a 10,000-share order versus a 100-share order is relatively small, yet the fixed-commission schedule used by NYSE member firms charged a much higher commission on the large order than on the small order. Thus, many institutional investors who traded in large quantities began to look for better (cheaper) ways of making large trades. A number of broker-dealers who were not members of the NYSE began to make markets in stocks which were listed on the exchanges, offering to execute large trades at much lower commissions. Trading in the third market reached its peak in 1972 when it accounted for 8½% of the volume traded on the NYSE.[11] Since 1972, third-market volume as a percentage of NYSE volume has steadily declined, presumably because the era of negotiated commissions has decreased the need for the third market.

2-8-2 The Fourth Market   The ultimate in reducing commission costs would be the complete elimination of the broker-dealer firm as a middleman. When one investor sells directly to another investor without going through a broker-dealer, they are said to be trading in the fourth market. For large trades, even in an era of negotiated commissions, this strategy might make sense. For example, if an institution negotiated a commission rate of ½ of 1% on a trade to sell 50,000 shares of XYZ at $65, the total value of the trade would be $3,250,000 and the commission would amount to $16,250. Of course, the buyer of the stock would also have to pay a similar commission. Thus, for institutions which make trades involving such large amounts of money, there is certainly an incentive to try to find a buyer of securities they are trying to sell and vice versa. To facilitate this, many institutions subscribe to an automated communications system called *Instinet* which provides quotations on a number of large, institutional stocks and automatically matches up buy and sell orders which have similar prices and quantities for a particular stock, without going through a broker-dealer firm.

2-9 REGULATION AND THE CENTRAL MARKET

A number of major changes in the securities markets have been the direct result of regulation. The current movement toward a "central market" is, in large part, due to

[11]*Statistical Bulletin*, Securities and Exchange Commission, Washington, D.C., 1978.

regulation, although competitive pressures and technological innovations have also pushed in this direction.

2-9-1 Regulation of the Securities Markets   A number of federal and state laws directly or indirectly impact upon the securities markets. The most important of these is the *Securities Act of 1933*. This act is sometimes called the ''truth in securities,'' or ''full disclosure'' law, as it requires the *registration of new issues and the disclosure of all information investors might need in order to make a decision as to whether or not to purchase the security*. As noted earlier, the prospectus is the primary document utilized to disclose information concerning the securities being offered.

The *Securities Exchange Act of 1934* was a companion piece to the 1933 act. The 1934 act extended the disclosure principles to the secondary markets and required that national exchanges and broker-dealers be registered with the Securities and Exchange Commission (SEC). The SEC is also the prime administrative agency for a number of other pieces of federal legislation. Among the more important of these are the *Investment Company Act of 1940* and the *Investment Advisors Act of 1940* which extended disclosure and registration requirements to investment companies and mutual funds, and investment advisors, respectively.

Another important piece of legislation is the *Banking Act of 1933*, known as the *Glass-Steagall Act*. This federal law separates commercial banking activities from investment banking—in general, a firm cannot engage in both activities. As a result, commercial banks have not played as prominent a role in the U.S. securities markets as they have in Europe and elsewhere. However, given the recent trend toward de-regulation of the banking industry, in the future commercial banks may become more important participants in the U.S. securities markets.

In addition to congressional statutes, federal securities laws rely heavily on the concept of self-regulation. For example, the regulation of trading on the NYSE is largely delegated to the members of the exchange; the regulation of OTC trading is largely delegated to the members of the NASD.

Prior to the Securities Act of 1933, the regulation of the securities markets was done by the states. Beginning in the early 1900s, many of the states began to pass what are known as *state blue-sky laws*. Today these blue-sky laws vary from state to state, but they are generally designed to prevent fraud and require the registration of broker-dealers and new issues of securities.

2-9-2 The Central Market   In 1975, Congress passed the *Securities Act Amendments* which mandated that the SEC should move as rapidly as possible toward the implementation of a single, nationwide and competitive securities market. In the proposed central market, the over-the-counter market and seven exchanges would be electronically linked together so that each floor specialist and market maker could see all the bid-ask quotes of their competitors, as could the trading department of any broker-dealer firm. This should enable the investor to get the best price available. In addition, the central market would eventually establish a single book for limit orders.

While the idea of a centralized market is conceptually sound, implementation has been slow, both because of technical problems and because of political infighting.[12]

---

[12]S. Crock, ''Experiment in Competitive Stock Trading Is Likely to Be Postponed by the SEC,'' *Wall Street Journal* (Apr. 20, 1981), p. 2.

Late in 1975 a consolidated stock ticker began to report trades which took place on the NYSE, and in the fourth market using the Instinet system. This information is used to produce the composite stock transactions reported in many financial newspapers. In 1978 the *composite quotation system* (CQS) was implemented which makes available the exchange specialists' bid-ask quotes to subscribers of the system. Progress on the final step of electronically linking the exchange specialists and all other market makers for a particular stock, and creating a single book for limit orders, has been slow. But such a centralized market seems inevitable in today's world of modern communications systems, especially since the forces of both regulation and competition are pointing in this direction.

2-10 SUMMARY

This chapter provided a brief description of the markets in which securities are traded. Knowledge of the securities markets is essential if one is to understand how securities are priced in these markets. As an introduction, the general characteristics of the three broad classes of securities (common stocks, preferred stocks, and bonds) were discussed.

The reader should by now understand the distinction between the primary and secondary markets. The primary markets deal with the issuance of *new* securities, and as a result, the issuing firm receives the proceeds from the sale of these securities. However, it is within the secondary markets that most trading takes place with one investor selling to another. While the NYSE dominates the secondary markets, considerable trading takes place over-the-counter as well as on the ASE and other smaller exchanges.

There are many types of trading arrangements the astute investor should be aware of, only a few of which were covered in this chapter. One should know the difference between market and limit orders, day orders and open orders, as well as the intricacies of buying on margin and short selling. Of course, every investor should be aware of the commissions associated with investing and how to minimize this expense.

Some recent innovations in the securities markets were discussed. These included the third and fourth markets, as well as the drive toward a centralized marketplace. Such a market seems inevitable in light of the technological progress being made in the field of communications and the regulatory pressure pointing toward the central market.

Finally, the Appendix to this chapter describes many of the more popular stock market indexes, such as the Dow Jones Industrial Average and the Standard & Poor's indexes. When investors ask "what is the market doing?" they are usually referring to one of these indexes. Thus, a description of the composition and computation of these indexes is included in the Appendix.

SUGGESTED READINGS

For general market statistics (trading volume, shares listed, etc.) good starting points are:
Fact Book, published by the New York Stock Exchange, Eleven Wall Street, New York, N.Y. 10005.
Amex Fact Book, published by the American Stock Exchange, 86 Trinity Place, New York, N.Y. 10006.

A good article on the cost of trading is:

T. F. Loeb, "Trading Cost: The Critical Link between Investment Information and Results," *Financial Analysts Journal* (May–June 1983).

Still one of the best references for a description of the many institutional aspects of the securities markets is:

G. A. Christy and J. C. Clendenin, *Introduction to Investments*, 8th ed., McGraw-Hill, New York, 1982.

An interesting article which describes how to pick a discount broker is:

M. D. Coler, "How to Choose a Discount Broker," *Barron's* (Oct. 17, 1983).

QUESTIONS

1. What roles do the securities markets play in allocating resources within an economy?
2. Name the general classes of securities and describe the basic characteristics of each group.
3. What is a primary market for securities and how does it differ from a secondary market?
4. Public offerings of securities can be categorized into seasoned and unseasoned issues. What is the difference between the two categories?
5. What three functions do investment bankers provide when they underwrite securities?
6. What would be the impact on the primary markets if active secondary markets did not exist?
7. As a general rule, which types of securities tend to be traded over-the-counter?
8. Define the third and fourth markets.
9. What type of investor would tend to trade in the third and fourth markets, and what is their incentive for doing so?
10. Describe the NASDAQ system.
11. What are the listing requirements for the NYSE and the ASE?
12. What are the advantages and disadvantages of placing a market order compared with a limit order?
13. Using Table 2-5, what would be the commission on a trade of 300 shares at $40? What would be the commission on 1000 shares at $20?
14. For the two trades in Question 13: (*a*) What is the commission expressed as a percentage of the money involved? (*b*) What would be the New York state tax and SEC fee for the sellers of the securities?
15. In your opinion, will the proposed central market benefit investors? If so, why hasn't it already been implemented? ~~investors~~
16. Assume an institutional portfolio has a value of $1 billion. The portfolio's trustees decide that the fund should not own more than 100 different stocks, nor should the fund own more than 5% of the outstanding stock of any one firm. (*a*) What will be the average market value of the common stock of the firms the fund invests in? (*b*) What does this suggest about the number of institutional analysts who follow the stocks of small companies?

APPENDIX: Market Indexes

"What's the market doing?" is frequently the first question investors ask their broker. This interest in market movements results from the fact that the prices of individual securities tend to vary together. Exceptions—securities which move against the general financial tide—are rare, and as a rule they do not persist on a contrary course for more than a few days or weeks at a time. This fact has long been known and accepted, and historic records confirm it.

The general movement of the stock market is usually measured by averages or indexes consisting of groups of securities that are supposed to represent the entire stock market or particular segments of it. The best-known indexes—the Dow Jones averages, the Standard & Poor's indexes, and the Value Line Composite Index—will be examined in detail in this Appendix. The NYSE, ASE, and NASDAQ indexes will be described in less detail.

2A-1 DOW JONES INDUSTRIAL AVERAGE (DJIA)

The DJIA is the oldest index of American stocks. Its origin dates back to 1884, when Dow Jones & Company began listing the average closing prices of 11 active stocks in the *Customer's Afternoon Letter*. This letter consisted of two pages of the day's financial headlines and was the forerunner of the *Wall Street Journal*.

First computed in May 1886, the DJIA was based on 12 stocks. In 1916, the list of stocks was expanded to 20, and in 1928 to 30 stocks. Since 1928 the number of stocks has remained at 30. Over time, a particular stock may be considered unrepresentative of its industrial sector, and substitutions are made. The stocks in the DJIA (as of June 1979) are listed in Table 2A-1, both before and after the June 29, 1979, change when Chrysler and Esmark were replaced by IBM and Merck.[13] The first column of numbers in this table, representing the weight of each stock on June 1, 1979, will be discussed later. The second column of numbers represents the weight of each stock in the average before the June 29 change, and the third column lists each stock's weight after the change. The fourth column lists the weight of each stock in the NYSE Composite Index. Note that the 30 DJIA stocks combined accounted for 24.2% of the market value of all stocks listed on the NYSE, which is a disproportionate amount relative to their number. (Based on aproximately 1300 individual companies being listed on the exchange, the 30 DJIA companies represent only about 2% of the total number of companies on the NYSE.) Thus, the typical DJIA stock is much larger than the typical NYSE stock and one of the criticisms of the DJIA is that the companies consist of a small number of blue-chip stocks which are not representative of the many medium- and small-sized firms that are traded on the exchange.

The DJIA is computed by adding the prices of the 30 securities and dividing by a denominator that is adjusted periodically to reflect changes such as stock splits and stock dividends. These events would distort the averages if no statistical adjustment were made. A very simple example illustrates this. Suppose we have three different stocks selling at $30, $20, and $10. Adding the share prices and dividing by 3 gives an average of $20. If the stock selling for $30 split two-for-one, the owner of the $30 share now has two shares worth $15 each. If the average were computed *without adjustment*, its new value would be $15. This represents a 25% decrease from the former average which obviously can't be right because the total dollar value of all shares in the average has not changed. Therefore, to adjust for the stock split, a new divisor is used that will yield an average of $20. Dividing the sum of the share prices by the initial average of $20 gives a new divisor of 2.25 ($45 ÷ $20 = 2.25); in turn, the new divisor results in an unchanged average of $20 ($45 ÷ 2.25 = $20). Over the years, each new stock split reduces

[13]The composition of the DJIA changes periodically as some securities are dropped from the index and others are added. Since the time of the study in Table 2A-1, Johns Manville and Standard Oil of California have been dropped from DJIA while American Express and Chevron Corp. have been added. From time to time the latest listing of the companies included in the Dow Jones averages will be published in the *Wall Street Journal*.

TABLE 2A-1   REPRESENTATION IN THE DJIA AND IN THE NYSE COMPOSITE
INDEX, PERCENT

	June 1, 1979	June 29, 1979		
	DJIA (old)	DJIA (old)	DJIA (new)	NYSE
Allied Chemical Corp.	2.6	3.1	2.9	0.10
Aluminum Co. of America	4.5	4.6	4.2	0.22
American Brands, Inc.	4.9	5.3	4.8	0.18
American Can Co.	3.2	3.5	3.2	0.09
American Telephone & Telegraph Co.	4.8	5.1	4.7	4.48
Bethlehem Steel Corp.	1.8	1.9	1.7	0.11
Chrysler Corp.	0.7	0.8	0.0	0.06
Du Pont, E.I., de Nemours	10.6	3.7	3.3	0.71
Eastman Kodak Co.	4.8	5.1	4.6	1.07
Esmark, Inc.	2.2	2.4	0.0	0.06
Exxon Corp.	4.2	4.8	4.4	2.55
General Electric Co.	4.1	4.4	4.1	1.29
General Foods Corp.	2.4	2.8	2.6	0.16
General Motors Corp.	4.9	5.3	4.8	1.91
Goodyear Tire and Rubber	1.4	1.4	1.3	0.14
Inco Limited	1.8	1.9	1.7	0.18
International Business Machines Corp.	0.0	0.0	6.0	5.13
International Harvester	3.2	3.5	3.2	0.13
International Paper Co.	3.5	4.0	3.6	0.23
Johns-Manville Corp.	2.0	2.2	2.0	0.06
Merck & Co., Inc.	0.0	0.0	5.5	0.55
Minnesota Mining and Mfg. Co.	4.7	5.0	4.6	0.75
Owens-Illinois, Inc.	1.7	1.7	1.6	0.07
Procter & Gamble Co.	6.8	6.8	6.2	0.77
Sears, Roebuck and Co.	1.6	1.7	1.6	0.71
Standard Oil Co. (Calif.)	3.8	4.3	4.0	0.89
Texaco Inc.	2.2	2.4	2.2	0.80
Union Carbide Corp.	3.1	3.3	3.0	0.28
United States Steel Corp.	1.9	1.9	1.8	0.22
United Technologies Corp.	3.1	3.3	3.0	0.18
Westinghouse Electric Corp.	1.5	1.8	1.6	0.17
Woolworth, F.W., Co.	2.1	2.3	2.2	0.08
	100.0	100.0	100.0	24.2*

*Based on the revised DJIA, which includes IBM and Merck, and excludes Chrysler and Esmark.
Source: Andrew T. Rudd, "The Revised Dow Jones Industrial Average," *Financial Analysts Journal*, November–December 1979, p. 59.

the divisor. In 1939, the divisor was 15.1; in 1950, it was down to 8.92; and by July 1981, the divisor was 1.314.

This method of calculating the DJIA makes it a *price-weighted average*. That is, a high-priced stock carries more weight in the average than a low-priced stock. If a $150 stock drops 10% in value, the corresponding drop in the average is much larger than that resulting from a 10% decrease in a $10 stock. These two events are illustrated at the top of the next page.

		Subsequent value assuming 10% decrease	
	Initial value	In High-priced stock	In low-priced stock
Stock X	$150	$135	$150
Stock Y	60	60	60
Stock Z	10	10	9
Sum	$220	$205	$219
Average	73.3	68.3	73
Percentage change		−6.8	−0.4

Note that a 10% decrease in the high-priced stock results in a 6.8% decrease in the average versus only a 0.4% decrease in the average assuming a 10% decrease in the low-priced stock. Thus, the weight of each stock in the average is proportional to its price and the DJIA is denoted as a price-weighted average.

Another problem with the DJIA is that the divisor is not adjusted for stock dividends of less than 10%. This policy creates a statistical bias against growth stocks that tend to split and to declare stock dividends more often than stable stocks. As a result, the averages are lower than they would otherwise be. Furthermore, adjustments for splits cause the relative price weightings of each stock in the average to change very rapidly. As noted earlier, Table 2A-1 gives the weights of the 30 companies that comprised the DJIA in June 1979, and their equivalent percentages in the New York Stock Exchange (NYSE) Composite Index. To examine the effect of a split on an individual stock, consider the case of Du Pont. Between June 1 and June 29, 1979 Du Pont's stock was split 3:1. Note that on June 1 Du Pont's weight in the DJIA was 10.6% whereas after the split it was 3.7%. Over time, these changes cause instability in the index and make long-term comparisons difficult.

On the positive side, the DJIA has a unique advantage. Its member stocks trade so frequently that new calculations of the average can be made almost every 5 minutes, providing timely readings of short-term market movements.

Besides the 30-stock industrial average, the Dow Jones Company compiles and publishes an average of 20 transportation stocks (DJTA), an average for 15 utility stocks (DJUA), and a composite average of all 65 stocks. Also computed are six bond price averages and an average of bond yields. These indicators are calculated in the same manner as the DJIA. However, the divisor for the transportation average is not changed if a stock split or stock dividend causes a change in the average of less than two points.

2A-2 STANDARD & POOR'S STOCK INDEXES

In 1923, the Standard & Poor's Corporation published a price index of 233 stocks and 26 separate group series. In February 1957, the list was expanded to include 500 stocks in the composite index and 95 subgroup indexes. Four of these subgroup indexes are well known among investors. As of July 1976, they consisted of 400 industrials, 40 public utilities, 20 transportation companies, and 40 financial institutions. Included in the other supplementary series are indexes on high-grade stocks, low-priced stocks, capital goods and consumer goods companies, and indexes covering many industry groups. As in the case of the Dow averages, changes are periodically made to the Standard & Poor's indexes to make them more representative.

Standard & Poor's indexes are not averages but rather are value-weighted indexes. That is, the price of each share in the index is multiplied by the number of shares outstanding to determine the market value. The market values of each stock in the index are then summed, and this aggregate market value is divided by the aggregate market value in the base period (1941–1943) and multiplied by 10. Expressed in a formula, the index calculation is

$$\text{Index} = \sum_{i=1}^{n} \frac{P_{it}Q_{it}}{P_{i0}Q_{i0}} \times 10$$

where P_{it} = current market price for ith stock

P_{i0} = market price in base period

Q_{it} = number of shares currently outstanding

Q_{i0} = number of shares outstanding in base period

Note that when multiplying by 10, the base period value of the index is set equal to 10.

As an illustration, let us suppose that the total market value of the stocks in the base year is $80,000 and that stocks A and B make up the current index with the following market value:

	Price per share	Shares outstanding	Market value
Stock A	60	1000	60,000
Stock B	50	1400	78,000
			138,000

The level of the index is 17.25, computed as follows:

$$\frac{138,000}{80,000} \times 10 = 17.25$$

Note that, unlike the Dow averages, the Standard and Poor's indexes are value-weighted. That is, both the price and the number of shares of each stock are recognized. Therefore, the stocks with the largest market value exert the most influence on the level of the index. For example, in 1979, IBM and Exxon, the two companies with the largest market value, accounted for about 7% and 3.5% of the Standard & Poor's 500, respectively.

The Standard & Poor's indexes have several advantages over other indexes. First, they cover a broad range of stocks and provide detailed data on specific industries. Second, because each stock's price is multiplied by the number of shares outstanding, value-weighted indexes automatically adjust for changes caused by stock splits and stock dividends. Third, the use of the value weights has intuitive appeal because a value-weighted index is more likely to track actual changes in the aggregate market value of common stocks than is a price-weighted or equally weighted index.

2A-3 VALUE LINE COMPOSITE INDEX (VLCI)

The VLCI is the most broadly based of the major security indexes. It is composed of approximately 1700 stocks (1500 industrials, 180 utilities, and 20 rails), comprising 85 to 90% of the stocks on the NYSE, and a portion of the AMEX, OTC, and a few Canadian securities. Together, this index covers 96% of the total dollar trading volume in American equity markets. The index includes all the Standard & Poor's 500 and all 30 DJIA stocks.

The VLCI is based on a *geometric average* of the individual stock price changes as opposed to the *arithmetic average* used for the DJIA and Standard & Poor's indexes. Recall that the method of calculating the DJIA results in its being a price-weighted average; i.e., for a given percentage change in stock price, a high-priced stock will have a larger impact than a low-priced stock. Also recall that the method of calculating the Standard & Poor's indexes results in value-weighted indexes; i.e., stocks with large market values have a relatively greater impact than stocks with small market values.

However, the use of a geometric average in calculating the VLCI results in each stock's being given approximately *equal* weight in the index and also results in a potential downward bias for the index over time. A geometric average of stock price changes is calculated by (1) dividing the current price of each stock by its price in the preceding time period; (2) computing the product of these ratios; (3) taking the nth root of this product, where n is the number of securities; and (4) subtracting 1.

A simple example will help illustrate this process. Suppose we have three stocks A, B, and C, which have the prices in time periods 0 and 1 as shown below:

| | Time period | | Ratio of |
Stock	0	1	prices
A	40	52	1.30
B	25	30	1.20
C	10	11	1.10
Total	75	93	

By observing the ratio of the two prices one can see that stocks A, B, and C provided returns of 30%, 20%, and 10%, respectively. Obviously an equally weighted average of the return for these three stocks would be 20%. The geometric average of the returns for these stocks is 19.7%, calculated as follows:

$$\text{Geometric average} = \sqrt[3]{(1.3)(1.2)(1.1)} - 1 = .197 = 19.7\%$$

Thus, the effect of using a geometric average is to give approximately equal weight to each stock.

Note that if the index was price-weighted (or if the index was value-weighted and there were an equal number of shares outstanding for each stock), then the average return would be 24%, calculated as the ratio of the sum of the prices in the two periods minus 1, i.e., 93/75 − 1 = .24. Thus, in this example, price weighting gives greater weight to the 30% return associated with the high-priced stock and results in a higher return (24%) than does the geometric average (19.7%), which gives roughly equal weight to each stock.

To see that there is a slight downward bias to a geometric average, assume that the price of each of the three stocks A, B, and C was $10, that each stock has one share outstanding, and that stock A still provided a 30% return, stock B 20%, and stock C 10%. Since each stock has the same beginning value ($10) and one share outstanding, both a price-weighted and a value-weighted index will generate an equally weighted average of 20%. However, the geometric average will still be 19.7%, as computed above.

In general, as long as the stock prices in the index do not change by the same amount, an index based on a geometric average will change relatively less than one based on an arithmetic average. In the case of the VLCI, however, two other factors influence its relative movements: breadth of base and composition. The 1700 companies that make up the index include many small, speculative stocks that tend to appreciate in price more than higher-priced, stable stocks. Thus, the downward bias of geometric indexes in general is somewhat less evident in the VLCI. On the other hand, the high volatility in individual stock performance—i.e., some increasing in price, others decreasing in price—inherent in a broad-based index like the VLCI exerts a downward pressure on the composite.

2A-4 OTHER U.S. STOCK INDEXES

The *NYSE composite* has been computed since 1966; it covers all the stocks listed on the exchange. Subsidiary indexes also exist for the big board stocks in utilities, transportation, industrials, and financial companies. Because it includes all stocks on the NYSE, this index is not subject to the criticisms of the other indexes concerning breadth of sample. Nevertheless, because it is value-weighted, its major movements are dominated by the stocks of larger companies. The NYSE composite is calculated by the same method as the Standard & Poor's 500. However, it uses December 31, 1965, as the base year, and the value for the base is 50.

The *ASE index* covers about 1000 stocks, warrants, and American depository receipts (ADRs) listed on the American Stock Exchange. The base period is August 31, 1973, and the index value was set at 100. The method originally used to compute this index differed from the methods described for the other composites and was severely criticized for a number of reasons. Consequently, in 1973 a value-weighted method of computing the index was adopted. The ASE index is greatly influenced by movements of small company stocks which are typical of those stocks listed on the ASE.

The *NASDAQ composite* covers more than 3000 over-the-counter stocks representing industrials, utilities, transportation, insurance, banks, and other financial companies. It is computed in a fashion similar to the NYSE index, using February 5, 1971, as the base year with a base value of 100. Like the ASE index, the NASDAQ composite is heavily influenced by movements of smaller stocks.

In addition to the major composites described so far, other indexes and averages are available to gauge the performance of various stock groups ranging in size from 5000 stocks (*Wilshire 5000 Equity Index*) to 16 regional stocks (*Pacific Northwest Stock Index*). A recent trend has been to compute indexes representing increasingly narrower sectors of the country or economy for special-purpose comparisons.

2A-5 FOREIGN INDEXES

Interest in international aspects of finance has increased substantially among U.S. scholars and practitioners in recent years. In an economic environment where international considerations are prominent, knowledge of foreign equity markets becomes important for several reasons. Individual investors are interested in the possibilities for diversification; economists are interested in the worldwide market structure as it influences capital flows between countries; and capital market theorists are concerned with, among other things, whether or not international equity markets are segmented or fully integrated.

The major foreign equity markets are:

Australia	Canada	Japan	Switzerland
Austria	France	Netherlands	United Kingdom
Belgium	Italy	South Africa	West Germany

Several studies that have been done on the movement of stock indexes in these countries are discussed in Chapter 22. The results seem to show that several international markets have higher degrees of similarity than the other markets. These markets (Canada, the Netherlands, Switzerland, West Germany, and Belgium) are relatively well developed and open to international capital flows. On the other hand, Austria and Italy tend to be the least similar markets. Values for worldwide stock indexes are published in *Barron's* and the *Wall Street Journal*.

2A-6 COMPARING STOCK MARKET INDICATORS

The question of which stock market indicator to use is difficult to answer because it depends on what the investor wants to know about the market. While most indicators tend to move together over the long run (see Figure 2A-1), there is something different to be learned and used from each. Thus, an investor may use the DJIA for a quick reading of the market trend but follow closely the ASE index when her holdings consist of smaller stocks traded on the ASE. Similarly, the manager of a large, well-diversified portfolio may use the S&P 500 as an indicator of overall performance since this index may come closest to encompassing the universe of large and small stocks he is investing in—at the same time, he may track several subgroups, or industry-specific averages representative of the individual securities in his portfolio.

FIGURE 2A-1   Stock market averages. (*Source: Summary of Advices and Index, the Value Line Investment Survey, Aug. 30, 1985, p. 40. Reprinted by permission.*)

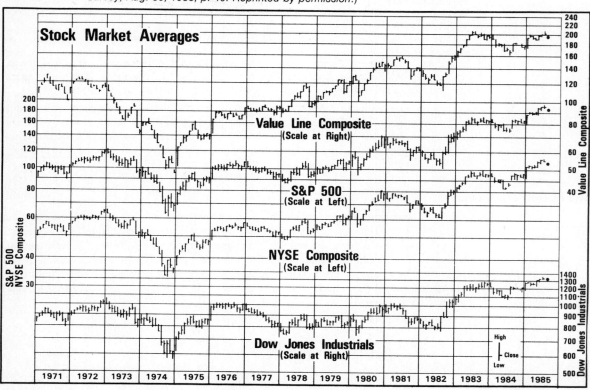

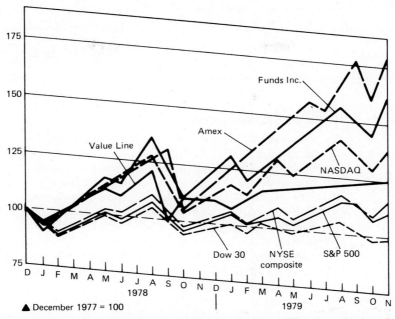

FIGURE 2A-2 How seven indexes tracked the market. [*Source: "Why One Index Isn't Enough," Business Week (Dec. 31, 1979). Reprinted by permission.*]

In addition, over shorter time periods, changes in the various indexes can be quite different, as Figure 2A-2 illustrates. Thus, for a number of reasons it is worthwhile to be aware of the many different indexes available, their composition, and how they are constructed.

CHAPTER 3

RISK AND RETURN

After reading this chapter, you should:

1 Understand the distinction between ex post (historical) returns and ex ante (expected) returns
2 Be able to calculate for individual securities the mean, variance, and standard deviation of either ex post or ex ante returns
3 Be able to calculate covariances and correlation coefficients
4 Be able to calculate the mean, variance, and standard deviation for portfolios
5 Understand the concepts of systematic (market-related) risk and nonsystematic risk and how diversification can reduce the nonsystematic risk of a portfolio
6 Develop an understanding of the magnitude and variability of historical rates of return generated by stocks and bonds

In order to objectively evaluate and compare various investment alternatives, we need to be able to quantify their risk and return characteristics. Simple generalities, such as "the semiconductors are risky stocks," or "small company stocks provide high returns," are not adequate for making investment decisions. How risky is "risky"? How high is "high"? Fortunately finance has made considerable progress in quantifying the concepts risk and return.

3-1 MEASURING HISTORICAL (EX POST) RETURNS

To properly measure the return generated by an investment, one must account for both the price change and the cash flow derived from the asset during the period the asset was held. In the case of common stocks, the analyst must consider the change in price and the dividends received. To illustrate, consider the data for the common stock of Boeing Company for the year 1984.

Boeing price as of December 31, 1983	$29 ⅛
Boeing price as of December 31, 1984	$37 ¾
Dividends paid during 1984	$ 0.93

Letting r stand for the rate of return on investment, P stand for price, and D stand for dividend, the return from holding Boeing Stock during 1984 is calculated[1] as:

---

[1]This calculation assumes, for the sake of simplicity, that a single dividend of $0.93 was received at the end of 1984. Actually, Boeing paid four quarterly dividends of $0.23 each. The method of adjusting for nonannual payments is discussed in Chapter 9.

$$r_{1984} = \frac{(P_{1984} - P_{1983}) + D_{1984}}{P_{1983}}$$

$$r_{1984} = \frac{37.75 - 29.13 + .93}{29.13} = .328 = 32.8\%$$

Thus, for stocks the return for a particular time period is equal to the sum of the price change plus dividends received, divided by the price at the beginning of the time period. For bonds, the holding-period return is equal to the price change plus interest received, divided by the beginning price.

In general, for the ith asset and the tth time period,

$$r_{it} = \frac{(P_{it} - P_{i,t-1}) + D_{it}}{P_{i,t-1}} \tag{3-1}$$

The subscript notation used in Equation (3-1) might seem complex at first. However, it is really a very useful method of keeping track of variables associated with different assets and different time periods. For example, consider Table 3-1, which lists hypothetical returns for three different stocks and 10 time periods. One can see that the return for the second stock in the fourth time period $r_{2,4}$ was -2%; the return for the third stock in the fifth time period $r_{3,5}$ was 32%; and so forth.

To compute the ex post, or historical, average return for the ith stock, we use the standard formula for computing arithmetic means:[2]

$$\bar{r}_i = \frac{1}{n}(r_{i1} + r_{i2} + \cdots + r_{in})$$

[2]In many cases, one is more interested in the geometric mean return rather than the arithmetic mean. The geometric mean is discussed in footnote 17 of this chapter, as well as in Chapter 8.

TABLE 3-1 HYPOTHETICAL EX POST RETURNS, PERCENT

Time period	Stock 1	Stock 2	Stock 3
1	10	11	-6
2	8	4	18
3	-4	-3	4
4	22	-2	-5
5	8	14	32
6	-11	-9	-7
7	14	15	24
8	12	13	-17
9	-9	-3	2
10	12	4	27
$\bar{r}_i$	6.20	4.40	7.20
σ^2	114.40	72.49	283.73
σ_i	10.70	8.51	16.84

where n equals the number of time periods. This can be written more succinctly as

$$\bar{r}_i = \frac{1}{n} \sum_{t=1}^{n} r_{it} \qquad (3\text{-}2h)$$

where the notation

$$\sum_{t=1}^{n} r_{it}$$

means that for the ith stock, the returns for time periods $t = 1, 2, \ldots, n$ are to be added. For example, the mean return for the first stock $\bar{r}_1$ in Table 3-1 is computed as

$$\bar{r}_1 = \frac{1}{10} \sum_{t=1}^{10} r_{1t} = \frac{1}{10}(10\% + 8\% + \cdots + 12\%)$$

$$\bar{r}_1 = \frac{1}{10}(62\%) = 6.20\%$$

Thus, calculating the arithmetic mean for historical returns is a relatively straightforward process. [Note that when numbering equations we will use the letter h, for example, $(3\text{-}2h)$, to indicate that we are dealing with historical returns; later we will use the letter e to denote equations dealing with expected returns.]

3-2 THE STANDARD DEVIATION

Risk has many connotations. Farming might be considered a risky business because of the large *changes* in farm product prices from year to year. Prospecting for gold might be considered risky because of the low *probability* of success.

In the field of investments, the concept of risk has slowly changed over many years. In the early 1900s analysts tended to concentrate on balance sheets in assessing the risk of securities—the more debt, the riskier the security. In the 1962 edition of *Security Analysis*, Graham, Dodd, and Cottle[3] defined one measure of risk as a "margin of safety." Their margin of safety was based not on financial statements but rather on the difference between market prices and "intrinsic values." Basically, they argued that the analyst should independently estimate the intrinsic value for the security without considering the current market price.[4] The difference between the intrinsic value and the current market price represented the margin of safety and a measure of risk—the larger the margin of safety, the lower the risk. At the same time, Graham and Dodd recognized the importance of the individual security's contribution to the risk of a

---

[3]B. Graham, D. Dodd, and S. Cottle, *Security Analysis*, McGraw-Hill, New York, 1962, p. 54.

[4]"Intrinsic value" can be described as the value an analyst would place on a security based on its earning power and financial characteristics, without regard to its current market price. See Graham, Dodd, and Cottle, p. 34.

well-diversified portfolio.[5] However, it was the work of Markowitz[6] and the subsequent development of the capital-asset pricing model which more clearly defined risk for portfolios and for individual securities.

Today, as a starting point, we tend to associate investment risk with the *variability of rates of return*. The more variable the return, the more risky the investment. The standard deviation represents one measure of this variability of returns. The notation σ (pronounced "sigma") will be used to represent the standard deviation:[7]

$$\text{Standard deviation} = \sigma$$

Another measure of variability which is directly related to the standard deviation and is of considerable importance in finance is the variance. The variance is simply the standard deviation squared, or the standard deviation is the square root of the variance:

$$\text{Variance} = \sigma^2$$

Equation (3-3h) is used to calculate the variance of historical returns:

$$\sigma^2 = \frac{1}{n-1} \sum_{t=1}^{n} (r_{it} - \bar{r}_i)^2 \tag{3-3h}$$

By taking the positive square root of the variance, one arrives at the standard deviation.

$$\sigma = \sqrt{\sigma^2} = \sqrt{\frac{1}{n-1} \sum (r_{it} - \bar{r}_i)^2} \tag{3-4h}$$

Let's examine these equations in more detail. To calculate the variance, one first calculates the average or mean return ($\bar{r}_i$). Then the difference between the return for each time period and the average return is determined. These differences, or *deviations from the average*, are squared[8] and added together. This sum is then divided by $n-1$

---

[5]Graham, Dodd, and Cottle, p. 55.

[6]H. Markowitz, "Portfolio Selection," *Journal of Finance* (March 1952) pp. 77–91.

[7]There are other measures of variability, such as the range, semivariance, and mean absolute deviation, which might be considered as a measure of risk. (See W. Sharpe, *Investments*, 2d ed., Prentice-Hall, Englewood Cliffs, N.J., 1981, pp. 119–122, for a discussion of these statistics.) In general σ is preferable analytically because knowledge of σ allows one to make probability statements for most types of distributions. Perhaps more importantly, as Sharpe (p. 121) notes: "The standard deviation of a portfolio's return can be determined from (among other things) the standard deviations of the returns of its component securities, no matter what the distributions. No other relationship of comparable simplicity exists for most other variability measures." Thus, there are a number of reasons for choosing σ as a measure of risk.

[8]The reason the deviations are squared is that the sum of the deviations will always equal zero, as the positive deviations cancel out the negative deviations. By squaring the deviations, a positive variance will always obtain.

(the number of observations minus 1).[9] Thus the variance can be thought of as the average square deviation from the mean return.

To illustrate how the variance is calculated, consider stock 1 in Table 3-1:

$$\sigma_1^2 = \frac{1}{10 - 1} \sum_{t=1}^{10} (r_{1t} - \bar{r}_1)^2$$

$$\sigma_1^2 = \frac{1}{9} [(10\% - 6.2\%)^2 + (8\% - 6.2\%)^2 + \cdots + (12\% - 6.2\%)^2]$$

$$\sigma_1^2 = \frac{1}{9} (1029.60) = 114.40$$

The standard deviation, which is the square root of the variance, turns out to be 10.70%.[10]

$$\sigma = \sqrt{\sigma^2} = \sqrt{114.40} = 10.70\%$$

Thus, *one can think of σ as the average deviation from the mean return*. Intuitively, one might consider this a reasonable measure of the variability, or risk, of a security.

When an investor is deciding whether or not to purchase a particular stock or bond, the asset's historical mean and standard deviation of return are certainly valuable information. However, the crucial set of information is the investor's *expectation* as to the *future* returns the asset may generate. For example, an investor may feel that there is a probability of .4 (a 40% chance) that oil prices may rise, in which case the investor expects Exxon's common stock to provide a 20% return. This same investor may associate a probability of .6 with the scenario that oil prices will fall, in which case he expects Exxon to provide a 6% return. Given these expectations, the investor will decide whether or not to purchase Exxon. *Thus, expectations about the future are the primary driving force behind security prices.* And it is possible, at least conceptually, to describe these expectations in terms of *probability distributions*, which is the subject of the next section.

Before continuing, you should be able to calculate the mean, variance, and standard deviation for ex post returns. As a check, see if you can calculate $\bar{r}$ and σ for stocks 2 and 3 in Table 3-1.

---

[9]When the observations (in this case, the returns) are considered to be a sample from the total population of observations, dividing by $n - 1$ provides an unbiased estimate of the true population variance and standard deviation. (See any textbook on statistics for a discussion of this.) If observations represent the entire population, the sum of the squared deviations is divided by n. Since in investments we are almost always sampling, $n - 1$ will be used in this text to calculate the variance and standard deviation, unless otherwise noted.

[10]If one expresses returns in decimal form (for example, .062 instead of 6.2%), σ will also be measured in decimal form (i.e., 0.1070 instead of 10.70%).

3-3 QUANTIFYING EX ANTE (EXPECTED) RISK AND RETURN

Suppose an analyst believes that there are four scenarios which describe the possible future "states of the world." One scenario is that there will be a recession plagued by high interest rates; a second scenario is that there will be a recession, but interest rates will fall; a third possibility is that there will be an economic boom accompanied by high interest rates; and the fourth possible state of the world is that there will be a boom in the economy coupled with low interest rates and also an oil shortage. The analyst associates a probability of .20 for the first scenario occurring, .25 for the second, .30 for the third, and .25 for the fourth. Since the probabilities sum to 1.00, the analyst has accounted for, in her own mind, all possible states of the world.

This particular analyst is responsible for following three stocks, denoted stocks 4, 5, and 6. After carefully considering the impact of each of these possible states of the world on the economic fortunes of these companies, she makes projections about the future dividend payments and future stock prices and arrives at expected rates of returns for each of these three stocks, *conditional upon* the four different states of the world. These expectations are presented in Table 3-2. We use the subscript s to denote which

TABLE 3-2   AN ILLUSTRATION OF EX ANTE PROBABILITY DISTRIBUTIONS

State of the world(s)	π_s	Conditional returns, % $r_{4,s}$	$r_{5,s}$	$r_{6,s}$
1. Recession and high interest rates	.20	− 18	− 13	− 4
2. Recession and low interest rates	.25	+ 16	+ 16	− 2
3. Boom and high interest rates	.30	+ 12	+ 32	+ 21
4. Boom, low interest rates, and oil shortage	.25	+ 40	+ 12	+ 20

Individual stock statistics	Stock 4	Stock 5	Stock 6
σ_i^2	376.00	245.00	136.50
σ_i, %	19.39	15.65	11.68
$E(r_i)$, %	14.00	14.00	10.00

Portfolio statistics	4 and 5	4 and 6	5 and 6	4, 5, and 6	4, 5, and 6
W_i, W_j	1/2,1/2	1/2,1/2	1/2,1/2	1/3,1/3,1/3	1/6,3/6,2/6
Cov_{ij}	150.00	142.00	124.00		
ρ_{ij}	.49	.63	.68		
σ_p^2	230.25	199.12	157.38	176.61	168.97
σ_p, %	15.17	14.11	12.55	13.29	13.00
$E(r_p)$, %	14.00	12.00	12.00	12.67	12.67

state of the world the return is conditional upon. For example, the conditional returns for stock 4 are denoted $r_{4,s}$. The specific return anticipated for stock 4, conditional upon the second scenario (recession and low interest rates), is denoted $r_{4,2}$ and is equal to $+16\%$, with an associated probability of .25.

To calculate the mean, or *expected value*, of these returns we use Equation (3-2e).

$$E(r_i) = \sum_{s=1}^{n} r_{is}\pi_s \qquad (3\text{-}2e)$$

where π_s is the probability of the s state of the world—for our purposes, the probability of a certain economic scenario occurring. For example, the expected return for stock 4 is:

$$E(r_4) = (-18\%)(.2) + (16\%)(.25) + (12\%)(.3) + (40\%)(.25)$$
$$E(r_4) = 14.00\%$$

Thus, the mean (expected value) of ex ante returns is simply a weighted average of the conditional returns where the weights are the probabilities of occurrence for each state of the world. This is similar to the mean, or average value, for historical (ex post) data, except that with historical data the relative frequency of each observation is used as the weight. (In the preceding section, the relative frequency for each return was $1/n$, or 1 out of 10 years.)

The variance of ex ante data is calculated according to Equation (3-3e):

$$\sigma_i^2 = \sum_{s=1}^{n} [r_{is} - E(r_i)]^2 \pi_s \qquad (3\text{-}3e)$$

For example, the variance for stock 4 is calculated as follows:

$$\sigma_4^2 = (-18\% - 14\%)^2(.2) + (16\% - 14\%)^2(.25)$$
$$+ (12\% - 14\%)^2(.3) + (40\% - 14\%)^2 (.25)$$
$$\sigma_4^2 = 376.00$$

Since the standard deviation is the square root of the variance, σ is calculated as

$$\sigma_4 = \sqrt{376.00} = 19.39\%$$

Thus, the ex ante standard deviation can be thought of as *a weighted average of the potential deviations from the expected return*. This, intuitively, would seem to be a reasonable measure of risk.

While investors may not go through this relatively explicit procedure of estimating returns and variances, they must have some expectations as to future returns. Why else would they buy a security? Why else would they postpone consumption if they didn't expect some positive rate of return on their investment? And they must have at least some subjective (if not explicit) measure as to how confident (how certain) they are about these future returns. A probability distribution (such as those in Table 3-2) with its expected return, associated variance, and standard deviation of return, is just one way of mathematically formalizing this procedure.

> Before continuing, you should be able to calculate the mean, variance, and standard deviation for ex ante returns. As a check, see if you can calculate $E(r_i)$ and σ for stocks 5 and 6 in Table 3-2.

The equations for quantifying the return, variance, and standard deviation of *individual* security returns for both ex post and ex ante data are summarized in Table 3-3. Now let's turn our attention to the problem of how to measure the risk and return of portfolios.

3-4 QUANTIFYING PORTFOLIO RISK AND RETURN

The foundation for portfolio theory can be traced to the 1952 paper published by Harry Markowitz.[11] Markowitz made the deceptively simple observation that investors do *not* necessarily try to maximize return. If investors were only interested in maximizing return, they would tend to hold only the *single* asset which they felt offered the highest future return. But instead, we know by simple observation that many investors hold portfolios of securities. The explanation for this behavior is that investors are concerned with both return and risk, and as we shall see, *diversification can reduce risk without any loss of return.*

Table 3-3   The return for a portfolio is simply a weighted average of the returns of the securities in the portfolio. For example, for ex post data the portfolio return for a particular time period is calculated as

[11]H. Markowitz, op. cit.

TABLE 3-3   QUANTIFYING INDIVIDUAL SECURITY RETURNS

Historical (ex post)		Expected (ex ante)	
Arithmetic mean return:		Expected return:	
$\bar{r}_i = \dfrac{1}{n} \displaystyle\sum_{t=1}^{n} r_{it}$	(3-2h)	$E(r_i) = \displaystyle\sum_{s=1}^{n} r_{is}\pi_s$	(3-2e)
Variance:		Variance:	
$\sigma_i^2 = \dfrac{1}{n-1} \displaystyle\sum_{t=1}^{n} (r_{it} - \bar{r}_i)^2$	(3-3h)	$\sigma_i^2 = \displaystyle\sum_{s=1}^{n} [r_{is} - E(r_i)]^2 \pi_s$	(3-3e)
Standard deviation:		Standard deviation:	
$\sigma_i = \sqrt{\dfrac{1}{n-1} \displaystyle\sum_{t=1}^{n} (r_{it} - \bar{r}_i)^2}$	(3-4h)	$\sigma_i = \sqrt{\displaystyle\sum_{s=1}^{n} [r_{is} - E(r_i)]^2 \pi_s}$	(3-4e)

r_{it} = historical (ex post) return generated by the *i*th stock in time period *t*.
r_{is} = expected (ex ante) return for the *i*th stock assuming the *s* state of the world occurs.
π_s = probability that the *s* state of the world will occur.

$$r_{pt} = \sum_{i=1}^{n} r_{it} W_{it} \tag{3-5h}$$

where W_{it} is the market value (at the beginning of the time period) of the ith asset divided by the market value of the entire portfolio, i.e., the asset's "weight" in the portfolio. For ex ante data,

$$E(r_p) = \sum_{i=1}^{n} E(r_i) W_i \tag{3-5e}$$

One might suspect that a portfolio's return is simply a weighted average of the returns associated with the individual stocks in the portfolio, and an example will demonstrate that this is, in fact, the case. Consider a portfolio consisting of two assets, stock A and stock B. At the beginning of the year the market value of stock A was $60 and the market value of stock B was $40. Thus, the total value of the portfolio was $100. Neither stock pays dividends, and at the end of the year stock A was worth $66 and stock B was worth $48, making the portfolio worth a total of $114. Thus, during this year the return on stock A was 10%, stock B's return was 20%, and the portfolio's return, which can be calculated in the standard way using Equation (3-1), was 14%:

$$r_{pt} = \frac{P_{pt} - P_{p,\,t-1}}{P_{p,t-1}} = \frac{\$114 - 100}{\$100} = 14\%$$

These results can be summarized as shown below:

	Stock A	Stock B	Portfolio
Beginning value	$60	$40	$100
Ending value	$66	$48	$114
Rate of return	10%	20%	14%

Now, to demonstrate the validity of Equation (3-5h), note that each stock's weight is calculated as its value at the beginning of the period divided by the beginning value of the portfolio. Thus, for stock A, $W_{at} = \$60/\$100 = .6$, and for stock B, $W_{bt} = \$40/\$100 = .4$. Using these weights, the portfolio return can be calculated, using Equation (3-5h), as follows:

$$r_{pt} = r_{at} W_{at} + r_{bt} W_{bt} = 10\%(.6) + 20\%(.4) = 14\%$$

This confirms that portfolio returns are simply a weighted average of the returns associated with the individual securities in the portfolio.

The variance of a portfolio is not so easy to calculate. The general equation for the variance of a portfolio is Equation (3-6),

$$\sigma_p^2 = \sum_{i=1}^{n} \sum_{j=1}^{n} \text{Cov}_{ij} W_i W_j \tag{3-6}$$

where Cov_{ij} represents the covariance between the returns of the ith and jth assets. (The term covariance will be defined in the next paragraph.) The double summation signs

$$\left(\sum_{i=1}^{n} \sum_{j=1}^{n} \right)$$

mean that all possible covariance terms are to be added. Since Equation (3-6) employs rather formidable notation, Equation (3-7), which is equivalent to (3-6), will be used instead.

$$\sigma_p^2 = \sum_{i=1}^{n} \sigma_i^2 W_i^2 + 2 \overset{*}{\sum} \text{Cov}_{ij} W_i W_j \tag{3-7}$$

The first half of (3-7),

$$\sum_{i=1}^{n} \sigma_i^2 W_i^2$$

indicates that the variance of each asset times its weight squared are to be added. The second half of Equation (3-7),

$$2 \overset{*}{\sum} \text{Cov}_{ij} W_i W_j$$

indicates that all the *unique* covariance terms (multiplied by the respective weights) are to be added and then multiplied by 2. The "*" above the summation sign indicates that there are $(n^2 - n)/2$ *unique* covariance terms for a portfolio of n securities.[12]

Table 3-4 summarizes the necessary mathematics for calculating portfolio returns and variances. The last two equations in this table are used to calculate covariances and correlation coefficients. An illustration will help explain covariance. Consider again the three-stock example in Table 3-2. The calculation of the expected covariance of 4 and 6 is as follows:

---

[12] As indicated by Equation (3-6), the variance of a portfolio is equal to the weighted sum of all possible covariances. In a portfolio of n securities, there are n^2 possible pairwise combinations, or covariances. For our three-stock example (4, 5, and 6) in Table 3-2, there would be 3^2, or nine possible pairwise combinations—4 and 4, 4 and 5, 4 and 6, 5 and 4, 5 and 5, 5 and 6, 6 and 4, 6 and 5, 6 and 6.

However, the covariance of an asset with itself (for example, 4 and 4) is its variance—this can be seen by comparing Equation (3-8e), which defines covariance, with Equation (3-3e), which defines variance. Thus, the first half of Equation (3-7) accounts for the n variance terms.

Also, in a portfolio of n securities, there will only be "*" *unique covariance terms, where* $* = (n^2 - n)/2$. In the three-stock example, the *unique* covariance terms will be 4 and 5, 4 and 6, and 5 and 6, since the covariance of 4 with 5 is the same as the covariance of 5 with 4, etc. The second half of Equation (3-7) accounts for two times the number of unique covariances. Therefore, Equation (3-7) includes the three variances and two times the three unique covariances, accounting for the total of nine ($n^2 = 9$) possible covariance terms. Thus, Equation (3-7) is equal to Equation (3-6).

TABLE 3-4 QUANTIFYING PORTFOLIO RETURNS

Historical (ex post)	Anticipated (ex ante)
Historical holding period return:	Expected holding period return:
$$r_{pt} = \sum_{i=1}^{n} r_{it} W_{it} \qquad (3\text{-}5h)$$	$$E(r_p) = \sum_{i=1}^{n} E(r_i) W_i \qquad (3\text{-}5e)$$
Variance:	Variance:
$$\sigma_p^2 = \sum_{i=1}^{n} \sum_{j=1}^{n} \text{Cov}_{ij} W_i W_j \qquad (3\text{-}6)$$	$$\sigma_p^2 = \sum_{i=1}^{n} \sum_{j=1}^{n} \text{Cov}_{ij} W_i W_j \qquad (3\text{-}6)$$
$$\sigma_p^2 = \sum_{i=1}^{n} \sigma_i^2 W_i^2 + 2 \overset{*}{\sum} \text{Cov}_{ij} W_i W_j \qquad (3\text{-}7)$$	$$\sigma_p^2 = \sum_{i=1}^{n} \sigma_i^2 W_i^2 + 2 \overset{*}{\sum} \text{Cov}_{ij} W_i W_j \qquad (3\text{-}7)$$
Covariance:	Covariance:
$$\text{Cov}_{ij} = \frac{1}{n-1} \sum_{t=1}^{n} (r_{it} - \bar{r}_i)(r_{jt} - \bar{r}_j) \qquad (3\text{-}8h)$$	$$\text{Cov}_{ij} = \sum_{s=1}^{n} [r_{is} - E(r_i)] [r_{js} - E(r_j)] \pi_s \qquad (3\text{-}8e)$$
Correlation coefficient:	Correlation coeff cient:
$$\rho_{ij} = \frac{\text{Cov}_{ij}}{\sigma_i \, \sigma_j} \qquad (3\text{-}9)$$	$$\rho_{ij} = \frac{\text{Cov}_{ij}}{\sigma_i \, \sigma_j} \qquad (3\text{-}9)$$

W_i = weight of the ith asset, defined as the market value of the ith asset divided by the market value of the portfolio.

$\overset{*}{\sum} \text{Cov}_{ij} W_i W_j$ = sum of the unique covariances (multiplied by their weights); when there are n assets in a portfolio, there are $(n^2 - n)/2$ unique covariances.

$$\text{Cov}_{4,6} = \sum_{s=1}^{4} [r_{4,s} - E(r_4)] [r_{6,s} - E(r_6)] \pi_s \qquad (3\text{-}8e)$$

$$= (-18\% - 14\%)(-4\% - 10\%)(.20) + (16\% - 14\%)(-2\% - 10\%)(.25)$$
$$+ (12\% - 14\%)(21\% - 10\%)(.30) + (40\% - 14\%)(20\% - 10\%)(.25)$$
$$\text{Cov}_{4,6} = 89.60 - 6.00 - 6.60 + 65.00 = 142.00$$

Note that *on average*, when the conditional return on 4 is greater than the expected return for 4, that is, when $r_{4,s} > E(r_4)$, the same is true for stock 6. Thus, the covariance is positive. If the opposite had been true—that is, if on average when the conditional return on 4 is above its expected value and for the same economic scenario the conditional return on 6 is below its expected value—then the covariance would be a negative number.

Equation (3-9) is used to calculate the correlation coefficient.

$$\rho_{ij} = \frac{\text{Cov}_{ij}}{\sigma_i \sigma_j} \qquad (3\text{-}9)$$

As one can see from Equation (3-9) the *correlation coefficient is simply the covariance standardized by dividing by the product of the two standard deviations of returns*. The calculation of the correlation coefficient for stocks 4 and 6 is as follows:

$$\rho_{4,6} = \frac{\text{Cov}_{4,6}}{\sigma_4 \sigma_6} = \frac{142}{(19.39)(11.68)} = .63$$

This indicates that the returns generated by the two stocks are, on balance, positively correlated—but not perfectly correlated. As we shall see, the fact that the returns are not perfectly correlated ($\rho_{4,6} < +1$) will allow part of their variance to be diversified away with no loss of return.

The correlation coefficient has the interesting and useful property of always being between -1 and $+1$, with the sign depending upon whether the covariance is positive or negative. If the returns on two assets are perfectly, positively correlated, ρ_{ij} will equal $+1$; if the returns are perfectly, negatively correlated, ρ_{ij} will equal -1. If there is no correlation between two assets' returns, both Cov_{ij} and ρ_{ij} will equal zero.

Figure 3-1 illustrates how the returns of stocks with varying degrees of correlation would plot on a graph. Each point on a graph represents the returns for stocks i and j for a particular time period. Figure 3-1a represents a plot of the returns from two stocks which are perfectly, positively correlated. In this highly unusual case, the points all plot on a straight, upward-sloping line, indicating that when the return on stock i is high, the return on stock j is also high, and vice versa. Figure 3-1b represents the equally unlikely case of two sets of security returns being perfectly, negatively correlated. In this case, the returns plot on a straight but downward-sloping line—thus

FIGURE 3-1   Correlation of security returns. (a) Perfect, positive correlation. (b) Perfect, negative correlation. (c) No correlation. (d) Partial, positive correlation.

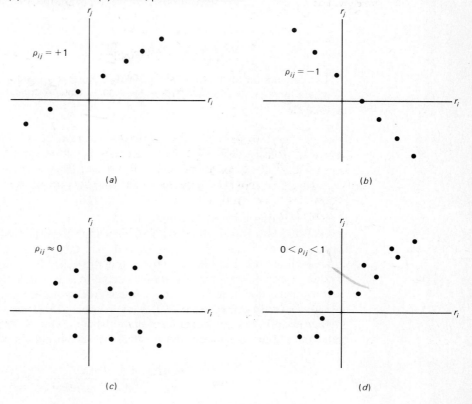

for a time period when the return on stock i is high, the return on stock j is low, etc. Figure 3-1c represents the case of no correlation. The observation points are scattered on the graph with no particular pattern. Thus, when the return on stock i is high, the return on stock j may be high, low, or anywhere in between. Finally, Figure 3-1d represents the more typical case where security returns are positively correlated, but not *perfectly* correlated. The return observations plot in an upward pattern, but not on a straight line. Thus, if the return on stock i is high, the return on stock j is also generally high, but one does not know *exactly* what r_j will be, given r_i.

Having determined the *unique* covariance terms, one can calculate the variance of the portfolio. For the three-stock portfolio consisting of 4, 5 and 6, $* = (n^2 - n)/2 = (9 - 3)/2 = 3$. Thus, there are three unique covariances, $\text{Cov}_{4,5}$, $\text{Cov}_{4,6}$, and $\text{Cov}_{5,6}$. Assuming equal weights ($W_4 = W_5 = W_6 = 1/3$), and using the data in Table 3-2, the ex ante variance is calculated as follows, using Equation (3-7):

$$
\begin{aligned}
\sigma_p^2 &= \sum_{i=1}^{n} \sigma_i^2 W_i^2 + 2 \sum^{*} \text{Cov}_{ij} W_{ij} \\
\sigma_p^2 &= \sigma_4^2 W_4^2 + \sigma_5^2 W_5^2 + \sigma_6^2 W_6^2 \\
&\quad + 2[\text{Cov}_{4,5} W_4 W_5 + \text{Cov}_{4,6} W_4 W_6 + \text{Cov}_{5,6} W_5 W_6] \\
&= (376.00)(1/3)^2 + (245.00)(1/3)^2 + (136.50)(1/3)^2 \\
&\quad + 2[(150.00)(1/3)(1/3) + (142.00)(1/3)(1/3) \\
&\quad + (124.00)(1/3)(1/3)] \\
\sigma_p^2 &= 41.77 + 27.22 + 15.17 + 2[46.22] = 176.61 \\
\sigma_p &= \sqrt{\sigma_p^2} = \sqrt{176.61} = 13.29\%
\end{aligned}
$$

The calculation of the expected portfolio return is straightforward. For the equal-weighted three-stock example, the expected return is calculated using Equation (3-5e) as follows:

$$
\begin{aligned}
E(r_p) &= \sum_{i=1}^{n} E(r_i) W_i \\
E(r_p) &= E(r_4) W_4 + E(r_5) W_5 + E(r_6) W_6 \\
E(r_p) &= (14\%)(1/3) + (14\%)(1/3) + (10\%)(1/3) = 12.67\%
\end{aligned}
$$

3-4-1 A Simple Proof of Equations (3-5e) and (3-7)   The portfolio's expected return could also be calculated by first calculating the conditional return for the port-folio, given each state of the world, and then taking the expected value of these conditional returns. Let's do this now in order to verify Equation (3-5e), which states that the expected return for a portfolio is equal to a weighted average of the expected returns for the stocks in the portfolio. In the process we can also verify that Equation (3-7) gives us the correct variance for a portfolio.

The portfolio's return conditional upon the first state of the world (recession and high interest rates) is a weighted average of the conditional returns for the three stocks:

$$
\begin{aligned}
r_{p1} &= r_{1,1} W_1 + r_{2,1} W_2 + r_{3,1} W_3 \\
&= -18\%(1/3) - 13\%(1/3) - 4\%(1/3) = -11.67\%
\end{aligned}
$$

In a similar fashion we can compute the portfolio's conditional return, given the second, third, and fourth states of the world as $r_{p2} = 10\%$, $r_{p3} = 21.67\%$, and $r_{p4} = 24\%$. Knowing the conditional returns and the probability of their occurrence (π_s), one can treat the portfolio as a single asset and compute its expected return by using Equation (3-2e):

$$
\begin{aligned}
E(r_p) &= \sum_{s=1}^{n} r_{ps}\pi_s \\
&= -11.67\%(.2) + 10\%(.25) + 21.67\%(.3) + 24\%(.25) \\
&= 12.67\%
\end{aligned}
$$

which is exactly the same answer we obtain using Equation (3-5e). Note that when Equation (3-5e) is used to calculate the portfolio's expected return, the conditional returns for the portfolio are not required.

In order to demonstrate that Equation (3-7) does, in fact, correctly compute the variance of a portfolio, consider the portfolio's conditional returns which we just calculated. Given these conditional returns, we can again treat the portfolio as a single asset and compute the variance in the conventional manner using Equation (3-3e):

$$
\begin{aligned}
\sigma_p^2 &= \sum_{s=1}^{n} [r_{ps} - E(r_p)]^2 \, \pi_s \\
&= (-11.67 - 12.67)^2 \, .2 + \cdots + (24 - 12.67)^2 \, .25 \\
&= 176.61
\end{aligned}
$$

Again, this is the same answer as was calculated previously using Equation (3-7). Thus, by using Equations (3-7) and (3-5e) we can calculate the variance and expected return for a portfolio *without* knowing the portfolio's conditional returns, as long as we know the expected returns, variances, and covariances for the individual securities in the portfolio.

> You have covered a lot of material in a relatively short space. Before continuing, you should be able to calculate the covariance and correlation between two securities and the expected return, variance, and standard deviation for a portfolio. As a check, calculate these statistics for stocks 4 and 5 in Table 3-2 using equal weights for the portfolio statistics.

Now that we have examined how to quantify the mean, or expected return, of a portfolio along with the variance and standard deviation, let's consider why investors hold portfolios.

3-5 PORTFOLIO THEORY AND THE BENEFITS OF DIVERSIFICATION

It is easy to see why diversification can reduce the variability of returns. Consider the hypothetical case of stocks A and B illustrated in Figure 3-2. The returns from both

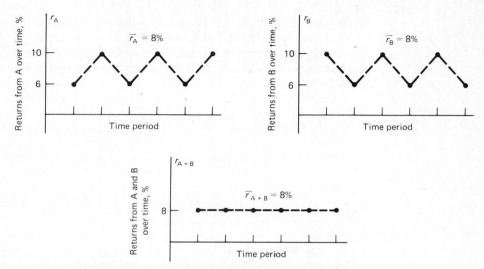

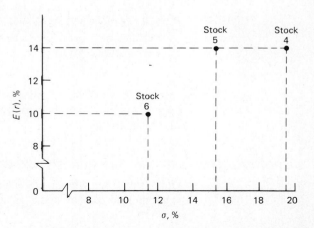

FIGURE 3-2   An example of perfectly negatively correlated returns and zero variance.

A and B vary between 6% and 10% and both average 8%. However, the two return streams are perfectly, negatively correlated. That is, when r_A = 10%, r_B = 6% and when r_A = 6%, r_B = 10%. Now, if one formed an equally weighted portfolio of A and B (W_A = W_B = 1/2), it is obvious that the portfolio return would *always* equal 8%. Thus, the variance of the portfolio would be *zero* and yet the return on the portfolio would equal the average return on the individual stocks.

Of course, this is a rather contrived example. Securities with perfectly, negatively correlated returns rarely, if ever, occur. A more realistic example would be stocks 4, 5, and 6 listed in Table 3-2. Figure 3-3 plots the expected return against the standard deviation of return for each of the three stocks. Stock 5 is said to "dominate" stock 4—that is, for the same level of expected return (14%), stock 5 has a lower standard

FIGURE 3-3   A plot of risk and return for stocks 4 and 5.

deviation of return (15.65% vs. 19.39%). This raises an interesting question: Why would anyone with this set of expectations concerning stocks 4 and 5 want to own stock 4? Of course, this is where the benefits of diversification come into play.

In Figure 3-4, stocks 4, 5, and 6 are plotted in addition to equally weighted portfolios of 4 and 5 and 5 and 6. (All the portfolio statistics are reported in Table 3-2.) Note in Figure 3-4 that 4, 5, and the portfolio of 4 and 5 all have the same expected return of 14%. But the standard deviation for the portfolio of 4 and 5 is less than the standard deviation for either 4 or 5 alone. By combining the two stocks 4 and 5 into a portfolio, the investor is able to "diversify away" some of the variability *without any loss of return*. Thus, for less risk the portfolio provides the same return.

As another example of the benefits of diversification consider the equally weighted portfolio consisting of stocks 5 and 6. Since the return for any portfolio is simply a weighted average of the individual security returns, the expected return for this portfolio is 12%, calculated as (1/2)(14%) + (1/2)(10%). But the standard deviation of a portfolio is *not* simply a weighted average of the individual securities' standard deviations (except for the unusual case when $\rho_{ij} = +1$).[13] Portfolio 5 and 6 plots to the left of a straight line connecting 5 and 6—again, there is less risk than a simple linear (weighted-average) combination would suggest. In general, since security returns are not perfectly, positively correlated, diversification tends to reduce or "push to the

[13]For the special case where security returns are perfectly, positively correlated ($\rho_{ij} = +1$), the standard deviation of the portfolio will be a simple weighted average of the standard deviations of the securities in the portfolio. This is easy to see for the two-security case—for example, 5 and 6. By substituting $\text{Cov}_{5,6} = \rho_{5,6}\sigma_5\sigma_6 = (1)\sigma_5\sigma_6$, the standard deviation of 5 and 6 is

$$\sigma_p^2 = \sigma_5^2 W_5^2 + \sigma_6^2 W_6^2 + (2)(1)\sigma_5\sigma_6 W_5 W_6$$
$$\sigma_p^2 = (\sigma_5 W_5 + \sigma_6 W_6)^2$$
$$\sigma_p = \sigma_5 W_5 + \sigma_6 W_6$$

Thus, the portfolio standard deviation is a linear function of the standard deviations of the individual securities in the portfolio when $\rho_{5,6} = +1$. In this special (and highly unusual) case, there is no benefit to diversification. Since the portfolio return is also a linear function of the individual stock returns, the portfolio will plot along a straight line connecting 5 and 6 on the return, standard deviation graph.

FIGURE 3-4   A plot of risk and return for portfolios.

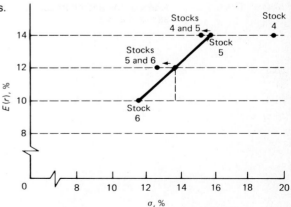

left'' the risk of potential investment opportunities available to investors, as illustrated in Figure 3-4.

We should also point out that securities in a portfolio do not necessarily have to be equally weighted. For example, in Table 3-2 statistics are reported for two different three-stock portfolios. One portfolio is equally weighted between stocks 4, 5, and 6. The other portfolio also consists of the same three stocks, but weights are arbitrarily set at 1/6, 3/6, and 2/6, respectively. In this particular case, both portfolios have the same expected return (12.67%), but they have slightly different standard deviations— 13.29% vs. 13.00%.

As one considers different weighting schemes and more securities, the *efficient portfolios* (those with the lowest standard deviation for a given level of return) plot farther and farther to the left on the expected return, standard deviation graph. That is, for a given level of return, the variability of return (σ) is reduced *because the returns generated by the securities held in the portfolio are not perfectly correlated.*

The risk-reducing benefit of diversification can be summed up by Figure 3-5, which shows the results of naive diversification using ''real-world'' data. (The term naive diversification means to diversify by simply picking stocks at random.) In this study by Evans and Archer,[14] portfolios were formed by randomly selecting NYSE stocks. Note in Figure 3-5 that as the number of securities in the portfolio is increased, the portfolio's standard deviation decreases until only what is termed *systematic* or *market-related risk* is left. As the number of stocks in the portfolio is increased, *the nonsystematic or residual risk of the individual securities is diversified away*, leaving only the market-related risk.

[14] J. L. Evans and S. H. Archer, ''Diversification and the Reduction of Dispersion: An Empirical Analysis,'' *Journal of Finance* (December 1968).

FIGURE 3-5   Reducing risk by diversification. [*Source: J. L. Evans and S. H. Archer, "Diversification and the Reduction of Dispersion: An Empirical Analysis,"* Journal of Finance *(December 1968), pp. 761–767.*]

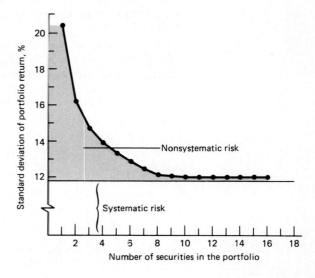

More specifically, the Evans and Archer study used as a data base the semiannual returns from 470 NYSE firms over the time period 1958–1967. The average standard deviation of returns for a single stock was approximately 21%, as can be seen in Figure 3-5. When portfolios of two randomly selected stocks were formed, the average standard deviation for these two-stock portfolios was approximately 16%. Similarly, the average standard deviation for three-stock portfolios was less than 15%, etc. Most of the benefit from diversification was achieved by the use of eight-stock portfolios, since the standard deviation leveled out at approximately 12% as the size of the portfolios was increased beyond eight. When all 470 stocks were grouped together into one portfolio, the standard deviation was 11.6%. Thus, for the stocks in this study, using semiannual returns, the *total risk* σ for an individual stock was about 21% on average. Of this 21%, approximately 9% represented nonsystematic risk which could be eliminated by diversification and the remaining 12% represented systematic risk which could not be diversified away.

Since the nonsystematic risk of individual securities can be eliminated by diversification, one might suspect that the total risk σ of individual securities is *not* what investors price in the marketplace. Rather, investors should be most concerned with the systematic, or market-related, risk of individual securities. Perhaps the most important contribution of the capital asset pricing model (CAPM) is the idea that market risk is the relevant measure of risk for securities. But the CAPM and its implications for investors is the subject of the next chapter.

3-6 THE HISTORICAL RECORD

It is important for the serious investor to develop a "feel for the numbers." That is, in addition to understanding how rates of return are calculated, it is important to have some idea as to the magnitude and distribution of actual returns generated by stocks, bonds, and other investment alternatives. Table 3-5 lists return statistics for the 20 stocks in the Dow Jones Industrial Average which have a continuous price record on the Chicago Center for Research in Security Prices (CRSP) tapes during the time period 1926–1978.

The first column in Table 3-5 lists the arithmetic mean return for the 636 months during this time period. For example, Allied Chemical generated a mean monthly return of 0.86% with an associated standard deviation of 7.45%. For these 20 companies, the average monthly return ranged from a low of 0.71% for Woolworth to a high of 1.52% for IBM. The third and fourth columns list the minimum and maximum return for any *single* month generated by each company. For example, the minimum return generated by Allied Chemical was a negative 26.68% while the maximum return was 38.93%. Considering all 20 stocks, Bethlehem Steel generated the most volatile return series with the largest standard deviation (10.94%), the most negative return for any single month (−38.46%), and the largest positive return for any single month (a whopping 99.04%).[15] Suffice it to say that owning Bethlehem Steel would have been exciting indeed over the years.

[15]As a historical anecdote, investors holding Bethlehem Steel stock suffered the 38.46% loss in May 1932. One year later, in May 1933, they enjoyed the 99.04% gain.

TABLE 3-5 SUMMARY STATISTICS, 20 INDIVIDUAL STOCKS, 1926–1978

Company*	636 monthly returns, %				53 annual returns, %			
	Arithmetic mean	Standard deviation	Minimum	Maximum	Arithmetic mean	Standard deviation	Minimum	Maximum
Allied Chemical (ACD)	-0.86	7.45	−26.68	38.93	9.78	27.83	−58.72	90.42
American Brands (AMB)	0.94	6.28	−29.47	37.98	11.09	22.08	−38.98	58.95
American Can (AC)	0.79	6.69	−33.74	48.74	9.62	24.16	−42.68	90.06
AT&T (T)	0.75	4.43	−22.47	27.58	9.57	16.38	−30.57	58.83
Bethlehem Steel (BS)	1.26	10.94	−38.46	99.04	14.64	38.03	−58.60	150.85
Du Pont (DD)	1.10	7.54	−37.19	56.62	15.31	35.51	−39.32	166.03
Eastman Kodak (EK)	1.02	6.51	−33.21	25.42	13.58	25.87	−44.40	72.85
Exxon (XON)	1.04	6.48	−27.49	36.95	12.98	24.23	−37.65	76.22
General Electric (GE)	1.07	8.36	−35.51	56.00	12.32	26.87	−44.88	76.05
General Foods (GF)	0.85	6.70	−33.87	31.47	9.72	21.21	−28.58	63.24
General Motors (GM)	1.36	8.65	−34.38	86.67	20.45	44.66	−48.77	186.43
IBM (IBM)	1.52	6.56	−22.92	35.11	21.01	30.57	−32.16	131.97
International Harvester (HR)	1.13	9.09	−34.46	68.35	13.26	31.07	−48.24	92.86
Owens-Illinois (OI)	0.91	7.59	−27.55	37.53	11.27	31.69	−33.40	150.79
Sears, Roebuck (S)	1.12	8.63	−37.71	60.49	15.20	36.20	−47.46	122.22
Standard Oil of California (SO)	1.02	6.81	−25.93	39.43	12.44	25.26	−41.31	74.93
Texaco (TX)	1.10	7.51	−36.45	46.67	13.28	26.70	−57.09	91.02
U.S. Steel (X)	0.90	9.41	−31.94	70.32	11.78	34.37	−70.53	97.72
Westinghouse (WX)	1.02	9.68	−34.42	73.08	12.91	37.44	−73.36	172.16
Woolworth (Z)	0.71	7.19	−32.37	35.20	9.12	31.92	−44.47	153.52
Average for all 20 companies	1.02	7.62	−31.81	50.58	12.97	29.60	−46.06	108.86

*Stock-ticker symbol in parentheses.
Source: Computed from CRSP tape data for the 20 Dow Jones Industrial stocks which have a complete price record for the period 1926–1978.

The last four columns of Table 3-5 present annual return data. As one would expect, the means for the annual returns are greater than for the monthly returns, but so too is the variability of returns. The means of the annual returns varied from a low of 9.12% for Woolworth to a high of 21.01% for IBM. The standard deviations of the annual returns for the 20 stocks varied from a low of 16.38% for AT&T (one might expect that AT&T would be a "stable" stock) to a high of 44.66% for General Motors. Taking all 20 stocks as a whole, the average annual return was 12.97%, while the average standard deviation of annual returns was 29.60%.

One should bear in mind that the statistics reported in Table 3-5 are presented here to help the reader develop a "feel" for the size and variability of historical *individual* stock returns. Because the fortunes of individual companies may change radically over time, ex post return data may be of little help in forecasting future returns for individual securities, other than providing a possible guide as to an upper and lower range for the forecast—a forecast of greater than 20% per year for a long time period should probably be viewed with extreme caution since IBMs do not come along very often.

Table 3-6 presents data on annual returns generated by five different types of assets and the inflation rate, as reported by Ibbotson and Sinquefield.[16] As an index for the

[16]*Stocks, Bonds, Bills, and Inflation: 1986 Yearbook*, Ibbotson Associates, Chicago, 1986.

TABLE 3-6   ANNUAL RATES OF RETURN AND CHANGES IN THE CPI, 1926–1985

Year	Common stocks	Small stocks	Long-term corporate bonds	Long-term goverment bonds	U.S. treasury bills	Consumer price index
1926	0.1162	0.0028	0.0737	0.0777	0.0327	−0.0149
1927	0.3749	0.2210	0.0744	0.0893	0.0312	−0.0208
1928	0.4361	0.3969	0.0284	0.0010	0.0324	−0.0097
1929	−0.0842	−0.5136	0.0327	0.0342	0.0475	0.0019
1930	−0.2490	−0.3815	0.0798	0.0466	0.0241	−0.0603
1931	−0.4334	−0.4975	−0.0185	−0.0531	0.0107	−0.0952
1932	−0.0819	−0.0539	0.1082	0.1684	0.0096	−0.1030
1933	0.5399	1.4287	0.1038	−0.0008	0.0030	0.0051
1934	−0.0144	0.2422	0.1384	0.1002	0.0016	0.0203
1935	0.4767	0.4019	0.0961	0.0498	0.0017	0.0299
1936	0.3392	0.6480	0.0674	0.0751	0.0018	0.0121
1937	−0.3503	−0.5801	0.0275	0.0023	0.0031	0.0310
1938	0.3112	0.3280	0.0613	0.0553	−0.0002	−0.0278
1939	−0.0041	0.0035	0.0397	0.0594	0.0002	−0.0048
1940	−0.0978	−0.0516	0.0339	0.0609	0.0000	0.0096
1941	−0.1159	−0.0900	0.0273	0.0093	0.0006	0.0972
1942	0.2034	0.4451	0.0260	0.0322	0.0027	0.0929
1943	0.2590	0.8837	0.0283	0.0208	0.0035	0.0316
1944	0.1975	0.5372	0.0473	0.0281	0.0033	0.0211
1945	0.3644	0.7361	0.0408	0.1073	0.0033	0.0225
1946	−0.0807	−0.1163	0.0172	−0.0010	0.0035	0.1817
1947	0.0571	0.0092	−0.0234	−0.0263	0.0050	0.0901
1948	0.0550	−0.0211	0.0414	0.0340	0.0081	0.0271
1949	0.1879	0.1975	0.0331	0.0645	0.0110	−0.0180
1950	0.3171	0.3875	0.0212	0.0006	0.0120	0.0579
1951	0.2402	0.0780	−0.0269	−0.0394	0.0149	0.0587
1952	0.1837	0.0303	0.0352	0.0116	0.0166	0.0088
1953	−0.0099	−0.0649	0.0341	0.0363	0.0182	0.0062
1954	0.5262	0.6058	0.0539	0.0719	0.0086	−0.0050
1955	0.3156	0.2044	0.0048	−0.0130	0.0157	0.0037
1956	0.0656	0.0428	−0.0681	−0.0559	0.0246	0.0286
1957	−0.1078	−0.1457	0.0871	0.0745	0.0314	0.0302
1958	0.4336	0.6489	−0.0222	−0.0610	0.0154	0.0176
1959	0.1195	0.1640	−0.0097	−0.0226	0.0295	0.0150
1960	0.0047	−0.0329	0.0907	0.1378	0.0266	0.0148
1961	0.2689	0.3209	0.0482	0.0097	0.0213	0.0067
1962	−0.0873	−0.1190	0.0795	0.0689	0.0273	0.0122
1963	0.2280	0.2357	0.0219	0.0121	0.0312	0.0165
1964	0.1648	0.2352	0.0477	0.0351	0.0354	0.0119
1965	0.1245	0.4175	−0.0046	0.0071	0.0393	0.0192
1966	−0.1006	−0.0701	0.0020	0.0365	0.0476	0.0335
1967	0.2398	0.8357	−0.0495	−0.0919	0.0421	0.0304
1968	0.1106	0.3597	0.0257	−0.0026	0.0521	0.0472
1969	−0.0850	−0.2505	−0.0809	−0.0508	0.0658	0.0611
1970	0.0401	−0.1743	0.1837	0.1210	0.0653	0.0549
1971	0.1431	0.1650	0.1101	0.1323	0.0439	0.0336
1972	0.1898	0.0443	0.0726	0.0568	0.0384	0.0341

TABLE 3-6 ANNUAL RATES OF RETURN AND CHANGES IN THE CPI, 1926–1985 (*Continued*)

Year	Common stocks	Small stocks	Long-term corporate bonds	Long-term goverment bonds	U.S. treasury bills	Consumer price index
1973	−0.1466	−0.3090	0.0114	−0.0111	0.0693	0.0880
1974	−0.2647	−0.1995	−0.0306	0.0435	0.0800	0.1220
1975	0.3720	0.5282	0.1464	0.0919	0.0580	0.0701
1976	0.2384	0.5738	0.1865	0.1675	0.0508	0.0481
1977	−0.0718	0.2538	0.0171	−0.0067	0.0512	0.0677
1978	0.0656	0.2346	−0.0007	−0.0116	0.0718	0.0903
1979	0.1844	0.4346	−0.0418	−0.0122	0.1038	0.1331
1980	0.3242	0.3988	−0.0262	−0.0395	0.1124	0.1240
1981	−0.0491	0.1388	−0.0096	0.0185	0.1471	0.0894
1982	0.2141	0.2801	0.4379	0.4035	0.1054	0.0387
1983	0.2251	0.3967	0.0470	0.0068	0.0880	0.0380
1984	0.0627	−0.0670	0.1639	0.1543	0.0985	0.0395
1985	0.3216	0.2466	0.3090	0.3097	0.0772	0.0377
Geometric mean	.098	.126	.048	.041	.034	.031
Arithmetic mean	.120	.183	.051	.044	.035	.032
Standard deviation	.212	.360	.083	.082	.034	.049

Source: *Stocks, Bonds, Bills, and Inflation: 1986 Yearbook*, Ibbotson Associates, Chicago, 1986, Exhibits 4 and 5.

common stock series, the Standard & Poor's 500 was used—the S&P 500 is a portfolio of 500 large New York Stock Exchange stocks. Note that while the arithmetic mean annual return generated by the S&P 500 of 12.0% was similar to the average return of 12.97% generated by the 20 Dow Jones stocks reported in Table 3-5, the standard deviation was significantly lower (21.2% vs. 29.6%). This is another illustration of the benefit to be gained by forming portfolios and diversifying away the nonsystematic risk of individual securities.

The other four asset classes represented in Table 3-6 are small stocks, long-term corporate bonds, long-term government bonds, and 90-day treasury bills. The small stock class generally consisted of the bottom 20% of all NYSE stocks ranked by size, where size was measured in terms of the market value of the stock. The small stocks, as one might suspect, provided the highest arithmetic mean return (18.3%) and were the riskiest. Note that the long-term bonds generated arithmetic mean returns of 5.1% and 4.4%, respectively, which were substantially lower returns than those generated by common stocks. However, the standard deviations associated with the bond returns (8.3% and 8.2%, respectively) were also substantially less than the standard deviation of 21.2% associated with the stock returns. Treasury bills provided similar annual returns (an average of 3.5%) and lower standard deviation of returns (3.4%). Finally, note that inflation, as measured by annual percentage changes in the consumer price index (CPI), averaged 3.2%.

Several interesting observations can be drawn from these data. First, there has been a strong tendency for higher returns to be associated with riskier assets, where risk was measured as the standard deviation of annual returns. In the past, stocks have provided substantially higher returns than bonds but have also been much riskier. Treasury bills provided the lowest returns but were also the least risky. It is also interesting to note that the rate of inflation was roughly equal to the return on treasury bills. Thus the real return provided by these securities was approximately zero. The best explanation for the zero real rate of return is that investors simply underestimated the rate of inflation during the time period of this study. Whether this will be the case in the future remains to be seen.

Table 3-7 is what is commonly referred to as a *diagonal table* of returns. This table lists for common stocks the compound annual rate of return[17] for any time period from the beginning of 1926 through 1978. For example, for the 2-year period from the beginning of 1926 through the end of 1927, the S&P 500 generated a compound annual rate of return of 23.9%. As another example, the compound annual rate of return for the 3-year period from the beginning of 1936 to the end of 1938 was 4.5%. Over the entire 60-year time period (1926–1985) common stocks generated a compound annual rate of return of 9.8%. One should note that all holding periods of a given length lie along a diagonal—hence the term ''diagonal table.'' For example, the 1-year holding period rates of return lie along the first diagonal. Thus, the 11.6%, 37.5%, etc., of the first diagonal in Table 3-7 correspond to the first column of annual returns for stocks in Table 3-6. The second diagonal line in Table 3-7 (23.9%, 40.5%, etc.) represents the compound annual rate of return for all 2-year holding periods, and so forth.

Finally, Table 3-8 presents correlation coefficients for the first 10 Dow Jones Industrial stocks listed in Table 3-5. Recall that for 10 stocks, there will be 45 unique covariance terms and correlation coefficients, i.e., $* = (n^2 - n)/2 = (10^2 - 10)/2 = 45$. Note that all 45 correlation coefficients are positive and fall in the .42 to .75 range. These results should not necessarily be considered typical, since all 10 of these companies are large, well-established industrial firms. Nevertheless, one will find that almost all stocks covary in a positive manner and a correlation coefficient of .3 to .6 is very typical.

---

[17]A compound rate of return is the same as the geometric mean rate of return, which is discussed in more detail in Chapters 8 and 9. The geometric mean return r_g is calculated as

$$r_g = \sqrt[n]{\prod_{t=1}^{n} (1 + r_t)} - 1$$

where r_t is the rate of return for the single time period t. The operator Π indicates that the product of the terms $(1 + r_t)$ is to be calculated. For example, the compound annual (geometric mean) return for the 2-year period of 1926–1927 is calculated as

$$r_g = \sqrt[2]{(1.116)(1.375)} - 1 = .239 = 23.9\%$$

Similarly, the compound annual return for the 3-year time period of 1936–1938 is calculated as

$$r_g = \sqrt[3]{(1.339)(.650)(1.311)} - 1 = .045 = 4.5\%$$

TABLE 3-7 COMMON STOCKS: COMPOUND RATES OF RETURN FOR ALL YEARLY HOLDING PERIODS FROM 1926 TO 1985
(Percent per annum compounded annually)

To the end of	From the beginning of																			
	1926	1927	1928	1929	1930	1931	1932	1933	1934	1935	1936	1937	1938	1939	1940	1941	1942	1943	1944	1945
1926	11.6																			
1927	23.9	37.5																		
1928	30.1	40.5	43.6																	
1929	19.2	21.8	14.7	8.4																
1930	8.7	8.0	-0.4	-17.1	-24.9															
1931	-2.5	-5.1	-13.5	-27.0	-34.8	-43.3														
1932	-3.3	-5.6	-12.5	-22.7	-26.9	-27.9	-8.2													
1933	2.5	1.2	-3.8	-11.2	-11.9	-7.1	18.9	54.0												
1934	2.0	0.9	-3.5	-9.7	-9.9	-5.7	11.7	23.2	-1.4											
1935	5.9	5.2	1.8	-3.1	-2.2	3.1	19.8	30.9	20.6	47.7										
1936	8.1	7.8	4.9	0.9	2.3	7.7	22.5	31.6	24.9	40.6	33.9									
1937	3.7	3.0	0.0	-3.9	-3.3	0.2	10.2	14.3	6.1	8.7	-6.7	-35.0								
1938	5.5	5.1	2.5	-0.9	0.0	3.6	13.0	16.9	10.7	13.9	4.5	-7.7	31.1							
1939	5.1	4.6	2.3	-0.8	0.1	3.2	11.2	14.3	8.7	10.9	3.2	-5.3	14.3	-0.4						
1940	4.0	3.5	1.3	-1.6	-1.0	1.8	8.6	11.0	5.9	7.2	0.5	-6.5	5.6	-5.2	-9.8					
1941	3.0	2.4	0.3	-2.4	-1.9	0.5	6.4	8.2	3.5	4.3	-1.6	-7.5	1.0	-7.4	-10.7	-11.6				
1942	3.9	3.5	1.5	-1.0	0.4	2.0	7.6	9.3	5.3	6.1	1.2	-3.4	4.6	-1.1	-1.4	3.1	20.3			
1943	5.0	4.7	2.9	0.6	1.3	3.7	9.0	10.8	7.2	8.2	4.0	0.4	7.9	3.8	4.8	10.2	23.1	25.9		
1944	5.8	5.5	3.8	1.7	2.5	4.8	9.8	11.5	8.3	9.3	5.7	2.6	9.5	6.3	7.7	12.5	22.0	22.8	19.8	
1945	7.1	6.9	5.4	3.5	4.3	6.6	11.5	13.2	10.4	11.5	8.4	5.9	12.6	10.1	12.0	17.0	25.4	27.2	27.8	36.4
1946	6.4	6.1	4.7	2.8	3.5	5.6	10.1	11.6	8.8	9.7	6.8	4.4	10.1	7.7	8.9	12.4	17.9	17.3	14.5	12.0
1947	6.3	6.1	4.7	3.0	3.7	5.6	9.8	11.2	8.6	9.4	6.7	4.5	9.6	7.5	8.5	11.4	15.8	14.9	12.3	9.9
1948	6.3	6.1	4.7	3.1	3.8	5.6	9.6	10.8	8.4	9.1	6.6	4.6	9.2	7.3	8.2	10.6	14.2	13.2	10.9	8.8
1949	6.8	6.6	5.3	3.8	4.5	6.3	10.1	11.2	9.0	9.7	7.4	5.6	10.0	8.3	9.2	11.5	14.8	14.0	12.2	10.7
1950	7.7	7.5	6.4	4.9	5.6	7.4	11.1	12.3	10.2	11.0	8.9	7.3	11.5	10.0	11.0	13.4	16.6	16.1	14.8	13.9
1951	8.3	8.1	7.1	5.7	6.4	8.2	11.7	12.9	11.0	11.7	9.8	8.4	12.4	11.1	12.1	14.3	17.3	16.9	15.9	15.3
1952	8.6	8.5	7.5	6.2	6.9	8.6	12.0	13.2	11.3	12.1	10.3	9.0	12.8	11.6	12.5	14.6	17.4	17.1	16.1	15.7

Year																			
1953	8.3	8.1	7.2	5.9	6.5	8.2	11.4	12.4	10.7	11.4	9.6	8.3	11.9	11.5	13.4	15.7	15.3	14.3	13.7
1954	9.6	9.5	8.6	7.4	8.1	9.7	12.9	14.0	12.4	13.1	11.6	10.4	13.9	13.9	15.8	18.2	18.0	17.4	17.1
1955	10.2	10.2	9.3	8.2	8.9	10.5	13.7	14.7	13.2	13.9	12.5	11.4	14.8	14.9	16.8	19.1	19.0	18.5	18.4
1956	10.1	10.1	9.2	8.2	8.8	10.4	13.4	14.4	12.9	13.6	12.2	11.2	14.4	14.4	16.1	18.2	18.1	17.5	17.3
1957	9.4	9.3	8.5	7.4	8.1	9.5	12.3	13.2	11.8	12.4	11.0	10.0	13.0	12.8	14.3	16.2	15.9	15.2	14.9
1958	10.3	10.2	9.5	8.5	9.1	10.6	13.3	14.3	12.9	13.6	12.3	11.4	14.3	14.3	15.8	17.6	17.5	16.9	16.7
1959	10.3	10.3	9.5	8.6	9.2	10.6	13.3	14.2	12.9	13.5	12.3	11.4	14.2	14.1	15.6	17.3	17.1	16.6	16.4
1960	10.0	10.0	9.3	8.3	8.9	10.3	12.8	13.7	12.4	13.0	11.8	10.9	13.5	13.5	14.8	16.4	16.1	15.6	15.3
1961	10.5	10.4	9.7	8.8	9.4	10.8	13.3	14.1	12.9	13.4	12.3	11.5	14.1	14.0	15.3	16.9	16.7	16.2	16.0
1962	9.9	9.9	9.2	8.3	8.8	10.1	12.5	13.2	12.1	12.6	11.4	10.7	13.0	12.9	14.1	15.5	15.3	14.7	14.4
1963	10.2	10.2	9.5	8.7	9.2	10.5	12.8	13.5	12.4	12.9	11.8	11.1	13.4	13.3	14.5	15.8	15.6	15.1	14.9
1964	10.4	10.4	9.7	8.9	9.4	10.6	12.9	13.6	12.5	13.0	12.0	11.3	13.5	13.5	14.5	15.8	15.6	15.2	14.9
1965	10.4	10.4	9.8	9.0	9.5	10.7	12.9	13.6	12.5	13.0	12.0	11.3	13.5	13.4	14.5	15.7	15.5	15.0	14.8
1966	9.9	9.8	9.2	8.4	8.9	10.1	12.2	12.8	11.8	12.2	11.2	10.5	12.6	12.4	13.4	14.5	14.3	13.8	13.6
1967	10.2	10.2	9.6	8.8	9.3	10.4	12.5	13.1	12.1	12.5	11.6	10.9	12.9	12.8	13.8	14.9	14.7	14.2	14.0
1968	10.2	10.2	9.6	8.9	9.3	10.4	12.4	13.1	12.1	12.5	11.6	10.9	12.9	12.8	13.7	14.7	14.5	14.1	13.9
1969	9.8	9.7	9.1	8.4	8.9	9.9	11.8	12.4	11.4	11.8	10.9	10.3	12.1	12.0	12.8	13.8	13.6	13.1	12.9
1970	9.6	9.6	9.0	8.3	8.7	9.7	11.6	12.2	11.2	11.6	10.7	10.1	11.9	11.7	12.5	13.5	13.2	12.8	12.5
1971	9.7	9.7	9.1	8.4	8.9	9.9	11.7	12.2	11.3	11.7	10.8	10.2	11.9	11.8	12.6	13.5	13.3	12.8	12.6
1972	9.9	9.9	9.3	8.7	9.1	10.1	11.9	12.4	11.5	11.9	11.0	10.5	12.1	12.0	12.8	13.7	13.5	13.0	12.8
1973	9.3	9.3	8.7	8.1	8.5	9.4	11.1	11.7	10.8	11.1	10.3	9.7	11.3	11.1	11.8	12.7	12.4	12.0	11.7
1974	8.5	8.4	7.8	7.2	7.5	8.4	10.1	10.6	9.7	10.0	9.1	8.5	10.1	9.8	10.5	11.2	10.9	10.5	10.2
1975	9.0	8.9	8.4	7.7	8.1	9.0	10.6	11.1	10.2	10.6	9.8	9.2	10.7	10.5	11.1	11.9	11.6	11.2	11.0
1976	9.2	9.2	8.7	8.0	8.4	9.3	10.9	11.4	10.5	10.9	10.1	9.5	11.0	10.8	11.5	12.2	12.0	11.6	11.3
1977	8.9	8.8	8.3	7.7	8.1	8.9	10.5	10.9	10.1	10.4	9.6	9.1	10.5	10.3	10.9	11.6	11.4	11.0	10.7
1978	8.9	8.8	8.3	7.7	8.0	8.9	10.4	10.8	10.0	10.3	9.6	9.0	10.4	10.2	10.8	11.5	11.3	10.9	10.6
1979	9.0	9.0	8.5	7.9	8.2	9.1	10.6	11.0	10.2	10.5	9.8	9.2	10.6	10.4	11.0	11.7	11.4	11.1	10.8
1980	9.4	9.4	8.9	8.3	8.7	9.5	11.0	11.4	10.6	10.9	10.2	9.7	11.1	10.9	11.5	12.2	11.9	11.6	11.4
1981	9.1	9.1	8.6	8.1	8.4	9.2	10.6	11.0	10.3	10.6	9.9	9.4	10.7	10.5	11.1	11.7	11.5	11.1	10.9
1982	9.3	9.3	8.8	8.3	8.6	9.4	10.8	11.2	10.5	10.8	10.1	9.6	10.9	10.8	11.3	11.9	11.7	11.4	11.2
1983	9.6	9.5	9.1	8.5	8.9	9.6	11.0	11.5	10.7	11.0	10.3	9.9	11.1	11.0	11.5	12.2	12.0	11.6	11.4
1984	9.5	9.5	9.0	8.5	8.8	9.6	10.9	11.3	10.6	10.9	10.3	9.8	11.0	10.9	11.4	12.0	11.8	11.5	11.3
1985	9.8	9.8	9.4	8.9	9.2	9.9	11.3	11.7	11.0	11.3	10.7	10.2	11.4	11.3	11.8	12.4	12.3	12.0	11.8

TABLE 3-7 *(Continued)* COMMON STOCKS: COMPOUND RATES OF RETURN FOR ALL YEARLY HOLDING PERIODS FROM 1926 TO 1985
(Percent per annum compounded annually)

To the end of	1946	1947	1948	1949	1950	1951	1952	1953	1954	1955	1956	1957	1958	1959	1960	1961	1962	1963	1964	1965
																	From the beginning of			
1946	-8.1																			
1947	-1.4	5.7																		
1948	0.8	5.6	5.5																	
1949	5.1	9.8	11.9	18.8																
1950	9.9	14.9	18.2	25.1	31.7															
1951	12.1	16.7	19.6	24.7	27.8	24.0														
1952	13.0	17.0	19.4	23.1	24.6	21.2	18.4													
1953	11.2	14.2	15.7	17.9	17.6	13.3	8.3	-1.0												
1954	15.1	18.4	20.4	23.0	23.9	22.0	21.4	22.9	52.6											
1955	16.7	19.8	21.7	24.2	25.2	23.9	23.9	25.7	41.7	31.6										
1956	15.7	18.4	19.9	21.9	22.3	20.8	20.2	20.6	28.9	18.4	6.6									
1957	13.2	15.4	16.4	17.7	17.6	15.7	14.4	13.6	17.5	7.7	-2.5	-10.8								
1958	15.3	17.5	18.7	20.1	20.2	18.8	18.1	18.1	22.3	15.7	10.9	13.1	43.4							
1959	15.1	17.1	18.1	19.3	19.4	18.1	17.3	17.2	20.5	15.0	11.1	12.7	26.7	12.0						
1960	14.0	15.8	16.6	17.6	17.5	16.2	15.3	14.9	17.4	12.4	8.9	9.5	17.3	6.1	0.5					
1961	14.8	16.5	17.3	18.3	18.3	17.1	16.4	16.2	18.6	14.4	11.7	12.8	19.6	12.6	12.9	26.9				
1962	13.3	14.8	15.4	16.1	15.9	14.7	13.9	13.4	15.2	11.2	8.5	8.9	13.3	6.8	5.2	7.6	-8.7			
1963	13.8	15.2	15.8	16.6	16.4	15.3	14.6	14.3	15.9	12.4	10.2	10.8	14.8	9.9	9.3	12.5	5.9	22.8		
1964	13.9	15.3	15.9	16.6	16.4	15.4	14.7	14.4	16.0	12.8	10.9	11.5	15.1	10.9	10.7	13.5	0.3	10.6	16.5	
1965	13.8	15.1	15.7	16.3	16.2	15.2	14.6	14.3	15.7	12.8	11.1	11.6	14.7	11.1	11.0	13.2	10.1	17.2	14.4	12.5
1966	12.6	13.7	14.2	14.7	14.4	13.4	12.7	12.4	13.4	10.7	9.0	9.2	11.7	8.2	7.7	9.0	5.7	9.7	5.6	0.6
1967	13.1	14.2	14.6	15.1	14.9	14.0	13.4	13.1	14.2	11.6	10.1	10.5	12.8	9.9	9.6	11.0	8.6	12.4	9.9	7.8
1968	13.0	14.0	14.5	14.9	14.7	13.8	13.3	13.0	14.0	11.6	10.2	10.5	12.7	10.0	9.8	11.0	8.9	12.2	10.2	8.6
1969	12.0	13.0	13.3	13.7	13.4	12.5	11.9	11.6	12.4	10.1	8.7	8.9	10.7	8.2	7.8	8.7	6.6	9.0	6.8	5.0
1970	11.7	12.6	12.9	13.2	13.0	12.1	11.5	11.1	11.9	9.7	8.4	8.6	10.2	7.8	7.5	8.2	6.3	8.3	6.4	4.8
1971	11.8	12.6	12.9	13.3	13.0	12.2	11.6	11.3	12.0	10.0	8.8	8.9	10.5	8.3	8.0	8.7	7.1	9.0	7.4	6.1
1972	12.0	12.9	13.2	13.5	13.3	12.5	12.0	11.7	12.4	10.5	9.4	9.5	11.0	9.0	8.8	9.5	8.1	9.9	8.6	7.6
1973	10.9	11.7	11.9	12.2	11.9	11.2	10.6	10.3	10.8	9.0	7.9	7.9	9.2	7.3	6.9	7.5	6.0	7.4	6.0	4.9
1974	9.4	10.1	10.2	10.4	10.1	9.3	8.7	8.2	8.7	6.9	5.7	5.7	6.7	4.8	4.3	4.6	3.0	4.1	2.5	1.2
1975	10.2	10.9	11.1	11.3	11.0	10.3	9.7	9.4	9.9	8.2	7.1	7.1	8.2	6.4	6.1	6.5	5.2	6.3	5.1	4.1
1976	10.6	11.3	11.5	11.7	11.5	10.8	10.3	9.9	10.4	8.8	7.8	7.9	9.0	7.3	7.1	7.5	6.3	7.5	6.4	5.6
1977	10.0	10.7	10.8	11.0	10.7	10.0	9.5	9.2	9.6	8.1	7.1	7.1	8.1	6.5	6.2	6.6	5.4	6.4	5.4	4.6
1978	9.9	10.5	10.7	10.9	10.6	9.9	9.4	9.1	9.5	8.0	7.1	7.1	8.0	6.5	6.2	6.6	5.5	6.5	5.4	4.7
1979	10.2	10.8	10.9	11.1	10.8	10.2	9.7	9.4	9.8	8.4	7.5	7.6	8.5	7.1	6.8	7.2	6.2	7.1	6.2	5.6
1980	10.7	11.3	11.5	11.7	11.5	10.9	10.4	10.2	10.6	9.2	8.4	8.5	9.4	8.1	7.9	8.3	7.4	8.4	7.6	7.1
1981	10.3	10.8	11.0	11.2	10.9	10.3	9.9	9.6	10.0	8.7	7.9	7.9	8.8	7.5	7.3	7.6	6.8	7.6	6.9	6.3
1982	10.6	11.1	11.3	11.5	11.2	10.7	10.2	10.0	10.4	9.1	8.4	8.4	9.3	8.1	7.9	8.2	7.4	8.3	7.6	7.1
1983	10.9	11.4	11.6	11.8	11.6	11.0	10.6	10.4	10.8	9.6	8.8	8.9	9.8	8.5	8.5	8.8	8.1	8.9	8.3	7.9
1984	10.7	11.3	11.4	11.6	11.4	10.9	10.5	10.2	10.6	9.4	8.7	8.8	9.6	8.4	8.4	8.7	8.0	8.8	8.2	7.8
1985	11.2	11.8	11.9	12.1	11.9	11.4	11.1	10.8	11.2	10.1	9.5	9.6	10.4	9.3	9.2	9.6	8.9	9.7	9.2	8.8

TABLE 3-7 (*Continued*) COMMON STOCKS: COMPOUND RATES OF RETURN FOR ALL YEARLY HOLDING PERIODS FROM 1926 TO 1984
(Percent per annum compounded annually)

To the end of	From the beginning of																			
	1966	1967	1968	1969	1970	1971	1972	1973	1974	1975	1976	1977	1978	1979	1980	1981	1982	1983	1984	1985
1966	-10.1																			
1967	5.6	24.0																		
1968	7.4	17.3	11.1																	
1969	3.2	8.0	0.8	-8.5																
1970	3.3	7.0	1.9	-2.4	4.0															
1971	5.1	8.4	4.8	2.8	9.0	14.3														
1972	7.0	10.1	7.5	6.7	12.3	16.6	19.0													
1973	4.0	6.2	3.5	2.0	4.8	5.1	0.8	-14.7												
1974	0.1	1.4	-1.5	-3.4	-2.4	-3.9	-9.3	-20.8	-26.5											
1975	3.3	4.9	2.7	1.6	3.3	3.2	0.6	-4.9	0.4	37.2										
1976	5.0	6.6	4.9	4.1	6.0	6.4	4.9	1.6	7.7	30.4	23.8									
1977	3.9	5.3	3.6	2.8	4.3	4.3	2.8	-0.2	3.8	16.4	7.2	-7.2								
1978	4.1	5.4	3.9	3.2	4.5	4.6	3.3	0.9	4.3	13.9	7.0	-0.5	6.6							
1979	5.1	6.3	5.0	4.5	5.9	6.1	5.1	3.2	6.6	14.8	9.7	5.4	12.3	18.4						
1980	6.7	8.0	6.9	6.5	8.0	8.4	7.8	6.5	9.9	17.5	13.9	11.6	18.7	25.2	32.4					
1981	5.9	7.1	6.0	5.6	6.9	7.2	6.5	5.2	7.9	14.0	10.6	8.1	12.3	14.3	12.2	-4.9				
1982	6.8	8.0	7.0	6.7	7.9	8.3	7.7	6.7	9.4	14.9	12.1	10.2	14.0	16.0	15.2	7.4	21.4			
1983	7.6	8.8	7.9	7.7	8.9	9.3	8.9	8.0	10.6	15.7	13.3	11.9	15.4	17.3	17.0	12.3	22.0	22.5		
1984	7.5	8.6	7.8	7.6	8.7	9.1	8.7	7.9	10.2	14.8	12.5	11.2	14.1	15.4	14.8	10.7	16.5	14.1	6.3	
1985	8.7	9.7	9.0	8.9	10.1	10.5	10.2	9.6	11.9	16.2	14.3	13.3	16.2	17.6	17.5	14.7	20.2	19.8	18.5	32.2

Source: Stocks, Bonds, Bills, and Inflation: 1986 Yearbook, Ibbotson Associates, Chicago, 1986, Exhibit A-1.

TABLE 3-8   CORRELATION COEFFICIENTS FOR 10 DOW JONES INDUSTRIAL STOCKS

Company	ACD	AMB	AC	T	BS	DD	EK	XON	GE	GF
Allied Chemical (ACD)	1.00									
American Brands (AMB)	.46	1.00								
American Can (AC)	.56	.53	1.00							
AT&T (T)	.58	.50	.55	1.00						
Bethlehem Steel (BS)	.64	.51	.53	.54	1.00					
Du Pont (DD)	.67	.48	.59	.61	.65	1.00				
Eastman Kodak (EK)	.56	.49	.48	.54	.49	.61	1.00			
Exxon (XON)	.56	.46	.49	.51	.57	.56	.56	1.00		
General Electric (GE)	.67	.55	.60	.61	.70	.70	.62	.58	1.00	
General Foods (GF)	.50	.53	.51	.51	.47	.49	.50	.42	.56	1.00

Correlation coefficients are based on 636 monthly returns over the time period 1926–1978.

3-7 SUMMARY

The problems associated with measuring returns are relatively straightforward. To measure the return for a single time period, we must take into account both the change in price and the cash flow received (dividends in the case of stocks, interest in the case of bonds). To measure the average return for ex post data, we use the familiar arithmetic mean or, in some cases, the geometric mean, which is discussed in Chapters 8 and 9. For ex ante data, the expected return is determined by the probability distribution of returns conditional upon different economic scenarios.

Risk is not so simple to quantify. While some disagreement remains, most analysts agree that risk should be measured by the variability of returns and the standard deviation is generally agreed upon as the best measure of this variability, *at least for portfolios.* However, diversification can eliminate most, if not all, of the nonsystematic risk of individual securities, leaving the portfolio with only market-related risk. Thus, many analysts argue that it is the systematic, or market-related, risk which is the relevant measure of risk for *individual securities.*

The tables in Section 3-6 presented data on historical rates of return. This should give the reader some idea as to magnitude and variability of returns generated by stocks and bonds in the past. While no one would expect the past to be a perfect proxy for the future, it nevertheless should provide some rough guidelines as to what returns one can expect from stocks and bonds.

SUGGESTED READINGS

A more rigorous treatment of portfolio theory and the value of diversification can be found in:
E. F. Fama, *Foundations of Finance*, Basic Books, New York, 1976.
H. Markowitz, "Portfolio Selection," *Journal of Finance* (March 1952).

The two most important records of historical rates of returns for U.S. securities are:
R. G. Ibbotson and R. A. Sinquefield, *Stocks, Bonds, Bills, and Inflation: The Past and the Future*, Financial Analysts Research Foundation, Charlottesville, Va., 1982. This study is updated each year by Ibbotson Associates in Chicago.

L. Fisher and J. H. Lorie, *A Half Century of Returns on Stocks and Bonds*, University of Chicago, Graduate School of Business, Chicago, 1977.

For an interesting study on the risk perceptions of institutional investors, see:

G. Farrelly and W. Reichenstein, "Risk Perceptions of Institutional Investors," *Journal of Portfolio Management* (summer 1984).

QUESTIONS

1 The standard deviation of expected returns was suggested as a good measure of risk. Discuss some of the arguments for using σ as a risk measure.

2 Ibbotson Associates reported that the arithmetic mean annual return for the S&P 500 index was 12.0% over the period 1926–1985. Given no other information, would you use this figure as a forecast of the return for the S&P 500 over the next 12 months? Are there any reasons why you might want to adjust your forecast up or down from 12%?

3 With respect to Question 2, would you have as much *confidence* in your forecast for the S&P index as you would in your forecast for any individual stock? Why or why not?

4 The correlation coefficients reported in Table 3-8 were for stocks from the Dow Jones Industrial Average. On average, would the correlations be higher or lower if some stocks from the Dow Jones Transportation and Utility Averages had been included? Why?

5 Based on the data in Table 3-6, in how many years did investors lose money in stocks? In how many years did investors lose money in long-term corporate bonds? What would you estimate to be the probability of losing money in stocks or bonds next year?

6 Using Table 3-7, determine how many 10-year periods occurred in which investors averaged less than a 5% rate of return from stocks.

PROBLEMS

1 First, pick your favorite stock and forecast the return the stock will provide over the next 30 days. Then, using data from such sources as the *Wall Street Journal* and *Standard & Poor's Stock Guide*, collect end-of-the-month price data for your favorite stock over the past 36 months. Also collect data on dividend payments (amounts and ex-dividend dates). Calculate the mean monthly return and the standard deviation of the returns. Given this new information, would you change your forecast of next month's rate of return? How confident do you feel about your forecast?

2 Table 3-6 indicates that 1931 was the worst year for stocks—a loss of 43.34%. 1974 was also a bad year with a negative return of 26.47%. In *real* terms, which year was the worst? (Hint: Subtract the inflation rate for the year from the stock returns.)

3 *Barron's* reports on a weekly basis the price level of stock indexes for several foreign countries. Calculate price changes for the British, Japanese, and U.S. indexes for 3 weeks. Do these results suggest anything about the potential for reducing risk by diversifying internationally?

4 Given the following data, calculate the one-period rate of return for ABC Inc. and XYZ Co.:

	ABC	XYZ
Beginning price	20	10
Ending price	15	15
Dividends	1	1

5 Listed below are the annual returns generated by IBM stock for the 10 years 1969–1978. Calculate the mean annual return and the standard deviation of these returns. Also, calculate the covariance and the correlation coefficient for the returns of IBM and those of the S&P 500 returns for this time period.

	Annual returns, %	
	IBM	**S&P 500**
1969	16.98	– 8.50
1970	– 11.36	4.01
1971	7.64	14.31
1972	21.12	18.98
1973	– 22.14	– 14.66
1974	– 30.01	– 26.48
1975	37.68	37.20
1976	28.27	23.84
1977	1.76	– 7.18
1978	13.93	6.56

6 Calculate the expected return and the standard deviation of return for a stock having the following probability distribution:

Conditional return, %	Probability of occurrence
– 24	.05
– 10	.15
0	.15
12	.20
18	.20
22	.15
30	.10

7 Given the information in Table 3-5 and Table 3-8, calculate the covariance between Allied Chemical and American Brands.

8 Use the following data to calculate the variance and standard deviation for a portfolio containing stocks 1 and 2:

$$\rho_{1,2} = 0.75 \quad \sigma_1 = 10 \quad \sigma_2 = 20$$
$$W_1 = 2/3 \quad W_2 = 1/3$$

9 Given the following ex post data for stocks X, Y, and Z, calculate all the unique covariances and correlation coefficients.

	Annual returns, %		
	X	**Y**	**Z**
1980	6.2	– 9.5	26.5
1981	3.6	– 11.7	– 12.3
1982	4.0	13.8	2.6
1983	2.4	– 5.3	10.5
1984	0.2	9.5	9.2

10 The economist employed by Northwest Investment Management recently forecast three economic scenarios, each of which she believes is equally likely to occur. Based on these scenarios, the firm's stock analyst made the following forecasts of the returns for stocks A and B:

Economic conditions	Conditional return		One-year T-bill
	Stock A	Stock B	
Recession	−10%	−15%	10%
Controlled growth	15%	10%	10%
Boom	40%	25%	10%

Compute the expected return, variance, and standard deviation for stocks A and B.

11 Refer to Problem 10. (*a*) Calculate the expected return, variance, and standard deviation for a portfolio consisting of 50% A and 50% B. (*b*) Calculate the expected return, variance, and standard deviation for a portfolio consisting of 20% T-bills, 40% A, and 40% B.

CHAPTER 4

THE MARKET MODEL AND SECURITY MARKET LINES

After reading this chapter, you should:

1 Understand the concept of the market model
2 Be able to calculate beta coefficients
3 Know how to interpret alphas
4 Be aware of how ex post security market lines are used to evaluate portfolio managers and test for market efficiency.
5 Be aware of how ex ante SMLs are used to identify underpriced stocks and measure the market price of risk

Investors have intuitively always understood the "market effect." When the overall market (as measured by, say, the S&P 500) is "up," most stocks experience price increases; when the market is "down," most stocks experience negative returns. Thus, at least part of the changes in individual security prices can be attributed to changes in the overall valuation of assets.

This phenomenon makes sense because there are many variables which influence the pricing of assets and *which are common to all assets.* For example, the overall level of interest rates would certainly affect the pricing of all bonds. If there is a general increase in interest rates, one would expect that the interest rate associated with a specific bond might also increase, resulting in a decrease in the bond's price. A similar relationship between interest rates and the prices of individual stocks can also be shown to exist. If a recession should occur, this will have a *general,* adverse impact on the profits of most corporations. One might expect that if a *consensus* forecast evolves which predicts a recession, stock prices in general will also fall.

Thus, *on an intuitive level,* there are a number of variables which might affect the prices of all securities, resulting in a "market effect." *At the theoretical level,* the capital asset pricing model (CAPM) suggests that the market effect is due to the relationship between individual security returns and the return on the "market portfolio." The CAPM argues that it is the "sensitivity" of individual securities to changes in the return from the "market portfolio" which determines the return one should expect for each security. Each security's sensitivity to changes in the market return is measured by its β (pronounced "beta"). And, according to the CAPM, the differences between the required returns associated with various securities are due *solely* to differences in the securities' betas. However, we will postpone until later chapters the discussion of the many assumptions, implications, and arguments pro and con concerning the CAPM. Rather, at this time, we will briefly explore the relatively simple concept of *systematic or market risk*—that is, risk associated with changes in securities' returns due to changes in the overall level of security returns.

4-1 THE MARKET MODEL

To derive what is commonly called the "market model" we need only two assumptions:[1]

1 Individual security returns are related to each other *only* through a common relationship with some basic underlying factor, which we will call the market index.[2] Typically we think of this underlying factor, or common source of security returns, as the "overall market," although it could be any efficient portfolio or a macroeconomic variable such as GNP.

2 Each security's relationship with the market index is linear.

The relationship between the return for a particular security and the market index return can then be expressed algebraically as

$$r_{it} = a_i + \beta_i r_{mt} + e_{it} \tag{4-1}$$

This equation indicates that the return r_{it} for the ith stock during time period t is a function of (depends upon) the return for the market index r_{mt} during the same time period. Further, this relationship between r_i and r_m is a simple linear function and can be graphed as illustrated in Figure 4-1.

---

[1]The market model, or what Sharpe termed the "diagonal model," was developed in W. F. Sharpe, "A Simplified Model for Portfolio Analysis," *Management Science* (January 1963) pp. 277–293.

[2]In order to distinguish between the "market model" and the capital asset pricing model (CAPM), we will refer to the common source of security returns as the "market index" when using the market model. In the market-model framework the S&P 500 is probably the most frequently used index, although any large, well-diversified portfolio could be used since the exact nature of the index is not specified by the market model. However, in the framework of the CAPM, the common source of security returns is specified as the "market portfolio," which is a theoretical portfolio consisting of all risky assets held in proportion to their market values. See Chapters 17 and 18 for further discussion.

FIGURE 4-1   A hypothetical regression (characteristic) line.

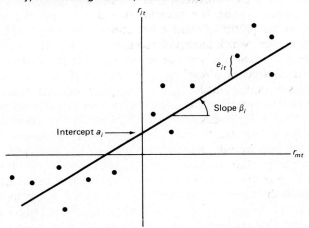

The straight line in Figure 4-1 represents the line of best fit between the actual observations of security returns and market returns. Since it is a linear model with *one independent variable r_{mt} and one dependent variable r_{it}*, simple linear regression is the empirical methodology used when dealing with the market model.[3] Thus, there are clear interpretations of the variables in Equation (4-1). The intercept term a_i can be interpreted as simply the average return on the ith security when the market index return is zero.[4] In regression analysis the e_{it} term in Equation (4-1) is a random-error term which will have a mean value of zero and is assumed to be uncorrelated with the market returns, the error terms of other securities, and the error terms of the same security over time.[5]

The most interesting parameter is the beta coefficient B_i. Beta is the slope of the regression line (sometimes referred to as the characteristic line)[6] and is calculated as

$$\beta_i = \frac{\text{Cov}_{im}}{\sigma_m^2} \tag{4-2}$$

That is, beta measures the covariance of r_i with r_m divided by the variance of r_m. Beta is frequently referred to as the measure of a security's systematic risk, or market risk, since it indicates the *manner in which a security's returns change systematically with changes in the market's returns*. For example, if the market's return increased by 10%, then for a stock with a beta of 1.5 we would expect the security's return to increase by 15% (1.5 × 10%).

To illustrate this, suppose that a stock has the following regression line:

$$r_{it} = a_i + \beta_i r_{mt} + e_{it}$$
$$r_{it} = 2\% + 1.5 r_{mt} + e_{it}$$

Since, on average, the error term e_{it} equals zero, we will ignore it here. Now, if the market index return was 4%, the return on the stock would be 8%, calculated as

$$r_{it} = 2\% + 1.5(4\%) = 8\%$$

If the market return increased by 10% (from 4% to 14%), the stock's return would increase by 15% (from 8% to 23%):

---

[3]We will cover linear regression in detail in Chapter 8.

[4]Readers should not confuse the intercept a_i from the regression of r_{it} against r_{mt} with the term "alpha." Alpha is associated with the security market line and is discussed in Section 4-3.

[5]More formally, the key assumptions in regression analysis regarding the error terms are

$$\text{Cov}(e_i, r_m) = 0$$
$$\text{Cov}(e_i, e_j) = 0$$
$$\text{Cov}(e_{it}, e_{i\tau}) = 0$$

In addition, by construction the regression model forces $E(e_i) = 0$.

[6]The term "characteristic line" was first used by J. L. Treynor, "How to Rate Management of Investment Funds," *Harvard Business Review* (January–February 1965), pp. 63–75. The term is used because it is the estimation of the characteristic (regression) line that enables one to determine the "characteristics" of a security or portfolio—these characteristics are its intercept a_i and its beta β_i.

$$r_{it} = 2\% + 1.5(14\%) = 23\%$$

Thus, the returns for a stock with a beta of 1.5 are said to be one and a half times as volatile as the returns for the market index.

To see that beta is a measure of *relative* market risk, note from Equation (3-8e) in Chapter 3 (the equation which defines covariance) that the covariance of a variable with itself is the variable's variance. That is, $Cov_{ii} = \sigma_i^2$. Thus, from equation (4-2), the beta for the market index has to be 1.0.

$$\beta_m = \frac{Cov_{m,m}}{\sigma_m^2} = \frac{\sigma_m^2}{\sigma_m^2} = 1.0$$

By using the market index's beta of 1.0 as a benchmark, one can classify the systematic risk of securities into two groups. Any stock which has a beta greater than 1.0 has above-average market-related, or systematic, risk. A stock with a beta of less than 1 has below-average systematic risk. Thus, beta provides a convenient measure of *relative* market risk.

> $\beta > 1$: above-average systematic risk
> $\beta < 1$: below-average systematic risk

4-2 ESTIMATING BETAS

Since betas are a measure of market-related risk, investors should be interested in the betas for individual securities and portfolios.[7] There are at least three methods of estimating betas: (1) estimating historical betas based strictly on ex post return data; (2) estimating ex ante betas based upon explicit probability distributions; and (3) estimating ex ante betas by adjusting historical betas, depending upon a variety of factors which may cause the security's beta to change in the future.

4-2-1 Historical Betas Historical betas are calculated using ex post data and Equation (4-2). To illustrate the procedure, the hypothetical ex post returns originally listed in Table 3-1 are reproduced in Table 4-1, along with a hypothetical return series for the market index. In addition to the mean, variance, and standard deviation of returns for each of the stocks and the market index, Table 4-1 reports the covariance and correlation coefficients between each security and the market index, and the beta for each security. The covariance between stock 1 and the market index is calculated using Equation (3-8h) from Chapter 3.

$$Cov_{1m} = \frac{1}{n-1} \sum_{t=1}^{n} (r_{1t} - \bar{r}_1)(r_{mt} - \bar{r}_m)$$

---

[7]It can be shown that the beta for a portfolio is a weighted average of the betas of the individual securities in the portfolio. That is,

$$\beta_p = \sum_i \beta_i W_i$$

$$Cov_{1m} = \frac{1}{9} [(10 - 6.2)(11 - 6.4) + (8 - 6.2)(7 - 6.4)$$

$$+ \ldots + (12 - 6.2)(10 - 6.4)]$$

$$Cov_{1m} = \frac{1}{9}(473.22) = 52.58$$

Once the covariance is calculated, stock 1's beta can be calculated using Equation (4-2):

$$\beta_{1m} = \frac{Cov_{1m}}{\sigma_m^2} = \frac{52.58}{34.27} = 1.53$$

Since stock 1's beta is greater than 1.0, it has above-average systematic risk and the stock would be classified as an aggressive security.

Another method of calculating beta is to make use of the fact that $Cov_{im} = \rho_{im}\sigma_i\sigma_m$. Substituting this relationship into Equation (4-2) yields

$$\beta_{im} = \rho_{im}\frac{\sigma_i}{\sigma_m} \tag{4-3}$$

Thus, beta is equal to the correlation coefficient for security i and the market index, multiplied by the ratio of the standard deviation of the security's beta to the standard deviation of the market index's returns. In words, a security's beta is a function of the correlation of the security's returns with the market index returns (ρ_{im}) and the variability of the security's returns relative to the variability of the index returns

TABLE 4-1   HYPOTHETICAL EX POST RETURNS AND THE CALCULATION OF BETAS

Time period	Stock			Market index
	1	2	3	
1	10%	11%	−6%	11%
2	8%	4%	18%	7%
3	−4%	−3%	4%	−2%
4	22%	−2%	−5%	8%
5	8%	14%	32%	9%
6	−11%	−9%	−7%	−5%
7	14%	15%	24%	12%
8	12%	13%	−17%	11%
9	−9%	−3%	2%	3%
10	12%	4%	27%	10%
$\bar{r}_i$	6.20%	4.40%	7.20%	6.40%
σ_i^2	114.40	72.49	283.73	34.27
σ_i	10.70%	8.51%	16.84%	5.85%
Cov_{im}	52.58	42.49	27.91	34.27
ρ_{im}	0.84	0.85	0.28	1.00
β_{im}	1.53	1.24	0.81	1.00

(σ_i/σ_m). Using the data from Table 4-1, and Equation (4-3), security 1's beta is calculated as

$$\beta_{1m} = \rho_{1m}\frac{\sigma_1}{\sigma_m} = (.84)\frac{10.70}{5.85} = 1.53$$

which, of course, results in the same beta as Equation (4-2).

Now, notice that the beta for stock 3 is considerably smaller than the beta for stock 1 (0.81 vs. 1.53). Yet the standard deviation of stock 3's returns is substantially larger than σ_1 (16.84% vs. 10.70%). Why does stock 3 have less systematic risk than stock 1? Looking at Equation (4-3) the answer becomes obvious. For stock 1, ρ_{1m} is 0.84; for stock 3, ρ_{3m} is only 0.28. Thus, the returns for stock 3 are not nearly as highly correlated with the market index as are stock 1's returns. Because of this low correlation, a large part of the variability of stock 3's returns can be eliminated by diversification. The remaining systematic risk is relatively small, resulting in a low beta.

The analyst generally does not have to perform the tedious task of calculating historical covariances and betas. Typically, a computer or some of the more advanced hand-held calculators are used to perform this task. Figure 4-2 illustrates a typical characteristic, or regression, line calculated by a computer. In this case the regression is for General Motors using 72 monthly returns over the period of 1973–1978 and using a value-weighted index of returns for all NYSE stocks as the market index. Each

FIGURE 4-2   Regression (characteristic) line for General Motors (72 monthly observations, 1973–1978, value-weighted index). (*Source: Computed from CRSP data.*)

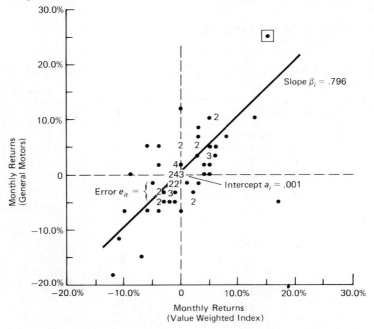

point on the graph represents the return for GM and the return for the market for a particular month. For example, consider the plot with a box around it in the uppermost right-hand corner of the graph. For that particular month, the return on the market was 15% and the return for GM was 25%—quite a month!

The analysis of variance (ANOVA) data printed below the graph are typical of the output one gets from the many computer statistical packages available for performing regressions. At this point it is not necessary for the reader to understand all the information in the ANOVA table. Right now we are interested in the regression coefficients a_i and β_i and the R^2, which have boxes drawn around them. The beta for GM based upon this particular regression is .796 and the intercept is .001. The R^2 of .410 means that the market index explained, or accounted for, 41% of the variance (changes) in the returns for GM over this time period. The R^2 statistic is simply ρ_{im} squared—thus, the correlation between GM's returns and the returns of the market index over this time period was 0.64.

4-2-2 Ex Ante Betas   Ex ante, or expected, betas can be estimated from explicit probability distributions, such as those presented in Chapter 3. Table 4-2 reproduces the ex ante probability distributions for stocks 4, 5, and 6 initially presented in Table 3-2, which were based on four different states of the world (four economic scenarios). Table 4-2 also presents the expected returns for the market index conditional upon these four economic scenarios. In addition, Table 4-2 lists the covariances and correlation coefficients of these three securities with respect to the market index and the securities' betas.

The ex ante covariance for stock 4 and the market index is calculated using Equation (3-8e):

$$\text{Cov}_{4m} = \sum_{s=1}^{n} [r_{4s} - E(r_4)][r_{m,s} - E(r_m)]\pi_s$$

TABLE 4-2   EX ANTE PROBABILITY DISTRIBUTIONS AND THE CALCULATION OF BETAS

State of the world, s	π_s	Conditional returns, %			
		$r_{4,s}$	$r_{5,s}$	$r_{6,s}$	$r_{m,s}$
1. Recession and high interest rates	.20	−18	−13	−4	−9
2. Recession and low interest rates	.25	+16	+16	−2	+8
3. Boom and high interest rates	.30	+12	+32	+21	+16
4. Boom, low interest rates, and oil shortage	.25	+40	+12	+20	+20

	Individual stock statistics			
	Stock 4	Stock 5	Stock 6	Market
σ_i^2	376.00	245.00	136.50	109.00
σ_i,%	19.39	15.65	11.68	10.44
$E(r_i)$,%	14.00	14.00	10.00	10.00
Cov_{im}	182.00	129.00	104.00	109.00
ρ_{im}	.90	.79	.85	1.00
β_{im}	1.67	1.18	.95	1.00

$$= (-18 - 14)(-9 - 10)(.20) + \ldots + (40 - 14)(20 - 10)(.25)$$
$$= 182.00$$

Given this covariance and the variance of the market index returns, stock 4's beta is calculated using Equation (4-2):

$$\beta_{4m} = \frac{\text{Cov}_{4m}}{\sigma_m^2} = \frac{182.00}{109.00} = 1.67$$

Given the information available in Table 4-2, stock 4's beta could also have been calculated using Equation (4-3):

$$\beta_{4m} = \rho_{4m}\frac{\sigma_4}{\sigma_m} = (.90)\frac{19.39}{10.44} = 1.67$$

4-2-3 Adjusted Betas   The purchase of an asset gives the investor a claim on the asset's *future* cash flows. Thus, investors are concerned with ex ante (expected) earnings, dividends, interest payments, etc. Likewise, investors are generally concerned with ex ante risk. The historical variability and systematic risk of a security is of use to an investor only if it provides some indication of the future variability and systematic risk of the security.

As discussed in the preceding section, ex ante betas can be calculated directly from explicit probability distributions such as those listed in Table 4-2. However, in many (if not most) cases, such explicit probability distributions are not available. Under these circumstances, one procedure for estimating future betas is first to measure the security's historical beta and then to adjust this estimate up or down, depending upon a number of factors. One of the most common adjustments is to correct for the tendency of individual security betas to "regress toward the mean" over time. Blume[8] found that very high betas, measured over a particular time period, tend to be lower (closer to 1.0) during the next time period and that very low betas tend to be higher when measured during the subsequent time period. For example, if a stock's measured beta for the 5-year time period 1980–1984 was 1.6, it might be measured as 1.4 during the next 5-year period, 1985–1989. Because of this tendency of betas to regress toward the mean beta (1.0) over time, many services which provide estimates of betas adjust upward very low historical betas and adjust downward very high historical betas.

A number of other adjustments are made to historical betas in order to arrive at a better estimate of a security's future beta. As just one example, if a firm substantially increases the amount of debt in its capital structure, one should consider adjusting its historical beta upward since betas have been shown to be a positive function of financial leverage.[9] Many of these adjustments will be discussed in more detail in Chapter 12. For now, the reader should simply be aware that the betas reported by many financial

[8]M. E. Blume, "Betas and Their Regression Tendencies," *Journal of Finance* (June 1975).

[9]The original theory linking betas and financial leverage was done by R. S. Hamada, "The Effect of a Firm's Capital Structure on the Systematic Risk of Common Stocks," *Journal of Finance* (May 1972). In general, Hamada demonstrated theoretically that the more leverage the firm uses, the higher the stock's beta. This relationship was then verified empirically.

TABLE 4-3   BETAS FOR THE 30 DOW JONES INDUSTRIALS

Company (stock symbol)	Estimated beta*
Allied Corporation (ALD)	1.05
Aluminum Company (AA)	1.10
American Brands (AMB)	.70
American Can (AC)	.95
American Express	1.40
AT&T (T)	.65
Bethlehem Steel (BS)	1.30
Chevron	1.15
Du Pont (DD)	1.20
Eastman Kodak (EK)	.80
Exxon (XON)	.80
General Electric (GE)	1.00
General Foods (GF)	.80
General Motors (GM)	1.10
Goodyear (GT)	1.10
Inco (N)	1.25
IBM (IBM)	1.05
International Harvester (HR)	.95
International Paper (IP)	1.10
Merck (MRK)	.80
Minnesota Mining & Manufacturing (MMM)	1.00
Owens Illinois (OI)	.80
Procter & Gamble (PG)	.70
Sears, Roebuck (S)	1.10
Texaco (TX)	.85
Union Carbide (UK)	1.15
U.S. Steel (X)	1.10
United Technologies (UTX)	1.15
Westinghouse Electric (WX)	1.25
Woolworth (Z)	.95
Average	1.01

*As estimated by *Value Line*, Sept. 13, 1985.

services are historical betas which have been adjusted in some fashion in hopes of providing a better estimate of the security's future beta.

4-2-4 Betas for the Dow Jones Industrials   In order to give the reader a feel for the distribution of betas across various stocks, the betas for the 30 Dow Jones Industrials, as calculated by *Value Line*,[10] are listed in Table 4-3. Note that the betas range from a high of 1.40 for American Express to a low of .65 for American Telephone and Telegraph. The betas tend to cluster around 1.0 and the arithmetic mean of these 30 betas is 1.01, which is close to the mean for all betas of 1.0. Of course, the Dow Jones 30 Industrials cannot be considered a representative group for all stocks, since it includes only large industrial firms which are listed on the New York Stock Exchange.

[10]*Value Line* reports betas based on 60 weeks of price changes (they do not include dividends in the weekly returns) using the NYSE composite as the market index. Adjustments are made for the regression tendency of betas, and all betas are rounded to the nearest .05.

Nevertheless, if a more representative sample was taken, one would find that the mean of the betas would still be close to 1.0; however, the distribution of the betas around 1.0 would be wider as there would be more very high and very low betas.

> Before continuing, you should:
>
> 1 Be able to describe the market model.
> 2 Be able to calculate both ex post and ex ante betas. As a check, see if you can compute the betas for stock 2 in Table 4-1 and stock 5 in Table 4-2.

4-3 SECURITY MARKET LINES

One of the contributions of modern portfolio theory to the field of investments is the concept of a security market line (SML). The SML simply represents the *average, or normal, trade-off between risk and return* for a group of securities, where risk is typically measured in terms of the securities' betas.[11] Figure 4-3 illustrates both an ex post and an ex ante SML.

In the ex post SML, average historical rates of return for securities are plotted against their betas for a particular time period. Typically, a straight line is fitted to

[11] The risk measure does not have to be limited to beta. For example, Kidder, Peabody and Co. constructs a SML using as its measure of risk what it terms its fundamental risk estimate (FRE). The FRE is a composite risk measure based on the securities' betas and other more traditional risk measures such as financial leverage.

FIGURE 4-3   (a) An ex post SML and (b) An ex ante SML.

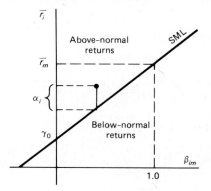

Normal Return, $N(\bar{r}_i) = \gamma_0 + \gamma_1 \beta_{im}$

where γ_0 = intercept of ex post SML

γ_1 = slope of SML

$\alpha_i = \bar{r}_i - N(\bar{r}_i)$

$= \bar{r}_i - (\gamma_0 + \gamma_1 \beta_{im})$

(a)

Required Return, $R(r_i) = r_f + [E(r_m) - r_f]\beta_{im}$

where r_f = risk-free interest rate

where $E(r_m) - r_f$ = slope of SML

$\alpha_i = E(r_i) - R(r_i)$

$= E(r_i) - \left\{ r_f + [E(r_m) - r_f]\beta_{im} \right\}$

(b)

the plots by regression, and this line is called the SML. Thus, the SML represents the "normal," or average, trade-off between return and risk. The SML can be written as:[12]

EX POST SML

Normal return, $N(\bar{r}_i) = \gamma_0 + \gamma_1\beta_{im}$ $\qquad$ (4-4)

where γ_0 = intercept of the SML
γ_1 = slope of the SML

Those securities which plot above the ex post SML generated above-normal returns for their risk (as measured by beta) for the particular time period used in constructing the SML. Those securities which plot below the SML generated below-normal rates of returns for their systematic risk.

The amount by which a security's return differed from the normal return for its level of risk is simply the vertical distance of the security's plot on the graph from the SML. This vertical distance is called the security's *abnormal return,* or its alpha (α). Thus, alpha is calculated as:

EX POST ALPHA

$$\alpha_i = \bar{r} - N(\bar{r}_i)$$
$$= \bar{r}_i - (\gamma_0 + \gamma_1\beta_{im})$$

$\qquad$ (4-5)

It is easy to see that securities with above-normal returns have positive alphas, while securities with below-normal returns have negative alphas.

$\alpha_i > 0$: above-normal return
$\alpha_i < 0$: below-normal return

To construct an ex ante SML, analysts must estimate the expected return and risk of individual securities. These return and risk estimates can then be plotted and a

---

[12]The reader should immediately note that the SML is *not* the same as the characteristic line for a single security. For a characteristic line the y axis represents the returns for a particular security and the x axis represents the returns for the market index. The slope of the characteristic line is the beta for the particular security involved. The y axis of the ex post SML represents the average returns for a number of different securities. (For the ex ante SML the y axis represents expected returns.) The x axis for the SML represents the betas for the different securities. Thus, a unique characteristic line is needed for each individual security in order to determine its beta. Then the average (or expected) returns for each security are plotted against their respective betas on a single security market line.

regression line fitted to the observations. In Figure 4-3*b* we have assumed that the assumptions of the CAPM are correct. Therefore, the intercept of the SML is equal to the risk-free rate r_f and the slope is equal to $[E(r_m) - r_f]$. We will use the term *required return,* denoted $R(r_i)$, to refer to the average, or normal, return implied by an ex ante SML.

EX ANTE SML

$$\text{Required return, } R(r_i) = \gamma_0 + \gamma_1 \beta_{im} \tag{4-6}$$

If the assumption of the CAPM are correct, then

$$R(r_i) = r_f + [E(r_m) - r_f]\beta_{im} \tag{4-6a}$$

Each security's ex ante alpha is calculated as the difference between the expected return and the "required" return implied by the SML.

EX ANTE ALPHA

$$\alpha_i = E(r_i) - R(r_i)$$
$$= E(r_i) - \{r_f + [E(r_m) - r_f]\beta_{im}\} \tag{4-7}$$

An example will help illustrate how alphas are calculated. Consider stocks 4 and 6 in Table 4-2. For stock 4, $E(r_4) = 14.00\%$ and $\beta_{4m} = 1.67$. For stock 6, $E(r_6) = 10.00\%$ and $\beta_{6m} = .95$. Now suppose the CAPM assumptions are valid, that $r_f = 3\%$ and that $E(r_m) = 10\%$. Then the following SML would be appropriate:

$$R(r_i) = 3\% + (10\% - 3\%)\beta_i \tag{4-8}$$

Given this SML and $\beta_{4m} = 1.67$, the required return for stock 4 would be 14.69%, calculated as

$$R(r_4) = 3\% + 7\%(1.67) = 14.69\%$$

Similarly, the required return for stock 6 would 9.68%. Given this information, the α for stocks 4 and 6 would be -0.69% and $+0.32\%$, respectively, calculated as follows:

	Stock 4	Stock 6
$E(r_i)$	14.00%	10.00%
Minus $R(r_i)$	(14.69%)	(9.68%)
Equals α_i	−0.69%	+0.32%

Thus, based on the set of expectations in Table 4-2 and the SML of Equation (4-8), stock 4 would be considered overpriced since it has a negative alpha and stock 6 would be considered underpiced because of its positive alpha. These relationships are illustrated in Figure 4-4. Note that stock 4 plots below the SML and stock 6 plots above. Note also that alpha is simply the vertical distance between the SML and the point where the stock plots on the $E(r_i)$, β_i graph.

4-4 APPLICATIONS OF SECURITY MARKET LINES

There are a number of applications of ex post SMLs. Among these are (1) evaluating the performance of portfolio managers; (2) tests of asset-pricing theories, such as the CAPM; and (3) tests of market efficiency. Some of the applications of ex ante SMLs are (1) identifying undervalued securities; and (2) determining the consensus "price of risk" implicit in current market prices.

FIGURE 4-4   Plotting of stocks 4 and 6 on an SML.

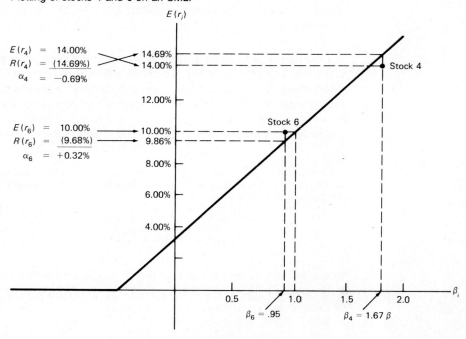

4-4-1 Applications of Ex Post SMLs   The performance of portfolio managers is frequently evaluated based on security market line criteria. Large, positive alphas indicate above-normal performance and negative alphas indicate below-normal performance. Unfortunately, the measurement of performance is not quite as simple as it might first appear. First, as Richard Roll has pointed out, the relative performance of a portfolio manager, as measured by alpha, can vary depending upon which index is used to determine the beta of the portfolio.[13] Perhaps more importantly, one would prefer a measure of performance which is predictive in nature. That is, if a portfolio manager performed well in the past, will he also perform well in the future? Unfortunately, no such consistency among portfolio managers has been demonstrated.[14] A more detailed discussion of these issues is presented in Chapter 5.

Many researchers have attempted to test the validity of the CAPM by constructing ex post SMLs.[15] However, these studies are particularly vulnerable to Roll's critique[16] since the CAPM specifies that betas are to be measured against the returns for the "market portfolio"—the value-weighted portfolio of *all* risky assets. Since the true "market portfolio" is not observable, proxies have to be used in its place, and these proxies may give results which are different from those that would be obtained if one was able to use the "market portfolio." Since the issues surrounding performance measurement and tests of the CAPM are fairly complex, a detailed discussion of these topics is deferred until Chapters 18 and 21.

Another area of inquiry utilizing ex post SMLs involves the testing of market efficiency. Broadly speaking, efficient markets imply the absence of abnormal returns—that is, all securities are correctly priced and provide a normal return for their level of risk. Tests of this nature require a model to specify what constitutes a normal return. Tests of market efficiency which utilize the market model assume that a normal return plots on the SML and that abnormal returns are measured by alpha. A number of tests of market efficiency have utilized this general technique, and many of the studies are reviewed in Chapter 5.

4-4-2 Applications of Ex Ante SMLs   The most obvious use of ex ante SMLs is for identifying under- and overvalued securities. Unlike some of the ad hoc methods of identifying mispriced securities which have traditionally been used in the securities industry, the use of a security market line allows one to *quantify how much a security is over- or underpriced*. The general procedure is for security analysts to estimate the expected return for individual securities over some future holding period—for example,

---

[13]See R. Roll, "A Critique of the Asset Pricing Theory's Tests," *Journal of Financial Economics* (March 1977), and R. Roll, "Ambiguity When Performance Is Measured by the Securities Market Line," *Journal of Finance* (September 1978).

[14]See R. J. Fuller, *Capital Asset Pricing Theories: Evolution and New Frontiers*, Financial Analysts Research Foundation, Charlottesville, Va., 1981, Chapter 3, for a summary of a number of issues concerning the measurement of portfolio performance, including Roll's critique and the lack of consistent performance over time. Also see J. M. Murphy, "Efficient Markets, Index Funds, Illusion and Reality," *Journal of Portfolio Management* (fall 1977).

[15]Among the better-known studies are: F. Black, M. C. Jensen, and M. Scholes, "The Capital Asset Pricing Model: Some Empirical Tests," in M. C. Jensen, ed., *Studies in the Theory of Capital Markets*, Praeger Publishers, New York, 1972; M. E. Blume and I. Friend, "A New Look at the Capital Asset Pricing Model," *Journal of Finance* (March 1973); and E. F. Fama and J. D. Macbeth, "Risk, Return, and Equilibrium: Empirical Tests," *Journal of Political Economy* (May–June 1973).

[16]Roll, "A Critique of the Asset Pricing Theory's Tests," *op. cit.*

the next 5 years. The analysts also estimate the risk associated with each security. The risk measure may be the security's ex ante beta, or it may be a more traditional measure of risk.[17] Figure 4-5 presents the results of an SML analysis done by the brokerage firm of Bache, Halsey Stuart, which utilizes a risk index based on each security's historical beta. One can see from Figure 4-5 that the observations are fairly evenly distributed about the market line. Table 4-4 lists data concerning the first 18 stocks (in alphabetical order) followed by the Bache analysis. The last column lists the alpha for each stock. Note that there are about as many positive alphas as there are negative alphas. For this particular group of stocks the alphas range from −1.89% (American Broadcasting) to +3.67% (Akzona). Thus, based on alpha, the most over-priced stock appears to be American Broadcasting and the most underpriced stock is Akzona.

Another application of ex ante security market lines is their use in determining the "market price of risk." For example, Wells Fargo Investment Advisors periodically has its analysts supply estimates of expected return and risk for a large number of

---

[17]In order for the SML concept to be valid, two conditions must be met: (1) security returns must be a function of a single factor; and (2) the functional relationship must be linear. One of the strongest arguments for constructing SMLs based on the market model is that there is a well-developed theory (the CAPM) which suggests that return is a linear function of beta. Thus, before using a risk measure other than beta in constructing a SML, one should have strong evidence supporting the alternative risk measure.

FIGURE 4-5 Market-line analysis, Bache research universe. Squares indicate individual stock data; the solid line is the S&P 500 market line. Slope of the market line is .210, and the *y* intercept is 15.620. (*Source: Bache, Halsey Stuart, "Quantitative Investment Strategies," Sept. 5, 1979.*)

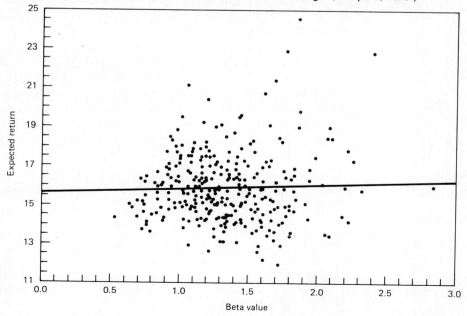

TABLE 4-4 DATA FOR SELECTED STOCKS COVERED IN BACHE'S MARKET LINE ANALYSIS*

Stock name	Earnings/dividends					Implied growth	Pers 1	2	Terminal payout	Terminal growth	Price	Expected return	Fund declared	Alpha
	1979	1980	1981	1982	1983									
A C F Inds Inc	5.50	5.75	6.00	6.50	7.00	10.0%E	10-	5	45.0%	8.8%	37.63	15.2%	3	-0.59
	2.24	2.24	2.50	2.75	2.80									
Am Intl Inc	0.95	2.50	3.75	4.50	5.50	15.0%E	7-	5	50.0%E	8.0%	17.13	17.3%	9	1.34
	0.28	0.36	0.50	0.64	0.80									
ARA Svcs Inc	5.20	5.75	6.35	7.00	7.85	10.7%	10-	5	50.0%	8.0%	38.13	15.8%	7	-0.15
	1.90	2.20	2.60	2.75	3.10									
Advanced Micro Devices	3.70	3.70	5.00	6.10	7.50	21.1%	5-	13	50.0%	8.0%	36.50	15.8%	10	-0.35
	0.0	0.0	0.15	0.30	0.50									
Aetna Life & Cas	7.00	6.75	6.00	7.00	8.00	8.0%E	5-	5	40.0%	9.9%	32.75	16.5%	7	0.53
	1.80	1.98	2.18	2.40	2.64									
Air Prods & Chems	3.45	3.60	4.00	4.50	5.00	12.0%E	12-	10	45.0%	8.8%	31.38	14.2%	5	-1.67
	0.65	0.80	1.00	1.20	1.50									
Akzona Inc	1.71	2.00	3.00	3.50	3.90	11.0%E	8-	5	50.0%	8.0%	12.63	19.5%	3	3.67
	0.80	1.00	1.25	1.50	1.75									
Albany Intl Corp	4.00	4.20	4.75	5.70	7.00	18.0%E	10-	5	45.0%	8.8%	40.75	15.9%	8	-0.04
	1.10	1.25	1.40	1.70	2.10									
Alexander & Alex	2.85	3.25	3.60	4.00	4.50	11.9%	5-	5	38.0%	9.9%	30.50	14.3%	9	-1.68
	1.40	1.57	1.76	1.97	2.20									
Allied Chem Corp	3.65	8.00	10.00	11.00	12.25	12.0%E	12-	10	50.0%	8.0%	36.75	19.1%	6	3.21
	2.00	2.40	2.80	3.50	4.00									
Alpha Inds Inc	1.36	1.70	2.05	2.50	3.15	22.9%	8-	7	50.0%	8.0%	13.38	17.5%	10	1.43
	0.10	0.15	0.25	0.35	0.45									
Amarex Inc	1.85	2.25	2.75	3.50	4.50	24.9%	7-	2	38.0%	9.9%	26.13	15.1%	8	-0.83
	0.0	0.25	0.50	0.75	1.00									
Amerada Hess	8.85	8.00	9.25	10.00	11.00	6.8%	5-	3	38.0%	9.9%	42.00	16.4%	7	0.44
	1.40	1.70	2.50	3.00	3.50									
Amcord Inc	4.00	3.50	4.50	5.00	6.00	10.0%E	9-	4	45.0%	8.8%	29.88	15.2%	5	-0.70
	1.40	1.50	1.60	1.75	2.10									
American Broadcasting	6.00	7.00	7.00	7.70	8.50	8.2%	10-	10	38.0%	9.9%	44.50	14.0%	7	-1.89
	1.20	1.40	1.70	2.00	2.30									
American Cyanamid	3.50	4.00	4.75	5.50	6.25	13.0%E	15-	10	50.0%	8.0%	29.88	17.9%	4	2.04
	1.60	1.80	2.10	2.50	2.85									
American Express	4.85	5.35	6.00	6.60	7.35	11.0%	5-	5	38.0%	9.9%	34.63	15.8%	9	-0.15
	1.80	2.00	2.22	2.46	2.73									
American Gen Ins	5.50	6.00	6.25	6.75	7.50	7.7%	5-	5	38.0%	9.9%	35.25	14.8%	8	-1.11
	1.00	1.10	1.21	1.33	1.46									

*Forecasts used in this report: risk-free rate = 10.30%; market return = 15.93%.
Source: Bache, Halsey Stuart, "Quantitative Investment Strategies," Sept. 5, 1979.

individual securities. A security market line is then fitted by regression to these expected return and risk (beta) estimates, producing an equation similar to Equation (4-6):

$$E(r_i) = \gamma_0 + \gamma_1\beta_1$$

One can see from this equation that the slope of the SML (γ_1) is a measure of the "market price of risk" in the sense that for each unit of beta, the expected return for a security increases by an amount equal to γ_1. By constructing SMLs in this manner at various points in time, one can observe how the price of risk changes with market cycles. The steeper the slope of the SML, the higher the price of risk, and vice versa. Expressed in other terms, the steeper the slope of the ex ante SML, the more averse investors (in the aggregate) are to assuming additional risk.

Figure 4-6 presents the ex ante SML, as estimated by Wells Fargo, at four different points in time.[18] One can see that the slopes of the SMLs varied from quite steep (June 30, 1970, and December 31, 1974) to quite flat (June 30, 1972). Since June 30, 1970, and December 31, 1974, were at the end of bear markets, one might expect that investors would be more risk-averse during these time periods. Similarly, June 30, 1972, was during a bull market when one might expect investors to be more optimistic and therefore more willing to tolerate risk. While it is unlikely that this type of analysis will enable one to pick market tops and bottoms, it may provide a guide as to approximately where one is in the current market cycle.

4-5 SUMMARY

In Chapter 3 methods for quantifying return and risk for individual securities were introduced. After these methods were extended to portfolios we were left with the tantalizing notion that the total risk of well-diversified portfolio σ_p was a function of the *systematic* risk of the individual securities making up the portfolio. Therefore, this chapter dealt with the market model which indicates that the return for a security is a function of its systematic risk, as measured by beta.

To estimate historical betas, the characteristic line is used. The characteristic line is a regression of the returns generated by a security over a number of time intervals against the returns associated with a market index over the same time intervals. Since security betas are known to change over time, adjustments to historical betas are frequently made when trying to estimate future, ex ante betas. In addition, future betas can be estimated directly if explicit ex ante probability distributions for securities are available.

Security market lines, generally based on the market model, have been applied to a number of investment problems. By utilizing alpha as a measure of abnormal returns, the SML concept has been applied to the problem of measuring portfolio performance and testing such theories as the CAPM and the efficient market hypothesis. In an ex ante sense, the SML concept can be used to identify over- and underpriced securities,

---

[18]W. L. Fouse, "Risk, Liquidity and Common Stock Prices," *Financial Analysts Journal* (May/June 1976).

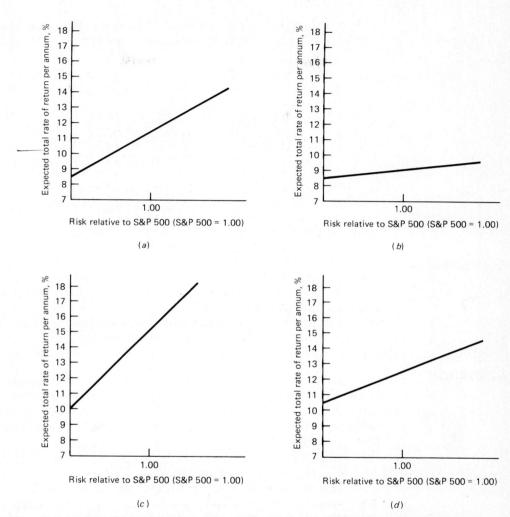

FIGURE 4-6   Ex ante SMLs for different time periods. (a) June 30, 1970; (b) June 30, 1972; (c) December, 31, 1974; and (d) June 30, 1975. [*Source: W. L. Fouse, "Risk, Liquidity and Common Stock Prices," Financial Analysts Journal (May/June 1976).*]

and to determine the current "market price of risk." While many of the applications of the SML concept are subject to criticism, the serious investor and analyst should become quite familiar with this useful tool.

SUGGESTED READINGS

Very readable discussions of portfolio theory, the market model, and the CAPM can be found in:

F. Modigliani and G. A. Pogue, "An Introduction to Risk and Return," *Financial Analysts Journal* (March–April, May–June 1974).

R. J. Fuller, *Capital Asset Pricing Theories—Evolution and New Frontiers,* The Financial Analysts Research Foundation, Charlottesville, Va., 1981.

For a more rigorous treatment of these topics, see:

E. F. Fama, *Foundations of Finance,* Basic Books, New York, 1976.

E. J. Elton and M. J. Gruber, *Modern Portfolio Theory and Investment Analysis,* Wiley, New York, 1981.

Interesting and readable discussions concerning performance measurement can be found in:

J. M. Murphy, "Efficient Markets," Index Funds, Illusion and Reality," *Journal of Portfolio Management,* (fall, 1977).

R. Roll, "Ambiguity When Performance Is Measured by the Securities Market Line," *Journal of Finance* (September 1978).

A nice discussion of some of the uses of security market lines can be found in:

W. L. Fouse, "Risk, Liquidity and Common Stock Prices," *Financial Analysts Journal* (May/ June 1976).

QUESTIONS

1. Graph a typical characteristic line. Graph a typical security market line. Explain the difference between the two lines and how they are related.
2. The S&P 500 is frequently used as the market index in the market model (and as a proxy for the "market portfolio" in the CAPM). Identify two other possible choices for a market index.
3. Is it possible for a security to have a very high standard deviation of returns and a low beta? Explain.
4. Graph a typical security market line and indicate where the overpriced and underpriced securities would plot. Also, indicate where the aggressive and defensive securities would plot.
5. Define, in words, the following: (*a*) market risk, (*b*) total risk, (*c*) unsystematic risk, (*d*) systematic risk.
6. Dreyfus Fund is a mutual fund which has over $1 billion in assets invested in more than 100 securities. How would you expect the total risk of this fund to be divided between systematic and unsystematic risk?
7. Give three potential applications of security market lines.
8. The market forecasting department of Bulls, Bears and Bucks, a brokerage firm, estimates that the slope of the SML will increase over the next 6 months and then stabilize at the steeper slope. What does this imply about the performance of high-beta stocks over (*a*) the next 6 months? (*b*) for the time period after the next 6 months?

PROBLEMS

1. Problem 1 at the end of Chapter 3 asked you to pick your favorite stock, collect 36 months of price and dividend data, and compute monthly returns and the mean and standard deviation of these returns. For the same stock, compute its beta by using the S&P 500 return data listed in Appendix VII (at the end of the book) as the market index. Is your favorite stock an "aggressive" or "defensive" security?
2. For your favorite stock (see Problem 1), compute its beta based on the first 18 months of data and then recompute its beta based on the last 18 months of data. Did the stock's beta change over this time period? If the beta did change, are you aware of any reason that may

have caused this to occur? (For example, did the company make an acquisition, issue substantial amounts of new debt, etc.?) Finally, if the stock's beta did change, do you believe that the change is significant, or just due to random sampling error?

3 Assume that the standard deviation of the returns for the market index is 20%. Given the information below, compute the betas for Auto Supplies, Inc., and Gold Diggers Corp. Explain why Gold Diggers Corp. has a lower beta, even though it has a higher σ.

	Auto Supplies	Gold Diggers
σ_i	25%	50%
ρ_{im}	.60	.20

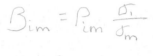

$$\beta_{im} = \rho_{im} \frac{\sigma_i}{\sigma_m}$$

4 Bulls, Bears and Bucks, a brokerage firm known in the trade as "Triple B," has estimated the following ex ante security market line:

$$R(r_i) = 8\% + 5\% \beta_{im}$$

(a) What is the estimated "market price of risk"? (b) The Triple B analysts estimate that Acme Inc. has a beta of 1.1 and an expected return of 15%. What is the ex ante alpha for Acme Inc.?

5 Given the explicit probability distributions shown below, (a) determine the equation for the security market line, assuming that the intercept γ_0 is 7%. (b) What does the SML tell you about the "market price of risk"? (c) Calculate the beta for security X. (d) Calculate the alpha for security X.

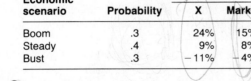

$E(X)$ 7.5

$COV = 24 - 7.5$

Economic scenario	Probability	Conditional returns	
		X	Market
Boom	.3	24%	15%
Steady	.4	9%	8%
Bust	.3	−11%	−4%

6 Given the following:

π	r_x	r_y	r_m
.20	−13%	−4%	−9%
.15	16%	−2%	8%
.40	32%	21%	16%
.25	12%	20%	20%

(a) What are the ex ante betas for X and Y? (b) If $r_f = 4\%$, calculate the ex ante alphas for stocks X and Y. Are these stocks under- or overpriced?

7 In the market model, $r_{it} = \alpha_i + \beta_i r_{mt} + e_{it}$. (a) Which is the dependent variable? (b) Given $\sigma_i^2 = 100$ and $Cov_{im} = 110$, calculate β_{im}. Would you classify this stock as defensive or aggressive? (c) If $\rho_{im} = .8$, what is the standard deviation of stock i?

CHAPTER 5

MARKET EFFICIENCY

After reading this chapter, you should:

1 Understand the concept of market efficiency and the role of competition
2 Be able to distinguish among the various forms of the efficient market hypothesis (EMH)
3 Understand the methodology of residual analysis used for event studies
4 Be aware of the empirical tests which support the weak- and semistrong-form EMH
5 Be aware of the empirical tests which do not support the semistrong- and strong-form EMH

Before one begins the process of security analysis and portfolio management, it is essential to understand the environment in which securities are priced. Chapter 2 described the securities markets and discussed the mechanics of these markets—that is, the institutions and the physical procedures involved in buying and selling securities.

This chapter describes *how effectively investor expectations are translated into security prices*. That is, are investor expectations regarding the future cash flows (and the risk associated with those cash flows) for a particular security *quickly and accurately* reflected in the price of the security? This is the concept of *market efficiency*. In an efficient market the current prices of securities represent unbiased estimates of the "fair," or "intrinsic," value of the securities.

If *all* securities are fairly valued, investors will earn a return on their investment which is appropriate for the level of risk assumed (i.e., a "normal return"), *regardless of which securities they purchase*. In other words, in a perfectly efficient market all securities are correctly priced—there are no under- or overpriced securities. Thus, the degree to which markets are efficient has important implications for investors. If markets are perfectly efficient, time, effort, and money spent on security analysis will be wasted. If some sectors of the securities markets are less efficient than others, efforts devoted to discovering mispriced securities should be directed to the less efficient sectors.

Before examining the concept of market efficiency in detail, one should be aware that some circularity of reasoning is involved. Almost all of those who argue that the securities markets are efficient agree that in order to have market efficiency there must be competent and well-informed analysts who continually evaluate the available information regarding any particular security. *It is the competition between these astute market participants which results in securities' being fairly and correctly priced*. And yet, in a perfectly efficient market these analysts immediately "compete away" any chance for earning abnormal profits. Thus, the marginal value of their analysis is zero in a perfectly efficient market. Yet it is obvious that a great deal of time and effort is spent on security analysis.

Fortunately, the paradox is not as perplexing as many originally thought. First, even if markets are perfectly efficient, some security analysis is still necessary to provide ex ante estimates of the risk characteristics of individual securities so that portfolios can be formed to match the risk preferences of different investors. Second, while the evidence is overwhelming that the securities markets are *reasonably efficient*, the evidence also suggests that they are not perfectly efficient. However, before examining the evidence, let's first consider why markets might be reasonably efficient.

5-1 GROCERY-STORE LINES, COMPETITION, AND MARKET EFFICIENCY

Consider the case of shoppers in a supermarket as they approach the checkout lines. The objectives of most shoppers are the same—to get through the checkout lines as quickly as possible. If the "market" for checkout lines is efficient, then all shoppers will spend roughly the same amount of time in line, *regardless of which line they choose*. However, if the situation is similar to that depicted in the left side of Figure 5-1, not all shoppers will spend an equal amount of time in line. Shopper 2 will obviously pick counter B since there is only one other shopper in line, compared with three shoppers in line at both counters A and C.

Figure 5-1   However, if the situation is similar to that depicted in the right side of Figure 5-1, it may not make any difference which line is chosen by any one of the four shoppers approaching the checkout counters. Although counter B has only one customer in its line, it is also obvious that shoppers 2 and 3 will choose to go to counter B. For shoppers 1 and 4, it probably does not make much difference which line they

FIGURE 5-1   Grocery-store lines and competition.

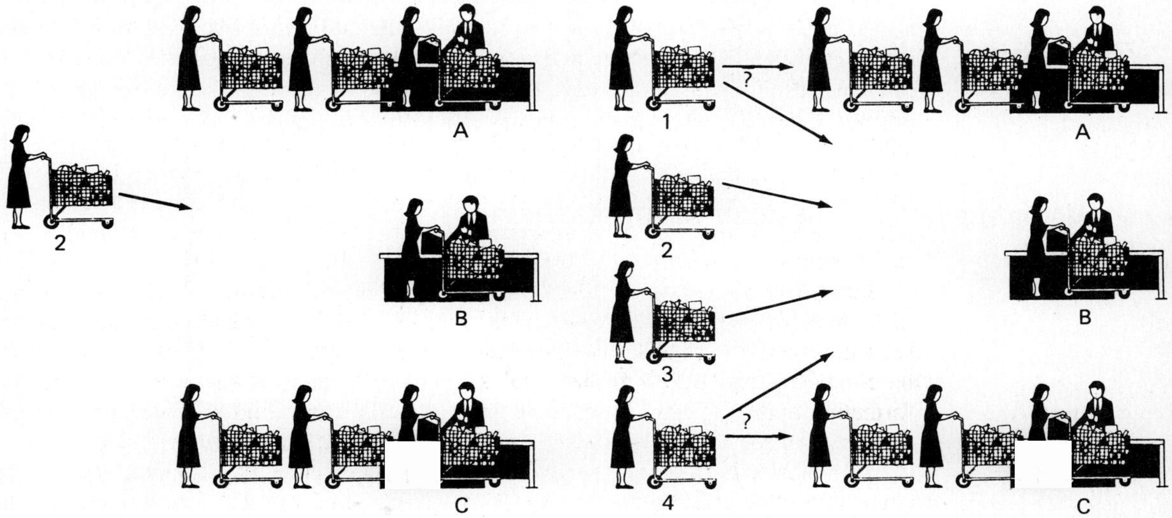

choose—shopper 1 can choose either counter A or B, and the odds are there will be three shoppers ahead of him—similarly, shopper 4 may choose either counter B or C and expect to spend the same amount of time in line.

What is the difference between the left side of Figure 5-1, where shopper 2 can easily identify a specific line which will minimize her wait time, and the right side of Figure 5-1 where the wait time is approximately the same, regardless of which line is chosen? The answer, of course, is obvious—there are more shoppers, *more competitors*, in the second situation. As long as there is a sufficient number of competitors, the wait times in any individual shopping line are likely to be equal.

The analogy to the securities markets is straightforward. Investors have similar objectives—they want to maximize their return for a given level of risk. If a security is obviously underpriced, investors will quickly identify it and rush to buy it, just as the shoppers rushed to counter B. In the process of bidding for the underpriced security, investors will drive up the price, thus reducing the return to a normal level. Superior performers will be only those investors who are talented enough to consistently identify underpriced securities, and agile enough to buy before the rest of the crowd.

As long as there is a reasonable number of competitors, it seems unlikely that securities will remain underpriced (or overpriced) for very long. In this type of environment, it will be quite difficult for anyone to consistently achieve superior performance. Most securities will be *correctly priced*, and one should be able to *earn a normal return by randomly choosing securities of a given risk level*. This is the essence of market efficiency. Since obviously a large number of competent competitors are involved in the securities markets, many observers have argued that these markets are efficient.

Before we leave the grocery-store analogy, one should bear in mind that investors have to be able to do more than simply count the number of shoppers in each line. The securities markets are considerably more complex than any set of grocery-store lines. But at the same time, there are potentially millions of competitors in the securities markets, including thousands of well-educated, well-trained, and highly motivated professionals whose primary job is to identify potentially mispriced securities. Thus, one might assume, at least as a first approximation, that the securities markets are efficient, despite their complexity. This is supported by the empirical evidence, which indicates that the markets are reasonably efficient—but perhaps not as efficient as was once believed to be the case.

5-2 FORMS OF THE EFFICIENT MARKET HYPOTHESIS (EMH)

Market efficiency is generally discussed within the framework presented in Fama's 1970 survey article.[1] We will likewise proceed within this framework with one or two exceptions. Fama defined efficient markets in terms of a "fair game" where security prices "fully reflect" the information available. That is, if markets are efficient, securities are priced to provide a normal return for their level of risk. (In the terminology of Chapter 4, the expected value of alpha is zero when securities are correctly priced.)

---

[1]E. F. Fama, "Efficient Capital Markets: A Review of Theory and Empirical Work," *Journal of Finance* (May 1970).

Fama suggested that the efficient market hypothesis (EMH) can be divided into three categories: the "weak form," the "semistrong" form, and the "strong" form. The distinctions among the weak, semistrong, and strong forms of the EMH are determined by the *level of information* being considered.

5-2-1 Weak-form EMH   In the weak-form EMH, the type of information being considered is restricted to only *historical prices*. If the weak-form EMH is correct, investors should not be able to consistently earn abnormal profits by simply observing the historical prices of securities. Technical analysis which relies on charts of stock prices over time is particularly vulnerable to the weak-form EMH, as are techniques which rely on moving averages of prices.

5-2-2 Semistrong-Form EMH   The semistrong-form EMH asserts that security prices adjust rapidly (and correctly) to the release of all *publicly available information*. Thus, under the semistrong form, current prices fully reflect not only all past price data but also such information as earnings reports, dividend announcements, annual and quarterly reports, and news items in the financial press. In short, any information that is available to the public should be quickly reflected in security prices so that investors cannot *consistently* earn abnormal returns by acting on such public information. Since a great deal of the information used by security analysts is available to the public at large, the semistrong-form EMH strikes at the very heart of the analyst profession.

Most tests of the semistrong form have dealt with the *speed* at which market participants react to public releases of new information. However, implicit in the semistrong-form EMH is that the public reacts quickly *and correctly* to public information. The empirical evidence generally supports the contention that the public reacts quickly to new information; but there is some evidence that the market does not always digest new information correctly.[2]

5-2-3 Strong-Form EMH   The strong-form EMH represents the most extreme case of market efficiency possible. Under the strong form it is argued that security prices fully reflect *all* information, including both public and private (monopolistic) information. In order to test the strong form, three groups of investors have been examined, each of which may have private information. These groups are corporate "insiders," stock exchange specialists, and mutual funds. Not many proponents of the efficient market hypothesis would argue that the strong form is a correct description of the securities markets. As Fama noted, the strong form "is obviously an extreme null hypothesis. And, like any other extreme null hypothesis, we do not expect it to be literally true."[3]

---

[2]Shiller has argued that changes in stock prices are too volatile, given changes in expected dividends. For example, declines in stock prices during bear markets are too severe given the decline in dividends during the subsequent recession or depression, and vice versa. This provides some indirect evidence that market participants may tend to overreact to new information concerning changes in dividends. See the suggested readings at the end of this chapter, and in particular R. J. Shiller, "Do Stock Prices Move Too Much to Be Justified by Subsequent Changes in Dividends?" *American Economic Review* (June 1981).

[3]Fama, op. cit., p. 388.

Before continuing, you should:

1 Understand the primary factor required in order to have efficient markets
2 Be aware of the implications of efficient markets for security analysis
3 Be able to distinguish among the three different forms of the efficient market hypothesis suggested by Fama

5-3 EMPIRICAL TESTS OF THE WEAK-FORM EMH

The genesis for the efficient market hypothesis was with the observation that stock price changes appeared to follow a random walk over time, creating patterns of stock prices similar to those in Figure 5-2. To say that a series of data follows a random walk over time means that each observation is *independent of the preceding observations*. If stock price changes follow a random walk, then the fact that yesterday's price was up, for example, provides no information as to what today's stock price change may be. The top half of Figure 5-2 displays a simulated stock price series which was generated by the use of a random-number table. The bottom half of Figure 5-2 displays a graph of the actual Friday closing prices for the Dow Jones Industrial Average during 1956. The point of this illustration is that charts generated by purely random outcomes bear a remarkable similarity to charts of actual stock prices.[4] Observations such as this provided the impetus for some researchers to formally investigate whether or not stock prices follow a random walk.

5-3-1 Tests for Serial Independence One method of testing for randomness in stock price changes is to measure their autocorrelations—that is, the correlation between price changes in one period and changes for the same stock in another period. If the autocorrelations are close to zero, the price changes are said to be serially independent.

A number of different studies[5] have analyzed the autocorrelations of stock price changes for time intervals ranging from 1 to 16 days and have reported similar results. Table 5-1 lists the autocorrelations for the 30 Dow Jones Industrial stocks as computed by Fama for the time period 1958–1962. The autocorrelations were generally found to be insignificant, with most falling in the range of $+.10$ to $-.10$. This is particularly damaging evidence for trading strategies which are based on stock price charts. If there is very little correlation of stock price changes over time, it is difficult to

---

[4]An easy way to randomly generate your own "stock charts" is by flipping a coin and recording the results on a blackboard or piece of paper. Represent a head by drawing a short upward-sloping line; for a tail draw a short, downward-sloping line; and connect each observation. After 30 or 40 flips of the coin, you will most likely begin to see head-and-shoulder and other patterns frequently utilized by "chartists." You know that the outcomes of successive flips of a fair coin are independent—that is, whether a head or tail is flipped on one toss does not change the probability of flipping a head or tail on the next toss. Thus, it is obvious that your chart will not help you predict the future outcomes. If, as the next section suggests, it can be shown that stock price changes are also independent over time, would you have much confidence in using stock price charts for predicting future stock price changes?

[5]The more important of these are S. Alexander, "Price Movements in Speculative Markets: Trends or Random Walks," *Industrial Management Review* (May 1961); E. F. Fama, "The Behavior of Stock Market Prices," *Journal of Business* (January 1965); and M. G. Kendall, "The Analysis of Economic Time Series," *Journal of the Royal Statistical Society* (1953). For an excellent summary of these articles, see E. F. Fama, "Efficient Capital Markets," op. cit.

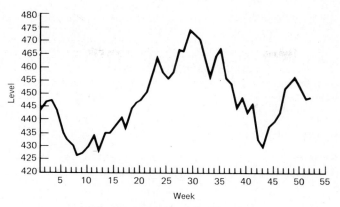

(a) Simulated market levels for 52 weeks

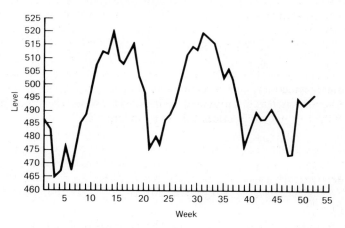

(b) Friday closing levels, December 30, 1955–December 28, 1956.
Dow Jones Industrial Index

FIGURE 5-2   Simulated and actual stock price returns. (a) Simulated market levels for 52 weeks. (b) Friday closing levels, Dec. 30, 1955, to Dec. 28, 1956, Dow Jones Industrial Index. [*Source: Harry Roberts, "Stock Market Patterns and Financial Analysis: Methodological Suggestions,"* Journal of Finance *(March 1959). Reprinted from Richard A. Brealey, An Introduction to Risk and Return from Common Stocks by permission of the M.I.T. Press, Cambridge, Mass. Copyright 1969 by the Massachusetts Institute of Technology.*]

understand how charts (which simply represent historical prices) can be of much use in predicting future price changes.

5-3-2 Tests of Filter Rules   Actually, to say that stock prices follow a random walk is a much stronger statement than the weak-form EMH.[6] The weak form does

---

[6]Strictly speaking, stock prices follow a random walk only if price changes are independent *and* identically distributed over time. This means that not only must the mean outcomes (returns) be constant over time, but the distribution of the outcomes about the mean must also be constant. For a discussion of the differences between the random walk model and the "fair game" implied by the weak-form EMH, see Fama, "Efficient Capital Markets," pp. 386–387.

TABLE 5-1 AUTOCORRELATIONS FOR THE 30 DOW JONES INDUSTRIAL STOCKS

Stock	Differencing interval, days			
	One	Four	Nine	Sixteen
Allied Chemical	.017	.029	−.091	−.118
Alcoa	.118*	.095	−.112	−.044
American Can	−.087*	−.124*	−.060	.031
A.T.&T.	−.039	−.010	−.009	−.003
American Tobacco	.111*	−.175*	.033	.077
Anaconda	.067*	−.068	−.125	.202
Bethlehem Steel	.013	−.122	−.148	.112
Chrysler	.012	.060	−.026	.040
Du Pont	.013	.069	−.043	−.055
Eastman Kodak	.025	−.006	−.053	−.023
General Electric	.011	.020	−.004	.000
General Foods	.061*	−.005	−.140	−.098
General Motors	−.004	−.128*	.009	−.028
Goodyear	−.123*	.001	−.037	.033
International Harvester	−.017	−.068	−.244*	.116
International Nickel	.096*	.038	.124	.041
International Paper	.046	.060	−.004	−.010
Johns Manville	.006	−.068	−.002	.002
Owens-Illinois	−.021	−.006	.003	−.022
Procter & Gamble	.099*	−.006	.098	.076
Sears	.097*	−.070	−.113	.041
Standard Oil (Calif.)	.025	−.143*	−.046	.040
Standard Oil (N.J.)	.008	−.109	−.082	−.121
Swift & Co.	−.004	−.072	.118	−.197
Texaco	.094*	−.053	−.047	−.178
Union Carbide	.107*	.049	−.101	.124
United Aircraft	.014	−.190*	−.192*	−.040
U.S. Steel	.040	−.006	−.056	.236*
Westinghouse	−.027	−.097	−.137	.067
Woolworth	.028	−.033	−.112	.040

*Coefficient is twice its computed standard error.
Time periods vary from stock to stock but usually run from about the end of 1957 to Sept. 26, 1962.
Source: E. F. Fama, "The Behavior of Stock Market Prices," *Journal of Business* (January 1965).

not state that stock price changes have to be serially independent; rather, it states that one cannot consistently earn abnormal rates of returns utilizing investment strategies based solely on historical prices. In order to test the weak-form EMH, many of the more popular "technical" trading strategies based on historical prices have been examined. One such strategy is the use of "filter rules." A 10% filter rule works in the following manner: suppose a stock has been decreasing in price. When the stock price ceases to decline and increases 10% above its low point, this triggers a buy signal; if the stock has been increasing in price and then begins to decline, once the price has declined 10% from its previous peak a sell signal is triggered. Several studies have examined this type of trading strategy, utilizing filters which ranged from as small as ½ of 1% to as large as 50%.[7] These studies found that, after adjusting for commissions, all such filter rules produced results that were below normal—in every case, a strategy of simply "buying and holding" a well-diversified portfolio outperformed the filter rules.

5-3-3 Other Tests   There probably are *at least* as many mechanical trading rules based on historical prices as there are technical analysts who attempt to forecast future prices. Thus, one can never conclusively state that all technical analysis is of no value since it would be impossible to test each "system." However, a large enough number of these mechanical systems have been tested so that one may draw reasonable conclusions about the general approach of technical analysis based on historical prices. Studies of chart patterns and moving averages have found trading strategies based on these techniques to be of little value. In addition, studies have been made of technical trading strategies based on information other than simply historical prices, such as odd-lot figures, advance-decline ratios, the volume of short sales and the size of short positions. Many of these studies were reviewed in an article by Pinches,[8] and the general conclusion was that such strategies have failed to outperform a naive strategy of buy-and-hold.

Thus, based on many different studies which considered different groups of stocks, different time periods, and many different technical trading strategies, it seems reasonable to conclude that the weak-form EMH is a valid description of the securities markets. This should come as no surprise. Since historical price information is the type of information regarding a security which is the easiest to obtain and understand, one might readily expect this type of information to be "fully reflected" in prices, given even minimal competition within the securities markets.

5-3-4 Why Do Technicians Exist?   Technical analysts generally attempt to forecast future market prices by using historical price information, as well as other market-related data such as trading volume. Since the available evidence overwhelmingly suggests that historical price data have no predictive value, one might reasonably wonder why investors are willing to pay for predictions based on such data. Why have technical analysts managed to survive and perhaps even prosper in the wake of the many negative findings by academic researchers regarding their services? One possible explanation is that it is impossible to test all the individual strategies used by each technician. Another factor is that many (if not most) technical analysts utilize, in addition to historical price data, other types of data which *may* have predictive value.

However, an intriguing explanation as to why technicians exist is suggested by the "arc sine law."[9] Consider a "fair game" where a coin is flipped many times in succession and one person is given a point if a head turns up and the other person

---

[7]See S. Alexander, "Price Movements in Speculative Markets: Trends or Random Walks, No. 2," *Industrial Management Review* (spring 1964); E. F. Fama and M. Blume, "Filter Rules and Stock Market Trading Profits," *Journal of Business* (January 1966 Supplement); and J. O'Hanlon and C. Ward, "How to Lose at Winning Strategies," *Journal of Portfolio Management* (spring 1986).

[8]G. Pinches, "The Random Walk Hypothesis and Technical Analysis," *Financial Analysts Journal* (March–April 1970).

[9]This section draws heavily on C. Dale and R. Workman, "The Arc Sine Law and the Treasury Bill Futures Markets," *Financial Analysts Journal* (November–December 1980).

wins a point if the result is a tail. One might expect that over the course of many successive flips, the lead would switch many times, back and forth, between the two players. The counterintuitive fact is that this is the *least likely outcome*. The odds overwhelmingly favor one player's being in the lead the vast majority of the time, *although we are unable to predict at the start of the game which player it will be.* Similarly, "according to the arc sine law, mechanical trading rules applied to price movements in financial assets will result in long periods of cumulative success, but equally long periods of cumulative failure."[10] Given the number of technical analysts plying their trade and the number of different "trading systems" each technician utilizes, the odds are very high that some of these systems will have "worked" for long periods in the past. The unsophisticated investor will have no way of determining which trading system worked because it has true predictive ability and which worked simply because of luck. Thus, many investors probably end up paying for technical trading strategies which have no better than a 50:50 chance of working in the future. Since there will always be a group of investors that are not well informed and since technicians and the "arc sine law" will continue to produce trading systems which appear to work, the prospects of technicians' continuing to exist are good.

5-4 EMPIRICAL TESTS OF THE SEMISTRONG-FORM EMH

Recall that the semistrong-form EMH argues that all *public information* is fully reflected in security prices. If the securities markets are efficient in the semistrong sense, then investors should not be able to earn abnormal rates of return utilizing trading strategies based on publicly available information. Public information includes not only such market-related data as historical prices and trading volume, but also data such as company financial statements, earnings and dividend announcements, and macro-economic data such as changes in monetary or fiscal policies and economic forecasts.

5-4-1 Residual Analysis and Event Studies

One of the first studies to examine the semistrong-form EMH was performed by Fama, Fisher, Jensen, and Roll (FFJR),[11] who analyzed the effect of stock splits on share prices. This is a particularly important study for several reasons. First, it provided some evidence on the efficiency of the securities markets. Second, it explored the question of whether stock splits increase shareholder wealth, an issue that is of interest in the study of both corporate finance and investments. Third, FFJR developed a research methodology for testing market efficiency which has been widely used by other researchers.

The method used by FFJR was to compute abnormal returns based on the market model in a fashion similar to the method of computing alphas demonstrated in Chapter 4. To estimate a "normal" return, security returns were regressed against the returns for an index constructed from all stocks listed on the New York Stock Exchange, utilizing Equation (5-1):

$$r_{it} = a_i + \beta_i r_{mt} + e_{it} \tag{5-1}$$

---

[10]Dale and Workman, p. 71. The reason for referring to this phenomenon as the "arc sine law" is that the probability associated with the last time the two players will be even in the coin-flipping game is calculated using an equation which can be approximated by the trigonometric arc sine function.

[11]E. F. Fama, L. Fisher, M. Jensen, and R. Roll, "The Adjustment of Stock Prices to New Information," *International Economic Review* (February 1969).

where r_{it} = realized return for the ith stock in time period t

$\quad r_{mt}$ = realized return for index in time period t

$\quad a_i, \beta_i$ = regression coefficients

$\quad e_{it}$ = error term, or residual, for time period t

The average, or normal, return for any time period, after adjusting for risk and changes in the market index, is then assumed to be

$$\text{Normal return} = a_i + \beta_i r_{mt} \qquad (5\text{-}2)$$

The error term e_{it} represents the residual, or abnormal, return AR_{it} for any particular time period, which is equal to the realized return r_{it} minus the normal return.

$$AR_{it} = e_{it} = r_{it} - (a_i + \beta_i r_{mt}) \qquad (5\text{-}3)$$

This method of estimating abnormal returns is frequently referred to as "residual analysis," since the regression equation represents a normal return and the residuals e_{it} in the equation represent the abnormal returns.

The other methodological innovation of FFJR was to measure the *cumulative average abnormal return* (CAAR) by adding the average abnormal returns AAR_t over time, with the time periods centered around the date of the event or the announcement data. (Studies which are concerned with measuring abnormal returns around the date of a particular type of event are frequently termed "event studies.") Mathematically,

$$AAR_t = \frac{1}{n} \sum_{i=1}^{n} AR_{it} \qquad (5\text{-}4)$$

where n equals the number of securities being studied and

$$CAAR = \sum_t AAR_t \qquad (5\text{-}5)$$

The CAAR is computed by adding the AAR_t for each time period with the time periods generally beginning several months before the "event" and ending several months after the event. Thus, the cumulative average abnormal return provides a picture of the average price behavior of securities over time. In general, if markets are efficient, the CAAR should be close to zero. Although a number of refinements have been made since the 1969 FFJR study, their general procedure for calculating and analyzing abnormal returns centered around the date of a particular event is still widely used today.[12]

---

[12] For some refinements in the FFJR methodology, see S. Bar-Yosef and L. D. Brown, "A Reexamination of Stock Splits Using Moving Betas," *Journal of Finance* (September 1977); G. Charest, "Split Information, Stock Returns and Market Efficiency—I," *Journal of Financial Economics* (June/September 1978); D. F. Larcker, L. A. Gordon, and G. E. Pinches, "Testing for Market Efficiency: A Comparison of the Cumulative Average Residual Methodology and Intervention Analysis," *Journal of Financial and Quantitative Analysis* (June 1980); and S. J. Brown and J. B. Warner, "Measuring Security Price Performance," *Journal of Financial Economics* (September 1980).

Before examining the FFJR results, first consider a hypothetical case. If stock splits (or some other event) provide additional, optimistic information about the company *and* the securities markets are semistrong efficient, then one of the following two scenarios should occur: (1) If the new, optimistic information has *not been anticipated* by investors, the stock should provide normal returns prior to the announcement, immediately react to the announcement by increasing in price thereby generating a ''one-shot'' positive abnormal return, and then provide normal returns thereafter. (2) If the optimistic information conveyed by the announcement has been gradually anticipated by investors, the stock should slowly rise in price before the announcement as more and more investors anticipate the company's improved prospects, show little or no reaction to the announcement, and provide normal returns from the announcement date forward.

Figure 5-3*a* illustrates the first case where the announcement is unanticipated. Notice that the cumulative average abnormal return (CAAR) drifts around zero until the announcement date when it immediately increases to, in this example, the +3% range. This is because the market reacted very rapidly to the new, favorable information by bidding up the stock price which resulted in a large, positive abnormal return on the announcement date. After this initial and immediate adjustment, the stock is once again ''fairly'' valued and ''fully reflects'' the new information. Thus, investors are not able to earn abnormal returns using this information and the CAAR fluctuates along a horizontal line. Of course, investors who happened to own the stock on the announcement date did reap the benefit of the price reaction, but since the information was assumed to be unanticipated, their good fortune can only be ascribed to luck— and luck, both good and bad, has a habit of evening out over time.

Figure 5-3*b* illustrates the second case where the favorable information is anticipated by investors before the official announcement date. Note that the CAAR rises as investors anticipate the good news, and bid up the stock price. By the announcement date it is too late—the news is already out and the CAAR again drifts along a horizontal line, indicating that investors cannot earn abnormal returns based on the now public information.

Of course, there is also the possibility that the markets are not efficient. Figure 5-3*c* illustrates the case where the favorable information is not anticipated and the market is semistrong *in*efficient. In this case the market reacts very slowly to the public announcement of good news, with the result that some investors are able to earn positive abnormal returns by purchasing the stock on the announcement date and then profiting as other less nimble investors bid up the stock price in the subsequent time periods. If this were the case, the CAAR would continue to rise for a number of periods after the announcement date, and one would be forced to reject the semistrong-form EMH.

5-4-2 The Fama, Fisher, Jensen, and Roll Results   FFJR examined 940 stock splits on the NYSE from 1927–1959 for which the split ratio was 5:4 or more. The price behavior for each of these stocks was examined for a period of 29 months before the date of the split and 29 months after the split.[13] The cumulative average abnormal

---

[13]When interpreting the FFJR results, the reader should be aware of two facts. First, the time periods are centered around the actual date of the stock split, not the announcement date. Typically, stock splits

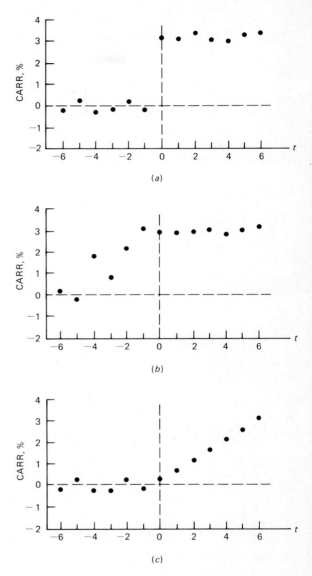

FIGURE 5-3 An illustration of the FFJR methodology. *(a)* Unanticipated favorable event in an efficient market. *(b)* Anticipated favorable event in an efficient market. *(c)* Unanticipated favorable event in an inefficient market.

returns are plotted in Figure 5-4. The first graph (Figure 5-4*a*) lists the CAAR for all 940 observations. One should first note that the actual act of splitting a stock did not have any impact on the wealth of the shareholders—the CAAR was essentially flat from the date of the split forward. This supports the theory that the act of splitting a stock does not create value. Likewise, a simple strategy of buying stocks after a stock

are announced a month or more before the date the stock is split. Second, this study used end-of-month prices, rather than daily prices. While both these factors make the FFJR results less precise than might be desired, nevertheless they probably do not qualitatively change them.

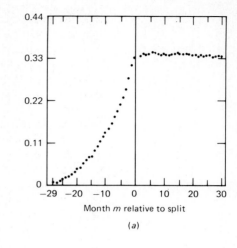

(a)

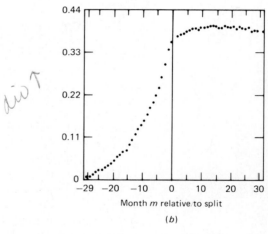

(b)

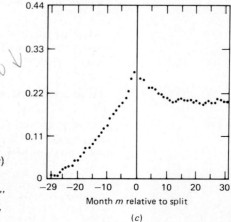

(c)

FIGURE 5-4 Fama, Fisher, Jensen, and Roll results of cumulative average abnormal returns for (a) all splits, (b) stocks with dividend increases, and (c) stocks with dividend decreases. [*Source: E. F. Fama, L. Fisher, M. Jensen, and R. Roll, "The Adjustment of Stock Prices to New Information,"* International Economic Review *(February 1969), p. 15.*]

split would not appear to produce abnormal returns. Thus, the FFJR results provide support for the semistrong-form EMH.

FFJR hypothesized that the reason the stocks provided positive abnormal returns *before* the split was that investors anticipated higher earnings and dividends, not the stock split itself. To test this, they divided their sample into stocks which provided increased cash dividends after the split and those which actually decreased their cash dividends. The CAARs for these two subsamples are shown in Figure 5-4*b* and *c*. Note that for those stocks which increased their dividends, the average CAAR was essentially flat subsequent to the stock split, which indicates that investors correctly anticipated the increased dividends. However, for those stocks which decreased their cash dividends, the CAAR declined after the split. In the latter case it appears that investors anticipated increased dividends and bid up the price of the stock; later (i.e., after the split) they found that the higher dividends were not forthcoming and, disappointed, they sold the stock. These results from the FFJR study are quite consistent with the behavior one would expect of rational investors competing in an efficient market.[14]

5-4-3 Other Studies Which Support the EMH In addition to the FFJR results, a number of other studies have supported the semistrong-form EMH. Ball and Brown[15] examined the effect of annual earnings announcements. They classified firms into two groups based on whether their earnings increased or decreased relative to the average corporate earnings. Ball and Brown found that *before* the earnings announcement stocks associated with increased earnings provided positive abnormal returns and stocks associated with decreased earnings provided negative abnormal returns. Both groups generated normal returns after the earnings were released, thus providing support for the semistrong-form EMH. The fact that the increased or decreased earnings were correctly anticipated also is evidence that security analysts do an effective job of anticipating future earnings.

Scholes[16] analyzed the price effects of large secondary offerings and found that the stock price tends to decline before the offering. Further, he found that the price decline was due nct to selling pressure created by the size of the offering but rather to an "information effect." This was because the largest price declines were associated with offerings made by corporate officers and smaller declines were associated with offerings made by groups which would not be considered "insiders." Even more interesting, while the identification of the seller does not have to be released to the public until 6 days after the offering, nevertheless the market, on average, *correctly identified the type of seller*. This is very strong evidence of market efficiency.

Many other studies have provided support for the semistrong-form EMH.[17] Thus, the preponderance of evidence from the earlier studies on market efficiency tended to

---

[14]However, a recent study of stock splits found that the market did not react efficiently to very small stock dividends (<6%). See J. R. Woolridge, "Ex-Date Stock Price Adjustment to Stock Dividends: A Note," *Journal of Finance* (March 1983).

[15]R. Ball and P. Brown, "An Empirical Evaluation of Accounting Income Numbers," *Journal of Accounting Research* (autumn 1968).

[16]M. S. Scholes, "The Market for Securities: Substitution versus Price Pressure and the Effects of Information on Share Prices," *Journal of Business* (April 1972).

[17]R. N. Waud, "Public Interpretation of Discount Rates Changes: Evidence on the 'Announcement Effect,' " *Econometrica*, vol. 38, no. 2; T. R. Archibald, "Stock Market Reaction to the Depreciation

support the semistrong-form EMH. However, more recently there has been a gradual accumulation of evidence which would suggest that the markets are not as efficient as was originally thought to be the case.

Before continuing, you should:

1 Understand the implications of serially independent stock price changes for "chart reading"
2 Be aware of the results of tests of technical trading rules
3 Understand the methodology of residual analysis
4 Be aware of the results of FFJR, and other tests of the semistrong-form EMH

5-5 EXAMPLES OF MARKET INEFFICIENCIES

In testing any hypothesis, a natural and correct procedure is to consider the simple and obvious examples first. If the hypothesis is proved to be incorrect for these cases, there is no point in testing the more complex and less obvious examples. In general, this is the manner in which testing of the efficient market hypothesis proceeded. Initial tests of the EMH generally dealt with the weak form, which utilizes relatively simple data. Attention then was focused on the semistrong form, and some of the more obvious types of trading strategies were examined, such as those based on stock splits, changes in annual earnings, and other examples, as described in the preceding section. As noted, these studies tended to support the semistrong-form EMH. However, as more complex examples have been examined and more detailed data have become available, the case for semistrong market efficiency has become considerably less clear-cut.

5-5-1 Quarterly Earnings Changes Recall that Ball and Brown examined the market reaction to annual earnings changes and concluded that the semistrong-form EMH was correct. However, a series of studies using quarterly earnings data came to a different conclusion.[18] One of these studies was performed by Joy, Litzenberger, and McEnally (JLM),[19] who examined prices and quarterly earnings over the period 1963–1968. The earnings for each quarter were compared with the earnings for the same quarter in the previous year. If the current quarter's earnings were 40% or more

---

Switch-Back," *Accounting Review* (January 1972); R. S. Kaplan and R. Roll, "Investor Evaluation of Accounting Information: Some Empirical Evidence," *Journal of Business* (April 1972); and S. Sunder, "Stock Price and Risk Related to Accounting Changes in Inventory Valuation," *Accounting Review* (April 1975).

[18]H. A. Latané, D. L. Tuttle, and C. P. Jones, "Quarterly Data: E/P Ratios vs. Changes in Earnings in Forecasting Future Price Changes," *Financial Analysts Journal* (January/February 1969); H. A. Latané, O. M. Joy, and Charles P. Jones, "Quarterly Data, Sort-Rank Routines, and Security Evaluation" *Journal of Business* (October 1970); C. P. Jones and R. H. Litzenberger, "Quarterly Earnings Reports and Intermediate Stock Price Trends," *Journal of Finance* (March 1970); and H. A. Latané and C. P. Jones, "Standardized Unexpected Earnings—A Progress Report," *Journal of Finance* (December 1977).

[19]O. M. Joy, R. H. Litzenberger, and R. W. McEnally, "The Adjustment of Stock Prices to Announcements of Unanticipated Changes in Quarterly Earnings," *Journal of Accounting Research* (autumn 1977). Chapter 11 discusses in more detail the relationship between changes in earnings and changes in stock prices.

above the earnings for the same quarter in the previous year, the earnings were classified as substantially better than expected. If the current quarter's earnings were 40% below the previous year's quarterly earnings, the earnings were classified as substantially worse than expected.

Figure 5-5 presents the JLM results. Abnormal returns were calculated from 13 weeks before the announcement of the earnings to 26 weeks after the announcement. Notice that stocks whose earnings were substantially greater than "expected" generated positive abnormal returns while those with earnings substantially below "expectations" generated negative abnormal returns. It is obvious from Figure 5-5 that the earnings' changes were not totally unexpected since a majority of the cumulative average abnormal returns occurred before the release of the earnings announcement. Again, it appears that investors were correctly anticipating the future earnings changes.

However, *after* the announcement of the earnings, stocks which reported earnings substantially above those of the previous year continued to generate positive abnormal returns. Since the announcement of the earnings makes the information public, this represents evidence against the semistrong-form EMH. According to the JLM results, investors could have earned positive abnormal returns of approximately 6.5% over the next 26 weeks by simply buying stocks which reported earnings 40% above the previous year's quarterly earnings. On the other hand, for those stocks with earnings substantially below the previous year there was no systematic market reaction after the announcement as the CAAR remained relatively stable.

The JLM results are well known to those in the academic community and presumably to professional investors as well. While a strategy such as that proposed by JLM may have worked in the past, such a strategy certainly *should not work now* if the markets are semistrong efficient. With modern computers and data bases, it is too easy to replicate their experiments. And yet a more recent study[20] using data for the period 1971–1980 documented results similar to those of JLM. Thus, the unexpected earnings effect on stock prices remains a puzzle.

[20]See C. P. Jones, R. S. Rendleman, Jr., and H. A. Latané, "Earnings Announcements: Pre- and Post-Responses," *Journal of Portfolio Management* (spring 1985).

FIGURE 5-5   Joy, Litzenberger, and McEnally results. [*Adapted from O. M. Joy, R. H. Litzenberger, and R. W. McEnally, "The Adjustment of Stock Prices to Announcements of Unanticipated Changes in Quarterly Earnings,"* Journal of Accounting Research *(autumn 1977), table 1 and fig. 3.*]

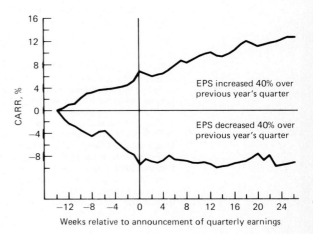

EPS increased 40% over previous year's quarter

EPS decreased 40% over previous year's quarter

CARR, %

Weeks relative to announcement of quarterly earnings

5-5-2 Other Tests Based on Earnings and Dividends   There have been a number of other tests which utilized earnings and dividend data and provided evidence contradictory to the semistrong-form EMH.[21] In a survey article, Ball[22] reviews over 20 different studies which reported abnormal returns, and agrees that "taken at face value, studies of the market reaction to earnings announcements reveal post-announcement excess returns." However, he argues that the results of these studies are probably not due to market inefficiency, but rather to methodological errors and, more importantly, *to a misspecification of the model that generates security returns*. Most of the studies reviewed by Ball utilized some version of the market model which suggests that security returns are a function of a single variable, which is the market index. However, it may be that there are several variables which determine security returns and by omitting these additional (and currently unknown) variables, the results of these studies were biased in favor of rejecting the semistrong-form EMH.

On the other hand, in the same issue of the *Journal of Financial Economics* in which Ball's survey appeared, there were several additional papers which reported results contrary to the EMH.[23] While all these new studies report market inefficiencies, they are all also based on the market model which argues that there is single factor r_m generating security returns. Thus, it is possible that Ball's hypothesis (that the market is efficient and that there is more than one factor generating security returns) is still correct. The studies of the small-firm effect may give us some clues as to the identity of the omitted factor(s).

5-5-3 The Small-Firm Effect   Banz[24] found that the size of the firm has been highly correlated with stock returns. In general, his results indicate that *the larger the market value of the firm's common stock, the lower the rate of return generated by the stock*. Specifically, Banz examined historical monthly returns for NYSE common stocks for the period 1931–1975 and the results are reported in Table 5-2.

To determine how much difference the size effect makes, Banz formed portfolios consisting of the 10 smallest firms and the 10 largest firms ($n = 10$), computed the average return for these portfolios, and then subtracted the large-firm portfolio return

[21]F. Black, "Yes Virginia, There Is Hope: Tests of the Value Line Ranking System," *Financial Analysts Journal* (September/October 1973). For an update on Black's study, see T. Copeland and D. Mayers, "The Value Line Enigma (1965–1978): A Cast Study of Performance Valuation Issues," *Journal of Financial Economics* (November 1982); R. L. Watts, "The Information Content of Dividends," *Journal of Business* (April 1973); S. Basu, "Investment Performance of Common Stocks in Relation to Their Price-Earnings Ratios: A Test of the Efficient Market Hypothesis," *Journal of Finance* (June 1977); and more recently, "The Relationship between Earnings' Yield, Market Value and Return for NYSE Common Stocks: Further Evidence," *Journal of Financial Economics* (June 1983); and D. A. Goodman and J. W. Peavy, "Industry Relative Price-Earnings Ratios as Indicators of Investment Returns," *Financial Analysts Journal* (July/August 1983).

[22]R. Ball, "Anomalies in Relationships between Securities' Yields and Yield-Surrogates," *Journal of Financial Economics* (June/September 1978).

[23]R. L. Watts, "Systematic 'Abnormal' Returns after Quarterly Earnings Announcements," *Journal of Financial Economics* (June/September 1978); R. Thompson, "The Information Content of Discounts and Premiums on Closed-End Fund Shares," *Journal of Financial Economics* (June/September 1978); D. Galai, "Empirical Tests of Boundary Conditions for CBOE Options," *Journal of Financial Economics* (June/September 1978); D. P. Chiras and S. Manaster, "The Information Content of Option Prices and a Test of Market Efficiency," *Journal of Financial Economics* (June/September 1978); and G. Charest, "Dividend Information, Stock Returns and Market Efficiency—II," *Journal of Financial Economics* (June/September 1978).

[24]R. W. Banz, "The Relationship between Return and Market Value of Common Stocks," *Journal of Financial Economics* (March 1981).

TABLE 5-2   BANZ's RESULTS ON TESTING THE SIZE EFFECT

Mean monthly returns on arbitrage portfolios

$$r_s - r_1 = \hat{\alpha}_i + \hat{\beta}_i (r_m - r_f)$$

	α_i		
	n = 10	**n = 20**	**n = 50**
Overall period:			
1931–1975	0.0152	0.0148	0.0101
5-year subperiods:			
1931–1935	0.0589	0.0597	0.0427
1936–1940	0.0201	0.0182	0.0089
1941–1945	0.0430	0.0408	0.0269
1946–1950	−0.0060	−0.0046	−0.0036
1951–1955	−0.067	−0.0011	0.0013
1956–1960	0.0039	0.0008	0.0037
1961–1965	0.0131	0.0060	0.0024
1966–1970	0.0121	0.0117	0.0077
1971–1975	0.0063	0.0108	0.0098

Equally weighted portfolios with n securities, adjusted for differences in market risk with respect to CRSP value-weighted index.
r_s = small-firm portfolio; r_1 = large-firm portfolio
Source: R. Banz, "The Relationship between Return and Market Value of Common Stocks," *Journal of Financial Economics* (March 1981), Table 3.

from the small-firm portfolio return. This procedure was repeated for the 20 smallest firms and the 20 largest ($n = 20$), and for the 50 smallest and 50 largest firms ($n = 50$). Note that for the overall period, the difference in return between the small-firm (r_s) portfolios and large-firm (r_l) portfolios ($n = 10$) was 0.0152 per month. If the 1.52% monthly difference in return is annualized, *the small-firm portfolio will have "outperformed" the large-firm portfolio by 19.8%.*

Since Banz constructed the portfolios so that they had the same beta, these results suggest that the CAPM, and/or the single-factor market model, are misspecified and that the return equation should contain an additional factor(s) which is highly correlated with firm size. The results could also be interpreted as an extreme case of market inefficiency, but given the fact that the return differential is so great between small and large firms, and the fact that this differential has persisted for so long, it seems unlikely that investors would not begin to identify the mispriced securities and "compete away" the abnormal profits.

Several other studies have confirmed the existence of a small-firm effect.[25] However, in the process of studying the size effect, these researchers have discovered a

[25] A partial list would include M. R. Reinganum, "Misspecification of Capital Asset Pricing: Empirical Anomalies Based on Earnings Yields and Market Values," *Journal of Financial Economics* (March 1981); M. R. Reinganum, "A Direct Test of Roll's Conjecture on the Firm Size Effect," *Journal of Finance* (March 1982); C. James and R. Edmister, "The Relation between Common Stock Returns, Trading Activity and Market Value," *Journal of Finance* (September 1983); and P. Brown, A. Kleidon, and T. Marsh,

number of things regarding this anomaly. First, the risk of small firms was underestimated in the earlier studies because the stocks of small firms do not trade as frequently as those of large firms, and Roll[26] has demonstrated that this results in the betas of small firms being systematically underestimated—which, in turn, results in their risk-adjusted returns being overstated. Second, Roll[27] and Blume and Stambaugh[28] have recently demonstrated that the method typically used to form portfolios in stock market studies results in the returns of small-firm portfolios being overstated. Correctly measuring the risk and return of small-firm portfolios appears to eliminate at least 50% of the small-firm effect.

Kiem[29] has documented that over half of the small-firm effect occurs in January and most of the abnormal return associated with January takes place during the first 5 days of trading. Stoll and Whaley[30] argue that a large portion of the small-firm effect can be explained by the fact that transaction costs (commissions and particularly the bid-ask spread) are higher for small firms. Another possible explanation is that of Arbel and Strebel,[31] who argue that the small-firm effect is really a "neglected-stock" effect. Neglected stocks are defined as those stocks which do not have a large number of analysts following them and are not owned by a large number of institutional investors. Arbel and Strebel find that abnormal profits are associated with neglected stocks and that the small-firm effect disappears after they control for the neglected-stock effect.

To date, the small-firm, and/or the neglected-stock, effect remains an unresolved issue. Much remains to be done in this area, on both a theoretical and an empirical basis, before we can reach any firm conclusions. At this point we can only speculate that firm size, or a variable highly correlated with size, is an omitted variable in the model for normal returns. However, it is probably safe to say that the single-factor market model does not completely account for the way returns are determined in the securities markets.

5-5-4 The Weekend Effect   It is conceivable that many of the previously discussed examples of market inefficiency can be explained because the model for determining

---

"New Evidence on the Nature of Size Related Anomalies in Stock Prices," *Journal of Financial Economics* (June 1983).

[26]R. Roll, "A Possible Explanation of the Small Firm Effect," *Journal of Finance* (September 1981).

[27]R. Roll, "On Computing Mean Returns and the Small Firm Premium," *Journal of Financial Economics* (September 1983).

[28]M. E. Blume and R. F. Stambaugh, "Biases in Computed Returns: An Application to the Size Effect," *Journal of Financial Economics* (September 1983).

[29]D. Kleim, "Size-Related Anomalies and Stock Return Seasonality," *Journal of Financial Economics* (June 1983). Also, see D. Givoly and A. Ovadia, "Year-End Tax-Induced Sales and Stock Market Seasonality," *Journal of Finance* (March 1983); M. Reinganum, "The Anomalous Stock Market Behavior of Small Firms in January: Empirical Tests for Tax-Loss Selling Effects," *Journal of Financial Economics* (June 1983); and P. Brown, D. Keim, A. Kleidon, and T. Marsh, "Stock Return Seasonalities and the Tax-Loss Selling Hypothesis: Analysis of the Arguments and Australian Evidence," *Journal of Financial Economics* (June 1983).

[30]H. Stoll and R. Whaley, "Transaction Costs and the Small Firm Effect," *Journal of Financial Economics* (June 1983). Also, see P. Shultz, "Transaction Costs and the Small-Firm Effect: A Comment," *Journal of Financial Economics* (June 1983).

[31]A. Arbel and P. Strebel, "The Neglected and the Small Firm Effects," *The Financial Review* (November 1982); A. Arbel and P. Strebel, "Pay Attention to Neglected Firms," *Journal of Portfolio Management* (winter 1983); and A. Arbel, S. Carvell, and P. Strebel, "Giraffes, Institutions and Neglected Firms," *Financial Analysts Journal* (May–June 1983).

normal returns is misspecified. However, a misspecified model for measuring normal returns cannot account for the ''weekend effect.''

In a fascinating study, French[32] examines the returns generated by the S&P 500 index for each day of the week over the time period 1953–1977. Ignoring holidays, the returns for Monday represent a three-calendar-day investment, from the close of trading Friday to the close of trading Monday. Returns for the other days of the week represent a 1-day period of investment. If expected return is a linear function of the period of investment, measured in calendar time, the mean return for Monday should be *three times* the mean return for the other days of the week. However, if the process generating returns operates in terms of trading days, the return for all 5 days of the week should be the same. Regardless of how returns are generated, one would not expect the returns for Mondays to be less than the returns for the other 4 days of the week. As it turns out, the returns for Mondays have not only been less than those for the other 4 days of the week, but *Monday returns have actually been negative*!

Since the returns are being compared for *the same portfolio* at different times of the week, the proper specification of the equilibrium model (single- or two-factor model, etc.) for determining normal returns is not an important issue. As French notes, ''It is difficult to imagine any reasonable model of equilibrium consistent with both market efficiency and negative expected returns to a portfolio as large as the Standard and Poor's Composite.''

One might be tempted to devise a trading strategy, based on the weekend effect, of purchasing the S&P 500 at the close on Monday, sell at the close on Friday, and hold cash over the weekend. Ignoring transaction costs, the trading rule would have generated an average annual return of 13.4% from 1953 to 1977, while a simple buy and hold would have yielded a 5.5% annual return. However, if transaction costs of only 0.25% per transaction were included, the buy-and-hold strategy would have provided a higher return. Nevertheless, knowledge of the weekend effect still is of value. Purchases planned for Thursday or Friday might be delayed until Monday, while sales planned for Monday might be delayed until the end of the week. Thus, the weekend effect provides an interesting counterexample to the efficient market hypothesis.

5-6 EMPIRICAL TESTS OF THE STRONG-FORM EMH

As noted earlier, the strong-form EMH argues that *all* information is fully reflected in security prices, which represents an extreme hypothesis most observers would not expect to be literally true. In addition, if there is some evidence suggesting that the semistrong form (which deals with public information) is not entirely valid, one might suspect that there will be considerably more evidence that the strong form (which deals with private information) is not valid.

5-6-1 The Near-Strong and Superstrong   Who might have private (monopolistic) information? One group would certainly be the top management of firms, or corporate ''insiders,'' since they have access to information regarding corporate strategies, investment opportunities, financing alternatives, and other information which is typically

---

[32]K. R. French, ''Stock Returns and the Weekend Effect,'' *Journal of Financial Economics* (March 1980).

not conveyed (at least immediately) to the public. Other individuals who have true monopolistic information are the specialists who make markets in stocks listed on the exchanges. The specialist is the only person who has access to the "book" of limit orders for a particular stock. Knowledge of the prices and quantities of the limit orders represents private information that would certainly be useful in devising trading strategies.

It has also been argued that professional money managers represent a third group which has private information. When the analysts for a large money-management organization develop their estimates of future earnings and other factors which are important in pricing securities, this information is frequently retained within the organization and not shared with the public. However, one should recognize that this type of information is fundamentally different from the monopolistic information of corporate insiders and exchange specialists. The analysts' estimates are based on *careful scrutiny of public information*. While a large investment organization may have information not generally available to the public, other professional investors may have developed similar private forecasts based on the same public information.[33] Thus, the private information generated by professional investors does not give them an advantage as strong as that afforded those who have true inside information, such as corporate officers and exchange specialists.

Therefore, we prefer to divide the strong-form EMH into two groups: (1) the "superstrong" form, which includes insiders and exchange specialists who have true monopolistic information; and (2) the "near-strong" form, which includes private estimates developed from public information. Intuitively it seems unlikely that the superstrong-form EMH would be valid. As it turns out, there is little, if any, evidence supporting the superstrong hypothesis. However, one can more easily argue a priori that the near-strong-form EMH is valid since the private estimates of professional investors are developed from public information. Unfortunately, it is very difficult, if not impossible, to devise definitive tests of the near-strong-form EMH.

5-6-2 Insider Trading   Corporate managers and anyone else who owns more than 10% of an issue of securities are deemed to be "insiders" under the Securities and Exchange Acts of 1933 and 1934. Insiders are required to report any transaction they make in their firm's securities to the Securities and Exchange Commission within 10 days following the month in which the transaction takes place. The information on insider trading is subsequently published in the SEC's *Official Summary of Securities Transactions and Holdings*. Thus, approximately 2 months elapse before information on insider transactions becomes publicly available.

A number of studies[34] have utilized the information in the *Official Summary* to examine the profitability of insider trading. In general, all these studies have found

---

[33]It would be naive to assume that there are no instances when an analyst is able to obtain true inside information through personal conversations with corporate insiders. However, an analyst in such a case would be considered a "tipee," and in the United States it is illegal for a tipee to engage in trading activity based on such inside information. Being against the law, of course, does not guarantee that such trading activity won't take place. But the threat of prosecution probably does limit this type of illegal trading activity to relatively minor amounts.

[34]J. H. Lorie and V. Niederhoffer, "Predictive and Statistical Properties of Insider Trading," *Journal of Law and Economics*, (April 1968); S. P. Pratt and C. W. DeVere, "Relationship between Insider Trading

TABLE 5-3   JAFFE'S RESULTS ON INSIDER TRADING

Length of time period	From month of insider trade		From month information became publicly available	
	CAAR	t value	CAAR	t value
1960s data; 861 cases; cutoff = 3 net purchasers or sellers				
1 month	0.98%	3.65	0.74%	2.53
2 months	2.09%	4.73	1.23%	3.96
8 months	5.07%	5.23	4.94%	4.77
1950s data; 293 cases; cutoff = 4 net purchasers or sellers				
1 month	0.94%	3.06	0.10%	0.28
2 months	1.74%	3.16	0.65%	1.80
8 months	5.14%	4.69	4.12%	3.71

Source: J. F. Jaffe, "Special Information and Insider Trading," *Journal of Business* (July 1974), Tables 3 and 5.

that insiders utilize their monopolistic information to their advantage and earn positive abnormal returns by trading in their firm's securities. Even more interesting is that several studies found that noninsiders could earn positive abnormal profits by utilizing the information published in the *Official Summary*—this represents additional evidence contrary to the semistrong-form EMH, since the *Official Summary* is available to the public.

For example, the results from a study by Jaffe[35] are reported in Table 5-3. Jaffe examined a trading strategy of identifying from the *Official Summary* stocks in which there was a net plurality of insiders buying or selling. The top half of Table 5-3 presents the results based on 1960s data when the cutoff for net purchaser or sellers was set at three (i.e., there must be at least three more insiders buying than selling, or vice versa). The bottom half of Table 5-3 presents results based on 1950s data when the cutoff was set at four or more net buyers or sellers. The column labeled "From month of insider trade" represents a test of the superstrong-form EMH since it measures how well the insiders fared on their own trades. And, as one might expect, insiders earned positive abnormal profits. According to Jaffe's results, the CAAR increased approximately 1% in each of the first 2 months following the date of the insider trade and reached a level of approximately 5% after 8 months. While these results are before

and Rates of Return for NYSE Common Stocks, 1960–1966," in J. H. Lorie and R. Brealey, eds., *Modern Developments in Investment Management*, 2d ed., Dryden Press, Hinsdale, Ill., 1978; J. E. Finnerty, "Insiders and Market Efficiency," *Journal of Finance* (September 1976); and J. E. Finnerty, "Insiders Activity and Inside Information: A Multivariate Analysis," *Journal of Financial and Quantitative Analysis* (June 1976).

[35] J. F. Jaffe, "Special Information and Insider Trading," *Journal of Business* (July 1974).

commissions, 5% would certainly exceed normal transaction costs on a round-trip trade.

The column labeled ''From month information became publicly available'' represents a test of the semistrong-form EMH, since investors presumably are able to devise trading strategies based on the publicly available information in the *Official Summary*. Notice that while the CAARs are not as large as for the insiders themselves, a strategy of buying (selling) stocks that insiders have bought (sold) would have produced positive abnormal profits of 4% or more after an 8-month holding period. Again, these abnormal profits would generally exceed brokerage commissions.

5-6-3 Specialist Trading   A number of studies have examined the issue of whether or not specialists earn abnormal returns. An SEC study[36] found that over 80% of the time specialists either sell above their last purchase price or buy below their last sale price. Niederhoffer and Osborne[37] reported that specialists earn positive abnormal returns, as did the Institutional Investor Study.[38] Finally, a study by Reilly and E. F. Drzycimiski[39] analyzed the impact of major unexpected world events and found that specialists typically made abnormal profits on trading centered around such events.

The results of all these studies seem quite consistent with the idea of specialists having monopolistic information. When one considers the research that has been done on both insider and specialist trading, it is apparent that the superstrong-form EMH is not valid. This is not surprising for such an ''extreme null hypothesis.''

5-6-4 Performance of Professional Money Managers   We define the near-strong-form EMH as dealing with private information (such as earnings forecasts) generated from public information. If this information remains private, it is possible to test the near-strong form only indirectly. The procedure most often used is to examine the performance of professional money managers over time, since they presumably base at least part of their trading activity on their internally generated private information.

A number of studies have examined the performance of mutual fund managers.[40] (Mutual fund managers have been the principal subject of this research because initially they were the only group of professional money managers for which return data were available.) Each of these studies concluded that mutual fund managers did *not* achieve abnormal returns and that the strong-form EMH was valid. (They did not distinguish between what we term the near-strong and the superstrong.)

However, a number of problems are associated with measuring the performance of money managers. These problems are serious enough to suggest that the results of

---

[36]*Report of the Special Study of the Security Markets*, Securities and Exchange Commission, Washington, D.C. (1963).

[37]V. Niederhoffer and M. F. Osborne, ''Market-Making and Reversal on the Stock Exchange,'' *Journal of American Statistical Association* (December 1966).

[38]U.S. Securities and Exchange Commission, *Institutional Investor Study Report*, 92nd Congress, 1st Session, House Document No. 92–64, Government Printing Office, Washington, D.C. (1971).

[39]F. K. Reilly and E. F. Drzycimiski, ''The Stock Exchange Specialist and the Market Impact of Major World Events,'' *Financial Analysts Journal* (July–August 1975).

[40]I. Friend, F. E. Brown, E. S. Herman, and D. Vickers, *A Study of Mutual Funds*, Government Printing Office, Washington, D.C. (1962); W. F. Sharpe, ''Mutual Fund Performance,'' *Journal of Business* (January 1966, Supplement); and M. C. Jensen, ''Risk, the Pricing of Capital Assets, and the Evaluation of Investment Portfolios,'' *Journal of Business* (April 1969).

these mutual fund studies may not be meaningful. We can classify these problems into three categories:

1 Specifying the correct model for estimating normal returns
2 Statistical measurement problems
3 A version of the Peter Principle

As noted earlier, if the model for determining normal returns is misspecified, one cannot identify abnormal returns or performance. It may be that normal returns should be a function of both systematic risk and liquidity, or firm size, or some other factor. In addition, even if the single-factor CAPM is correct, Roll[41] has pointed out that the rankings of individual money managers may be sensitive to the index chosen as a proxy for the market portfolio. For example, a money manager ranked above average based on a value-weighted index may be ranked below average if an equally weighted index is chosen.

Another problem is that there is so much "noise," or variability in the return data. A money manager may be superior over the long term, but during shorter intervals her performance will almost certainly vary, as she might produce returns that are either above or below average in any single period. This variability makes it difficult to identify performance that is significantly different (in the statistical sense) from average performance.[42] For example, Murphy examined the results reported in one study and found:

> The only fund that did well enough to be significant at the 95% confidence level had to outperform the market by 5.82% *per year* for fourteen years. Responsible investment professionals might aim for 2.0% per year over a long period. One of the funds in Jensen's study outperformed the market by 2.1% per year for twenty years, yet this performance was not statistically significant even at the 62% level. In all, thirteen of the 115 funds added at least 1% per year incremental value after paying all expenses but did not achieve statistical significance.[43]

Based on his own simulations of performance data, Murphy reported:

---

[41]R. Roll, "Ambiguity When Performance Is Measured by the Securities Market Line," *Journal of Finance* (September 1978); also R. Roll, "A Critique of the Asset Pricing Theory's Test," *Journal of Financial Economics* (March 1977).

[42]The test to determine whether a manager's performance is statistically different from average performance usually involves a t statistic calculated as

$$ t = \frac{\overline{AR_i}}{\sigma/\sqrt{n}} $$

where $\overline{AR_i}$ = mean abnormal return for fund i

σ = standard deviation of abnormal returns for fund i

n = number of observations, or time periods

If the fund has, on average, positive abnormal performance, but the performance varies substantially from period to period, σ will be large. This will cause the t statistic to be small and not statistically significant, unless n (the number of time periods) is very large.

[43]J. M. Murphy, "Efficient Markets, Index Funds, Illusion, and Reality," *Journal of Portfolio Management* (fall 1977), pp. 10–11.

Given a reasonable level of average annual outperformance and variability, it takes about *seventy years* of quarterly data to achieve statistical significance at the 95% level. [Italics added.]

Brown and Warner[44] and Valentine[45] also examined whether superior performance can be detected and drew conclusions similar to those of Murphy.

Still another problem associated with identifying outstanding money managers is associated with a modified version of the Peter Principle.[46] A successful manager, by virtue of her success, will increase the amount of money under management and undoubtedly will attract additional, outside funds to manage. It seems inevitable that as the amount under management becomes larger and larger, the performance will be forced closer and closer to the market averages. In addition, the successful money manager is frequently promoted within her organization, which increases her responsibilities beyond that of strictly managing money. It is unlikely that a truly superior manager will be in the same position, or with the same organization, long enough to identify his or her superior performance.

For all these reasons, the results of the earlier mutual fund studies are suspect. It may be that we will never have any conclusive evidence regarding the performance of professional money managers and the near-strong EMH.

> Before continuing, you should:
> 1 Be aware of several counterexamples to the semistrong-form EMH
> 2 Be able to distinguish between the near-strong and superstrong forms
> 3 Know that most studies have rejected the superstrong-form EMH
> 4 Understand some of the problems involved in identifying above- and below-average portfolio performance

5-7 PASSIVE VS. ACTIVE INVESTMENT MANAGEMENT

Approaches to investment management can be classified into two broad categories, passive and active. Passive investment managers generally believe that the markets are efficient and therefore all securities are priced to yield a normal return. While passive managers may tailor portfolios to meet the risk and return preferences of their individual clients, they nevertheless do not engage in a strategy of trying to "beat the market." Rather than searching for underpriced securities, they assume that each stock or bond is correctly priced. Consequently, they tend to select a well-diversified group of securities which have the appropriate risk characteristics of their client and then hold these securities for relatively long periods of time, thus minimizing transaction costs. This passive strategy is frequently referred to as "indexing."

[44]S. J. Brown and J. B. Warner, "Measuring Security Price Performance," *Journal of Financial Economics* (September 1980).

[45]J. L. Valentine, *Investment Analysis and Capital Market Theory*, Occasional Paper Number 1, The Financial Analysts Research Foundation, Charlottesville, Va. (1975), p. 17.

[46]The Peter Principle basically argues that competent managers will be successively promoted to higher and higher positions in the organization until they reach a level at which they are no longer competent. See L. J. Peter and R. Hall, *The Peter Principle*, William Morrow, New York, 1969.

Active managers, on the other hand, do not believe that the markets are perfectly efficient, and they tend to devote considerable effort to searching out mispriced securities. Since securities are unlikely to be mispriced for very long, these managers tend to be relatively active traders, buying and selling at frequent intervals, in an attempt to achieve abnormal returns and "beat the market."

5-7-1 Is Active Management Worth the Effort?

Before engaging in an active investment-management strategy, one should first determine whether or not the additional time, effort, and cost associated with an active strategy compared with a passive strategy will be well spent. Based on the material presented in the previous sections of this chapter, it should be obvious that the securities markets are competitive and, as a minimum, reasonably efficient. Even those studies which examined and rejected the superstrong-form EMH did not report exceedingly large abnormal returns. For example, the Jaffe study on insider trading reported that insiders earned abnormal returns on the order of 4 to 5% over a period of 8 months *before transaction costs*.

Nevertheless, it appears that if one is able to consistently identify market inefficiencies, an active strategy will provide large enough abnormal returns to justify the additional costs. A particularly interesting study along these lines was performed by Hodges and Brealey.[47] They simulated the results for various active strategies using stock returns and variances similar to the historical distributions of stock returns. Figure 5-6 presents the simulated results for strategies of forming portfolios of "underpriced" securities assuming different abilities for identifying mispriced stocks. The ability to identify mispriced stocks was measured by the correlation between the

[47]S. D. Hodges and R. A. Brealey, "Portfolio Selection in a Dynamic and Uncertain World," *Financial Analysts Journal* (March–April 1973).

FIGURE 5-6 The impact of the ability to forecast individual security abnormal returns on portfolio performance; M = market index; R = correlation between expected and actual abnormal returns for individual securities. [*Source: S. D. Hodges and R. A. Brealey, "Portfolio Selection in a Dynamic and Uncertain World," Financial Analysts Journal (March/April 1973), fig. 1.*]

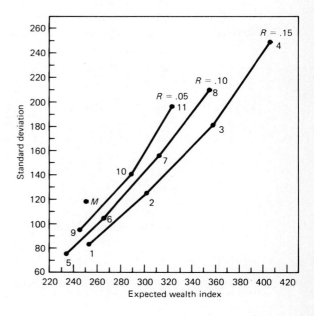

analysts' forecasts of individual security abnormal returns and the actual abnormal returns generated by the securities. Point M in Figure 5-6 represents the results of a naive strategy of buying and holding a market index. Each line represents the results of a number of simulations for each level of assumed forecasting ability. Note that even when the correlation between expected and actual abnormal returns was only 0.05, the active strategy "beat" the passive strategy—the line for $R = .05$ is to the right of M, indicating that even a relatively minor ability to forecast security returns can be utilized to form portfolios which generate more return than a passive strategy for the same level of risk. In this case, return was measured as the level of terminal wealth after 8 years and risk is measured as the standard deviation of the portfolio returns. As the forecasting ability improves (as the correlation between expected and actual abnormal returns increases), the active stock-selection strategies provide increasingly superior returns relative to the passive strategy.

Of course, it only stands to reason that to the extent investors can correctly forecast the abnormal returns of securities they can improve their portfolios' relative performance—obviously, investors will buy those securities which they perceive to have positive abnormal returns and avoid those with expected negative abnormal returns. However, the impressive point of this study is that the simulations suggest one is able to achieve substantially better performance with relatively little ability to forecast abnormal returns. These results are particularly interesting since Hodges and Brealey assumed a relatively high commission rate of 2½% for each transaction—for example, the process of selling one stock and replacing it with another would generate a total commission cost of 5%.

Hodges and Brealey also examined the impact of forecasting ability with respect to changes in the overall market. Again, the presence of forecasting ability produced results which were superior to those of a naive buy-and-hold strategy. However, forecasting ability with respect to market timing was not as valuable as forecasting ability with respect to individual stock selection. Nevertheless, *if* one has the ability to forecast either abnormal returns for individual securities or changes in the overall level of the market, then active strategies are clearly worth the effort.

Sharpe[48] also examined active strategies based on market timing. Basically, he assumed that investors decided at the beginning of each year whether or not the return on the S&P 500 would exceed the return for treasury bills for the same year. If the S&P 500 return was expected to exceed the treasury bill return, "market timers" bought the S&P index; if not, they invested in treasury bills. A commission of 2% was charged each year the portfolio was shifted from one asset to the other. Table 5-4 presents the results which would have been achieved by three different strategies: (1) buying only treasury bills, denoted "cash equivalents" in Table 5-4; (2) buying and holding the S&P 500, denoted "stocks"; and (3) correctly forecasting the return on the S&P 500 relative to the treasury bill rate each year, denoted "perfect timing."

As one would expect, a market-timing strategy based on perfect foresight would generate returns superior to a naive buy-and-hold strategy and a lower standard deviation of returns, although the gains are not as large as one might expect. For example, over the entire time period of the study, perfect market timing generated an average

---

[48] W. F. Sharpe, "Likely Gains from Market Timing," *Financial Analysts Journal* (March–April 1975).

TABLE 5-4   OVERALL PERFORMANCE: CASH EQUIVALENTS, STOCKS, AND A POLICY WITH PERFECT TIMING

	Cash equivalents	Stocks	Perfect timing
1929–1972			
Average return, %	2.38	10.64	14.86
Standard deviation of annual returns	1.96	21.06	14.58
Geometric mean return	2.36	8.49	13.99
1934–1972			
Average return, %	2.40	12.76	15.25
Standard deviation of annual returns	2.00	18.17	13.75
Geometric mean return	2.38	11.23	14.46
1946–1972			
Average return, %	3.27	12.79	14.63
Standard deviation of annual returns	1.83	15.64	12.46
Geometric mean return	3.25	11.73	13.99

Source: W. F. Sharpe, "Likely Gains from Market Timing," *Financial Analysts Journal* (March–April 1975), Table 2.

annual return of 14.86% with a standard deviation of 14.58% compared with the buy-and-hold strategy which generated a lower average annual return of 10.64% and a higher standard deviation of 21.06%.

However, when one allows for less than perfect market timing, the comparisons change dramatically, primarily because of the transaction costs associated with shifting from stocks to treasury bills in the market-timing strategy. Sharpe found that for the market-timing strategy to produce returns equivalent to the buy-and-hold strategy, the investor had to correctly identify whether or not the forthcoming year was "good" or "bad" *at least 74% of the time*. This represents a substantial challenge to those who attempt to time the market.

5-7-2 Implications for Active Management   The many studies on the concept of market efficiency provide a number of implications for active investment management. First, one should not underestimate the degree of competition within the securities markets. There are thousands of well-educated, intelligent, and hard-working analysts and portfolio managers, most of whom have the same objective—to earn abnormal profits. In such an environment it would be foolish to believe that earning those elusive abnormal profits will be an easy task.

Second, the active manager striving for abnormal profits should search in the least efficient sectors of the securities markets. The less efficient sectors are likely to be those areas which have the least competition or are the most complex areas to analyze. Thus, the potential for abnormal profits may be greater for the stocks of smaller firms traded over-the-counter, than for the stocks of large companies listed on the NYSE. Perhaps greater potential for abnormal returns is associated with the stocks of firms involved in very complex and sophisticated business operations such as biogenetic engineering, or computer applications. Or perhaps complex investment strategies such as option writing and warrant or convertible bond hedges offer the potential for abnormal returns. However, before getting too excited about delving into some of these potentially less efficient sectors of the securities markets, bear in mind that *abnormal returns can be either positive or negative*. Thus, some active managers may earn abnormal profits while others suffer abnormal losses.

A third implication of the efficient markets literature is that market timing may be the "hardest game in town" simply because it involves the most competitors. Practically every investor utilizes, either explicitly or implicitly, some projection of the future level of the overall market. In addition, the study by Sharpe suggests that one has to have correct forecasts of future market returns a surprisingly high percentage of the time before an active strategy based on market timing will produce better results than a simple buy-and-hold strategy. Also, the Hodges and Brealey study indicated that the potential for gain was greater for a strategy based on security selection than for a strategy based on market timing. Thus, while a market-timing strategy may well be worth the effort *if successful*, the odds of success are not great and the payoff is potentially not as large as for an active strategy based on security selection.

5-8 SUMMARY

As noted at the beginning of this chapter, it is important for investors to understand the market environment in which they compete. Market efficiency implies that securities are correctly priced so that they will provide a fair or normal level of return, given their risk characteristics. The most important factor causing securities to be efficiently priced is competition. The more competitors, the less likely abnormal profit opportunities will exist.

Traditionally the efficient market hypothesis (EMH) has been divided into three forms, depending upon the level of information being considered. The weak-form EMH suggests that all historical price data are "fully reflected" in current prices and therefore one cannot earn abnormal profits using trading strategies based on historical prices. The empirical evidence overwhelmingly supports the weak-form EMH, which implies that most technical analysis (particularly chart reading) is of little value.

The semistrong-form EMH suggests that all publicly available information is fully reflected in current prices. The empirical evidence with respect to the semistrong form is mixed. Most of the earlier studies considered relatively simple types of information and found the markets to be semistrong efficient. However, a number of recent studies have found that either the markets are not semistrong efficient or the model used to determine normal returns is misspecified or both. It does appear that positive abnormal returns are associated with smaller firms when a single-factor market model is used to determine normal returns. There may also be opportunities for earning positive abnormal returns by reacting to quarterly earnings "surprises."

The strong-form EMH deals with nonpublic information. We choose to subdivide the strong form into the near-strong and the superstrong forms. The near-strong form deals with private information generated from data available to the public. A good example of such private information would be the earnings forecasts made by analysts working for a large investment management organization. Such forecasts are typically not made available to all investors but are determined after analyzing information that is available to the public. Tests of the near-strong form generally have involved examining the performance of professional investment managers, such as mutual fund organizations. For a number of reasons, the results of such tests are inconclusive and it may be that we will never be able to make definitive statements regarding portfolio performance.

The superstrong-form EMH deals with truly monopolistic information, such as that available to the "insiders" of the firm and specialists on the exchanges. Almost all empirical studies of the trading activities of insiders and specialists have rejected the superstrong-form EMH. This should not be surprising, since it is asking a great deal of the securities markets to "fully reflect" information that most market participants do not know about.

Given that the securities markets are reasonably efficient, passive investment strategies are viable options for many investors. For example, the manager of an index fund does not attempt to identify mispriced securities. Rather, the manager buys securities in the same proportions as the market value of the securities in a specified index. To illustrate, if a manager is trying to index his fund to the S&P 500 index and IBM represents 2% of the market value of the S&P 500, then the manager would allocate 2% of the fund's portfolio to IBM. In general, passive managers select a well-diversified group of securities based on the risk preferences of their client. These securities are then held for relatively long periods of time, thus minimizing transactions costs and taxes.

Finally, there are a number of implications for those who choose to pursue active investment strategies designed to capitalize on market inefficiencies. First, the active investor should be aware of the difficulty of the task. Second, *if* one is able to consistently exploit market inefficiencies, the potential rewards are great enough to compensate for the additional effort involved in active strategies. Third, it appears that there is more potential reward associated with individual security selection than with market timing. Further, one has to be *very* consistent in timing the market to outperform a simple buy-and-hold strategy.

SUGGESTED READINGS

The following are excellent survey articles on the topic of market efficiency:

E. Fama, "Efficient Capital Markets: A Review of Theory and Empirical Work," *Journal of Finance* (May 1970).

R. Ball, "Anomalies in Relationships between Securities' Yields and Yield-Surrogates," *Journal of Financial Economics* (June/September 1978).

J. Murphy, "Efficient Markets, Index Funds, Illusion and Reality," *Journal of Portfolio Management* (fall 1977).

The following is an excellent article dealing with the technical aspects of measuring abnormal returns:

S. Brown and J. Warner, "Measuring Security Price Performance," *Journal of Financial Economics* (September 1980).

A new field of study concerning market efficiency deals with "variance bound tests." Essentially, these studies generally conclude that the variance of security returns is too large given the variance of such factors as the dividend stream. This may be a very fruitful area of research over the next few years, and seminal articles on this topic are:

S. Grossman and R. Shiller, "The Determinants of the Variability of Stock Market Prices," *American Economic Review* (May 1981).

S. LeRoy and C. LaCivita, "Risk Aversion and the Dispersion of Asset Prices," *Journal of Business* (October 1981).

S. LeRoy and R. Porter, "The Present-Value Relation: Tests Based on Implied Variance Bounds," *Econometrics* (May 1981).

R. Michener, "Variance Bounds in a Simple Model of Asset Prices," *Journal of Political Economy* (February 1982).

R. Shiller, "Do Stock Prices Move Too Much to Be Justified by Subsequent Changes in Dividends?" *American Economic Review* (June 1981).

R. Shiller, "The Use of Volatility Measures in Assessing Market Efficiency," *Journal of Finance* (May 1981).

A few of the more recent articles documenting market inefficiencies are:

J. Jaffe and R. Westerfield, "The Week-End Effect in Common Stock Returns: The International Evidence," *Journal of Finance*, vol. 40 (June 1985), pp. 433–454.

B. Rosenberg, K. Reid, and R. Lanstein, "Persuasive Evidence of Market Inefficiency," *Journal of Portfolio Management*, vol. 11, no. 3 (spring 1985), pp. 9–17.

C. P. Jones, R. J. Rendleman, Jr., and H. A. Latane, "Earnings Announcements: Pre- and Post-Responses," *Journal of Portfolio Management*, vol. 11, no. 3 (spring 1985), pp. 28–33.

QUESTIONS

1. Define an efficient market in the context of a "fair game."
2. What single factor is the most important in order to ensure efficient capital markets?
3. Describe the differences among the weak, semistrong, near-strong and superstrong forms of the efficient market hypothesis.
4. Describe two different types of tests of the weak-form EMH and their results.
5. In general, what have been the results of tests of the weak-form EMH, and what does this imply for most forms of technical analysis?
6. Describe the research methodology known as residual analysis.
7. Describe and discuss the results of two studies which support the semistrong-form EMH.
8. Describe and discuss two studies which do not support the semistrong-form EMH.
9. Ray Ball has argued that many of the "anomalies" in the efficient market studies are actually due to the fact that the model for determining normal returns is misspecified. Discuss his arguments and summarize at least one study which identified a possible market inefficiency but which may in fact be consistent with Ball's argument.
10. What is the difference between the near-strong and superstrong forms of the EMH?
11. What are some of the problems involved in testing the near-strong-form EMH?
12. What groups of individuals have true monopolistic information, and what have been the results of empirical studies of the trading activities of these groups?
13. A priori, would you expect the superstrong-form EMH to be a correct description of the securities markets?
14. In general terms, describe active investment management and passive investment management.

15 What are some of the implications regarding active management which can be drawn from the empirical studies of the efficient market hypothesis? Be specific.

16 Assume that securities markets are semistrong efficient. Is it still possible for superior analysts to consistently earn positive abnormal returns?

17 Professor Fumble was studying the impact of "budget crises on the returns of Washington-based stocks." Using historical data, he found the following "normal" relationships between the returns of two stocks and a market index:

$$r_{it} = a_i + \beta_i r_{mt} + e_{it}$$
$$r_{it} = 2\% + 1.5\, r_{mt}$$
$$r_{1t} = 3\% + 0.8 r_{mt}$$

For three time periods following the most recent budget crisis (the "event"), he observed the following returns:

t	r_{1t}	r_{2t}	r_{mt}
1	14%	4%	10%
2	−7%	−8%	−5%
3	24%	7%	12%

a Using the "residual analysis method," what were the abnormal returns (residuals) for stocks 1 and 2 for each time period?

b What was the average abnormal return (AAR_t) for each time period?

c What was the cumulative average abnormal return (CAAR) for each time period?

d Based on these data, can you suggest a trading strategy utilizing the announcements of "budget crises"?

TWO

ANALYTICAL TOOLS
AND VALUATION
CONCEPTS

The previous five chapters, which constituted Part One of this book, provided a description of U.S. capital markets and an introduction to the notions of risk, return, and market efficiency. These topics represent essential background material for the serious student of investments. Before beginning to analyze individual securities, it is also essential that the investor master a number of analytical tools as well as thoroughly understand valuation concepts. Part Two of this book, which consists of Chapters 6 through 10, introduces the reader to some of these topics.

One of the most important sources of information regarding any firm is its financial statements. Consequently, it is important that investors understand how financial statements are prepared as well as how to analyze the statements. Chapter 6 presents what for many readers will be a review of basic accounting concepts. Chapter 7 introduces a number of techniques for analyzing financial statements, such as common size and trend statements, as well as the very important topic of ratio analysis.

Chapter 8 presents a number of analytical tools, including a discussion on computing historical growth rates, which is not as simple as one might expect, and a discussion of regression analysis. In addition, a number of forecasting techniques are presented.

To set the groundwork for studying the principles of valuation, Chapter 9 reviews the mathematics of solving various time value of money problems. Then Chapter 10 introduces the fundamental principle of valuation—the concept that current prices are equal to the present value of the cash flows expected to be derived from the ownership of the asset. While this is a relatively short chapter, most of the material in subsequent chapters builds upon this fundamental concept.

CHAPTER 6

UNDERSTANDING
FINANCIAL STATEMENTS*

After reading this chapter, you should:

1 Understand the basic accounting model and the financial statements it generates
2 Understand the role of financial statements as a starting point for formulating expectations about the future
3 Understand the type of information communicated in financial statements prepared using generally accepted accounting principles (GAAP)
4 Understand the potential impact of estimates, judgments, and accepted alternative accounting methods on financial statement comparability

Financial statements are a primary source of information for evaluating the investment prospects of various companies. Therefore, it is critical that the investor or security analyst understand the information communicated in these statements which accountants prepare. Unfortunately, the body of accounting knowledge is too large to be adequately covered in one chapter of an investments text—this is why students are almost always required to take one or more accounting courses before they take courses in finance and investments. Consequently, we assume the reader has already been exposed to accounting, and the purpose of this chapter is to alert the reader to some of the major problems investors have in interpreting financial statements. The aspiring security analyst may want to build on this background by taking additional courses in financial accounting.

In order for the investor to understand the information communicated in financial statements, she must understand the framework underlying accounting—the basic accounting concepts, the types of estimates and judgments, and the accounting methods used in preparing financial statements. Perhaps the auditor's report which often accompanies a set of financial statements best identifies the framework that dictates the information content of these statements. The auditor's report for Bandag, Inc., for the year ended December 31, 1984, concludes as follows:

> In our opinion, the financial statements referred to above *present fairly* the consolidated financial position of Bandag, Incorporated and subsidiaries at December 31, 1984, 1983 and 1982, and the consolidated results of their operations and changes in their financial position

*We gratefully acknowledge the considerable assistance of Professor Albert Frakes, Department of Accounting, Washington State University, on this chapter.

for the years then ended, *in conformity with generally accepted accounting principles applied on a consistent basis.* [Emphasis added.]

The auditor's report reflects their opinion as to the conformance of the financial statements with *generally accepted accounting principles.* When the auditor speaks of the fairness of the financial statements, he is speaking of fairness in the context of the concepts, rules, and procedures which constitute generally accepted accounting principles (GAAP) at that particular point in time. *Just as the auditor must be well versed in accounting principles in order to attest to the fairness of financial statements, so must the investor who will use those statements for decision-making purposes.*

6-1 ROLE OF FINANCIAL STATEMENTS

In order to place financial statements in perspective, consider the M Company, a small manufacturing corporation. Suppose you are contemplating the acquisition of this company as of December 31, 1986. What would be the maximum price you would be willing to pay for the entire firm? To assist you in your decision-making efforts, the controller of M Company has provided you with three sets of data which are shown in Table 6-1. The data include a December 31, 1986, balance sheet, a summary of net income and dividend distributions for the last 5 years, and a set of projections regarding future cash distributions to shareholders through annual dividends and eventual liquidation on December 31, 1996. Also assume that you are able to earn 8% compounded annually on alternative investments having similar risk.

After contemplating the situation for several minutes and satisfying yourself that the controller's projections are reliable, you conclude that the maximum price to be

TABLE 6-1   M COMPANY EXAMPLE

Data Set 1—Balance Sheet

M Company
Balance Sheet
12/31/86

Assets:		Liability and owners' equity:	
Current assets	$ 20,000	Liabilities	$ 30,000
Long-term assets ...	80,000	Owners' equity	70,000
Total	$100,000	Total	$100,000

Data Set 2—Net Income and Dividends

Summary of past activity:

	1986	1985	1984	1983	1982
Net income	8,000	6,000	5,000	5,000	3,000
Dividends paid	3,000	3,000	1,500	1,500	1,500

Data Set 3—Dividends and Liquidation Value

Expectations regarding future cash distributions to owners:
  a. 1987 through and including 1996—$4,000 dividends per year on 12/31 of each year
  b. 12/31/96—$200,000 liquidation value

---

paid would be determined by finding the present value of the 10 future dividend payments and the lump-sum liquidation value. An interest rate of 8% would be used in the present-value calculations. The maximum price you might pay, based on the present value of the estimated future cash flows, is $119,479 determined as follows:[1]

$$\text{Present value at } 12/31/86 = \frac{4000}{1.08} + \frac{4000}{(1.08)^2} + \cdots + \frac{4000}{(1.08)^{10}} + \frac{200,000}{(1.08)^{10}}$$
$$= \$119,479$$

You review your computations and are satisfied that the potential investment has been valued properly. However, you are bothered by the fact that only one of the three data sets (Data set 3, dividends and liquidation value) was utilized in your valuation effort. Does this mean that the historical financial statements produced by accountants are of no value for these types of decisions? You are also concerned by the large apparent discrepancy between your $119,479 estimate of the worth of the company and the balance sheet's $70,000 valuation of the owners' equity. If the balance sheet is attempting to portray financial position at December 31, 1986, why does the reported owners' equity differ so significantly from your estimate of the firm's current value?

The answer to your first concern regarding the relevance of historical financial statements lies in the fact that dividend and liquidation value estimates were *given* in this example. In most situations, such projections are not readily available and it is up to the investor to formulate his or her own expectations regarding the firm's future cash flows. Or, if the projections are provided, the investor probably would be somewhat skeptical and would want to gain some satisfaction as to their reasonableness.

Historical financial statements provide a starting point in formulating expectations regarding the future. The income statement's summary of past revenues and expenses provides a starting point for estimating future revenues, expenses, and net income. The accountant even attempts to aid the investment analyst by disclosing in the income statement information about discontinued operations and unusual and/or nonrecurring revenue and expense items. Revenue and expense items that are both unusual and nonrecurring are described as extraordinary items. Revenues and expenses that are either unusual or nonrecurring, but not both, are usually highlighted through footnote disclosure. Information about past dividend decisions sheds light on future dividend policy, thus enabling the analyst to convert net income estimates into dividend estimates.

The balance sheet provides information about assets currently held by the firm as well as its obligations so that the firm's financial structure and liquidity can be assessed. The information about the past gleaned from the financial statements is then combined with other available information about the plans of the business and the economy, and expectations are formulated. Thus, the financial statements are a valuable source of information for these types of decisions. *But it should be clear that they are not a sufficient source, and in many cases they may not be the most important information*

---

[1]Most readers should be familiar with present-value calculations. For those who are not, the mathematics are reviewed in Chapter 9.

source. They do, however, provide a logical starting point for understanding the financial characteristics of a business.

The answer to the second concern regarding the difference between the owners' equity reported on the balance sheet and the investor's estimate of the firm's value is found in generally accepted accounting principles (GAAP). There are at least three distinct reasons for the difference. They include (1) the impact of basic accounting concepts such as the historical cost principle and the objectivity principle, (2) the impact of estimates and judgments, and (3) the existence of alternative accounting methods. These differences will be explained and illustrated in subsequent sections as we discuss generally accepted accounting principles and their impact on the information content of financial statements.

6-2 FINANCIAL STATEMENTS AND THE ACCOUNTING EQUATION

The preparation of financial statements can be likened to the development of a financial model of the business. The basic reference part for the model is the familiar accounting equation

$$\text{Assets} = \text{liabilities} + \text{owners' equity} \tag{6-1}$$

In order to understand financial statements, we must understand the relationship of financial statements to the equation and the model building rules (GAAP) that accountants follow in accumulating financial information using the equation.

TABLE 6-2   JANUARY 1986 TRANSACTIONS FOR EXAMPLE COMPANY

			Assets					
		Cash		Accounts receivable		Equipment		Accumulated depreciation
Balances, Jan. 1, 1986		$10,000	+	$20,000	+	$50,000	−	$14,000
1/5	Purchase equipment	− 5,000				+ 5,000		
1/8	Collect accts. rec.	+ 20,000		− 20,000				
1/10	Declare and pay div.	− 2,000						
1/15	Paid taxes	− 2,000						
1/20	Pay A. P.	− 6,000						
1/31	Make payment on bank loan including $100 interest	− 2,100						
1/31	Op. expense for Jan. to be paid in Feb.: rent, salaries, etc.							
1/31	Customers billed for Jan. service revenue			+ 22,000				
1/31	Est. taxes for Jan.							
1/31	Jan. depre. exp.							− 1,000
Balances, Jan. 31, 1986		12,900	+	$22,000	+	$55,000	−	$15,000
				$74,900				

There are two general types of financial statements that can be prepared from the accounting equation. The first is a *position statement* showing the status of the equation at a *particular point in time*. The balance sheet or statement of financial position is the most prominent example of this type of report. The other type of report is a *flow report,* which shows changes in selected elements of the equation *over a period of time*. The income statement, statement of changes in retained earnings, and statement of changes in financial position are all examples of flow reports. Flow reports can be thought of as linking successive balance sheets by showing how selected elements of financial position have changed over the reporting period.

The information from which financial statements are prepared is accumulated by analyzing the impact of the economic activity of the business on the accounting equation. GAAP guides the accountant in identifying relevant economic activity, analyzing and measuring the impact of that activity on the equation, and developing financial statements and related footnotes. To refresh the reader's memory regarding the nature of financial statements and their relation to the accounting equation, consider Table 6-2. Table 6-2 presents the status of the accounting equation for Example Company as of January 1, 1986. The results of the analysis of the company's January transactions are shown in tabular form and, when combined with the initial January 1, 1986, balances, produce the updated equation as of January 31, 1986. The January 1 and January 31 balance sheets that can be prepared from these data are presented in Table 6-3. Notice that we've classified the assets into current assets and noncurrent or fixed assets in an effort to provide information about their liquidity. Current assets are those assets that will be converted into cash within a relatively short time period,

TABLE 6-2   (Continued)

	Liabilities			+	Owners' equity		
	Accounts payable		Taxes payable	Bank loan		Capital stock	Retained earnings
=	$6,000	+	$2,000	+ $20,000	+	$30,000 +	$8,000
							−2,000
			−2,000				
	−6,000						
				−2,000			−100
	+7,000						−7,000
							+22,000
			+3,900				−3,900
							−1,000
=	$7,000	+	$3,900	+ $18,000	+	$30,000 +	$16,000
=				$74,900			

TABLE 6-3
Example Company Balance Sheet

Assets

	January 1, 1986		January 31, 1986	
Current assets:				
Cash		$10,000		$12,900
Accounts receivable		20,000		22,000
Total current assets		$30,000		$34,900
Noncurrent assets:				
Equipment	$50,000		$55,000	
Less: accumulated depreciation	<14,000>	36,000	<15,000>	40,000
Total assets		$66,000		$74,000

Liabilities & Owners' Equity

	January 1, 1986		January 31, 1986
Current liabilities:			
Accounts payable		$ 6,000	$ 7,000
Taxes payable		2,000	3,900
Total current liabilities		$ 8,000	$10,900
Noncurrent liabilities:			
Bank loan		$20,000	18,000
Total liabilities		$28,000	$28,900
Owners' equity:			
Capital stock		30,000	30,000
Retained earnings		8,000	16,000
Total liabilities & owners' equity		$66,000	$74,900

usually 1 year. Similarly, liabilities are classified into those that will require payment in a relatively short time period (current liabilities) and those that will not require payment so soon (noncurrent liabilities). Again, the critical time period is usually 1 year. Since Example Company is organized as a corporation, the owners' equity is divided into subclassifications for capital stock and retained earnings.

As noted earlier, the flow reports show selected dimensions of the changes that occur in the company's accounting equation (balance sheet) over time. In this sense the income statement, retained earnings statement, and statement of changes in financial position are all similar. They differ, however, in that each statement reports on changes in different elements of the company's accounting equation (balance sheet).

Consider first the income statement. Income is reflected in the change in the retained earnings element of owners' equity. All changes in retained earnings except owner withdrawals in the form of dividends are included in the measurement of business income. The retained earnings changes entering into the determination of income are broken down into revenue and expense transactions. The income statement for Example Company for January 1986 is shown in Table 6-4.

As the name implies, the statement of changes in retained earnings summarizes the changes in the retained earnings element of owners' equity. Since the revenue and expense transactions have already been presented in the income statement, it is not

TABLE 6-4
Example Company Income Statement
January 1986

Revenue from services		$22,000
Less expenses:		
Operating expense	$7000	
Interest expense	100	
Depreciation expense	1000	
Tax expense	3900	
		12,000
Net income		$10,000

necessary to present them in detail again in the retained earnings statement. Thus, this statement shows the net income and dividends for the period—which lead from the beginning retained earnings balance to the ending retained earnings balance. Example Company's statement of changes in retained earnings for January 1986 is presented in Table 6-5.

The third flow report, the statement of changes in financial position (SCFP), differs from the income and retained earnings statements by shifting focus from the retained earnings element of owners' equity to selected assets and liabilities grouped as a pool of liquid resources. The income statement reflects the impact of business operations on the owners and is used to evaluate profitability. The SCFP helps users understand how the business is generating and using the liquid resources required to carry on operations so that profits can be earned. The SCFP helps users assess the firm's liquidity and understand its important financing and investing activities.

The format of the SCFP will vary depending upon the composition of the pool of liquid resources used as a basis for the statement. Cash and working capital (current assets minus current liabilities) are the two most commonly used liquidity concepts. While working capital has historically been the more commonly used basis for the SCFP, a push to use cash as the basis for the statement has been under way since the early 1980s. Cash flows are considered to be more meaningful than working capital flows.

Table 6-6 presents the Example Company's SCFP for January 1986 prepared using the cash concept of liquidity. It shows how the company generated cash (its financing activities) and how it spent cash (its investing activities). In this case, Example Company's operations generated $11,900 of cash, there were no additional (nonoperating) sources of cash, and a total of $9000 of cash was spent to purchase equipment ($5000),

TABLE 6-5
Example Company Statement of Changes in
Retained Earnings January 1986

Retained earnings, January 1, 1986	$ 8,000
Add: January net income	10,000
Less: January dividends	2,000
Retained earnings, January 31, 1986	$16,000

TABLE 6-6
Example Company
Statement of Changes in Financial Position—Cash Basis
January 1986

Source of cash:		
Operations:		
Collection of accounts receivable		$20,000
Payment of accounts payable	$6,000	
Interest payment	100	
Tax payment	2,000	8,100
Net source from operations		$11,900
Other sources:		
None		0
Total sources		$11,900
Other uses:		
Purchase of equipment	$5,000	
Paid dividend	2,000	
Paid loan principal	2,000	9,000
Net increase in cash		2,900
Cash balance January 1, 1986		10,000
Cash balance January 31, 1986		$12,900

pay dividends ($2000), and pay off debt ($2000). As a result the cash balance increased during January by $2900.

    The discussion of Example Company's financial statements illustrates the unique purpose of each of the statements and the manner in which they relate to one another. All the statements are necessary for a complete understanding of the firm's financial activities. In fact, whenever financial statements are presented to show both financial position and results of operations, GAAP requires that a balance sheet, income statement, statement of changes in retained earnings, and statement of changes in financial position must all be presented along with necessary footnotes and other explanatory materials.

Before continuing, you should:

1 Understand the role of financial statements as a starting point for making predictions of future financial activity
2 Be able to explain each of the four basic financial statements in terms of their relationship to the basic accounting equation and to peach other
3 Be able to prepare the four basic financial statements when given simple transaction data

6-3 BASIC ACCOUNTING CONCEPTS

The impact of basic accounting concepts was one of the explanations offered in Section 6-1 for the difference that existed between the balance sheet valuation of M Company and the investor's valuation of its shares. Recall that the owners' equity reported on the balance sheet was $70,000 whereas the present value of the expected cash flow was computed to be $119,479.

There are numerous alternative approaches that could be taken in measuring economic activity and constructing financial statements. GAAP represents one of these approaches, and it has specific implications for the information content of the financial statements. Several basic concepts are particularly relevant in helping investors understand GAAP-based financial statements.

6-3-1 The Historical Cost Principle In order to provide the investor with a situation that highlights relevant basic accounting concepts in an understandable way, particularly the historical cost principle, let's consider an accounting question a merchandising firm would face in valuing its inventory. Suppose our company acquired one unit of inventory on November 30, 1986, and still held it on December 31, 1986, at the time of preparing its year-end balance sheet. How would this asset be valued in the December 31, 1986, balance sheet? Consider the possible alternatives:

1 Actual acquisition cost on November 30, 1986, $70
2 Retail selling price on December 31, 1986, $120
3 Estimated replacement cost if purchased from suppliers on December 31, 1986, $80
4 Estimated value in forced liquidation on December 31, 1986, $90
5 Actual acquisition cost adjusted for inflation based on an index of the general price level which was 100 on November 30, 1986, and 108 on December 31, 1986,

$$\frac{108}{100} \times \$70 = \$75.60$$

The alternatives presented result in a range of possible values from $70 to $120. The *historical cost principle* dictates that alternative 1, the actual acquisition cost, be used in GAAP-based financial statements. The concept of *objectivity*, which asserts that accounting measurements should be as factual as possible, is used to rule out alternatives 2 and 3. On December 31, 1986, it is not clear when a sale will occur and at what price. Likewise, the inventory item has not been replaced and the actual replacement cost cannot be known until the replacement transaction is executed.

The *going concern* assumption is used to rule out alternative 4. Unless the accountant has strong evidence to the contrary, the business will be assumed to be a going concern having an indefinite life. Liquidation is not viewed as a possible occurrence; hence, liquidation values are not considered to be relevant. Alternative 5, original cost adjusted for the impact of inflation, is eliminated by the *stable monetary unit assumption*. This assumption argues that the dollar can be viewed as a stable monetary unit, thus allowing the accountant to ignore the impact of inflation. From the accountant's perspective, 1930 dollars are viewed as being equivalent to 1980 dollars, and they can be added and subtracted without adjustment.

The *historical cost principle* argues that the most *objective* measure of the value of the inventory to the *going concern* is its actual acquisition cost. Therefore, the accountant initially records the inventory at its acquisition cost and carries the asset at that value in subsequent balance sheets until a change in value is documented through a sale or other exchange transaction.

For valuation purposes, assets can be classified as either monetary or nonmonetary. The distinction between monetary and nonmonetary assets is important because each of the asset classifications is accounted for in its own way. *Monetary assets include cash and claims to fixed amounts of cash and are valued on the basis of the number of dollars held (in the case of cash) or the estimated dollars to be collected (in the case of accounts receivable).* The valuation of monetary assets is not particularly controversial, since these valuations usually correspond quite well with current values. This is not to say, though, that estimates and judgments are not required to value these assets. Significant judgment is required, for example, in estimating bad debts in order to value accounts receivable.

Because their cash generation capacity is uncertain, *nonmonetary assets are all valued according to the historical cost principle* as illustrated by the merchandise inventory example above. However, the valuation of nonmonetary assets tends to be more controversial because balance sheet valuations for those items may not correspond well with current market values. As a result informal adjustments may be made to the balance sheet valuations of these assets by investors in making their determinations of the firm's current value. Nonmonetary assets include investments in marketable equity securities, land, buildings, equipment, and intangibles such as patents and copyrights. Suppose one of M Company's long-term assets was a piece of land which was acquired in 1948 at a cost of $3000. Because of inflation and market conditions, the land is currently appraised at $28,000. The land would be reflected in the balance sheet at its historical cost of $3000. Under GAAP, no adjustments would have been made to recognize either the effects of inflation or market conditions. In order to bring the balance sheet current, both asset and owners' equity totals would have to be increased by $25,000.

Examples of hidden or undervalued assets are not difficult to find. As one example, the annual report of Hershey Foods Corporation fails to disclose a balance sheet asset to reflect the value of the Hershey's trade name which has become synonymous with the chocolate bar. Obviously the name Hershey has considerable value.

As another example, in the 1980 annual report of Weyerhaeuser Company and Subsidiaries, supplementary disclosures present the net assets of Weyerhaeuser as measured according to GAAP in comparison with inflation-adjusted net assets and net assets restated in terms of current replacement costs.[2] The current replacement cost

---

[2]Financial Accounting Standards Board Statement 33 requires large publicly held companies to disclose certain financial statement information adjusted to reflect the impact of inflation and current replacement costs. This information is supplementary to the financial statements and the related footnotes and, as such, does not come directly under the scope of the independent auditor's opinion. However, it should be of use to investors in helping them to assess the impact of inflation on the entity being analyzed. The article ''Who's Afraid of Current-Cost Earnings'' in *Value Line: Selection and Opinion* (Oct. 26, 1984) clearly outlines the usefulness of FASB Statement 33 disclosures and suggests that investors zero in on the information. This research, based on the 1983 earnings of the 30 Dow Jones Industrials, indicated that inflation-adjusted return on net worth was more highly correlated with the ratio of price to inflation-adjusted net worth than was the case using unadjusted return on net worth to predict the unadjusted ratio of price to net worth.

measure of net assets was 1.90 times higher than GAAP-based measures appearing in the financial statements. Property and equipment were 1.50 times higher while timber and timberlands were 2.50 times greater. These disclosures clearly illustrate the possible impact of the historical cost principle and the stable monetary unit assumption.

The impact of the historical cost principle and stable monetary unit assumption on the valuation of nonmonetary assets also extends to the income statement. As inventory is sold, the historical cost becomes expense. Likewise, as long-term nonmonetary assets such as buildings, equipment, and patents are used, expense is recognized through the depreciation, depletion, or amortization of the asset's historical cost.

Because the measurement of many expenses is tied to the historical cost valuation of assets, expenses will also be measured in acquisition-year dollars. The matching process will generate a nominal or dollar income measure, as revenues denominated in current dollars are compared with expenses which are denominated in acquisition-year dollars. But the comparison of dollar units of different value or purchasing power makes the resulting income difficult to interpret during periods of inflation (or deflation). If the inventory item above were sold in January 1987 for $130, income of $60 would be reported since the $70 acquisition cost of the merchandise would be charged to expense.

A logical interpretation of the reported income is that the business' command over goods and services has increased by the $60 net income. But this is not necessarily the case. If inflation of 8% were realized between the date of acquisition and sale of the merchandise, the historical cost of the merchandise in terms of current purchasing power would be $75.60 (1.08 × $70). The real income of the firm is reflected by matching the inflation-adjusted historical cost of $75.60 with the $130 revenue and is $54.40, not $60.

Likewise, if the replacement cost of the merchandise increased faster than the general price level so that it was $80 at the time of sale, it might be argued that a "truer" measure of income is $50, the difference between revenue of $130 and the $80 replacement cost at the time of sale. If the business is to continue in the same line of work, $80 must be retained from the $130 revenue in order to replace the consumed asset and maintain capital in terms of the specific goods and services which are used by this business. The relevant point is that *income reported under GAAP cannot necessarily be interpreted as the real gain the business has made over the reporting period*. The business could not necessarily distribute that income and maintain its same position in terms of either general or specific purchasing power. Management usually recognizes this attribute of reported income and adjusts dividend policy accordingly. Indicative of this is the fact that dividend payout ratios (dividends/earnings) have tended to decrease during periods of high inflation. For example, during the period 1960–1969, the payout ratios for the DJIA firms averaged 60% while inflation averaged 2.3%. During the period 1970–1979, inflation increased to a 7.1% average rate while payout ratios decreased to a 47% average rate for the DJIA firms.

When investors use the term *quality of earnings* in reference to a firm's reported net income, *one of the factors* influencing their evaluation of quality is the perceived differences between reported GAAP-based income and general price level adjusted or current replacement cost income. If many of the reported expenses such as cost of goods sold, depreciation, and amortization are based on prior years' acquisition costs which are significantly out of date because of inflation, then income will be overstated in real terms, will be considered to be of low quality, and will be discounted. This was the case in the mid-1970s when double-digit inflation was the rule for several years.

6-3-2 The Objectivity Principle and the Recognition of Assets In order for an economic event to be recognized, some element of the accounting equation must be changed. And objective evidence must exist to prompt the accountant to recognize change. In many cases the supporting evidence is a by-product of an exchange transaction, such as a sale. Change in the market value of land not realized through sale is an example of economic activity which is *not* generally recognized by the accountant.

In accounting for assets, some interesting recognition and classification issues arise. Suppose that over the years M Company had carried on an extensive effort to train its managers. The effort was very successful and most observers agree that one of M Company's most important resources was its superior management team. In all likelihood this resource would not be listed on the balance sheet among the firm's assets. At the time expenditures were made for management training programs, the extent of future benefits was probably uncertain. It was not clear whether an asset existed and, if so, what its cost or useful life was. Consequently, the accountant did not have sufficient objective evidence to recognize an asset, and the expenditures were expensed.

The existence of a significant intangible asset may become clear over a number of years. However, the accountant still will not recognize the asset if there is not an exchange transaction which would objectively support the asset's existence and valuation. Examples of unreported intangibles include trade names, technical expertise, special processes and formulas, and loyal customers, all of which are developed by numerous expenditures made over a long period of time.

The only way that these intangible assets become recognized is if they are acquired either individually or through the acquisition of an entire business. When an entire business is acquired, the accountant will value all identifiable tangible and intangible assets at their current market value. The extent to which the price paid for the business as a whole exceeds the identified assets is attributed to unidentified intangible assets such as loyal customers, superior management, and unusual expertise and is lumped into a catchall intangible called *goodwill*. Therefore, when a business is valued for sale, all previously unrecognized intangibles will be included, thus departing from the accountant's presale balance sheet.

Before leaving this section, it is important to note that the assets which are listed in the balance sheet constitute *a selected listing* of the reporting entity's resources. Because of the accountant's objectivity principle, some important resources may not be recognized in the financial statements.

6-3-3 The Objectivity Principle and Liabilities The valuation and reporting of liabilities reflects, for the most part, the basic concepts used in accounting for assets. The concept of objectivity governs the recognition of liabilities, although the concept of conservatism is also relevant. Before an obligation can be listed as a liability, there must be objective evidence as to the existence and value of the debt. The existence of the debt is established by the occurence of the event creating the liability. The critical event is usually an exchange transaction, but it could also be the signing of a contract or some other event. The documentation related to the critical event usually establishes the amount of the obligation. In some cases, the amount to be paid is not determined until some time after the critical event and timely accounting for the liability requires estimates.

Liabilities are often divided into three groups. A *definite liability* is one where the critical event has occurred and the amount of the obligation is known. A trade payable associated with a purchase in the current period is an example. An *estimated liability* is similar to a definite liability except that the amount owed is not yet determined. If past experience can be used to produce reasonable estimates of the amount to be paid, the liability can be recognized. The liability for estimated product warranty costs is an example of an estimated liability. The sale of a warranted product is the event creating the warranty expense and obligation. The exact amount to be paid cannot be known with certainty until customers return the product for warranty service. However, experience under warranty agreements can usually be used as a basis for estimating and accounting for the liability at the time of sale.

A *contingent liability* is the third liability category. Depending on the likelihood that a claim exists and the existence of evidence to support the amount, the contingency may be accounted for in one of three ways. It may be treated like an estimated liability and recorded in the financial statements; it may be omitted from the financial statements but disclosed in a footnote; or it may be omitted entirely from the statements and related footnotes. If a company had violated a patent agreement in 1986 and suit was brought against it, a potential liability exists. If the facts indicate that the violation occurred in 1986 and it is *probable* that the court will find for plaintiff, and if the amount of loss can be estimated, the contingency would be recognized in the balance sheet as an estimated liability. If, however, it is not possible to estimate the amount, or the existence of a claim is only *reasonably possible,* the criteria for recognition of a liability would not be met and the possible liability would not be recorded. It would, however, be disclosed in the financial statement footnotes.[3] If the existence of a claim was only remotely possible, the contingency would be neither recorded nor disclosed. It is interesting to note that the accountant will recognize estimated and contingent liabilities when the existence of a claim is probable and the amount to be paid is reasonably estimable, when more objective evidence is required to justify recognition of an asset. This disparity illustrates the influence of the principle of *conservatism.*

---

[3]D. Kieso and J. Weygandt, *Intermediate Accounting*, 4th ed. 1983 (Wiley, New York) identify some of the more common sources of loss contingencies that *would not* ordinarily be accrued as estimated liabilities. They are:

1 Guarantees of indebtedness of others
2 Obligations of commercial banks under standby letters of credit (commitments to finance projects under certain circumstances)
3 Guarantees to repurchase receivables (or any related property) that have been sold or assigned
4 Disputes over additional income taxes for prior years
5 Pending lawsuits whose outcomes is uncertain

A possible obligation resulting from a lawsuit illustrates why the investor may not consider the liabilities as presented in the GAAP-based balance sheet a complete listing of a firm's obligations. If M Company had been sued in 1986 and if it were possible, but not probable, that M Company would be required to pay the $10,000 in damages being sought, the accountant would not recognize the obligation as a liability. The possible obligation would, however, be disclosed in the financial statement footnotes. The investor may very well want to include this possible obligation in valuing the business.

The valuation of liabilities also parallels the valuation of assets. Since most liabilities require the payment of cash at some future date, they are considered monetary items and are valued in terms of the cash to be paid. If interest is associated with the debt, it is added to the liability as the interest accrues. The interest cost is measured based on the *effective rate* at which the transaction was negotiated. To the extent interest rates fluctuate subsequent to the data of the transaction, the market value of the obligation will vary from its initial or historical value. Accountants stick with the historical effective interest rate, and as a result, *the accountant's valuation of monetary liabilities may not correspond with current market values*.

Nonmonetary liabilities arise from obligations to perform services such as would exist if a customer paid for a product in advance of delivery. A nonmonetary liability is valued at its historical amount established at the time the advance payment is made.

As we've noted, the application of basic accounting principles to the measurement of liabilities also results in a selective listing of the business' obligations. For the liabilities that are listed, current market values may differ from the balance sheet valuations, although these differences do not seem to receive the same attention as is the case for assets.

6-3-4 Revenue Recognition, Matching, and Income

Under GAAP, income is measured using the *accrual basis of accounting*. Income is determined by matching the revenues earned during the period with the cost of goods and services consumed to produce those revenues. The *realization principle* provides guidance in determining when revenues are earned. The *matching principle* relates to the measurement of expenses.

For a merchandising or manufacturing business the process of acquiring, marketing, and selling an inventory item (or service) is called the earning process and is illustrated as follows:

EARNING PROCESS FOR A MERCHANDISING BUSINESS

Acquisition of facilities	Acquisition of product	Marketing of product	Sale of product on credit	Collection of cash

The realization principle says that revenue is not considered earned and hence recognizable until the earning process is essentially complete (i.e., the revenue is "realized"). This principle is clearly rooted in the objectivity principle. The accountant will not recognize revenue until he has objective evidence as to (1) the existence of revenue and (2) the amount to be received.

In a manufacturing or merchandising business, revenue is generally recognized at the point of sale. In a service business, revenue is generally recognized as the service is performed. However, there are circumstances which lead some businesses to recognize revenue at different point in the earning process. If, for example, a merchandising business sells under conditions where collection of the cash is not assured at the point of sale, the realization concept may dictate that revenue not be recognized until cash is actually collected. In this case revenue is recognized by either the *installment* or *cost recovery* methods. By contrast, if a manufacturer produces a custom product under a firm contract at an agreed-upon price, the realization criteria may be met before the point of sale so as to permit the earlier recognition of revenue during production. From the investor's perspective, it is critical to know how a particular business recognizes revenue in order to utilize its financial statements.

Before continuing, you should:

1 Be able to explain how assets and liabilities are valued in financial statements
2 Be able to explain the shortcomings of the income statement in measuring net income during a period of inflation
3 Be able to explain how the accountant's concern for objectivity affects the recognition of assets and liabilities in the financial statements
4 Be able to explain why reported revenue and the resulting net income may not be comparable between firms

6-4 ESTIMATES AND JUDGMENT

Many people view accounting as a very precise activity. When they get into the study of accounting, they are startled to realize that accounting involves numerous estimates and judgments in determining financial position and operating results. With respect to the example of M Company, the estimates and judgments required in preparing financial statements represent a second potential source of the difference between the reported owners' equity on M Company's balance sheet of $70,000 and the estimated market value of $119,479.

6-4-1 Some Areas Requiring Estimates   Significant estimates are required to account for a number of transactions. In valuing accounts and notes receivable at the amount of cash expected to be collected, provision must be made for possible uncollectible accounts or bad debts. Accountants look at past loss experience and current and expected future economic conditions in an effort to estimate the portion of current receivables that will ultimately be uncollectible. Estimated uncollectibles are recorded by recognizing a bad debt expense in the income statement, offset by a reduction in the value of accounts receivable in the balance sheet.

The measurement of bad debts in valuing accounts receivable can be controversial. The financial difficulties of banks in recent years has brought the issue of providing for uncollectible loans into sharp focus. Because of the volume of loans receivable, bad debts expense has a significant impact on a bank's income statement. Modest variations in bad debt estimates can have a significant impact on net income and earnings per share. Many banks in financial difficulty have been criticized for being too optimistic in accruing bad debts expense.

Some banks have also been criticized for using bad debt estimates as an income-smoothing device. During periods of growth and prosperity when net income is at or above expected levels, more pessimistic bad debt estimates are made by management because the income statement can absorb the expense and still reflect desired income growth. In years when the income prospects are bleak, more optimistic bad debt expense estimates are made in order to keep income and income growth as close to desired levels as possible. Over time loans receivable may be properly valued but bad debt expense is not being reported in the proper accounting period, thus obscuring real earnings performance. Because of the subjective nature of bad debt expense estimates, auditors will accept a range of possible estimates. Based on the concept of conservatism, most auditors would not object to pessimistic estimates if within reason. As a result, bank managements may be able to manage earnings to some extent through bad debt estimates.[4]

In the case of M Company, differences in opinion over important financial statement estimates may cause an investor to adjust the accountant's balance sheet in order to place a value on the business. For example, based on past loss experience, M Company estimated that ½% of credit sales will eventually prove to be uncollectible. If the investor forecasts difficult economic times, she may believe that a more realistic estimate of bad debts is 1½% of credit sales, resulting in lower overall valuation of both accounts receivable and the business as a whole.

Other areas where estimates are important are summarized as follows:

Depreciation, Depletion, and Amortization In order to compute depreciation, depletion, or amortization of tangible and intangible fixed assets, estimates of salvage value and economic life must be made. While engineering data and prior experience can provide guidance, these estimates are subject to management's influence. A variation in estimated useful life from 8 to 10 years, for example, has the effect of reducing depreciation expense by 20% in each of the first 8 years of the asset's life when straight-line depreciation methods are used.

Recognizing Impairment in the Value of an Asset GAAP requires that significant and permanent declines in the value of an asset be recognized immediately. Recognition of such a decline reduces the value of the asset and produces a loss that

---

[4]Worth reports that Allied Bancshares, after turning in a string of 31 consecutive quarterly earnings increases before a decline in the final quarter of 1983, admitted to income smoothing through its bad debt estimates. Allied Bancshares' management acknowledged the belief that it was appropriate to build reserves in periods of good earnings to assure earnings growth in down periods. They also believed that there was really no benefit to showing extraordinarily large earnings increases and that it was more important to maintain a trend. While the outside auditors expressed some concern over the unusually large bad debt expense estimates, they accepted the estimates because they were conservative. See F. S. Worthy, "Manipulating Profits: How It's Done," *Fortune* (June 25, 1984).

is reflected in the income statement. Determination of such declines requires estimates, and significant variation is possible depending on the optimism of management. It is not unreasonable to expect management to attempt to put such write-downs off as long as possible, especially if they are facing adverse economic conditions.

In 1981, Litton Industries, Inc., settled charges of improper reporting by the SEC in connection with postponement to 1978 of the recognition of $330 million in losses on shipbuilding contracts incurred over the period 1972–1977. Litton was overly optimistic in believing that contract disputes with the Navy would be settled in their favor. The SEC also censured Litton's auditors for failure to require the write-downs in order for the financial statements to comply with GAAP.[5]

Distinguishing Capital Expenditures from Expense   Many expenditures made by the business give rise to potential future benefits. The accountant is faced with the decision as to whether the expenditure should be expensed or capitalized as an asset. The uncertainty surrounding many of these expenditures provides management with an opportunity to manage income. Different philosophies regarding capitalizing vs. expensing such expenditures can also impair financial statement comparability. One of the greatest problem areas in the past was in accounting for research and development costs. The FASB now requires that such expenditures be expensed as incurred in most situations.

Estimated Liabilities and Contingencies   The accrual of liabilities for which the amount of the obligation is not yet determined, such as the estimated product warranty liability, requires estimates like those required for bad debts. Because of the uncertainties involved, estimates can be influenced by management, and the investor needs to watch for significant revisions and changes in procedures for making estimates. GAAP requires that changes in estimates be disclosed in the footnotes to the financial statement if the change has a significant impact on financial statement comparability.

Estimated liabilities are one type of the more general loss contingency or contingent liability. Diversity in practice exists in reporting contingencies because of the varied interpretations that are possible of the terms "probably," "reasonably possible," and "remote" which determine whether the item is accrued, disclosed, or omitted entirely. Investors should pay particular attention to contingencies that are disclosed but not accrued.

Pensions   GAAP requires that employers with pension plans accrue their obligation for retirement benefits over the service lives of their employees. However, because

---

[5]See the article "SEC Censures Touche Ross in Litton Audit" in the Nov. 15, 1983, *Wall Street Journal*. Other examples illustrate how estimates and judgments of managements of different firms in the same industry can result in widely different accounting for a common event. When the Washington Public Power Supply System suspended construction of a nuclear plant, two Oregon utilities had to decide how to value their investments in the project. Pacific Power & Light, coming off a strong operating performance in 1983, wrote off over half of its $292 million investment. Portland General Electric, which posted flat earnings in 1983, kept its full $266 million investment in the balance sheet intact. Investors would be hard-pressed to make valid comparison of the two utilities without adjusting financial statements so that the event is handled in a comparable manner. See Worthy, op. cit.

there are several actuarial cost methods by which a firm can compute their obligation, and because numerous estimates are required, pension expenses of firms with similar pension obligations may not be readily comparable. In addition, the rate at which the employer actually funds their pension obligation may differ from the actuarily determined obligation. If the funding trails the accrual of the obligation, an unfunded pension liability accumulates on the employer's books. If funding leads the accrual, an asset called prepaid pension costs appears. Investors can get a handle on the adequacy of a company's expense accruals and funding policies by examining footnote disclosures. The pension footnote should explain both accounting and funding policies as well as important changes in assumptions, estimates, and actuarial cost methods. In addition, the note should disclose the actuarial present value of accumulated plan benefits in comparison with available plan assets which reflect on the adequacy of funding policies · as well as the employer's reported pension obligation.

6-4-2 Judgments on the Nature, the Timing, and the Form of Transactions
Management can influence financial statements not only via required estimates but also through judgments on the *nature of certain transactions*, the *timing of transactions*, and the *form of transactions*. Income statement classification and disclosure require rules that unusual and nonrecurring revenue and expense activities be identified. If a revenue or expense item is judged to be both unusual and nonrecurring in nature, it will be set out separately as an extraordinary item and reported apart from income from operations. Items that are judged to be either unusual or nonrecurring but not both will usually be disclosed and will be separately classified as an ''other'' operating item. Investors should be alert to a natural bias which might lead management to consider significant losses as extraordinary while significant gains are considered to be part of normal operations. Items labeled as extraordinary or set out as ''other'' items should be carefully scrutinized in evaluating profitability.

Management can also influence reported net income by the timing of transactions. In most instances, gains and losses from changes in the value of assets or liabilities are recognized when a sale or exchange transaction occurs. A firm which owns assets that have appreciated in value or owes liabilities which have decreased in value has a pool of profits which can be tapped at management's discretion. Management can sell the appreciated assets so that the gain would be recognized entirely in the period of sale. Similarly, if long-term debt which (because of rising interest rates) has decreased in value can be repurchased and retired at current market value, the gain will be recognized in the period of retirement. Investors should be alert to the unusual and/or nonrecurring nature of these gains in evaluating profitability and in predicting the future. Likewise, because of their discretionary nature, the timing of such gains may obscure the real trend in earnings.

Closely related to the timing of transactions is the *form of transactions*. In a number of situations, management can structure the transactions so as to make appropriate a form of accounting which significantly affects the reporting of the transaction in the financial statements. These situations are illustrated by *in-substance defeasance of debt transactions* and by transactions which fall under the heading of *off-balance-sheet financing*.

In-substance defeasance of debt transactions is undertaken as a means of effectively reacquiring debt which has decreased in value so that a gain on its retirement can be realized. However, to accomplish this in situations where it is either not possible or expensive to reacquire the debt in the market, transactions have been structured whereby relatively riskless securities are purchased in sufficient amounts to fully fund the remaining interest and principal due on the debt. The securities are placed in an irrevocable trust to be used solely for the purpose of serving and retiring the outstanding debt. Under GAAP, if the trust is properly structured and the securities are adequate to cover the outstanding debt, it is permissible to offset the securities against the debt and effectively remove both the asset and liability from the balance sheet as though the debt were reacquired and retired. The debt equity ratio is improved, and because at the current higher interest rates the debt can be funded for less than its book value, a gain on retirement can be reported on the income statement. Because the company is still responsible for the debt, investors may want to include the debt as a liability in computing debt equity ratios and return on total assets.[6]

The whole topic of off-balance-sheet financing illustrates how transactions can be structured to accomplish an economic objective without reflecting the substance of the transaction in the financial statements. For years, accountants have been required under GAAP to capitalize long-term noncancelable lease transactions of lessee companies if the lease was *in substance an installment purchase*. Capitalization entails recognizing both an asset and a liability equal to the present value of future lease payments. The asset represents the equity in the leased property and is depreciated over the useful life of the property. The liability represents the obligation under the lease and is liquidated as payments of interest and principal are made.

However, because of the vague nature of the criteria for determining whether the lease was *in substance an installment purchase*, most companies accounted for the lease as a rental agreement. Neither an asset nor a liability was recognized and lease payments were charged to rent expense as they were made. The borrowing and investing substance of the lease transaction was therefore omitted from the financial statements again with probable salutary effects on the debt/equity ratio and return on investment. In 1976, the Financial Accounting Standards Board (FASB) issued Statement of Financial Accounting Standards 13 in an effort to correct this problem. The standard outlined very specific and detailed criteria for determining whether a long-term noncancelable lease transaction should be capitalized by the lessee company. Shortly after issuance of the standard, leasing transactions were structured so as to avoid the capitalization criteria so that the lessees could continue to account for the lease as a rental agreement, thus omitting the "borrowing" from the balance sheet. If an investor is attempting to compare two companies, one of whom purchases its capital assets while the other obtains its assets under long-term, noncancelable lease agreements that *do*

---

[6]Worthy, op. cit., notes that investment bankers have been hawking various defeasance packages ever since they sold Exxon on the idea in 1982. Exxon defeased $151 million of debt, reporting a gain of $132 million, and improving its debt/equity ratio. He also notes that this tactic may not be in shareholders' best interests since the bondholders will be earning an interest return reflecting the riskiness of the company's bonds when in fact the bonds are backed by risk-free government securities.

not require capitalization, allowances should be made for the understated debt of the lessee company.

Numerous other transactions have been structured to effectively obtain long-term financing without recording a long-term liability. Dieter and Wyatt identify several techniques which result in off-balance-sheet financing. They include finance subsidiaries, sale of receivables with recourse, project and product financing arrangements, through-out arrangements, and take-or-pay contracts.[7]

In making required estimates and judgments and in timing and structuring transactions, management can demonstrate various tendencies. They can be uniformly optimistic or pessimistic; they can take whatever action is appropriate to achieve some desirable financial reporting objective such as smoothing trends in income or earnings; or they could be as realistic and objective as possible. If management is consistently optimisitic or manipulative in resolving these matters, investors generally view this as a negative signal in assessing the quality of the firm's earnings.

6-5 ALTERNATIVE ACCOUNTING METHODS

A third potential source of difference between M Company's estimated market value of $119,479 and its balance sheet equity of $70,000 is the existence of alternative accounting methods affecting the measurement of financial statement elements. GAAP does not contain definitive accounting rules for each and every account or transaction. In a number of situations, accountants have been able to rationalize alternative accounting concepts. Although the accounting profession has taken steps to specify criteria for choosing among alternative accounting methods, depending upon their interpretation of the situation and the applicability of basic accounting methods, there are some alternative methods for which the criteria for choice are rather vague.

Suppose that M Company is involved in construction work. In valuing a partially completed construction contract, M Company can choose between the *completed contract* and *percentage completion* accounting methods. The completed contract method values the contract at the sum of the costs incurred to date, and *all income or profit from the contract is deferred until the contract is finished*. Under the percentage completion method, the construction contract is valued at costs to date *plus a portion of the anticipated income or profit* corresponding to the percentage of the work completed to date. If the M Company were using the completed contract method to prepare its balance sheet, differences could arise if the investor who is estimating the value of the business believes the percentage completion method to be more appropriate.

The existence of acceptable alternative accounting methods is particularly troublesome from the investor's viewpoint because it impairs financial statement comparability. How can financial statements be used to assess the relative profitability of two companies when their financial statements contain differences which are due solely to

[7]See R. Dieter and A. R. Wyatt, "Get It Off the Balance Sheet!" *Financial Executive* (January 1980).

the selection of different methods of accounting and do not reflect real economic differences?

Accountants have recognized this problem and have attempted to narrow the range of choice among alternative methods over the last 25 years. However, acceptable alternative methods still exist in a number of instances including the measurement of inventory cost, depreciation of plant and equipment, reporting of the investment tax credit, measurement of revenue, and the accounting for drilling and exploration costs in the gas and oil industry. In these instances, accountants rely on footnote *disclosures* to alert the investor to the methods being used. They also insist that the method be used *consistently* from year to year to ensure comparability over time. However, disclosures may not provide enough information to permit the investor to convert reported results to reflect the effect of an alternative accounting method.

6-5-1 Alternative Inventory Methods   To illustrate the potential impact of alternative accounting methods, let's consider the problem of determining the cost of inventory sold and on hand. Suppose Wholesale Supply, Inc., begins operations in 1986. The company deals in a single product which shows the following activity during that year:

	Units	Unit cost	Total cost
Inventory, 1/1/86	0	0	0
Purchases 1/15/86	100	$10	$1000
6/25/86	200	11	2200
10/17/86	200	12	2400
Goods available	500		$5600
Units sold	300		
Inventory, 12/31/86	200		

In order to prepare financial statements, the accountant must determine the cost of goods sold and the ending inventory—that is, what portion of the $5600 cost of goods available for sale should be associated with the 300 units sold, and what portion should be reported on the balance sheet as the cost of the 200 units in the December 31, 1986, inventory?

One way of allocating the cost would be to use a *specific identification* approach and determine the costs *actually paid* for the 300 units that were sold and the 200 units that remain on hand. However, it is generally not feasible to keep such detailed records to permit specific identification. Rather than allocating costs based on the *actual movement or flow* of inventory, accountants allocate costs based on an *assumed flow* of inventory. Three commonly used assumed flow methods are the *first-in, first-out method (FIFO), weighted average method (AVG),* and the *last-in, first-out method (LIFO).* The impact of each of these methods on cost of goods sold and inventory is summarized as follows:

	1986 cost of goods sold	December 31, 1986 ending inventory
FIFO	100 @ $10 = $1000 200 @ $11 = 2200 $3200	200 @ $12 = $2400
AVG	$\dfrac{\$5600}{500} \times 300 = \$3360$	$\dfrac{\$5600}{500} \times 200 = \$2240$
LIFO	200 @ $12 = $2400 100 @ $11 = 1100 $3500	100 @ $11 = $1100 100 @ $10 = 1000 $2100

Under GAAP, management would be free to select one of these alternative methods, provided that it is used consistently from period to period and the same method is also used for income tax purposes. Notice that under FIFO, cost of goods sold will be $300 less than under LIFO, causing FIFO income to be $300 higher. Likewise, the FIFO ending inventory will be $300 higher than the LIFO inventory. As long as prices are rising and inventory levels do not decrease, the FIFO method will report higher net incomes and inventory values than the LIFO method. The weighted average method will produce a result somewhere between FIFO and LIFO. If two companies were being analyzed by an investor, the use of alternative inventory methods would impact the comparability of current ratios, asset and inventory turnover ratios, debt/equity ratios, income as a percentage of sales, and return on investment. In addition, a LIFO company's inventory values are apt to be significantly outdated since the LIFO method relegates old costs to inventory. In fact, it would be possible for a LIFO company that had been organized in the 1940s to be carrying its inventory at the 1940 costs.

Notice that the impact of the different inventory methods depends on the volume of acquisitions, the size of the inventory, and the rate of change in inventory costs. In the mid-1970s significant numbers of companies switched to the LIFO method in an effort to suppress the impact of inflation-caused ''inventory profits.'' The switch to LIFO reduced the firm's reported income, but more importantly, it also reduced their taxable income and consequently their tax liability. *Accounting Trends and Techniques* reports that the percentage of firms using LIFO increased from about 25% in 1973 to 56% in 1978. In that time period the wholesale commodity price index increased from about 125 to 210.[8]

For larger companies which are also SEC registrants, sufficient information may be available in footnote and supplementary FASB Statement 33 disclosures to convert from one inventory method to another. The SEC requires that LIFO companies disclose

---

[8]Morse identifies several factors that could explain why a higher percentage of firms don't use LIFO. Some industries such as electronics have experienced deflationary cost trends. In this situation the FIFO method reports the lower income and tax liability. The expectation of increasing tax rates and widely fluctuating inventory levels may also cause managers to conclude that taxes would be minimized under FIFO rather than LIFO. The costs associated with conversion as well as the impact of LIFO on reported income may also make management reluctant to switch even in the face of potential tax savings. See D. Morse, ''LIFO . . . or FIFO?'', *Financial Executive* (February 1980).

the excess of the replacement cost (FIFO cost can be used if not materially different) of inventory over its stated LIFO cost. The stated LIFO cost of goods sold (COGS) can be recomputed on the FIFO basis by utilizing the general relationship

$$COGS = \text{beginning inventory} + \text{purchases} - \text{ending inventory} \qquad (6\text{-}2)$$

Reported LIFO cost of goods sold would be adjusted as follows if both beginning and ending inventories were higher under replacement cost (FIFO):

$$\text{FIFO COGS} = \text{LIFO COGS} + \text{FIFO excess for beginning inventory}$$
$$- \text{FIFO excess for ending inventory} \qquad (6\text{-}3)$$

Using the example of Wholesale Supply Company, there would be no FIFO excess for beginning inventory since inventories were zero at the beginning of the year, but there would be $300 of FIFO inventory in excess of LIFO inventory at the end of the year ($2400 − $2100). Thus, we could compute FIFO cost of goods sold as

$$\text{FIFO COGS} = 3500 + 0 - 300 = 3200$$

The results of a FIFO firm can similarly be converted to LIFO by recognizing that FASB Statement 33 requires disclosure of cost of goods sold at current replacement cost, which should generally approximate LIFO results. The approximation may not be very good in situations where costs have changed rapidly over the year or where inventory levels have decreased, releasing old LIFO costs into cost of goods sold.[9]

6-5-2 Depreciation methods   Alternative methods also exist for depreciating the cost of plant and equipment. Four decisions are required in order to compute depreciation. The cost of the asset must be determined; the salvage value must be estimated; the economic life of the asset must be estimated; and, finally, the pattern of receipt of benefits over the asset's life must be established. For most plant and equipment items, it is hard to determine the manner in which benefits flow from the asset. Therefore, it is difficult to specify criteria for the selection of a depreciation method. GAAP only requires management to select a depreciation method that produces a *systematic and rational allocation* of cost over the asset's economic life. All the commonly used depreciation methods such as the straight-line, sum-of-the-years'-digits, and declining balance methods meet these criteria and are considered acceptable. Management is therefore free to choose among these methods at will, restricted only by the requirement that the method be used consistently from period to period for that

---

[9]One disadvantage of LIFO is the fact that old costs may be released into income if the units sold exceed the units purchased. In this situation, some of the units sold are assumed to have come from the beginning inventory and are valued at the old LIFO costs. As a result, inventory profits caused by inflation are released into income and the result may be an income well in excess of comparable FIFO-based results. Worthy, op. cit., notes that U.S. Steel has reported $1.7 billion in LIFO inventory profits since 1976, as a result of drawing down inventories while business has been shrinking. Whether these draw-downs reflect the real trend in U.S. Steel's operations or have been done to bolster sagging profits is not clear.

particular type of asset. Unlike accounting for inventories, the IRS also permits the company to use a different depreciation method for federal income tax purposes.

From the investor's viewpoint, financial statement comparability may again be impaired. Suppose a manufacturer acquires a new piece of machinery at a cost of $100,000. The machine is estimated to have a 5-year life with zero salvage value. Consider the impact on depreciation expense of the commonly used methods illustrated in Table 6-7.

Over the asset's 5-year life, depreciation expense and income will be the same. However, income before tax can vary as much as $20,000 in any one of the 5 years, depending on the method selected. The choice of depreciation methods will impact asset turnover ratios, net income as a percentage of sales, return on investment, and debt/equity ratios.

If the investor is attempting to analyze two similar companies, and financial statement disclosures indicate that different depreciation methods are being used, how might the investor convert depreciation expense to a common base? If the balance sheet shows that the aggregate cost of equipment is $1,000,000 and the footnote disclosures indicate an average useful life of 10 years for equipment, then straight-line depreciation for 1 year can be estimated to be $100,000 ($1,000,000 × 1/10) and income can be adjusted accordingly to put the income statements of both companies on a comparable straight-line basis. This approach to estimating straight-line depreciation is only an approximation, as it assumes that no equipment items in the $1,000,000 total are fully depreciated and that acquisitions and disposition occurred on the first day of the year.

6-5-3 Deferred Income Taxes   The existence of alternative accounting methods also has income tax implications. For several different transactions, companies are able to use a different accounting method for book (financial statement) purposes than they use for preparing their income tax return. In most cases, the use of alternative methods simply alters the timing of revenue and expense recognition for tax purposes vs. book purposes. For example, a company may use the accelerated cost recovery system[10] to depreciate a piece of machinery over 5 years for tax purposes while depreciating the machine over a 10-year life using the straight-line method for the financial statements. The total depreciation taken under either method will be the same. However, the tax depreciation will be recorded over the first 5 years of the asset's life while book depreciation will extend over 10 years. These differences in the rec-

---

[10]The Economic Recovery Tax Act of 1981 initiated a new approach to recognizing depreciation on capital assets, called the accelerated cost recovery systems (ACRS). Rather than basing depreciation on wear and tear and economic lives, this new depreciation system emphasized periods for the recovery of capital so as to encourage capital investment. The ACRS allows the rapid recovery of an asset's cost using fixed recovery schedules over prescribed statutory periods. Four classes and schedules are established for tangible personal property while one schedule is established for real estate. For example, 5-year personal property includes most forms of machinery equipment and furniture previously depreciated for tax purposes over 5 or more years. The fixed depreciation schedule for 5-year property is 15% of cost in year 1, 22% in year 2, and 21% in each of years 3, 4, and 5. Because ACRS allows such rapid depreciation relative to the asset's economic life, the method is not generally consistent with GAAP and would only be used for tax purposes.

TABLE 6-7   IMPACT OF ALTERNATIVE DEPRECIATION METHODS

Year	Straight-line	Sum-of-the-years'-digits		Double-declining-balance	
1	$20,000	5/15 × 100,000 =	$33,333	.4 × 100,000 =	$40,000
2	20,000	4/15 × 100,000 =	$26,667	.4 × 60,000 =	$24,000
3	20,000	3/15 × 100,000 =	$20,000	.4 × 36,000 =	$14,400
4	20,000	2/15 × 100,000 =	$13,333	.4 × 21,600 =	$ 8,640
5	20,000	1/15 × 100,000 =	$ 6,667	Remainder =	$12,960
5-year total	$100,000		$100,000		$100,000

ognition of depreciation expense for tax vs. book purposes are called temporary timing differences.

Table 6-8 provides an example of comparative depreciation schedules based on accelerated cost recovery for tax purposes and straight-line depreciation for book purposes. Column 3 shows the difference in book income vs. taxable income over the asset's life. GAAP requires that when temporary timing differences like those that are illustrated exist, income tax expense will be measured based on the book income even though the tax liability is determined by the taxable income shown on the tax return. If book income were $12,000 in year 1 and the tax rate was 40%, tax expense for

TABLE 6-8   COMPARATIVE DEPRECIATION SCHEDULES AND THE DEFERRED INCOME TAX LIABILITY

Year	Tax purposes: accelerated cost recovery (1)	Book purpose: straight-line (2)	Excess of book income over taxable income (3)	Excess of tax expense over tax liability Col. 3 × 40% (4)	Accumulated deferred tax liability (5)
1	1,500	1,000	500	200	200
2	2,200	1,000	1,200	480	680
3	2,100	1,000	1,100	440	1,120
4	2,100	1,000	1,100	440	1,560
5	2,100	1,000	1,100	440	2,000
6	0	1,000	(1,000)	(400)	1,600
7	0	1,000	(1,000)	(400)	1,200
8	0	1,000	(1,000)	(400)	800
9	0	1,000	(1,000)	(400)	400
10	0	1,000	(1,000)	(400)	0
Total	10,000	10,000	0	0	

Assumptions: Asset is a machine which qualifies as a 5-year asset for accelerated cost recovery depreciation.

Initial cost = $10,000
Estimated life = 10 years
Estimated salvage value = 0
Tax rate = 40%

book purposes would be .4 × \$12,000 = \$4800 while the actual tax liability would only be .4 × (\$12,000 − \$500) = \$4600. The \$200 difference would be the tax effect of the temporary timing differences in recognizing depreciation expense. The excess of book income that will eventually be taxable over current taxable income would give rise to a deferred tax liability. Over the first 5 years the deferred tax liability would grow as book income exceeded currently taxable income (column 3, Table 6-8), causing the income tax expense to exceed the actual income tax liability (columns 4 and 5, Table 6-8). In the last 5 years of the asset's life, book depreciation catches up with tax depreciation, the temporary timing difference reverses, and the deferred tax liability is liquidated.

Deferred tax liabilities have been a subject of controversy particularly when they are generated by firms using accelerated depreciation for tax purposes and straight-line depreciation for book purposes. If the investment in plant and equipment is growing, then in the aggregate, book depreciation may never exceed tax depreciation. The timing differences never reverse and the deferred tax liability does not require payment. Critics argue that if the liability does not require payment, by definition it is not a liability. They argue that a more realistic accounting for income tax expense would be to measure tax expense based on the tax return and ignore the reporting of a deferred tax liability unless it is clear that the timing differences will reverse in the near future resulting in an actual tax liability. Studies conducted on the behavior of deferred income tax liability accounts for companies during the periods 1954–1973 and 1973–1982 support the critics' argument by showing that deferred income tax liability accounts seldom decreased as a result of tax payments arising from the reversal of depreciation timing differences.[11] Investors and analysts may want to discount the deferred income tax liability account, especially where it results from depreciation timing differences and has been growing over the years. This is particularly true if the reversal of the timing difference is only expected to occur under adverse economic conditions where losses would be likely to eliminate any potential tax liability.

6-5-4 Alternative Accounting Methods and Stock Prices   Management's approach to the selection of alternative accounting methods also influences investors' assessments of the quality of earnings. If management selects methods that uniformly favor reported earnings by accelerating the recognition of revenues and deferring the recognition of expenses then, depending on the circumstances, earnings quality may be assessed as being low. The question that has been raised in the finance and accounting literature is whether or not the use of alternative accounting methods influences stock prices. Does the company that switches to a more liberal accounting method so as to increase reported income achieve an advantage?

[11]S. Davidson, S. F. Rasch, and R. Weil, "Behavior of the Deferred Tax Credit Account, 1973–1982," *Journal of Accountancy* (October 1984), found that in the period 1973–1982, 76.3% of the 22,559 changes in the deferred tax credit (liability) account were increases while only 23.7% were decreases. Dollar amounts of increases exceeded decreases by 8 times. Only 7.5% of the decreases resulted from reversals of depreciation timing differences. In the period 1954–1973, 78.6% of the changes were increases while 21.4% were decreases. Dollar amounts in increases exceeded decreases by 6.5 times. Less than 3% of the decreases were due to reversals of depreciation timing differences. T. D. Skekel and C. Fazzi, "The Deferred Tax Liability: Do Capital Intensive Companies Pay It?" *Journal of Accountancy* (October 1984), report the rate of reversal of depreciation timing differences was even lower for capital-intensive companies.

In summarizing the relevant empirical research, Lev and Ohlson preface their analysis by noting that in an efficient market, rational investors should not be concerned with the "packaging" of information.[12] Investors' beliefs about future events should be unaffected by the form of disclosure and, if there are no effects on a firm's cash flows, then it follows that market values should be unperturbed by firms' choices of, or changes in, accounting methods.

Lev and Ohlson note that empirical research tends to support the rationality of the market, although the study of this topic is still in its infancy. Beaver and Dukes studied firms using accelerated depreciation for tax purposes and *either* straight-line *or* accelerated depreciation for financial reporting purposes.[13] They determined that once the earnings of the straight-line firms were adjusted to accelerated depreciation, the average *P/E* ratios of the straight-line and accelerated depreciation firm samples were almost identical. Studies of the effect of switching from accelerated to straight-line depreciation (while not changing the depreciation method used for tax purposes) disclosed no significant impact on stock prices in the month of earnings announcement even though reported earnings increased by about 10%.[14]

Research results are more mixed regarding the impact of changes in inventory methods. Early studies by Sunder were consistent with market efficiency in that an examination of switches to LIFO during the inflationary period of the early 1970s showed that the market correctly perceived the increased after-tax cash flow even though reported income decreased.[15] More recent studies by Ricks[16] and by Brown[17] which controlled for unusual earnings increases of LIFO adopting firms during the periods prior to the switch (1974–1975) found that LIFO adopters experienced significantly below normal returns in the month of changing to LIFO. Thus, it appears that the market's reaction to the LIFO switches was adverse and therefore seemingly inconsistent with market efficiency and investor rationality.

Lev and Ohlson suggest that answers to the conflicting results for changes in inventory methods may be found by more sensitive research designs. Alternatively, hidden but real cash flow consequences may be associated with all changes through, for example, management compensation schemes and contractual provisions such as bond covenants. Study of manager's motives in selecting alternative accounting meth-

---

[12]B. Lev and J. A. Ohlson, "Market-Based Empirical Research in Accounting: A Review, Interpretation, and Extension," *Journal of Accounting Research,* vol. 20, Supplement (1982).

[13]W. H. Beaver and R. E. Dukes, "Interperiod Tax Allocation and Delta-Depreciation Methods: Some Empirical Results," *The Accounting Review* (July 1973).

[14]T. R. Archibald, "The Return to Straight-Line Depreciation: An Analysis of a Change in Accounting Methods," *Empirical Research in Accounting: Selected Studies, 1967,* Supplement to *Journal of Accounting Research* (1967), and "Stock Market Reaction to the Depreciation Switch-Back," *The Accounting Review* (January 1972).

[15]S. Sunder, "Relationship between Accounting Changes and Stock Prices: Problems of Measurement and Some Empirical Evidence," *Empirical Research in Accounting: 1973,* Supplement to *Journal of Accounting Research* (1973), and "Stock Price and Risk Related to Accounting Changes in Inventory Valuation," *The Accounting Review* (April 1975).

[16]W. Ricks, "The Market's Response to the 1974 LIFO Adoptions," *Journal of Accounting Research* (autumn 1982).

[17]R. M. Brown, "Short-Range Market Reaction to Changes in LIFO Accounting Using Preliminary Earnings Announcement Dates," *Journal of Accounting Research* (spring 1980).

ods may provide insights as to the more indirect impact of accounting method changes on a firm's future operations.

6-6 EXAMPLE OF ADJUSTING REPORTED EARNINGS

It should be obvious by now that the choice of various accounting alternatives as well as the estimates and judgments involved in preparing financial statements can have a significant influence on reported earnings. The term *quality of earnings* refers to this problem. Firms that are considered to report low-quality earnings are those firms which consistently utilize optimistic estimates and choose the accounting alternatives which result in the highest level of reported earnings. High-quality earnings are associated with firms which utilize conservative estimates, judgments, and accounting alternatives.

As the example in Table 6-9 illustrates, the accounting options available to management can have a significant impact on reported EPS. In the example, ITT is used to illustrate how changes in estimates, judgments, and accounting methods affect both the level and the comparability of its 1982 and 1983 earnings. While ITT had reported earnings of $4.50 per share in 1983 and $4.47 in 1982, adjustments to eliminate the impact of various changes affecting comparability disclose quite a different earnings picture. Table 6-9 summarizes the various estimate and method changes and other nonrecurring items for which adjustments were made.

In an effort to make 1982 comparable with 1983, 1982 EPS was adjusted downward by $0.57 to remove nonrecurring items. The adjustment resulted from removing the $0.85 per share effect of two nonrecurring gains that were reported in 1982 from the sale of a 60% owned U.K. subsidiary ($0.61) and an AT&T antitrust settlement ($0.24). Netted against the gains was $0.28 per share which was due to either a change in accounting method or accounting estimates for oil and gas which accelerated expensing of costs in 1982 but which had the opposite effect in 1983.

Likewise, 1983 results were adjusted for 16 different revenue and expense items which, because of their nonrecurring nature, were considered by the author to be obscuring the trend in income from continuing operations. A policy decision was apparently made by ITT in 1983 to temporarily reduce or defer R&D expenditures, thus reducing expense and increasing income by $0.40 per share in 1983. Changed circumstances or revised estimates resulted in deferring in 1983 $0.14 per share in software costs that would have been expensed in 1982. Changed conditions led to lower technology restructuring expense of $0.28 per share in 1983 as well as higher tax rates which decrease 1983 results by $0.27/share. Other large adjustments to 1983 income were for two nonrecurring gains reported in 1983 from Hartford Insurance ($0.24) and the sale of facilities and companies ($0.24). The combined effect of these 16 items was to increase 1983 EPS over 1982 EPS by a net amount of $1.13. The author adjusted reported EPS by this amount to achieve comparability with the adjusted EPS for 1982. Note that allowing for all the author's adjustments, EPS *declined* in 1983 ($3.37 vs. $3.90), whereas reported EPS showed a slight *increase* ($4.50 vs. $4.47).

While differences of opinion might exist as to whether or not all the adjustments are appropriate, the ITT example clearly indicates the importance from the investor's

TABLE 6-9 ADJUSTING ITT's NET

"In 1983, ITT reported earnings of $4.50 a share, vs. $4.47 in 1982. However, on a more 'normalized' basis, 1983's earnings would have been $3.37, vs. $3.90 the prior year."

	Aided (+) or penalized (−) estimated per-share impact	
	1983	**1982**
Items affecting1983–1982 earnings comparisons:		
Increased other net	+ $0.08	
Lower R&D expenditures	+ $0.40	
Change in oil and gas accounting	+ $0.05	− $0.28
Increased capitalized software	+ $0.14	
Gain of issuance of U.K. affiliates stock	+ $0.07	
Lower pension expense	+ $0.07	
Gain on sale of majority interest in U.K.		+ $0.61
Gain on AT&T antitrust settlement		+ $0.24
Lower percentage allowance for doubtful accounts	+ $0.05	
Lower technological restructuring expense	+ $0.28	
Increased deferred business development expenses	+ $0.10	
Increased capital gains—Hartford Insurance	+ $0.24	
Net gain on sale of facilities and companies	+ $0.24	
Lower capitalized interest	− $0.04	
Lower gains on retirement of debt	− $0.07	
Lower gains on sale of tax benefits	− $0.13	
Unfavorable foreign currency swing	− $0.08	
Higher tax rate	− $0.27	
Net positive incremental contributions	+ $1.13	+ $0.57
Earnings as reported	$4.50	$4.47
Less net positive contributions	− $1.13	− $0.57
Adjusted earnings	$3.37	$3.90

Source: R. Olstein, "Quality of Earnings: The Keys to Successful Investing," *Barron's* (July 2,1984).

perspective of understanding financial statements and of knowing enough about GAAP to know when to question the reported numbers and possibly to adjust them before conducting your analysis.

6.7 SUMMARY

We have seen that the basic financial statements are a useful starting point for analyzing the financial affairs of a business. In order to use GAAP-based financial statements intelligently, the investor must have an understanding of generally accepted accounting principles. Of the basic accounting concepts, the historical cost principle, the stable monetary unit assumption, the rules for revenue recognition, and the objectivity principles were shown to have significant impact on the information reported in the balance sheet and income statement.

Accounting numbers are not as factual as they might seem at first glance. Numerous estimates and judgments are required of management and the firm's accountants in developing financial statements. Investors must be alert to estimates and judgments, especially significant changes therein. While most managements try to be realistic in making estimates and judgments, it is natural to be overly optimistic, especially in the face of declining income and deteriorating financial position.

Finally, the impact of accepted alternative accounting methods was discussed. The impact of different accounting methods on inventories, depreciation, and deferred taxes was specifically illustrated. However, the reader should be aware that there are many other areas for which different accounting methods can be chosen.

Where GAAP permits alternative accounting methods, the criteria for choice is often vague. Management is free to adopt a method that meets their pragmatic reporting objectives. Acceptable alternative methods can impair financial statement comparability for investment decisions. Financial statement footnotes must be examined to identify situations where alternative methods are in use or changes in methods have occurred. Where alternative accounting methods are used by two or more companies which the investor is attempting to analyze and compare, financial statement footnotes and other supplementary materials *may produce* adequate information to allow the investor to put the companies on a comparable basis. Where changes in methods occur for a single company between years, footnote disclosures will indicate the impact of the switch for the year of change to facilitate comparison with previous years.

Empirical evidence regarding the impact of changes in accounting methods generally supports the notion that investors see through changes in accounting methods, although some conflicting results and opinions exist. In any case, it is imperative that the investor and analyst be aware of the potential effects of alternative accounting methods, estimates, judgments, and basic accounting concepts and principles on financial statements. While it may be difficult or impractical to build the accounting expertise needed to assess the impact of these factors, investors should be sufficiently informed so as to identify problem areas which should be investigated further, possibly with the help of an accounting expert, before investment decisions are made from GAAP-based financial statements.

SUGGESTED READINGS

Numerous texts are available for extending your understanding of financial statements. The following texts are oriented toward the needs of investors and are suggested as general references for readers who have an introductory and/or dated background in accounting.

M. H. Granof, *Accounting for Managers and Investors,* Prentice-Hall, Englewood Cliffs, N.J., 1983.

G. Shillinglaw and P. E. Meyer, *Accounting: A Management Approach,* 7th ed., Irwin, Homewood, Ill., 1983.

For those readers who already have an extensive background in accounting, the following provides a complete discussion of GAAP and financial accounting:

D. E. Kieso and J. J. Weygandt, *Intermediate Accounting,* 4th ed., Wiley, New York, 1983.

The following book provides a particularly detailed discussion of GAAP and its impact on financial statements and financial analysis.

L. A. Bernstein, *Financial Statement Analysis: Theory, Application and Interpretation,* 3d ed., Irwin, Homewood, Ill., 1983.

For the analyst who wants to explore the effect of inflation on GAAP-based financial statements, the following book is particularly relevant:

S. Davidson, C. P. Stickney, and R. L. Weil, *Inflation Accounting: A Guide for the Accountant and Financial Analyst,* McGraw-Hill, New York, 1976.

Articles frequently appear in the finance and business literature which discuss specific accounting issues investors should consider in using financial statement information for investment decisions. The following are some of the articles which should be of interest to investors:

W. Beaver and S. Ryan, "How Well Do Statement No. 33 Earnings Explain Stock Returns?," *Financial Analysts Journal* (September–October 1985).

R. Brammer, "Something Doesn't Compute," *Barron's* (Oct. 10, 1983).

C. G. Callard and D. C. Kleinman, "Inflation-Adjusted Accounting: Does It Matter?," *Financial Analysts Journal* (May–June 1985).

E. E. Comiskey and M. Ghosal, "Tax Analysis of the Operating Loss Company," *Financial Analysts Journal* (November–December 1984).

C. J. Loomis, "The Earnings Magic at American Express," *Fortune* (June 25, 1984).

R. Olstein, "Quality of Earnings: The Keys to Successful Investing," *Barron's* (July 2, 1984).

T. W. Pratt, "Who's Afraid of Current-Cost Earnings?," *Value Line: Selection and Opinion* (Oct. 26, 1984).

F. S. Worthy, "Manipulating Profits: How It's Done," *Fortune* (June 25, 1984).

QUESTIONS

1 "Accounting is of little value for the investor. About all it's good for is meeting tax requirements. The sole focus of accounting is on the past. An investor wants to know about the future. I just don't see why such a fuss is made about financial statements!" Do you agree? Explain.

2 Why might the value of the owners' equity as portrayed in the balance sheet differ from the value placed on the business and its shares by investors?

3 What are generally accepted accounting principles (GAAP)? Where do they come from?

4 State the accounting equation and explain its elements.

5 What do an income statement and a statement of changes in financial position have in common? How do they differ?

6 Distinguish between a current and a noncurrent asset. Give examples of each type of asset.

7 Distinguish between current and noncurrent liabilities. Give examples of each type of liability.

8 Explain the historical cost principle. How does it affect the valuation of nonmonetary assets like an auto, merchandise inventory, land, and marketable equity securities?

9 Explain why merchandise inventory is not valued in the balance sheet at its expected selling price.

10 Explain the stable monetary unit assumption and discuss its implications for valuing assets and measuring income.

11 Explain the going concern concept and discuss its implications for valuing assets.

12 Discuss the shortcomings of GAAP-based income during a period of inflation. How do managements take these problems into account in making dividend decisions?

13 How do general price level accounting and current replacement cost accounting methods differ from GAAP-based historical cost accounting?

14 What does the term "quality of earnings" mean as it is used by investors?

15 "The balance sheet is a complete listing of all of our firm's assets and liabilities." Do you agree? Explain.

16 Give some examples of intangible assets a firm might have but which will not be reported on the balance sheet because of the accountant's objectivity principle.

17 Section 6-6 identified a number of areas where estimates made by management and accountants can have a significant impact on the firm's financial statements. Discuss one of these areas and identify a real-life example which illustrates the problem area you chose.

18 How is a bond liability valued in the balance sheet? What is the impact of fluctuations in the market rate of interest on (a) the valuation of the bond in the balance sheet and (b) the value of the bond traded in the securities markets?

19 Explain the differences among definite, estimated, and contingent liability. What types of contingent liabilities would be omitted from the balance sheet?

20 "Conservative accounting is good accounting!" What is meant by the concept of conservation? Do you agree with the statement? Explain.

21 A lawsuit has been filed against Felmar Company alleging violations of federal antitrust laws and claiming damages which, when trebled, total $2.2 billion. Felmar Company denies the charges and intends to contest the suit vigorously. Legal counsel advises the company that the litigation will last for several years and that a reasonable estimate of the final outcome cannot be made at this time.

Should Felmar Company include in its current balance sheet a liability for the damages claimed in this lawsuit? Explain fully.

22 Explain the realization and matching principles and discuss how they are important to the implementation of accrual accounting.

23 Why should an investor give particular attention to items in the financial statements listed as unusual or extraordinary?

24 What is meant by off-balance-sheet financing? Give an example of off-balance-sheet financing and discuss its impact on the financial statements.

25 What is in-substance defeasance? Why should the investor be concerned about the impact of such a transaction?

26 What are the attractions of the LIFO inventory method in a period of rising prices? What are its disadvantages?

27 What are inventory profits? Compare the FIFO and LIFO inventory methods in terms of their treatment of inventory profits in a period of rising prices.

28 "One area of accounting that is pretty much cut and dried is the measurement of depreciation on plant and equipment items. All that's required is to divide the asset's cost by its useful life. What could be easier?" Do you agree? Explain.

29 What is a deferred tax liability? How does it come into being? Why might the investor want to discount this liability in certain situations?

30 Should the use of alternative accounting methods have an impact on stock prices? Under what conditions? What have been the results of empirical research directed at this question?

PROBLEMS

1 Use the information given to determine the amount that should appear in *each* of the blanks below. Each situation is independent of the others unless specifically stated otherwise.

a Assume owners' equity is $80,000 on 12/31/87. In addition, on the same date:

Total Assets	_____
Capital stock	_____
Liabilities	30,000
Retained earnings	20,000

b The Fandango Corporation reports total assets of $20,000, liabilities of $6500, and stockholders' equity of $13,500 as of 12/31/87. The accountant discovers that supplies on hand of $500 and an electricity bill payable of $1000 have been omitted from these listings of assets and liabilities. Prepare revised asset, liability, and stockholders' equity totals as of 12/31/87 to correct for these errors. All other assets and liability accounts are properly stated as of 12/31/87.
Total assets _____
Liabilities _____
Stockholder's equity _____

c The Smith Corp. reported a current ratio of 4:1. Current liabilities were $12,000, while total assets were $85,000. What amount was reported for noncurrent assets?
Noncurrent assets _____

d

	Case A	Case B
Stockholders' equity, Jan. 1	$20,000	$50,000
Stockholders' equity, Dec. 31	30,000	40,000
Capital stock sold during year	5,000	0
Dividends declared during year	15,000	5,000
Net income for year (loss)	$_____	$_____
Revenues for year	$_____	93,000
Expenses for year	60,000	$_____

e During 1987, the assets of the Ram Corporation increased by $73,000 while the liabilities increased by $91,000. During the year dividends were paid to stockholders in the amount of $14,000. No additional shares of stock were sold. In its published financial statements for 1987 the firm should report net income (or net loss) of how much?
1987 net income (or net loss) $ _____

2 The following letter symbols represent the elements of the balance sheet equation for a corporation: A = assets, L = liabilities, CS = capital stock, RE = retained earnings. Use the appropriate letter symbols and a (+) for increases or a (−) for decreases to indicate how elements of the balance sheet equation would be affected by each transaction described below. The first item is completed as an example.

a Capital stock was issued for cash. [Answer: A(+), CS(+)]
b Purchased supplies on account.
c Paid office rent in advance.
d Billed customers for services rendered.
e Paid for supplies purchased earlier on account.

    f Paid employees' wages for the current month.

    g Collected cash from credit customers.

    h Declared and paid a cash dividend.

3 Early this year Bill Butler began a new business, called Butler's Delivery Service, with a motorcycle having a $500 fair market value and $100 in cash. He has kept no accounting records and now, at the year-end, has engaged you to determine the service's net income or loss for the year. You find that Butler's Delivery Service has a year-end bank balance of $760; there is $15 in the office cashbox; and The Bon, a local department store, owes the concern $110 for delivering packages during the past month. The concern still has the motorcycle, but it has depreciated $100 during the year. In addition, it has a new delivery truck that cost $3000 and has depreciated $150 since its purchase; the delivery service still owes the finance company $1700 on it. When the truck was purchased, Bill borrowed $1000 from his father-in-law for the down payment. The loan was made in the name of the delivery service and was interest-free. It has not been repaid. Finally, Bill has withdrawn $100 per week from the business (48 weeks) to be used for personal living expenses.

    a Prepare a balance sheet as of the end of the current year.

    b Compute the net income or loss earned by the business in its first year of operations.

4 In each of the situations described below indicate whether generally accepted accounting principles have been violated. If they have, indicate the accounting concept or principle that has been violated and explain the nature of the violation. If you conclude that the situation is consistent with generally accepted accounting principles, so indicate and defend your position.

    a In 1986, Ball Company reported $2000 of service revenue, which represented a cash advance for services to be performed in 1987.

    b Zeb Company follows the practice of charging the cost of merchandise purchased to expense before it is sold in order to report a less favorable financial position.

    c Wellman Corporation has used the declining-balance method of depreciation for both its income tax return and its GAAP-based financial statements. During the current year the company changed to the straight-line method of depreciation for financial reporting purposes but retained the declining-balance method for the income tax return. The change was disclosed in the financial statement footnotes and was approved by the outside auditors Zell, Nick, and Co., CPAs.

    d Marketable equity securities which cost $300,000 are reported in the balance sheet at $650,000, which represents the year-end selling price of the securities less estimated brokerage commission and other selling costs.

    e Because of a highly trained and cohesive management team that Zabell Company has groomed over the last 15 years, the company has been able to earn returns significantly in excess of other firms in their industry. In view of this accomplishment, management elects to establish an asset called goodwill on its book at an initial value of $92,500.

    f The Lynn company has purchased a computer for $1.5 million. The company expects to use the computer for 5 years, at which time it will acquire a larger and faster computer. The new computer is expected to cost $3.5 million. During the current year the company debited $700,000 to the depreciation expense account to "provide for one-fifth of the estimated cost of the new computer."

    g Richmond Company was established in the early 1900s. One of its assets, a piece of land, was acquired in 1918 at a cost of $25,000. Because the general level of prices had increased approximately fivefold by 1987, the controller, after consulting with the board of directors, increased the value of the land in the balance sheet to $125,000. The controller argued that the change is necessary to make the historical cost based financial statement more reflective of economic reality.

5 Evaluate each of the following independent situations relating to the reporting of assets and liabilities:

    a On 1/1/87 Q Co. acquired a plot of land for a building site for a factory. The W Co. paid $100,000 to the previous owner, $10,000 commission to the real estate broker who handled the deal, and $500 to the title company for transfer of title to Q Co. On 12/31/87 the site had an appraised market value of 120,000.

        (1) What amount would be associated with the land in the Q Co. balance sheet prepared as of 1/1/87?

        (2) What amount would be associated with the land in a balance sheet prepared as of 12/31/87?

    b Guido's Lombardy House is a fashionable restaurant specializing in northern Italian food. One resource owned by this firm is described below. Indicate whether or not the resource is an asset (from the accountant's viewpoint). Explain your answer. If you are uncertain, indicate instead what you would need to know in order to answer decisively.

        The firm rents its premises from another company. One year ago it signed a 5-year lease. At the same time it paid $10,000 for the right to renew its lease for another 5 years on the same terms when the current lease expires. Rental rates on properties of this kind have been increasing. Did this $10,000 payment result in an asset?

    c Sparks Company sells a product called "Flaz." The trade name Flaz was developed by advertising and other expenditures made over the last 20 years. The president of Sparks Company, Sparky Sparks, says, "Our most valuable resource is our trade name Flaz. The public knows and respects the name, giving us a considerable advantage over competitors." The balance sheet for Sparks Company, supposedly prepared based on generally accepted accounting principles, does not report the trade name as an asset. Is it possible that the balance sheet conforms to GAAP? Explain briefly.

6 Land was acquired by Bishop Company on Jan. 1, 1970, at a cost of $1 million. At that time the general price level, as measured by a popular index, was at 120. By Dec. 31, 1985, the general price level had risen to 360 and the land was appraised at $4,100,000. On January 4, 1986, the land was sold for $4,102,000.

    a Describe how the land sale would be reported in the 1986 income under generally accepted accounting principles.

    b How much better off is Bishop Company as a result of its investment in the land in real terms?

    c Critique the reporting of the gain on sale of land under GAAP. Consider both the timing of the gain and the amount. Suggest an alternative method.

7. The Johnson Company, which recently completed its second year of operations, now uses the FIFO inventory method. The management wishes to see what effect other inventory methods would have had on income and financial position, because another inventory method may be used in the future.

    The controller has presented the following information:

	1987	1986
Sales	$1,200,000	$800,000
Purchases	515,000	640,000
All other expenses	150,000	100,000
Ending inventory:	187,000	200,000
FIFO		
LIFO	168,000	188,000

   a Prepare the income statements for 1986 and 1987 using the FIFO inventory method.
   b Prepare the income statements for 1986 and 1987 using the LIFO inventory method.
   c Analyze the differences between the income statements in **a** and **b** and explain the likely cause.
   d Which method will result in higher total assets at the end of 1987? Higher total owners' equity? Explain.

8 The Advance Corporation began business on Oct. 1, 1986. Its purchases and sales of merchandise for the first 3 months of operation are shown below:

	Purchases			
Month	**Pounds**	**Price**	**Amount**	**Sales in pounds**
October	17,000	2.00	$34,000	4,000
November	5,000	2.30	$11,500	4,500
December	4,000	2.50	$10,000	4,800
	26,000		$55,500	13,300

12/31/86 inventory 12,700

   a Calculate cost of goods sold for 1986 and inventory as of 12/31/86 under both the FIFO and LIFO inventory methods.
   b Determine the inventory profits (due to price increases) included in 1986 income if the FIFO method of inventory valuation is used.
   c What method of inventory valuation would you recommend that Advance Corporation adopt assuming that the effect of inventory profits on income was to be minimized? Explain.
   d What guidance do generally accepted accounting principles offer Advance Corporation in choosing among the alternate inventory costing methods? What are the implications for the usefulness of financial statements based on generally accepted accounting principles? How are the concepts of consistency and disclosure related?

9 For one of its large pieces of machinery, Dantly Corporation uses an accelerated depreciation method for both financial statements and income taxes. In the first 5 years of operation, accelerated depreciation on this piece of machinery amounted to $2,376,000. The machine appears in the current year-end balance sheet as follows:

Machine	$4,250,000
Less: accumulated depreciation	2,376,000
Net book value	$1,874,000

   a Assuming the machine is expected to last 15 years with no salvage value at the end of year 15, estimate the depreciation that would have been taken to date under the straight-line depreciation method.
   b If the company had used the straight-line rather than the accelerated depreciation method, how would its current balance sheet differ? Its current year's income statement? (ignore income taxes.)
   c If the company had used accelerated depreciation for tax purposes, but straight-line depreciation for financial statements, and if the average income tax rate over the last 5 years was 40%, what amount, if any, would be shown currently as a deferred income tax liability? When would the company have to pay this liability? Explain.

10 Given the information below, prepare an income statement in as much detail as possible for 1987.

Balance Sheet

Assets:	12/31/86	12/31/87
Cash	200	300
Accounts receivable	100	150
Merchandise inventory	200	250
Prepaid insurance	100	150
Fixed assets (net of depreciation)	500	600
Total assets	1100	1450

Liabilities:		
Accounts payable to creditors for merchandise	300	500
Taxes payable	200	300
Bonds payable	300	200
Common stockholder equity	300	450
Total liabilities	1100	1450

Cash Flow Statement for 1987

Collections from customers		1200
Less: Payments for merchandise	350	
Wages	200	
Insurance	100	
Taxes	100	
Retirement of bonds	100	
Dividends paid	50	
Purchase of fixed assets	200	1100
Cash balance increase		100

APPENDIX: Computing Earnings per Share

In 1966, the Accounting Principles Board recommended in APB Opinion 9 that firms include an earnings per share (EPS) computation as part of the basic financial statement disclosures. The board recommended an *actual EPS* figure which would be computed by dividing actual net income to common stockholders by the weighted average outstanding common shares. In 1969, the Accounting Principles Board issued Opinion 15, which required public companies to include EPS computations as part of basic financial statement disclosures. However, the EPS concept was changed somewhat for companies having commitments to issue additional common shares through the conversion or exercise of convertible bonds, convertible preferred stock, stock warrants, stock options, etc. (potentially dilutive securities). Rather than disclose actual EPS for businesses with so-called complex capital structures, a pro forma EPS concept was adopted. The pro forma EPS differs from actual EPS in that the EPS computation is based on the *estimated* common shares that *could be outstanding* as a result of the potentially dilutive securities rather than the *actual* number of common shares that are outstanding. Pro forma EPS is calculated under two assumptions concerning the exercise. *Primary EPS* is computed based on a restrictive assumption about the exercise of conversion privileges and options while *fully diluted EPS* is computed based on the assumed *exercise of all existing* conversion privileges and options which have a dilutive effect. Thus, fully diluted EPS presents the maximum possible dilution in EPS.

6A-1 ACTUAL EPS

Under APB Opinion 15, companies not having potentially dilutive securities outstanding are said to have a "simple capital structure." Actual EPS is presented for these companies. *Note too that actual EPS will be presented for companies with complex capital structures as long as the potentially dilutive securities do not reduce actual EPS by at least 3%.* To illustrate the calculation of actual earnings per share, consider the following data for Zelbeck Incorporated:

Common stock, par $10, authorized 400,000 shares:	180,000 shares	$1,800,000
Outstanding 1/1/86		
Issued 6/1/86	12,000 shares	$ 192,000
Preferred stock, par $20, 6% nonconvertible, authorized:	5,000 shares	$ 100,000
Issued and outstanding		
From the 1986 income statement:		$ 240,000
Income before extraordinary item		
Extraordinary gain (net of 46% tax)		$ 20,000
Net Income		$ 260,000
Marginal tax rate = 46%		

Computation of Income to Holders of Common Shares

Annual preferred dividend requirement = .06 × $100,000 = $6000
    Income figures adjusted for payment of preferred stock dividend:

(1) Income before extraordinary items $240,000 − $6000	= $234,000
(2) Extraordinary gain (net of 46% tax)	20,000
(3) Net income $260,000 − $6000	= 254,000

Computation of Weighted Average Outstanding Common Shares

	Months		Shares		Product
January 1 to May 31	5	×	180,000	=	900,000
June 1 to December 31	7	×	192,000	=	1,344,000
Totals	12				2,244,000

Weighted average shares = 2,244,000 ÷ 12 = 187,000 shares

Computation of Actual EPS

(1) Income before extraordinary items $= \dfrac{\$234,000}{187,000} = \$1.25/\text{share}$

(2) Extraordinary gain $\dfrac{\$20,000}{187,000} = \$0.11/\text{share}$

(3) Net income $\dfrac{\$254,000}{187,000} = \$1.36/\text{share}$

6A-2 PRIMARY AND FULLY DILUTED EPS

To illustrate computation of EPS for a company with a complex capital structure, let's assume the same facts as above for Zelbeck Incorporated. In addition, assume that Zelbeck had the following potential dilutive securities outstanding during all of 1986:

(A) Common stock warrants for 10,000 shares
Exercise price: $15
Average market price for common stock during the year: $40/share
Market price of common stock, 12/31/86: $50/share
(B) Convertible bonds, 8%, $500,000
Conversion rate: Each $1000 bond is convertible into 40 shares
of common stock
Issued at 100 in 1980 when the prime rate was 9%.

6A-2-1 Common Stock Equivalents Primary EPS is computed by dividing the income available to holders of common shares by the weighted average outstanding shares plus *common stock equivalents*. Common stock equivalents (CSE) include securities which are in substance equivalent to common stock. A stock warrant or option would be considered a CSE if the exercise is highly likely because the option or exercise price has been less than the current market price for at least the last 3-month period. Convertible securities are considered a CSE if the convertible securities are held primarily for their stock-appreciation potential. The test used to determine if substantial value is placed on the conversion privilege is to compare the cash yield with normal lending rates as represented by the yield in Aa corporate bonds for securities issued after March 1, 1982, and the prime rate for securities issued before March 1, 1982. If the cash yield based on market price at issuance is less than 66 2/3% of the normal lending rate at that time, the convertible security is considered a CSE.

Are Zelbeck's stock warrants and convertible bonds considered CSE for the 1986 EPS computations? The stock warrants are a CSE because the option price of $15 is significantly below the average market price of $40 for 1986. However, the convertible bonds are not a CSE. The cash yield (for convertible bonds, the coupon rate if the bonds were issued at par) at issuance was 8.0%, which is greater than 66 2/3% of the then existing prime rate of 9%. Therefore, the stock warrants as a CSE will enter the computation of both primary and fully diluted EPS. The convertible bonds, because they are not a CSE, will only enter into the computation of fully diluted EPS.[18]

6A-2-2 Primary EPS In order to compute Zelbeck's primary EPS we must determine the CSE shares that would result from exercise of the warrants. If the warrants were exercised as of the first day of the current year, 10,000 additional common shares would be outstanding during the year and Zelbeck would have $10,000 \times \$15 = \$150,000$ in additional capital at its disposal. An assumption must be made as to the manner in which this capital will be employed in order to assess the impact on outstanding shares and net income. In order to avoid having to impute a return to the capital, the *treasury stock method* is used to determine the CSE of the 10,000 shares issued upon exercise of the warrants. The $150,000 proceeds from the warrants is assumed to be used to reacquire and retire shares of common stock at their average price for

---

[18]Note that the CSE status of a convertible security is determined once and for all at its issuance date. Note too that options and warrants are always CSE but will only have a dilutive effect and thus will be included in primary and fully diluted EPS computations when the exercise price is below the option price.

the year. The difference between the issued and reacquired shares is the CSE of the warrants. In this case the CSE $= 10,000 - (150,000 \div 40) = 10,000 - 3750 = 6250$ shares.[19] Since the exercise of the warrants and subsequent repurchase of shares does not change the capital of the firm, no adjustment of net income is required beyond the preferred dividend. Primary EPS is computed as follows:

Income before extraordinary item: $\dfrac{\$240,000 - \$6000}{187,000 + 6250} = \dfrac{\$234,000}{193,250} = \$1.21/\text{share}$

Extraordinary gain: $\dfrac{\$20,000}{193,250} = \$0.10/\text{share}$

Net income: $\dfrac{\$260,000 - \$6000}{193,250} = \dfrac{\$254,000}{193,250} = \$1.31/\text{share}$

The primary EPS represents a dilution of

$$4.4\% \left(\frac{1.31 - 1.37}{1.37} = -4.4\% \right)$$

from the actual EPS, and consequently primary EPS would be reported in the financial statements.

6A-2-3 Fully Diluted EPS
In determining the CSE for the warrants for the fully diluted EPS computation, treasury shares purchased is determined by dividing the proceeds from the exercise of the warrants by the greater of the average share price for the year or the year-end share price. In the Zelbeck example the year-end price ($50) is greater than the average price ($40). CSE for fully diluted EPS $= 10,000 - (150,000 \div 50) = 7000$ shares. In addition, the convertible bonds will be assumed to have been converted to common stock as of the beginning of the year. The assumed conversion will have two effects. First, 20,000 additional shares of common stock will be outstanding over the year (500 bonds $\times$ 40 shares/bond). Second, net income will be increased by the elimination of the bond interest expense for the year. The after-tax effect of eliminating the interest expense is $21,600 [(0.08 $\times$ $500,000) $(1 - 0.46) = \$21,600$]. Fully diluted EPS would be computed as follows:

Income before extraordinary item: $\dfrac{\$240,000 - \$6000 + \$21,600}{187,000 + 7000 + 20,000} = \dfrac{\$255,600}{214,000} = \$1.20$

Extraordinary gain: $\dfrac{\$20,000}{214,000} = \$0.09$

Net income: $\dfrac{\$260,000 - \$6000 + \$21,600}{214,000} = \dfrac{\$275,600}{214,000} = \$1.29/\text{share}$

[19]If the number of common shares issuable exceeds 20% of the common shares outstanding at the end of the period, the treasury stock method is modified. The proceeds from the exercise of warrants are first assumed to be used to repurchase 20% of the outstanding common shares, and the excess is assumed to be used to purchase and retire short-term or long-term borrowings. Any remainder would be assumed to be invested in United States government securities.

The fully diluted EPS reflects a 6.2% dilution of the actual EPS of $1.37. Zelbeck would then disclose on the 1986 income statement both primary and fully diluted EPS for net income, extraordinary items, and income before extraordinary items, as follows:

	1986
Primary earnings per share (Note X):	
Income before extraordinary items	$1.21
Extraordinary item	0.10
Net income	$1.31
Fully diluted earnings per share (Note X):	
Income before Extraordinary item	$1.20
Extraordinary item	0.09
Net income	$1.29

Note X—A note to the financial statement describing the computation of EPS and describing the options and convertible bonds.

In addition, APB Opinion 15 requires that a description of the various securities be included, in summary form, sufficient to explain all pertinent rights and privileges of the various outstanding securities.

6A-3 SUMMARY

The preceding illustration was designed to illustrate how EPS is computed for businesses with both simple and complex capital structures. The examples were realistic but not extremely complex. There are a number of factors which might further complicate the determination of both primary and fully diluted EPS. They include stock dividends and stock splits; issuance of potentially dilutive securities during the current year; actual exercise of conversion privileges, options, or warrants during the current year; existence of multiple convertible securities; and antidilutive securities. The analyst who is faced with these complications could consult the texts on intermediate accounting and financial statement analysis listed among the suggested readings for this chapter. In addition, the article by S. Matulich, L. A. Nikolai, and S. K. Olson, "Earnings per Share: A Flow Chart Approach to Teaching Concepts and Procedures," *The Accounting Review* (January 1977) is suggested.

QUESTIONS RELATING TO APPENDIX ON COMPUTING EPS

A1 What is a common stock equivalent? How is it used in determining EPS?

A2 Distinguish among actual, primary, and fully diluted EPS.

A3 In computing a price/earnings ratio for a firm having a complex capital structure, would you use actual, primary, or fully diluted EPS? Explain.

PROBLEM RELATING TO APPENDIX ON COMPUTING EPS

A1 Information concerning the capital of the Modoc Corporation is as follows:

	December 31	
	1985	1986
Common stock	90,000 shares	90,000 shares
Convertible preferred stock	10,000 shares	10,000 shares
8% convertible bonds	$1,000,000	$1,000,000

During 1986, Modoc paid dividends of $1.00 per share on its common stock and $2.40 per share on its preferred stock. The preferred stock is convertible into 20,000 shares of common stock, but is not considered a common stock equivalent. The 8% convertible bonds are convertible into 30,000 shares of common stocks and were issued in 1980 when the prime rate was 13%. The net income for the year ended December 31, 1986, was $285,000. Assume that the income tax rate was 50%.

a Determine actual EPS, primary EPS, and fully diluted EPS for 1986.

b What EPS amounts would be shown on Modoc Corporation's 1986 income statement? Explain briefly.

CHAPTER 7

ANALYZING FINANCIAL STATEMENTS

After reading this chapter, you should:

1 Understand how "common size" and "trend" financial statements are constructed and used
2 Know how to compute the basic financial ratios
3 Be aware of the strengths and weaknesses of the return on investment ratios—ROA, ROE, and EP
4 Understand the linkage between stock price and financial ratios based on the constant growth model and the DuPont system
5 Understand why industry averages are typically used as benchmarks in ratio analysis
6 Be aware of several sources of industry ratios

To evaluate securities, projections must be made concerning the prospects of the firm and the risk associated with the securities. For example, the common stock valuation models developed in Chapter 13 require estimates of future growth rates of earnings and dividends as well as the appropriate rate of return to be used in discounting the expected cash flows.

While many factors are considered in making projections of the key variables which determine security prices, the starting point is typically an analysis of the firm's financial statements. This chapter will discuss two of the techniques most commonly used to analyze financial statements: constructing common size and trend statements, and the most important analytical tool, ratio analysis. But before we begin, we need to present a simplified view of the financial statements, as well as the abbreviations we will use throughout this text for various items on the financial statements.

7-1 A REVIEW OF FINANCIAL STATEMENTS

As a rule, the most important source of information regarding a company is its financial statements. And, of the four basic financial statements, by far the most important are the income statement and the balance sheet. Table 7-1 presents the 1982, 1983, and 1984 income statements for Bandag, Inc., as they appeared in the company's 1984 annual report. Bandag (BDG) is the world's largest manufacturer of tread rubber, equipment, and supplies for the tire retreading industry.

The first two items on Bandag's income statement (net sales and other income) represent the total revenues of the firm. For exposition purposes we will generally

TABLE 7-1
Income Statements for Bandag, Inc.
Consolidated Statement of Earnings
(In thousands, except per share data)

	Year ended Dec. 31		
	1984	**1983**	**1982**
Income:			
Net sales	$318,842	$303,498	$285,954
Other income	9,965	10,852	12,641
	$328,807	$314,350	$298,595
Costs and expenses:			
Cost of products sold	(193,117)	(182,556)	(181,359)
Engineering, selling, administrative, and			
other expenses	(52,124)	(51,082)	(46,988)
Interest	(3,249)	(3,832)	(2,681)
Earnings from continuing operations before			
income taxes and extraordinary credit.........	80,317	76,880	67,567
Income taxes	(35,665)	(37,748)	(32,691)
Earnings from continuing operations	$44,652	$39,132	$34,876
Discontinued operations, less applicable			
income taxes:			
Earnings (loss) from operations	—	—	(2545)
Earnings before extraordinary credit	44,652	39,132	32,331
Extraordinary credit, net of applicable			
taxes	2,261		
Net earnings	$46,913	$39,132	$32,331
Per common and common equivalent			
share:			
Earnings from continuing operations	4.83	3.88	3.07
Earnings (loss) from discontinued			
operations	—	—	(.22)
Earnings from extraordinary credit	.24		
Net earnings	$5.07	$3.88	$2.85

Source: Bandag 1984 Annual Report.

combine these two items under the notation ''sales'' or simply *S*. However, the analyst frequently will want to consider these two items separately, as they may give important clues concerning the performance of various segments of the firm's operations. (In BDG's case, other income represents 3% of total sales and thus little information is lost by considering only total sales.) Table 7-2 presents a simplified 1984 income statement for Bandag. For this table net sales and other income, added together under the notation Sales, or *S*, amounted to $328,807,000 for 1984.

There are three major expense items which the analyst will usually be interested in—cost of goods sold (COGS), a catchall category called general administrative and selling expenses (GAS), and interest (*I*). The income statement presented in Bandag's

TABLE 7-2
Simplified 1984 Income Statement for Bandag, Inc.
(In $000s, except for EPS)

		1984
S:	Sales	$328,807
COGS:	Cost of goods sold	(193,117)
GP:	Gross profit	$135,690
GAS:	General administration and selling expense	(52,124)
EBIT:	Earnings before interest and taxes	$ 83,566
I:	Interest	(3,249)
EBT:	Earnings before taxes	$ 80,317
TAX:	Income taxes	(35,665)
EAT:	Earnings after taxes	$ 44,652
EPS:	Earnings per share	$ 4.83

annual report (see Table 7-1) divides expenses into these three categories and uses almost identical titles for these expense items. However, this will frequently not be the case. For example, many companies will report marketing expenses separately. Other firms may separately identify depreciation expense, etc. When analyzing a company in detail, the analyst will be interested in all the various expense items reported in the income statement. However, for our purpose the simplified income statement presented in Table 7-2 does account for the major expense items which are applicable to most firms and will be used to illustrate many of the analysts' tools discussed in this and subsequent chapters.

Sales minus cost of goods sold is usually termed *gross profit* (GP), which in the case of Bandag was $135,690,000 in 1984, as shown in Table 7-2. Gross profit minus general administrative and selling expenses will be termed *earnings before interest and taxes* (EBIT). Many writers refer to EBIT as either *operating earnings* or *operating profit*. For Bandag, EBIT amounted to $83,566,000 in 1984.[1] Subtracting interest expense (*I*) from EBIT leaves *earnings before taxes (EBT)*, or *pretax income*. Bandag's 1984 EBT amounted to $80,317,000. Finally, deducting income taxes (TAX) from the pretax income leaves *earnings after taxes (EAT)*. This is generally the amount used in computing *primary earnings per share* unless the firm has preferred stock outstanding, in which case the preferred stock dividends are subtracted from EAT, leaving "earnings available to common shareholders." In Bandag's case, there is no preferred stock outstanding and the EAT of $44,652 is used to compute earnings per share (EPS). As a general rule, EPS are computed by dividing EAT by a weighted average of the number of common shares outstanding during the year.[2] For 1984, Bandag's EPS amounted to $4.83.

[1]Since Bandag does not expressly report EBIT, one has to add back interest expense ($3,249,000) to earnings before taxes ($80,317,000) to arrive at EBIT.
[2]Calculating EPS may not be this straightforward. The Appendix at the end of Chapter 6 provides a detailed explanation of how to calculate EPS.

The alert reader may have noticed by comparing Tables 7-1 and 7-2 that the simplified income statement in Table 7-2 is based on *earnings from continuing operations*. In general, this will be the procedure followed throughout this text. If a firm has disposed of a business segment during the year, then the earnings generated by the part of the firm no longer owned at the end of the year will be reported as *earnings from discontinued operations*. Concentrating on the ongoing operations of the firm (income from continuing operations) will generally provide a better picture of the firm's future operations. However, some firms seem to have the habit of discontinuing part of their business *each year*. In such cases one might be better advised to concentrate on net earnings, as opposed to earnings from continuing operations, if the discontinued earnings or losses seem to be a regular occurrence.

Table 7-3 presents the 1982, 1983, and 1984 balance sheets for Bandag as they appeared in BDG's 1984 annual report. One can immediately see that current assets ($139,958,000 in 1984) represent the majority of total assets ($190,348,000). This is because Bandag licenses its proprietary tire retreading process to franchised dealers. Thus, BDG itself does not have a large requirement for fixed assets such as property, plant, and equipment. One can also see that BDG is conservatively capitalized with stockholders' equity representing $128 million of the total $190 million of liabilities and equity.

Note the decrease in stockholders' equity from 1983 to 1984. Since Bandag was quite profitable, this was not the result of losses, but rather the result of the company buying back and retiring its shares. The common stock account had a balance of $8,629,000 in 1984 vs. $9,967,000 in 1983. Recall that, in general, the common stock account balance is equal to the number of shares issued multiplied by the par value of the stock. In Bandag's case, par value is $1. Thus, the company repurchased and retired a little over 1.3 million shares in 1984 (9,967,138 minus 8,628,823). The fewer shares outstanding in 1984 had a positive impact on EPS. Note that while EAT increased 14% in 1984 ($44,652,000 vs. $39,132,000), EPS increased 24% ($4.83 vs. $3.88) based on the smaller number of shares outstanding.

A simplified balance sheet is presented in Table 7-4 to illustrate the abbreviations which will be used for the major balance sheet items. As a general rule we will lump cash and short-term marketable securities under the heading CASH. Accounts and notes receivable are also grouped together and denoted AR. All types of inventories are grouped together and denoted INV. For most firms the bulk of current assets (CA) will be comprised of receivables and inventories—in Bandag's case AR plus INV represent 82% of current assets.

We will generally group property, plant, equipment, and other tangible fixed assets under the heading of fixed assets (FA). Intangible assets[3] and occasionally some miscellaneous assets will be denoted as other fixed assets (OFA).

On the liabilities side, current liabilities (CL) will generally be divided into two groups—accounts and notes payable (AP) and other current liabilities (OCL). Current liabilities for BDG amounted to $46,951,000.

---

[3]Intangible assets include items such as patents, copyrights, trademarks, and goodwill. Goodwill is the excess of the purchase price of an acquired company over the specific values assigned to the acquired assets. See Section 6-3.

TABLE 7-3
Balance Sheet for Bandag, Inc.
(In thousands)

	December 31		
	1984	**1983**	**1982**
Assets			
Current assets:			
Cash, principally time deposits	$ 13,296	$ 24,806	$ 31,798
Marketable securities, at cost which approximates market	10,000	26,205	14,426
Accounts receivable, less allowance (1984—$3, 482; 1983—$3, 484; 1982—$2, 612)	80,821	82,453	78,548
Amounts receivable from sale of discontinued operations	—	—	1,454
Insurance claim receivable	3,492	3,742	—
Inventories:			
Finished products	19,521	18,048	16,731
Material and work in process	10,745	10,461	11,109
	$ 30,266	$ 28,509	$ 27,840
Prepaid expenses and other current assets	2,083	3,600	6,456
Total current assets	$139,958	$169,315	$160,522
Property, plant, and equipment, on the basis of cost:			
Land	1,253	1,452	1,488
Buildings and improvements	26,711	26,117	24,378
Machinery and equipment	52,567	49,225	47,728
Construction and equipment installation in progress	3,604	1,085	2,835
	$ 84,135	$ 77,879	$ 76,429
Less allowances for depreciation and amortization	(40,687)	(37,790)	(36,744)
	$ 43,448	$ 40,089	$ 39,685
Other assets	6,942	10,046	12,888
Total assets	$190,348	$219,450	$213,095
Liabilities and stockholders' equity			
Current liabilities:			
Accounts payable	$ 14,387	$ 14,479	$ 13,034
Employee compensation, taxes, and other accrued expenses	18,520	20,778	15,796
Dividend payable	2,373	2,492	2,354
Income taxes currently payable	5,477	—	10,504
Deferred income taxes	5,331	4,892	—
Short-term notes payable and current portion of long-term debt and capital lease obligations	863	2,193	5,169
Total current liabilities	$ 46,951	$ 44,834	$ 46,857
Long-term debt and other noncurrent liabilities	6,232	6,828	8,031
Capital lease obligations	2,672	2,959	3,236
Deferred income taxes	5,569	2,815	—
Stockholders' equity:			
Common stock, $1 par value; authorized—25,000,000 shares; outstanding—8,628,823 shares in 1984; 9,967,138 shares in 1983; 10,460,138 shares in 1982	8,629	9,967	10,460
Additional paid-in capital	4,877	6,962	8,073
Retained earnings	127,723	149,778	139,859
Equity adjustment (reduction) from foreign currency translation	(1,021)	(4,693)	(3,421)
	$128,924	$162,014	$154,971
	$190,348	$219,450	$213,095

Source: Bandag 1984 Annual Report.

TABLE 7-4
Simplified 1984 Balance Sheet for Bandag, Inc.
(In $000s)

Assets

CASH:	Cash and marketable securities	$ 23,296
AR:	Net accounts receivable and notes receivable	84,313
INV:	Inventories	30,266
OCA:	Other current assets	2,083
CA:	Current assets	$139,958
FA:	Net fixed assets	43,448
OFA:	Other fixed assets	6,942
A:	Total assets	$190,348

Liabilities and equity

AP:	Accounts payable	$ 14,387
OCL:	Other current liabilities	32,564
CL:	Current liabilities	$ 46,951
LTD:	Long-term debt	6,232
LEASES:	Capitalized leases	2,672
OLTL:	Other long-term liabilities	5,569
PS:	Preferred stock	0
EQ:	Total stockholders' equity	128,924
		$190,348

We will generally divide long-term liabilities into three categories—long-term debt (LTD), such as bonds, debentures, and other formal debt obligations; capitalized leases (LEASES); and other long-term liabilities (OLTL) such as deferred taxes. For Bandag, LTD amounted to $6,232,000; LEASES amounted to $2,672,000; and OLTL amounted to $5,569,000 and represented deferred taxes (see Table 7-3). Bandag has not issued any preferred stock, which we denote PS in Table 7-4. Common stockholders' equity (EQ) totaled $128,924,000 at the end of 1984.

Having reviewed the notation we will use for financial statement items, we can now consider some of the tools used by investors in analyzing financial statements.

7-2 COMMON SIZE AND TREND STATEMENTS

There are two basic approaches to analyzing a set of financial variables: (1) *cross-sectional techniques* and (2) *time-series techniques*. Cross-sectional techniques involve a comparison of the same financial variable for a *number of different firms at the same point in time*. Time-series techniques involve a comparison of a financial variable *for the same firm over a series of different time periods*. An example of a cross-sectional analysis would be a comparison of the after-tax profit margins of several tire manufacturers (Bandag, Firestone, Goodyear, etc.) for a single year, say 1984. An example of a time-series analysis would be a comparison of the profit margin of a single company over a series of years, say 1974 through 1984. Generally both cross-sectional and time-series techniques are required to thoroughly investigate a potential investment.

7-2-1 Common-Size Statements Common-size statements can be used as either a cross-sectional or a time-series technique. The basic procedure is to convert income statement and balance sheet variables into percentages. In the case of income statement variables, each item on the income statement is presented as a percentage of sales. Common-size balance sheets present each balance sheet variable as a percentage of total assets.

Consider first Table 7-5, which presents a cross section of common-size income statements and balance sheets for three companies—Bandag, Armstrong Rubber Company, and Firestone Tire & Rubber Company. Note how the common-size statements facilitate the comparison of a cross section of companies. For example, it is easy to see that the COGS for Armstrong (80.0%) is substantially higher than it is for Bandag (58.7%). This is probably because Armstrong sells a large percentage of its tires to major retailers such as Sears. In general, this type of business is characterized by lower gross profit margins. On the other hand, Armstrong's general administration and selling expenses (13.2%) are lower than Bandag's (15.9%). This is not surprising, since one would expect selling (and perhaps administrative) expenses to be lower for a firm which sells to fewer, but larger customers.

Comparing EAT as a percentage of sales indicates that Bandag has a considerably higher after-tax profit margin (13.6%) than either Armstrong (3.8%) or Firestone (1.6%). This result primarily stems from the fact that BDG controls a proprietary process (a more efficient method of retreading tires) while Firestone and Armstrong compete in the well-established replacement tire market. Most commodity businesses are characterized by low profit margins, and tires have many of the characteristics of a commodity.

One can also observe differences among the three firms when comparing the common-size balance sheets listed in Table 7-5. For example, Bandag has a larger current asset component (73.5% of total assets) than either Armstrong or Firestone. As noted earlier, most of the actual production process associated with Bandag is done by the franchised dealers; thus BDG does not have a large fixed-asset (plant and equipment) requirement. On the other hand, Armstrong and Firestone are primarily manufacturers and therefore they do have a substantial investment in plant and equipment. On the liabilities and equity side, the major difference among the three firms is that Bandag is primarily capitalized with equity (67.7% of total assets), whereas Armstrong and Firestone use more debt financing.

Common-size statements can also be used in a time-series fashion to analyze changes in financial variables for a particular company over time. Table 7-6 presents common-size financial statements for Bandag for the years 1982 through 1984. One can quickly see that after-tax profits (EAT) as a percentage of sales increased from 11.7% to 13.6%. Most of this increase in the after-tax profit margin can be attributed to an improved gross margin. Note that gross profit (GP) as a percentage of sales increased from 39.3% to 41.3%, while expenses as a percentage of sales, such as GAS and *I*, were quite stable over the 3-year period.

TABLE 7-5   COMMON-SIZE FINANCIAL STATEMENTS FOR 1984

Common-size income statements, %

	Bandag*	Armstrong*	Firestone*
S	100.0	100.0	100.0
COGS	(58.7)	(80.0)	(80.0)
GP	41.3	20.0	20.0
GAS	(15.9)	(13.2)	(18.2)
EBIT	25.4	7.2	3.7
I	(1.0)	(1.2)	(1.2)
EBT	24.4	6.3	2.6
TAX	(10.8)	(2.5)	(1.0)
EAT	13.6	3.8	1.6

Common-size balance sheets, %

	Bandag†	Armstrong†	Firestone†
Assets			
CASH	12.2	5.6	4.9
AR	44.3	23.1	20.5
INV	15.9	29.8	21.5
OCA	1.1	0.6	3.2
CA	73.5	59.1	50.1
FA	22.8	37.8	44.0
OFA	3.6	3.1	5.9
A	100.0	100.0	100.0
Liabilities and equity			
AP	7.6	10.3	13.9
OCL	17.1	15.1	22.4
CL	24.7	25.4	36.3
LTD, LEASES, and OLTL	7.6	19.3	15.6
PS	0.0	0.0	0.0
EQ	67.7	55.4	48.1
	100.0	100.0	100.0

*Percentages based on the following 1984 total revenues: Bandag = $328,807,000; Armstrong = $665,630,000; Firestone = $4,001,000,000.
†Percentages based on the following 1984 total assets: Bandag = $190,348,000; Armstrong = $376,960,000; Firestone = $2,571,000,000.
Source: Computed from company annual reports.

An analysis of the balance sheet items reveals a number of interesting changes. First note that CASH as a percentage of total assets decreased from 21.7% to 12.2%, while both AR and INV increased. The investor would want to determine why these changes occurred. Given that Bandag was quite profitable during these years, the decrease in cash and marketable securities is probably not cause for alarm—it may be that in 1982 Bandag simply had excess cash which it employed in other assets such as receivables and inventories over the next 2 years, while part of the stock repurchases discussed earlier was probably financed with CASH. In addition, the fact that Bandag is very conservatively capitalized reduces concerns regarding the decrease in CASH.

TABLE 7-6 COMMON-SIZE FINANCIAL STATEMENT FOR BANDAG
OVER TIME

	1982	1983	1984
Income statement:			
Sales	100.0	100.0	100.0
COGS	(60.7)	(58.0)	(58.7)
GP	39.3	42.0	41.3
GAS	(15.7)	(16.3)	(15.9)
EBIT	23.5	25.7	25.4
I	(0.9)	(1.2)	(1.0)
EBT	22.6	24.5	24.4
TAX	(10.9)	(12.0)	(10.8)
EAT	11.7	12.4	13.6
Sales ($000s)	$298,595	$314,350	$328,807
Balance sheet:			
Assets:			
CASH	21.7	23.2	12.2
AR	37.5	39.3	44.3
INV	13.0	13.0	15.9
OCA	3.0	1.6	1.1
CA	75.2	77.1	73.5
FA	18.6	18.3	22.8
OFA	6.0	4.6	3.6
A	100.0	100.0	100.0
Liabilities and equity:			
AP	6.1	6.6	7.6
OCL	15.9	13.8	17.1
CL	22.0	18.2	24.7
LTD	5.3	5.7	7.6
EQ	72.7	73.8	67.7
	100.0	100.0	100.0
Total assets ($000s)	$213,095	$219,450	$190,348

Source: Computed from company annual reports.

For example, note that LTD is less than 8% of total assets and owners' equity is equal to nearly 68% of total assets. Nevertheless, the alert investor should always try to determine the reasons for such a sharp change in the cash position, as well as any other significant changes in the balance sheet.

7-2-2 Trend Statements   Trend statements are generally considered to be a time-series technique, although they can also be used to make cross-sectional comparisons. The basic procedure in preparing trend statements is to designate one year as a base year and then, for each financial variable, express the values for subsequent years as a proportion of the base-year value. These ratios (values in subsequent years divided by the base-year value) are referred to as *trend values* or *value relatives*.

Table 7-7 presents trend statements for the years 1979 through 1984 for Bandag, Armstrong, and Firestone. To illustrate how the trend statements are constructed, note

TABLE 7-7 TREND STATEMENTS FOR SELECTED FINANCIAL VARIABLES: 1979–1984

	1979 $ value ($000s)	Value relatives					
		1979	1980	1981	1982	1983	1984
Bandag:							
Net sales	$ 216,283	1.000	1.204	1.360	1.322	1.403	1.474
EBIT	49,430	1.000	1.198	1.399	1.421	1.633	1.691
EBT	48,078	1.000	1.192	1.391	1.405	1.599	1.670
EAT	25,261	1.000	1.167	1.370	1.380	1.549	1.767
Total assets	193,047	1.000	0.998	1.135	1.104	1.137	0.986
LTD and LEASES	13,312	1.000	1.087	0.933	0.846	0.735	0.669
EQ	147,938	1.000	1.054	1.213	1.046	1.095	0.871
Armstrong:							
Net sales	393,700	1.000	1.019	1.424	1.463	1.510	1.690
EBIT	19,300	1.000	def	2.016	1.984	2.119	2.503
EBT	10,900	1.000	def	2.771	2.771	3.110	3.881
EAT	8,500	1.000	def	2.047	2.000	2.212	2.988
Total assets	295,500	1.000	0.949	1.155	1.159	1.271	1.276
LTD and LEASES	86,300	1.000	0.958	0.984	0.890	0.757	0.626
EQ	120,000	1.000	0.838	1.021	1.137	1.561	1.739
Firestone:							
Net sales	5,132,000	1.000	0.914	0.850	0.754	0.753	0.780
EBIT	NA	1.000	NA	NA	NA	NA	NA
EBT	NA	1.000	NA	NA	NA	NA	NA
EAT	63,000	1.000	def	1.524	0.032	1.587	1.619
Total assets	3,587,000	1.000	0.874	0.860	0.772	0.761	0.717
LTD and LEASES	701,000	1.000	0.974	0.715	0.633	0.544	0.342
EQ	1,460,000	1.000	0.916	0.977	0.892	0.884	0.847

NA = not available; def = deficit.
Source: Company annual reports.

that 1979 was chosen as the base year—thus, all value relatives for 1979 are equal to 1.00. To complete the illustration, note that Bandag's 1979 net sales were $216,283,000. Net sales for 1982 (see Table 7-1) were $285,954,000. Thus 1982 net sales were equal to 132.2% of the base year's sales and the value relative was 1.322. Similarly, 1982 EAT was $34,876, which is equal to 1.380 times the base-year EAT of $25,261.

One of the most useful attributes of trend statements is that they allow one to quickly see which financial variables have changed the most rapidly over time. For example, BDG's net sales in 1984 were 1.474 times 1979 net sales, while 1984 EAT was 1.767 times 1979 EAT.

Trend statements also allow one to quickly compare the change in financial variables over time for different companies. For example, by comparing the 1984 EAT value relatives for Bandag (1.767), Armstrong (2.988), and Firestone (1.619), it is obvious that over the period 1979 through 1984, Armstrong experienced the highest growth rate in profits. Similar comparisons can be made for the other income statement and balance sheet items reported in Table 7-7.

Before continuing, you should:

1 Be aware of the major components of the income statement and balance sheet
2 Understand how common-size statements are constructed and how they are used in both a cross-sectional and time-series fashion
3 Understand how trend statements are constructed and how they can also be used in either cross-sectional or time-series fashion

7-3 RATIO ANALYSIS

A ratio simply expresses the proportional relationship between two variables. For example, in 1984 Bandag's current assets equaled $140.0 million while its current liabilities equaled $47.0 million. Thus, Bandag's current ratio for 1984 was 3.0, where the current ratio is defined as current assets divided by current liabilities. For the same year Firestone's current ratio was 1.4, based on current assets of $1.29 billion and current liabilities of $0.93 billion. This illustrates one of the advantages of analyzing ratios. A ratio allows one to make comparisons across companies, even though their scale of operations may be substantially different—Bandag's assets and liabilities were measured in millions of dollars whereas Firestone's were measured in billions.

Since most ratios simply involve the division of one variable by another, the calculation of ratios is a straightforward process. However, the interpretation of ratios is a much more difficult matter. In the first place, the ratio must make economic sense. For example, most would agree that total assets divided by stockholders' equity is a reasonable measure of the financial leverage of the firm, and for a number of reasons investors should be interested in the firm's financial leverage. Thus, the assets/equity ratio makes sense. On the other hand, it is also possible to calculate a ratio of, say, deferred taxes paid to total debt. But, one would be hard pressed to find constructive ways of utilizing such a ratio in the analysis of a potential investment. Such a ratio simply does not make economic sense.

The interpretation of ratios will nearly always be complicated by factors which influence the variables involved in the ratio. Consider an example outside the investments field—an example from politics. One ratio frequently analyzed in the political arena is the winning candidate's percentage of the vote—that is, a ratio defined as the number of votes cast for the candidate divided by the total number of votes cast in the election. Suppose two Republican candidates from different states were both elected to the U.S. Senate with a winning percentage of 60%. One would not want to interpret these identical winning percentages as equally impressive without first considering a number of other factors. For example, were both candidates from traditionally Republican states? Were either of the candidates incumbents? If they were incumbents, what were their winning percentages in the previous elections? Thus, in addition to the winning percentage, there are a number of other factors one might want to consider in interpreting the results of an election.

Similarly, there are many factors one needs to consider in interpreting financial ratios. For example, when interpreting current ratios, investors want to consider the composition of the current assets and liabilities, particularly the composition of the assets. Are the current assets composed primarily of accounts receivables or of inventories? Since inventories have yet to be sold, their actual monetary value has not yet been determined. On the other hand, while accounts receivables represent actual sales, one needs to determine whether or not an adequate bad-debt reserve has been established.

Another factor to consider is the trend of the ratio over time. For example, if firms A and B both reported a current ratio of 2.5 in the most recent period, but in the previous period firm A's current ratio was 1.8 while firm B's current ratio was 4.3, investors would feel more comfortable about the trend of firm A's current ratio.

In addition, the investor needs to be alert to the fact that ratios can be manipulated. For example, it is a relatively simple matter for management to increase the firm's current ratio. One method would be to issue long-term debt (which is not included among current liabilities) and pay off short-term liabilities. This will have the effect of increasing the current ratio as current liabilities are decreased, yet the total amount of debt in the firm remains the same. The current ratio can also be increased by selling the firm's accounts receivable to a collection agency and using the cash received to pay off current liabilities.[4] Yet, if the receivables are sold at too large a discount from their reported amount, this may be a poor decision on the part of management.

Finally, the purpose of ratio analysis is primarily to assist in making *forecasts* of future variables such as revenues, expenses, profits, dividends, and capital structure. This is where the investor's skillful and subjective judgment utilized in analyzing ratios becomes most important. Such judgment comes from experience, common sense, and the careful study of ratio analysis. The first step in studying ratio analysis is to become familiar with some of the more common ratios—how they are calculated and used. To do this, we divide ratios into five general categories which are discussed in the next section.

7-4 TYPES OF RATIOS

We will group ratios into five categories: (1) liquidity ratios, (2) capital structure/ coverage ratios, (3) profit margins, (4) turnover ratios, and (5) return on investment ratios. The reader should bear in mind that, like any grouping procedure, the choices are somewhat arbitrary and some ratios might be placed in two or more of the groups. For example, inventory turnover is quite properly placed in the turnover group—yet this ratio is frequently used to analyze the liquidity of a firm since the speed at which the firm turns over (sells) its inventory indicates how quickly the inventory is converted into cash.

We should also point out that the ratios presented in the following sections do not represent an exhaustive list of all possible ratios. Rather, these ratios are only meant to be illustrative of the more commonly used ratios. In practice, there may be as many ratios as there are security analysts. However, the definition of a particular ratio is

---

[4]This assumes that the current ratio is greater than 1.0. As an exercise to demonstrate that you understand these relationships, construct a hypothetical current ratio that is less than 1, and then show that in this case selling receivables and using the proceeds to pay off accounts payables will result in a *lower* current ratio.

not as important as whether the investor: (1) understands how the ratio is calculated; (2) uses the ratio on a consistent basis; and (3) does not use a single ratio in isolation but rather considers a number of ratios which provide a picture of the firm's entire operations.

7-4-1 Liquidity Ratios   The term *liquidity* generally refers to the ability of the firm to meet its short-term obligations. Short-term obligations are typically defined as those which are due and payable within 1 year or less. The most frequently used liquidity ratio is the *current ratio*, which is calculated as current assets (CA) divided by current liabilities (CL).

$$\text{Current ratio} = \frac{\text{CA}}{\text{CL}} \tag{7-1}$$

To illustrate the calculation of the current ratio and all the ratios which will be discussed shortly, we will use the simplified financial statements for Bandag which are presented in Tables 7-2 and 7-4. As noted earlier, Bandag's current ratio for 1984 was 3.0, calculated as follows:

$$\text{Current ratio} = \frac{139,958}{46,951} = 3.0$$

While the current ratio is the ratio most frequently used to measure liquidity, it is possible that inventories may not be sold within a year and that when sold they may bring a selling price that is less than the value at which they are carried on the balance sheet. Prepaid expenses (for example, prepaid insurance premiums) may not be convertible into cash in order to pay off the firm's short-term liabilities. Consequently, another ratio frequently used to measure liquidity is the *quick ratio* (also referred to as the *acid-test ratio*). The numerator of the quick ratio is defined as cash (where cash includes short-term marketable securities such as treasury bills and certificates of deposits) plus accounts receivable, and the divisor remains as current liabilities.

$$\text{Quick ratio} = \frac{\text{CASH} + \text{AR}}{\text{CL}} \tag{7-2}$$

The 1984 quick ratio for Bandag is

$$\text{Quick ratio} = \frac{23,296 + 84,313}{46,951} = 2.3$$

Based on a current ratio of 3.0 and a quick ratio of 2.3, Bandag would be considered by most observers to be a very liquid company. A more typical current ratio would be closer to 2 and a more typical quick ratio would be close to 1.[5] However, one

---

[5]See, for example, Appendix 5.A in G. Foster, *Financial Statement Analysis*, Prentice-Hall, Englewood Cliffs, N.J., 1978.

needs to be very careful about generalizations such as these. One reason is that ratios will vary substantially from industry to industry. For example, an electric utility will frequently have a current ratio that is *less than 1*. Does this mean that the utility is illiquid, that it is nonsolvent? Obviously not. Utilities can operate with fewer current assets than current liabilities because their accounts receivable are converted into cash each month as their customers pay their utility bills, while the accounts payable of the utility on average are not due in 30 days or less. Also, bear in mind that the current ratio and the quick ratio for an electric utility are nearly identical since the utility tends to have very little invested in inventories and prepaid expenses.

For these and other reasons, one cannot generalize what a typical ratio is for all firms in the economy. As a result, most analysts compare the ratios for a particular firm with the average for all firms in the same industry.

7-4-2 Capital Structure/Coverage Ratios   There are many reasons for analyzing capital structure and coverage ratios. For example, creditors are concerned with the ability of the firm to meet interest and principal payments when due. Equity shareholders are interested in the amount of financial leverage employed by the firm and its impact on after-tax profits. As a result, a number of ratios have been developed over time to analyze the leverage position of the firm. We will consider only three: the leverage ratio, the long-term debt/equity ratio, and the times interest earned ratio.

We will define the *leverage ratio (L)* as total assets (A) divided by equity (EQ).

$$L = \frac{A}{EQ} \tag{7-3}$$

The leverage ratio simply indicates how many dollars of assets the firm employs for each dollar of equity. This ratio has a number of attributes. First, it is easy to calculate and to understand. Second, as will be shown later, it can be directly incorporated into an analysis of the firm's return on equity.

The 1984 leverage ratio for Bandag (based on the data in Table 7-4) is calculated as follows:

$$L = \frac{190,348}{128,924} = 1.48$$

A leverage ratio of 1.48 is quite low. (Obviously, the lowest possible leverage ratio is 1.0 for a firm the finances 100% of its assets with equity—this is an extremely unlikely situation as almost every firm will at least have some current liabilities.) More typically, the leverage ratio is above 2 for industrial firms, although again one has to be careful about such generalizations, as the typical leverage ratio will vary substantially from industry to industry.

Another commonly used capital structure ratio is the *long-term debt/equity ratio*. This is defined as long-term debt (LTD) plus capitalized leases (LEASES) divided by common shareholders' equity (EQ).

$$\text{LTD to equity ratio} = \frac{\text{LTD} + \text{LEASES}}{\text{EQ}} \qquad (7\text{-}4)$$

The 1984 long-term debt/equity ratio for Bandag is .069, calculated as follows:

$$\text{LTD to equity ratio} = \frac{6232 + 2672}{128,924} = .069$$

As noted earlier, many different capital structure ratios are used by analysts. We should point out that considerable ambiguity is also associated with the definition of ratios, and this is especially true of capital structure ratios. In particular, the definition of debt varies from source to source. For example, some analysts include deferred liabilities such as deferred taxes in their definition of debt; some do not include capitalized leases as part of long-term debt as we do. Also, some authors suggest that the market value of liabilities and equity should be used instead of book values. We use book values and define long-term debt as we do partially for the sake of convenience and partially because these definitions are consistent with the conceptual framework for ratio analysis presented in the next section of this chapter.

A coverage ratio which focuses directly on the firm's ability to service its interest payments is the *times interest earned ratio*. This ratio is based on the earnings generated by operations and is defined as earnings before interest and taxes (EBIT) divided by annual interest payments (I).

$$\text{Times interest earned ratio} = \frac{\text{EBIT}}{I} \qquad (7\text{-}5)$$

Because this ratio measures the earnings available to pay interest (EBIT) divided by the interest payments, the times interest earned ratio is said to measure how well interest payments are covered by earnings. Consequently, this ratio is also frequently referred to as the interest coverage ratio. For Bandag the 1984 times interest earned ratio was 25.7, calculated as follows:

$$\text{Times interest earned ratio} = \frac{83,566}{3249} = 25.7$$

Seeing that interest was covered 25.7 times by earnings, one would obviously conclude that Bandag should have no difficulty meeting its interest payments.

When the firm has issued junior debt that is subordinated to a senior debt issue, a separate times interest earned ratio may be calculated for both issues.[6] For example,

---

[6]In the event of bankruptcy or liquidation of the firm, interest and principal payments cannot be made on junior debt until all interest and principal payments are made in full on the senior debt. Thus, senior debt holders are more likely to receive their promised payments than are holders of subordinated debt. Because the senior debt is less risky than the junior debt, we would logically expect the times interest earned ratio to be higher for the senior debt. Calculating the ratios in the manner illustrated here will give this result.

suppose a firm has issued $1,000,000 of first mortgage bonds at a 10% interest rate which are senior to a $500,000 issue of subordinated debentures which have a 12% coupon. Thus, the firm has annual interest payments which total $160,000 ($100,000 interest on the senior debt and $60,000 interest on the junior debt). To calculate the times interest earned ratio for the senior debt one simply divides EBIT by the interest on the senior debt. To calculate times interest earned on the junior debt, divide EBIT by the interest payments on *both* the senior debt and the junior debt. This will result in a lower times interest earned ratio for the junior debt than for the senior debt, which is the appropriate relationship since senior debt is more assured of interest and principal payments than debt which is subordinated to it. Assuming EBIT equals $500,000 for this firm, the following illustrates how the interest coverage ratios would be calculated for the senior and junior issues of debt:

Type of debt	Annual interest	Times interest earned
Senior debt: $1,000,000 @ 10%	$100,000	$\dfrac{500,000}{100,000} = 5.0$
Junior debt: $500,000 @ 12%	$ 60,000	$\dfrac{500,000}{100,000 + 60,000} = 3.1$

By successively adding the fixed charges in the denominator as one considers successively more junior issues, the times interest earned ratio will become smaller— thus, the most junior issue will have the lowest times interest earned ratio, which is the appropriate result.

We do not want to overstate the importance of the distinction between junior and senior debt. The fact is, most firms which default on their subordinated debt also default on their senior debt. Thus, the probability of default is nearly the same for both senior and subordinated debt for any particular company. This would argue for use of a single, overall coverage ratio which, of course, would be the coverage ratio for the most junior debt issue. On the other hand, when distributions are made to the various debt holders during bankruptcy proceedings, the senior debt holders will almost always receive a greater proportion of their claims than will the junior debt holders. This fact supports the argument for computing different coverage ratios in the manner illustrated above for senior vs. subordinated debt.

There are a number of variations of the basic times interest earned ratio. One of these is the *fixed charge coverage ratio*, which is defined as earnings before fixed charges divided by fixed charges.

$$\text{Fixed charge coverage ratio} = \frac{\text{earnings before fixed charges}}{\text{fixed charges}} \qquad (7\text{-}6)$$

The disadvantage of this ratio is that there is no generally accepted definition of fixed charges. Most agree that fixed charges include interest on debt and captalized leases, as well as the implicit interest charge on noncapitalized leases. Other fixed charges may include preferred stock dividends, sinking fund and principal repayments, and the noninterest portion of lease payments. Another problem is that data on many of these items are not readily available to outside investors. On the other hand, because of its more comprehensive nature, the fixed charge coverage ratio is potentially a better indicator of the firm's ability to meet its interest and other fixed charge requirements than is the times interest earned ratio.

7-4-3 Profit Margins   Probably the most familiar ratios are *profit margins*. Profit margins simply express profits (however defined) as a percentage of sales. Thus, *gross profit margin* refers to gross profits (GP) divided by sales (*S*), *operating profit margin* refers to operating profits (EBIT) divided by sales, *pretax profit margin* refers to earnings before tax (EBT) divided by sales, and *after-tax profit margin* refers to earnings after-tax (EAT) divided by sales.

The various profit margins for Bandag based on its 1984 income statement are shown below.

$$\text{Gross margin} = \frac{GP}{S} = \frac{135,690}{328,807} = 41.3\% \tag{7-7}$$

$$\text{Operating margin} = \frac{EBIT}{S} = \frac{83,566}{328,807} = 25.4\% \tag{7-8}$$

$$\text{Pretax margin} = \frac{EBT}{S} = \frac{80,317}{328,807} = 24.4\% \tag{7-9}$$

$$\text{After-tax margin} = \frac{EAT}{S} = \frac{44,652}{328,807} = 13.6\% \tag{7-10}$$

Bandag's pretax and after-tax profit margins are considerably higher than those of the typical firm. For example, Bandag's 1984 after-tax profit margin of 13.6% compares with 3.8% for Armstrong and 1.6% for Firestone (see Table 7-5).

7-4-4 Asset Turnover Ratios   Turnover ratios (also called activity ratios) are computed by dividing sales by the value of an asset, as reported on the balance sheet. In general, the higher the level of sales per dollar of asset, the higher the return on invested capital (assuming profit margins are positive). Consequently, investors have always been interested in various asset turnover ratios.

It is generally better to use average assets employed by the firm during the year in the denominator of the turnover ratio, rather than simply using the year-end balance sheet amount. For example, it may be that the firm made a large investment during the last part of the year. While the firm would not have had the use of these assets throughout the year (and consequently the assets could not have been used to generate sales), these new assets would nevertheless be reported on the year-end balance sheet. As a result, a turnover ratio based on year-end asset values might distort the true relationship between sales and assets. The best solution would be to use, say, a monthly average of the asset values. Unfortunately, investors generally do not have access to such data. Consequently, the practice of using an average of the beginning and ending asset balances has evolved. While we agree with this practice, we will use only the ending balance sheet value of the asset in order to simplify the examples.

The total asset turnover ratio, or what we will refer to as simply the *asset turnover ratio (ATO)*, is defined as sales (*S*) divided by total assets (*A*).

$$\text{Asset turnover ratio (ATO)} = \frac{S}{A} \qquad (7\text{-}11)$$

The 1984 asset turnover ratio for Bandag was 1.73, calculated as follows:

$$\text{ATO} = \frac{\$328,807}{\$190,348} = 1.73$$

Of course, one can compute as many different types of asset turnover ratios as there are different types of assets on the balance sheet. The more commonly used turnover ratios are associated with fixed assets, inventories, and accounts receivable, in addition to the total asset turnover ratio discussed above. The equations for calculating these ratios are straightforward and listed below as well as the calculation of the 1984 ratios for Bandag.

$$\text{Fixed asset turnover ratio} = \frac{\text{sales}}{\text{FA}} = \frac{328,807}{43,448} = 7.57 \qquad (7\text{-}12)$$

$$\text{Inventory turnover ratio} = \frac{\text{sales}}{\text{INV}} = \frac{328,807}{30,266} = 10.86 \qquad (7\text{-}13)$$

$$\text{Accounts receivable turnover ratio} = \frac{\text{sales}}{\text{AR}} = \frac{328,807}{84,313} = 3.90 \qquad (7\text{-}14)$$

Ceteris paribus, the higher the activity ratio, the more profitable the firm. However, in practice the interpretation of turnover ratios can be rather complex. An extremely high fixed asset turnover ratio may indicate that the firm is up against the capacity limits of its plant and equipment, and therefore provide a warning signal that the firm may have to expand its capacity. The purchase of additional plant and equipment may require additional outside financing—new issues of stocks or bonds, for example. This, in turn, may indicate future dilution of the current shareholders' position if new common stock is issued, or higher interest charges if bonds are issued.

The inventory turnover ratio is closely watched by financial analysts, particularly credit analysts. A high inventory turnover rate means that the firm's inventories are being converted into sales at a rapid pace, and therefore concerns about the value of the inventories are not as great as for a firm whose inventories are very slowly converted into sales. On the other hand, a high inventory turnover ratio may indicate that the firm simply is not carrying enough inventory and consequently is losing sales the firm might otherwise have had. For example, a retailer of men's apparel may be able to increase its inventory turnover ratio by limiting the number of different colors of shirts it carries. But, it will also lose a sale to the customer who wants a shirt color not carried in the store.

Since inventories are generally stated on the balance sheet at cost, a more accurate method of measuring the turnover of inventories is to use cost of goods sold (COGS) in the numerator of the ratio, rather than sales, because COGS is also stated at cost. Using this method, the 1984 inventory turnover ratio for Bandag would be

$$\text{Inventory turnover} = \frac{\text{COGS}}{\text{INV}} = \frac{193{,}117}{30{,}266} = 6.38 \qquad (7\text{-}15)$$

The difference between the inventory turnover ratio based on sales vs. cost of goods sold will be a function of the firm's gross profit margin. In Bandag's case the inventory turnover ratio based on sales (10.86) is substantially higher than the ratio based on cost of goods sold (6.38). As noted earlier, Bandag also has high gross profit margins (41.3% in 1984). For firms which do not have relatively high gross margins (for example, grocery stores) it will not make as much difference whether sales or COGS are used in calculating the inventory turnover ratio.

Many of the same observations made about the inventory turnover ratio can also be applied to accounts receivable. A high turnover of receivables, *ceteris paribus*, will result in a higher return on invested capital. In addition, a high turnover ratio indicates a more liquid firm because the receivables are being converted into cash more quickly. On the other hand, an extremely high accounts receivable turnover ratio may indicate that the firm is following too restrictive a credit policy for its customers. As a result, the firm may be losing sales to competitors who have more lenient credit terms.

Another ratio frequently used to analyze accounts receivable is called the *average collection period*. This ratio is calculated by dividing the firm's accounts receivable by its sales per day, as shown below for Bandag.

$$\text{Average collection period} = \frac{\text{AR}}{\text{sales/day}} = \frac{84{,}313}{328{,}807/365 \text{ days}} = 94 \text{ days} \quad (7\text{-}16)$$

This ratio indicates the number of days of sales that are outstanding in the form of accounts receivable and thus is a rough estimate of the number of days between the date a credit sale is made and the date the receivable is collected, i.e., the average collection period. As a rule, the lower this ratio, the better. However, the same problems of interpretation which apply to accounts receivable turnover also apply to the average collection period.

7-4-5 Return on Investment Ratios   The most important category of ratios are the return on investment ratios. This relative importance is due to the fact that these ratios are most closely analogous to the shareholders' objective of maximizing their return on investment (subject to an acceptable level of risk). If the managers of the firm, acting as agents for the holders of the firm's securities, maximize the return on the capital invested by the firm, then presumably this will be reflected in the market prices of the firm's securities—again, subject to an acceptable level of risk. We will consider three return on investment ratios: *return on assets, return on (common) equity*, and *earning power*.

Return on assets (ROA) is defined as earnings after taxes (EAT) divided by total assets (A).

$$\text{ROA} = \frac{\text{EAT}}{A} \qquad (7\text{-}17)$$

This ratio provides an indication as to how efficiently the total assets of the firm are being utilized. As with the turnover ratios, it is probably better to use an average of the beginning and ending balance sheet amounts of total assets. However, we will again use only the ending balance sheet amount in order to simplify the presentation. For 1984, Bandag's return on assets was 23.5%, calculated as follows:

$$\text{ROA} = \frac{44,652}{190,348} = 23.5\%$$

From the viewpoint of the holders of common stock, return on equity may be the single most informative ratio, since it represents the return earned on the capital invested in the firm by the equity shareholders. Return on equity (ROE) is defined as earnings after taxes divided by common stockholders' equity (EQ).

$$\text{ROE} = \frac{\text{EAT}}{\text{EQ}} \qquad (7\text{-}18)$$

For 1984, Bandag's ROE amounted to 34.6%, calculated as follows:

$$\text{ROE} = \frac{44,652}{128,924} = 34.6\%$$

Bandag's ROA and ROE are relatively high, compared with all industrial firms and compared with tire companies. Table 7-8 compares the 1984 ROA and ROE figures for Bandag, Armstrong Rubber, Firestone, and the Fortune 500.[7] In general, over the past 10 years or so, Bandag has managed to generate an above-average ROA and ROE. And Bandag tended to sell at a higher price/earnings (P/E) ratio than the average

---

[7]*Fortune* provides statistical data on the Fortune 500 companies on an annual basis, usually in an April or May issue.

TABLE 7-8   1984 ROA AND ROE RATIOS

	ROA, %	ROE, %
Fortune 500	6.1	13.6
Bandag	23.5	34.6
Armstrong	6.7	12.2
Firestone	4.0	8.3

Source: *Fortune* (April 1985) and company annual reports.

firm over this same time period. In the next section we will demonstrate why one would expect higher price/book value and *P/E* ratios to be associated with firms earning higher rates of return on invested capital. In particular, higher *P/E*s and price/book value ratios should be associated with higher return on equity ratios, *ceteris paribus*.

However, at this point we should also point out a potential problem associated with the ROE ratio which is due to the use of leverage. It is possible for a firm with a relatively low return on assets to generate a high return on equity if it can use financial leverage favorably. Another problem with ROE, and any other ratio based on after-tax earnings, is that in any particular year a firm may temporarily reduce its tax rate below the rate it normally pays by, for example, utilizing a large investment tax credit based on a major purchase of new assets. This has the effect of increasing EAT, and in turn, return on investment ratios based on after-tax earnings will be higher than if the firm had paid its normal tax rate.

One return on investment ratio which avoids the problems associated with financial leverage and tax rates is the ratio we term *earning power*. Earning power (EP) is defined as earnings before interest and taxes divided by total assets.

$$EP = \frac{EBIT}{A} \qquad (7\text{-}19)$$

By utilizing earnings before interest and taxes divided by total assets, EP avoids the problems mentioned above concerning the use of leverage and different tax rates. For 1984, Bandag's EP was 43.9%, calculated as follows:

$$EP = \frac{83,566}{190,348} = .439$$

Table 7-9 will be used to compare the three return on investment ratios ROA, ROE, and EP. In this illustration, three hypothetical companies all have the same total assets, $1000. In addition, all three firms generate $200 of earnings before interest and taxes. Thus, the earning power of each firm is 20%—that is, each firm is able to generate a 20% return on assets before taxes and leverage considerations.

However, the use of leverage causes significant differences in the return on assets and return on equity ratios for firms A and B. Note that firm B has $500 of debt (at 10%) and $50 dollars of interest, while A has no debt and no interest expense. As a

TABLE 7-9   COMPARISON OF ROA, ROE, AND EP RATIOS

	A	B	C
Debt	0	500	500
Equity	1000	500	500
Total assets	1000	1000	1000
EBIT	200	200	200
I	(0)	(50)	(50)
EBT	200	150	150
TAX	(80)	(60)	(15)
EAT	120	90	135
ROA, %	12	9	13.5
ROE, %	12	18	27
EP, %	20	20	20

result, earnings before taxes for firm A are $200 while EBT is equal to $150 for firm B. Both firms have an average tax rate of 40%. Thus, EAT is $120 for firm A and $90 for firm B. This results in a return on assets of 12% for A and 9% for firm B. However, the effect of leverage on the return on equity is just the opposite—firm A's ROE is 12% (the same as its ROA since it is an all-equity firm), while the ROE for firm B is leveraged up to 18%.

Based on this illustration, one can generalize the relationship between leverage and the two ratios ROA and ROE as follows: (1) The use of debt will always reduce the return on assets when ROA is defined as EAT/A.[8] (2) If the firm's earning power (20% in this example) is greater than the cost of debt (10% in this example), the use of debt will result in favorable financial leverage and the firm's return on equity will be increased. If EP is less than the interest rate on debt, unfavorable financial leverage will result and the use of debt will decrease the return on equity. (This second point will be illustrated later in this chapter.)

To analyze the effect of different tax rates, consider firms B and C. Both use the same amount of debt and therefore have the same pretax income of $150. However, firm C's tax rate is only 10% vs. B's 40% tax rate. This has the obvious effect of

---

[8]Another method of measuring the return on assets which reduces the effect of leverage on the ratio is the following:

$$ROA = \frac{EAT + I(1 - T)}{A}$$

where T is the firm's tax rate and I is the interest expense. Because this ratio adds back the after-tax interest payments to EAT, the use of debt will not affect the return on assets. In fact, one can show that ROA, as defined above, is simply an after-tax version of earning power, i.e., $EP(1 - T)$. However, this definition of ROA is still affected by the tax rate (T). Thus, we consider the EP ratio to be a better measure of the profitability of total assets.

making firm C's after-tax income greater than firm B's, resulting in a higher ROA (13.5% vs. 9%) and a higher ROE (27% vs. 18%).

When comparing companies in the same industry it is unlikely that similar firms will be able to maintain substantially different tax rates over a period of years. For example, during any single year one firm may utilize a large investment tax credit and report a tax rate that is substantially lower than that of other firms within its industry. However, the use of such tax breaks is likely to even out among firms in the same industry over time. Thus, one wants to view with skepticism a high return on equity reported by a firm which also reports an unusually low tax rate for its industry.

To a certain extent the same arguments about tax rates within an industry also apply to the use of debt. The leverage ratios for firms within an industry tend to be fairly uniform because of the common operating characteristics of the firms. For example, all public utilities are able to borrow large amounts of debt relative to their equity base, primarily because of the stable demand for their services. Consequently, if one observed a public utility with a relatively low debt ratio, it would be reasonable to assume that over time the company would increase its debt ratio until it was more in line with the ratios of other firms in its industry.

This example should serve to illustrate the point that when comparing the return on assets and return on equity ratios for different companies, one needs to consider both the amount of leverage used by the firms and their tax rates. However, neither leverage nor tax rates affect the earning power of the firm. (Note in the example EP was 20% for all three firms.) This is a strong argument for the use of the EP ratio in comparing firms.

To summarize, the return on investment ratios are the most important group of ratios since they provide an indication as to how effectively management is utilizing the assets of the firm. Return on equity, since it is most closely related to the shareholders' objective of maximizing the return on their investment, is potentially very useful to the analyst. (In fact, ROE is generally the starting point in ratio analysis, as we show in the next section.) However, both ROA and ROE can be affected by differing financial structures and tax rates across firms. Earning power, on the other hand, is not influenced by either interest expense or tax rates, since it deals with earnings before interest and taxes. As a result, EP is a very useful ratio for comparing how well managements of firms are utilizing the assets of the firm.

Before continuing, you should:
1 Know how to compute current ratios and quick ratios and understand how they are used to analyze the short-term liquidity position of the firm
2 Know how to compute the capital structure ratios and be aware of some of the more complicated aspects of the times interest earned ratio
3 Know how to compute profit margins and turnover ratios
4 Know how to compute the return on investment ratios ROA, ROE, and EP
5 Understand how leverage and tax rates can affect ROA, ROE, and EP

7-5 A CONCEPTUAL FRAMEWORK FOR RATIO ANALYSIS

For many years investors have incorporated the analysis of financial ratios into the process by which they identified underpriced and overpriced securities. In fact, it is probably fair to say that the cornerstone of Graham and Dodd's classic textbook, *Security Analysis*,[9] was the careful evaluation of various financial ratios. Yet it is probably also fair to say that many investors only vaguely understood why they should be interested in a particular ratio. For example, one might intuitively suspect that return on equity is an important factor in determining stock prices but still not know what the specific relationship should be between ROE and stock prices. In the sections which follow, we will develop a conceptual framework for analyzing some of the key financial ratios and their relationships to stock prices. Interestingly, we find that many of the ratios which investors have used in the past have a logical connection to stock prices and rates of return.

7-5-1 Stock Prices and ROE   To develop a framework for ratio analysis, we will start with the constant growth dividend discount model which is derived in Section 10-4 and is probably familiar to those readers who have previously taken an introductory finance course. This model states that the current stock price P_0 is equal to the expected dividend in the first year D_1, divided by the difference between the appropriate risk-adjusted discount rate r and the expected long-term growth rate g.

$$P_0 = \frac{D_1}{r - g} \tag{7-20}$$

(To simplify the notation, from now on the subscripts will be dropped from P_0 and D_1.) This model of stock prices is based on the principle of discounting all future dividends, which is a conceptually sound approach. However, to simplify the model to Equation (7-20), one has to assume that dividends grow at a constant rate of g *forever*, which is an unrealistic assumption for individual common stocks. Therefore, one should bear in mind that the framework for ratio analysis which follows does not describe the *exact* functional relationships between various ratios and stock prices. Because of the dynamic nature of the securities markets and the valuation process, we will probably never know the exact nature of these relationships. However, we can develop a framework for describing the general relationship between prices and financial ratios.

To do this, we define the following additional variables:

E = earnings per share = EAT divided by the number of shares outstanding

b = payout ratio = D/E

BV = book value per share = common stockholders' equity (EQ) divided by the number of shares outstanding

[9]B. Graham, D. Dodd, and S. Cottle, *Security Analysis*, 4th ed., McGraw-Hill, New York, 1962.

Substituting $D = E \cdot b$, we have

$$P = \frac{E \cdot b}{r - g} \tag{7-21}$$

We can further expand this equation by noting that $E = \text{ROE} \cdot \text{BV}$ and substituting for E in the above equation.

$$P = \frac{\text{ROE} \cdot \text{BV} \cdot b}{r - g} \tag{7-22}$$

Thus, stock prices are a positive function of ROE, BV, b, and g,[10] and a negative function of r. That is, everything else held constant, the higher the return on equity the higher the stock price, and similar *ceteris paribus* arguments hold for book value, the payout ratio, and the growth rate. Conversely, everything else held constant, the higher the required discount rate, the lower the stock price.

7-5-2 Growth and Return on Equity This same general framework can be used to develop an estimate of the long-run dividend growth rate. To do this, we need to make three simplifying assumptions: (1) ROE is constant over time and is defined as earnings after taxes divided by beginning stockholders' equity. On a per share basis, $\text{ROE} = E_1 / \text{BV}_0$. (2) The payout ratio b is constant over time. (3) The firm finances new assets through retained earnings and therefore does not issue any new debt or shares of common stock. Given these assumptions, it can be shown that the dividend growth rate, and also the earnings growth rate, will be[11]

---

[10]In the dividend discount model the stock price is equal to the present value of all *expected* future dividends. Thus, in this analysis, the stock price should be a positive function of the *expected* ROE, BV, b, and g. However, in the constant growth dividend discount model g is assumed to be constant and for this analysis we also assume ROE and b to be constant. In this spirit historical averages of E, D, b, ROE, etc., can be used.

[11]By definition, the growth rate for dividends in any year is

$$g = \frac{D_1 - D_0}{D_0}$$

Assuming a constant payout ratio b, $D_1 = bE_1$ and $D_0 = bE_0$. Substituting for D_1 and D_0,

$$g = \frac{E_1 - E_0}{E_0}$$

By assuming ROE is constant and defining ROE as earnings per share E_t divided by beginning book value BV_{t-1}, we have $E_1 = \text{ROE} \cdot \text{BV}_0$ and $E_0 = \text{ROE} \cdot \text{BV}_{-1}$. Substituting for E_1 and E_0,

$$g = \frac{\text{BV}_0 - \text{BV}_{-1}}{\text{BV}_{-1}}$$

Assuming no outside financing, the change in book value $(\text{BV}_0 - \text{BV}_{-1})$ is equal to $E_0 - D_0 = E_0(1 - b)$. Substituting, we have

$$g = \frac{E_0(1 - b)}{\text{BV}_{-1}} = \text{ROE}(1 - b)$$

$$g = \text{ROE}(1 - b) \tag{7-23}$$

That is, the long-run growth rate of dividends and earnings is equal to the firm's return on equity multiplied by the quantity 1 minus the payout ratio. This estimate of the firm's long-run growth rate is also referred to by some analysts as the *sustainable growth rate*, or the *plow-back ratio*.

For example, suppose a firm's long-run ROE is estimated to be 15% and its payout ratio is estimated to be 40%. In this case, a reasonable estimate of its long-run growth rate of earnings and dividends would be 9%, calculated as follows:

$$g = (15\%)(.6) = 9\%$$

This model for estimating g has several pleasing features. First, it is simple to calculate and therefore represents an easy *starting point* in the process of estimating growth rates. In addition, by assuming no additional outside financing and holding the return on equity constant, this model does not allow for increases in ROE (and consequently the growth rate) by the increased use of leverage. In the long run this is reasonable, since there are practical limits as to how much debt the firm can issue.

On the other hand, this model is based on obviously unrealistic assumptions. Return on equity is not constant for firms but varies from year to year, and firms do engage in outside financing. Thus, when utilizing historical data and Equation (7-23) to estimate the growth rate, one should probably use an average of the firm's ROE over a period of years, rather than simply the most recent year's ROE. Similar observations can be made concerning the assumption of a constant payout ratio.

7-5-3 ROE, P/BV, and P/E Ratios   It is now easy to see the relationship between ROE and the ratios of price to book value (*P*/BV) and price to earnings (*P*/E). By rearranging the terms in Equation (7-22) and substituting $g = \text{ROE}(1 - b)$ we have

$$\frac{P}{\text{BV}} = \frac{\text{ROE} \cdot b}{r - \text{ROE}(1 - b)} \tag{7-24}$$

Thus, the *P*/BV ratio is a positive function of ROE and a negative function of r, the discount rate. It is not clear what effect the payout ratio b has on the *P*/BV ratio, since an increase in b will simultaneously increase the numerator and the denominator.

A similar analysis can be applied to *P*/E ratios. By substituting $g = \text{ROE}(1 - b)$ into Equation (7-21) and rearranging terms we have

$$\frac{P}{E} = \frac{b}{r - \text{ROE}(1 - b)} \tag{7-25}$$

Again, the *P*/E ratio is a positive function of ROE and a negative function of the discount rate, and the relationship with the payout ratio is ambiguous.

7-5-4 ROE and the DuPont System   To further analyze the relationship between stock prices and return on equity, we will use what has become known as the *DuPont system*. This is based on the fact that the firm's return on equity is equal to its return on assets multiplied by its leverage ratio L.

$$\text{ROE} = \text{ROA} \times L = \frac{\text{EAT}}{A} \times \frac{A}{\text{EQ}} \qquad (7\text{-}26)$$

Thus, ROE results from the interaction of the return on assets and leverage. Everything else held constant, the higher either ROA or L, the higher ROE.

In addition, return on assets can be divided into two components—the after-tax profit margin (PM) and the asset turnover ratio (ATO).

$$\text{ROA} = \text{PM} \times \text{ATO} = \frac{\text{EAT}}{S} \times \frac{S}{A} \qquad (7\text{-}27)$$

Thus, in analyzing a stock, one of the key ratios is ROE. Using the DuPont system, ROE can be formulated in terms of return on assets and leverage. In turn, ROA can be formulated in terms of profit margin and asset turnover. Finally, the analyst can compare various levels of profit margins (after-tax margins up to gross margins) and all the various asset turnover ratios.

A hypothetical example will help illustrate this process. Table 7-10 presents an income statement and a balance sheet for Hiroe Company. The bottom half of Table 7-10 lists the key ratios in the DuPont system for Hiroe and for the average firm in the same industry. (Before continuing, make sure that you can compute all the ratios for Hiroe based on its income statement and balance sheet.)

First note that Hiroe's ROE of 20% is considerably higher than the industry average of 15%. In order to determine why Hiroe has a higher ROE, the first step is to look at the two major determinants of ROE using the DuPont system, i.e., ROA and L. Hiroe's ROA (15%) is also substantially above the industry average of 10%, while its leverage ratio (1.33) is actually slightly below the industry average of 1.5. Thus, Hiroe's relatively high ROE is the result of a high ROA and not the result of the use of leverage.

To further analyze the return on assets, we consider both profit margins and asset turnover. Looking first at the turnover ratios, note that the total asset turnover (ATO) is actually lower for Hiroe (.50) than for the industry average (.60). In general, all the various asset turnover ratios for Hiroe are either approximately equal to, or less than the industry average. Thus, Hiroe's relatively high return on equity does not come from high asset turnover—rather, the high ROE must come from high profit margins. And this is immediately obvious when one observes that Hiroe's after-tax profit margin is 30.0% vs. 17.5% for the industry average.

However, one does not want to stop at the after-tax profit margin, as a great deal can be learned about a firm by analyzing the other profit margins and the various expense ratios which can be computed from its income statement. For example, note

TABLE 7-10 RATIO ANALYSIS FOR HIROE COMPANY
USING THE DU PONT SYSTEM

Income statement		Balance sheet	
Sales	$1000	CASH	$ 100
COGS	(350)	AR	350
GP	650	INV	50
GAS	(100)	CA	500
EBIT	550	FA	1500
I	(50)	Total assets	$2000
EBT	500		
TAX	(200)	CL	100
EAT	$ 300	EQ	1500
			$2000

Comparative ratios		
	Hiroe	Industry average
ROE, %	20.0	15.0
ROA, %	15.0	10.0
L	1.33	1.50

Turnover ratios		
ATO	.50	.60
FA TO	.67	.64
INV TO	7.00	9.30
AR TO	2.86	3.40

Profit margins and expense ratios (as a % of sales)		
After-tax margin	30.0	17.5
Average tax rate	40.0	39.8
Pretax margin	50.0	29.1
Interest expense	5.0	6.2
Operating margin	55.0	35.3
GAS expense	10.0	9.3
Gross margin	65.0	44.6
COGS	35.0	55.4

that the average tax rate (TAX/EBT) for Hiroe is 40.0% vs. 39.8% for the industry average. Thus, Hiroe's high after-tax profit margin is not the result of simply having a lower tax rate. Likewise, Hiroe's relatively high pretax margin (50.0% vs. 29.1%) is not the result of having lower interest expense, since the interest expense ratio (I/S) is roughly the same as that of the industry average (5.0% and 6.2%).

A similar statement can be made concerning operating margins—Hiroe's high operating margin (55.0% vs. 35.3%) is not the result of having lower administrative and selling expenses. In fact, Hiroe's GAS expense as a percentage of sales is actually higher than the industry average—10.0% vs. 9.3%. It is when we come to gross margins and cost of goods sold that the difference between Hiroe and the industry average becomes dramatically clear. Hiroe's high gross margin (65.0% vs. 44.6% for the industry) is the result of a correspondingly lower COGS expense ratio (35.0% vs. 55.4%). Thus, using the DuPont system we have been able to trace the firm's high ROE to its high gross margin.

This is the point at which ratio analysis might end and additional security analysis begin. We want to know *why* Hiroe has such a high gross margin. Perhaps the firm has a proprietary product with brand-name recognition and therefore can charge a higher price; perhaps the firm has been able to negotiate a more favorable labor agreement than its competitors; perhaps Hiroe has geographic and distribution advantages; or perhaps Hiroe was able to lock in a favorable raw materials purchase agreement. The investor would certainly want to know whether the reasons for Hiroe's low COGS expense ratio will persist into the future. If so, and assuming all the other factors affecting Hiroe's profitability remain roughly the same, then one might expect that Hiroe will continue to earn a higher rate of return on its equity than the industry average.

7-5-5 Earning Power, Leverage, and ROE   Return on equity can also be analyzed by considering the interaction of earning power and leverage. To do this, we first formulate the equation for return on assets as follows:

$$\text{ROA} = \frac{(1 - T)(\text{EBIT} - I)}{A} \tag{7-28}$$

where T = firm's average tax rate. Note that the numerator is simply EAT, but rewritten in terms of EBIT. By formulating ROA in this manner and then multiplying this quantity by L, we can express return on equity in terms of earning power and leverage, as follows:[12]

---

[12]Total interest payments I can be written as iD where i = average interest rate on total debt and D = total debt = $A - \text{EQ}$. Substituting $i(A - \text{EQ})$ for I in Equation (7-28), we have

$$\text{ROA} = \frac{(1 - T)[\text{EBIT} - i(A - \text{EQ})]}{A}$$

Dividing through by A leaves

$$\text{ROA} = (1 - T)\left(\text{EP} - i + i\,\frac{\text{EQ}}{A}\right)$$

Substituting this for ROA in the equation $\text{ROE} = \text{ROA} \times L$, we have

$$\text{ROE} = (1 - T)\left(\text{EP} - i + i\,\frac{\text{EQ}}{A}\right)L$$

Since $L = A/\text{EQ}$, we can simplify this expression to Equation (7-29).

$$ROE = (1 - T)[i + L(EP - i)] \tag{7-29}$$

where i = average interest rate on firm's debt

Note that if earning power (i.e., the rate of return earned on assets before interest and taxes) is greater than the interest rate on debt, then ROE increases as leverage increases. This is termed *favorable financial leverage*. If earning power is less than the interest rate on debt, ROE will decrease as leverage increases.

> If EP > i, ROE increases with L
> If EP < i, ROE decreases with L

Table 7-11 illustrates the relationship among EP, leverage, and ROE. Two firms are involved in this illustration, one with favorable financial leverage and one with unfavorable leverage. Both firms start with a leverage ratio equal to 2.0 and subsequently increase L to 3.0. Note that the first firm's EP is equal to 20% while its interest rate on debt is 10%. Consequently, this firm has favorable financial leverage and the increase in its leverage ratio results in its ROE increasing from 18% to 24%. However, the second firm has unfavorable financial leverage—its EP is equal to only 9% while i is equal to 10%. Consequently, the increased use of debt results in a decrease in its ROE, from 4.8% to 4.2%.

TABLE 7-11   ILLUSTRATION OF EARNING POWER, LEVERAGE, AND ROE

	Favorable financial leverage		Unfavorable financial leverage	
	Before	After additional debt	Before	After additional debt
Debt	500	1000	500	1000
Equity	500	500	500	500
Total assets	1000	1500	1000	1500
EBIT	200	300	90	135
I	(50)	(100)	(50)	(100)
EBT	150	200	40	35
TAX @ 40%	(60)	(80)	(16)	(14)
EAT	90	120	24	21
L	2.0	3.0	2.0	3.0
EP, %	20	20	9	9
i, %	10	10	10	10
ROE, %	18	24	4.8	4.2

Before continuing, you should:
1 Understand the general relationship among stock prices, ROE, BV, the payout ratio, growth, and the discount rate
2 Know how to analyze ROE using the DuPont system
3 Understand the relationship among earning power, interest rates, leverage, and return on equity
4 Know how to estimate the firm's long-run growth rate based on its payout ratio and return on equity

7-6 THE USE OF INDUSTRY AVERAGES

It has been standard practice for many years to make comparisons of ratios for firms that are in the same industry. There are several good reasons for this practice. First, in order to classify a ratio as either high or low, one needs a benchmark. One possible choice for such a benchmark might be the average ratio for all firms in an economy. However, there may be substantial differences in average ratios for various industries because the economic environments in which they operate may be substantially different. For example, the profit margins for grocery stores will be quite low compared with those of a typical jewelry store, but the inventory turnover of the grocery store will be much higher. A second reason for using industry norms as a benchmark in ratio analysis is that there is some evidence that the ratios of firms within the same industry tend to gravitate toward the industry average ratio over time.

On the other hand, a number of problems are associated with making cross-sectional comparisons of ratios for firms within an industry. First, one needs to avoid the temptation of assuming that the industry average, or norm, is "good." (For example, it may be that the average ROE for a particular industry is quite poor.) Instead, analysts typically view deviations from the industry norm as a signal to investigate the reasons why the firm's ratio deviates from the average for the industry—as opposed to simply assuming, say, that because a firm's ROE is higher than the industry norm, the firm is utilizing its assets well.

Another problem with using industry norms as benchmarks is that many firms have diversified across many different product lines. For example, a substantial portion of General Tire's sales are derived from aerospace products; a substantial portion of B. F. Goodrich's sales come from chemical products; etc. Nevertheless, despite these problems, it is still probably better to make industry comparisons of ratios than to use an economywide norm, or to give up on the use of benchmarks entirely.

7-6-1 Sources of Industry Averages   There are several possible sources of industry norms, several of which are discussed in the Appendix to Chapter 8. One of the most frequently used sources is Dun & Bradstreet's *Key Business Ratios in 125 Lines*. Table 7-12 presents a sample page from this publication. A number of key ratios are reported for each industry classification. For each ratio, three numbers are reported. The middle number represents the median ratio for the firms in the particular industry. For example, the median current ratio for the agricultural chemicals industry

TABLE 7-12   AN EXAMPLE OF DUN & BRADSTREET RATIOS

Line of business (and number of concerns reporting)	Current assets to current debt (times)	Net profits on net sales (percent)	Net profits on tangible net worth (percent)	Net profits on net working capital (percent)	Net sales to tangible net worth (times)	Net sales to net working capital (times)	Collection period (days)
2871–72–79[a]	3.71	4.46	11.13	25.05	4.69	13.45	28
Agricultural Chemicals	1.88	2.17	6.90	10.43	3.08	5.98	56
(41)	1.34	0.79	1.45	3.95	1.67	3.91	107
3722–23–29	2.26	7.01	22.67	44.41	4.82	9.37	29
Airplane Parts &	1.78	4.44	16.67	26.26	3.23	5.22	39
Accessories (53)	1.36	2.92	8.10	14.98	2.35	4.35	55
2051–52	2.39	4.46	16.54	67.52	5.59	28.67	13
Bakery Products (2)	1.84	2.37	10.21	34.41	4.15	16.40	18
	1.39	0.94	3.79	12.75	2.98	10.32	24
3312–13–15–16–17 Blast	3.65	6.08	11.85	26.47	2.53	5.10	29
Furnaces, Steel Works	2.58	4.07	8.01	19.18	1.90	4.21	35
& Rolling Mills (63)	2.02	3.00	5.38	11.44	1.41	3.19	43
2331	2.64	2.01	17.21	22.70	13.18	15.24	27
Blouses & Waists,	1.73	0.69	7.86	9.28	8.58	9.80	36
Women's & Misses' (71)	1.41	0.19	1.33	1.47	6.32	8.00	50
2731–32	3.52	8.14	17.52	25.20	3.18	5.02	41
Books: Publishers	2.63	5.20	10.44	16.13	2.32	2.86	58
Publishing & Printing (43)	2.01	2.65	5.63	8.19	1.69	1.95	78
2211	4.32	5.67	10.90	22.49	2.11	5.35	26
Broad Woven Fabrics,	3.00	3.96	7.34	15.84	1.82	4.03	53
Cotton (38)	2.24	2.58	4.09	7.50	1.43	3.10	58
2031–32–33–34–35–36–37	2.40	6.16	17.28	43.40	4.91	13.41	15
Canned & Pres. Fruits,	1.63	2.80	11.25	20.02	3.13	7.45	24
Vegetables & Sea Foods (75)	1.25	1.75	6.23	11.21	2.06	4.31	40

[a]Standard Industrial Classification (SIC) categories.
Source: Key Business Ratios in 125 Lines, Dun & Bradstreet, New York. Reprinted by permission of Dun & Bradstreet.

was 1.88. The upper and lower numbers represent the interquartile range—that is, the middle 50% of the firms in the industry. For example, the interquartile range for the agricultural chemical industry's current ratio was 3.71 to 1.34. That is, 25% of the firms in the industry had current ratios greater than 3.71, 25% had current ratios less than 1.34, and 50% had current ratios between 3.71 and 1.34. The size of the interquartile range provides an indication of the dispersion of a ratio within an industry—the larger the interquartile range, the greater the dispersion, and vice versa.

Looking down the columns of Table 7-12, one can see that there is considerable variation in ratios across industries. For example, the median net profit margin (second column) for the agricultural chemicals industry was 2.17% vs. 4.44% for the airline parts and accessories industry vs. 0.69% for the blouses and waists industry. Similar observations can be made with respect to the other ratios. This variation in median industry ratios provides some evidence in support of the practice of using industry averages in analyzing ratios.

7-6-2 Industry Averages as Target Ratios Another argument for using an industry average is suggested by the results of a study by Lev.[13] This study examined the hypothesis that firms attempt to change their financial ratios to closely match the average ratio for their industry. A rationale for this hypothesis is that firms whose ratios are substantially different from the industry average will be viewed with concern by investors, unless there are valid reasons for the deviation. Thus, on average, firms will attempt to change their ratios over time to more closely conform to the industry average. That is, firms consider the industry average to be a target ratio.

In order to test this hypothesis, Lev examined several ratios for 245 firms over the period 1947–1966. In general Lev found a statistically significant tendency for the ratios of individual firms to change over time toward the industry average. For example, he found that the difference between the current ratio of an individual firm and the average current ratio for the industry decreased by roughly 50% in one year's time. Similarly, the difference between the equity/total debt ratio of individual firms and the industry ratio decreased by roughly 30% within a year.

Of course, whether or not this tendency is the result of conscious decisions on the part of firms is debatable. For example, it seems unlikely that the management of a firm generating an above-average ROE would consciously try to lower the firm's ROE to the industry average. Rather, it is more likely that there are economic forces which tend to drive the financial ratios of firms within an industry toward the average ratios of the industry. However, regardless of the true cause, this observed tendency of individual firm ratios moving over time toward the industry average provides strong justification for the practice of making comparisons of firms *within an industry* and using the industry average ratio as a benchmark for ratio analysis.

7-7 SUMMARY

The key determinant of security prices is expectations concerning the firm's earnings and dividends and their associated risk. The starting point for forming projections of earnings, etc., is an analysis of the firm's financial statements. Some of the approaches used by investors in analyzing financial statements are common-size and trend statements.

Ratio analysis is the most frequently used analytical technique in the investor's toolbox. Consequently, it is important, perhaps essential, for the investor to understand ratios and know how they are used. In this text we have grouped ratios into five categories: (1) liquidity ratios, (2) capital structure/coverage ratios, (3) profit margins, (4) turnover ratios, and (5) return on investment ratios.

Properly used, ratios can provide many helpful insights into the past and prospective fortunes of a firm and how the firm's operating prospects might be translated into future stock returns. As with other types of financial analysis, ratios should be examined in both a cross-sectional and a time-series fashion. That is, investors should compare the relevant ratios of a particular firm with those of other firms—generally with other firms in the same industry. One also wants to examine how a firm's ratio has changed over time. By examining some of the key ratios from each of the five general categories

---

[13]B. Lev, "Industry Averages as Targets for Financial Ratios," *Journal of Accounting Research* (autumn 1969).

of ratios mentioned above, in both a cross-sectional and a time-series fashion, a great deal can be learned about the financial and operating characteristics of a firm.

In order to provide some intuition as to how the firm's characteristics (as measured by ratios) are linked to stock prices and shareholder returns, a conceptual framework for ratio analysis was presented. The reader should bear in mind that this framework is based on strong assumptions which greatly simplify the real world of investments. Nevertheless, some useful insights can be gained from this framework. Perhaps the most important of these insights is the positive relationship between ROE and stock prices. In addition, the DuPont system provides a useful framework for determining the sources of the firm's profitability, or lack of profitability, whichever the case may be.

Traditionally, investors have used industry average ratios as benchmarks for several reasons. First, there are substantial differences in the operating and financial characteristics of firms in different industries. Consequently, comparisons of the ratios of firms in different industries can be very misleading. In addition, there appears to be a tendency for the ratios of an individual firm to trend over time toward the industry average ratio. In general, if a particular ratio for a firm is, say, above the industry average for that ratio, then over time the firm's ratio frequently will decline and approach the industry average. For these reasons it is good practice to make comparisons of the firm's ratio with the average ratios for its industry.

SUGGESTED READINGS

For additional information on ratio analysis, the following book should be particularly helpful:
G. Foster, *Financial Statement Analysis*, Chapters 3–6, Prentice-Hall, Englewood Cliffs, N.J., 1978.

Some other books which deal with ratio analysis are:
L. Bernstein, *Financial Statement Analysis: Theory, Application and Interpretation*, rev. ed., Irwin, Homewood, Ill., 1978.
B. Graham, D. Dodd, and S. Cottle, *Security Analysis*, McGraw-Hill, New York, 1962.
B. Lev, *Financial Statement Analysis: A New Approach*, Prentice-Hall, Englewood Cliffs, N.J., 1974.

QUESTIONS

1 Simplified financial statements were developed in this chapter. In order to do this, several income statement and balance sheet variables had to be combined. The COMPUSTAT tapes also combine financial statement items in order to present the accounting items of all firms in a consistent manner. What problems might an analyst face when using data for different companies presented in such standardized formats?

2 It was argued that, as a general rule, it is better to concentrate on ''earnings from continuing operations'' as opposed to net earnings (earnings after adding or subtracting profits or losses from discontinued operations). Based on the income statements for Bandag presented in Table 7-1, can you make an argument for concentrating on net earnings?

3 Explain how common-size statements can be used in a time-series fashion.

4 Explain how trend statements can be used to make cross-sectional comparisons.

5 Based on the information in Tables 7-5 and 7-7, which of the three stocks would you expect to sell at the highest *P/E* ratio? Which would you expect to sell at the lowest *P/E* ratio? Justify your answers.

6 What are the advantages of using ratios as opposed to the actual values of various financial variables?

7 Ratios were arbitrarily classified into five groups. Identify two ratios (other than inventory turnover and times interest earned) which could be listed in two or more of these groups and discuss the reasons why.

8 Identify two ratios which you believe provide the most information concerning the overall performance of the firm and justify your choices.

9 Under what circumstances would it not make much difference whether the inventory turnover ratio is calculated using sales vs. cost of goods sold in the denominator?

10 Using the DuPont system, what are the key components of return on equity?

11 Under what conditions will financial leverage increase ROE?

12 As a general rule, would you expect a firm with low profit margins to have a high or low turnover of assets?

13 How is the times interest earned ratio computed for senior debt vs. subordinated debt?

14 What problems are involved in computing fixed charge coverage ratios?

15 Given no other information, what would you estimate the long-run growth rate to be for a firm that pays out an average of 30% of its earnings and averages a 12% return on its equity?

16 Industry averages are typically used as benchmarks in ratio analysis. Justify this practice.

17 Under what circumstances might a firm's current ratio suggest the firm is highly liquid when its quick ratio indicates the opposite?

18 Under what circumstances might a firm have a low LTD/equity ratio but a high leverage ratio? Is the high leverage ratio necessarily bad?

19 What are the principal arguments for using EP as opposed to ROE in analyzing the overall profitability of the firm? What are some arguments for ROE?

20 List three possible sources of industry average ratios.

PROBLEMS

1 Compute common-size and trend statements for Cooper Tire's income statements shown below:

| | (In $000,000) | | | |
	1981	1982	1983	1984
Net sales	393.9	430.3	457.8	555.4
COGS	337.7	366.6	390.1	482.3
Interest	4.0	4.3	3.1	2.6
EBT	31.2	34.9	39.8	41.9
EAT	17.3	19.0	21.4	24.6

2 Based on the income statement data presented in Question 1, answer the following questions:
   a What was the dollar amount of general administrative and selling expenses in 1981?
   b What was the effective tax rate (TAXES/EBT) in 1982 and 1983? What might have caused the difference in the tax rates?
   c What has been the most important factor in the improvement of after-tax profit margins from 1981 to 1984?

3 a Given the information below for Fluor Corporation, compute the basic financial ratios and analyze the profitability of the firm.
   b By checking standard sources, such as Value Line or Standard & Poor's, can you identify any reason for the substantial change in Fluor's ratios from 1980 to 1981?

| | ($000,000's) | |
	1980	1981
SALES	4826	6073
COGS	(4557)	(5698)
GAS	(45)	(42)
I*	20	(44)
TAXES	(112)	(130)
EAT	132	159
EPS	$2.73	$2.83
CASH	217	187
AR	242	497
INV	466	672
OCA	32	64
CA	956	1420
FA	601	2504
OFA	148	503
A	1705	4427
CL	775	1255
LTD and LEASES	378	1484
EQ	552	1688
	1705	4427

*I = interest expense minus interest income.

4 In 1985, Value Line listed the 12 companies shown below in its "Home Appliance Industry."

| Company | 1984 financial variable ($000,000) | | | |
	Sales	EAT	EQ	A
Black & Decker	1533	95	684	1368
Hoover	683	26	190	335
Magic Chef	1054	55	246	477
Maytag	643	63	229	305
National Presto	90	16	155	180
Ranco	178	8	54	111
Rival	111	9	55	70
Robertshaw	416	24	138	218
Roper	572	18	103	378
Toro	280	8	75	172
Whirlpool	3138	190	1096	1525
White Consolidated	1906	47	512	1089

   a Compute the after-tax profit margin, ROE, ROA, and leverage ratio for each firm.
   b Determine a <u>benchmark</u> for each of these four ratios.
   c Are your benchmarks based on the mean or the median industry ratio? Why?
   d Read the Value Line report on each of these companies. Can you see any problems in using the mean or median ratios for this group of stocks as benchmark ratios?
5 Which of the 12 stocks in Problem 4 would you expect to sell at higher *P/E* ratios and why? What additional information would you like to have in order to answer this question?

CHAPTER 8

ANALYTICAL TECHNIQUES

After reading this chapter, you should:

1 Know how to calculate geometric mean growth rates
2 Understand the principles of regression analysis
3 Be able to construct several simple time-series forecasting models
4 Understand how regression analysis can be used as a forecasting tool
5 Be aware of some of the ways computers can be utilized in the analysis of securities
6 Know how to use the appendix to this chapter which lists many sources of information and data which may be useful to investors

A number of techniques that investors have developed over the years have proved useful in analyzing securities. Certainly the most commonly used technique is ratio analysis, which was the subject of the preceding chapter. This chapter will discuss some additional tools which are frequently used by professional security analysts and which the serious investor should understand.

8-1 CALCULATING GROWTH RATES

As should be obvious to the reader by now, growth rates of such variables as sales, earnings, and dividends are essential inputs for the security valuation process. Therefore, it is important to be able to calculate historical growth rates, as historical growth rates are frequently the starting point for estimating future growth rates.

8-1-1 The Geometric Mean Growth Rate   Those readers familiar with the principles of compound interest will recall that the future value of the dollar is equal to $1 multiplied by the quantity 1 plus the rate of return raised to the tth power, where t is equal to the number of years over which the compound annual rate of return is achieved.[1] The same principle applies to the growth rate of any variable. Let V_0 equal the value of the variable in year 0 (the base year) and V_t equal the value of the variable t years later. Further, let g equal the *average compound* annual growth rate. Then,

$$V_0(1 + g)^t = V_t \tag{8-1}$$

[1] If the mathematics of compounding and discounting are unfamiliar or only a hazy memory, you may want to skip ahead and read Section 9-1 before continuing.

The compound annual growth rate is easily solved for as follows:[2]

$$(1 + g)^t = \frac{V_t}{V_0}$$

$$g = \left(\frac{V_t}{V_0}\right)^{1/t} - 1 \tag{8-2}$$

Note in Equation (8-2) that the ratio V_t/V_0 is a value relative. Thus, the value relatives in trend statements lend themselves directly to the calculation of compound growth rates. Simply take the tth root of the value relative[3] and subtract 1 to determine the growth rate expressed in decimal form.

For example, the average compound (geometric mean) annual growth rate over the 5 years from the end of 1979 to the end of 1984 for Bandag's net sales was 8.1%, calculated as follows:

$$g = \left(\frac{V_t}{V_0}\right)^{1/t} - 1 = \left(\frac{\$318,842}{\$216,283}\right)^{1/5} - 1$$
$$= (1.474)^{1/5} - 1$$
$$= 1.081 - 1 = .081 = 8.1\%$$

Note that we simply took the fifth root of the 5-year value relative for sales (1.474) in Table 7-7 and subtracted 1.

8-1-2 Geometric vs. Arithmetic Mean This is a good time to consider the difference between the arithmetic mean growth rate and the geometric mean growth rate. The geometric mean growth rate is equivalent to the compound growth rate calculated using Equation (8-2). Consequently, we will use the terms *geometric mean growth rate* and *compound growth rate* interchangeably.

---

[2]One can also express growth rates as *continuously* compounded rates, as opposed to annually compounded rates, as follows:

$$V_0 e^{gt} = V_t$$
$$e^{gt} = \frac{V_t}{V_0}$$
$$g = \frac{1}{t} \ln\left(\frac{V_t}{V_0}\right)$$

Thus, the continuously compounded growth rate is equal to the natural log of the value relative divided by the number of years between the two observations. The interested reader may want to review Section 9-5, which deals with continuous compounding.

[3]There are two simple methods of finding the tth root of a variable with a calculator. If the calculator has a y^x key, simply key in the variable (in this case, the value relative), key in $1/t$, and press the y^x key. If the calculator has a log and an antilog key, first take the log of the variable, divide this number by t, and then take the antilog of this quotient.

The data below regarding Bandag's net sales for the years 1977–1981 will be used to illustrate the difference between the arithmetic mean and the geometric mean.

BANDAG'S NET SALES (1979–1984)

Year	Net sales ($000s)	Annual growth rates g_t
1979	216,283	
1980	260,404	20.4%
1981	294,145	13.0%
1982	285,954	−2.8%
1983	303,498	6.2%
1984	318,842	5.1%

The annual growth rates g_t listed above are simply the sales in a particular year divided by the sales in the previous year, minus 1. We previously determined that the geometric mean annual growth rate g over the 5-year period was 8.1%.[4] However, the arithmetic mean of the five annual growth rates $\bar{g}$ is 8.4%, calculated in the usual fashion for an arithmetic mean:

$$\bar{g} = \frac{1}{n} \sum g_t$$
$$= \frac{1}{5} (20.4 + 13.0 - 2.8 + 6.2 + 5.1) = 8.4\%$$

The fact that the arithmetic mean (8.4%) is greater than the geometric mean (8.1%) is not unusual. In fact, it will always be the case that the arithmetic mean is greater than the geometric mean.[5]

---

[4]Formally, the geometric mean growth rate g is expressed as

$$g = \left[\prod_{t=1}^{n} (1 + g_t) \right]^{1/n} - 1$$

where the $\prod$ operator indicates that the quantities $(1 + g_t)$ are to be multiplied. For the example above concerning BDG's sales, the geometric mean g of the individual annual growth rates g_t would be calculated as follows:

$$g = [(1 + g_1)(1 + g_2)(1 + g_3)(1 + g_4)(1 + g_5)]^{1/5} - 1$$
$$= [(1.204)(1.130)(0.972)(1.062)(1.051)]^{1/5} - 1$$
$$= (1.474)^{1/5} - 1 = .081$$

Notice that the product of the $(1 + g_t)$'s is equal to 1.474, which, of course, is the 5-year value relative for BDG's sales over the years 1979–1984. Thus, to calculate the geometric mean of individual growth rates, one can simply use Equation (8-2), which utilizes the value relative.

[5]Only for the case when the individual growth rates g_t are constant will the arithmetic mean and the geometric mean be the same. Otherwise, the arithmetic mean will always be greater than the geometric mean.

For many investment problems which deal with rates of return, we are interested in the geometric mean as opposed to the arithmetic mean.[6] To see this, consider the case of an individual who invests $1 for a period of 2 years. During the first year the investor earns 100% on his money and during the second year he suffers a 50% loss. Thus, the value of his investment changed from an initial $1 to $2 and back again to $1. Obviously the rate of return on his investment over the 2 years was equal to zero, and using Equation (8-2), the geometric mean growth rate would also be calculated as zero. However, the arithmetic mean return was equal to (100% − 50%)/2, or a *positive 25%*. There are two points to be learned from this short story. First, this demonstrates again that the arithmetic mean will always be greater than the geometric mean. Second, since investors are primarily interested in compound rates of return or growth over a period of years, it is the geometric mean that we are primarily interested in, as opposed to the arithmetic mean. One would be hard pressed to convince the investor in the above example who started with $1 and ended with $1 that he had earned an average return of 25% per year!

8-1-3 Normalizing Growth Rates   When growth rates are calculated using Equation (8-2), only two observations are used, V_0 and V_t. Thus, all the intermediate values are ignored and this may distort the estimates of the underlying growth rate for the variable in question. To illustrate this potential problem, consider the hypothetical EPS record of the XYZ Company shown in Table 8-1. Over the entire 12-year time period the geometric mean annual growth rate was 20.0%. (You should verify this number, using Equation (8-2), as well as the 10-year growth rates mentioned below). However, suppose that one was interested in 10-year growth rates and that a 10-year growth rate was calculated at the end of 1981 and then again at the end of 1982. For the 10 years from 1971 through 1981, the compound annual growth rate was 15.2%.

[6]For a good discussion of the issues concerning the geometric vs. the arithmetic mean, see R. W. McEnally, ''Latané's Bequest: The Best of Portfolio Strategies,'' *Journal of Portfolio Management* (winter 1986).

TABLE 8-1   XYZ CO. EPS

Year	EPS	% change
1970	$1.00	
1971	1.41	41.0
1972	0.65	−53.9
1973	1.73	166.2
1974	2.10	21.4
1975	2.45	16.7
1976	3.00	22.4
1977	3.60	20.0
1978	4.25	18.1
1979	5.16	21.4
1980	6.20	20.2
1981	5.80	−6.5
1982	8.95	54.3

However, for the years 1972 through 1982, the compound annual growth rate was 30.0%—quite a difference!

What caused such a large difference in the 10-year growth rates? Notice that during 1971 EPS increased 41%, while in 1981 EPS decreased 6.5%. Thus, for the 10 years 1971–1981 the base year (1971) was a year of unusually strong EPS growth for XYZ Company, while the ending year was an unusually weak year. This combination of a high base year with a low ending year resulted in a 10-year geometric mean growth rate that was probably below the "normal" growth pattern for the firm. On the other hand, the 10-year period of 1972–1982 produced just the opposite result. The base year (1972) was a year of depressed earnings, while the ending year (1982) was a year of unusually strong earnings growth. This combination resulted in a 10-year geometric mean growth rate of 30.0%, which is probably above the "normal" growth pattern for the firm.

In order to reduce distortions such as these, analysts frequently calculate "normalized" growth rates. One method of doing this is to adjust the value of the variable (EPS in this example) for any particular year associated with an unusual event. For example, suppose that EPS for XYZ were depressed in 1972 because of a strike. The analyst might then want to adjust upward the 1972 EPS to a more "normal" level, say to the $1.50 area. Using an adjusted 1972 EPS estimate of $1.50 would result in a 10-year (1972–1982) compound annual growth rate of 19.6%.

Another commonly used method of computing normalized growth rates is to use 3-year averages for the starting and ending points, rather than a single year. For example, for the 3 years of 1970, 1971, and 1972 EPS averaged $1.02 and for the 3 years of 1980, 1981, and 1982 EPS averaged $6.98. The geometric mean annual growth rate over the 10 years between these two periods was 21.2%, using the average earnings of $1.02 for the base year and $6.98 for the ending year. The diagram below illustrates the procedure of averaging earnings for the purpose of estimating normal growth rates.

	1970	1971	1972		1980	1981	1982
EPS	1.00	1.41	.65		6.20	5.80	8.95
Average EPS		1.02				6.98	

10 years

$g = 21.2\%$

While the use of 3-year averages may have produced a reasonable estimate of the underlying growth rate, the reader should recognize that any technique for "normalizing" growth rates is based on arbitrary procedures. For example, why is a 3-year average more appropriate than a 2-year or 4-year average? There are no hard-and-fast answers to such questions. However, when performed by experienced analysts, the value of the information gained by normalizing growth rates probably exceeds any drawbacks associated with such arbitrary procedures.

There is another procedure for estimating growth rates which utilizes all the information available concerning a particular variable, as opposed to just a beginning and ending observation or averages of observations around a beginning and ending point. This procedure involves regressing the natural logarithm of the variable against time and is a very useful tool. But, to use this procedure, the reader must first become more familiar with regression analysis, which is the subject of the next section of this chapter.

8-2 REGRESSION ANALYSIS

Regression analysis is one of the most frequently used and one of the most valuable of the analyst's tools. Like any powerful tool, regression analysis can yield many useful insights *when properly used*. But, in the hands of someone not properly trained to use this tool, regression analysis may cause more harm than good. Thus the reader should be aware that this section is meant only as an introduction to this important topic—there is much more to be learned about regression than we can devote space to here. Nevertheless, you should be able to compute and interpret simple regression equations after completing this section. And, because regression is so widely used in finance, mastery of this introductory material should prove of value to the investor.

As noted, regression is used in many ways in the field of investments. One of the most obvious and important uses is to compute ex post betas for individual securities. Frequently both ex post and ex ante security market lines are computed using regression. (The use of regression to compute betas and SMLs was briefly discussed in Chapter 4.) Another use of regression is to examine the cross-sectional relationship between two or more variables. For example, many analysts have attempted to explain the variation in a cross section of *P/E* ratios by performing regressions of *P/E*s against growth rates, payout ratios, measures of risk, and other variables. Still another useful application of regression is for estimating the growth rate of a variable over time. And there are many more possible applications of regression analysis to investment problems. Therefore, let us examine how regression equations are calculated.

8-2-1 Estimating a Regression Equation   Suppose that we are willing to assume that a variable Y is a linear (straight-line) function of a variable X. We call Y the *dependent variable* and X the *independent variable* since Y depends upon (is a function of) X. Now suppose that the relationship between Y and X is not perfect and there is an element of random error. In this case we have a model of the following form:

$$Y_i = A + BX_i + e_i \tag{8-3}$$

where A = intercept
B = slope of straight line describing relationship between Y and X
e_i = *random error or residual term* which has an expected value of zero

Linear regression is a procedure for estimating parameters A and B of this equation. We will denote these estimates $\hat{A}$ and $\hat{B}$. Regression uses the technique called *ordinary least squares* (OLS) to compute $\hat{A}$ and $\hat{B}$. The OLS technique will also, by construction, force the mean of the estimated error terms $\hat{e}_i$ to be zero. Therefore, the *expected, or predicted*, value of Y_i, given a value of X_i, can be written as

$$\hat{Y}_i = \hat{A} + \hat{B} X_i \tag{8-4}$$

where the hat (^) above the variable or parameter indicates that it is an estimate of the true value of the variable or parameter. Thus, Equation (8-4) represents an estimate of the true, but unobservable, relationship expressed in Equation (8-3). Note that the predicted value of Y_i, given X_i, is denoted $\hat{Y}_i$ and frequently referred to as ''Y-hat.''

The interpretation of the estimated residual or error term is straightforward: $\hat{e}_i$ is the difference between Y_i (the actual or observed value of the dependent variable) and $\hat{Y}_i$ (the predicted value of Y_i, given X_i). That is,

$$\hat{e}_i = Y_i - \hat{Y}_i = Y_i - (\hat{A} + \hat{B}X_i) \tag{8-5}$$

The purpose of the ordinary least squares technique is to determine the linear model which best describes the relationship between Y_i and the independent variable X_i. The best relationship, frequently referred to as the *line of best fit*, is defined as the linear model which *minimizes the sum of the squared error terms*—thus the terminology ''least squares.'' One can think of this process as minimizing the prediction errors, that is, minimizing the difference between the actual value of Y_i and the predicted value $\hat{Y}_i$. In order to determine the line of best fit, OLS calculates $\hat{A}$ and $\hat{B}$ as follows:[7]

$$\hat{A} = \bar{Y} - \hat{B} \bar{X} \tag{8-6}$$

$$\hat{B} = \frac{\text{Cov}(Y,X)}{\sigma^2(X)} \tag{8-7}$$

Equation (8-7) should look familiar. Recall from Chapter 4 that a stock's historical beta was taken from a regression of the individual stock returns r_i against the returns for a market index r_m and that beta was calculated as $\beta_{im} = \text{Cov}(r_i, r_m)/\sigma^2(r_m)$. Thus, for a market model regression, β_{im} and $\hat{B}$ are identical. We will use the notation β_{im} to specifically denote the slope coefficient for a regression of security returns against the returns of a market index; we will use $\hat{B}$ as a more general term to denote the slope coefficient for any regression involving two variables.

To illustrate the calculation of the regression parameters $\hat{A}$ and $\hat{B}$, consider the following example. Suppose a security analyst responsible for following housing-related stocks wanted to estimate the number of housing starts. One of the key variables influencing housing starts is the level of interest rates on home mortgages. High mortgage rates reduce the consumer's ability to purchase houses since the higher the mortgage rates, the higher the monthly payments required to purchase a given house.

---

[7]The derivation of the equations for $\hat{A}$ and $\hat{B}$ can be found in almost any introductory statistics textbook which covers regression.

Thus, one would expect *an inverse or negative relationship between mortgage rates and housing starts*.

This analyst decided to use linear regression to investigate the relationship between housing starts and mortgage rates. Table 8-2 lists housing starts (the dependent variable) and mortgage rates (the independent variable) for the 10 years 1972–1981. Housing starts (Y) are expressed in millions of units per year, while mortgage rates (X) are expressed as a percentage and represent the annual yield on conventional new-home mortgages.

Recall from Chapter 3 that the equations for covariance and variance are as follows:

$$\text{Cov}(Y, X) = \frac{1}{n - 1} \sum_i (Y_i - \bar{Y})(X_i - \bar{X}) \tag{8-8}$$

$$\sigma^2(X) = \frac{1}{n - 1} \sum_i (X_i - \bar{X})^2 \tag{8-9}$$

When calculating $\hat{B}$, note that $1/(n - 1)$ in the covariance and variance terms in Equation (8-7) will cancel out, leaving

$$\hat{B} = \frac{\text{Cov}(Y, X)}{\sigma^2(X)} = \frac{\sum_i (Y_i - \bar{Y})(X_i - \bar{X})}{\sum_i (X_i - \bar{X})^2} \tag{8-7a}$$

Recall that $(Y_i - \bar{Y})(X_i - \bar{X})$ is called the cross-product term. Thus, to calculate $\hat{B}$, we need to divide the sum of all the cross-product terms by the sum of the squared

TABLE 8-2 AN ILLUSTRATION OF REGRESSION: HOUSING STARTS AND MORTGAGE RATES

	(1) Housing starts, millions	(2) Mortgage rate, %	(3)	(4)	(5)	(6)	(7)	(8)	(9)	(10)
Year	Y_i	X_i	$(Y_i - \bar{Y})$	$(X_i - \bar{X})$	$(Y_i - \bar{Y})^2$	$(X_i - \bar{X})^2$	$(Y_i - \bar{Y})(X_i - \bar{X})$	$\hat{Y}_i$	$\hat{e}_i$	$\hat{e}_i^2$
1972	2.4	7.6	0.73	−2.32	0.533	5.382	−1.694	1.976	0.424	0.180
1973	2.1	8.0	0.43	−1.92	0.185	3.686	−0.826	1.923	0.177	0.031
1974	1.4	8.9	−0.27	−1.02	0.073	1.040	0.275	1.804	−0.404	0.163
1975	1.2	9.0	−0.47	−0.92	0.221	0.846	0.432	1.791	−0.591	0.349
1976	1.5	9.0	−0.17	−0.92	0.029	0.846	0.156	1.791	−0.291	0.085
1977	2.0	9.0	0.33	−0.92	0.109	0.846	−0.304	1.791	0.208	0.043
1978	2.0	9.5	0.33	−0.42	0.109	0.176	−0.139	1.725	0.275	0.076
1979	1.7	10.5	0.03	0.88	0.001	0.774	0.026	1.554	0.146	0.021
1980	1.3	12.7	−0.37	2.78	0.137	7.728	−1.029	1.303	−0.003	0.000
1981	1.1	14.7	−0.57	4.78	0.325	22.848	−2.725	1.040	0.060	0.004
Sums	16.70	99.20	0.00	0.00	1.721	44.176	−5.824	16.700	0.000	0.953

Source: 1982 Economic Report of the President, Government Printing Office, Washington, D.C.

deviations from the mean for X. Using the data from columns 3 to 5 of Table 8-2, we see that the sum of the squared deviations for X (column 6) is 44.176 and the sum of the cross-product terms (column 7) is -5.824. Therefore, $\hat{B}$ is -0.132, calculated as follows using Equation (8-7a):

$$\hat{B} = \frac{-5.824}{44.176} = -0.132$$

There is a straightforward economic interpretation of $\hat{B}$. The negative slope coefficient of -0.132 suggests that for every 1% *increase* in mortgage rates, housing starts will *decrease* by .132 million (132,000) units.

The intercept for the regression line is estimated using Equation (8-6):

$$\hat{A} = \bar{Y} - \hat{B}\,\bar{X} = 1.670 - (-.132)(9.920) = 2.979$$

($\bar{Y}$ and $\bar{X}$ can be obtained directly from the sums for Y_i and X_i in Table 8-2). Having solved for $\hat{A}$ and $\hat{B}$, the estimated regression equation is

$$\hat{Y}_i = 2.979 - .132X_i$$

For this particular problem there is no economic interpretation of the intercept $\hat{A}$. Normally, we think of the intercept as being the predicted value of Y if the value of X is zero. However, we would never expect mortgage rates (X) to be zero. Thus, in this example, $\hat{A}$ is simply an artifact of the regression and has no economic meaning. When analyzing the intercept term of a regression, ask the question, "Does it make any sense for the independent variable X to have a value of zero?" If so, the interpretation of the intercept is that $\hat{A}$ represents the best estimate of Y when X equals zero. Otherwise, the intercept has no economic meaning.

Figure 8-1 plots the values for housing starts and mortgage rates, as well as the regression line. Note that it is conventional to plot the Y values on the vertical axis and the X values on the horizontal axis. Simple observation of Figure 8-1 suggests that there is not a perfect fit between housing starts and mortgage rates—that is, all the observations do not plot on the regression line. This is another way of saying that knowledge of X (mortgage rates) will not allow one to make perfect predictions of Y (housing starts)

The statistic most commonly used to measure the "goodness of fit" is denoted R^2 and pronounced "r-squared." R^2 is also termed the *coefficient of determination*. The equation for computing R^2 is

$$R^2 = \frac{\sum(Y_i - \bar{Y})^2 - \sum \hat{e}_i^2}{\sum(Y_i - \bar{Y})^2} \tag{8-10}$$

Recall that the error term $\hat{e}_i$ is equal to the actual value of Y_i minus the predicted value of Y_i for a given value of X_i. That is, $\hat{e}_i = Y_i - \hat{Y}_i$. The error terms are frequently

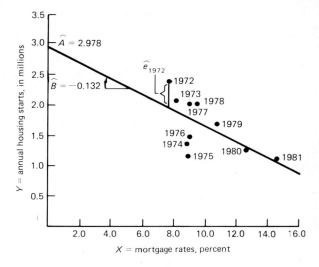

FIGURE 8-1 Plot of housing starts and mortgage rates.

described as the variation in Y which is not explained by the regression. In this sense there is a nice intuitive interpretation of R^2. From Equation (8-10), we see that the numerator for R^2 is equal to $\sum(Y_i - \bar{Y})^2$ (the total variation in Y) minus $\sum \hat{e}_i^2$ (the variation of Y that is not explained by the regression), which leaves the explained variation. In other words, the numerator is equal to the variation of Y that is explained by the regression. The denominator is equal to the total variation of Y. Thus, R^2 is equal to the percentage of the total variation of Y that is explained by the regression equation

$$R^2 = \frac{\text{explained variation of } Y}{\text{total variation of } Y}$$

Columns 8 to 10 of Table 8-2 provide the necessary data for computing R^2 for the regression of housing starts against mortgage rates. One first has to calculate the predicted value of Y_i for a given value of X_i. (The $\hat{Y}_i$'s are reported in column 8.) For example, $\hat{Y}_i$ for 1972 is 1.976, computed as follows:

$$\hat{Y}_{1972} = 2.979 - 0.132 \, X_{1972} = 2.979 - .0132(7.6) = 1.976$$

The error term for 1972 is then computed to be 0.424.

$$\hat{e}_{1972} = Y_{1972} - \hat{Y}_{1972} = 2.400 - 1.976 = 0.424$$

(The error terms and the squared error terms are reported in columns 9 and 10.) Once all the error terms are computed, squared, and summed, one can calculate the R^2, which turns out to be .446.

$$R^2 = \frac{\sum(Y_i - \bar{Y})^2 - \sum \hat{e}_i^2}{\sum(Y_i - \bar{Y})^2} = \frac{1.721 - 0.953}{1.721} = .446$$

The R^2 of .446 suggests that roughly 45% of the variation in the level of housing starts over the time period 1972–1981 can be "explained" by the regression.

We are also frequently interested in whether the slope coefficient B is significantly different from zero—that is, whether the $\hat{B}$ we estimated occurred by chance, assuming the true (but unobservable) slope coefficient B is zero. If this is true, there is no relationship between Y and X.[8]

To test whether $\hat{B}$ is different from zero in the statistically significant sense, we need to calculate what is called the t *statistic* or t value for $\hat{B}$. This is done using Equation (8-11):

$$t(\hat{B}) = \frac{\hat{B}}{\sigma(B)} \tag{8-11}$$

The denominator $\sigma(\hat{B})$ is termed the standard error of $\hat{B}$ and is estimated as follows:

$$\sigma(\hat{B}) = \left[\frac{(\sum \hat{e}_i^2)/(N - K)}{\sum(X_i - \bar{X})^2} \right]^{1/2} \tag{8-12}$$

where N = number of observations in sample
$N - K$ = number of degrees of freedom

In a regression, K is equal to 1 plus the number of independent variables. In this example there is only one independent variable (X) and therefore K equals 2. Using the data in Table 8-2, the t statistic for $\hat{B}$ is calculated as follows:

$$\sigma(\hat{B}) = \left[\frac{(0.953)/(10 - 2)}{44.176} \right]^{1/2} = 0.052$$

$$t(\hat{B}) = \frac{-.132}{.052} = -2.54$$

As a rule of thumb, if the absolute value of the t statistic is equal to or greater than 2.0, the variable is generally considered to be statistically significant at the 5% (or less) level. This means that there is less than a 5% chance that one would observe a t value as large as 2.0 when the true value of B is zero. Thus, if the t statistic was 2

---

[8]To see this, note that if $\hat{B}$ equals 0, then from Equation (8-6) $\hat{A}$ must equal $\bar{Y}$. In this case the predicted value for any individual Y_i is *always* $\bar{Y}$, regardless of the value of X_i. The regression equation becomes $\hat{Y}_i = \bar{Y}$. Thus, there is no relationship between Y and X if $\hat{B}$ equals 0.

or larger we would reject the hypothesis that B is equal to zero and instead conclude that there is a relationship between Y and X. However, this rule of thumb applies to large samples (generally considered to be 30 observations or more), and care has to be taken when dealing with small samples, as in this example, which is based on only 10 observations.[9]

Before leaving our example, we should consider some of the potential problems with this regression model. First and foremost, there is no theory which suggests that housing starts are a linear function of mortgage rates. Common sense would suggest that there should be an inverse (negative) relationship between housing starts and mortgage rates. However, this does not mean that the relationship is necessarily *linear*. Nor is there any theory to suggest that the mortgage rate is the *only* variable which influences the level of housing starts. Some other plausible factors which may affect housing starts are: the level of unemployment, changes in real personal income, and the demographic makeup of the population.

Another potential problem concerning the housing starts regression is that the data may violate the assumptions underlying the OLS technique. *The principal OLS assumptions are*: (1) the error terms are normally distributed, (2) the error terms are not correlated with each other or with the independent variable, and (3) the error terms have a constant variance. There are statistical tests to determine whether or not these assumptions are violated, but such tests are beyond the scope of this text. Nevertheless, the reader should be aware that if the data do not conform to the OLS assumptions, a regression may provide poor predictions, even if the R^2 is quite high.

Finally, bear in mind that in this example the independent and the dependent variables were contemporaneous. That is, the levels of housing starts and of mortgage rates were observed as of the *same year*. Thus, even if this example generated a very good regression model with a high R^2, predictions of *future* housing starts would depend upon the accuracy of predictions for future mortgage rates. Like any other model, the quality of the output is no better than the quality of the input.

8-2-2 Using Regression to Compute Growth Rates A very useful application of linear regression is for calculating "normalized" growth rates. The advantage of using regression to calculate growth rates is that all the observations in the time series are considered, as opposed to calculating the geometric mean growth rate by considering only the beginning and ending values.

To compute growth rates using linear regression one must first formulate the problem in terms of continuous compounding. Those readers familiar with the mathematics of

---

[9]Since $t(\hat{B})$ was -2.54 in this example, one can safely conclude that B is different from zero, despite the small sample size. If more precision is required, one can look up the significance level of the t value in a t table, which most introductory statistics books will have. (For example, see the table for the t distribution at the end of this text.) Or, if the regression was performed using one of the many standard computer software packages, the results provided in the computer output will more than likely provide the significance level associated with the calculated t statistics. In this example, a t statistic of -2.54 for eight degrees of freedom is associated with a significance level of approximately 3%. Thus, because of random sampling error there is a 3% probability of observing a $t(\hat{B})$ equal to -2.54 if there is no actual relationship between housing starts and mortgage rates, i.e., assuming the true, but unobservable, slope coefficient is equal to zero. In almost all cases, observers would accept the 3% chance of being wrong and conclude that there is, in fact, a negative relationship between housing starts and mortgage rates.

compound interest will recall that the future value of a variable V_t continuously compounded at the rate of $\hat{g}$ for t periods can be written[10]

$$V_t = V_0 e^{\hat{g}t} \qquad (8\text{-}13)$$

where V_0 is the beginning value and e is the natural logarithm ($e \cong 2.718$). If we take the natural log (ln) of both sides, we have

$$\ln(V_t) = \ln(V_0) + \hat{g}t \qquad (8\text{-}14)$$

Note that the equation is now in linear form. On the left-hand side of the equation is the natural log of the variable being considered. On the right-hand side is the natural log of V_0, which will be constant since there is only one starting point; also on the right-hand side is the product of $\hat{g}t$, where $\hat{g}$ is the continuously compounded growth rate and t is the number of time periods from the beginning time period. Thus, Equation (8-14) is exactly the form of a linear regression model—$\hat{A}$ is equal to $\ln(V_0)$ and $\hat{B}$ is equal to $\hat{g}$. Consequently, in order to measure a continuous growth rate, one can simply regress the natural log of the variable against t. As we shall see, this method has the advantage of being much less sensitive to the choice of the starting and ending points for the variable and, as a result, is a good method of estimating a normalized historical growth rate for the variable.

To illustrate this technique, we will reconsider the problem of estimating the growth rate of earnings per share for XYZ Corporation. Table 8-3 reproduces the EPS over the time period 1970–1982 for XYZ. The top half of this table also lists ln(EPS), which is the Y variable in the regression and t, which is the X variable. Three regressions were performed using a standard computer statistical package.[11] The first regression utilized the 12 observations during the entire time period, 1970–1982; the second regression utilized the 10 observations during the time period of 1971–1981; and the third regression utilized the 10 observations during the time period 1972–1982.

The bottom half of Table 8-3 lists the results of these regressions. First notice that the R^2's are quite high. The intercepts $\hat{A}$ require some explanation. Since these regressions were done in log form, to interpret the intercept one needs to take the antilog of $\hat{A}$. If the regression was perfect, this value should equal the EPS for the beginning year of the time period covered, i.e., for $t = 0$. For example, for the first regression the intercept is $-.105$, the antilog of which is .90, which is reasonably close to the actual EPS of \$1.00 in 1970.

Of course, it is the slope coefficient which is of most interest. First notice that the t statistics for $\hat{B}$ are all well above 2, suggesting that there is a highly significant relationship between EPS and time. The actual value of $\hat{B}$ is a measure of the contin-

---

[10]Once again, if you are unfamiliar with the mathematics of compounding and discounting, you may want to skip ahead to Section 9-5, which deals with continuous compounding and discounting.

[11]The reader may estimate the regression equations by hand by setting up the appropriate columns of numbers in a fashion similar to Table 8-2. Such an exercise should quickly convince the reader of the advantages of using computers for solving problems such as these.

TABLE 8-3   ESTIMATING THE GROWTH RATE OF XYZ's EPS USING LINEAR REGRESSION

Regression: $\ln(EPS_t) = \hat{A} + \hat{B}t$

Data

Year	EPS	$\ln(EPS_t) = Y_i$	$t = X_i$
1970	$1.00	0.000	0
1971	1.41	0.344	1
1972	0.65	−0.431	2
1973	1.73	0.548	3
1974	2.10	0.742	4
1975	2.45	0.897	5
1976	3.00	1.099	6
1977	3.60	1.281	7
1978	4.25	1.447	8
1979	5.16	1.641	9
1980	6.20	1.825	10
1981	5.80	1.758	11
1982	8.95	2.192	12

Regression results

Time period	R^2	$\hat{A}$	antilog of $\hat{A}$	Continuous growth rate $\hat{B} = \hat{g}$	$t(\hat{B})$
1970–1982	.908	−.105	.90	.189	10.43
1971–1981	.865	−.141	.87	.192	7.58
1972–1982	.903	−.284	.75	.209	9.18

uously compounded rate of growth $\hat{g}$. Note that continuous growth rates $\hat{g}$ converted to compound annual growth rates g as follows:

$$g = e^{\hat{g}} - 1 \qquad (8\text{-}15)$$

For example, in the first regression for which $\hat{B} = .189$, the compound annual growth rate would be estimated as .208, or 20.8%.

$$g = 2.718^{.189} - 1 = .208 = 20.8\%$$

We can now compare the annual growth rates calculated using regression with the geometric mean annual growth rates calculated earlier (Section 8-1-3) using only the starting and ending points. The comparisons are in the following table.

COMPARISON OF ESTIMATED GROWTH RATES, PERCENT

Time period	Regression		Geometric mean
	Continuous	Annualized	
1970–1982	18.9	20.8	20.0
1971–1981	19.2	21.2	15.2
1972–1982	20.9	23.2	30.0

As we observed earlier, the geometric mean growth rates are very sensitive to the choice of starting and ending points. Over the entire time period (1970–1982) the geometric mean growth rate was computed to be 20.0%. Unfortunately, when slightly different 10-year time periods were considered, the geometric mean varied from 15.2% to 30.0%. However, this is not the case with the regression technique. Notice that the estimated annualized growth rate only varied between a range of 20.8% to 23.2% when the different time periods were considered. A simple explanation of this is that the regression technique gives approximately equal weight to *all* the observations within the time period chosen and therefore the results are not affected as much by an unusually high or low observation. Thus, the regression technique is a nice method of measuring "normal" historical growth rates.

An important caveat is in order at this time. One should *not* think that the use of regression to measure normal growth rates which have occurred in the past will solve the problem of forecasting *future* growth rates. The regression in this example was based on historical data. To use the measured historical growth rate as an estimate of the future growth rate one has to assume that past economic conditions and the firm's relationship to those past conditions will be similar in the future. The hallmark of the truly superior security analyst is the ability to forecast *changes* in historical relationships between the firm and the economy. Nevertheless, frequently the best starting point in the process of estimating future growth rates is the firm's historical growth rates. The analyst can then adjust the estimated future growth rate up or down from the historical growth rate, depending upon her assessment of the potential for changes in the firm's operating and financial characteristics. Thus, the more reliable the starting point (the historical growth rate), the better the chances of making good forecasts of future growth rates.

Before continuing, you should:

1 Know how to calculate geometric mean growth rates
2 Be aware of several methods for "normalizing" growth rates
3 Know how to calculate the regression coefficients $\hat{A}$ and $\hat{B}$
4 Understand the meaning of R^2 and know how to use this statistic
5 Know how to calculate the t statistics for the $\hat{B}$ coefficient and understand its meaning
6 Know how to estimate historical growth rates using regression

8-3 STATISTICAL METHODS OF FORECASTING

There are many statistical techniques the investor may use as aids in forecasting. We will describe the use of a few time-series techniques and also regression analysis. The simple time-series techniques which we will discuss *rely solely on historical data for the variable to be forecast.*[12] These techniques do not consider any interrelationships between the forecast variable and other factors which may influence the behavior of the forecast variable. Because these simple time-series techniques do not account for any cause-and-effect relationships, they are not likely to produce forecasts as good as more complex models which do consider the interrelationships between the forecast variable and other factors.

On the other hand, these basic time-series techniques have a number of attributes: (1) They are relatively simple models and therefore easy to implement. (2) If the only information available is the historical data (the time series) for the forecast variable, then time-series techniques are the only choice. (3) Simple time-series forecasts can serve as useful benchmarks for evaluating the forecasts of other techniques. If a more complex forecasting model does not produce better forecasts than a simple time-series technique, then there is no point in using the more complex model.

On the other hand, *regression, when properly used, does try to capture the cause-effect relationship between the forecast variable and other variables.* Since regression analysis utilizes data for the forecast variable as well as data for one or more "explanatory" variables, we might expect this technique to generate better forecasts than simple time-series techniques. And, in fact, this seems to be the case. However, let's first examine some of the time-series techniques before proceeding to an analysis of how regression might be used as a forecasting tool.

8-3-1 Time-Series Techniques The simplest time-series model is frequently referred to as the *random walk model*. This model assumes that there will be no change in the forecast variable from the previous period's level. For example, we might forecast that the current year's sales will be the same as the previous year's sales. Thus, the random walk model's forecast can be expressed as

$$\hat{Z}_t = Z_{t-1} \tag{8-16}$$

where $\hat{Z}_t$ is the predicted value of the variable to be forecast for time period t, and Z_{t-1} is the actual value of the forecast variable in the previous time period. As another example, if the previous period's EPS were \$1.50, this model would forecast the next period's EPS to also be \$1.50.

To understand time-series models it is necessary to understand the term *autocorrelation*. An autocorrelation of lag 1 refers to the correlation between changes in adjacent time periods, i.e., $\rho(\Delta Z_t, \Delta Z_{t-1})$, where ΔZ_t refers to the change in Z during

---

[12]In this chapter we present only simple, *univariate* time-series techniques, i.e., techniques which utilize only data for a single variable, such as a company's sales. *Multivariate* time-series techniques utilize data for several variables—for example, company sales or changes in GNP and interest rates. Multivariate techniques are more complex and potentially more powerful but are beyond the scope of this text.

time period t, etc. An autocorrelation of lag 2 refers to $\rho(\Delta Z_t, \Delta Z_{t-2})$. The random walk model assumes that the forecast variable changes in a random fashion. Consequently, the autocorrelations between changes in one time period with changes in another time period must be zero for all lags. Assuming that there is a seasonal pattern to the forecast variable, the random walk model must be adjusted accordingly. If quarterly data are being used, then the expected value of the forecast variable is equal to the value of the variable in the same quarter of the previous year. That is,

$$\hat{Z}_t = Z_{t-4} \tag{8-17}$$

For a *seasonal random walk model*, based on quarterly data, we would expect the autocorrelations of lags 1, 2, and 3 to be small (and generally negative) and the autocorrelation for lag 4 to be large and positive.

Another simple time-series model is what we will refer to as the *average-growth model*. In this model the expected value of the forecast variable is equal to the value of the variable in the previous time period multiplied by 1 plus the average growth rate of the variable in the past.[13] Mathematically,

$$\hat{Z}_t = (1 + g)Z_{t-1} \tag{8-18}$$

where g represents the historical growth rate of the forecast variable. For example, if sales have, on average, increased 10% per year over a number of years, we might forecast that this year's sales will be 10% higher than the previous year's sales.

Both the random walk and the average-growth models are time-series models in the sense that the only information these models consider is the historical time series of the forecast variable. A third, and perhaps the simplest model at all, is what we will call the *arithmetic mean model*. This model simply states that the best estimate of the forecast variable is its historical mean value. For this model,

$$\hat{Z}_t = \bar{Z} \tag{8-19}$$

where $\bar{Z}$ is the arithmetic mean of the time series of the forecast variable.

These three models (random walk, average growth, and arithmetic mean) are all very simple models and, as such, can be used as benchmarks for evaluating more

---

[13]This is similar to the conventional time-series model referred to as a "random walk with a drift." The forecast of this model is generally expressed as

$$\hat{Z}_t = Z_{t-1} + \delta$$

where δ is the constant "drift" factor. This formulation implies that the change over time is linear, as opposed to Equation (8-18), which assumes that the change is equal to a compound growth rate. For example, a conventional random walk with a drift model might forecast that sales in the next time period will equal the current period's sales plus a constant (say $50,000), whereas Equation (8-18) would indicate that sales in the next period will be a certain percentage (say 10%) greater than the previous period's sales. Of course, Equation (8-18) can be expressed as a linear function by taking the logs of both sides, i.e.,

$$\ln(\hat{Z}_t) = \ln(1 + g) + \ln(Z_{t-1})$$

complicated models. A comprehensive method of analyzing time-series data has been developed by Box and Jenkins (BJ)[14] which allows one to search for more complicated patterns in the time series. Frequently the BJ technique will identify patterns which fit the historical data better and can be used to generate better forecasts than these three benchmark models.

A discussion of how the BJ technique is actually applied to time-series data is beyond the scope of this text. However, an example will help illustrate the procedure. Table 8-4 presents data for a hypothetical time series of EPS. Figure 8-2 plots the data over time, and one can quickly see that the EPS fluctuate in what appears to be a cyclical pattern.

Using BJ techniques, the model which best fits these data turns out to be what is called a second-order autoregressive process, denoted AR(2). This means that the best forecast of the EPS in time period t is based on the level of EPS in the two previous time periods. The specific model that was fitted to these data was:[15]

$$\hat{EPS}_t = 1.62 + 1.52\ EPS_{t-1} - .84EPS_{t-2} \qquad (8\text{-}20)$$

[14]G. Box and G. Jenkins, *Time-Series Analysis: Forecasting and Control*, rev. ed., Holden-Day, Inc., San Francisco, 1976.

[15]To see how this particular equation was derived, see S. Makridakis and S. Wheelwright, *Forecasting Methods and Applications*, Wiley, New York, 1978, chapter 9.

TABLE 8-4   AN ILLUSTRATION OF TIME-SERIES MODELS

Time period	Hypothetical EPS	Time period	Hypothetical EPS
1	$4.20	11	$3.63
2	5.80	12	5.18
3	6.90	13	7.11
4	7.62	14	8.26
5	5.57	15	7.96
6	3.34	16	6.78
7	2.00	17	5.07
8	1.70	18	5.04
9	2.02	19	6.02
10	2.71	20	7.61

Type of model	Equation	Mean square error*
Arithmetic mean	$\hat{EPS}_t = \overline{EPS}$	4.62
Random walk	$\hat{EPS}_t = EPS_{t-1}$	1.64
Average growth	$\hat{EPS}_t = (1 + g)EPS_{t-1}, g = .03178$	1.68
Box Jenkins, AR(2)	$\hat{EPS}_t = 1.62 + 1.52EPS_{t-1} - .84EPS_{t-2}$	0.51

*Based on 18 predictions.
Source: Adapted from S. Makridakis and S. Wheelwright, *Forecasting Methods and Applications*, Wiley, New York, 1978, chapter 9, table 9-1.

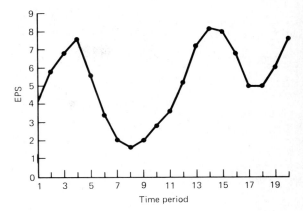

FIGURE 8-2   Plot of hypothetical EPS over time.

To evaluate how well a model forecasts, the *mean square error* (MSE) is typically used. The MSE is calculated as

$$\text{MSE} = \frac{\sum\limits_{t=1}^{n'} e_t^2}{n'} \tag{8-21}$$

where e_t is the forecast error for a particular time period (that is, the difference between the actual outcome and the outcome predicted by the model), and n' is the number of predictions. [Notice that for this problem, which has 20 EPS observations, n' for the Box Jenkins AR(s) model is 18, since the first possible forecast is for time period 3 based on the observations for time periods 1 and 2.] The bottom of Table 8-4 lists the MSE for the three benchmark models and for the Box Jenkins AR(2) model. For this particular time period, the BJ model has a MSE of 0.51, which is substantially lower than the MSEs for the three benchmark models. For time-series data which have a pattern similar to that of Figure 8-2, BJ models will generally provide the smallest MSE. However, for time series which exhibit other types of patterns, this may not be the case. Nevertheless, the important point is that if one has only time-series data available, the BJ techniques may generate the best forecasting models. Thus, the serious forecaster should be aware of this methodology. The references at the end of the chapter will provide a good introduction to the subject.

8-3-2 Regression Analysis   Since the only information utilized by these time-series models is the historical data for the variable to be forecast, these models are *extrapolative models*. That is, they simply extrapolate into the future what has occurred in the past—albeit the extrapolation may sometimes be a rather complicated procedure, such as Equation (8-20).

On the other hand, when properly used, regression is based on a *cause-effect* relationship. That is, the variable to be predicted (dependent variable) is assumed to depend upon the explanatory (independent) variable. There is good evidence that if one understands the relationships between the forecast variable and the factors which cause it to change, then one's predictions can be improved significantly. For example, Chant[16] examined the problem of forecasting earnings per share. For a sample of 218 firms he constructed three simple models which forecast the percentage change in EPS for the next year to be equal to: (1) the percentage change in the current year's money supply; (2) the percentage change in the S&P 500 in the current year; and (3) the percentage change in bank loans for the current year. In equation form,

$$(\%\Delta \text{ EPS})_t = (\%\Delta \text{ money supply})_{t-1}$$
$$(\%\Delta \text{ EPS})_t = (\%\Delta \text{ S\&P 500})_{t-1}$$
$$(\%\Delta \text{ EPS})_t = (\%\Delta \text{ bank loans})_{t-1}$$

Thus, these three models assumed a simple one-for-one relationship between EPS changes for individual companies and changes in the three explanatory variables. (For example, if this year's money supply increases 10%, the first model would forecast next year's EPS to be up 10% for each company.) The forecast errors were then computed for each model and compared with the forecast errors generated by the random walk and the average growth time-series models. Chant found that the model based on changes in the current year's money supply generated, on average, the smallest forecast error and that the average forecast error of the other two causal models was similar to that of the extrapolative models.

Note that the causal models developed by Chant were very simple—the changes in EPS for all companies in the sample were assumed to be affected in the same one-for-one way by the explanatory variable. If forecasts can be improved by the use of such simple causal models,[17] then a more careful application of this approach might prove to be quite useful. Therefore, let's examine regression as a forecasting tool.

As noted earlier, regression analysis should be based on a causal relationship—that is, the variable to be forecast (the dependent variable) depends upon the explanatory (independent) variable. Thus, the first step in regression analysis is to try to determine the appropriate cause-effect relationship. In some cases a well-established theory may exist which indicates the appropriate relationship. For example, the capital asset pricing model is a theory which argues that the returns of individual securities should be a linear function of the returns of the "market portfolio." Consequently, we often use linear regression to estimate the relationship between stock returns and some broadly based index, such as the S&P 500.

Unfortunately, when forecasting such variables as sales and earnings, we generally do not have a well-defined theory regarding their behavior over time. As a result, the investor is frequently forced to search for an appropriate causal relationship before using regression to forecast the desired variable. There are two primary methods of conducting this search: (1) using common sense; and (2) searching for strong correlations.

[16]P. Chant, "On the Predictability of Earnings per Share Behavior," *Journal of Finance* (March 1980).
[17]For example, Eckel also finds that incorporating macroeconomic variables into simple causal models improves the accuracy of EPS forecasts. See N. Eckel, "An EPS Forecasting Model Utilizing Macroeconomic Performance Expectations," *Financial Analysts Journal* (May/June 1982).

Common sense will generally start the search in the right direction. For example, if we were interested in forecasting sales for the steel industry, common sense would suggest that the demand for steel is related to overall economic activity. Consequently, we might consider changes in GNP as an explanatory variable. Or, since a large amount of steel is used in the manufacture of automobiles, auto sales might also be considered as an independent variable. The analyst who carefully considers the characteristics of the industry within which a firm operates should be able to develop a reasonable list of candidates for the independent variable in the regression equation.

Once a reasonable set of candidates for the independent variable has been identified, we can examine the historical correlation between these candidates and the variable to be forecast. Bear in mind, however, that over relatively short time periods variables may have high correlations simply because of chance when, in fact, there is no causal relationship between them. *Thus, the first and overriding criterion for selecting an independent variable should be a well-established theoretical relationship and/or the analyst's best judgment as to the factors upon which the forecast variable depends.*

Now, let's illustrate how one might use regression analysis as a forecasting tool. Suppose at the end of 1981 we were interested in forecasting the 1982 sales for Louisiana Pacific Corporation. Louisiana Pacific (LP) grows, harvests, and converts timber into forest products which are used primarily in construction—both residential and commercial. Thus, reasonable candidates for the independent variable might be housing starts, the level of new construction, or even the overall level of economic activity as measured by GNP.

However, when forecasting variables which are prone to cyclical fluctuations, it is better to first compute the *percentage change* in each period and then perform the regression using percentage changes, rather than the actual levels of the variables. This is because regression essentially fits a straight line through observations and as a result will not be able to identify turning points in a series which has cyclical fluctuations. (We will illustrate this point later.)

Using data on these three variables for the years 1969 through 1981, percentage changes were computed and the correlation coefficients with respect to changes in LP's sales were found to be:[18]

$$\rho(\%\Delta \text{ LP sales}, \%\Delta \text{ GNP}) = .605$$
$$\rho(\%\Delta \text{ LP sales}, \%\Delta \text{ new construction}) = .858$$
$$\rho(\%\Delta \text{ LP sales}, \%\Delta \text{ housing starts}) = .572$$

Based on these correlation coefficients it would appear that the change in new construction is the best explanatory variable for changes in LP's sales. And common sense would support this conclusion since most of Louisiana Pacific's products are used in construction.

Table 8-5 presents the data for LP's sales and new construction, along with the percentage change for both variables for each year. The bottom part of this table

---

[18]The data were taken from the 1982 issue of the *Economic Report of the President*, Government Printing Office, Washington, D.C.

TABLE 8-5   FORECASTING LOUISIANA PACIFIC'S SALES USING REGRESSION

Year	Louisiana Pacific		Total new constitution	
	Sales (millions)	% change	Amount (billions)	% change
1969	$ 177.3	—	$ 94.3	
1970	155.3	− 12.4%	95.2	1.0%
1971	209.8	35.1	110.3	15.9
1972	272.6	29.9	124.4	12.8
1973	416.9	52.9	138.4	11.3
1974	460.1	10.4	139.2	0.6
1975	386.7	− 16.0	135.2	− 2.9
1976	562.3	45.4	151.1	11.8
1977	794.5	41.3	173.8	15.0
1978	1042.1	31.2	205.6	18.3
1979	1301.9	24.9	230.8	12.3
1980	1195.6	− 8.2	230.3	− 0.2
1981	1023.1	− 14.4	236.3	2.6

Regression results

Dependent variable = % change in LP's sales
Independent variable = % change in total new construction

Intercept $\hat{A}$ = −5.68 $t(\hat{A})$ = −0.94
Slope $\hat{B}$ = 2.93 $t(\hat{B})$ = 5.28
R^2 = .74

presents the results of regressing the percentage change in LP's sales against the percentage change in new construction. Note that the slope coefficient $\hat{B}$ is 2.93 and statistically significant. (The t statistic for $\hat{B}$ is 5.28.) Thus, for a 1% change in new construction, LP's sales change approximately 2.93%. The R^2 is .74, which is quite high for a regression involving variables that represent percentage changes.

This particular regression equation would have provided a remarkably good forecast of LP's 1982 sales *if we had been able to accurately forecast the percentage change in new construction for 1982*. Specifically, 1982 sales for LP were $872.2 million, which was a decrease of 14.75% from 1981 sales of $1023.1 million. During 1982 total new construction declined 3.1%. Had we accurately forecast this decline in the level of construction activity, our forecast of the percentage change in LP's sales for 1982 would have been computed as follows:

$$\%\Delta \text{ LP sales} = -5.68\% + 2.93(\%\Delta \text{ new construction}) \qquad (8\text{-}22)$$
$$\%\Delta \text{ LP sales} = -5.68\% + 2.93(-3.1\%) = -14.76\%$$

Our forecast would have almost exactly equaled the actual decline in LP's sales of 14.75%.

Of course, a forecast this accurate is due partly to luck. But, more importantly, it is due to *knowing in advance* what the actual decline in construction activity for 1982 would be. Obviously, investors would not know this at the beginning of 1982. If, for example, we had estimated a 1% decline in new construction, the regression equation would indicate an 8.61% decline in LP's sales; if we had estimated a 4% increase in new construction activity, the regression equation would indicate a 6.04% increase in LP's sales. Thus, this type of model is like any other model—it depends upon the quality of the inputs.

Before leaving this topic, let's examine what would have been the case had we not formulated the regression in terms of percentage changes. Recall that the correlation coefficient based on the percentage change in LP's sales and the percentage change in new construction was .858. If, instead, we had used the *level* of LP sales and the *level* of new construction, we would have found the correlation coefficient between these two variables to be .980. Regressing the level of sales against the level of new construction would have produced the following equation:

$$\text{LP sales} = -615.83 + 7.75(\text{new construction}) \tag{8-23}$$

where LP sales are expressed in millions of dollars and new construction is expressed in billions of dollars. For 1982 new construction activity declined to $232.0 billion. If we had been able to forecast this perfectly, the above regression equation would have predicted LP's 1982 sales to be $1182.2 million, which represents an *increase* of 15.55% over 1981 sales of $1023.1 million. As we have already seen, LP's 1982 sales actually decreased 14.75%! This reinforces the point we made previously—when dealing with variables that have cyclical fluctuations over time, formulate the regression in terms of percentage changes rather than the actual levels of the variables. Otherwise your model may produce very large errors around turning points.

Before continuing, you should:

1 Be able to construct three simple time-series models which might be used as benchmarks for more complicated models
2 Be aware that the Box Jenkins methodology for analyzing time-series data is a potentially valuable tool for the analyst
3 Understand that the critical step in using regression as a forecasting tool is identifying the correct cause-effect relationship

8-4 COMPUTERS AND SECURITY ANALYSIS

It should be obvious from the previous sections that modern computers are an extremely valuable tool available to investors. While one can determine regression equations using pencil, paper, and pocket calculator, this task is much more easily done by a computer. In general, when there are large amounts of data to deal with or when statistical computations are required, the task is more easily accomplished using computers.

Statistical software packages are available for most computers, from the smallest personal computer to the largest mainframe computer. These packages relieve the analyst of the tedious calculations involved with most statistics. However, they do not relieve the analyst of the responsibility for determining the correct statistical procedure and checking to see if the data fit the assumptions underlying the procedure. Nor do computers relieve the analyst of the most important responsibility of all—that of properly interpreting the results.

One of the biggest advantages offered by computers is their ability to access large data bases. Many data bases contain far more data than a human being can comprehend in any reasonable period of time. Thus, computers are a powerful tool for screening large data bases to identify securities which have predetermined characteristics. Once the initial screening is completed by the computer, the investor can then more thoroughly analyze those securities which met the initial selection criteria.

A number of machine-readable data bases are commercially available. Four of the more important of these are: the CRSP tapes produced by the Center for Research in Security Prices at the University of Chicago; the COMPUSTAT tapes produced by Standard & Poor's Corporation in New York; the Value Line Data Base produced by Arnold Bernhard & Co. in New York; and the Media General Data Base produced by Media General in Richmond, Virginia.

The CRSP tapes provide monthly and daily return data. The monthly tapes cover all NYSE stocks from 1926 to the present and provide monthly prices, dividends, and returns for each stock, as well as some descriptive statistics such as the number of shares outstanding and industry classifications. The daily CRSP tapes basically provide the same type of information, only on a daily basis from 1962 to the present, and for both ASE and NYSE companies.

The COMPUSTAT tapes provide financial statement data on over 3000 U.S. companies. The data are taken from annual reports and quarterly reports and cover the past 20 years. In addition, the COMPUSTAT tapes have month-end prices and dividends for the companies' common stock.

The Value Line Data Base essentially provides all the information available in the Value Line Investment Service, which covers some 1700 companies. The data consist of both financial statement data as well as market-related data such as prices and P/E ratios. In addition, the Value Line Data Base contains the forecasts of sales, earnings, dividends, etc., made by the Value Line analysts.

The Media General Data Base provides both financial statement data and market data on nearly 4000 companies.

There are a number of time-sharing services which the investor can use to access the COMPUSTAT, Value Line, Media General, and other data bases. These time-sharing services allow the investor with a microcomputer and a telephone modem to retrieve information from these data bases quickly, easily, and at a reasonable cost. Three of the more important of these time-sharing services are CompuServe, the Dow Jones New Retrieval, and The Source.

Finally, numerous software packages have been developed for microcomputers. Many of these allow the user to screen data bases of securities for any number of criteria the user specifies. An updated data base may be mailed to the user periodically (typically monthly) on a floppy diskette, or the user may create his own data base by accessing the large data bases available on a time-sharing system. It is impossible for a textbook to be current on the most recent developments in the rapidly changing microcomputer area. Investors will simply have to read the advertisements in the financial and software press to identify the specific software and data base services that fit their needs.

8-5 SUMMARY

This chapter has presented some of the tools used by investors and security analysts. Several techniques for calculating historical growth rates were presented. First, the simple mechanics of calculating the geometric mean growth rate of a variable between two points in time were reviewed. Unfortunately, the growth rate determined by this procedure is very sensitive to the choice of the starting and ending points. Consequently, "normalized" growth rates are frequently utilized instead. These normalized growth rates are generally based on using average values for the starting and ending points, where the averages are based on three or four observations centered around the starting and ending points, respectively. In addition, a comparison between the geometric mean growth rate and the arithmetic mean growth rate was presented. It was shown that the geometric mean will always be equal to or less than the arithmetic mean. Also, for most problems which deal with growth rates and rates of return, the geometric mean growth rate or rate of return is more appropriate than the arithmetic mean.

Certainly one of the most useful tools available to the analyst is regression analysis, which is based on a model of the following form:

$$Y_i = \hat{A} + \hat{B}X_i + \hat{e}_i$$

The Y variable is said to depend upon the X variable—that is, changes in X can explain changes in Y. While procedures for calculating the regression coefficients $\hat{A}$ and $\hat{B}$ are not conceptually difficult, the actual computations can become tedious. Therefore, most regressions are performed by computers.

The regression model itself has many useful applications in finance. For example, a security's historical beta is equal to the $\hat{B}$ based on a regression of the security's returns against the returns for a market index. Other applications include trying to identify the structural relationship between two variables—for example, the relationship between housing starts and mortgage rates presented in the text. Regression was also shown to be a useful method of estimating normal growth rates. However, we should point out that this powerful tool, like any tool, must be properly used in order for it to provide meaningful results.

Finally, three simple time-series models were introduced: the random walk model, the average-growth model, and the arithmetic mean model. These models are useful as benchmarks for evaluating the predictions of more complex models such as the Box Jenkins models or regression models. If the more complex models do not provide better forecasts than these simple benchmark models, it makes sense to use the simpler model.

Before any analysis of securities can begin, the investor must have access to a variety of information. The starting point is the company's financial statements. However, there are many types of information which may be important in the overall analysis. Therefore, the Appendix to this chapter lists a number of different sources of information. This appendix will at least put the investor on the right path for finding the necessary information.

SUGGESTED READINGS

Good textbooks dealing with regression analysis are:

J. Neter, W. Wasserman, and M. Kutner, *Applied Linear Regression Models*, Irwin, Homewood, Ill., 1983.

R. Fogler and S. Ganapathy, *Financial Econometrics*, Prentice-Hall, Englewood Cliffs, N.J., 1982.

The following are good references on time-series forecasting:

C. R. Nelson, *Applied Time Series Analysis for Managerial Forecasting*, Holden-Day, San Francisco, 1973.

G. Box and G. Jenkins, *Time-Series Analysis: Forecasting and Control*, rev. ed., Holden-Day, San Francisco, 1976.

After you have become reasonably proficient at these statistical forecasting techniques, but before you attack a real-life forecasting problem, read:

F. Black, "The Trouble with Econometric Models," *Financial Analysts Journal* (March/April 1982).

Many new software packages are being developed for microcomputers which have investment applications. Some of the more common applications are charting (technical analysis), portfolio management, and accessing data bases for fundamental data such as sales, earnings, and *P/E* ratios. The latter packages generally provide methods for screening stocks based on a number of criteria—for example, you might want to screen out all stocks that have low *P/E* ratios and high dividend yields. To find the most recent investment software packages, the following sources will be useful:

Wall Street Computer Review, published bimonthly, 150 Broadway, New York, N.Y. 10038.

W. F. Sharpe, "Microcomputer Perspectives," a regular column in the *Financial Analysts Journal*.

PC World, published monthly, P.O. Box 4700, Bergenfield, N.J. 07621.

PC Magazine, published monthly, P.O. Box 13848, Philadelphia, Pa. 19601.

Softalk, published monthly, Box 60, North Hollywood, Calif. 91603.

QUESTIONS

1 Can you calculate a geometric mean growth rate if either the starting or ending value is a negative number?

2 In calculating the rate of change in the consumer price index over time, would you want to consider the arithmetic mean or geometric of annual CPI changes? Why?

3 In calculating the average inflation rate from 1973 to 1983, what special problems might you encounter and how might you attempt to solve them? (Hint: 1973 included the last phases of Nixon's wage and price controls.)

4 Describe three different techniques for normalizing growth rates.

5 In a linear regression model, define the dependent variable, the independent variable, and the regression coefficients.

6 What assumptions does OLS make concerning the error terms?

7 Show that if $\hat{B} = 0$, then R^2 must also equal zero. Interpret this result.

8 In many statistics textbooks the equations for $\hat{A}$ and $\hat{B}$ (called the "normal equations") are frequently written as

$$\hat{A} = \frac{\sum Y_i - \hat{B}\sum X_i}{N}$$

$$\hat{B} = \frac{N\sum Y_i X_i - \sum Y_i \sum X_i}{N\sum X_i^2 - (\sum X_i)^2}$$

Show that these two equations are equivalent to Equations (8-6) and (8-7) in the text.

9 What does a beta of 1.3 mean?

10 How might you estimate an ex ante beta? (Hint: You might want to review Chapter 4.)

11 Suppose you performed two regressions. The first regression involved inflation against government deficits and resulted in an intercept term of 2%. The second regression involved daily beer consumption as a function of age and resulted in an intercept term of two beers. What is your interpretation of the intercept terms for these two regressions?

12 If the $t(\hat{B})$ values for the two regressions in Question 11 were 2.4 and 1.3, respectively, what conclusions might you draw about the relationships between inflation v. deficits and beer consumption v. age? (Assume both regressions were based on large samples.)

13 In what sense does R^2 measure how well the regression explains changes in the dependent variable?

14 In using regression to compute growth rates, why is $\hat{B}$ equal to the continuously compounded growth rate?

15 Suppose you wanted to use regression to estimate the growth rate of EPS and the EPS series included deficit earnings. Does this present any special problems? How might you solve these problems?

16 What are some of the uses of computers in security analysis?

17 What functions of the analyst can computers not perform?

18 What is the difference between the MSE for the arithmetic mean model and the variance of the time series itself?

19 Describe how a large investment organization might utilize time-series techniques to evaluate the forecasting ability of their security analysts.

20 Frequently, cause-effect relationships are contemporaneous—that is, the outcome for the forecast variable depends upon the outcome for the explanatory variable in the same time period. What problems does this create for the person trying to predict the forecast variable?

21 Can you think of any cause-effect relationships that might be lagged as opposed to contemporaneous?

PROBLEMS

1 Based on the data presented in Table 7-7 in Chapter 7,
   a Compute the geometric mean growth rate for Armstrong's EBIT from 1979 through 1982.
   b Compute the geometric mean growth rate for Armstrong's net sales for the 2 years from the end of 1980 through 1982.

2 Listed below are the annual rates of return generated by the S&P 500 for the 10 years 1969 through 1978 as reported by the Ibbotson and Sinquefield study (see Table 3-6):

Year	S & P 500 annual return, %
1969	−8.50
1970	4.01
1971	14.31
1972	18.98
1973	−14.66
1974	−26.48
1975	37.20
1976	23.84
1977	−7.18
1978	6.56

a Compute the value relative for an investment in the S&P 500 index over the 10-year period 1969–1978 and the geometric mean over this time period. (Hint: Make the starting value at the *beginning* of 1969 equal to 1.0.)

b Compute the arithmetic mean of the returns for the S&P 500 over this time period.

c Which is the better estimate of the average return an investor would have earned from stocks during this time period, the arithmetic mean or the geometric mean return?

3 Performance Measurement Inc. (PMI) is evaluating six portfolio managers. Listed below are the average returns $\bar{r}_p$ generated by these managers and the betas of their portfolios:

Fund manager	Average portfolio return $\bar{r}_p$, %	Portfolio beta β_p
1	10	.9
2	12	1.1
3	9	.9
4	6	.6
5	13	1.2
6	14	1.5

PMI has decided to evaluate these managers by regressing their portfolio's average return against the portfolio's beta, i.e.,

$$\bar{r}_p = \hat{A} + \hat{B}\beta_p + \hat{e}_p$$

a Compute the regression equation.

b What is your interpretation of $\hat{A}$ and $\hat{B}$?

c Compute the residuals $\hat{e}_p$ for each portfolio and calculate the R^2 for the regression. What is your interpretation of the R^2?

d Is the relationship between average portfolio return and portfolio beta statistically significant?

e Based on this analysis, which portfolio manager demonstrated the best performance?

4 Listed below are the sales (in $ billions) of American International Steel for the years 1971–1983.

Year	Sales	Year	Sales
1971	10.5	1978	16.3
1972	11.3	1979	17.8
1973	12.7	1980	17.9
1974	10.4	1981	14.2
1975	11.5	1982	10.7
1976	14.2	1983	16.8
1977	15.7		

    a What is the geometric mean and the arithmetic mean growth rate for the entire time period 1971 through 1983?

    b What is the geometric mean growth rate for the 10 years 1973–1983 and for the 10 years 1972–1982?

    c Estimate a "normal" growth rate of sales using the 3-year average method and the regression method for the entire time period.

5 Listed below are the EPS for General Jump Co. for the years 19X0 through 19X6.

    a Compute a forecast for each year beginning with 19X1 using the random walk model and the average-growth model.

    b For each model compute the forecast error by year and the mean square error. (Use 16.5% for the growth rate in the average-growth model.)

    c Which model works better and why?

Year	19X0	19X1	19X2	19X3	19X4	19X5	19X6
EPS	1.00	0.60	0.55	0.55	0.50	2.70	2.50

6 Repeat Problem 5 using the data listed below for General Gro, Inc.

Year	19X0	19X1	19X2	19X3	19X4	19X5	19X6
EPS	1.00	1.20	1.45	1.78	2.01	2.20	2.50

7 Listed below are disposable personal income in billions of dollars (DPI) and unit auto sales in millions for the 1970s.

    a Estimate a regression equation where auto sales is the dependent variable and DPI is the independent variable.

    b Given the *actual* DPI for 1980, what would be your forecast for auto sales for 1980?

    c What additional information might you want to consider in forecasting auto sales?

Year	DPI	Auto sales	Year	DPI	Auto sales
1970	685.3	6,547	1976	1194.4	10,110
1971	751.8	8,585	1977	1311.5	11,185
1972	810.3	8,824	1978	1462.9	11,312
1973	914.5	9,658	1979	1641.7	10,669
1974	998.3	7,331	1980	1821.7	?
1975	1096.1	8,640			

8 Pick a stock followed by Value Line that is of interest to you. Analyze Value Line's EPS estimate for the upcoming year. Compare this estimate with an estimate based on the average-growth model using the last 5 years' EPS data to estimate the growth rate. Does Value Line's estimate differ significantly from the forecast of the average-growth model, and if so, are there any obvious reasons why?

APPENDIX: Sources of Information

One of the first steps in the process of analyzing securities and forming portfolios is assembling the relevant information. This appendix is designed to aid this process by identifying potential sources of information. These sources are divided into four general categories: macroeconomic information, industry-specific information, general market information, and company-specific information. The reader should bear in mind that this appendix is not meant to be an exhaustive listing of all possible sources of information. Rather, the sources cited represent some of the more commonly used references and should at least direct the reader to the right section of the library where many more references may be found.

8A-1 SOURCES OF MACROECONOMIC DATA

Many of the sources of information on macroeconomic data are prepared by various government agencies. Some of these are:

Economic Indicators   This is a monthly publication prepared by the President's Council of Economic Advisors. It provides both monthly and annual data on GNP accounts, employment, production, various price indexes, and a number of other macroeconomic variables.

Federal Reserve Bulletin   This is a monthly publication of the Board of Governors of the Federal Reserve System. It provides the most thorough coverage of monetary data, such as the various definitions of the money supply, aggregate member-bank reserves, federal open-market transactions, and other statistics regarding commercial banks. It also provides data on corporate profits, corporate finance, interest rates, and some stock market data. In addition, it provides data on GNP accounts, employment, and international finance. The *Federal Reserve Monthly Chart Book* presents graphs of many of the data series contained in the *Federal Reserve Bulletin.*

Each of the Federal Reserve district banks also publishes monthly reviews in addition to other periodic reports. The most widely followed of these monthly reviews is produced by the St. Louis Federal Reserve Bank. Other sources of monetary data and comments on monetary policy are the periodic reports published by the major commercial banks, such as Chase Manhattan and Citicorp (both of New York) and the Continental Illinois Bank and Harris Trust and Savings Bank (both of Chicago). Interested investors can get on the mailing lists of the Federal Reserve district banks as well as those of the large commercial banks and receive their reports free of charge.

Survey of Current Business   This is a monthly publication of the U.S. Department of Commerce. It provides data on all segments of GNP and national income accounts, as well as employment, interest rates, and foreign economic statistics. It also provides data on industrial production for various segments of the economy—thus, it is an excellent source for industry data. Every other year a supplement called *Business Statistics* is published which contains more extensive historical data.

Business Conditions Digest   This is a monthly publication of the Department of Commerce's Census Bureau. Its most notable feature is that it provides data on the economic indicator series developed by the National Bureau of Economic Research. These indicator series contain the well-known index of 12 leading indicators, as well as the index of coincident indicators and the index of lagging indicators.

8A-2 SOURCES OF INDUSTRY DATA

In addition to the *Survey of Current Business* mentioned above, there are a number of sources of industry data. By far the most important source is *Standard & Poor's Industry Survey*. This publication provides data on approximately 70 different industries. In addition to historical data, the *Industry Survey* provides an analysis of each industry's current prospects and information on the leading companies in each industry.

Although better known for information concerning individual companies, the *Value Line Investment Survey* also provides some industry data as well as a current analysis of the industry's prospects. This information can be found at the beginning of each section of *Ratings and Reports* just before the individual reports on each company in the industry. However, the aggregated industry data are somewhat sketchy.

For those investors who have the time and the interest, a great deal of industry data can be collected from trade associations and industry publications. Most industries have formed a trade association which gathers data for the industry. Frequently the trade association will publish these data as well as articles of current interest concerning the industry in a monthly or quarterly magazine. One example would be the banking industry's American Banker's Association, which publishes the *American Banker*. The easiest way to find out about such publications is to ask the management of the company you are interested in if the firm belongs to such a trade association.

In addition, an excellent starting point for collecting data may be an in-depth industry report prepared by a major brokerage firm. These reports will frequently present historical industry data, give references to sources of industry information, provide a current analysis of the industry's prospects, and discuss the leading firms in the industry.

8A-3 SOURCES OF GENERAL MARKET DATA

Several of the macroeconomic data sources mentioned earlier contain information on the securities markets—the most important being the *Federal Reserve Bulletin* (particularly interest rate, bond, and money market data) and the *Survey of Current Business*. There are, however, a number of other important sources of general market data.

Wall Street Journal   This is the world's largest-circulation daily newspaper. In addition to excellent news coverage, the *Journal* provides complete daily listings of prices for all NYSE, ASE, and OTC stocks, as well as money market rates, corporate and government bond prices, option prices, mutual fund prices, and the levels of all the major stock market indexes. It also reports the latest dividend and earnings announcements.

Barron's This is a weekly publication which has the most complete listing of weekly prices for all financial markets. It provides information on many stock market indicator series, as well as information on commodities, foreign securities, and options.

New York Stock Exchange Fact Book This is an annual publication of the NYSE. It is an excellent source of information concerning NYSE trading activity.

Amex Databook This book has been published sporadically (e.g., 1969, 1973, and 1976). The latest edition (1983) is titled the *Amex Statistical Review*. These publications contain a variety of information on ASE trading activity.

Statistical Bulletin This is a monthly publication of the SEC that contains data on the securities markets. It includes trading volume on all the exchanges as well as the OTC market. In addition, it includes data on prices, volatility, liquidity, and new issues.

Annual Report of the SEC This publication contains historical data for many of the items included in the *Statistical Bulletin*, as well as comments on the SEC's regulatory activities during the year.

There are a number of other sourcess of general market data. Among these are: *Standard & Poor's Trade and Security Statistics*; *Standard and Poor's Daily Stock Price Record*; *Barron's Market Laboratory*; the *Dow Jones Investor's Handbook*, the *Dow Jones Commodities Handbook*, and the *Dow Jones Stock Options Handbook*. Finally, one should not overlook the general market reports issued by brokerage firms. These will frequently provide hard data on the security markets as well as soft opinions as to the direction of the markets.

8A-4 SOURCES OF COMPANY-SPECIFIC DATA

The most important sources of data on individual companies are the firm's annual and quarterly reports as well as any recent prospectus. Additional information can be found in the 10-K report, 10-Q report, and other reports which the company must file with the SEC. Most, if not all, of these reports can be obtained directly from the company by writing the company treasurer. The address of the company can be found in a variety of sources, including the *Value Line Investment Survey*, *Standard & Poor's Stock Reports*, and *Moody's* manuals (all of which are discussed below), as well as *Standard & Poor's Register of Corporations, Directors and Executives*.

The annual report contains the firm's financial statements for the year. In addition, annual reports generally contain a description of the company's operations and a summary of historical financial data. The quarterly reports provide an income statement for the most recent quarter as well as comments from management regarding recent operations and occasionally forecasts concerning the next quarter's operations. A prospectus is required when the firm wishes to issue additional securities. This document will contain the most recent financial statements as well as a great deal of information regarding the firm's operations, key management personnel, and other items of potential interest to investors.

A number of commercial publications provide information on individual companies. The more important of these publications are generally available in your local library and are described below.

Standard & Poor's Stock Guide This is a monthly publication which provides selected information on most publicly traded stocks. Figure 8A-1 illustrates this information. While the information on each company is relatively limited, the *Stock Guide* does provide a quick and easy reference for nearly all actively traded stocks.

96 Gam-Gen

Standard & Poor's Corporation

¶S&P 500 ●Options Index	Ticker Symbol	Name of Issue (Call Price of Pfd. Stocks)	Market	Com. Rank. & Pfd. Rating	Par Val.	Inst. Hold Cos	Inst. Hold Shs. (000)	Principal Business	Price Range 1971-83 High	1971-83 Low	1984 High	1984 Low	1985 High	1985 Low	May Sales in 100s	May, 1985 Last Sale Or Bid High	Low	Last	%Div. Yield	P-E Ratio
1	GAMBY	Gambro AB Cl'B'ADR	OTC	NR	[51]....	1	18	Devices/sys for medical indus	47¼	22½	30	8⅞	10⅛	7¾	553	9⅜	8	8⅜B	0.3	1
2	GAMA	Gamma Biologicals	OTC	NR	10¢	9	257	Blood transfusion prod	17¼	2⅞	10½	6½	11½	7¼	3848	11½	9½	11B	0.9	48
3	GANDF	Gandalf Technologies	OTC	NR	No	16	1444	Electr data communic prod	21¾	8⅝	14	9¼	12¾	5½	4097	8	5½	6¾B	...	12
¶4	GCI	Gannett Co	NY,B,M,Ph	A+	1	388	61124	Newspapers: TV/radio:adv	48	7¼	50¾	33⅜	62⅛	47	28851	61½	56½	61¼	2.4	19
5	GPS	Gap Stores[54]	NY,M,P	B+	5¢	43	2977	Apparel specialty stores	45¼	3¾	23⅝	17½	27¼	20½	3980	27¼	24	26⅝	1.9	21
6	GAN	Garan Inc	AS	B+	1	21	775	Knitted/woven apparel	32¼	3¾	33	24⅜	30⅛	25½	730	29¼	26	27½	4.4	10
7	GMEX	Garcia's of Scottsdale	OTC	NR	1¢	3	177	Mexican food restaurants	15⅞	5¾	8⅜	1⅝	3⅝	1¾	5476	3	2	2⅞B	...	d
8	GLJ	Gates Learjet	AS	↓B—	1	13	1238	Mfr business jet aircraft	27¾	⅞	18⅞	10	13¾	7⅞	1287	10⅛	7⅞	9⅛	...	d
9	GMT	GATX Corp	NY,B,M,Ph	B	62½¢	85	8365	Railcar leas'g/mfg:shipping	65	20½	34½	25¾	37½	27¾	3153	30¼	27¾	29⅜	4.1	10
10	Pr	$2.50 cm Cv Pfd (63)vtg	NY,M	BBB+	1	2	.3	cap eq fin'g:ind'l eq:tank	80	28½	44	33¼	47¼	36¾	62	39	36¾	38¼B	6.5	..
11	Pr A	Adj[56]9.50%cm Cv Pfd([57]50)	NY	BBB+	1	2	105		50	50	51⅝	49¼	51½	50	3110	51½	50½	50⅜B	9.4	..
12	GYL	Gaylords National[59]	AS	B—	10¢	2	44	Discount dept/retail stores	20	¾	10⅝	7	10¾	7	1086	9	8½	8¾B	...	15
13●[1]	GCA	GCA Corp	NY,M	B	60¢	73	5846	Semiconductor prod'n eq:lab	39¼	⅜	41¼	19⅛	32⅛	17⅞	20172	25⅞	17⅞	18½	...	7
14	GOI	Gearheart Ind	NY,B,M,Ph	A—	50¢	43	6709	Oil wireline svs & equip	60¾	⅞	30⅝	10⅝	13¾	10⅜	6823	11⅝	10½	11⅛	3.6	22
15	GEC	GEICO Corp	NY,M	B+	1	100	12107	Direct writer of auto insur	64	2⅛	65⅝	48⅞	77¾	57⅛	10425	77¼	68	76⅜	1.3	15
16	GEL	Gelco Corp	NY,M	B+	50¢	51	10008	Fleet management service	37	3⅛	23¼	13⅜	19⅞	14¾	4856	19¾	17	19⅝	2.9	13
17	GSC	Gelman Sciences	AS	B	10¢	7	331	Lab health devices: filters	20	1	16¼	9¾	12⅝	10¼	514	12⅝	11	12⅛	...	17
18	GNL	Gemco Nat'l	AS	B	50¢	2	69	Metal/glass,hosp supl,headwr	11¾	⅛	6¼	2⅝	4⅝	2¾	528	3¾	3⅛	3½	...	d
19	GMI	Gemini II	NY,M	NR	1	...	....	Dual purpose investment co	....	....	....	....	12¼	9⅞	5330	12¼	10¼	11¾	...	..
20	Pr	cm Income share	NY	NR	1	...	....	Com-cap gains:Pfd-income	....	....	....	....	12	10	3532	12	11⅜	11⅞	6.7	..
21	GETC	Gemtec Corp[63]	OTC	B	1	1	26	Jewelry mfg: R.E. contr mgmt	6⅝	⅛	3⅝	2¾	4½	2¾	50	3⅞	3⅝	3⅝B	...	32
22	GY	GenCorp	NY,B,C,M,P,Ph	B—	30¢	107	9119	Tires, plastics, chemicals:TV	38⅛	7⅞	38½	29⅝	47⅞	32⅝	16197	47¼	43	45¾	s3.3	11
23●[2]	GENE	Genentech, Inc	OTC	NR	2¢	72	2339	Health care pr-gene splic'g	59⅜	17⅜	42¼	28¾	56½	34¼	6461	51½	45½	45¾B	...	..
24	GAM	Gen'l Amer Investors	NY,M	NR	1	17	594	Medium sized closed end	24	6⅞	22⅝	15⅞	17¾	15⅛	1418	17¾	16¼	17⅛	1.6	..
25	GBS	General Bancshares	NY,M	A—	2	19	588	Bank hldg: St. Louis, Missouri	38¾	7¾	45¾	29¾	46¼	38½	1791	44¼	40¾	43⅜	2.3	8
26	GBND	General Binding	OTC	B	12½¢	15	858	Mfr business machines & sup	37	7	13¾	7½	15	11	842	15	13¼	15B	2.4	13
¶27	GCN	General Cinema	NY,B,M	A	1	132	13676	Soft drinks:theatre chain	22⅞	⅝	28	16¾	34¾	24¼	6799	32¾	29¾	32⅛	1.2	14
28	Pr A	[68]Ser A cm[69]Cv Stk (NC)	NY,M	NR	1	27	1134	TV & radio stations	22¼	12¾	27	16¾	33½	24⅜	117	31½	29½	31	1.5	..
29	GDC	Gen'l DataComm Ind	NY,M	B	10¢	60	6291	Data communic'n: netwk/eq	16	⅛	21	12½	20½	13	10844	16¼	13½	15	...	14
30	GDF	General Defense	AS	B+	10¢	31	2215	Mfr tank ordnance	25⅛	4⅛	20¾	12½	17¼	13⅝	9154	17¼	13¾	16⅞	5.2	9
31	GDIC	General Devices	OTC	C	1¢	2	13	Engr & tech svs: personnel	7½	1/16	2⅜	1⅝	2⅞	1⅝	503	2¼	2⅛	2⅛B	...	19
¶32●[3]	GD	General Dynamics	NY,B,C,M,P,Ph,Mo	B+	1	283	14872	Aerospace: sub mfr: bldg mtl	61¾	2¾	69¾	42	84	65¾	35626	73¼	67	71¾	1.4	8
¶33●[4]	GE	General Electric	NY,B,C,M,P,Ph	A+	1¼	1126	223751	Lgst mfr electrical eq,mining	58⅞	15	59⅜	48	65¼	55⅝	147027	61¾	58	60⅝	3.6	11
34	JOB	Gen'l Employ Enterpr	AS	B	No	1	30	Personnel placement service	9¾	¾	5¼	2⅝	5	2¾	305	4⅞	4⅜	4⅜	4.6	14
¶35●[3]	GF	General Foods	NY,B,C,M,P,Ph	A	1	385	28849	Leading mfr packaged foods	53½	16	59⅞	45⅛	69¾	53½	24727	69¾	61⅜	69½	3.6	10
36	GGP	Gen'l Growth Pr SBI	NY,M	NR	1	41	2803	Real estate investment trust	47	8¼	31½	23	31¼	5¾	4921	7⅝	6½	7⅜	8.1	7
37	Pr	$1.90cm Cv A Pfd([77]22.71[78]:SF21)	[5]	NR	No	5	158		27½	21¾	31¼	26⅛	30¾	27	3	28	28	27¼B	7.0	..
38	GHO	General Homes	NY	NR	1¢	16	926	Builds single-family homes	19½	9¼	11¾	5¾	9¾	6¼	1540	7¼	6¼	6⅝	...	12
39	GH	General Host	NY,M,P,Ph	B	1	65	10357	Spec food retail/processor	11¾	⅞	14¾	8⅛	14⅛	11¼	14099	14	13	13⅞	2.2	3
40	GHW	General Housewares	NY,M,Ph	B	33⅓¢	13	515	Mfr cookware & giftware	29¾	¼	19½	8⅞	12⅞	8½	1152	10⅞	8½	10	2.4	d
41	GHYD	Gen'l Hydrocarbons	OTC	NR	10¢	2	85	Oil/gas lease acq,dev:mgmt	6⅞	¼	1	¼	½	¼	1194	⅜	¼	¼B	...	d
¶42●[6]	GRL	General Instrument	NY,B,C,M,P,Ph	B+	1	151	15548	Electronic components & sys	66⅞	1⅜	34⅝	15½	22⅞	15¾	22111	19	16⅜	16⅞	1.5	22
43	GMCC	General Magnaplate	OTC	B+	No	2	203	Corrosion/wear-proof coating	16¾	¼	10	8	12⅜	9¼	431	12⅜	11¼	12B	0.4	11
44	GMW	General Microwave	AS	B+	1¢	11	556	Electron measure/control eq	18¼	⅜	17¾	11½	17⅜	13⅛	873	14⅞	13⅜	14½	0.7	12
¶45	GIS	General Mills[85]	NY,B,C,M,P,Ph	A+	75¢	332	27198	Consumer foods,apparel,toys	57¾	14 1/16	60	41⅝	60⅝	47¾	48950	60⅝	52	60	3.7	18

Uniform Footnote Explanations—See Page 1. Other: [1]AS:Cycle 2. [2]CBOE:Cycle 1. [3]CBOE:Cycle 2. [4]CBOE:Cycle 3. [5]NY. [6]Ph:Cycle 3. [51]Par 10 SKR. [52]Approx. [53]⊙$0.50,'84. [54]Name chge to Gap Inc:eff Jun 3. [55]□$9.06,'83. [56]Thru 7-15-85:min 6%,max 12%. [57]Fr 1-15-87. [58]On 7th business day before divd pay date. [59]Zayre Corp offer for com,$8.50 to Jun 5. [60]Subsid pfd in $M. [61]□$1.17,'83. [62]□$0.22,'82. [63]Vote Jul 23 on liquid'n. [64]△$1.72,□$0.30,'81. [65]Excl 0.73M conv restricted stk. [66]⊙$1.35,'85. [67]⊙$2.38,'84. [68]Divd rt $0.06 plus amt pd on com. [69]Cv limit 10% of amt issued. [70]□$0.78,'82. [71]Incl $25 fr sale of shop'g ctrs. [72]$0.11416 cap gains:$0.29175. [73]△$0.09,'81. [74]△$0.32,'82. [75]△$0.45,'83. [76]□$0.05,'84. [77]Restr to 9-30-86(com price equals150%Cv price). [78]To 9-30-85,scale to $21 in'93. [79]Fiscal Feb'82 & prior. [80]△$0.07,□$0.09,'82. [81]Yr Dec'83 & prior. [82]⊙$0.32,'84. [83]Fiscal Jun 82 & prior. [84]⊙$1.13,'84. [85]Plan sell fashion units & spinoff toy group. [86]□$0.35,'82.

Common and Preferred Stocks — Gam-Gen 97

Splits ◆ Index	Cash Divs. Ea. Yr. Since	Dividends Latest Payment Per$	Date	Ex. Div.	Total $ So Far 1985	Ind. Rate	Paid 1984	Financial Position Mil-$ Cash& Equiv.	Curr. Assets	Curr. Liab.	Balance Sheet Date	Capitalization Lg Trm Debt Mil-$	Shs. 000 Pfd.	Com.	Earnings $ Per Shr. Years End	1981	1982	1983	1984	1985	Last 12 Mos.	Interim Earnings Period	$ Per Shr. 1984	1985	Index
1◆	1984	[52]0.024	6-18-85	5-20	[52]0.024	0.02½	0.032	46.1	151.	47.3	12-31-83	21.6	...	±16344	Dc	....	0.79	0.87	P6.68	....	6.68				1
2◆	1977	Q0.02½	4-5-85	3-19	0.05	0.10	0.10	1.50	15.3	3.93	12-31-84	2.71	...	4483	Mr	0.29	0.31	0.30	....	....	0.23	9 Mo Dec△	0.20	0.13	2
3	.....	None Since Public			....	Nil	....	12.2	48.5	15.2	j1-26-85	6.34	...	9916	Jl	0.53	0.73	0.38	[53]0.51	E0.55	j0.61	6 Mo Jan	0.15	0.25	3
4◆	1929	Q0.37	7-1-85	6-10	1.11	1.48	1.28	57.9	393.	277.	3-31-85	247.	...	80165	Dc	2.11	2.26	2.40	2.80	E3.30	2.88	3 Mo Mar	0.44	0.52	4
5◆	1976	Q0.12½	6-17-85	6-3	0.37½	0.50	0.47½	11.7	136.	69.2	5-4-85	26.7	...	8442	Ja	1.55	2.33	2.52	1.45	....	1.24	3 Mo Apr	0.08	d0.13	5
6◆	1963	Q0.30	5-30-85	5-13	0.90	1.20	1.20	38.9	83.7	19.9	12-31-84	9.86	...	3277	Sp	2.91	2.51	3.32	3.63	....	2.86	6 Mo Mar	1.59	0.82	6
7	.....	None Since Public			....	Nil	....	0.63	3.48	8.79	12-31-84	4.79	...	5991	Dc	d0.43	■d0.20	d0.48	d0.33	....	d0.23	16 Wk Apr	d0.03	0.07	7
8◆	1977	0.05	4-27-84	4-10	....	Nil	0.05	4.69	188.	184.	3-31-85	80.6	...	12100	Dc	1.86	1.21	0.04	d0.88	....	d1.06	3 Mo Mar	d0.14	d0.32	8
9	1919	Q0.30	6-28-85	6-6	0.60	1.20	1.20	70.8	782.	221.	3-31-85	1238	1003	13275	Dc	j5.26	2.41	[58]□1.22	2.37	E2.90	2.23	3 Mo Mar	0.74	0.60	9
10	1969	Q0.62½	6-3-85	5-7	1.25	2.50	2.50	Conv into 1.25 shares common				....	203	...	Dc	b1.50	b1.19	b0.33	n/a	....	....				10
11	1984	1.18¾	7-15-85	6-10	3.57½	4.75	3.980	Cv into com of $50 mkt val[58]				....	800	...	Dc	....	....	b0.33	n/a	....	....				11
12	.....	0.05	5-2-79	4-16	....	Nil	....	1.43	43.2	33.0	10-27-84	9.82	...	1288	Ja	▲0.38	0.07	0.87	....	....	0.57	9 Mo Oct△	d0.69	▲d0.99	12
13◆	.....	0.066	3-31-82	3-4	....	Nil	....	3.15	213.	96.1	12-30-84	89.2	...	13741	Dc	1.73	d1.18	0.10	2.10	E2.60	2.04	3 Mo Mar	0.21	0.15	13
14	1960	Q0.10	5-20-85	5-3	0.20	0.40	0.40	27.5	333.	173.	1-31-85	158.	[60]110	★27208	Ja	2.05	1.03	0.40	0.66	E0.50	0.66				14
15	1977	Q0.25	6-28-85	6-3	0.50	1.00	0.88	Equity per shr $22.12			12-31-84	p197.	...	18766	Dc	△3.11	□3.80	△4.48	△5.11	E5.05	4.95	3 Mo Mar	△1.20	△1.04	15
16	1974	Q0.14	4-19-85	3-28	0.28	0.56	0.56	Equity per shr $3.78			1-31-85	2127.	...	13816	Jl	4.67	2.51	■[81]d1.36	•0.94	....	1.53	9 Mo Apr	•0.59	1.18	16
17◆	.....	None Paid			....	Nil	....	1.09	18.0	5.95	1-31-85	9.18	...	2471	Jl	•▲■2.49	0.01	•0.65	•■0.66	....	0.73	6 Mo Jan	•0.12	0.19	17
18	.....	0.12	3-7-70	2-17	....	Nil	....	5.24	36.2	24.3	12-31-84	5.16	...	2534	Dc	0.44	□[82]0.50	0.68	0.05	....	d0.07	3 Mo Mar	d0.07	d0.19	18
19	1985	....			....	Nil	....	....				....	10000	10000	Dc	....	....	....	....	....	....				19
20	1985	Q0.20	6-3-85	4-25	0.20	0.80	....	To Redeem 1-31-97 at $9.30				....	10000	...	Dc	....	....	....	....	....	....				20
21	.....	None Since Public			....	Nil	....	0.94	7.10	3.16	10-31-84	0.39	...	806	Ja	0.22	0.30	0.28	P0.11	....	0.11				21
22◆	1937	Q0.37½	5-31-85	5-9	s0.737	1.50	s1.470	109.	894.	524.	2-28-85	279.	36	21897	Nv	□△[64]2.82	□▲1.09	□▲3.16	0.32	E4.00	0.30	3 Mo Feb	0.06	0.04	22
23◆	.....	None Since Public			....	Nil	....	106.	136.	20.0	3-31-85	14.5	...	[65]16351	Dc	•0.02	0.05	0.08	0.19	....	0.21	3 Mo Mar	0.03	0.05	23
24	1939	⊙[66]0.28	3-5-85	1-15	0.28	⊙0.28	[67]0.67	Net Asset Val $18.18			5-24-85	....	...	14355	Dc	§20.51	§18.84	§21.41	§16.72	....	....				24
25	1913	Q0.25	7-29-85	6-24	0.50	1.00	1.00	Book Value $43.23			3-31-85	38.3	35	2963	Dc	4.80	▲4.41	4.84	■5.04	....	5.37	3 Mo Mar	0.94	1.27	25
26	1975	Q0.09	6-24-85	5-20	0.18	0.36	0.34	2.01	80.4	31.1	3-31-85	19.3	...	±4899	Dc▲■	±1.50	±0.83	±d0.03	±1.30	....	1.18	3 Mo Mar	0.32	0.20	26
27◆	1953	Q0.10	4-30-85	4-2	0.20	0.40	0.34	22.1	122.	173.	1-31-85	302.	...	±p37743	Oc	⊙1.00	⊙1.19	△⊙1.51	⊙△1.95	E2.25	⊙2.07	3 Mo Jan	⊙0.26	⊙0.38	27
28◆	1982	Q0.11½	4-30-85	4-2	0.23	0.46	0.40	Cv into com shr/shr				....	...	p4731	Oc	....	....	....	....	....	....				28
29◆	.....	None Since Public			....	Nil	....	1.05	111.	23.9	12-31-84	★63.6	...	14824	Sp	▲0.14	d0.09	0.25	0.80	E1.10↓	0.94	6 Mo Mar	0.36	0.50	29
30◆	1980	Q0.22	5-21-85	5-1	0.44	0.88	s0.70	19.3	85.4	52.3	1-31-85	★183.	...	★8208	Ja	0.88	1.13	▲1.45	1.74	....	1.82	3 Mo Apr	0.36	0.44	30
31	.....	None Paid			....	Nil	....	0.23	10.4	8.73	3-31-85	4.58	...	2721	Dc	0.11	d0.52	▲■d0.17	•0.12	....	0.11	3 Mo Mar	•0.02	0.01	31
32	1979	Q0.25	5-15-85	4-9	0.50	1.00	1.00	16.8	1675	1074	3-31-85	15.3	...	43206	Dc	2.25	2.41	5.30	8.08	E9.30	8.75	3 Mo Mar	1.52	2.19	32
33◆	1899	Q0.55	7-25-85	5-31	1.65	2.20	2.00	1702	10983.	8517	3-31-85	770.	...	454876	Dc	3.63	4.00	4.45	5.03	E5.50	5.08	3 Mo Mar	1.07	1.12	33
34◆	1984	Q0.05	6-13-85	5-22	0.10	0.20	0.20	1.82	3.65	2.08	12-31-84	0.26	...	1447	Sp	0.87	d0.21	d0.36	0.33	....	0.31	12 Mo Mar	0.19	0.31	34
35	1922	Q0.62½	6-5-85	5-14	1.25	2.50	2.47½	288.	2378	1403	3-30-85	725.	...	p47684	Mr	[70]□4.83	5.73	6.10	□P6.96	E6.95↑	6.96				35
36	1971	Q0.15	7-25-85	6-24	[71]25.45	0.60	[72]0.60	Equity per shr $7.80			3-31-85	13.3	24	10549	Sp	[73]△0.24	[74]△0.03	△[75]0.42	[76]□0.32	....	1.01	6 Mo Mar	△0.11	□△0.80	36
37	1984	S0.95	3-31-85	2-25	0.95	1.90	1.90	Cv into 1 shr com				....	468	...	Dc	....	....	....	b1.05	....	....	Mand SF 300,000 fr Sep'94			37
38	.....	None Since Public			....	Nil	....	Equity per shr $8.92			12-31-84	★276.	...	15000	Sp	d0.04	[79]1.42	1.52	0.75	....	0.53	6 Mo Mar	0.10	d0.12	38
39◆	1974	Q0.07½	4-16-85	3-26	0.141	0.30	0.266	205.	311.	139.	1-27-85	155.	...	18895	Ja	•1.05	[80]□△0.65	[81]0.93	4.87	....	4.87				39
40	1981	Q0.06	6-28-85	6-10	0.12	0.24	0.24	0.42	34.5	14.6	3-31-85	7.52	...	2332	Dc	1.55	1.71	1.76	[82]0.33	....	d0.08	3 Mo Mar	0.29	d0.12	40
41	.....	None Since Public			....	Nil	....	0.36	2.92	2.82	12-31-84	6.87	...	p20213	Dc	•0.01	•[83]0.01	d0.11	△d0.02	....	d0.02				41
42◆	1977	Q0.06¼	6-28-85	5-24	0.31¼	0.25	0.50	71.7	481.	166.	2-28-85	35.6	...	32407	Fb	3.01	3.34	[84]1.16	d0.30	E0.75	d0.30				42
43◆	1984	0.05	10-1-84	9-10	....	0.05	0.05	1.79	3.30	0.69	12-31-84	2.64	...	1076	Je	0.57	0.57	0.05	0.45	....	1.08	9 Mo Mar	Nil	0.63	43
44	1973	S0.05	3-1-85	2-8	0.05	0.10	0.10	0.04	6.69	2.05	12-1-84	6.00	...	1309	Fb	0.54	0.73	1.12	P1.21	....	1.21				44
45	1898	Q0.56	5-1-85	4-3	1.12	2.24	2.14	93.3	1463	1024	2-24-85	446.	...	p44291	My	▲3.90	□▲[86]4.81	▲4.89	4.98	E△3.40	1.69	9 Mo Feb	4.08	0.79	45

◆ **Stock Splits & Divs By Line Reference Index** [1]5-for-4,'84. [2]4-for-3,'81:3-for-2,'82. [4]3-for-2,'81(wi'80),'84(wi'83). [5]3-for-2,'83. [6]6-for-5,'83. [8]2-for-1,'81:Adj for 5%,'83. [13]3-for-2,'81,'83. [17]6-for-5,'81(ex,'80). [22]Adj to 2%,'85. [23]3-for-2,'83. [27]100% dstr of Cv A Pfd'82:2-for-1,'84. [28]2-for-1,'84. [29]2-for-1,'84. [30]3-for-2,'81,'83:Adj to 5%,'84. [33]2-for-1,'83. [34]10%,'81. [35]3-for-2,'85. [42]3-for-1,'81. [43]3-for-1 twice,'81.

FIGURE 8A-1 Sample page from the S&P Stock Guide.

CORPORATE BONDS — **Iow-Iow 71**

Title-Industry Code & Co. Finances (In Italics) / Individual Issue Statistics, Exchange	Ind / Interest Dates	Chgs. 1976 / S&P Quality Rating	Eligible	Times Earn. 1977 / Bond Form	1978 Yr. End / Legality C M N N N t a H J Y	Cash & Eqv / Redemption Provisions: Refund Earliest/Other	Current Assets / Call Price For S.F.	Liabs Date / Call Price Regular	L. Term Debt (Mil $) / Out-st'd'g (Mil $)	Debt % Prop / Underwriter Firm	Year	Interim Times Earn. Period / Price Range 1960-77 High	1960-77 Low	1978 / 1978 High	1979 / 1978 Low	1979 High	1979 Low	Mo. End Price Sale(s) or Bid	Curr Yield	Yield to Mat.
Iowa Beef Processors	*27e*	*7.46*		*10.13*	*11.70 Oc*	*51.0*	*251*	*87.0 8-79*	*86.6*	*60.5*										
Sec Bonds 9⅞s '95	mS15	BBB	X	R	- - - - -	[1]104½	100	±104½	13.3	N4	'70	108	85	101½	96	97	94	94	10.51	10.66
Iowa Elec. Lt. & Pwr.	*75*	*1.89*		*2.24*	*2.23 Dc*	*1.03*	*74.9*	*84.6 6-79*	*195*	*39.7*		*12 Mo Aug*		*2.21*	*2.27*					
1st J 6¼s '96	mS	A	X	R	√- √√√	....	±101.37	±104.43	15.0	M5	'66	106	61¼	77⅝	68⅞	69¼	59½	59¼	10.55	11.91
1st K 8⅝s '99	mN	A	X	R	√- √√√	....	±100.24	±105.83	20.0	S1	'69	109¾	80¼	98⅜	87⅝	88⅛	74½	74⅝	11.56	11.99
1st L 7⅞s 2000	jD	A	X	R	√- √√√	....	100	105.43	15.0	S1	'70	103¾	73⅜	91	81	81¼	68⅛	68⅛	11.56	12.08
1st M 7⅝s 2002	Mn	A	X	R	√- √√√	....	100	±105.78	30.0	E7	'72	101½	71	88¼	78⅜	78⅞	65⅝	65⅝	11.62	12.10
1st R 8¼s 2007	jD	A	X	R	√- √√√	[2]106.83	100	107.68	25.0	F2	'77	97¼	96⅝	97	83⅛	83⅝	68¾	68¾	12.00	12.20
Iowa-Illinois Gas & Elec.	*75*	*2.81*		*2.66*	*3.05 Dc*	*6.16*	*78.7*	*70.6 6-79*	*★252*	*40.1*		*12 Mo Jun*		*4.18*	*4.35*					
1st 3⅜s '83	Jj15	AA	X	CR	√- √√√	....	±100.47	±100.56	8.00	K5	'53	88	60⅛	82⅞	78⅞	83⅛	78¾	80	4.22	10.95
1st 5s '90	Ao15	AA	X	CR	√- √√√	....	±100.51	±102.07	14.6	M5	'60	107	57	74½	68¾	71¾	62¼	64⅛	7.80	10.81
1st 4⅞s '91	Mn	AA	X	CR	√- √√√	....	±100.68	±102.30	14.7	H2	'61	106¾	55	72⅛	66⅛	69¼	59½	61⅜	7.94	10.82
1st 5⅞s '97	jJ15	AA	X	R	√- √√√	....	±100.28	±103.65	22.0	M5	'67	100⅜	58⅞	75⅞	67	69	58	60	9.79	11.07
1st 7⅝s '99	Ao	AA	X	R	√- √√√	....	±100.88	±105.66	15.0	G1	'69	103	71½	91½	81⅜	83⅛	70⅛	72½	10.52	11.10
1st 7⅞s '99	fA15	AA	X	R	√- √√√	....	±100.76	±105.73	20.0	W7	'69	103⅞	73⅝	93⅞	83½	85¼	72	74⅜	10.59	11.10
1st 8¾s 2000	mS	AA	X	R	√- √√√	....	±100.97	±106.77	20.0	M5	'70	111	79⅜	101½	91	92¾	78¼	81	10.80	11.10
1st 9⅜s 2005	jJ	AA	X	R	√- √√√	[3]107.76	100	±108.09	20.0	F2	'75	113	94⅞	105¾	96½	98⅜	81⅜	84¼	11.13	11.26
1st 8¾s 2006	Ao	AA	X	R	√- √√√	[4]108.07	101	±108¾	20.0	S6	'76	107¼	97⅜	101⅝	90½	92⅜	76	78⅝	11.13	11.30
1st 8¼s 2007	Jj15	AA	X	R	√- √√√	[5]106.83	100	±107.69	30.0	M5	'77	101⅛	97⅜	97⅜	85⅝	87⅜	71⅞	74⅜	11.09	11.29
1st 8¾s 2008	mS	AA	X	R	- - √√√	[6]107¼	[7]100	±108.45	20.0	S1	'78	....	....	100	90⅜	92	75¾	78⅜	11.16	11.30
SF Deb 7¼s '93	Jd	A	X	R	√- √√-	....	±100.44	±104.24	16.5	M5	'68	104⅞	65⅞	89	80⅛	80⅝	70¾	71⅞	10.09	11.36
Iowa Power & Light Co.	*75*	*2.84*		*3.29*	*3.61 Dc*	*3.20*	*53.1*	*91.4 6-79*	*457*	*81.4*		*12 Mo Jun*		*3.59*	*3.06*					
1st 2¾s '79	jD	A	X	CR	√√√√√	....	100	100	6.37	H2	'49	91⅝	61⅜	94⅜	91⅛	99⅝	93½	99⅝	2.76	Mat
1st 3¼s '82	Mn15	A	X	CR	√√√√√	....	±100.20	±100.34	8.48	H2	'52	87½	60⅛	84¼	80¾	85	80¾	82¾	3.93	11.27
1st 3⅜s '83	jD	A	X	CR	√√√√√	....	±100.28	100.51	7.25	F2	'53	91⅜	58¼	78⅞	74¾	78⅞	74⅝	75⅜	4.48	11.03
1st 3⅝s '86	Jd	A	X	CR	√√√√√	....	±100.51	±101.12	6.57	H2	'56	91⅜	53⅜	72⅝	68¼	71	66⅛	66⅛	5.48	10.99
1st 3⅝s '88	Jj15	A	X	CR	√√√√√	....	±100.18	±101.13	8.91	F2	'58	90⅜	50¼	69	64	66½	60⅝	60⅝	5.98	11.04
1st 4⅝s '91	Jj	A	X	CR	√√√√√	....	±100.22	±101.91	9.05	F2	'61	105½	53⅜	70⅛	64½	66¼	58⅛	59	7.84	11.13
1st 6⅝s '98	Jj	A	X	R	√√√√√	....	±101.32	±105.13	14.1	F2	'68	103⅛	65	82	72½	74⅛	62⅝	63¾	10.39	11.39
1st 9s 2000	Jj	A	X	R	√√√√√	....	±101.87	±107.66	14.0	F2	'69	111	81⅝	102	92½	94¼	79¾	81⅛	11.09	11.41
1st 7⅝s 2001	jD	A	X	R	√√√√√	....	±100.48	105.89	14.4	F2	'71	101½	71	89¾	80	81⅝	68	69⅛	11.03	11.50
1st 10¾s 2004	fA	A	X	R	√√√√√	[8]107.05	100	±108.90	[9]19.0	D1	'74	116	95¾	112	104½	104⅛	90½	90½	11.88	11.95
1st 8¾s 2006	Ms	A	X	R	√√√√√	[10]108.07	[11]101	±108¾	30.0	S1	'76	104⅛	93⅛	101	89⅝	91⅛	75⅜	76¾	11.40	11.59
1st 8¼s 2007	mS15	A	X	R	√√√√√	[12]106.83	[13]100	±107.69	30.0	K2	'77	100¼	95⅝	98	84¾	86½	71⅛	72⅜	11.40	11.59
1st 9¾s 2009	Jj15	A	X	R	√√√√√	[14]107.28	[15]99.09	±108.79	30.0	L5	'79	....	....	....	....	100¼	85	85	11.47	11.55
SF Deb 4⅝s '89	Ao	BBB	X	CR	√- √√-	....	±100.44	±102.04	7.70	W7	'64	102¾	52	70¾	66½	67⅝	60⅛	60¼	7.68	11.70
Iowa Public Service Co.	*75*	*2.35*		*2.71*	*3.14 Dc*	*6.96*	*66.6*	*57.2 6-79*	*★296*	*40.3*		*12 Mo Jun*		*3.06*	*3.78*					
1st 3½s '81	jJ	AA	X	CR	√√√√√	....	±100.04	±100.12	5.00	H2	'51	91	62½	88½	85½	89½	85⅛	87¾	3.99	11.84
1st 3s '84	Mn	AA	X	CR	√√√√√	....	100	±100.19	7.50	H2	'54	82¼	54	76½	72	75¾	71⅞	72	4.17	11.06
1st 4¼s '88	Ms	AA	X	CR	√√√√√	....	100	±101.38	10.0	H2	'58	98¾	55⅛	72⅜	67⅜	69¾	63⅝	63⅝	6.68	11.03
1st 4⅞s '93	mS	AA	X	CR	√√√√√	....	100	±101.97	12.0	H2	'63	100	49½	65	58⅜	60	51¾	52¾	8.29	11.15
1st 10¾s '95	Mn	AA	X	R	√√√√√	[16]105.10	100	108.49	20.0	B9	'75	121¾	100	113	104¼	105	92½	92½	11.62	11.81
1st 9s 2000	Ao	AA	X	R	√√√√√	....	±100.95	±106.93	25.0	B1	'70	111⅛	86	103	92½	94¼	79¾	81	11.11	11.42
1st 8s 2001	mS	AA	X	R	√√√√√	....	100	±105.80	15.0	H18	'71	105¼	77⅜	94½	83⅜	85⅛	71⅛	72⅜	11.05	11.47
1st 7⅞s 2002	Jd	AA	X	R	√√√√√	....	100	±105.60	17.0	E1	'72	99¼	72	88	77½	79¼	65⅞	67	11.01	11.50
1st 10⅛s 2005	jD	AA	X	R	√√√√√	[17]108.38	100	108.73	25.0	D1	'75	117	99¼	108⅞	101	101⅞	88	88½	11.44	11.52
1st 9s 2006	Mn	AA	X	R	√√√√√	[18]107.45	100	±108.07	25.0	B1	'76	109⅜	98	103⅛	92	93¾	77⅜	78¾	11.43	11.59
1st 8s 2007	fA	AA	X	R	√√√√√	[19]106.63	100	±107.45	25.0	H18	'77	98⅞	94¾	94¾	82⅜	84⅛	69⅛	70⅜	11.37	11.59

Uniform Footnote Explanations—See Page 1. Other: [1]Fr 9-15-80. [2]Fr 12-1-82. [3]Fr 6-1-82. [4]Fr 4-1-81. [5]Fr 1-15-82. [6]Fr 9-1-83. [7]Fr 9-1-81. [8]Fr 8-1-84. [9]Call $0.20M 8-1-79. [10]Fr 3-1-81. [11]Fr 3-1-82. [12]Fr 9-15-82. [13]Fr 9-15-83. [14]Fr 1-15-84. [15]Fr 1-15-85. [16]Fr 5-1-85. [17]Fr 12-1-80. [18]Fr 5-1-81. [19]Fr 8-1-82.

FIGURE 8A-2 Sample page from the S&P Bond Guide.

Standard's & Poor's Bond Guide Figure 8A-2 illustrates the *Bond Guide*. Like its stock counterpart, the *Bond Guide* represents a quick and easy reference for many publicly traded bonds.

Standard & Poor's Stock Reports These are a series of two-page reports on several thousand companies, including all NYSE and ASE traded firms as well as many OTC traded firms. Figure 8A-3 presents a copy of one of these reports. As the reader can see, the *Stock Reports* list key financial statements for a number of years, as well as recent quarterly earnings reports. In addition, an assessment of the firm's current prospects is included.

Value Line Investment Survey This survey provides coverage of approximately 1700 companies. A separate report is provided for each firm, and Figure 8A-4 illustrates one report. In addition to over 15 years of historical financial statement data, Value Line provides forecasts of sales, earnings, and other items for the next 1 or 2 years plus a long-range forecast of 3 to 5 years. Each report includes the Value Line ranking for performance (timeliness) which was mentioned in both Chapter 5 and discussed in more detail in Chapter 13, as well as rankings for safety, financial strength, price stability, price growth persistence, and earnings predictability.

Hart Schaffner & Marx 1102

NYSE Symbol HSM

Price	Range	P-E Ratio	Dividend	Yield	S&P Ranking
Nov. 6'80 14⅜	1980 16-9¾	6	1.00	7.0%	B+

Summary

This leading manufacturer of men's tailored clothing also operates about 275 specialty apparel stores under some 44 recognized names throughout the U.S. Sales and earnings have made good progress in recent periods, and continued favorable demand for the traditional lines and growing emphasis on sportswear and fashion apparel should lead to further moderate growth.

Current Outlook

Earnings for fiscal 1981 should compare favorably with the $2.60 a share estimated for fiscal 1980.

Dividends are at $0.25 quarterly.

Sales for fiscal 1981 should advance moderately from the approximately $675 million anticipated for fiscal 1980. Orders for spring merchandise are ahead of the year-earlier level on both a unit and dollar basis. The planned addition of new retail units should also be beneficial. Margins should be fairly well maintained.

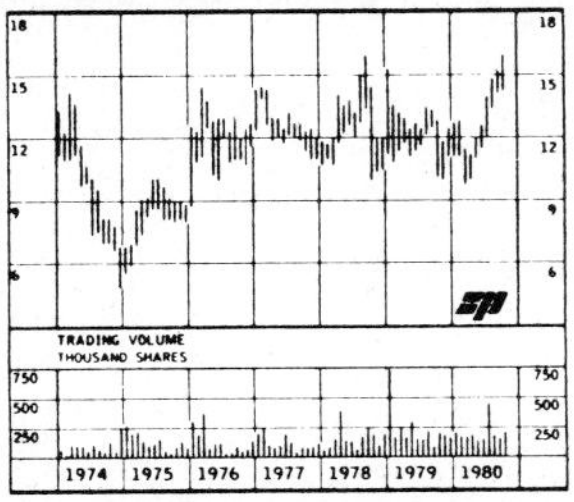

Net Sales (Million $)

Quarter:	1979-80	1978-9	1977-8	1976-7
Feb.	184.6	171.3	165.6	147.8
May	143.3	138.6	133.3	128.0
Aug.	161.3	149.8	146.8	131.3
Nov.		171.0	160.9	160.9
		630.7	606.6	568.0

Sales for the nine months ended August 31, 1980 rose 6.4%, year to year. Net income was up 8.4%, to $1.88 a share from $1.73.

Common Share Earnings ($)

Quarter:	1979-80	1978-9	1977-8	1976-7
Feb.	0.90	0.79	0.68	0.55
May	0.53	0.51	0.44	0.36
Aug.	0.45	0.43	0.38	0.32
Nov.		0.72	0.59	0.57
		2.45	2.09	1.80

Important Developments

Sep. '80—HSM acquired Bishop's, a men's specialty store in Salem, Ore., for an undisclosed amount of cash. This was the first such acquisition following the expiration in June of a consent decree which restricted such moves. The acquisition of Bishop's brings HSM's total number of retail units to 275. Some 12-15 units are planned to be opened in fiscal 1981.

Sep. '80—HSM signed a definitive agreement to acquire Country Miss, a manufacturer of women's apparel in the moderate-to-better price range, for some $12.5 million in cash. Country Miss earned $2.1 million in fiscal 1979 on $35.2 million in sales. This would be HSM's first manufacturing acquisition outside the men's apparel field.

Next earnings report due in late December.

Per Share Data ($)

Yr. End Nov. 30	1980	1979	1978	1977	1976	1975	1974	1973	1972	1971
Book Value	NA	24.70	23.10	21.78	20.68	19.69	19.27	18.66	17.65	16.72
Earnings	NA	2.45	2.09	1.80	1.61	0.97	1.36	1.84	1.61	1.18
Dividends	0.97	0.88	0.80	0.72	0.63	0.60	0.88	0.86	0.80	0.80
Payout Ratio	NA	35%	38%	39%	39%	62%	64%	46%	49%	67%
Prices[1]—High	16	15⅜	16	14½	14½	10⅛	14¼	29¼	32½	31½
Low	9¾	10	10	11	8¾	5½	4⅞	9¾	23¾	25½
P/E Ratio—	NA	6-4	8-5	8-6	9-5	10-6	10-4	16-5	20-15	27-22

Data as orig. reptd. 1. Cal. yr. NA-Not Available.

Standard NYSE Stock Reports Vol. 47/No. 221/Sec. 9 — November 13, 1980 — Standard & Poor's Corp. 25 Broadway, NY, NY 10004

Copyright © 1980 Standard & Poor's Corp. All Rights Reserved

1102 Hart Schaffner & Marx

Income Data (Million $)

Year Ended Nov. 30	Revs.	Oper. Inc.	% Oper. Inc. of Revs.	Cap. Exp.	Depr.	Int. Exp.	Net Bef. Taxes	Eff. Tax Rate	Net Inc.	% Net Inc. of Revs.
1979	631	42.4	6.7%	[1]12.4	9.13	5.11	[2]40.2	47.8%	21.0	3.3%
1978	607	42.2	7.0%	[2]6.7	8.79	5.77	[2]36.0	49.9%	18.0	3.0%
1977	568	37.4	6.6%	11.7	8.30	5.52	30.7	49.6%	15.5	2.7%
1976	535	33.5	6.3%	9.7	7.51	4.27	28.1	50.6%	13.9	2.6%
1975	487	25.5	5.2%	4.9	7.72	6.61	16.3	49.1%	8.3	1.7%
1974	495	32.5	6.6%	9.6	7.71	6.98	23.2	49.2%	11.8	2.4%
1973	469	38.5	8.2%	14.0	6.91	4.87	[2]30.4	47.0%	16.1	3.4%
1972	423	34.1	8.1%	8.0	6.38	4.00	[2]27.2	47.9%	14.2	3.4%
1971	372	26.2	7.0%	9.4	5.90	3.73	19.7	47.5%	10.4	2.8%
1970	363	27.9	7.7%	10.8	5.33	4.19	21.8	47.8%	11.4	3.1%

Balance Sheet Data (Million $)

Nov. 30	Cash	——Current—— Assets	Liab.	Ratio	Total Assets	Ret. on Assets	Long Term Debt	Common Equity	Total Cap.	% LT Debt of Cap.	Ret. on Equity
1979	5.6	281	83.3	3.4	351	6.1%	54.2	207	267	20.3%	10.4%
1978	7.8	279	84.9	3.3	339	5.3%	53.7	194	254	21.2%	9.4%
1977	14.5	279	90.0	3.1	341	4.7%	61.8	183	251	24.7%	8.6%
1976	16.3	259	83.8	3.1	318	4.6%	55.0	174	234	23.4%	8.1%
1975	14.3	231	56.6	4.1	289	2.7%	61.1	166	232	26.3%	5.0%
1974	8.2	261	79.7	3.3	323	3.8%	75.3	163	243	30.9%	7.2%
1973	3.3	238	79.8	3.0	301	5.7%	56.0	160	221	25.3%	10.3%
1972	6.1	210	54.9	3.8	268	5.4%	55.1	153	213	25.8%	9.4%
1971	10.2	196	48.6	4.0	250	4.2%	51.9	143	202	25.7%	7.2%
1970	13.4	194	40.2	4.8	244	4.6%	58.0	140	204	28.4%	8.1%

Data as orig. reptd. 1. Net of curr. yr. retirement and disposals. 2. Incl. equity in earns. of nonconsol. subs.

Business Summary

The company is a major operator of men's and women's apparel stores and the leading manufacturer of men's tailored clothing. Sales and pretax earnings in fiscal 1979 were derived as follows:

	Sales	Profits
Retailing	62%	44%
Manufacturing	38%	56%

The Retail Stores division owns and operates about 241 men's and 29 women's retail apparel stores under names such as Wallachs, Hasting's, Silverwoods, Baskin and Chas. A. Stevens. More than half of the men's units also have sections for women's clothing, (virtually all manufactured by others). Total stores at Nov. 30:

1979	1978	1977	1976	1975	1974
272	274	276	261	249	252

The Hart Schaffner & Marx Clothes division produces men's tailored clothing under the HS&M, Society Brand, Sterling & Hunt and Graham & Gunn brands. It also makes British-designed clothing under the Austin Reed of Regent Street brand, a collection bearing the Jack Nicklaus name, and tailors the Christian Dior collection.

Other manufacturing divisions include Hickey-Freeman, the largest U.S. maker of high-quality men's tailored clothing, and M. Wile, a producer of Johnny Carson Apparel, the Rue Royale Collection by Nino Cerruti, and private label clothing. Jaymar-Ruby, the largest manufacturer of men's high-quality tailored slacks, also makes sportswear.

Dividend Data

Dividends have been paid since 1939.

Amt. of Divd. $	Date Decl.	Ex-divd Date	Stock of Record	Payment Date
0.22	Jan. 15	Jan. 28	Feb 1	Feb. 15'80
0.25	Apr. 8	Apr. 25	May 1	May 15'80
0.25	Jul 16	Jul. 28	Aug 1	Aug 15'80
0.25	Oct 15	Oct. 28	Nov 3	Nov. 17'80

Next dividend meeting: mid-Jan. '81.

Capitalization

Long Term Debt: $53,273,000.

$2 Cum. Conv. Pfd. Stk.: 82,006 shs. ($1 par); conv. into 1.8 com.

Common Stock: 8,408,166 shs. ($2.50 par). Institutions hold approximately 34%. Shareholders: 9,000.

Office—36 South Franklin St., Chicago, Ill 60606 **Tel**—(312) 372-6300 **Pres & CEO**—J. S. Gore **VP-Secy**—C. L. Stewart **VP-Treas & Investor Contact**—M. J. Lies **Dirs**—J. D. Gray (Chrmn), A. R. Abboud, L. S. Bickmore, J. F. Chambers, Jr., P. A. Conley, J. E. Devitt, S. Gore, A. Gunzberg, R. P. Hamilton, D. P. Jacobs, C. Marshall, J. R. Meinert, B. B. Ruby, E. Schlesinger **Transfer Agent & Registrar**—First National Bank of Chicago. **Incorporated** in New York in 1911.

Information has been obtained from sources believed to be reliable, but its accuracy and completeness are not guaranteed. J F K

FIGURE 8A-3 Sample report from the S&P Stock Reports.

Other information provided includes ex ante betas, indexes of insider trading, institutional holdings, and annual growth rates. Suffice it to say, a wealth of information is provided in each report. The report for each company is updated once every 13 weeks, while the performance ranking is updated weekly and can be found in the weekly index to the company reports.

Value Line also produces several other services. The *Value Line OTC Special Situations Service* provides information on smaller companies which are not followed in its main service, the *Investment Survey*. The *Value Line Options and Convertibles* service provides information and recommendations on options and convertible securities.

Moody's Manuals Another major source of information on individual companies is the *Moody's Manuals*. These manuals divide their coverage as follows: major industrial firms; OTC industrial firms; public utilities; transportation firms; banking- and finance-related firms; and one manual covers local, state, and federal government agencies, as well as foreign governments and international agencies.

FIGURE 8A-4   Sample page from the Value Line Investment Survey.

There are a number of other sources of information on individual companies. One such source is the reports produced by brokerage firms which generally contain both historical data, comments on current operations of the firm, and a recommendation as to whether the stock or bond should be bought or sold.

Many magazines provide coverage of publicly traded firms. Among these are *The Wall Street Transcript, Media General Financial Weekly, Forbes*, and *Financial World*. In addition, the investment profession has several trade journals which publish interesting articles. Among these are *Institutional Investor, Pension and Investment Age*, and the *C.F.A. Digest*.

Among the academic journals, the two that are specifically oriented toward investments are the *Financial Analysts Journal* and the *Journal of Portfolio Management*. Other scholarly journals that may be of interest to investors, depending upon their level of academic training, are the *Journal of Finance*, the *Journal of Financial and Quantitative Analysis*, the *Journal of Business*, and the *Journal of Financial Economics*.

As noted at the start of this appendix, no attempt was made to discuss all the possible sources of information. There are simply too many. However, Table 8A-1 lists a number of sources of information and classifies these sources by type of information. This may give the reader additional clues as to where the desired information can be found.

TABLE 8A-1 SOURCES OF INFORMATION

Publication	Frequency of publication	General business information	Industry information	Company information	General security market information	Security price quotations	Data on foreign companies	Data on money markets	Data on mutual funds
American Banker	Daily newspaper	X	X						
American Investor	Monthly periodical	X							
An Analytical Record of Yields and Yield Spreads	Annual							X	
Annual Review of the Bond Market								X	
Audit's Housing and Realty Investor			X						
Audit's Realty Trust Review			X						
Bank and Quotation Record	Monthly				X				
Bank Stock Quarterly	Quarterly		X	X					
Barron's	Weekly newspaper	X	X	X	X	X	X	X	X
Bond Market Review	Quarterly							X	
Bond Market Roundup	Weekly							X	
Business Condition Digest	Monthly	X							
Business Week	Weekly	X	X	X	X		X		
California Business	Weekly	X		X					
Capital International Perspective							X		
Chase Manhattan International Finance	Biweekly	X							

Publication	Frequency	1	2	3	4	5	6	7
Comments on Audit	Weekly							X
Comments on Values	Monthly							X
Commercial and Financial Chronicle	Weekly	X		X	X			
Conference Board Record	Monthly	X						
Conference Board Statistical Bulletin	Monthly	X						
Corporate Financing	Bimonthly	X						
Daily Stock Price Index	Daily					X		
Disclosure Journal			X	X				
Dow Jones Investor's Handbook	Annual				X			
Dun's	Monthly	X	X	X				
Dun and Bradstreet Key Business Ratios	Annual			X				
Economic Indicators	Monthly	X						
European Mutual Funds	Monthly							X
F&S Index of Corporate Change			X					
F&S Index of Corporations and Industries			X					
Federal Reserve Bulletin	Monthly	X		X				X
Federal Reserve Monthly Chart Book	Monthly	X						
Finance	Monthly	X						
Finance World	Weekly	X						
Financial Analysts Journal	Bimonthly	X		X			X	

TABLE 8A-1 SOURCES OF INFORMATION (*Continued*)

Publication	Frequency of publication	General business information	Industry information	Company information	General security market information	Security price quotations	Data on foreign companies	Data on money markets	Data on mutual funds
Financial Dynamics				X					
Financial Executive	Monthly	X		X					
Financial Planner	Bimonthly	X							
Financial Post (Canadian)	Weekly	X							
Financial Times (British)	Daily	X		X	X		X		
Financial Times Yearbook	Annual	X							
Forbes	Biweekly	X							
Fortune	Bimonthly	X							
Growth Stock Digest	Quarterly	X							
Handbook of Basic Economic Statistics		X							
Harvard Business Review	Bimonthly	X							
Institutional Investor	Monthly	X			X				X
International Fund Year Book	Annual								X
Investment Companies International Yearbook	Annual			X					X
Investment Dealers' Digest	Weekly	X							X
Japan Stock Journal	Weekly	X			X				
Johnson's Investment Company Charts									X
Journal of Business	Quarterly	X							
Journal of Commerce	Daily	X							
Journal of Finance	Quarterly	X							

Publication	Frequency							
Journal of Financial and Quantitative Analysis	Quarterly	X						
Journal of Money, Credit and Banking	Quarterly	X						
Journal of Portfolio Management	Quarterly	X						
Key Figures of European Securities	Quarterly					X		
La Vie Française	Weekly	X						
Mergers and Acquisitions	Quarterly	X						
Money Manager	Weekly	X						
Moody's Bond Record			X	X				
Moody's Bond Survey	Weekly		X	X			X	
Moody's Dividend Record			X	X				
Moody's Handbook of Common Stocks			X	X				
Moody's Manuals	Annual		X	X			X	
Moody's Stock Survey				X				
Mutual Fund Performance Monthly								X
National Bond Summary (OTC)					X			
National Observer	Daily	X						
Nation's Business	Monthly	X						
Newsweek	Weekly	X						
New York Times	Daily	X			X		X	X
OTC Market Chronicle	Daily	X						

TABLE 8A-1 SOURCES OF INFORMATION (Continued)

Publication	Frequency of publication	General business information	Industry information	Company information	General security market information	Security price quotations	Data on foreign companies	Data on money markets	Data on mutual funds
Over-the-Counter Securities Handbook				X					
Over-the-Counter Securities Review	Monthly	X							
Penny Stock Handbook				X					
Pocket Data Book		X							
Public Affairs Information Service Bulletins			X						
Retail Automation Report			X	X					
Robert Morris and Associates Statement Studies				X					
S&P's Analysts' Handbook	Annual with monthly supplements			X					
S&P's Bond Guide				X	X	X			
S&P's Called Bond Record				X	X				
S&P's Commercial Paper Reports					X			X	
S&P's Dividend Record				X	X	X			
S&P's Earnings Forecaster				X	X				
S&P's Fixed Income Investor					X				
S&P's Industry Surveys			X	X	X				
S&P's Stock Report				X					
S&P's Outlook	Weekly		X		X				

Publication	Frequency						
S&P's Standard Corporation Descriptions	Daily						X
S&P's Stock Guide					X		X
S&P's Trade and Securities Statistics					X		X
S&P's Transportation Securities					X		
Smith Security Risk Evaluation						X	
Spectrum		X					
Stanford Research Institute Long Range Planning Service Reports						X	
Statistical Abstracts of the U.S.						X	X
U.S. Bureau of the Census						X	
Stock Market Magazine	Monthly					X	
Supply and Demand for Credit	Annual		X				
Survey of Current Business	Monthly			X		X	
The M/G Financial Weekly	Weekly	X			X	X	
Treasury Bulletin	Monthly					X	
U.S. Bureau of Domestic Commerce U.S. Industrial Outlook	Annual					X	
U.S. Business Service United Business & Investment Report							X
U.S. Business Service United Mutual Fund Selector		X					

TABLE 8A-1 SOURCES OF INFORMATION *(Continued)*

Publication	Frequency of publication	General business information	Industry information	Company information	General security market information	Security price quotations	Data on foreign companies	Data on money markets	Data on mutual funds
U.S. Census Bureau Annual Survey of Manufacturers			X						
U.S. Congress Joint Economic Report	Annual	X							
U.S. Mines Bureau Mineral Yearbook	Annual		X						
U.S. News and World Report	Weekly	X							
U.S. Office of Business Economics Business Statistics	Biennial	X							
U.S. President Economic Report . . . together with the annual report of the Council of Economic Advisors	Annual	X							
United Mutual Fund Selector			X	X					
Value Line Convertible Survey			X	X	X				
Value Line Investment Survey		X	X	X	X				
Vickers Guide to Insurance Company Portfolios			X						
Walkers' Manual of Far-Western Securities				X					
Wall Street Journal	Daily	X	X	X	X	X	X	X	X
Wall Street Transcript	Weekly	X	X	X	X	X	X	X	X
Weekly Bond Buyer	Weekly							X	

CHAPTER 9

THE TIME VALUE
OF MONEY

After reading this chapter, you should:

1 Understand the concept of the time value of money
2 Be able to solve compounding and discounting problems for single cash flows
3 Be able to solve time value of money problems involving multiple cash flows
4 Know how to solve problems involving nonannual and continuous rates of return

Most readers should be familiar with the time value of money concept and should already know how to solve compounding and discounting problems. For them, this chapter will merely be a review. However, our experience has been that it never hurts to review this important topic. Readers for whom this material is new will want to study this chapter carefully because the time value of money concept is central to understanding security prices.

The time value of money concept simply argues that a *dollar received today is worth more than a dollar received tomorrow.* This follows from the idea (introduced in Chapter 1) that investors will postpone current consumption and invest only if their future consumption opportunities will be larger as a result of their investment.

Alternatively, a dollar today *must* be worth more than a dollar tomorrow given the fact that one can invest the dollar today and start earning interest immediately. Consequently, it takes more future dollars to equal the value of a current dollar.

While the time value of money is a relatively simple idea, we need to be able to quantify this concept. To do this the mathematical procedures of *compounding and discounting* are used. While students sometimes have difficulties with time value of money problems, these are actually relatively easy problems to solve once one correctly identifies the sequence of the cash flows—as we shall see, the mathematics of compounding or discounting cash flows is not particularly difficult.

9-1 COMPOUNDING A SINGLE CASH FLOW

Suppose you invest $100 today. If your investment earned *simple interest* at the rate of 10% per year, the future value of your investment would be the original $100 plus $10 for every year the money was invested at 10% simple interest. Thus, if you invested the $100 for 3 years, you would have $130 at the end of the time period.

Compounding works differently. When investments are made at *compound interest rates*, one earns "interest on interest." That is, interest is paid in one period on interest that has been earned in previous periods. To see this, consider the example of investing $100 for 3 years, but now at 10% interest compounded annually. The calculation of the annual interest and the future value of the investment is as follows:

Time period	Beginning amount	Interest earned	Ending amount
1	$100.00	$100.00 × .10 $ 10.00	$100.00 +10.00 $110.00
2	$110.00	$110.00 × .10 $ 11.00	$110.00 +11.00 $121.00
3	$121.00	$121.00 × .10 $ 12.10	$121.00 +12.10 $133.10

Thus, at the end of 3 years the $100 initial investment compounded at 10% annually would be worth $133.10. Note that this is $3.10 more than the $130 ending amount if the investment had been made at 10% simple interest. This "extra" $3.10 represents interest earned on interest.

There is a very simple formula for calculating the future value (ending value) of an investment made at some compound rate of interest. Note in the example above that the value of the initial investment at the end of 1 year was $110.00. This amount can be written as $100(1.10). The $121 amount at the end of 2 years can be written as $110(1.10), or as $100(1.10)(1.10), or as $100(1.10)^2$. Similarly, the $133.10 amount at the end of 3 years can be written as $121(1.10)$, or as $100(1.10)(1.10)(1.10)$, or as $100(1.10)^3$. The pattern should be obvious. One can generalize the procedure for calculating the future value of a single cash flow compounded annually as follows:

Let C_0 = initial cash flow or investment

r = stated annual rate of interest or return

n = life of investment

C_n = value of C_0 at end of n years

Then,

$$C_n = C_0(1 + r)^n \tag{9-1}$$

While there may not be much difference between simple interest and compound interest for short time periods, there can be a substantial difference if the life of the investment is long. For example, $100 invested at 10% simple interest would be worth

$240 at the end of 14 years (the initial $100 plus $140 of interest). By comparison, $100 invested at 10% compounded annually would be worth $379.75 at the end of 14 years. Using Equation (9-1),

$$C_{14} = \$100(1.10)^{14} = \$379.75$$

The computations involved in compounding problems are not difficult. One simply has to solve for $(1 + r)^n$ and then multiply this amount times the initial cash flow C_0. The amount $(1 + r)^n$ will be called the *future-value compound factor* ($FVCF_{r,n}$), where the subscripts r and n denote the rate and the number of time periods.

$$FVCF_{r,n} = (1 + r)^n \qquad (9\text{-}2)$$

Thus, Equation (9-1) can be written as

$$C_n = C_0 \cdot FVCF_{r,n} \qquad (9\text{-}1a)$$

With the advent of hand-held calculators, the FVCF is easy to calculate. If one has a calculator with a y^x key, simply key in $(1 + r)$ first, then the number of years, and push the y^x key.[1] Thus the future-value compound factor for 14 years at 10% is

$$FVCF_{10\%,14} = (1.10)^{14} = 3.7975$$

Given the $FVCF_{10\%,14}$, the previous problem of determining the future value of $100 invested at 10% compounded annually for 14 years could be solved using Equation (9-1a).

---

[1] If you do not have a y^x key but do have a logarithm and antilog key, the problem can be solved using logarithms, as follows.

$$FVCF_{r,n} = (1 + r)^n$$
$$\ln(FVCF_{r,n}) = n \ln(1 + r)$$
$$FVCF_{r,n} = \text{antiln}[n \ln (1 + r)]$$

Thus, using a calculator, first take the log of $(1 + r)$, multiply this by the number of compounding periods n, and then take the antilog of the product. (The procedure is the same whether one uses natural logarithms or logarithms to the base 10.)

Using natural logarithms, the FVCF for 10% compounded for 14 time periods would be calculated as follows:

$$FVCF_{10\%,14} = (1.10)^{14}$$
$$\ln(FVCF_{10\%,14}) = 14 \ln(1.10) = 14(.0953) = 1.3343$$
$$FVCF_{10\%,14} = \text{antiln}(1.3343) = 3.7975.$$

Using logarithms to the base 10,

$$FVCF_{10\%,14} = (1.10)^{14}$$
$$\log (FVCF_{10\%,14}) = 14 \log(1.10) = 14(.0414) = .5795$$
$$FVCF_{10\%,14} = \text{antilog}(.5695) = 3.7975.$$

$$C_{14} = C_0 \cdot \text{FVCF}_{10\%,14}$$
$$= (\$100)(3.795) = \$379.75$$

For those who do not have access to a calculator, Table I at the end of the text lists the FVCFs for a number of different interest rates and time periods. However, we recommend that these tables not be used, as long as you have a calculator with a y^x key, for several reasons. First, you are just as likely to make an error in locating and recording the number from the table as you are in entering the numbers into a calculator. Second, when working a problem, it is actually faster to use a y^x key than to use the tables. Third, and most important, when tables are used, it is easy to forget how compounding problems are solved mathematically, which will present difficulties when you encounter a situation which requires an interest rate or number of compounding periods which are not listed in the tables.

9-2 DISCOUNTING A SINGLE CASH FLOW

Investors are more frequently interested in determining the current or present value of future cash flows. For example, the present value (current price) of a stock should be equal to the present value of all the future cash flows the investor will receive by owning the stock. To convert future cash flows into present values, we use the procedure of *discounting*. To discount a future cash flow to the present, simply rearrange terms in Equation (9-1) and solve for C_0:

$$C_0 = \frac{C_n}{(1 + r)^n} \tag{9-3}$$

Thus, discounting is the opposite of compounding. When compounding, one *multiplies* current cash flows by $(1 + r)^n$. When discounting, one *divides* future cash flows by $(1 + r)^n$. Frequently, Equation (9-3) is written as

$$C_0 = C_n \times \frac{1}{(1 + r)^n}$$

where the quantity $\dfrac{1}{(1 + r)^n}$ is referred to as the *present-value discount factor* $(\text{PVDF}_{r,n})$.

$$\text{PVDF}_{r,n} = \frac{1}{(1 + r)^n} \tag{9-4}$$

Thus, Equation (9-3) can also be written as

$$C_0 = C_n \cdot \text{PVDF}_{r,n} \tag{9-3a}$$

It is easy to see that the discount factor (PVDF) is simply the reciprocal of the compound factor (FVCF). Thus, one can solve for the discount factor using either a y^x key or logarithms in a fashion similar to solving for the compound factor. In addition, Table II at the end of the text presents various discount factors in a fashion similar to the compound factors presented in Table I. A comparison of these two tables reinforces the notion that the discount factor is the reciprocal of the compound factor. For example, the compound factor for $1 compounded at 8% annually for 4 years is 1.360. The discount factor for $1 received 4 years from the present, discounted at 8%, is .735, which is the reciprocal of 1.360.

To illustrate the procedure for discounting a future cash flow to its present value, consider the following example. Mr. Jones has an offer to buy a piece of paper. This document gives him the right to receive $500 in cash 5 years from now. Mr. Jones, after considering the risk associated with this claim on future cash, decides that 12% is an appropriate rate of return for such an investment. How much will Mr. Jones pay for this claim on the future $500? The answer is $283.71, calculated as follows using Equation (9-3):

$$C_0 = 500 \times \frac{1}{(1.12)^5} = \$500(.567) = \$283.71$$

Alternatively, using Equation (9-1) one can see that $283.71 invested at 12% compounded annually will yield $500 at the end of 5 years:[2]

$$C_4 = \$283.71(1.12)^5 = \$283.71(1.762) = \$500$$

As another example, consider the following problem. You are offered an investment which promises to pay $2000 seven years from now. The cost of the investment today is $1000. What compound annual rate of return will this investment provide? Using Equation (9-3),

$$C_0 = C_n \times \frac{1}{(1 + r)^n}$$

$$1000 = 2000 \times \frac{1}{(1 + r)^n}$$

$$\frac{1}{2} = \frac{1}{(1 + r)^7} = \text{PVDF}_{r,7}$$

One needs to know what rate of return for 7 years results in a discount factor of 0.5. Looking at the 7-year row in Table II, one sees

[2]You may have noticed that some ''rounding off'' is involved in the above illustrations. For example, $500 × .567 equals $283.50, not the $283.71 reported above. This difference occurs because the above examples were worked out by a calculator with nine-digit precision. The $\text{PVDF}_{12\%,5}$ is equal to .567426856, which multiplied by $500 gives the correct answer of $283.71. Thus, still another argument for solving time value of money problems using a calculator instead of tables is the greater precision of the calculator.

	PVDF	
	10%	**11%**
7 years	.513	.482

Thus, this investment promises a return of between 10% and 11%, and closer to 10%. To solve for the exact rate of return, a y^x key can be used by noting that

$$(1 + r)^7 = 2$$
$$(1 + r) = 2^{1/7} = 1.1041$$
$$r = .1041 = 10.41\%$$

Simply find the reciprocal of 7 and use the y^x key to raise 2 to the 1/7 power.

If you do not have access to logarithms or a y^x key, an approximate solution can be determined by *interpolation*. Interpolation is a method of finding a proportionate distance between two points. In this case, the correct answer is between 10% and 11% and occurs when $PVDF_{r,7} = .500$. There is a 1% distance between 10% and 11%; there is a .031 distance between the $PVDF_{10\%,7}$ of .513 and the $PVDF_{11\%,7}$ of .482; and there is a distance of .013 between the $PVDF_{10\%,7}$ of .513 and the $PVDF_{r,7}$ of .500. Given these data, interpolation can be used to determine the proportionate distance between 10% and 11% as follows:

$$1\% \begin{bmatrix} \begin{bmatrix} \text{at } 10\%, \ PVDF_{10\%,7} = .513 \\ \text{at } r, \quad\ \ PVDF_{r,7} \ \ = .500 \\ \text{at } 11\%, \ PVDF_{11\%,7} = .482 \end{bmatrix} .013 \end{bmatrix} .031$$

$$r = 10\% + \frac{.013}{.031}(1\%) = 10.42\%$$

While interpolation will not produce an exactly correct answer (in this example, 10.42% vs. the correct answer of 10.41%), generally it will be close enough.[3]

We can also solve for n, the number of compounding periods, in time value of money problems. For example, at a compound annual rate of 11%, how long does it take for a dollar to quadruple? (This is the same as asking how many years at 11% are required for the compound factor to be 4 or for the discount factor to be .25.) Thus, to solve for n, either Equation (9-1) or Equation (9-3) can be used. Using (9-1),

$$C_n = C_0(1 + r)^n$$
$$\$4 = \$1(1.11)^n$$

---

[3]Interpolation provides only an approximate solution because it assumes that the compounding or discounting function is linear—thus, it solves for the proportionate distance between two points. Since compounding and discounting are exponential functions, interpolation will always yield a higher rate than the true rate. (Can you demonstrate graphically why this is the case?)

Thus, $FVCF_{11\%,n} = 4.0$. Looking down the 11% column of Table I one can see that the number of years is between 13 and 14, and closer to 13 years.

	FVCF 11%
13 years	3.883
14 years	4.310

To solve for n exactly, logarithms can be used.[4]

$$(1.11)^n = 4$$
$$n \ln(1.11) = \ln(4)$$
$$n = \frac{\ln(4)}{\ln(1.11)} = \frac{1.386}{.104} = 13.284 \text{ years}$$

Before continuing, you should

1 Understand the difference between simple and compound interest
2 Know that the compound factor is $(1 + r)^n$ and that the discount factor is simply the reciprocal of this number
3 Be able to construct Tables I and II yourself. To prove you can, generate a 4½% column for Table I
4 Be able to solve for C_0, C_n, r, or n in any compounding or discounting problem for single cash flows

9-3 MULTIPLE CASH FLOWS

So far we have only considered problems associated with compounding or discounting a single cash flow. However, most financial problems are concerned with multiple cash flows. Multiple cash flow problems, in principle, are no different from those we have already considered. One can simply discount (or compound) each individual cash

[4] Solving for n by interpolation yields

$$1 \text{ year} \left[\begin{array}{l} \text{at 13 years, } FVCF_{11\%,13} = 3.883 \\ \text{at } n \text{ years, } FVCF_{11\%,n} = 4.000 \\ \text{at 14 years, } FVCF_{11\%,14} = 4.310 \end{array} \right] .117 \Bigg] .427$$

$$n = 13 \text{ years} + \frac{.117}{.427} (1 \text{ year}) = 13.27 \text{ years}$$

Again, interpolation does not provide the exact answer, but it is probably "close enough." (Can you demonstrate graphically why interpolation will always yield a solution for n which is smaller than the correct answer?)

flow involved in the project and then add the present values (or future values) for all the cash flows. Thus, the procedures are the same, but they can become tiresome as the number of cash flows increases. Fortunately, many types of problems involving multiple cash flows can be substantially simplified. But first, let us look at the general case.

9-3-1 The General Case   First, consider the problem of discounting multiple cash flows. Let P_0 equal the present value (price) of an investment which has n cash flows, each of which occurs at the end of a discounting period. If r is the appropriate discount rate,

$$P_0 = \frac{C_1}{(1 + r)^1} + \frac{C_2}{(1 + r)^2} + \cdots + \frac{C_n}{(1 + r)^n}$$

To illustrate, suppose a potential investment promises to pay $200 at the end of the first year, $300 at the end of the second year, and $600 at the end of the third year. If 13% compounded annually is an appropriate discount rate, what should be the price of this investment? The answer is $827.77, calculated as follows:

$$P_0 = \frac{\$200}{(1.13)^1} + \frac{\$300}{(1.13)^2} + \frac{\$600}{(1.13)^3}$$
$$= \$200(.885) + \$300(.783) + \$600(.693)$$
$$= \$176.99 + \$234.94 + \$415.83 = \$827.77$$

Compounding problems involving multiple cash flows can be handled in a similar fashion. Suppose a person decides to place $150 in a savings and loan association at the beginning of the current year, $200 at the beginning of the second year, and $250 at the beginning of the third year. If the savings and loan pays 6% compounded annually, how much will be in the savings account at the end of the third year? Letting FV_n equal the future value of the savings account, the solution is calculated as follows:

$$FV_n = C_0(1 + r)^n + C_1(1 + r)^{n-1} + \cdots + C_{n-1}(1 + r)^1$$
$$FV_3 = \$150(1.06)^3 + \$200(1.06)^2 + \$250(1.06)^1$$
$$= \$150(1.191) + \$200(1.124) + \$250(1.06) = \$668.37$$

9-3-2 Present Value of Annuities   An annuity consists of a *constant* payment received at the end of each year. If we let P_0 equal the present value of an annuity which pays C dollars at the end of each year for n years,

$$P_0 = \frac{C}{1 + r} + \frac{C}{(1 + r)^2} + \cdots + \frac{C}{(1 + r)^n}$$

where r is the appropriate discount rate.

For example, consider an *annuity* which pays $2500 at the end of each year for 20 years. To find the present value of this annuity would require solving the following equation:

$$P_0 = \frac{2500}{(1 + r)^1} + \frac{2500}{(1 + r)^2} + \cdots + \frac{2500}{(1 + r)^{20}}$$

Solving this would become tedious fast! Fortunately, the above equation can be re-written as

$$P_0 = 2500\left[\frac{1}{(1 + r)^1} + \frac{1}{(1 + r)^2} + \cdots + \frac{1}{(1 + r)^{20}}\right]$$

The sequence of numbers within the brackets represents a *geometric progression*, which is a type of mathematical problem frequently encountered in finance. (Consequently, the Appendix at the end of this chapter illustrates the necessary steps for solving geometric progressions.) The geometric progression in the brackets will be referred to as the *present-value annuity factor* ($PVAF_{r,n}$) at r rate and n years. Using this notation, we can express the present value of any annuity as

$$P_0 = C \cdot PVAF_{r,n} \tag{9-5}$$

where C is the amount of the constant payment. In the Appendix we show that the present-value annuity factor can be simplified to

$$PVAF_{r,n} = \frac{1 - [1/(1 + r)^n]}{r} \tag{9-6}$$

In the above example, where there are 20 payments, and using an 8% discount rate, the PVAF is

$$PVAF_{8\%,20} = \frac{1 - [1/(1.08)^{20}]}{.08} = 9.818$$

Since the annual payments C in the example are $2500, the present value of this annuity would be

$$P_0 = C \cdot PVAF_{r,n} = \$2500(9.818) = \$24,545$$

For those who do not have access to a calculator, Table III at the end of the text lists the $PVAF_{r,n}$ for various discount rates and time periods. It is instructive to note that Table III can be derived from Table II by simply adding the single cash flow PVDFs in a particular column for n years. For example, note in Table III that the present-value discount factor for a 3-year annuity at 10% is 2.487, which is equal to the sum of the first three numbers in the 10% column of Table II. That is:

From Table III		From Table II		
$PVAF_{10\%,3}$	=	$PVDF_{10\%,1}$ +	$PVDF_{10\%,2}$ +	$PVDF_{10\%,3}$
2.487	=	.909 +	.826 +	.751

Of course, this is because the present value of an annuity is simply the sum of the present values of each of the individual cash flows.

9-3-3 Perpetuities

There are some financial assets which promise to pay a constant periodic amount indefinitely or in perpetuity. Many preferred stocks fall into this category as they promise to pay a fixed dividend for the life of the company, which is presumably unlimited.

Under these conditions Equation (9-5), the general equation for annuities, can be written

$$P_0 = C \cdot PVAF_{r,n} = C \frac{1 - [1/(1 + r)^\infty]}{r}$$

Since

$$\frac{1}{(1 + r)^\infty}$$

approaches zero (assuming r is positive), the equation for perpetual annuities becomes

$$P_0 = \frac{C}{r} \tag{9-7}$$

Thus, if a preferred stock pays a $6 annual dividend and the appropriate discount rate is 8%, the price of the preferred stock should be[5]

$$P_0 = \frac{\$6}{.08} = \$75$$

9-3-4 Future Value of an Annuity

Suppose you put $100 into a savings account at the *beginning of each year* for 8 years and the savings account paid 7% compound annual interest. How much would you have in your savings account at the end of the eighth year? The future value of an annuity (FVA) can be expressed as

$$FVA = C(1 + r)^n + C(1 + r)^{n-1} + \cdots C(1 + r)^1$$

---

[5]Most preferred stocks pay dividends quarterly, rather than annually. The adjustments necessary for nonannual discounting and compounding will be taken up in the next section.

Again, we have a geometric progression. Letting the *future-value annuity factor* ($FVAF_{r,n}$) represent the geometric progression, as shown in the Appendix, we can express the future value of an annuity as

$$FVA = C \cdot FVAF_{r,n} \qquad (9\text{-}8)$$

where

$$FVAF_{r,n} = \frac{(1 + r)[(1 + r)^n - 1]}{r} \qquad (9\text{-}9)$$

To solve the above problem, substitute .07 for r and 8 for n so that

$$FVAF_{.07,8} = \frac{(1.07)[(1.07)^8 - 1]}{.07} = 10.978$$

Thus, in our example, the future value of the annuity with $100 payments is

$$FVA = \$100(10.978) = \$1097.80$$

Table IV, at the end of the text, lists the $FVAF_{r,n}$ for various time periods and rates of return.[6]

9-4 NONANNUAL COMPOUNDING AND DISCOUNTING

All the examples we have considered so far have assumed that each cash flow occurred either at the end of a year (discounting problems) or at the beginning of the year (compounding problems). There are, of course, many situations where nonannual cash flows are involved. For example, if a local bank advertises that it pays 8% compounded quarterly on savings deposits, interest will be computed every 3 months. In such cases adjustments must be made to the standard formulas for computing present or future values on an annual basis. Fortunately, the adjustments necessary for nonannual compounding are not difficult to make.

Consider the example of 8% compounded quarterly. The *stated annual rate* is 8%. However, if the stated annual rate of 8% is compounded quarterly, this means that

---

[6]Table IV lists the FVAFs for *beginning of the period compounding*. Some texts will present tables for FVAFs based upon *end of the period compounding*. Each cash flow, based on end of the period compounding, will have one less compounding period than our example. Therefore, the FVAF for end of the period compounding will be less than the FVAF for beginning of the period compounding by a factor of $(1 + r)$. Thus, for *end of the period* compounding,

$$FVAF = \frac{(1 + r)^n - 1}{r}$$

To convert the beginning of period future-value annuity factors listed in Table IV into end of period FVAFs, simply divide the number in Table IV by $(1 + r)$.

the bank will pay 2% compound interest ($\frac{1}{4} \times 8\%$) on deposits held for 3 months. Thus, if a saver deposited $100 at the beginning of the year, after the end of 1 year, or four quarters, the savings account would be worth $108.24, calculated as follows:

1st quarter	$100.00(1.02) = $102.00
2nd quarter	$102.00(1.02) = $104.04
3rd quarter	$104.04(1.02) = $106.12
4th quarter	$106.12(1.02) = $108.24

Thus, 8% compounded quarterly provides an *effective annual rate* of 8.24%. We can generalize the procedures to be used for nonannual compounding or discounting as follows:

Let r = stated annual rate
m = number of compounding periods in a year
n = number of years

Then Equation (9-1), which is used to calculate the future value of money earning compound interest, can be adjusted for nonannual compounding as follows:

$$C_n = C_0(1 + r)^n \qquad \text{annual compounding} \qquad (9\text{-}1)$$

$$C_n = C_0\left(1 + \frac{r}{m}\right)^{mn} \qquad \text{nonannual compounding} \qquad (9\text{-}10)$$

Similarly, Equation (9-3), which is used to calculate the present value of future cash flows discounted at annual rates, can be adjusted for nonannual discounting as follows:

$$C_0 = \frac{C_n}{(1 + r)^n} \qquad \text{annual discounting} \qquad (9\text{-}3)$$

$$C_0 = \frac{C_n}{(1 + r/m)^{mn}} \qquad \text{nonannual discounting} \qquad (9\text{-}11)$$

To illustrate nonannual compounding, suppose that you have $1000 to invest and that you can earn 12% compounded annually at one bank for 10 years and 12% compounded monthly at another bank. How much difference will the monthly compounding make? Not a great difference, as shown below, but nevertheless large enough to make shopping for the best *effective annual rate* worthwhile.

Annual compounding $\qquad\qquad $1000(1.12)^{10} = 3105.85

Monthly compounding $\qquad $1000\left(1 + \frac{.12}{12}\right)^{120} = 3300.39

To calculate the effective annual rate r_e for a stated annual rate r, compounded m times per year, use Equation (9-12) below. For example, the effective annual rate for 10% compounded semiannually is 10.25%, calculated as follows:

$$r_e = \left(1 + \frac{r}{m}\right)^m - 1$$

$$r_e = \left(1 + \frac{.10}{2}\right)^2 - 1 = 1.1025 - 1 = 10.25\%$$

(9-12)

9-5 CONTINUOUS COMPOUNDING AND DISCOUNTING

For a stated annual rate, the effective annual rate increases as the compounding interval decreases. Table 9-1 lists the effective annual rates for various compounding periods for a 10% stated annual rate.

At the limit, the shortest compounding period can be achieved by paying interest continuously, i.e., making the compounding period infinitely small. While continuous compounding may sound complex, there is a simple solution to such problems. This is because from calculus it can be shown that as m approaches infinity (as we approach continuous compounding), the quantity $(1 + r/m)^m$ approaches e^r. That is:

$$\lim_{m \to \infty} \left(1 + \frac{r}{m}\right)^m = e^r \cong 2.718^r$$

where e is the base for natural, or Napierian, logarithms. Thus, for continuous compounding, e^r is equal to 1 plus the effective annual rate where r is the stated annual rate.[7] In the previous example the stated annual rate is 10% and the effective annual rate for 10% continuously compounded is 10.517%.

TABLE 9-1 EFFECTIVE ANNUAL RATES FOR A 10% STATED ANNUAL RATE

Compounding period	Effective annual rate, %
Year	10.000
Semiannual	10.250
Quarter	10.381
Month	10.471
Day	10.516
Continuous	10.517

[7]To show that e^r is equal to 1 plus the effective annual rate for continuous compounding, let

$$f(m) = \left(1 + \frac{1}{m}\right)^m$$

$$e^r = (2.718)^{.10} = 1.10517$$
$$r_e = 1.10517 - 1 = .10517 = 10.517\%$$

Consequently in terms of continuous compounding, Equation (9-1) can be rewritten as

$$C_n = C_0 e^{rn} \tag{9-13}$$

Similarly, for continuous discounting, Equation (9-3) can be rewritten as

$$C_0 = \frac{C_n}{e^{rn}} \tag{9-14}$$

A simple example will help illustrate how one solves time value of money problems using continuous compounding, or discounting. Suppose that you can invest $1 at 13% compounded continuously for 4 years. At the end of the 4 years your $1 investment would be worth $1.682, calculated as follows:

$$C_4 = \$1\ e^{(.13)(4)} = \$1(2.718)^{.52} = \$1.682$$

Note that the $1.682 compares with $1.630 for 13% compounded annually over 4 years. Thus, continuous compounding can make a difference, particularly as holding period n increases.

By definition,

$$e \equiv \lim_{m \to \infty} f(m) = \lim_{m \to \infty} \left(1 + \frac{1}{m}\right)^m = 2.71828$$

Now, let

$$V(m) = \left(1 + \frac{r}{m}\right)^m = \left[\left(1 + \frac{r}{m}\right)^{\frac{m}{r}}\right]^r$$

and

$$w = \frac{m}{r}$$

Then,

$$V(m) = \left[\left(1 + \frac{1}{w}\right)^w\right]^r$$

Since $w \to \infty$ as $m \to \infty$,

$$\lim_{m \to \infty} V(m) = e^r \text{ and } \lim_{m \to \infty} \left(1 + \frac{r}{m}\right)^m = e^r$$

To illustrate continuous discounting for a single cash flow, assume that $3 is to be received 5 years from now and that an appropriate discount rate is 10% discounted continuously. The present value of the $3 is $1.82, calculated as follows:

$$C_0 = \frac{\$3}{e^{(.10)5}} = \frac{\$3}{(2.718)^{.5}} = \$1.82$$

9-6 SUMMARY

For many readers this chapter merely represents a review of material they have studied in previous finance, accounting, or economics courses. However, the time value of money concept is central to most theories of how assets are valued. Thus, it is critical that the reader become familiar with the procedures for solving time value of money problems. This will be of benefit not only for the chapters to come but also for many other applications in the field of finance.

SUGGESTED READINGS

An excellent book for further developing your skills in solving time value of money problems is:

G. Clayton and C. Spivey, *The Time Value of Money*, Saunders, Philadelphia, 1978.

PROBLEMS

1 What is the $FVCF_{4\frac{1}{2}\%,3}$?

2 What is the $PVDF_{7\frac{1}{4}\%,4}$?

3 If the discount rate is 8%, find the present value of the following cash flows:
   a $200 three years from now.
   b $100 two years from now and $200 three years from now.
   c $150 at the end of each of the next 5 years.

4 Assume that the government agrees to loan you $3000 to complete your last year of college if you will agree to repay the government $3374.59 three years from now. What is the compound annual rate of interest for this loan?

5 If you can invest at 13%, what is your future wealth if you:
   a Invest $75 and leave it for 6 years.
   b Invest $25 at the beginning of the current year and at the beginning of each of the next 3 years (for a total of four investments) and withdraw the money at the end of the fourth year.

6 At a growth rate of 6%, how long does it take a sum to double?

7 Acme Corporation is establishing a sinking fund to retire a $1 million dollar debenture issue over a period of 10 years. The company plans to put a fixed amount into the fund at the *end* of each of the next 10 years, and the company anticipates that the fund will earn 8% compounded annually. What annual contributions must be made to accumulate the $1 million by the end of the 10 years?

8 Richard Dixon is considering an offer from Jacob the Liquidator calling for 15 payments of $5000 each. The first payment will be 5 years from today, while there will be no payment at the end of the sixth year. The remaining 14 payments will each be paid at the end of the next 14 years, i.e., years 7 through 20. What is the present value of this stream of payments if the discount rate is 12% compounded annually?

9 Assume that you need $100,000 at the end of 10 years, and that your only investment opportunity is a savings account paying 6% compounded quarterly.

    a What amount must you invest at the beginning of each of the next 10 years to achieve your goal of $100,000?

    b What amount must you invest today as a lump sum if you are to achieve your objective of $100,000 at the end of 10 years?

10 Prove algebraically that semiannual compounding results in a higher future value at the end of 1 year than does annual compounding. Your proof should be general—that is, it should hold for all r, including negative rates.

11 What is the present value of a 3-year annuity consisting of $150 annual payments discounted continuously at 6%?

12 What is the present value of a 77-year annuity consisting of $1 payments discounted continuously at 6%? Hint! Solve the geometric progression, letting $X = 1/e^{.06}$.

13 If Acme Corporation's earnings per share were $2.00 in 1974 and $7.17 in 1981, what was the compound annual rate of growth in EPS over this time period?

14 XYZ Company paid a $1 dividend last year. Dividends are expected to increase at a rate of 10% for each of the next 4 years.

    a Calculate the expected dividend for each of the next 4 years and their present value using a 12% annual discount rate.

    b Assume that the stock can be sold for $20 four years from now. What is the present value of this future sales price, again using a 12% discount rate?

    c How much would you be willing to pay for this stock?

APPENDIX: Solving Geometric Progressions

A geometric progression is a sequence of numbers in which each successive number is obtained by multiplying the preceding number by a constant factor. Many financial instruments can be described mathematically as a geometric progression and, as a result, simplified significantly. To illustrate, consider the case of an annuity where the payments C are received at the *end of the period*, there are n periods, and the discount rate is r. The present value of this annuity can be written as

$$P_0 = \frac{C}{(1 + r)^1} + \frac{C}{(1 + r)^2} + \cdots + \frac{C}{(1 + r)^n}$$

$$= C \left[\frac{1}{(1 + r)^1} + \frac{1}{(1 + r)^2} + \cdots + \frac{1}{(1 + r)^n} \right]$$

The sequence of terms within the brackets represents a geometric progression because each successive term is equal to the preceding term *multiplied* by a constant factor of $1/(1 + r)$. To simplify any geometric progression, the following steps should be followed:

STEPS FOR SOLVING GEOMETRIC PROGRESSIONS

Let

$$V = CX + CX^2 + \cdots + CX^n \tag{9A-1}$$

Step 1   Identify X as the constant "geometric" factor and isolate the geometric progression.

$$V = C(X + X^2 + \cdots + X^n) \tag{9A-2}$$

Step 2   Multiply both sides of Equation (9A-2) by X.

$$VX = C(X^2 + X^3 + \cdots + X^{n+1}) \tag{9A-3}$$

Note that the right-hand sides of Equations (9A-2) and (9A-3) are identical except for the first term (X) of (9A-2) and the last term (X^{n+1}) of (9A-3). Thus, if Equation (9A-3) is subtracted from (9A-2), all the intermediate X terms will cancel out, leaving only X and $-X^{n+1}$ on the right-hand side.

Step 3   Subtract Equation (9A-3) from Equation (9A-2)

$$V - VX = C(X - X^{n+1}) \tag{9A-4}$$

Step 4   Solve for V

$$V = C\frac{X - X^{n+1}}{1 - X} \tag{9A-5}$$

Step 5   If X represents a more complex variable, such as $1/(1 + r)$, substitute for X and simplify.

To solve for the present value of an annuity, let $\text{PVAF}_{r,n}$ represent the geometric progression:

$$\text{PVAF}_{r,n} = \frac{1}{(1 + r)^2} + \frac{1}{(1 + r)^2} + \cdots + \frac{1}{(1 + r)^n}$$

Now, using step 5, we can simplify the expression as follows:

Step 5   Substitute $1/(1 + r)$ for X and simplify.

$$\begin{aligned}
\text{PVAF}_{r,n} &= \frac{[1/(1 + r)] - [1/(1 + r)^{n+1}]}{1 - [1/(1 + r)]} = \frac{[1/(1 + r)] - [1/(1 + r)^{n+1}]}{(1 + r - 1)/(1 + r)} \\
&= \frac{1 - [1/(1 + r)^n]}{r}
\end{aligned}$$

which is Equation (9-6) of the text.

As another example, to solve for the *future* value of an annuity where payments are made at the *beginning* of the period, let $\text{FVAF}_{r,n}$ represent the geometric progression.

$$FVAF_{r,n} = (1 + r)^n + (1 + r)^{n-1} + \cdots + (1 + r)^1 \qquad (9A\text{-}6)$$

Note that the constant factor is $(1 + r)^{-1}$. Multiply (9A-6) by $(1 + r)^{-1}$.

$$FVAF_{r,n} (1 + r)^{-1} = (1 + r)^{n-1} + (1 + r)^{n-2} + \cdots + 1 \qquad (9A\text{-}7)$$

Subtracting (9A-7) from (9A-6) and solving for $FVAF_{r,n}$ leaves

$$FVAF_{r,n} = \frac{(1 + r)^n - 1}{1 - (1 + r)^{-1}} = \frac{(1 + r)\,[(1 + r)^n - 1]}{r} \qquad (9A\text{-}8)$$

which is Equation (9-9) of the text.

PART THREE

ANALYZING EQUITY SECURITIES

It is probably true that when the term "investments" is mentioned, more people think of the stock market than of any other segment of the capital markets, and rightfully so. The equities markets represent the largest segment of the U.S. capital markets.

This part of the book represents only an introduction to the process of analyzing equities. While some aspects of security analysis can be taught in a classroom setting, the most valuable lessons will be learned in the real school of actual experience. As many investors have learned, the cost of such an education can be quite high. We hope the next four chapters will provide a solid base upon which real-world experiences can be gained at not too high a price.

Before beginning to analyze securities it is essential to understand the determinants of value. Therefore, Chapter 10 introduces the basic valuation principles which are simply an extension of the time value of money concepts presented in Chapter 9.

Since the driving force behind stock prices is the profitability of the firm, Chapter 11 is devoted to the behavior of earnings, dividends, and cash flow and the relationship of stock prices with these three variables. As even the most inexperienced investor might suspect, changes in stock prices are frequently associated with changes in earnings, dividends, and cash flow.

Chapter 12 is devoted to analyzing the risk of stocks. Both the capital market theory concept of risk (beta) and more traditional risk measures are discussed, and considerable emphasis is put on predicting future levels of risk, as opposed to just measuring what happened in the past.

Chapter 13 presents several valuation models which try to put together estimates of future cash flows (such as earnings and dividends) with estimates of risk. The end product of these valuation models is an estimate of a model price which can be compared with the stock's current market price. Model prices that are higher than current market prices identify stocks that are undervalued and should be bought; model prices that are lower than current market prices identify stocks that are overpriced and presumably should be sold. In a perfectly efficient market current market prices should represent fair prices, and valuation models should not be able to identify winners and losers. However, there is some evidence which suggests that markets are not perfectly efficient and that the use of valuation models may help the investor achieve above-normal returns.

Both authors of this text have spent the majority of their professional careers involved with problems in analyzing stocks and forming equity portfolios. We have found the work always challenging, frequently humbling, and very enjoyable. We suspect your experience will be similar to ours and hope that the next four chapters will get you off on the right foot.

CHAPTER 10

PRINCIPLES OF VALUATION

After reading this chapter, you should:

1 Be able to calculate the price of a bond, given the appropriate discount rate
2 Be able to calculate the price of a common stock, given its expected dividend stream and the appropriate discount rate
3 Understand the constant growth, dividend discount model

Bonds represent one of the most clear-cut examples of how the principles of the time value of money are applied to security prices. If one knows the appropriate discount rate, it is a relatively simple matter to determine the present value (current price) of a bond.

10-1 CALCULATING BOND PRICES

The typical bond pays a specified amount of interest (called the *coupon*) twice a year, and at the end of the life of the bond pays the *principal*, which is usually $1000 per bond. Thus, calculating a bond price represents a special type of semiannual discounting problem. The coupons represent an annuity of payments received twice a year for the life of the bond, and the principal amount represents a single lump sum received at the end of the life of the bond. This can be expressed mathematically as

$$P_0 = \frac{C_1}{(1 + r/2)^1} + \frac{C_2}{(1 + r/2)^2} + \cdots + \frac{C_{2n}}{(1 + r/2)^{2n}} + \frac{\$1000}{(1 + r/2)^{2n}} \quad (10\text{-}1)$$

where C = semiannual coupon
n = number of years to maturity
r = appropriate stated rate, discounted semiannually

Since the coupon is the same amount each period, Equation (10-1) can be rewritten as

$$P_0 = C \cdot \text{PVAF}_{r/2, 2n} + \$1000 \cdot \text{PVDF}_{r/2, 2n} \quad (10\text{-}2)$$

when PVAF represents the present-value annuity factor and PVDF represents the present-value discount factor, as discussed in Chapter 9.

As an example, assume that Acme Inc. issued 8% bonds in 1980 with a 30-year maturity. Since the *coupon rate* is 8%, these bonds will pay $80 per year (8% × $1000). Thus, each semiannual coupon will be $40. At the end of the 30 years (in the year 2010), the principal amount of $1000 will be paid in addition to the last coupon. If the appropriate market interest rate for these bonds was also 8% at the time of their issue, the bonds would have been offered to the public at face value, or par value ($1000), calculated using Equation (10-1) or (10-2) as follows:

$$P_0 = \frac{\$40}{(1.04)^1} + \frac{\$40}{(1.04)^2} + \cdots + \frac{\$40}{(1.04)^{60}} + \frac{\$1000}{(1.04)^{60}}$$

$$P_0 = \$40 \text{ PVAF}_{.04,60} + \$1000 \text{ PVDF}_{.04,60}$$

$$= \$40(22.623) + \$1000(.095) = \$1000.00$$

Note that any time the discount rate equals the coupon rate, the bond price will always equal $1000, or par value.

Now assume that exactly 5 years after the Acme 8% bonds of 2010 have been issued, interest rates have changed and the appropriate discount rate for the bonds is now 9% discounted semiannually. The price of the bonds, which now have 25 years to maturity, would be calculated as follows:

33.95

$$P_0 = \frac{\$40}{(1.045)^1} + \frac{\$40}{(1.045)^2} + \cdots + \frac{\$40}{(1.045)^{50}} + \frac{\$1000}{(1.045)^{50}}$$

$$= \$40 \text{ PVAF}_{.045,50} + \$1000 \text{ PVDF}_{.045,50}$$

$$= \$40(19.762) + \$1000(.111) = \$901.19$$

Thus, the increase in interest rates caused the Acme bonds to fall in price to $901.19. It should be obvious that *whenever the current market interest rate is above a bond's coupon rate, the price of the bond will be less than $1000. Conversely, when the current market interest rate is below the coupon rate for a bond, the price will be above $1000.* For example, if in 1990 the appropriate discount rate for the Acme bonds fell to 7% discounted semiannually, the price of the Acme 8% bonds of 2010 would be $1106.78. (The reader should ensure that he understands how to calculate bond prices by confirming this price.)

10-2 COMMON STOCKS AND THE PRESENT VALUE OF DIVIDENDS

Let us now turn our attention to the principles underlying the valuation of common stocks. In general, there are two basic approaches to determining the value of a share of common stock. One approach is to determine an appropriate multiplier of the firm's earnings—a price/earnings (*P/E*) ratio. Estimating an appropriate *P/E* ratio has long been a favorite approach among security analysts for deciding whether stocks are under- or overpriced. The other approach is to estimate the present value of the expected dividends associated with the common stock. We will show in Chapter 13 that the two approaches are generally consistent with each other. For now, we concentrate on the present value of dividends.

The value of any financial asset is determined by the cash flow the asset ultimately provides its owners. In the case of common stocks, this cash flow is the cash dividend stream, including any liquidating dividend when the firm ceases operations. The present value of the expected dividend stream can be written as

$$P_0 = \frac{E(D_1)}{(1 + r)^1} + \frac{E(D_2)}{(1 + r)^2} + \cdots + \frac{E(D_n)}{(1 + r)^n} = \sum_{t=1}^{n} \frac{E(D_t)}{(1 + r)^t} \qquad (10\text{-}3)$$

where P_0 = current stock price

$E(D_t)$ = expected dividend in year t

n = number of years the firm operates

r = appropriate risk-adjusted discount rate

This equation assumes that investors hold the stock for the life of the firm. Of course most investors do not have this long a holding-period horizon. For an investor who intends to hold the stock for, say, 2 years, her return will be based on the dividends received over the 2-year period plus the sale price of the stock at the end of the second year. For this investor, the price of the stock would be calculated as

$$P_0 = \frac{E(D_1)}{(1 + r)^1} + \frac{E(D_2)}{(1 + r)^2} + \frac{E(P_2)}{(1 + r)^2} \qquad (10\text{-}4)$$

where $E(P_2)$ = expected price at end of second year

Since most investors' holding periods are not equal to the life of the firm, one might be tempted at first glance to conclude that the current price of a stock is not based on the expected dividend stream over the life of the firm. However, it is easy to show that Equation (10-4) is the same as Equation (10-3). Simply assume that at the end of the second year the new purchaser of the stock will offer a price based on the remaining dividends $(D_3, D_4, \ldots, D_n)$ and that the expectations regarding dividends and the discount rate are the same for both the seller and the purchaser of the stock. In this case, the expected price at the end of the second year would be

$$E(P_2) = \frac{E(D_3)}{(1 + r)^1} + \frac{E(D_4)}{(1 + r)^2} + \cdots + \frac{E(D_n)}{(1 + r)^{n-2}}$$

Substituting this value for $E(P_2)$ into Equation (10-4) gives

$$P_0 = \frac{E(D_1)}{(1 + r)^1} + \frac{E(D_2)}{(1 + r)^2} + \frac{1}{(1 + r)^2}\left[\frac{E(D_3)}{(1 + r)^1}\right.$$
$$\left. + \frac{E(D_4)}{(1 + r)^2} + \cdots + \frac{E(D_n)}{(1 + r)^{n-2}}\right]$$

which is exactly the same as Equation (10-3).

Admittedly most stocks are held by a series of investors over the life of the firm. Each investor, in turn, is concerned only with the price he paid for the stock, the dividends received while holding the stock, and the price at which the stock is sold. But for every seller there must be a buyer. As shown above, the intermediate prices agreed upon by these buyers and sellers can be dropped out of the equation, leaving only dividends (and the discount rate) as the determinants of stock values.

10-3 THE CONSTANT GROWTH DIVIDEND DISCOUNT MODEL

Unfortunately, Equation (10-3) is not very practical since one is forced to estimate each dividend paid over the life of the firm. What is needed is a simplified model. One such model is the constant growth dividend discount model, which is sometimes referred to as the Gordon model.[1] As we shall soon see, the assumptions underlying this model are extremely strong and, as a result, the constant growth dividend discount model is not particularly useful for estimating *individual* stock prices. Nevertheless, the model is a very helpful aid in understanding the primary determinants of stock prices, and it may be a useful model for estimating the price of large groups of stocks such as the S&P 500 index or the Dow Jones Industrial Average.

To simplify the problem of estimating the long stream of dividends in Equation (10-3), the constant growth dividend discount model makes three assumptions:

1 The stream of dividends is perpetual $(n \rightarrow \infty)$.
2 Dividends grow at a constant rate of g forever.
3 The discount rate is greater than the growth rate $(r > g)$.[2]

Given the first two assumptions, Equation (10-3) can be rewritten as

$$P_0 = \frac{D_0(1 + g)^1}{(1 + r)^1} + \frac{D_0(1 + g)^2}{(1 + r)^2} + \cdots + \frac{D_0(1 + g)^\infty}{(1 + r)^\infty}$$

[1] See M. J. Gordon, *The Investment, Financing and Valuation of the Corporation*, Irwin, Homewood, Ill., 1962; also M. J. Gordon, "Dividends, Earnings and Stock Prices," *Review of Economics and Statistics* (May 1959). An equivalent relationship was actually derived earlier in J. B. Williams, *The Theory of Investment Value*, Harvard University Press, Cambridge, Mass., 1938.

[2] The assumption that the discount rate exceeds the constant growth rate is reasonable for several reasons. First, if r is equal to or less than g, the price calculated using Equation (10-6) becomes infinitely large, and we know that stocks do not sell for infinite prices. Second, there are physical and political factors which eventually constrain long-run growth rates. For example, sheer size can become a constraint. Consider the case of IBM. In 1984, IBM's after-tax profits were $6.6 billion and its profits had increased at a 14% compound annual rate over the past 20 years or so. In 1984, total after-tax profits of U.S. corporations were approximately $196 billion. Thus, IBM's profits represented 3.4% of total corporate profits in 1984. If total corporate profits continued to increase at their historical 5% growth rate over the next 40 years, then in the year 2024 total corporate profits would be $1.38 trillion. If, over the same 40 years, IBM's profits continued to increase at its historical, and above-normal, growth rate of 14%, then IBM's profits would be $1.25 trillion in the year 2024, or *90%* of total corporate profits. This is a highly unlikely result. More likely, IBM's growth rate will decrease over time toward the average growth rate for all firms. This is one way of illustrating that the long-run growth rate for most firms will probably be close to the average growth rate for total corporate profits. In the past, this growth rate has been approximately 5%. And, in the past, the discount rate r has averaged about 9%. Thus, in the aggregate, r has comfortably exceeded g, and this must also be true for individual firms.

$$P_0 = D_0\left[\left(\frac{1 + g}{1 + r}\right)^1 + \left(\frac{1 + g}{1 + r}\right)^2 + \cdots + \left(\frac{1 + g}{1 + r}\right)^\infty\right] \qquad (10\text{-}5)$$

This is now in the form of a geometric progression, where the constant "geometric" factor is the ratio $(1 + g)/(1 + r)$. Using the steps for solving geometric progressions listed in the Appendix to Chapter 9, we can rewrite Equation (10-5) as follows:[3]

$$P_0 = \frac{D_1}{r - g} \qquad (10\text{-}6)$$

where $\quad D_1$ = dividend to be received over next 12 months

While the assumption of constant, perpetual growth is quite strong, Equation (10-6) is nevertheless a very useful model for analyzing the primary determinants of stock prices and stock returns.

---

[3] To simplify the geometric progression in Equation (10-5) we follow the steps illustrated in the Appendix to Chapter 9.

Step 1 Let $X = (1 + g)/(1 + r)$.

$$P_0 = D_0(X + X^2 + \cdots + X^n) \qquad (1)$$

Step 2 Multiply Equation (1) by X.

$$P_0 X = D_0(X^2 + X^3 + \cdots + X^{n+1}) \qquad (2)$$

Step 3 Subtract Equation (2) from (1).

$$P_0 - P_0 X = D_0(X - X^{n+1}) \qquad (3)$$

Step 4 Solve for P_0.

$$P_0 = \frac{D_0(X - X^{n+1})}{1 - X} \qquad (4)$$

Step 5 Substitute $(1 + g)/(1 + r)$ for X and simplify.

$$P_0 = \frac{D_0[(1 + g)/(1 + r) - [(1 + g)/(1 + r)]^{n+1}]}{1 - [(1 + g)/(1 + r)]} \qquad (5)$$

At this stage we utilize the assumption that r (the discount rate) is greater than g (the growth rate), in conjunction with the assumption of a perpetual dividend stream. Since $r > g$, as $n + 1$ approaches infinity the quantity $[(1 + g)/(1 + r)]^\infty$ approaches zero. Thus, Equation (5) can be simplified as follows:

$$P_0 = \frac{D_0[(1+g)/(1+r)]}{(1 + r - 1 - g)/(1 + r)} = \frac{D_0(1 + g)}{r - g}$$

Noting that $D_0(1 + g) = D_1$, we get the familiar equation for the constant growth dividend discount model:

$$P_0 = \frac{D_1}{r - g}$$

For example, the terms in Equation (10-6) can be rearranged as follows:

$$r = \frac{D_1}{P_0} + g \qquad (10\text{-}7)$$

Thus, the total return investors receive from common stocks can be broken down into two components, the dividend yield D_1/P_0 and growth g. If one assumes that r, the capitalization rate, remains constant, the growth in the stock price will equal the growth rate of dividends. While capitalization rates obviously change over time, Equation (10-7) is still a useful approximation of the actual experience of investors. For example, recall from Table 3-7 that the Ibbotson Sinquefield study reported that the S&P 500 generated a *total* return of approximately 10% per year over the time period 1926–1985. Of this 10% total return a little more than half (approximately 5%) came from the stocks' dividends. The other 5% was the result of capital appreciation—that is, the share prices grew at a rate of around 5% per year. Interestingly, but not surprisingly, the growth rate of dividends over this time period for the S&P 500 index was also very close to 5%. Thus, Equation (10-7) provides a useful model for analyzing long-run stock returns, at least for large portfolios of stocks such as the market indexes.

As another example, consider the S&P 500. Toward the end of 1985 the S&P 500 was selling at 210 and estimates of its next 12-month dividend were in the $8 area. *Assuming* that investors anticipated the growth rate of dividends to be 5%, the expected return implicit in the price of the S&P 500 at this time was 8.8%, calculated using Equation (10-7):

$$r = \frac{D_1}{P_0} + g = \frac{8}{210} + 5\% = 8.8\%$$

Thus, this analysis suggests that at this time the S&P 500 was priced to provide a return that was slightly below its long-run, historical return.

It is always fun, and sometimes enlightening, to ask questions such as ''what will happen to prices if investors change their required rates of return?'' For example, what if the required discount rate for the S&P 500 should increase to, say, 11% and investors' expectations regarding next year's dividend and the growth rate of dividends remain the same? Using Equation (10-6) we see that the price of the S&P 500 would fall to 133!

$$P_0 = \frac{D_1}{r - g} = \frac{\$8}{.11 - .05} = 133$$

In a similar fashion, one can analyze the impact on prices of changes in estimates of the next year's dividend or the long-run growth rate of dividends. Thus, even though the constant growth dividend discount model represents a strong abstraction of reality, it is still a very useful model.

10-4 VALUATION BASED ON EARNINGS, DIVIDENDS, AND CASH FLOW

In the past there has been a controversy over whether or not the value of a common stock is determined by its earnings, dividends, or cash flow. Financial theorists generally argue that ultimately it is the dividends investors receive which determine the value of a stock. This is because cash dividends can be spent on consumption, whereas earnings and cash flow are simply accounting concepts. However, this is not to say that earnings and cash flow are of no value in analyzing securities—*they are very useful concepts* for several reasons.

First, it has been shown that valuation models based on dividends, earnings, and cash flow are equivalent, when earnings and cash flow are properly defined and measured.[4] This should come as no surprise since the firm's ability to pay dividends is predicated in the short run upon its current cash position and in the long run upon the earning power of its assets.

Second, in many situations it is more convenient to use valuation models based upon earnings. One obvious example is the case of stocks which currently do not pay dividends. Thus, in the subsequent chapters we will consider both dividend- and earnings-based valuation models.

10-5 SUMMARY

The price of any asset can be viewed as the present value of the cash payment received by the owners of the asset, where the payments are discounted at the appropriate risk-adjusted rate. Thus, the keys to the valuation process are estimating the future cash payments and determining the appropriate discount rate.

Estimating the cash payments associated with bonds is a relatively simple problem compared with estimating the cash payments associated with common stocks. For bonds, the semiannual coupon payments and the principal payment are fixed. This does not mean that investors know with certainty the bond's cash flows since there is always the risk of default, in which case the promised payments may not be made. Still, estimating the cash payment stream for a bond is an easier task than estimating the dividend stream for common stocks. However, determining the appropriate discount rate for bonds can be nearly as troublesome as it is for common stocks. Many of the problems involved in analyzing bonds are discussed in Chapters 14, 15 and 16.

The basic valuation model for common stocks is predicated upon the price being equal to the present value of all future dividends paid by the firm, including any liquidating dividend when the firm ceases operations. The constant growth dividend discount (Gordon) model was derived and shown to be useful as a general model for analyzing the primary determinants of stock prices and stock returns. However, the assumption of a perpetual, constant growth rate of dividends is probably too strong

---

[4]For an excellent demonstration of the equivalence of earnings, dividend, cash flow, and "investment opportunity" valuation models, see J. C. T. Mao, *Quantitative Analysis of Financial Decisions*, Macmillan, Toronto, 1969, pp. 464–476. Also, see W. F. Sharpe, *Investments*, 2d ed., Prentice-Hall, Englewood Cliffs, N.J., 1981, pp. 369–371.

for this model to be utilized in analyzing *individual* stock prices. In fact, the analysis of individual common stocks is a very complex process. Chapters 11, 12, and 13 discuss a number of the issues in analyzing equity securities.

SUGGESTED READINGS

Some of the classic works on the theory of value which are still well worth reading are:

M. J. Gordon, *The Investment, Financing and Valuation of the Corporation*, Irwin, Homewood, Ill., 1962.

F. Modigliani and M. H. Miller, ''The Cost of Capital, Corporation Finance, and the Theory of Investment,'' *American Economic Review* (June 1958).

J. B. Williams, *The Theory of Investment Value*, Harvard University Press, Cambridge, Mass., 1938.

QUESTIONS

1 Why might the constant growth dividend discount model *not* be useful for evaluating individual common stock prices?

2 The Gordon model assumes that $r > g$. Why is this a necessary assumption?

3 In recent years the dividend yields of most common stocks have been less than the interest rate on government bonds. Does this mean that corporations can raise equity capital at lower cost than the government can borrow?

4 In showing that valuation based on short-term holdings [Equation (10-4)] is the same as valuation based on holding the stock for the life of the firm [Equation (10-3)], we invoked some assumptions. What are they? Were any implicit, but unstated, assumptions also used? Can you imagine circumstances under which these assumptions might fail to apply?

PROBLEMS

$P_0 = 1098$

1 A bond with a 7% coupon is selling to yield 6% (discounted semiannually) to maturity. The bond has 15 years to maturity. What is the bond's price?

$P_0 = 53.00$

2 XYZ Corp. paid a $3 dividend which is expected to grow at a 6% rate for the foreseeable future. If investors require a 12% return to purchase XYZ stock, what is a good estimate of the price of the stock?

$P_0 = 14.06$

3 Western Holdings Inc. recently paid a $1 dividend which is expected to grow at a 6% rate for the next 3 years. What is a good estimate of the current stock price if investors require a 10% return to purchase shares of Western Holdings and expect the stock price to be $15 at the end of 3 years?

$r = 24.35\%$

4 If the current price of Western Holdings is $10 and expectations with respect to dividends and price at the end of 3 years are the same as in Question 3, what is the return investors require to purchase Western Holdings at its current price of $10?

5 NoGro Inc. pays an annual dividend of $5. The company has stated that it does not intend to change its dividend.

$P_0 = 62.50$

a If investors require an 8% return to purchase NoGro shares, what is the current price per share?

$Div\ Yld = 8\%$

b What is the current dividend yield of NoGro shares?

$P_0 = 41.67$

c If the required discount rate should change to 12%, what would be the current price of NoGro shares?

CHAPTER 11

EARNINGS, DIVIDENDS, AND CASH FLOW

After reading this chapter, you should:

1 Understand why earnings are important
2 Be aware of the random nature of annual earnings changes and the seasonal nature of quarterly earnings changes
3 Be aware that the earnings of many firms are heavily influenced by economywide and industry factors
4 Know that changes in the current level of dividends may cause investors to revise their expectations regarding future dividends and consequently may affect stock prices
5 Understand why many investors analyze cash flow in addition to earnings and dividends
6 Be aware of the evidence concerning the ability of analysts to forecast future earnings and future prices

In previous chapters we argued that the price of a security represents the present value of the future cash flows the owners of the security expect to receive, where the discount rate is appropriately adjusted for the risk associated with the cash flow stream. For common stocks, these future cash flows consist of the dividends the investor expects to receive and the expected selling price at the end of his holding period. Since future prices of the stock will depend upon the expected dividend stream at future points in time, it is possible to show, at least conceptually, that stock prices are solely a function of the expected dividend stream (see Section 10-3). As a result, dividend discount models have a great deal of support, both by theoreticians and by investment professionals.

On the other hand, earnings are considered to be an important factor influencing stock prices by many, if not most, investors. In addition, some analysts pay a great deal of attention to cash flow. Consequently, this chapter will discuss a number of issues concerning earnings, dividends, and cash flow.

11-1 THE IMPORTANCE OF EARNINGS

It is sometimes argued that earnings, as measured by the accountant, are irrelevant. As we saw in Chapter 6, it is relatively easy to change the accounting earnings of a firm by choosing different, but perfectly acceptable, accounting treatments of such items as inventories, depreciation, and revenue recognition. Since accounting earnings can be changed at the discretion of the firm's management and accountants, one might question whether earnings have any economic value. But perhaps more fundamental to the issue of the relevance of earnings is the fact that the firm cannot deposit its reported earnings in its bank account. The firm cannot pay bills or buy assets with its accounting earnings. It can only do these things with cash. Likewise, the stockholder cannot spend the earnings reported by the company. Shareholders can only spend cash, and the cash received from investing in common stocks comes only from cash dividends. (Here we define dividends to include any liquidating dividend including the sale of the stock.) Thus, it is possible to argue that earnings are irrelevant.

How can we reconcile the fact that, theoretically, only dividend streams and their associated risk should determine stock prices with the fact that investors clearly pay a great deal of attention to earnings? Perhaps the easiest explanation of this question is that both reported earnings and earnings forecasts help investors forecast the future dividend stream. For example, if earnings are expected to grow at 10% a year, it might be reasonable *in some cases* to also expect dividends to grow at 10% a year. As another example, if a company reports a large decrease in its most recent quarterly earnings, it might be reasonable for investors to change their expectations as to the future long-run growth rate of dividends.

Simple observation of the security markets will quickly confirm the notion that earnings are important determinants of stock prices. The sometimes dramatic drops in the stock prices of companies which report unexpectedly poor earnings provide casual evidence that earnings do matter. As just one example, on July 21, 1983, Hewlett-Packard announced that its third-quarter earnings would be less than the previous year's third quarter. This came as a surprise to analysts, most of whom were projecting a third-quarter earnings *increase* of 10 to 15%. The market reaction was swift—on the same day the price of Hewlett-Packard stock dropped over six points, from 93 3/8 to 87 1/4.

A specific test of the relationship between earnings and stock prices was performed by Niederhaffer and Regan.[1] Figure 11-1 illustrates the results of their analysis of 650 stocks over the 5-year time period 1966–1970. Note that the 50 stocks which provided the largest change in stock price (the Top 50) over the 5 years also experienced large increases in EPS over the same time period. (For the Top 50 the median change in EPS was +199.4% and the median change in price was +181.9%.) Similarly, those stocks which suffered large declines in price (the Bottom 50) also tended to have experienced large decreases in EPS.

Niederhaffer and Regan also considered analysts' forecasts of EPS compared with the actual earnings which were reported for the single year 1970. Figure 11-2 presents these results. The Top 50 represents the 50 stocks among all stocks listed on the NYSE which provided the largest percentage change in price during 1970. (The median change in price for this group was +48.4%.) The Bottom 50 stocks suffered a median percentage decrease in price of 56.7%.

[1] V. Niederhaffer and P. Regan, "Earnings Changes, Analysts Forecasts, and Stock Prices," *Financial Analysts Journal* (May/June 1972).

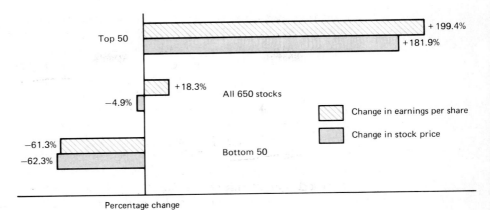

FIGURE 11-1 Earnings changes and stock prices (5-year horizon, 1966–1970). [*Source: V. Niederhaffer and P. J. Regan, "Earnings Changes, Analysts Forecasts, and Stock Prices,"* Financial Analysts Journal *(May/June 1972), fig. 3.*]

Similar to the 5-year results, the change in stock price for 1970 was highly correlated with the change in 1970's reported EPS. The median change in EPS for the Top 50 was +21.4%, whereas it was −83.0% for the Bottom 50. Note, however, that this was not the case for the forecasted EPS. For the Top 50 performing stocks the median forecast of EPS change was +7.7%, which was actually less than the +15.3% median

FIGURE 11-2 Earnings changes, analysts forecasts, and stock prices (1-year horizon, 1970). [*Source: V. Niederhaffer and P. J. Regan, "Earnings Changes, Analysts Forecasts, and Stock Prices,"* Financial Analysts Journal *(May/June 1972), fig. 1.*]

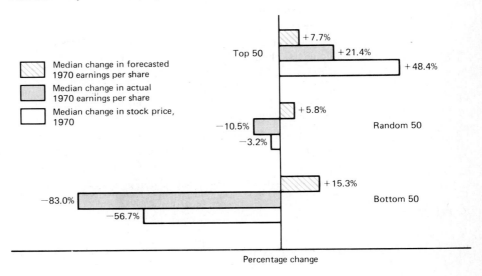

forecast for the Bottom 50 stocks. What apparently happened was that those stocks which performed most poorly during the year were also those stocks for which analysts most overestimated their earnings for the year. On the other hand, pleasant surprises (those cases where actual EPS exceeded estimated EPS) were quite rewarding.[2] The Top 50's median price change of $+48.4\%$ came during a year when stock prices in general performed relatively poorly—note that a randomly selected group of stocks experienced a price decline of 3.2%.

The inescapable conclusion to be drawn from Figures 11-1 and 11-2 is that changes in stock prices are highly correlated with changes in earnings. And investors with superior earnings forecasts are more likely to enjoy pleasant surprises and avoid disappointing earnings reports and stock performance. Thus, the ability to generate superior earnings forecasts is one key to investment success.[3] Chapter 8 presented some techniques for forecasting earnings, and the Appendix at the end of this chapter provides a case example of how one analyst forecasted earnings. But, before one begins to make earnings forecasts, it is important to understand the general behavior of earnings over time, which is our next topic.

11-2 THE RANDOM NATURE OF EARNINGS CHANGES

Recall from our discussion of market efficiency in Chapter 5 that stock prices, by and large, tend to follow a random walk. More specifically, stock prices tend to change in a random fashion with an upward drift over time. If stock prices are heavily influenced by changes in earnings, as the evidence presented in the preceding section suggests, then one might suspect that changes in earnings could also be approximated by a random walk.

A number of studies have investigated the behavior of earnings over time—the first being Little's 1962 study of British companies which had the intriguing title "Higgledy Piggledy Growth."[4] However, we will limit our discussion to studies of U.S. companies and will first consider annual earnings changes, then quarterly earnings changes, and finally common influences in earnings changes.

11-2-1 Annual Earnings Changes   It is often argued that some firms are able to sustain above-average and predictable growth rates of earnings over a period of many

---

[2]Another interesting observation made by Niederhaffer and Regan, op. cit., had to do with how fast companies reported their earnings. They found that 88% of the Top 50 companies in 1970 reported earnings within 2 months of the end of their fiscal year, vs. only 40% of the Bottom 50 companies. This supports the notion that the poorer the earnings, the longer the company takes to report the bad news.

[3]The positive relationship between changes in earnings and stock prices has been documented by a number of other researchers. Some of these studies were discussed in Sections 5-4 and 5-5.

[4]A partial list of some of the earlier studies on the behavior of earnings would include: I. M. D. Little, "Higgledy Piggledy Growth," *Bulletin of the Oxford Institute of Economics and Statistics* (November 1962); I. M. D. Little and A. C. Rayner, *Higgledy Piggledy Growth Again*, Blackwell's, Oxford, 1966; R. A. Brealey, "The Statistical Properties of Successive Changes in Earnings," a paper presented to the Seminar on the Analysis of Security Prices, University of Chicago (May 1967) and summarized in Chapter 5 of R. A. Brealey, *An Introduction to Risk and Return from Common Stocks*, 2d ed., MIT Press, Cambridge, Mass., 1983; and J. Lintner and R. Glauber, "Higgledy Piggledy Growth in America," a paper presented to the Seminar on the Analysis of Security Prices, University of Chicago (May 1967) and reprinted in J. Lorie and R. A. Brealey, *Modern Developments in Investment Management*, Praeger, New York, 1972.

years. This superior earning power is generally attributed to some sort of monopoly condition, such as a proprietary product, superior management, or large capital costs which act as a barrier to entry by new firms. If such firms exist, we would expect to observe them consistently producing above-average earnings gains.

A simple test of this was conducted by Brealey,[5] who examined 610 companies over the 14-year period 1953–1966. Table 11-1 lists Brealey's results. The companies were grouped according to the number of years in which their growth rate of earnings in a particular year was above the average earnings growth rate for all 610 companies in that year. The second column in the top half of Table 11-1 shows these results. Note that no company's earnings growth was below average in all 14 years, nor was any single company's growth above average in all 14 years. Only one company out of the 610 in the sample experienced above-average growth in 13 out of the 14 years and only two companies were above average in 12 of the years.

The third column lists the number of companies one would expect to observe in each group if earnings growth was distributed by random chance among companies. For example, if earnings growth was distributed randomly, then for a sample of 610 firms one would expect to find one firm with only 1 year of above-average growth, three firms with only 2 years of above-average growth, and at the other end of the spectrum, three firms with 12 years of above-average growth and one firm with 13 years of above-average growth—all simply due to random chance. Note the striking similarity between the second column (the actual number of companies in each group) and the third column (the number expected if earnings changes are distributed randomly).

Using what is called a *runs test*, Brealey also considered whether or not years of above- or below-average growth tended to bunch up for individual firms. To illustrate, suppose we let a " + " indicate a year of above-average growth and a " − " indicate a year of below-average growth. A "run" consists of a change in the sign, that is, a change from above-average growth to below-average growth and vice versa. Suppose that an individual firm had the following sequence of earnings growth: + + + − + + − − − − + − − −. This firm would have experienced six runs, three runs of above-average growth and three runs of below-average growth. Brealey determined the number of runs for all the firms in his sample, which are reported in the second and third columns of the lower half of Table 11-1. Again, the actual results are compared with the results one would expect if earnings changes were distributed randomly, which is the fourth column of numbers. And again, notice the similarity between the actual results and those that would be expected to occur by random chance.

A comment on statistical methodology is appropriate here. The above results do not *prove* that earnings change in a random fashion. In fact, classical statistical tests can never prove that a hypothesis is correct; they can only reject the hypothesis. In this case, Brealey's results and the results of other studies are *consistent with* the hypothesis that earnings changes are randomly distributed. However, this does not prove that, in fact, earnings change in a random fashion. It probably is the case that there are certain characteristics of firms which largely determine changes in earnings

---

[5]Brealey, "The Statistical Properties of Successive Earnings Changes," op. cit.

TABLE 11-1   STATISTICAL PROPERTIES OF EARNINGS CHANGES

Number of companies experiencing a given number of years of above average growth in earnings

Number of good years	Actual number of companies	Expected number of companies*
0	0	0
1	0	1
2	1	3
3	6	14
4	34	37
5	84	75
6	114	112
7	139	128
8	115	112
9	68	75
10	30	37
11	16	14
12	2	3
13	1	1
14	0	0

Runs of successive years with growth greater or less than average

Length of run, years	Actual number of runs of good years	Actual number of runs of bad years	Expected number of runs of good or bad years*
1	1152	1102	1068
2	562	590	534
3	266	300	267
4	114	120	133
5	55	63	67
6	24	20	33
7	23	12	17
8	5	6	8
9	3	3	4
10	6	0	2
11	2	0	1
12	1	0	1
13	0	0	0
14	0	1	0

*Expected number assuming earnings are randomly distributed.
Source: R. A. Brealey, *An Introduction to Risk and Return from Common Stocks*, 2d ed., MIT Press, Cambridge, Mass., 1983, Tables 5.3 and 5.4.

over time. For example, it seems very unlikely that IBM's superior earnings record is simply due to luck.

Brealey's results illustrate the difficulty of identifying a firm with those characteristics which will enable it to generate superior earnings growth over any reasonable period of time. As noted earlier, only one company out of 610 produced above-average earnings in 13 out of 14 years and only two companies were above average in 12 years. Nor were companies, in general, able to produce even relatively short runs of good years. Note in the second column of the bottom half of Table 11-1 how quickly the number of runs of good (above-average) years decreases as the length of the run increases. For example, in the total sample the number of runs of 2 good years was 562, whereas there were only 266 runs of 3 good years and 114 runs of 4 good years. Thus, even if earnings changes are not due to random chance, the actual distribution of earnings changes is very similar to that of a random distribution, and it should be obvious that the likelihood of an individual company's achieving above-average earnings growth over a reasonably long period of time is small.

Ball and Watts performed a study[6] that was similar to Brealey's and found similar results. Their study covered the 20-year period 1947–1966 and a sample of more than 700 firms. Table 11-2 lists the results of the part of their study which dealt with the *autocorrelation of earnings*. When we speak of the autocorrelation of earnings, we are referring to the relationship between the present earnings of a particular company and its own earnings in previous time periods. (This is in contrast to the cross-sectional results in Table 11-1, where a company's earnings growth was compared with the average earnings growth for a large sample of firms.) The question is, can we forecast the earnings of a particular company by looking at its earnings growth rates in previous years? If we can, then changes in earnings over time will be correlated. An autocorrelation coefficient of lag 1 refers to the correlation of the earnings changes in adjacent years. An autocorrelation coefficient of lag 2 refers to the correlation coefficient of the earnings change in a particular year with the earnings change 2 years before, etc.

Notice in Table 11-2 that the autocorrelations for both net income and EPS for lags of 1 to 5 years are very close to zero. The most extreme autocorrelation was $-.200$ for adjacent year EPS changes. If we think of this in terms of regressing EPS changes in year t against EPS changes in year $t - 1$, the R^2 would be only .04. (Recall from

[6]R. Ball and R. Watts, "Some Time Series Properties of Accounting Income," *Journal of Finance* (June 1972).

TABLE 11-2   MEAN AUTOCORRELATION
COEFFICIENTS OF ANNUAL
EARNINGS CHANGES

| Lag | Autocorrelation for | |
	Net income	EPS
1	$-.030$	$-.200$
2	$-.040$	$-.076$
3	.006	$-.061$
4	$-.007$	.023
5	.005	.010

Source: R. Ball and R. Watts, "Some Time Series Properties of Accounting Income," *Journal of Finance* (June 1972), Tables 3 and 4.

Chapter 8 that R^2 is equal to the correlation coefficient squared.) Thus, knowing the change in the previous year's EPS would have explained only 4% of the change in the current year's EPS—and this was for the most extreme autocorrelation shown in Table 11-2.

Other studies have found a similar lack of autocorrelation in earnings as well as other financial variables such as sales, operating earnings, and earnings before taxes.[7] Thus, it appears that forecasts of future growth rates based on simply extrapolating historical growth rates are unlikely to be of much value. While the historical growth rate may provide a convenient point of departure, better-than-average forecasts will have to be based on a large variety of economic variables—among these would be the political and economic environment the firm is expected to operate in, the firm's expected competitive position, the expected cost of labor and raw materials, and the quality of management. Forming these expectations has been, and will continue to be, one of the most important responsibilities of the security analyst.

11-2-2 Quarterly Earnings Changes   While there does not appear to be any systematic autocorrelation for annual earnings changes, there does appear to be significant autocorrelation in quarterly earnings. Because of seasonality factors, we might expect that this would be the case. For example, we would expect that a retail store which sells only fireworks would generate most of its sales in June and July. We would expect that a toy manufacturer would ship a disproportionate amount of its annual sales in the months preceding Christmas. Thus, there are definite seasonal factors associated with the activities of many firms, and these systematic relationships should result in quarterly earnings being autocorrelated.

To illustrate, consider the following hypothetical series of quarterly EPS for a firm whose earnings peak in the second and third quarters and decline substantially in the fourth quarter.

HYPOTHETICAL SERIES OF
QUARTERLY EPS

Quarter	Quarterly EPS	Change in EPS $EPS_t - EPS_{t-1}$
1st	1.00	
2nd	2.50	+ 1.50
3rd	2.75	+ .25
4th	.25	− 2.50
1st	1.10	+ .85
2nd	3.00	+ 1.90
3rd	3.05	+ .05
4th	.30	− 2.75
1st	1.25	+ .95

[7]For example, see Brealey, op cit.; Lintner and Glauber, op. cit.; and W. H. Beaver, "The Time Series Behavior of Earnings," *Empirical Research in Accounting: Selected Studies 1970,* supplement to *Journal of Accounting Research* (1970).

TABLE 11-3   AUTOCORRELATIONS COEFFICIENTS
OF QUARTERLY EPS CHANGES

Lag	Mean autocorrelation
1	−.296
2	−.125
3	−.153
4	.408
5	−.162
6	−.076
7	−.139
8	.344

Source: G. Foster, "Quarterly Accounting Data:
Time Series Properties and Predictive-Ability Results," *The Accounting Review* (January 1977).

Notice that there is a very strong seasonal pattern in the changes in EPS. The second quarter has a large increase compared with the first, the fourth quarter has a large decrease compared with the third quarter, and the pattern repeats itself every four quarters. Thus, we would expect to see a strong autocorrelation for EPS changes that are lagged by four quarters.

Table 11-3 presents the autocorrelations found by Foster.[8] He examined the quarterly earnings of 69 NYSE firms over the 1946–1974 period. Notice that the autocorrelations for lags 4 and 8 are positive and quite large. This suggests that there is, on average, a seasonal factor to earnings. Thus, the practice of comparing the current quarter's earnings with the earnings of the same quarter in the previous year is a more meaningful comparison than comparing the current quarter's results with the immediately preceding quarter.

11-2-3 Common Factors in Earnings Changes   It is well established that, on average, the earnings of firms fluctuate with changes in the overall level of economic activity. In fact, aggregate corporate profits are considered a coincident indicator of economic activity and are used to identify turning points in the business cycle. In addition, we might suspect that characteristics unique to an industry would cause some common covariation of the earnings of firms within the industry, over and above the variation due to economywide factors.

Several studies have attempted to measure the amount of variation in firms' earnings which can be explained by economywide and industry factors.[9] Table 11-4 summarizes

[8]G. Foster, "Quarterly Accounting Data: Time Series Properties and Predictive-Ability Results," *The Accounting Review* (January 1977).

[9]The two studies referenced in Table 11-4 are from Chapter 5 of R. A. Brealey, *An Introduction to Risk and Return from Common Stocks*, op. cit., and Chapter 5 of G. Foster, *Financial Statement Analysis*, Prentice-Hall, Englewood Cliffs, N.J., 1978. Other studies on this topic include: P. Brown and R. Ball, "Some Preliminary Findings on the Association between the Earnings of a Firm, Its Industry, and the Economy," *Empirical Research in Accounting: Selected Studies, 1977*, supplement to *Journal of Accounting Research* (1967); N. J. Gonedes, "Properties of Accounting Numbers: Models and Tests," *Journal of Accounting Research* (autumn 1973); and R. P. Magee, "Industry-Wide Commonalities in Earnings," *Journal of Accounting Research* (autumn 1974).

the results of two of these studies. The two studies differ with respect to the time periods covered and how industries were defined. Thus, we should expect some differences in their results. Nevertheless, one can draw some general conclusions.

First, it appears that, *on average*, a little over 20% of the variation in a firm's earnings can be attributed to economywide factors and another 20% or so can be attributed to industry factors. Second, as one might suspect, different industries tend to be more sensitive to economywide factors than are other industries. The auto industry appears to be one of the most sensitive, as economywide factors explained 48% of the variation in the earnings of auto manufacturers. This is a reasonable result, since the purchase of an automobile will be heavily influenced by the level of discretionary income available to consumers, which in turn is largely influenced by the business cycle. It also appears that oil company earnings are heavily influenced by industry

TABLE 11-4 PROPORTION OF EARNINGS CHANGES ATTRIBUTED TO ECONOMYWIDE AND INDUSTRY FACTORS

Industry	Brealey's study			Foster's study		
	Economy	Industry	Combined	Economy	Industry	Combined
Aircraft	.11	.05	.16	.15	.01	.16
Air transport				.27	.05	.32
Autos	.48	.11	.59			
Auto parts				.13	.21	.34
Beer	.11	.07	.18			
Building materials				.12	.15	.27
Cement	.06	.32	.38			
Chemicals	.41	.08	.49	.29	.27	.56
Cosmetics	.05	.06	.11			
Department stores	.30	.37	.67	.34	.26	.60
Drugs	.14	.07	.21	.05	.51	.56
Electric utilities	.24	.08	.32	.35	.17	.52
Food	.10	.10	.20			
Food chains	.06	.33	.39	.23	.12	.35
Machinery	.19	.16	.35			
Natural gas				.22	.09	.31
Nonferrous metals	.26	.25	.51			
Office equipment	.14	.06	.20	.16	.20	.36
Oil	.13	.49	.62	.31	.49	.80
Paper	.27	.28	.55	.37	.40	.79
Tin and rubber	.26	.48	.74	.22	.29	.51
Steel	.32	.21	.53	.20	.16	.36
Textiles and clothing	.25	.29	.54	.39	.19	.58
Tobacco	.08	.19	.27			
Averages	.21	.21	.42	.24	.22	.46

Source: Adapted from R. A. Brealey, *An Introduction to Risk and Return from Common Stocks*, 2d ed., MIT Press, Cambridge, Mass., 1983, Table 5.6, and G. Foster, *Financial Statement Analysis*, Prentice-Hall, Englewood Cliffs, N.J., 1978, Table 5.5.

factors—in both studies industry factors explained 49% of the changes in oil company earnings. And, at the other extreme, some companies' earnings do not appear to be substantially influenced by either economywide or industry factors. For example, these two factors *combined* explained only 18% of the total variation of the earnings of beer companies and 11% of the earnings variation of cosmetic companies.

Thus, while some companies may be more impacted than others, the typical firm's earnings tend to be heavily influenced by economywide and industry factors. Consequently, good forecasts of individual firm earnings are going to depend, in no small part, on good forecasts of the prospects for the general economy and for the firm's industry. As a natural result of this, many investment organizations have their own economic forecasters and/or purchase economic forecasts from outside sources. In addition, many investment firms organize their security analysts along industry lines. These analysts frequently develop a great deal of knowledge and understanding of the industry they follow—so much so that the managements of firms within an industry often look to industry security analysts as a source of information concerning the supply and demand conditions within their industry.

Before continuing, you should:
1 Be able to cite several studies which document the importance of earnings in determining stock prices
2 Know that the distribution of annual earnings changes is similar to a random distribution
3 Know that quarterly earnings tend to follow a seasonal pattern
4 Be aware of the importance of economywide and industry influences on earnings changes

11-3 DIVIDENDS AND STOCK PRICES

From a theoretical viewpoint, the importance of dividends in determining stock prices is obvious—stock prices should equal the present value of all future expected dividends. And there is a growing body of empirical evidence which supports the theory.

11-3-1 Dividend Changes and Stock Returns   A number of studies have examined the impact that changes in dividends have on stock returns.[10] The results of a careful study by Aharony and Swary[11] are summarized in Figure 11-3. They examined the quarterly dividend announcements of 149 firms over the period 1963–1976.

After controlling for other factors which might affect stock returns around the announcment date, the sample was divided into two groups—those announcements associated with dividend decreases and those announcements associated with dividend

---

[10]One of the first studies was by R. R. Petit, "Dividend Announcements, Security Performance and Capital Market Efficiency," *Journal of Finance* (December 1972). A more recent study is: J. Cole, "Are Dividend Surprises Independently Important," *Journal of Portfolio Management* (summer 1984).

[11]J. Aharony and I. Swary, "Quarterly Dividend and Earnings Announcements and Stockholders' Returns: An Empirical Analysis," *Journal of Finance* (March 1980).

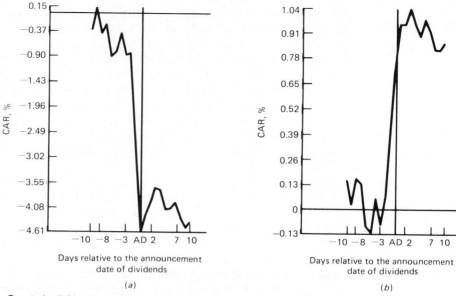

FIGURE 11-3 Quarterly dividend announcements and stock returns. (a) Dividend decrease: (b) dividend increase. [*Source: J. Aharony and I. Swary, "Quarterly Dividend and Earnings Announcements and Stockholders' Returns: An Empirical Analysis,"* Journal of Finance *(March 1980), fig. 1.*]

increases. Notice in Figure 11-3 that the cumulative abnormal return (CAR)[12] dropped sharply for several days before the announcement date and on the announcement date itself. The total decline in the CAR was 4.6%. Conversely, the stocks of companies which announced dividend increases experienced positive abnormal returns, although the absolute amount of the change in the CAR was only about 1%.

These results support the notion that stock prices are affected by changes in current dividend rates and that current dividend changes cause investors to revise their expectations concerning the long-run dividend stream. A similar study by Charest[13] provides further evidence on the latter point. Figure 11-4 illustrates his results. In this figure the CAR is graphed for 24 months before and after the dividend announcement. Notice that there is a substantial decline in the CAR (-26%) prior to announcements of dividend decreases, and an increase in the CAR ($+9\%$) prior to announcements of dividend increases.

This is another example of competitive security markets at work. Good analysts apparently anticipated the positive (negative) dividend changes and investors bought (sold) the stocks before the actual public announcement of the changes. Since the actual size of the dividend changes is relatively small in dollar terms compared with

---

[12]For a discussion of event study methodology, see Section 5-4-1. Aharony and Swary use the abbreviation CAR for cumulative average residual, which is equivalent to the abbreviation CAAR for cumulative average abnormal return used in Chapter 5.

[13]G. Charest, "Dividend Information, Stock Returns and Market Efficiency—II," *Journal of Financial Economics* (June/September 1979).

the stock price, analysts must revise their expectations concerning the entire future dividend stream in order to justify changes in stock prices on the order of -26% for stocks which cut their dividends and $+9\%$ for stocks which increased their dividends.

Both the Aharony and Swary study and the Charest study found larger abnormal returns associated with dividend decreases than with dividend increases. This is consistent with the notion that the managers of firms are reluctant to cut dividends, and we will present evidence to support this notion in the next section. Given a reluctance on the part of management to cut dividends, investors apparently view dividend cuts as a much stronger indicator of the company's future fortunes than dividend increases. Consequently, there has been a much larger market reaction to dividend cuts than to dividend increases.

The Charest study has also been cited as evidence of a market inefficiency. Notice that for dividend increases the cumulative abnormal return increases another 4% over a period of 24 months *after* the announcement date, while for dividend decreases the CAR continues to decline another 6%. Since the dividend change is publicly known after the announcement date, the CAR should immediately level off if prices fully reflect public information. However, one needs to be careful in interpreting these results. First, the abnormal returns in the postannouncement period were not nearly as large as those in the preannouncement period. Second, an abnormal return of -6% or $+4\%$ is not as large as it might initially appear to be when one considers that this occurred over a 2-year time period. And, it *may* be that other factors, besides the information on dividend changes, affected the returns of these stocks. Nevertheless, given Charest's results, it would seem prudent for investors to pay close attention to changes in dividends, particularly if the change involves a cut in the dividend.

11-3-2 The Nature of Dividend Changes   One important distinction between earnings and dividends is that managers can arbitrarily determine, at least in the short run, the level of dividends. Aside from the issue of "managing earnings" by choosing among various accounting conventions, the level of earnings is largely determined by supply-and-demand conditions within the firm's markets. And management has relatively little control over these variables.

FIGURE 11-4   Abnormal returns before and after dividend changes. [*Source: G. Charest, "Dividend Information, Stock Returns and Market Efficiency—II,"* Journal of Financial Economics *(June/September 1978), table 3.*]

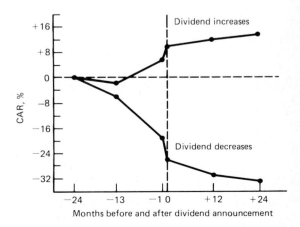

TABLE 11-5   DISTRIBUTION OF DIVIDEND CHANGES

	Firms that increased dividends, %	Firms that decreased dividends, %	No change
All firms, all years	56.4	28.1	15.5
Firms classified by earnings change:			
Single year of increased earnings	65.8	20.3	13.9
2 consecutive years of increased earnings	74.8	13.8	11.4
Single year of decreased earnings	42.8	39.5	17.9
2 consecutive years of decreased earnings	31.8	48.8	19.4

Source: E. Fama and H. Babiak, "Dividend Policy: An Empirical Analysis," *American Statistical Association Journal* (December 1968).

However, as long as the firm has cash or the ability to borrow cash, the current level of dividends is determined by management. Of course, in the long run the amount of cash available to pay dividends will be determined by the profitability of the firm. But this may not necessarily be the case in the short run. Frequently, earnings will decline and management will maintain or even increase the current level of dividends.

It is often argued that managers generally have a *target payout ratio* of dividends to earnings. This target payout ratio represents the amount of the firm's "normal earnings" that can be paid out and still maintain a desired level of capital investment and a desired growth rate over the longer term. Thus, if reported earnings over time fluctuate around what management considers to be the firm's normal earnings, the payout ratio of dividends to current (reported) earnings may fluctuate. For example, if reported earnings drop to a level that is less than management's estimate of the firm's normal earnings, management may choose to not cut the current dividend. Likewise, if earnings should increase to a level above managment's estimate of normal earnings, the dividend may not be increased. Only when management is certain that earnings are permanently higher or lower will the dividend be raised or lowered, acccording to the target payout argument.

A study by Fama and Babiak[14] considered the issue of whether or not firms try to maintain a target payout ratio of dividends to normal earnings. Their sample included dividend and earnings changes for 392 firms during the period 1946–1964, and the results are summarized in Table 11-5. Note that when all firms and all years are considered, 56.4% of the time the dividend was increased. However, when firms are classified as to whether their earnings increased or decreased during the year, we notice a substantial difference in the distribution of dividend changes. For example, 65.8% of the firms with increased earnings in the current year also increased their dividends. Of the firms whose earnings had increased for 2 years in a row, 74.8% increased their dividends and only 13.8% cut their dividend. Apparently the managers of these firms believed that earnings were at a permanently higher level.

[14]E. Fama and H. Babiak, "Dividend Policy: An Empirical Analysis," *American Statistical Association Journal* (December 1968).

Of those firms whose earnings declined from the previous year, 39.5% cut their dividend payments. If earnings had declined for 2 years in a row, almost half (48.8%) of the firms cut their dividend. Taken as a whole, these results provide support for the argument that in the short run dividends are "sticky" and do not fluctuate as much as earnings. And it appears that managers are much less likely to cut dividends than they are to increase them. But over the longer term, dividend changes tend to track earnings changes.

Another study by Fama[15] examined dividend changes using a different approach. Let b^* equal a target payout ratio of earnings and E_t equal the firm's reported earnings. Now, for the time being, assume that E_t also equals management's estimate of the firm's normal earnings. Then in any particular year t, the target dividend payment would be

$$\text{Target dividend} = b^*E_t$$

Given these definitions, D_t, the actual dividend in year t, can be written as

$$D_t = D_{t-1} + p(b^*E_t - D_{t-1}) \tag{11-1}$$

where D_{t-1} represents the dividend in the previous year. Note that $(b^*E_t - D_{t-1})$ represents the difference between the current year's target dividend and the previous year's dividend, i.e., the *target change in dividend*. Fama called p the "speed of adjustment coefficient," since it measures how quickly firms adjust their dividends to the target level. Note that if $p = 1$, the current dividend would be equal to the target dividend (i.e., the previous year's dividend plus the target change), and the "speed of adjustment" would be immediate.

Of course, it is unlikely that reported earnings E_t will represent management's estimate of normal earnings in any particular year, even though this may be, on average, a reasonable assumption over a period of years. Thus, we wouldn't expect firm managers to immediately adjust the dividend level to b^*E_t. To see how quickly firms do adjust dividends to changes in reported earnings, Fama first estimated b^* for each of 298 firms over the period 1946–1968. Then p was estimated by regression analysis. For the typical firm he estimated b^* to be .58 (i.e., the typical target payout ratio was 58%), and p was estimated to be .251 for the typical firm. This suggests that, on average, firms adjusted their dividends by about one-fourth of the change in earnings each year.

While the relationship was not perfect (on average, this procedure explained 42% of the variation in dividends over time), the results are strong enough to suggest that this may be a useful procedure for estimating changes in the current level of dividends, given the current period's earnings. For example, the analyst might first estimate a target payout ratio by calculating the average payout ratio over a period of years, or by simply asking the firm's management what its target payout ratio is. Then p might

---

[15]E. Fama, "The Empirical Relationship between the Dividend and Investment Decision," *American Economic Review* (June 1974).

be set at .25, or *p* might be estimated from a regression using the firm's historical data and Equation (11-1). Given estimates of *b** and *p*, and the firm's current earnings, the forthcoming dividend payment could be estimated. Similarly, given estimates of future earnings, one could estimate a series of future dividends.

11-4 CASH FLOW

In addition to earnings and dividends, many investors also pay close attention to cash flow. For example, the *Value Line Investment Survey* plots a line on the price chart of each stock they follow. In most cases this line is equal to cash flow per share multiplied by some appropriate number.[16] Referring back to the Bandag example in the Appendix to Chapter 8, one can see that the line on the price chart portion of Figure 8A-4 is equal to 14 times cash flow per share. Thus, this type of analysis of determining an appropriate cash flow multiple is similar to the more conventioanl method of trying to determine an appropriate *P/E*, or earnings multiple.

Unfortunately, there is no single, agreed-upon definition of cash flow. One definition of cash flow is the firm's earnings after taxes (EAT) plus noncash charges, where the noncash charges are typically viewed to be depreciation (Depr). However, the sum of earnings after taxes and depreciation really only measures the amount of *working capital provided by operations*. It may be that the earnings and noncash charges are being used to finance increased levels of inventories or accounts receivable and not increasing the actual cash available to the firm. Thus, a broader definition of cash flow from operations would be

$$\text{Cash flow} = \text{EAT} + \text{Depr.} - \Delta\text{WC} \tag{11-2}$$

where ΔWC stands for the change in the *noncash* components of working capital during the accounting period.[17]

The serious investor will want to examine the firm's cash flow carefully, as there are times when an analysis of cash flow may provide some valuable insights into the company's profitability—insights that an analysis of earnings might not reveal. One classic example of this was the case of W.T. Grant, which was the nation's largest retailer when it filed for bankruptcy in 1975.

W.T. Grant's profitability, turnover, and liquidity ratios had trended downward over the 10 years prior to its bankruptcy, although most analysts apparently did not consider the trend alarming as the firm's stock price held up well. Nor was there a marked decline in working capital provided by operations, i.e., EAT + Depr. However, an analysis of cash flow as defined in Equation (11-2) would have shown that for many years preceding bankruptcy, the company's operations were a net user of

[16]As an aside, the term "value line" was coined by Arnold Bernhard, the founder of the *Value Line* advisory service. Value line referred to a line, representing the stock's intrinsic value, drawn on a price chart. One could look at the chart to see if the stock price was above or below the value line.

[17]For example, an increase in accounts receivable would be subtracted, a decrease in inventories would be added, an increase in accounts payable would be added, etc.

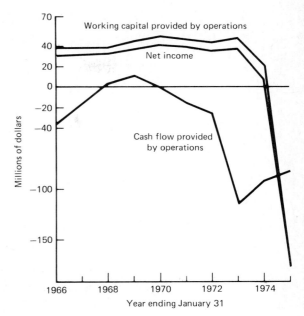

FIGURE 11-5 W. T. Grant Company net income, working capital, and cash flow from operations for fiscal years ending January 31, 1966 to 1975. [*Source: S. Largay and C. Stickney, "Cash Flows, Ratio Analysis and the W. T. Grant Company Bankruptcy,"* Financial Analysts Journal *(July/August 1980), exhibit III.*]

cash, not a generator of cash. Figure 11-5 illustrates these results.[18] Notice that while Net Income and Working Capital Provided by Operations remained positive in the decade prior to bankruptcy, cash flow as defined in Equation (11-2) was negative in 8 out of the 10 years and dropped precipitously in 1973 and 1974. With the advantage of hindsight, investors would have been well served in the case of W.T. Grant to have paid close attention to cash flow, in addition to earnings.[19]

11-5 CAN ANALYSTS FORECAST?

Investors use many different techniques to forecast growth. The various methods can be broadly divided into two groups—statistical techniques and subjective approaches. By their nature, the statistical techniques are well defined and consequently can be learned in classroom situations. In fact, many business schools offer an entire course on forecasting techniques within their statistics or quantitative methods curriculum. We discussed some of these techniques in Chapter 8, although obviously not in the detail one would receive in a formal statistics course on forecasting.

On the other hand, the subjective approaches used by many professional security analysts are too eclectic and complex and incorporate too many different sources of information to be distilled down into a few pages of a textbook. One can only learn

[18]These results are taken from S. Largay and C. Stickney, "Cash Flows, Ratio Analysis and the W.T. Grant Company Bankruptcy," *Financial Analysts Journal* (July/August 1980). Another recent and interesting article dealing with cash flow is M. Gombola and J. Ketz, "A Caveat on Measuring Cash Flow and Solvency," *Financial Analysts Journal* (September/October 1983).

[19]For references to additional studies dealing with forecasting bankruptcy, see Section 15-2-2.

TABLE 11-6   A COMPARISON OF ANNUAL EARNINGS FORECASTS

Magnitude of forecast error, %	Percentage of forecasts with a smaller error	
	Box-Jenkins	Value Line analysts
± 5	15.0	18.0
± 10	26.5	32.0
± 25	54.5	63.5
± 50	81.0	86.5
± 75	87.5	90.5
± 100	89.5	92.0

Source: Adapted from Table 2 of L. D. Brown and M. S. Rozeff, "The Superiority of Analyst Forecasts as Measures of Expectations," *Journal of Finance* (March 1978).

these approaches through the school of experience. In order to acquaint the reader with some of the possible subjective methods of forecasting growth, the Appendix presents an example of how one analyst approached an actual forecasting problem. This example should be worth reading because the evidence suggests that the answer to the question "can analysts forecast?" is yes. The earnings forecasts of analysts have been shown to be superior to the forecasts generated by purely statistical models. In addition, it appears that analysts also have some ability to forecast stock price performance.

11-5-1 Earnings Forecasts   Brown and Rozeff[20] compared the earnings forecasts made by Value Line analysts with the forecasts generated by purely statistical models. Their study considered both annual and quarterly earnings forecasts for 50 firms over the 4-year period 1972–1975. Value Line analysts, like most security analysts, utilize a large variety of techniques and information sources in making their earnings estimates. As a comparison, Brown and Rozeff utilized three different statistical techniques to estimate earnings, including the Box-Jenkins (BJ) technique, which was discussed in Section 8-3-1. In this study the BJ technique proved to be the best of the statistical methods of forecasting earnings.

However, Brown and Rozeff found that the analysts consistently made better forecasts than any of the statistical methods for both quarterly and annual earnings. For example, Table 11-6 presents a comparison of the Value Line forecasts with the BJ forecasts for annual earnings. Notice that 18% of the forecasts were within ±5% of the actual earnings, vs. 15% for the best of the statistical models. Similarly, 32% of the analysts' forecasts were within ±10% of the actual earnings, vs. 26.5% for the BJ technique, and so on.

It should also be noted that two of the statistical models analyzed by Brown and Rozeff were (1) no change in earnings and (2) a change in earnings equal to the previous

---

[20]L. D. Brown and M. S. Rozeff, "The Superiority of Analyst Forecasts as Measures of Expectations," *Journal of Finance* (March 1978). Also see A. Fisher, "How Good Are Wall Street's Security Analysts?" *Fortune* (Oct. 1, 1984).

period's change. The first model is analogous to earnings following a random walk. The analysts' forecasts were consistently superior to these two models. Thus, while on the surface earnings may appear to be randomly distributed, there obviously must be fundamental factors influencing earnings which analysts are able to identify and utilize in their forecasts.

Consequently, the more complex, subjective methods used by analysts appear to be superior to the strictly statistical methods. Another interesting question, of course, is can analysts forecast stock price performance in addition to earnings? Again, the answer appears to be yes.

11-5-2 Stock Price Forecasts   In two studies,[21] Ambachtsheer reported on the ability of analysts to forecast stock price performance by measuring what he referred to as the *information coefficient*. First, analysts ranked stocks from 1 to 5, with a rank of 1 signifying the poorest expected price performance over a specified time period and a rank of 5 signifying the best expected performance. At the end of the time period the stocks were again ranked from 1 to 5, this time based on the actual performance. *The information coefficient (IC) is the correlation coefficient between the expected ranks and the actual rankings.* If analysts were perfect forecasters of relative stock price performance, the IC would be 1; if they had no forecasting ability the IC would be zero.

In the first study, the rankings of analysts from one financial institution who followed 250 stocks were examined. In the second study, analysts from 16 different financial institutions ranked 150 stocks and 25 industries for relative price performance. The ICs varied, of course, between the two studies and depending upon the length of time over which price performance was measured. However, for time periods of approximately 6 months, the ICs tended to be about .15, and statistically significant. (Recall that if markets are perfectly efficient, investors should not be able to predict relative price performance and ICs should be zero.) While a correlation coefficient of .15 may, at first glance, seem small, it does show that analysts have some ability to forecast relative price performance.[22] And, as the study by Hodges and Brealey (see Figure 5-7) demonstrated, relatively low forecasting ability can improve portfolio performance substantially.

This raises an interesting question. If, in fact, analysts do have some ability to forecast relative stock price performance, why isn't this ability translated into superior portfolio performance? (Recall from Chapter 5 that the studies on portfolio performance

---

[21]K. P. Ambachtsheer, "Portfolio Theory and the Security Analyst," *Financial Analysts Journal* (November–December 1972); and K. P. Ambachtsheer, "Profit Potential in an 'Almost Efficient' Market," *Journal of Portfolio Management* (fall 1974). This same approach was also used to assess the forecasting ability of two investment advisory services, Value Line and Wells Fargo. See K. P. Ambachtsheer and J. L. Farrell, "Can Active Management Add Value?" *Financial Analysts Journal* (November/December 1979).

[22]Other studies have confirmed that analysts have some ability to forecast stock price performance. See J. Bjerring, J. Lakonishok and T. Vermaelen, "Stock Prices and Financial Analysts' Recommendations," *Journal of Finance* (March 1983); D. Givoly and J. Lakonishok, "The Information Content of Financial Analysts' Forecasts of Earnings: Some Evidence on Semi-Strong Inefficiency," *Journal of Accounting and Economics* (December 1979); and R. Groth, W. Lewellan, G. Schlarbaum, and R. Lease, "An Analysis of a Brokerage House Securities Recommendations," *Financial Analysts Journal* (February 1979).

were not able to identify superior portfolio managers.) It may be that portfolio managers do not realize the value of analysts' price forecasts and consequently do not utilize this information. However, this seems unlikely since the typical portfolio manager depends upon the analysts' judgment in determining which stocks to include in a portfolio. Perhaps portfolio managers overreact to analysts' recommendations and eliminate the profit potential by excessive trading. Or it may be that in the process of correctly reacting to analysts' recommendations by buying and selling securities, a signal is sent to other investors who compete away the potential profits. At least the latter conjecture is consistent with the notion of competition and efficient markets.

11-6 SUMMARY

There is a sound theoretical basis for believing that changes in dividends should influence changes in stock prices, and the empirical evidence supports the theory. Empirically, there is equally strong support for the importance of earnings. Stock prices of companies which report higher earnings also tend to experience above-normal returns, and vice versa. Thus, the investor who can generate superior earnings forecasts may also achieve above-normal returns.

However, forecasting earnings is likely to prove difficult, since earnings changes tend to be distributed as if they were randomly determined. Thus, simply extrapolating historical growth rates into the future is not likely to lead to better than average earnings forecasts. The truly superior analyst will most likely have a better understanding and forecast of the economywide and industry factors which influence the earnings of individual firms, as well as a superior understanding of the characteristics unique to the firm.

In addition to analyzing earnings and dividends of firms, investors will be well served by investigating the firm's ability to generate cash. Cash flow analysis will occasionally provide insights into the true profitability of the firm that cannot be gained by considering only the firm's reported earnings.

Despite the difficulty of the task, it does appear that the forecasts of analysts are superior to forecasts generated by purely statistical models. Perhaps even more interesting is the fact that the evidence suggests analysts also have some predictive ability concerning future stock price performance. Surely this ability is based, at least in part, on the analysts' ability to forecast earnings and dividends. Consequently, the Appendix to this chapter, which presents an example of how one analyst went about the problem of forecasting earnings, should be of interest to the reader.

SUGGGESTED READINGS

Excellent summaries of the literature concerning the relationship among earnings, dividends, and stock prices can be found in:

R. A. Brealey, *An Introduction to Risk and Return from Common Stocks*, 2d ed. MIT Press, Cambridge, Mass., 1983.

G. Foster, *Financial Statement Analysis*, Prentice-Hall, Englewood Cliffs, N.J., 1978.

Of the original research published on these topics, the following articles might be the most useful to read:

V. Niederhoffer and P. Regan, ''Earnings Changes, Analysts Forecasts, and Stock Prices,'' *Financial Analysts Journal* (May/June 1972).

G. Foster, ''Quarterly Accounting Data: Time Series Properties and Predictive-Ability Results,'' *The Accounting Review* (January 1977).

J. Aharony and I. Swary, ''Quarterly Dividend and Earnings Announcements, and Stockholders' Returns: An Empirical Analysis,'' *Journal of Finance* (March 1980).

A good summary article on the topic of how well analysts forecast earnings and the related topic of whether above-normal profits can be achieved by the superior forecaster, is:

D. Givoly and J. Lakonishok, ''The Quality of Analysts' Forecasts of Earnings,'' *Financial Analysts Journal* (September/October 1984).

The following are recent articles related to the problem of forecasting earnings:

R. D. Arnott, ''The Use and Misuse of Consensus Earnings,'' *Journal of Portfolio Management* (Spring 1985).

L. D. Brown and M. S. Rozeff, ''The Superiority of Analyst Forecasts as Measures of Expectations,'' *Journal of Finance* (March 1978).

W. A. Collins and W. S. Hopwood, ''A Multivariate Analysis of Annual Earnings Forecasts Generated from Quarterly Forecasts of Financial Analysts and Univariate Time Series,'' *Journal of Accounting Research* (autumn 1980).

J. G. Cragg and B. G. Malkiel, ''Expectations and the Valuation of Shares,'' Working Paper 471, National Bureau of Economic Research (April 1980).

E. J. Elton, M. J. Gruber, and M. H. Gultekin, ''Professional Expectations: Accuracy and Diagnosis of Errors,'' *Journal of Financial and Quarterly Analysis* (December 1984).

D. Fried and D. Givoly, ''Financial Analysts' Forecasts of Earnings: A Better Surrogate for Earnings Expectations,'' *Journal of Accounting and Economics* (October 1982).

D. Givoly and J. Lakonishok, ''The Information Content of Financial Analysts Forecasts of Earnings,'' *Journal of Accounting and Economics* (winter 1979).

T. J. Kerrigan, ''When Forecasting Earnings, It Pays to Watch Forecasts,'' *Journal of Portfolio Management* (summer 1984).

R. C. Klemkosky and W. P. Miller, ''When Forecasting Earnings, It Pays to Be Right,'' *Journal of Portfolio Management* (summer 1984).

QUESTIONS

1 Discuss some of the arguments for the point of view that earnings are not important determinants of stock prices. What evidence can you cite that supports the importance of earnings?

2 Are the actual changes in earnings more important than deviations from expected earnings? What are the implications of your answer for investment management?

3 What does the phrase ''dividends are sticky'' mean? If dividends are ''sticky,'' what does this imply for short-run forecasts of dividends? for long-run forecasts?

4 Would you expect the quarterly earnings of a grocery store chain to be autocorrelated? What about the quarterly earnings of H&R Block?

5 If you were assigned the problem of determining which of three variables (earnings, dividends, or cash flow) were most closely linked to stock prices, how might you approach this problem?

6 The W.T. Grant example illustrated one case where an analysis of cash flow would have been very beneficial to the investor. Can you think of any situations where cash flow might be misleading concerning a firm's profitability?

7 The Charest study suggested that investors might be able to earn abnormal profits by simply buying stocks after an announcement of an increase in the dividend payment. Can you think of any reasons why such a strategy might not work?

8 If earnings, in fact, are *not* randomly generated, but rather earnings are determined by fundamental economic factors, why might earnings still appear to be randomly distributed?

9 Is it possible for markets to be efficient and for analysts to be able to accurately forecast earnings changes? Explain.

10 Is it possible for markets to be efficient and for analysts to be able to forecast relative stock price performance? Explain.

PROBLEMS

1 Given the information below:
   a Calculate the first-order autocorrelation coefficient for changes in EPS.
   b Calculate the fourth-order autocorrelation coefficient for changes in EPS.

t	E_t	D_t	b
1	1.00	.40	.400
2	1.10	.40	.364
3	1.50	.50	.333
4	1.60	.55	.344
5	1.55	.60	.387
6	1.80	.60	.333
7	1.85	.65	.351
8	2.00	.65	.325
9	2.00	.70	.350
10	2.25	.75	.333

2 Using the information in Problem 1:
   a Estimate b^* for Equation (11-1) of the text.
   b If the company just reported EPS of $2.30 for time period 11, using Equation (11-1) what would be your estimate of D_{11}, the next dividend payment which has not yet been announced? Assume $p = .4$.
   c If EPS for time period 12 are forecast to be $2.75, what would you expect D_{12}, the dividend for time period 12, to be?

3 Assume you have followed the methodology suggested by Fama and have estimated b^* to be .3 and p to be .6 for No-Cut, Inc. No-Cut's last dividend D_0 was $1.00 and its current period's earnings E_1 are $2.00.
   a Using Fama's methodology, what is your estimate of D_1, No-Cut's dividend for the current period?
   b Based on the company's name, what do you think the dividend will be?

4 Given the income statement and balance sheet shown at the top of page 303:
   a Calculate cash flow using the traditional definition of EAT + Depr.
   b Calculate cash flow using Equation (11-2).
   c Discuss your findings.

Income Statement	
Revenues	2000
Cost of goods sold	(1200)
Gross profit	800
Selling and administration expense	(300)
Depreciation	(100)
Earnings before taxes	400
Taxes	(160)
Earnings after taxes	240

Assets and Liabilities	Start of year	End of year
Cash	200	100
Accounts receivable	200	400
Inventory	200	440
Current assets	600	940
Fixed assets	700	800
Accumulated depreciation	(100)	(200)
Total assets	1200	1540
Accounts payable	200	200
Notes payable	300	300
Current liabilities	500	500
Long-term debt	200	300
Equity	500	740
	1200	1540

5 Pick a stock followed by Value Line that is of interest to you. Analyze Value Line's EPS estimate for the upcoming year. Compare this estimate with an estimate based on the average growth model (see Chapter 8) using the last 5 years' EPS data. Does Value Line's estimate differ significantly from the forecast of the average growth model and, if so, are there any obvious reasons why?

APPENDIX: An Example of Estimating EPS

As noted at the beginning of this chapter, the various approaches used by practicing security analysts to estimate earnings and other financial variables are too eclectic and too complex to be neatly summarized in one chapter of a textbook. Most analysts utilize a combination of statistical techniques and subjective methods in arriving at their forecasts, and frequently the subjective approaches are unique to the analyst. Consequently, we will only attempt to expose you to some of these approaches by reprinting parts of an actual research report produced by a highly competent analyst.

In early 1984, Jeffrey Atkin, an analyst at the Seattle-based brokerage firm of Cable, Howse & Ragen, wrote a research report on Trus Joist Corporation. Trus Joist is a well-managed firm headquartered in Boise, Idaho, which produces wood-based products for the construction markets. Since residential and commercial construction are highly cyclical, forecasting earnings for firms supplying products to these markets is no easy task. The following is a condensed version of Mr. Atkins' report in which he predicted that Trus Joist's 1984 EPS would be $2.60 compared with the $1.62 the company had earned in 1983.

Notice that Mr. Atkin not only analyzes the historical financial performance of Trus Joist in considerable detail, but he also tries to anticipate future changes in Trus Joist's profitability. For example, he anticipates a change in the company's product mix due to increased industrial sales. He carefully considers the impact that past research and development expenditures may have on future profit margins. And notice in the last table of the report that he forecasts a decline in the tax rate to 35.0% for 1984 vs. 41.0%. As you read the report, see if you can determine his reasons for expecting a lower tax rate. As we've said before, *the hallmark of the truly superior analyst is the ability to anticipate changes in historical relationships.*

TRUS JOIST CORPORATION (TJCO-OTC)
Fiscal Year Ends: Dec.
($28 3/4)

52-week price range	Earnings per share			P/E ratio			Indicated dividend	
	1982	1983	1984E	1982	1983	1984E	Rate	Yield
$40 1/2–$27 1/4	$1.17	$1.62	$2.60	24.6X	17.7X	11.1X	$0.36	1.3%

Market Capitalization	Shares Outstanding	Estimated Float
$106.1 million	3,690,000 shs.	2,300,000 shs.
Average Daily Volume	**Return on Average Equity**	**Est. EPS Growth/3 Yrs.**
5,000 shares	20.2%–5 yrs.	18%–20%

SUMMARY AND RECOMMENDATION

Trus Joist Corporation can simply be described as a wood technology company. Its products, which are almost exclusively geared toward the construction markets, are highly proprietary. In large part this proprietary feature is due to the use of MICRO=LAM^R lumber, a veneer lumber made by laminating many layers of dried veneer into long, wide pieces of dimensionally stable, structural lumber. Five series of open web trusses and certain of the I-configured all-wood joists are manufactured for the light commercial construction market (37% of 1983 sales). Three series of I-configured all-wood joists for floor and roof supports are directed primarily at the residential construction industry (58% of 1983 sales). Finally, about 5.0% of last year's sales consisted of MICRO=LAM lumber sales to non-construction, industrial customers.

While we believe that Trus Joist clearly qualifies as a growth company, it has not been immune to the cyclical swings of the construction industry. Table I shows TJCO's operating record begining in 1970 when sales totaled only $11.3 million. Sales and earnings per share have declined in only three of these 12 years, once during the 1974–75 construction downturn and twice during the recent dip of 1980–82. On a peak-to-peak basis, that is, the five-year period, 1974–79, sales showed compounded annual growth of 19.6%. Over this same cycle (except for the peak earnings year being on the 1973 base year), earnings per share increased at a compounded annual rate of 26.6%. Also impressive, in our view, is that Trus Joist's pretax margin has been quite stable in a business prone to wide cyclical swings. This is especially true when looking at the Company's performance during the recent downturn. Housing starts totaled 1.3 million in 1980, 1.1 million in 1982, and 1.0 million in 1982, in contrast to an average annual level of 1.8 million for the prior years. During this three-year period Trus Joist was able to maintain its pretax margin while keeping its sales performance well ahead of the housing-start decline. From another perspective, we are impressed that TJCO produced an 11.6% pretax margin in 1982 while also earning 11.3% on average equity. We believe that this testifies to the proprietary features of the Company's product line and also underscores its market potential.

With housing activity this year expected slightly to exceed 1983 and with a much better environment projected for the light commercial construction industry, we anticipate a healthy improvement in TJCO's earnings. Specifically, we are estimating earnings of $2.60 per share this year, up 60.5% from 1983. This estimate, however, is still far from reflecting what we believe is the Company's true earnings power. This is primarily due to the continued under-utilization of the capacity devoted to products intended for light commercial construction ap-

TABLE I   OPERATING RECORD ($ in 000)

	Sales		Pretax income			Tax rate	Net income		Earnings per share	
	Amount	% change	Amount	% change	Margin	rate	Amount	% change	Amount	% change
1984E	$125,000	30.3%	$15,250	46.6%	12.20%	35.0%	$9,910	61.4%	$2.60	60.5%
1983	95,950	44.7%	10,405	35.8%	10.84%	41.0%	6,141	40.3%	1.62	38.5%
1982	66,322	(22.9)%	7,663	(32.9)%	11.55%	42.9%	4,376	(34.5)%	1.17	(34.3)%
1981	86,009	4.6%	11,413	(5.5)%	13.27%	41.5%	6,677	1.7%	1.78	1.1%
1980	82,247	(19.2)%	12,071	(14.2)%	14.68%	45.6%	6,563	(10.5)%	1.76	(11.1)%
1979	101,849	29.9%	14,069	34.1%	13.81%	47.9%	7,332	31.8%	1.98	31.1%
1978	78,422	39.0%	10,492	60.4%	13.38%	47.0%	5,564	71.7%	1.51	67.8%
1977	56,430	40.5%	6,541	65.1%	11.59%	50.5%	3,241	64.7%	0.90	60.7%
1976	40,171	20.7%	3,963	51.5%	9.86%	50.3%	1,968	42.1%	0.56	43.6%
1975	33,271	(20.1)%	2,616	19.5%	7.86%	47.1%	1,385	19.7%	0.39	18.2%
1974	41,641	1.7%	2,190	(31.1)%	5.26%	47.2%	1,157	(31.5)%	0.33	(31.3)%
1973	40,929	51.7%	3,177	60.9%	7.76%	46.8%	1,689	63.0%	0.48	60.0%
1972	26,989	52.6%	1,975	37.8%	7.32%	47.5%	1,036	42.1%	0.30	36.4%
1971	17,684	56.6%	1,433	60.5%	8.10%	49.1%	729	62.0%	0.22	46.7%
1970	11,293		893		7.91%	49.6%	450		0.15	

plications. Typically, the turn in light commercial construction lags that of the residential side by six to nine months. We anticipate that this lag will hold true for the present recovery, though we do not believe that the turnaround will be as dramatic as what is currently happening in residential construction. Regardless, 1984 should find both of Trus Joist's major lines in a solid trend upward. If all of the Company's plants were producing at their maximum output, Trus Joist, in our opinion, could well earn perhaps 80%–100% above our 1984 estimate.

At its current level, TJCO common sells at 11.1 times our 1984 projection. This represents only a 19.4% premium to the S & P 400. We recommend PURCHASE of Trus Joist common for the reasons given above as well the following:

● **Trus Joist's products for the most part are highly proprietary,** reflecting the technology-orientation of the Company. Most important, in our view, are the high-strength, light-weight characteristsics of MICRO = LAM lumber, which allow the Company to offer significant productivity benefits to both builders and industrial customers. Patents have been obtained for certain features of the MICRO = LAM lumber manufacturing process and the machinery involved. In addition, the company owns patents applying to some of the open-web series joists and the "I" joists as well as related machinery and processes. While we consider these patents to be of some importance, **a key priority of the Company is to reduce the cost of MICRO = LAM lumber by improving the manufacturing process.** The construction of a 4-foot-wide MICRO = LAM lumber press, now out of the developmental stage, will be a large factor in helping TJCO accomplish this goal. Trus Joist has been successful in selling its products in the past in spite of its prices having been above those of (conventional solid-sawn lumber) competing products. **The ability to reduce product costs would tremendously aid future selling efforts and, we believe, have a dramatic impact on the Company's bottom line.**

● **Trus Joist is a very profitable company.** For the five-year period, 1979–83, TJCO's pretax margin averaged 12.8% while return on equity averaged 20.2%. Even in 1982, a miserable year for the construction industry, these figures reached 11.6% and 11.3%, respectively. We consider this to be an outstanding performance considering that the company's manufacturing plants were operating at an average of about **35% of effective capacity** throughout the year. This speaks highly of the proprietary qualities of the Trus Joist products. In addition, we feel that it reflects the high quality of the individuals who are running the Company.

● **A sharp increase in earnings is projected for 1984 with trendline growth of 18%–20% per year anticipated for the next three to five years.** Trus Joist has barely made a dent in the residential joist market. We estimate that its share of this market is about 1%–2%. The Company's stocking lumber dealer program in California and the northeastern and midwestern sections of the United States never really got off the ground due to the severe downturn in the construction industry. With improved housing activity, we believe that Trus Joist will have a fair chance of penetrating these regions. An important point is that in the Northwest and Southeast, where TJCO first concentrated its stocking lumber dealer effort and was able to establish itself, residential-related sales have held up significantly better than in the Northeast and Midwest.

● **The Company is now beginning a far more intense effort to market MICRO=LAM lumber to non-construction, industrial customers.** This category represented 9% of sales in 1982. While management has always acknowledged that there were broader applications for MICRO=LAM lumber, the company's marketing effort never equalled the perceived potential. This imbalance has changed, and we expect industrial sales to grow far more rapidly than construction-related (both commercial and residential) revenues, perhaps reaching one-fourth to one-third of the corporate total over the next three to five years.

● **Trus Joist has barely begun to penetrate the residential market.** As mentioned above, best estimates indicate that the Company's current TJI volume represents only a very small fraction of the available residential market, and geographic penetration has been quite uneven in the U.S. As a result, we believe market-share opportunities are substantial.

● **International sales, excluding Canada, have been nil.** A licensing agreement signed with a Swedish company in 1980 never came to fruition as that company backed out mainly because of the declining European construction market and the increasing strength of the U.S. dollar. However, Trus Joist and a Japanese concern last year formed a joint venture in Japan. This represents another attractive long-term growth possibility for the Company.

● **At Trus Joist there is continuing emphasis on manufacturing products more efficiently in order to price more competitively.** We feel that TJCO has proven that it is a highly innovative company in its field and, while new products are always receiving attention, there is just as much emphasis on reducing manufacturing costs. Trus Joist currently is working out the "bugs" in a press that will manufacture MICRO=LAM lumber in 4-foot widths, twice the width of MICRO=LAM lumber produced by the Company's 13 existing presses. The economics of the 4-foot-wide press are such that it will reduce the per-foot cost of manufacturing MICRO=LAM lumber, thereby allowing TJCO to price its product more competitively and further penetrate the market.

● **Trus Joist is in very sound financial condition.** At Dec. 31, 1983, long-term debt represented 21.8% of the total capitalization. At this same date, its current ratio was 3.8:1. Unrestricted cash and equivalents of $21.8 million were almost equal to the total current liabilities and long-term debt of $23.0 million.

PRODUCT MIX

As shown in the table below, light commercial and construction applications in 1978 accounted for 62% of total sales. The severe downturn in this sector of the construction industry, plus the additional penetration on the residential side, has reduced this percentage to where it represented

37% of total sales last year. For the future, we project that residential sales will account for a still increasing portion of the total.

TABLE II   ($ in millions)

	1978	1979	1980	1981	1982	1983	1984E
Light commercial	$48.6	$65.2	$50.2	$43.0	$29.8	$35.5	$48.7
Residential	26.7	31.6	26.3	34.4	30.5	55.7	67.5
Non-construction industrial	3.1	5.1	5.8	8.6	6.0	4.8	8.8
Total	$78.4	$101.8	$82.2	$86.0	$66.3	$96.0	$125.0
Percent of total							
Light commercial	62%	64%	61%	50%	45%	37%	39%
Residential	34%	31%	33%	40%	46%	58%	54%
Non-construction industrial	4%	5%	6%	10%	9%	5%	7%
Total	100%	100%	100%	100%	100%	100%	100%

MICRO=LAM LUMBER

MICRO=LAM lumber, in our view, stands as the single most significant technological element of the Company, as well as one of the most significant breakthroughs in wood technology. By 1971, after about 10 years of rapid growth, the Company had to deal with a shortage of raw material for its unique open-web and I-joists. Both of these product lines required high-strength structural lumber which is available only in limited quantities in North America. In response to this problem, Troutner invented **MICRO=LAM lumber, a precision-engineered, laminated veneer lumber.** This product was a major technological development in the wood products industry and became the basis for the Company's third major product line. Using a fully proprietary process that larger companies have been unable to replicate exactly, Trus Joist produces this product by gluing sheets of wood veneer together under heat and pressure. The process is conducted in a large, continuous press which produces 80' × 2' billets of laminated lumber in ¾ to 2½-inch thicknesses.

MICRO=LAM lumber uses less raw material than its sawn lumber counterpart requires; and it can be made from smaller, more abundant second-growth logs, as well as from a variety of wood species. At the same time, however, MICRO=LAM lumber assumes several quality advantages over natural lumber. Each sheet of veneer is laid with all grains parallel and electronically graded into four strength categories before being fed into the presses. The result is that MICRO=LAM lumber is more predictable in its strength specifications since the manufacturing process randomizes knots and other natural defects found in trees.

Another key factor in evaluating MICRO=LAM lumber is that it uses small, second-growth trees. Large, old-growth lumber, which comes from first-growth trees, has become scarcer due to more modern and scientific management of forests. The rate of growth declines as trees grow older, making it uneconomical to allow trees to grow more than 10 to 15 inches in diameter before being harvested. Lumber from small, second-growth logs is filled with knots and tends to be less dense and less strong than the old-growth lumber that was once available in much greater supply. This trend fully benefits the manufactured laminated veneer lumber of Trus Joist, and we anticipate that it will also help alleviate the current price spread between TJIs and competing products.

Trus Joist today manufactures MICRO = LAM lumber on 13 presses located at two plants—Eugene, Ore. (8 presses) and Junction City, Ore. (5). A ninth press will be added in Eugene this year. With all of its MICRO = LAM lumber capacity in the Northwest and a strong and still-growing demand for its TJIR line in the Southeast, TJCO has been moderately hindered by the cost of shipping MICRO = LAM lumber across the country. This has been costing the Company roughly $0.60 per billet-foot to ship MICRO = LAM lumber to the Southeast. This problem will be alleviated when Trus Joist opens its new MICRO = LAM lumber plant at Natchitoches, La. This facility, an unused plant purchased from Willamette Industries, will be upgraded at a cost of about $9.0 million and will receive the first 4-foot-wide press when it opens late this year. When a second 4-foot press is installed, perhaps about mid-1985, it will increase TJCO's MICRO = LAM lumber capacity by 35%–40%.

INDUSTRIAL SALES

One of the challenges facing Trus Joist has been to broaden the applications for its product lines. In particular, finding additional uses, preferably non-construction ones, for MICRO = LAM lumber has been a key priority. A wide range of industrial applications has been identified by TJCO's MICRO = LAM lumber division and is currently being developed. One of these uses is concrete-forming and shoring. The unique length, strength and reliability of MICRO = LAM lumber make it ideal for supporting and keeping in place the forms used to pour concrete in high-rise buildings, highway overpasses, bridges, retaining walls and dams. Management believes this is a $100 million market. A second application is planking for scaffolding. To date, the Company's greatest success in this area has been with the shipbuilding industry. Other applications include manufactured housing, furniture manufacture, and break-away highway signposts.

Perhaps the most promising opportunity for Trus Joist rests in the electric utility market. The major application at this time is for cross-arms, transformer racks and power transmission towers used across long distances and for residential distribution systems that link customers and substations. MICRO = LAM lumber cross arms are stronger and lighter than conventional sawn lumber products; they are also available in the extended lengths required by the utilities. The consistency of the MICRO = LAM lumber cross arms and their combination of strength and lightness results in considerable labor savings for the utilities. MICRO = LAM lumber cross arms also carry appearance advantages. Their reduced weight and tapered shape mean that fewer obtrusive supporting braces are required.

In addition to the utility cross arms, Idaho Power has been exploring the potential of three other MICRO = LAM lumber products:

- **Transformer platforms.** Carrying up to three 10,000-pound transformers apiece, utility platforms have generally required five poles for support. With the stronger MICRO = LAM lumber platforms, only two poles are required, which leads to significant time and labor savings.
- **Major transmission towers.** MICRO = LAM lumber allows these towers to be redesigned into a simpler, streamlined shape, which offers significant labor savings. Another major advantage of these MICRO = LAM-lumber towers is their weather-resistance potential in a variety of climates.
- **Streetlight poles.** While the trend is to move telephone poles underground, the process is too costly for the electric utilities. Most of the systems will remain overhead, which offers a future market possibility for MICRO = LAM lumber.

RESEARCH AND DEVELOPMENT

Research and development has been perhaps the key factor behind Trus Joist's success. The development of new and proprietary products is only half of this effort. The other half relates to productivity. First, all materials consumed in a product are used to their best advantage with minimum or no waste. Second, manufacturing productivity is maximized through highly efficient layout and proprietary machinery. Trus Joist, we believe, has accumulated a tremendous bank of knowledge on the subject of wood fiber and on its structural applications. This has been fueled by the growing scarcity of large logs and increasing stumpage costs. Some 55 professionals, including engineers, wood technologists, machine designers and machinists, make up the R&D staff.

Extending MICRO = LAM Lumber

One effort which could well provide major benefits is the development of and, at this point, limited production from a press for the manufacture of 4-foot-wide MICRO = LAM lumber material. The 13 presses currently operated by the Company manufacture material in 2-foot widths. **Manufacturing efficiency is one of the primary benefits of the 4-foot-wide machine.** While it is capable of producing twice as much product as the present 2-foot-wide machine, we believe that the non-raw-material costs such as for labor and power, run only 50%–75% more. The result is lower cost per foot of output. Adding further benefit is the fact that the new machine will be fed by computer, and there will be hydraulic cylinders in place to allow for automated conversion from one product to another. Previously, this had to be done by hand. There will also be significant enhancements in quality control. **A second benefit of the 4-foot-wide machine is that it will allow Trus Joist to broaden its raw-material requirements—** notably, it can now use 54-inch veneer. This is in contrast to what has solely been the need for 24- or 27-inch veneer. Since there is a much larger supply of 54-inch veneer, Trus Joist should see more price stability and perhaps a lower cost basis on its raw material input. **A third benefit is that a 4-foot-wide billet allows for more economical cutting** into customer-specified products.

Other Directions

Outside of the major new products discussed earlier (TJI, MICRO = LAM lumber), most of Trus Joist's efforts have been upgrades and refinements of existing products. In 1982, it introduced the TJLx truss, the TJI/35x joist and rough sawn MICRO = LAM lumber lumber. Both the TJLx and TJI/35x provide significant increases in load-carrying capacity versus previous products, without corresponding increases in costs. The addition of a rough sawn surface to MICRO = LAM lumber allows the product to serve both as a non-skid scaffold plank and as an appearance-grade beam in structural applications. In 1981, TJCO introduced the tapered TJI joist, which can be used principally in minimum-slope roof applications. We believe that most of the new-product activity over the next three to five years will continue to represent upgrades and new applications for MICRO = LAM lumber.

In 1981, Trus Joist moved into a new new-products facility in Boise. We believe that a move such as this in the middle of a severe building downturn reflects the Company's commitment to research and development. At 70,000 square feet, the building is a little over three times the size of the older facility. About 40 people work at the plant and are responsible for checking out new manufacturing processes and supporting test marketing and new-product introductions.

TABLE III   RESEARCH & DEVELOPMENT
EXPENSES

	R&D spending	% of sales
1983	$1,501,000	1.6%
1982	994,000	1.5%
1981	711,000	0.8%
1980	845,000	1.0%
1979	891,000	1.0%
1978	686,000	0.9%
1977	515,000	0.9%

As the above table shows, until 1982 the Company had spent about 1.0% of its sales on R&D. This did rise to 1.5% in 1982 and 1.6% in 1983 as the absolute dollar amount spent increased by 40% and 51%, respectively. This reflects costs associated with the new-products facility and an increased effort to develop additional products as the Company headed into what it believed was an upturn in construction. **We believe that much of the money spent to develop new products over the past several years has not had any real impact on the top and bottom lines due to the weak construction market. In addition, significant leverage should accrue to the Company from these efforts during the current upturn.**

We would also add that the increased R&D spending also reflects a greater effort to come up with new non-construction, industrial applications for MICRO=LAM lumber, such as products for the electric utility industry.

Research and development costs are expected to rise sharply over the next several years, though this will likely not show up as a percentage of sales, as the revenue base is estimated to improve dramatically because of a cyclical upturn in construction.

RETURN-ON-EQUITY ANALYSIS

During reasonably good years for the construction industry, Trus Joist has been able to generate an excellent return on equity. This is evidenced by ROEs of 26.21%, 34.03% and 32.88% for 1977, 1978, and 1979, respectively. It is significant that the ROEs in excess of 30% were accomplished in years when balance-sheet leverage dropped sharply. The key components of the fine performance were high asset turnover and an improved pretax margin. During the construction downturn, which began in 1980, the asset turnover fell substantially, while the pretax margin held up rather nicely. We attribute this performance to the Company's strategy of keeping its pricing structure as close to "normal levels" as possible, even at the risk of losing some volume. At the same time, sales were coming under pressure, and the Company's asset base was expanding with total assets up 34.3% in 1980 and 12.2% in 1981 before falling a modest 1.1% in 1982. (Last year, total assets rose 15.9%.) These asset increases in 1980 and 1981 were largely a function of a buildup of cash and fixed assets (plant and equipment) and not of inventories and receivables, both of which have declined in each of the three years from 1980 to 1982.

As a result of these events, Trus Joist today finds itself with $21.8 million in cash and equivalents and increased capacity as the Company continues to benefit from a construction upturn. Trus Joist has proven that it can generate an excellent return on its assets in good years (23.0% to 23.6% in 1978 to 1979 versus 6.9% in 1982), effectively manage its expenses in accordance with the swings in the construction cycle, and it can maintain its pricing structure during adverse periods. Given that the newer capacity is inherently more efficient and utilization rates have begun to rise, we feel that beginning in 1984 Trus Joist should again be earning a healthy return on equity. Specifically, we are projecting a 20.9% return this year with further improvement in 1985. In light of the Company's larger size today, we feel it is unlikely that Trus Joist could earn more than 30% on average equity in a peak earnings year. To approach this figure would require that TJCO use a larger amount of its unused capacity, which would have the effect of bringing asset turnover up to the 2.7 level attained in 1978 and 1979.

TABLE IV RETURN-ON-EQUITY ANALYSIS

	Sales / Avg. assets	×	Pretax margin	×	Avg. assets / Avg. equity	×	1 − tax rate	=	Return on avg. equity
1983	1.4020	×	.1084	×	1.5901	×	.5902	=	14.27%
1982	1.0406	×	.1155	×	1.6396	×	.5711	=	11.26%
1981	1.4198	×	.1327	×	1.7621	×	.5850	=	19.42%
1980	1.6516	×	.1468	×	1.7412	×	.5437	=	22.95%
1979	2.7268	×	.1381	×	1.6751	×	.5211	=	32.88%
1978	2.6927	×	.1338	×	1.7813	×	.5303	=	34.03%
1977	2.3994	×	.1159	×	1.9025	×	.4954	=	26.21%
1976	2.0186	×	.0986	×	1.9889	×	.4965	=	19.65%
1975	1.8239	×	.0786	×	2.1732	×	.5294	=	16.50%
1974	2.5370	×	.0526	×	2.3336	×	.5283	=	16.45%

1983 RESULTS

As expected, 1983 was a year of greatly improved earnings for Trus Joist. While sales increased 44.7% and earnings per share 38.5%, these figures did not begin, we believe, to reflect the Company's real earnings power. Sales to light commercial construction customers rose by only 19%, as many of these markets remained severely depressed for the major part of the year. Typically, this segment of the construction industry tends to lag residential construction which more closely tracks the overall economy. Industrial sales fell 20% and were disappointing in light of the greatly enhanced marketing effort expended in this area. This implies a large jump on the residential side, which totaled 83%. More important, sales to stocking lumber dealers increased well over 100%. In light of the 70% rise in housing starts in the U.S. last year (1.7 million versus 1.0 million), this reflects an encouraging increase in market share in 1983.

In spite of the healthy increase in sales, the pretax margin for the full year fell moderately from 11.55% in 1982 to 10.84% in 1983. Several factors account for this decline. First the Company switched to LIFO accounting beginning in 1983. The LIFO charge for the year totaled $553,000, or $0.08 per share after-tax. On a FIFO basis, the gross margin for 1983 was 32.54%, or equal to the 32.57% posted in 1982. The Company also faced a sharp increase in research and development costs in 1983. The gain of 51.5% was greater than the 44.7% growth in sales. Also hindering gross margin progress, in our estimation, was the competitive pricing environment which existed for over half of the year in open-web joists for the light commercial construction industry. **In fact, we do not feel that Trus Joist made a great deal of money in this business for 1983 as a whole.** It was only heading into the fourth quarter that pricing and backlogs began to firm and this did not exert much of an impact on the final period.

In looking at other expense categories, both selling and general and administrative expenses fell as a percentage of sales, though not dramatically. Selling expenses totaled 10.98% in 1983 versus 11.89% in 1982. We believe that there would have been more improvement if not for a very heavy investment in additional sales personnel, sales management and spending, designed to automate the sales force more completely. General and administrative expenses, which fell from 12.35% of sales in 1982 to 11.63% last year, also would have shown more improvement, we believe, if there had been more uniform sales growth in all product lines.

Interest income also exerted a major influence on the corporate profit margin and earnings comparisons. In that Trus Joist has a healthy cash position and all of its debt is at fixed rates, the Company does accrue some benefits from high interest rates. In 1982, net interest income of $2.2 million produced a bottom-line impact of $0.32 per share (see Table V). The year 1983 saw lower rates and the absence of a favorable arbitrage of funds slated for the initial Stayton expansion bring net interest income down to $1.0 million, or $0.16 per share.

A quarterly breakdown of interest income and expense is shown below:

TABLE V   QUARTERLY INTEREST INCOME AND EXPENSE ($ in 000)

	Interest income				Interest expense			
	1983	**1982**	**1981**	**1980**	**1983**	**1982**	**1981**	**1980**
Q1	$406	$974	$834	$286	$274	$398	$335	S87
QII	539	1,009	766	534	236	502	335	232
QIII	599	1,063	800	516	246	500	318	306
QIV	503	784	922	501	266	294	368	327
Year	$2,047	$3,830	$3,322	$1,837	$1,022	$1,694	$1,356	$952

	Net interest income				EPS impact			
	1983	**1982**	**1981**	**1980**	**1983**	**1982**	**1981**	**1980**
QI	$132	$576	$499	$199	$0.02	$0.08	$0.07	$0.03
QII	303	507	431	302	0.05	0.07	0.07	0.04
QIII	353	563	482	210	0.05	0.09	0.08	0.03
QIV	237	490	554	174	0.04	0.08	0.09	0.03
Year	$1,025	$2,136	$1,966	$885	$0.16	$0.32	$0.31	$0.13

Other items having a negative impact on profit margins in 1983 include start-up costs relating to the new Valdosta, Ga., plant; operating problems connected with the change in managers at TJCO's Junction City plant; and the development of CAD systems for the entire network of manufacturing facilities.

OUTLOOK

For 1984, we project a 25%–35% rise in sales to $120–$130 million. We are looking for housing starts in the U.S. to total about 1.75 million (up slightly from 1983) with commercial construction activity greatly improved. Industrial sales are expected to benefit from what we believe will be 4.5% growth in the GNP. Under these assumptions, the trend of sales growth among TJCO end-markets should reverse itself this year with the strongest gains coming on the light commerical construction side (projected to rise 37%) and industrial sales (83%). We expect the sale of residential products to increase about 21%, which would still be above the rate of growth projected for housing activity. We feel that Trus Joist will continue to benefit from the increased number of stocking lumber dealers carrying its product, as well as from the increasing penetration of the existing dealer base.

Further profit margin improvement is anticipated in 1984. A slight increase in the LIFO charge to $600,000 is factored into our estimate, owing to higher inventory levels and a 6%–7% rate of inflation. In spite of this 62.7% gain, we look for a rise in the gross margin to 33.2% primarily due to our expectation of a firmer pricing environment in the light commercial construction products area. Selling expenses are expected to fall only moderately as a percentage of sales. In contrast, general and administrative costs should decline more dramatically relative to sales. We feel that G&A costs will total 11.00% of sales versus 11.63% in 1983 as the Company accrues further benefits from its strong revenue growth. Interest income is projected to fall as the unexpended funds related to the Valdosta facility have been put to use and will not be generating income this year. We believe that there will be higher cash balances throughout 1984, though not enough to prevent a 7%–8% decline in interest income. We look for a similar increase in interest expense because of the financing charges related to the Natchitoches facility. At this point, this plant is scheduled to be financed with an industrial development bond (IDB).

These assumptions result in a pretax margin of 12.2% of the full year. While this is an improvement over the 10.84% posted in 1983, it still does not equal 1980–81 levels. Admittedly this tax rate will be a key variable in the final outcome for the 1984 EPS. We are currently using a 35% effective tax rate. Depending upon the timing of the Natchitoches opening, the tax rate could be 30% for 1984, which would bring full-year earnings to above our $2.60 per share estimate.

For the longer term, earnings per share are expected to grow at a compounded annual rate of 18%–20%. We believe that the proprietary features of the TJI line will result in further market growth in the U.S., particularly as Trus Joist progresses further in expanding its dealer base and better educating both the stocking lumber dealer personnel and the building community as to the advantages of its products. Finally, we see the international market for industrial MICRO = LAM lumber applications and new products as being major growth factors in the future. In reference to profit margins, the productivity benefits discussed earlier give TJCO the opportunity to increase margins and price more aggressively and enhance sales growth.

FINANCIAL

Trus Joist's financial condition is very sound. At the close of 1983, long-term debt of $12.7 million represented only 21.8% of the total capitalization. Most of this debt comes from industrial revenue bond (IRB) financing at rates ranging from 6.9%–10.2%. There is $3.2 million on the books at a rate of 8.8%.

Cash and short-term investments at this date totaled $21.8 million. Given capital spending plans for 1984, the Company should be able to add another $4.0–$6.0 million to this position by the close of the year.

Capital expenditures this year will total about $18–$20 million. With IDB financing likely for Natchitoches and Stayton, TJCO can easily internally finance the remaining $2–$3 million of other expenditures.

Trus Joist has a $3.5 million line of credit which could be used if dictated by seasonal needs. At this point, we do not anticipate that any external financing will be required through at least 1984, and probably 1985. Should Trus Joist be as successful as we expect with its residential products and industrial MICRO = LAM efforts, then further capacity additions will be necessary in 1985. However, this may not require external financing.

Trus Joist initiated cash dividends in 1977 and, as indicated below, declared steady increases until the construction downturn put pressure on earnings. The payout has been maintained at

$0.075 per quarter beginning in the first quarter of 1980 and continuing through all of 1983. Effective with the first quarter of 1984, the quarterly payout was increased 20% to $0.09 per share. Over the past five years, TJCO's payout ratio averaged 22.0%. During an economic upturn we would expect it to trend lower (a 13.4% rate is projected for the year) and believe that a 15%–20% payout ratio is reasonable for a company with Trus Joist's growth potential. We anticipate that this rate will continue through 1984 and feel there is a good chance of another dividend increase in 1985.

TABLE VI   DIVIDEND RECORD & ESTIMATE

	Dividend per share	Dividends declared	Net income	Payout ratio
1984E	$0.36	$1,330	$9,910	13.4%
1983	0.30	1,107	6,141	18.0%
1982	0.30	1,104	4,376	25.2%
1981	0.30	1,103	6,677	16.5%
1980	0.30	1,091	6,563	16.6%
1979	0.18	646	7,332	8.8%
1978	0.22	784	5,564	14.1%
1977	0.08	283	3,240	8.7%

TABLE VII   SOURCES AND USES OF FUNDS ($ in 000)

	1984E	1983	1982	1981
Sources				
Net income	$9,910	$6,141	$4,376	$6,677
Depreciation & amortization	3,000	2,637	2,330	2,271
Deferred income tax expense	1,000	805	716	229
Total from operations	13,910	9,583	7,422	9,177
Realization of purchased tax benefits, net of change in invest.	–0–	1,484	86	
Additions to long-term debt	16,000	–0–	6,000	550
Increase (decrease) in deferred inc. taxes	300	242	(116)	289
Decrease in unexpended funds–IDB	200	5,154	451	523
Total sources	30,410	16,463	13,843	10,539
Uses				
Additions to property & equip., net	19,000	9,704	2,185	7,104
Dividends declared	1,330	1,106	1,104	1,103
Payments and changes in current maturities of long-term debt	600	544	7,986	568
Other, net	500	301	796	5
Total uses	21,430	11,655	12,071	8,780
Increase (decrease) in working capital	**$8,980**	**$4,808**	**$1,772**	**$1,759**

TABLE VIII   BALANCE SHEET ($ in 000)

	12/31/83	1/01/83	1/02/82
Assets			
Current assets:	$21,756	$18,639	$18,604
Cash and equivalents			
Receivables	8,870	6,373	6,452
Inventories	7,851	5,910	6,075
Other	977	764	1,636
Total	39,454	31,686	32,767
Property, plant and equipment	50,320	40,794	38,844
Accumulated depreciation	18,254	15,795	13,700
Net property, plant and equipment	32,066	24,999	25,144
Unexpended funds (IRB)	187	5,341	5,792
Other assets	1,771	1,373	372
Total assets	$73,478	$63,399	$64,075
Liabilities and stockholders' equity			
Current liabilities:	$553	$586	$568
Current maturities - LTD			
Accounts payable	3,668	2,334	2,497
Accrued liabilities	5,961	4,265	6,091
Income taxes payable	91	128	1,010
	10,273	7,313	10,166
Long-term debt	12,693	13,237	15,223
Deferred income taxes	4,898	2,380	1,409
Stockholders' equity	45,614	40,469	37,277
Total liabilities and stockholders' equity	$73,478	$63,399	$64,075

VALUATION

As can be discerned from the accompanying table, over the past five years Trus Joist has sold at a premium price/earnings multiple relative to the market. This has been the case in years of both good and poor earnings. Based upon estimates for 1984, the current premium stands at 19.4%. Given our view that TJCO earnings this year could well surpass our $2.60 per share estimate, plus strong earnings per share growth projected for beyond 1983, we do not feel that this premium is at all excessive. PURCHASE is recommended.

TABLE IX VALUATION HISTORY

| | TRUS JOIST | | | | | | S & P 400 | | | | | |
| | Price range | | | P/E range | | | Price range | | | P/E range | | |
	Hi	Low	EPS	Hi	Low	Mean	Hi	Low	EPS	Hi	Low	Mean
1984E	286		$2.60	11.1			$177.24		$19.00	9.3		
1983	394 –	274	1.62	24.4 –	17.0	20.7	194.84	154.95	15.20	12.8 –	10.2	11.4
1982	29 –	176	1.17	24.8 –	15.2	20.0	159.66 –	114.08	14.90	10.7 –	7.7	9.2
1981	302 –	172	1.78	17.0 –	9.7	13.3	157.02 –	125.93	16.56	9.5 –	7.6	8.5
1980	264 –	114	1.76	15.1 –	6.5	10.8	160.96 –	111.09	16.13	10.0 –	6.9	8.4
1979	262 –	124	1.98	13.3 –	6.3	9.8	124.49 –	107.08	16.21	7.7 –	6.6	7.1
1978	272 –	7	1.51	18.0 –	4.6	11.3	118.71 –	95.52	13.12	9.0 –	7.3	8.2

TJCO P/E relative to S&P 400

	Hi	Low	Mean
1984E	1.194		
1983	1.906 –	1.667	1.816
1982	2.318 –	1.974	2.174
1981	1.789 –	1.276	1.565
1980	1.510 –	0.942	1.286
1979	1.727 –	0.955	1.380
1978	2.000 –	0.630	1.378

TABLE X TRUS JOIST CORPORATION EARNINGS RECORD & ESTIMATE ($ in 000)

	Fiscal years ending December 31							
	1977	1978	1979	1980	1981	1982	1983	1984E
Net sales	$56,430	$78,422	$101,849	$82,247	$86,009	$66,322	$95,950	$125,000
LIFO charge	–0–	–0–	–0–	–0–	–0–	–0–	553	600
Gross profit	19,369	26,167	$34,150	28,121	27,873	21,603	30,673	41,500
Gross margin	34.32%	33.37%	33.53%	34.19%	32.41%	32.57%	31.97%	33.20
Selling expense	6,248	7,864	9,648	8,697	9,238	7,888	10,516	13,300
% of sales	11.07%	10.03%	9.47%	10.57%	10.74%	11.89%	10.96%	10.65%
Admin. expense	6,061	7,403	10,427	8,238	9,188	8,188	11,161	13,750
% of sales	10.74%	9.44%	10.24%	10.01%	10.68%	12.35%	11.63%	11.00%
Interest exp. (income)				(885)	(1,966)	(2,136)	(1,025)	(800)
% of sales				(1.08)%	(2.29)%	(3.22)%	(1.07)%	(0.65)%
Gain on sale of assets	–0–	–0–	–0–	–0–	–0–	–0–	(384)	–0–
Pretax income	6,541	10,492	14,069	12,071	11,413	7,663	10,405	15,250
Pretax margin	11.59%	13.38%	13.81%	14.68%	13.27%	11.55%	10.84%	12.20%
Tax provision	3,300	4,928	6,737	5,508	4,736	3,287	4,264	5,340
Tax rate	50.5%	47.0%	47.9%	45.6%	41.5%	42.9%	41.0%	35.0%
Net income	3,241	5,564	7,332	6,563	6,677	4,376	6,141	9,910
Earnings per share	$0.90	$1.51	$1.98	$1.76	$1.78	$1.17	$1.62	$2.60
Book value per share	$3.91	$5.29	$7.14	$8.63	$10.14	$10.97	$12.36	$14.65
Average shares (outstanding (000)	3,581	3,694	3,711	3,730	3,752	3,750	3,800	3,810

DJIA: 1154.63
S&P 400: 177.33

B1 Aggressive purchase recommended; stock is expected to outperform the market significantly.
B2 Purchase recommended; stock is expected to outperform the market moderately.
B3 Accumulate long-term position.
H Additional purchase not recommended at this time.
S Sell

CHAPTER 12

ESTIMATING THE RISK
OF COMMON STOCKS

After reading this chapter, you should:

1 Be able to compare the traditional view of the risk premium with the capital market theory view of risk
2 Understand how total risk (variance of return) can be decomposed into market factors, industry and other common factors, and security-specific factors
3 Develop an understanding of the historical relationship between risk and return
4 Understand some of the problems in computing ex post betas
5 Know some of the techniques for estimating ex ante betas
6 Be aware of some of the methods used in computing traditional measures of risk

The most fundamental tenet of finance is that there is a trade-off between risk and return. The return from holding equity securities is derived from the dividend stream and price changes. The preceding chapter dealt primarily with estimating future dividends and earnings, and implicitly with estimating future stock prices. This chapter will deal with estimating the risk associated with equity securities.

Recall in Chapter 3 we argued that the standard deviation of return is an appropriate measure of risk for *portfolios*. In Chapter 4 the market model was introduced which argues that the measure of risk *for an individual security* is the security's systematic risk, or its beta. On the other hand, professional investors have long used other variables as risk measures, such as financial leverage or variability of earnings. As we shall see, these two approaches to estimating risk are not incompatible. Before examining some of the techniques for estimating risk, it is appropriate to review how risk is incorporated into discount rates and consequently into security prices.

12-1 RISK AND THE DISCOUNT RATE

At the very beginning of this text, we suggested that the return investors require to postpone consumption and invest is equal to a real risk-free rate plus expected inflation plus a risk premium. That is, the required return $R(r)$ can be written as

$$R(r) = \text{risk-free real rate} + \text{expected inflation} + \text{risk premium} \quad (12\text{-}1)$$

The term *required return* is synonymous with the discount rate used to discount future dividends and selling prices back to the current price of the stock.

12-1-1 The Risk-Free Real Rate   Frequently, when economists refer to the ''real rate,'' they are actually referring to the *risk-free* real rate. This is the rate of return earned, after adjusting for changes in price levels, on an investment which has no uncertainty associated with its cash flows. Typically, we associate risk-free investments with U.S. government obligations. Because of its power to create money, it is extremely unlikely that the U.S. government will fail to meet its monetary obligations. Thus, the risk of default is generally assumed to be zero for treasury bonds, notes, and bills.

Conceptually, we can describe the risk-free real rate as being determined by the safest investment opportunities generally available to investors. Unfortunately, we cannot directly observe real returns, at least in the ex ante sense, because interest rates and security prices are stated in nominal terms and we generally do not know what rate of inflation investors expect.

12-1-2 The Risk-Free Nominal Rate   The interest and principal payments associated with treasury bills (T-bills) and other treasury obligations are expressed in dollar amounts, that is, *in nominal terms, not in real terms*. For a specified future time period, say the next year, the usual working assumption is that the risk-free nominal rate is equal to the return on a 1-year U.S. Treasury obligation, and that this 1-year nominal rate can be decomposed into an expected risk-free real rate of return plus the expected rate of inflation. Thus, if we know the rate for a 1-year treasury note and we have an estimate of the expected rate of inflation, we can subtract the two and come up with an estimate of the risk-free real rate.[1] For example, if a 1-year treasury note yields 10% and the expected inflation rate over the next year is 6%, then an estimate of the risk-free real rate would be 4%.

Given this framework, the nominal interest rates we observe for U.S. Treasury obligations represent the sum of the risk-free real rate plus the expected rate of inflation. Therefore, the required return for a security can be written as

$$R(r) = \text{risk-free nominal rate } + \text{ risk premium} \qquad (12\text{-}2)$$

Note that for *any* security, part of its required return is determined by the level of the risk-free nominal rate. Thus, changes in the level of interest rates on government securities could cause required returns, and consequently prices, of all securities to change. Consequently, changes in interest rates account for at least part of the observed co-movement of security prices—the ''market effect'' discussed in Chapter 4. On the

---

[1]This analysis ignores the risk of uncertain inflation. Even though the risk of default on nominal payments of interest and principal for U.S. government obligations is nil, there is still uncertainty regarding future inflation rates, which in turn, makes the real rate of return uncertain. Consequently, what is referred to as the risk-free nominal rate actually includes a risk premium associated with the uncertainty of future inflation. This uncertain inflation risk premium has traditionally been ignored, presumably because in the past (say, before 1970) it was assumed to be small. Whether this assumption holds now is debatable.

other hand, while the risk-free nominal rate is common to the required return of all securities, the risk premiums could be, and generally are thought to be, unique to each security.

To illustrate how Equation (12-2) might be used, suppose that the nominal rate on long-term government bonds is 10% and an analyst believes 4% is an appropriate risk premium for a particular stock. A rate of 14% would then be used as the discount rate in, say, a dividend discount model where all the expected dividends and perhaps an estimated future selling price are discounted back to the present. The present value of all the expected future cash flows associated with the security could then be compared with the current stock price to determine if it is over- or undervalued.

In the above situation the analyst would not have any trouble determining the nominal risk-free rate since the yield to maturity of treasury bonds can be found in daily newspapers. The difficult aspect of this problem is determining the appropriate risk premium.

12-1-3 The Risk Premium   Discussion of the risk premium can be divided into two schools of thought: (1) the capital market theory view and (2) the traditional view. Capital market theory suggests that the risk premium should be solely a function of the systematic risk of a security. In the framework of the Sharpe-Lintner CAPM,[2] the required return for the ith security should be

$$R(r_i) = r_f + \beta_i[E(r_m) - r_f] \qquad (12-3)$$

where r_f = risk-free nominal rate

$E(r_m)$ = expected return on the "market portfolio"

$[E(r_m) - r_f]$ = "excess market return," that is, expected return

on the market in excess of the risk-free rate

Note that in the CAPM framework *the risk premium for a security is equal to its beta multiplied by the excess market return.* Thus, the only thing unique to a particular security which influences the security's required rate of return is its beta. And recall from Chapter 4, beta is a measure of the security's systematic risk. Securities with betas greater than 1.0 have above-average systematic, or market-related, risk; securities with betas less than 1.0 have below-average systematic risk.

On the other hand, the traditional view has generally argued that the risk premium is a function of three factors: (1) business risk, (2) financial risk, and (3) liquidity. *Business risk* deals with the uncertainty of the firm's operating income, where the uncertainty is created by changes in the firm's underlying business. We typically measure operating income as earnings before interest and taxes (EBIT). The more EBIT fluctuates, the more business risk is associated with the firm. This is easy to see from the point of view of a lender, or a bondholder. Obviously, if earnings before

---

[2]See Chapter 4 for a brief introduction and Chapter 17 for a more detailed discussion of capital market theory and the CAPM.

interest and taxes should decrease, the lenders will be less likely to receive their promised interest and principal payments on time.

Financial risk refers to the additional risk associated with the use of debt. In Section 7-4-5 we illustrated how financial leverage can magnify the changes in the firm's after-tax earnings. According to the traditional view, the more debt employed by the firm, the more volatile its earnings stream and the riskier its common stock. As we will discuss in more detail later, this is perfectly consistent with the CAPM— the more debt, the higher the stock's beta.

Liquidity risk is not as well defined as business risk and financial risk. Investors typically refer to liquidity in such terms as *the easier it is to buy or sell an asset quickly and without any significant change in price, the more liquid the asset.* The greater the uncertainty concerning how quickly a stock can be bought or sold, and the greater the uncertainty concerning how much stock can be bought or sold, the greater the liquidity risk. Treasury obligations, particularly 30- to 90-day T-bills, have practically no liquidity risk—investors can buy and sell these securities in minutes in very large amounts while giving up almost no price concessions. At the other extreme, large positions in the stocks of smaller companies may take days or weeks to buy or sell and large price concessions may have to be made. We have long suspected that at least part of the small-firm effect discussed in Chapter 5 is really a risk premium compensating for the lack of liquidity associated with the stocks of small firms.

12-2 THE DECOMPOSITION OF RISK

In Chapter 3 we defined the risk of an asset to be the variance associated with its return. Recall from Chapter 4 that the variance of return can be subdivided into two components, *systematic (market-related) risk and unsystematic (non-market-related) risk*. What allowed us to make this tidy two-part subdivision of risk was the market model's simplifying assumption that the returns of individual securities are related to each other *only* through their common covariation with the market index.

The real world does not appear to be quite so simple. In fact, several sources of *extramarket covariation* have been empirically identified. One possible source which might immediately come to mind is an industry factor, and this appears to be the case. Other extramarket factors might be such things as dividend yield, size of firm, and other characteristics of broad groups of securities which are not captured by industry factors. Figure 12-1 illustrates the decomposition of risk along these lines. The first bar in this figure represents the decomposition of total risk for a typical common stock. Systematic, market-related risk represents perhaps 30% of the total variance of the stock's returns, while unsystematic risk represents the remaining 70%. The unsystematic risk is determined by industry factors, other common factors, and factors specific or unique to the stock.

The second bar in Figure 12-1 represents the decomposition of total risk for a well-diversified portfolio. Since most, if not all, of the unsystematic risk can be eliminated by proper diversification, the portfolio's variance of return is almost totally determined by the market factor. The security specific risk can be eliminated by simply diversifying across a number of different securities. The industry-related risk can be eliminated by

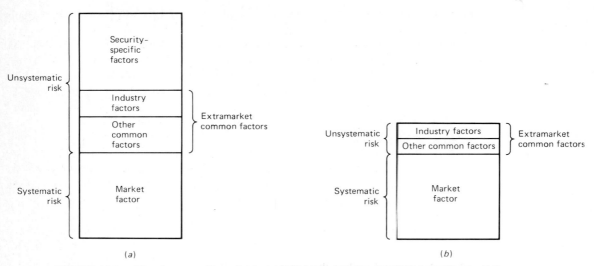

FIGURE 12-1 The decomposition of risk. (*a*) Individual security; (*b*) Well-diversified portfolio.

holding securities which are in a number of different industries. The risk associated with other common factors can be reduced by holding a number of securities which have different levels of the common factor. For example, if the common factor is dividend yield, this common factor risk can be reduced by diversifying across stocks with different dividend yields. To eliminate all unsystematic risk, the portfolio would ideally be constructed so that it held all securities in proportion to their market values. This, of course, would be a passive strategy similar to holding an index fund.

To the extent an investor chooses not to hold an index fund, he or she will be assuming some unsystematic risk. Why would an investor do this? Presumably because the investor feels that actively managing the portfolio will generate additional returns sufficient to offset the additional unsystematic risk associated with the active strategy.

12-2-1 Industry Factors   A number of problems are involved in classifying stocks into industries—the primary problem being that many companies are involved in a variety of different activities, each of which might be thought of as being in a separate industry. One of the first studies to determine whether or not an industry factor exists was performed by King.[3] In this study, returns for a sample of 63 stocks in six different industries were examined over the time period 1927–1960. King used two-digit Standard Industrial Codes (SIC Codes) published by the Securities and Exchange Commission.[4]

The first step in this study involved estimating the market's effect on each security's return. Once the market factor had been determined, the remaining unsystematic return

[3]B. F. King, "Market and Industry Factors in Stock Price Behavior," *Journal of Business* (January 1966).

[4]Securities and Exchange Commission, "Directory of Companies Filing Annual Reports with the Securities and Exchange Commission," Government Printing Office, Washington, D.C.

component was examined to determine if there was an industry factor. Using a statistical technique known as cluster analysis, King found that the stock returns did, in fact, tend to group together along industry lines. The results varied, depending upon which security and which time period was involved. However, as a generalization, King found that the market factor accounted for about 30% of the variance of an individual stock's return and that industry factors accounted for another 10% of the variance.[5]

12-2-2 Group Factors A study by Farrell[6] was designed to determine if there is extramarket covariation of stock returns that is not due to industry factors. In this study, returns for 356 stocks were analyzed over the period 1970–1977. Since these stocks represented 90 different industries, any industry effect was largely neutralized. In a fashion similar to King, the market factor was first removed and then the unsystematic portion of the stock returns was analyzed using cluster analysis.

Farrell found that the stock returns tended to cluster in four groups. Farrell defined the four groups as follows:

1 *Growth stocks*—"earnings of these companies are expected to show a faster rate of secular expansion than the average company."

2 *Cyclical stocks*—"these companies have an above-average exposure to the economic cycle."

3 *Stable stocks*—"these companies have a below-average exposure to the economic cycle."

4 *Energy stocks*—"energy companies supply energy to both producers and consumers."

Farrell found that the market factor accounted for approximately 30% of the variance of individual stock returns. The group factor accounted for 10 to 15% of the variance for the growth, stable, and cyclical stocks. For energy stocks, the group factor was even more important, accounting for roughly 30% of the individual stock variance.

In order to illustrate the importance of group factors, Farrell compared the returns for two mutual funds and the S&P 500 for the period December 31, 1972, through July 31, 1974. These comparisons as well as the composition of each portfolio are shown in Table 12-1. This time period was obviously a bear market, as the S&P 500 declined 29%. In a bear market we would expect a well-diversified portfolio to decline in value by an amount roughly equal to the portfolio's beta multiplied by the market decline. However, for these two mutual funds this was not the case. Notice that Affiliated Fund declined by 16%, much less than what we might expect given its beta

---

[5]These findings are consistent with the results reported by Brealey and Foster with respect to earnings (see Section 11-2-3). Brealey and Foster reported that roughly 20% of the variance of earnings for individual companies could be attributed to economywide factors and another 20% could be attributed to industry factors. Since stock returns are highly correlated with earnings changes, it follows that stock returns would be influenced by both economywide factors (a market effect) and industry factors.

[6]These results are described in Chapter 8 of J. L. Farrell, *Guide to Portfolio Management*, McGraw-Hill, New York, 1983. The original research was reported in J. L. Farrell, "Analyzing Covariation of Returns to Determine Homogeneous Stock Groupings," *Journal of Business* (April 1974) and J. L. Farrell, "Homogeneous Stock Groupings: Implications for Portfolio Management," *Financial Analysts Journal* (May/June 1975).

TABLE 12-1 GROUP WEIGHTINGS: S&P 500 AND MUTUAL FUNDS

Stock group	Percentage of portfolio by group		
	S&P 500	**Affiliated Fund**	**T. Rowe Price**
Growth stocks	39.8	10.5	80.2
Cyclical stocks	24.0	57.5	8.7
Stable stocks	20.0	18.0	4.1
Energy (oil) stocks	16.2	14.0	7.0
Total	100.0	100.0	100.0
Portfolio beta	1.00	1.09	1.11
Fund performance, (12/31/72–7/31/74), %	−29	−16	−42

Source: J. L. Farrell, Jr., "Homogeneous Stock Groupings: Implications for Portfolio Management," *Financial Analysts Journal* (May/June 1975).

of 1.09—a beta of 1.09 multiplied by the market decline of 29% would suggest a decline of 32%. On the other hand, T. Rowe Price Fund produced a greater than expected decline of 42%, given its beta of 1.11.

The reason the two funds performed so much differently than one might expect, given their similar betas, becomes clear upon examining the composition of their portfolios. Notice that Affiliated Fund was substantially "underweighted" with respect to growth stocks—only 10.5% of Affiliated Fund was invested in growth stocks, compared with 39.8% in the S&P 500. By contrast, T. Rowe Price was substantially overweighted in this group with 80.2% invested in growth stocks.

The point of this analysis was not to show that the T. Rowe Price fund performed poorly in the bear market of 1973–1974. (In fact, as Farrell pointed out, this fund was one of the premier performers in the 1960s and early 1970s.) Rather, the point is that when a portfolio contains assets in substantially different proportions for the market index, results can be obtained that are substantially different from what one might expect simply based on the portfolio's beta—even if the portfolio contains a large number of stocks, as these funds did. And the results can be either good or bad, depending upon whether the correct "bets" were made by over- or underweighting various groups of stocks. In order to eliminate most of the unsystematic risk, simply diversifying across a number of different securities is not enough—the portfolio must be diversified across industries and broad groups of securities, such as the four groups described by Farrell.

12-2-3 Other Common Factors There may be other common factors affecting security returns besides the industry and group factors discussed above. Two additional possibilities might be dividend yield and size of the firm. The rationale behind dividend yield being a common factor is not based on yield being a risk factor but rather is based on taxes. Dividend income is considered to be ordinary income and, as such, is taxed at a higher rate than capital gains. Stocks which have high dividend yields generally have lower earnings growth rates and, as a rule, less capital gain potential. Consequently, it might be reasonable to assume that high dividend yield stocks, on average, would be priced to provide higher *pre*tax returns than otherwise comparable low dividend yield stocks to offset the higher tax rate associated with the dividend yield component of the total return.

This tax-induced relationship between high (low) dividend yield stocks and high (low) pretax returns would result in dividend yield being another extramarket factor determining security returns. However, there is considerable debate concerning this issue, some of which is discussed in Chapters 17 and 18. On the surface the tax-induced dividend yield factor may be appealing. However, consider the fact that there are numerous tax-free investors, some of which are major competitors in the securities markets—for example, most pension, profit-sharing, and endowment plans are essentially tax-free investors. If dividend yield is a common factor in determining security returns, what is to prevent these tax-free investors from arbitraging this dividend effect by buying high-yield stocks and selling low-yield stocks of equivalent risk? The effect of dividends on security returns continues to be one of the most perplexing and hotly debated issues in finance.[7]

Perhaps another common factor in security returns is firm size. Recall from Chapter 5 that many empirical studies have shown that small-firm stocks have provided above-normal returns and large-firm stocks below-normal returns. These studies adjusted for risk by using betas in the market model, or CAPM sense. It may be that firm size is a proxy for risk that is not captured by beta. For example, it may be that the smaller the firm, the less liquid the stock, and that investors require a higher return before investing in the less liquid stocks of smaller firms. Or it may be that firm size is proxying for some other risk factor which has not yet been identified. Whatever the case, the empirical evidence does suggest that firm size is another extramarket common factor, or at least a proxy for an unidentified common factor.

12-3 HISTORICAL RISK-RETURN RELATIONSHIPS

If there is no trade-off between risk and return, there is no point in being concerned about risk. Therefore, before beginning our discussion on how to estimate risk, we will first examine some evidence regarding the historical relationship between risk and return to see if, in fact, investors should be concerned with risk.

Figure 12-2 presents some evidence by Sharpe and Cooper[8] concerning the relationship between risk and return. In this figure, the vertical axis represents the arithmetic average annual return for each of 10 risk classes of NYSE common stocks over the period 1931–1967. The risk classes were determined by estimating the beta of each stock at the beginning of each year. Betas were estimated by regressing a stock's

---

[7]The fact that the relationship between dividend yield and security return mentioned above is an unresolved issue in finance should not be confused with arguments made earlier in this book that stock prices represent the present value of all future dividends. The latter argument refers to any type of dividend. For example, a stock could pay zero dividends for a number of years and then pay one final liquidating dividend—the stock price would then be the present value of the liquidating dividend. When we refer to the relationship between dividend yield and security return in this chapter, we are referring to the payment of regular (typically quarterly) cash dividends. Whether or not increasing or decreasing the current dividend yield affects security prices is not well established.

[8]W. F. Sharpe and G. M. Cooper, "Risk-Return Classes of New York Stock Exchange Common Stocks, 1931–1967," *Financial Analysts Journal* (March/April 1972).

monthly returns over the previous 5 years against an equally weighted index of all NYSE stock returns. Then a portfolio was formed consisting of the 10% of all the stocks which had the lowest betas; a second portfolio was formed consisting of the next 10% of the remaining stocks with the lowest betas, and so on, until the tenth portfolio consisting of the highest-beta stocks was formed.

Notice in Figure 12-2 that there is a consistent relationship between risk (measured as beta) and return. The least risky portfolio with the lowest beta (0.58) also had the lowest average return—11.58%. The most risky portfolio had a beta of 1.42 and also had the highest return—22.67%.[9]

Another study looked at the relationship between risk and return in a different manner. In this study, risk was measured by "quality ratings" provided by Fitch, Inc., an advisory service. Stocks are classified by Fitch into six classes, where class 1 represents the highest-quality, lowest-risk stocks and class 6 represent the lowest-quality, highest-risk stocks. Analysts at Fitch place stocks into one of these six risk classes based upon a fundamental analysis of such company characteristics as debt ratios, stability of sales and earnings, size of the firm, and industry characteristics. Figure 12-3 shows the results of this study. The vertical axis represents the total percentage increase in value, on average, for each risk class over eight different 5-year holding periods. Again, it is apparent that there was a strong positive relationship between risk and return during the time period of this study, which was 1926–1971. The lowest-risk class of stocks generated the lowest average return and the highest-risk class generated the highest returns.

[9]The very clear-cut relationship indicated by Figure 12-2 is somewhat misleading. For example, Sharpe and Cooper found that when the geometric mean return is used instead of the arithmetic mean return, group 7 stocks actually provided the highest return. For a discussion of some of these nuances, the reader should refer to the original study.

FIGURE 12-2   Risk-return classes. [*Source: W. F. Sharpe and G. M. Cooper, "Risk-Return Classes of New York Stock Exchange Common Stocks, 1931—1967,"* Financial Analysts Journal *(March/April 1972).*]

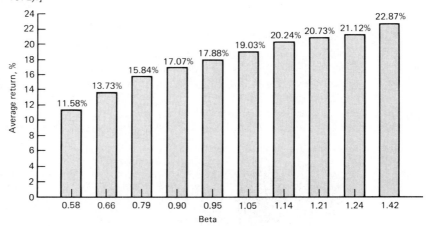

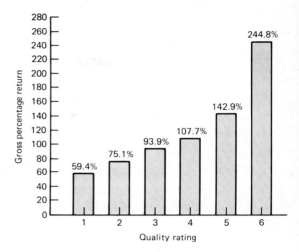

FIGURE 12-3   Performance of Fitch quality classes. [*Source: M. E. Blume and I. Friend, Risk, Investment Strategy, and the Long-Run Rates of Return,"* Review of Economics and Statistics *(August 1974).*]

These results are particularly interesting since the risk measure was not the stocks' betas but rather an assessment by the analysts at Fitch of the companies' fundamental characteristics. Since these results are similar to those of studies using beta as the risk measure, it appears that the more traditional, fundamental approach used by analysts in assessing risk is reasonably consistent with the capital market (beta) approach suggested by financial theory. In Section 12-5, we will analyze the relationship between systematic risk and company fundamentals more closely. It turns out that estimates of betas can be improved by considering such fundamental variables as debt ratios and earnings stability.

A number of other studies have confirmed the basic trade-off between risk and return.[10] While the preponderance of the historical evidence does suggest that higher returns are associated with riskier securities, *the relationship isn't perfect, particularly over relatively short time periods.* Figure 12-4 presents the results of a study which placed stocks into 10 risk classes (based on the stocks' betas) at the beginning of each year. The return for each of these 10 portfolios was computed for the year, and the process of forming new portfolios and measuring returns was repeated for each of the years 1956–1972.

Each portfolio is represented by an x. The dashed, horizontal line represents the return on the overall sample of stocks which we will refer to as the *market return.* For example, the market return was approximately +10% in 1956, −10% in 1957, and +50% in 1958. When the market return is above the risk-free rate, we would expect stocks with high betas to have higher returns than low-beta stocks. When the market return is below the risk-free rate, we would expect high-beta stocks to have

---

[10]Some of the more important of these studies are: F. Black, M. C. Jensen, and M. Scholes, "The Capital Asset Pricing Model: Some Empirical Tests," in M. C. Jensen, ed., *Studies in the Theory of Capital Markets,* Praeger, New York, 1972; E. F. Fama and J. D. Macbeth, "Risk, Return, and Equilibrium: Empirical Tests," *Journal of Political Economy* (May–June 1973); and W. H. Wagner and S. C. Lau, "The Effect of Diversification on Risk," *Financial Analysts Journal* (November/December 1971). These are discussed in more detail in Chapter 18.

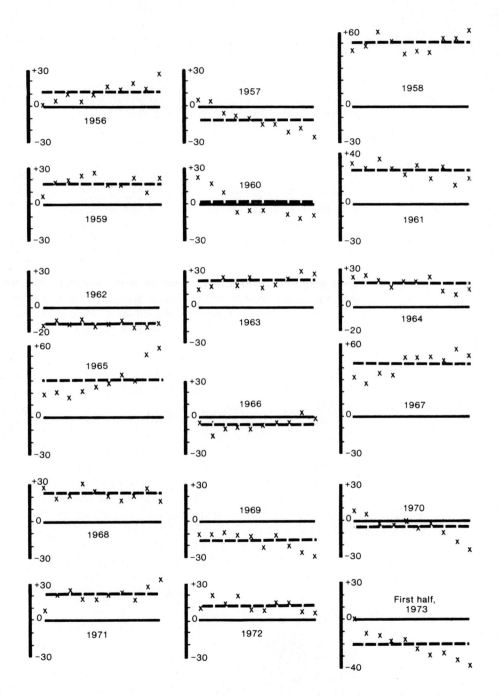

FIGURE 12-4 Annual returns by beta deciles. [*Source: W. L. Fouse and B. Rosenburg, "Is Beta Phlogiston?"* Financial Analysts Journal *(January/February 1974).*]

lower returns than low-beta stocks. This was generally the case. For example, in 1956, the market return was positive and high, and high-beta stocks generally provided higher returns than low-beta stocks. In 1957, the market return was negative and high-beta stocks provided lower (more negative) returns than did low-beta stocks.

However, there were years that proved to be exceptions to the conventional risk-return trade-off. For example, in 1961, the market return was quite high (approximately 28%) and yet low-beta stocks generally provided higher returns than high-beta stocks. Similar contradictory results were observed for the years 1964, 1966, 1968, and 1972.

What conclusions can we draw from these studies of the historical relationship between risk and return? First, the relationship has generally been positive—that is, higher-risk securities have generally provided higher returns. Second, this relationship appears to be robust with respect to how risk is measured—that is, whether the measure of risk was beta or more traditional "quality ratings," the same general trade-off between risk and return was observed. Finally, the relationship is not perfect and the shorter the time period, the weaker the trade-off between risk and return. Apparently, in the short run, anything can happen, as the 1-year results in Figure 12-4 illustrate. Over long time periods, say 5 years or more, it appears that higher risk is generally compensated by higher returns. Thus, investors clearly need to consider risk, and to do so, they must have a method of estimating risk, which is the next subject.

Before continuing, you should:

1 Once again be aware that required returns are equal to the risk-free nominal rate plus a risk premium

2 Recall that in a CAPM framework, the risk premium is equal to the security's beta times the expected return on the market minus the risk-free rate, i.e., $\beta[E(r_m) - r_f]$

3 Be aware that the more traditional view divides risk into three categories—business risk, financial risk, and liquidity risk

4 Know that when risk is measured as the variance of return, it can be decomposed into a market factor, industry factors, other common factors, and security-specific factors

5 Be aware of some of the empirical evidence regarding the trade-off between risk and return

6 Review Section 8-2, which deals with regression analysis, since regression is the primary statistical tool for estimating betas

12-4 ESTIMATING HISTORICAL BETAS

Since investors buy securities based on their *future* prospects, generally we are more interested in ex ante betas than in historical, or ex post, betas. Chapter 4 illustrated how one might go about estimating ex ante betas using a formal probability distribution of future states of the world (economic scenarios), and the returns of various stocks given those states of the world. However, most investors do not form such explicit probability distributions, even though they implicitly may do so. Consequently, the most commonly used procedure for estimating ex ante betas is to use the security's historical beta as a starting point. Adjustments are then made to this ex post beta based on recent or estimated future changes in the company's fundamental characteristics. These adjustments will be discussed in later sections. For now, we will concentrate on the starting point of this process, which is the security's historical beta.

It might seem that estimating ex post betas is a relatively straightforward procedure—simply regress the security's returns against the returns for some appropriate index. However, a number of issues must be resolved before one begins the regression. Some of these are: (1) Over what interval should returns be computed? Should the return interval be daily, weekly, monthly, or quarterly? (2) How should the returns be computed? Should the return include dividends or simply price changes? (3) What should be the length of the time horizon? Should the regression utilize returns over the past year, over the most recent 5 years, etc.? (4) What is the most appropriate index to use for the market returns? (5) Finally, another issue that might not be immediately apparent but which can be quite important deals with how frequently the security trades—this is referred to as the nonsynchronous trading problem.

12-4-1 The Return Interval   In order to perform a regression, we need a number of paired observations. With respect to computing betas, the paired observations are the returns for the security in question and the return for a market index, where the returns for each are measured over the same time interval. We will refer to the length of the individual time periods over which returns are computed as the *return interval*. When we refer to the *time horizon*, we are referring to the total time period over which the betas are to be estimated. For example, if we estimate betas over the 2 years 1983 and 1984, and we use monthly return intervals, the time horizon is 2 years and the number of monthly return intervals (which will also be the number of observations or data points for the regression) is 24.

It is an empirical question as to what is the most appropriate return interval. The obvious candidates are daily, weekly, monthly, quarterly, and annual intervals since prices are typically reported as of the end of the day, week, month, quarter, or year. It turns out that there are trade-offs between using shorter vs. longer return intervals. The shorter the return interval, the greater will be the number of observations within a particular time horizon. For example, within a time horizon of 1 year, there would be approximately 250 daily return intervals, but only 52 weekly and 12 monthly return intervals. Regression, like many statistical procedures, is a method of estimating a population parameter (in this case, the security's beta) from a sample of observations. In general, the larger the sample of observations, the more reliable the estimate. This would argue for the use of the shortest return interval (say, daily) since within a given time horizon, this will give the most observations.

However, some problems are associated with using short return intervals. One is the practical issue concerning data availability. For example, the CRSP (Chicago Center for Research in Security Prices) tapes have monthly data going back to 1926 on all NYSE stocks, whereas they have daily data going back to only 1962. Another serious problem has to do with nonsynchronous trading. The securities of many smaller companies do not always trade on each day, and consequently the returns on those days have to be either estimated or ignored. It turns out that the use of daily data can cause serious biases in the estimates of betas for securities which do not trade continously. This problem is reduced as the return interval is increased to, say monthly, as most securities will trade during each month.

Consequently, we recommend that monthly return intervals be used. Monthly data are readily available, are not as susceptible to nonsynchronous trading problems, and still will result in an acceptable number of observations—for example, over a 5-year time horizon, there will be 60 observations; over a 3-year time horizon, there will be 36 observations.

12-4-2 Computing Returns   To compute returns over a particular interval, say, the month of January, we use the following familiar equation, which was first introduced in Chapter 1:

$$r_t = \frac{P_t - P_{t-1} + D_t}{P_{t-1}} \tag{12-4}$$

One question that is frequently asked is "does it make any difference when estimating betas whether dividends are included in the return calculations?" That is, can reliable beta estimates be made using only price changes, rather than using total return, which includes dividends? The answer is a qualified yes. If the only purpose of the regression is to obtain an estimate of beta, it does not make any significant difference whether or not dividends are included in the return calculations. However, *if one is interested in other statistics, such as the security's alpha, the total return including dividends must be used.*

Listed below are two beta estimates for General Motors, Mobil Oil, and Time, Inc., based on monthly return intervals over the 10-year time period 1974–1983, using the CRSP value-weighted index of all NYSE stocks as the market index. One beta was estimated using total returns and the other was estimated using only price changes, i.e., excluding dividends:

	Beta		
Type of return	GM	Mobil	Time
Dividends included	.687	.913	.995
Dividends excluded	.683	.893	.995

From these three examples it does not appear that there is any significant difference between the beta estimates based on returns which include dividends and the beta estimates based on returns which do not include dividends. Of course, three examples do not prove the point. However, a study by Sharpe and Cooper[11] examined over 1500 stocks and found the correlation, between betas computed with dividends in the return

---

[11]W. F. Sharpe and G. M. Cooper, op. cit.

equation and betas computed without considering dividends, to be in excess of .99; i.e., the two sets of betas were almost perfectly correlated.

Given this information, should dividends be included when estimating betas? We would argue they generally should. In the first place, betas are measures of the relationship between returns, not just price changes. Second, many readily available computer data bases have total returns series, in which case there is no reason not to include dividends. However, when it is prohibitively time-consuming to collect dividend information, it is comforting to know that good beta estimates can be obtained by just considering the change in price.

12-4-3 Choice of Index Another issue that must be resolved before performing regressions to estimate betas is *what index should be used as the source of market returns*. It is unlikely the returns for a particular security will be correlated in exactly the same way with two different indexes. Consequently, the beta estimate will depend upon which index is chosen. To illustrate this consider the three stocks mentioned earlier, General Motors, Mobil Oil, and Time, Inc. Listed below are two sets of estimates for their betas. Each set of estimates is based on the same 10-year time horizon (1974–1984), the same return interval (monthly), and the same method of computing returns (dividends are included). The only difference between the two sets of beta estimates is the choice of the market index. The first set uses the CRSP value-weighted index of all NYSE stocks while the second set uses the CRSP equal-weighted index of all NYSE stocks:

Type of index	Beta		
	GM	**Mobil**	**Time**
CRSP value-weighted	.687	.913	.995
CRSP equal-weighted	.618	.576	.791

In the case of GM, the choice of index did not make much difference. But for the other two stocks, and particularly for Mobil, the index choice makes a significant difference in the beta estimate.

Thus, we have a dilemma—which index should be chosen from among the many indexes available? Capital market theory argues that the index should be a good proxy for the "market portfolio," which is defined as a portfolio consisting of all risky assets with weights in proportion to their market value. Unfortunately, such an index is not readily available.[12] As a result, the index choice is generally made on the basis of convenience. The S&P 500, which is a value-weighted index of 500 large NYSE

[12]Recently some attempts have been made to construct such an index. For example, First Chicago Investment Advisors (a subsidiary of First National Bank of Chicago) has constructed a multiple market index which includes various categories of stocks and bonds, as well as venture capital investments, real estate, and other assets. Also see R. F. Stambaugh, "On the Exclusion of Assets from Tests of the Two Parameter Model: A Sensitivity Analysis," *Journal of Financial Economics* (November 1982).

TABLE 12-2   SENSITIVITY OF ALPHA TO CHOICE OF INDEX

Indexes	Portfolio size	Rank correlation coefficient
S&P 500 vs. CRSP equal weighted	1	.969
	10	.977
	30	.980
	100	.975
S&P 500 vs. DJIA	1	.982
	10	.997
	30	.987
	100	.990
CRSP equal weighted vs. DJIA	1	.950
	10	.975
	30	.966
	100	.973

DJIA = Dow Jones Industrial Average.

The rank correlation coefficient is for alphas of portfolios formed from all NYSE stocks over the period 1963–1977. Betas and alphas were computed for each portfolio three different times using three different indexes. The above results were for portfolios which were rebalanced daily. The results were similar for buy-and-hold portfolios and beta-sorted portfolios.

Source: R. Roll, "The Sensitivity of Performance Measurement," unpublished paper summarized in R. J. Fuller, *Capital Asset Pricing Theories—Evolution and New Frontiers*, Financial Analysts Research Foundation, Charlottesville, Va., 1981.

stocks, is probably the most frequently used index primarily because information on this index is readily available. Since it is so widely used, Table VII at the end of this text lists S&P 500 monthly returns. The CRSP value-weighted index (which is highly correlated with the S&P 500 index) is also frequently used, particularly by researchers utilizing the CRSP tapes as their source of data for individual security returns.

Fortunately, when *portfolios* are considered, the index choice is not as important as the previous example of three stocks might indicate. It appears that both portfolio betas *and alphas* are relatively insensitive to the index choice. Table 12-2 lists the results of a study by Roll[13] which examined the degree of correlation between portfolio alphas based on different indexes. In general, the correlations are all well above .9, which suggests that, at least for portfolios, the choice of index does not have a significant effect on the relative ranking of betas and alphas.

On the other hand, since the index choice can have a significant impact on estimates of betas and alphas for *individual securities*, we recommend that either the S&P 500 or the CRSP value weighted index be used. While no conceptual argument can be

[13]R. Roll, "The Sensitivity of Performance Measurement," unpublished paper summarized in R. J. Fuller, *Capital Asset Pricing Theories—Evolution and New Frontiers*, Financial Analysts Research Foundation, Charlottesville, Va., 1981.

made that either of these is the most appropriate choice, they have the advantage of being the most widely used, thus making comparisons easier.

12-4-4 The Time Horizon   Another issue which must be decided prior to estimating historical betas is the time horizon over which observations are to be made. Should the return for the stock and the market index be computed over the past year, the past 5 years, the past 10 years, etc.?

To illustrate that betas can differ depending upon the chosen time horizon, consider again the three stocks, General Motors, Mobil Oil, and Time, Inc. Listed below are two beta estimates for each stock. Each of these betas was calculated using the CRSP value-weighted index, monthly return intervals, and returns including dividends. What distinguishes the two beta estimates for each stock is the time horizon. The first beta is estimated over the 5-year period 1974–1978, while the second is estimated over the 5-year period 1979–1983:

Time horizon	Beta		
	GM	Mobil	Time
5 years, 1974–1978	.726	.856	.839
5 years, 1979–1983	.647	.999	1.227

The time horizon does not appear to make any significant difference in the beta estimate of General Motors, and to a lesser extent, one might make the same argument for Mobil Oil. However, this is not the case for Time's beta estimates—note that the estimated beta increased from .839 for the 1974–1978 time horizon to 1.227 for the 1979–1983 time horizon. Not only did the beta estimate change from below-average market risk to above-average risk, but the difference is also significant in the statistical sense.[14]

Upon reflection, it should be obvious that betas for individual securities can change over time. A security's systematic risk is ultimately determined by certain fundamental characteristics of the firm, some of which are discussed in the next section of this chapter. One of these firm characteristics is the amount of financial leverage—the more highly leveraged the firm, the higher the stock's beta, *ceteris paribus*. Obviously, the firm can change its financial structure over time, and consequently we would expect its beta to also change.

We might also expect the risk characteristics of a stock to change if the firm changed its basic business by, say, making a major acquisition. This, in fact, was the case for Time, Inc. During the period 1974–1978, Time was primarily in the publishing business. However, in 1979, Time's product mix was substantially changed when it ac-

---

[14]A formal statistical test as to whether the beta estimates are significantly different is the t test for the difference between two means—in this case, the two means are the two beta estimates for each stock. The t statistic for GM was .50 and for Mobil it was .808, neither of which would be considered statistically significant. However, for Time the t statistic was 1.95, which would be considered significant at the 5% level.

quired Inland Container, a forest products concern.[15] While this acquisition may not have been the only reason the beta for Time changed, it most likely was at least partially responsible.

Given the fact that individual security betas can and do change over time, we are left with the question: What is the most appropriate time horizon over which the beta is to be estimated? The answer will depend upon our purpose. If we are interested in a particular ex post time period, say for the purpose of evaluating performance during a specific time period, then the appropriate time horizon is the same as the ex post time period in question.

More likely, however, we will be interested in estimating a future beta. In this case we want to use the ex post time horizon which will produce a historical beta that is the most reliable predictor of the security's future beta. The most commonly used time horizon is 5 years.[16] If monthly return intervals are used, a 5-year time horizon results in 60 return observations, which is generally a large enough sample size to produce statistically reliable results. However, if a significant change has occurred in the company's fundamental characteristics, such as a major acquisition or a substantial change in the firm's capital structure, we may want to use only the time period since the change. If the change has occurred within the past 30 months or less, and consequently not enough return observations are available to get reliable estimates from the regression, then we will be forced to arbitrarily "adjust" the historical beta measured over, say, the past 5 years, based on the change in the firm's fundamental characteristics. Such adjustments are discussed in Section 12-5.

12-4-5 Nonsynchronous Trading   When securities do not trade at the end of each return interval, problems associated with what is termed "nonsynchronous trading" arise. In particular, the security's beta will generally be underestimated. To see this, first recall from Chapter 4 that beta can be expressed as follows:

$$\beta_{im} = \rho_{im} \frac{\sigma_i}{\sigma_m} \qquad (12\text{-}5)$$

where ρ_{im} = the correlation coefficient between security's returns and market index returns

σ_i = standard deviation of security's returns

σ_m = standard deviation of market index's returns

Now, to illustrate the problems associated with nonsynchronous trading, suppose we have a security that has the following "true" relationship with the market index: it is perfectly, positively correlated with the market and has a beta of 1.0. However, this security does not trade every period, and we need to *estimate* its beta based on the three most recent return intervals. The prices for the security and the market index

---

[15]Interestingly, in 1984, Time spun off its forest products division, and as a result the remaining businesses of the firm were again involved primarily in publications.

[16]For example, Standard & Poor's, Value Line, and Merrill Lynch all generally use a 5-year time horizon in estimating betas.

for these three time periods are shown below, as well as the computed return for each interval. To simplify this illustration, we'll assume that neither the security nor the index pays dividends:

Time period	Security		Market index	
	Price	Return, %	Price	Return, %
0	1.00	—	1.00	
1	1.10	10.0	1.10	10.0
2	No trade	?	1.05	−4.5
3	1.20	?	1.20	14.3

In the first period, the index was up 10% and since the security traded and is perfectly correlated with the index, it was also up 10%. In the second period the index was down 4.5%, but the security did not trade. If the security had traded, it would also have been down 4.5%, but since we can only observe market prices and do not know what the "true" correlation is between the security and the index, we do not know what the correct return is for the second time period. During the third period the index is up 14.3% to 1.20. During this period the security trades, and its price also rises to 1.20.

The analyst, who does not know the "true" relationship between the security and index, is faced with the problem of what return should be computed for the security during the second and third period. Typically, this problem is handled in one of two ways: (1) The second period can simply be ignored and the security's return in the third period computed based on the first- and third-period prices. This would result in a computed security return of 9.1% for the third period (1.20/1.10 − 1). In this case there are only two paired observations of security and market index returns—the first and third periods. (2) A second, and the more commonly used approach, is to average the security's price change over the second and third period. This results in a return of approximately 4.4% for the security in each period.[17] The returns for both methods are summarized below.

Time period	Ignore second period		Average second and third period	
	Security return, %	Index return, %	Security return, %	Index return, %
1	10.0	10.0	10.0	10.0
2	—	—	4.4	−4.5
3	9.1	14.3	4.4	14.3

[17]One method of averaging the return over the second and third period would be simply to compute the return based on the first- and third-period prices and divide by 2: (1.20/1.10 − 1)/2 = 4.5%. Another, and better, method would be to compute the geometric mean return over the two periods: $(1.20/1.10)^{1/2} - 1 = 4.4\%$.

TABLE 12-3   THE IMPACT OF NONSYNCHRONOUS TRADING
ON BETA ESTIMATES

Portfolio	Beta	Aggregated coefficients beta
MV1	0.75	1.69
MV2	0.87	1.64
MV3	0.90	1.55
MV4	0.96	1.50
MV5	0.98	1.46
MV6	0.97	1.39
MV7	0.95	1.31
MV8	0.97	1.24
MV9	0.95	1.13
MV10	0.98	0.97

Source: M. Reinganum, "A Direct Test of Roll's Conjecture on the Firm Size Effect," *Journal of Finance* (March 1982).

* WAY of correct for non synchro trading

It should be obvious that regardless of which procedure is used to deal with the second period during which the security did not trade, the estimated correlation coefficient between the security and the index will be less than its "true" value of 1.0. From Equation (12-5) it can be seen that, everything else held constant, underestimating the correlation coefficient results in underestimating the true beta.[18]

From this simple illustration we can make the following general statement: *the betas for securities which do not trade frequently will tend to be underestimated if standard regression techniques are used to estimate the betas.* What types of securities are more likely to not trade in every time period and therefore are more susceptible to nonsynchronous trading problems? Roll has pointed out that the stocks of smaller capitalization companies tend to trade less frequently, and therefore, their betas will be underestimated using standard regression techniques.[19]

To correct for the nonsynchronous trading problem, two methods have been proposed, one by Scholes and Williams[20], and the other by Dimson.[21] These techniques are complex and beyond the scope of this text. However, researchers examining the risk and return characteristics of securities which do not trade frequently will have to master either the Scholes/Williams or Dimson techniques because, as the results listed in Table 12-3 demonstrate, nonsynchronous trading can cause serious biases when ordinary least-squares (OLS) regression is used to estimate betas. In this study, Rein-

[18]In addition, the procedure of averaging the returns over the period the security did not trade results in an observed standard deviation for the security which is also lower than the security's true standard deviation, which in turn will cause the estimated beta to be less than the true beta. The procedure of ignoring return intervals during which the security did not trade may or may not decrease the estimate of the security's standard deviation. Regardless of which treatment of missing observations is used, the most serious error results from the underestimation of the correlation coefficient and consequently the underestimation of beta.

[19]R. Roll, "A Possible Explanation of the Small Firm Effect," *Journal of Finance* (September 1981).

[20]M. Scholes and J. Williams, "Estimating Betas from Nonsynchronous Data," *Journal of Financial Economics* (December 1977).

[21]E. Dimson, "Risk Measurement When Shares Are Subject to Infrequent Trading," *Journal of Financial Economics* (June 1979).

ganum[22] estimated betas using OLS regression and "aggregated coefficients," which is the method proposed by Dimson. Portfolios were formed based on market value, and portfolio betas were computed for each portfolio using both methods. Note that for the portfolio containing the smallest firms (MV1), the OLS beta was 0.75, whereas when the "aggregated coefficients" method was used to correct for nonsynchronous trading, the portfolio beta was 1.69! For the largest market value portfolio (MV10) there was no nonsynchronous trading problem—the OLS beta was 0.98 and the "aggregated coefficients" beta was a nearly identical 0.97. This confirmed Roll's conjecture that nonsynchronous trading will cause OLS betas to be underestimated for small-firm stocks but not for large-firm stocks.[23] And it should serve as an incentive to researchers and those commercial services providing beta estimates to utilize the methods provided by Scholes and Williams or Dimson when estimating the betas for thinly traded securities.

> Before continuing, you should:
> 1 Understand some of the decisions which have to be made concerning the return interval and time horizon when computing ex post betas
> 2 Be aware of the issues surrounding the choice of market index to be used in regressions for computing betas
> 3 Be aware of the problem nonsynchronous trading creates when estimating betas, particularly for smaller-firm stocks

12-5 PREDICTING BETAS

Just as *expected* earnings and dividends are determinants of today's stock prices, so are *expectations concerning risk*. While there are many occasions when historical betas per se are of interest, more often investors are interested in predicting betas. In the preceding section we indicated that typically the starting point for predicting betas is the security's historical beta. This raises the question of how well historical betas serve as predictors of future betas.

The Sharpe and Cooper study provides some evidence on this point. In this study every stock on the NYSE was classified into one of 10 risk classes based upon their betas for each year during the period 1931 through 1967. (Betas were computed using monthly return intervals over the previous 5 years and the CRSP equal-weighted index for the market returns). Table 12-4 lists the results. The first column indicates the

---

[22]M. Reinganum, "A Direct Test of Roll's Conjecture on the Firm Size Effect," *Journal of Finance* (March 1982).

[23]Both Roll, op. cit. and Reinganum, op. cit., were interested in testing for the small-firm effect, which is discussed in more detail in Section 5-5-3. The small-firm effect argues that small-capitalization stocks provide above-normal risk-adjusted returns. Roll suggested that because of nonsynchronous trading, the risk of small firms might have been underestimated in earlier studies and consequently their risk-adjusted returns might have been overstated. Both Roll and Reinganum found that, in fact, the risk (betas) of small firms had been underestimated. However, they both also found that, even after adjusting for nonsynchronous trading, small firms still provided above-normal risk-adjusted returns, although the amount of the small-firm effect was reduced roughly by one-half after adjusting for nonsynchronous trading.

TABLE 12-4   HISTORICAL BETAS AS A PREDICTOR OF FUTURE BETAS

Beta class	Percentage of stocks in same beta class 5 years later	Percentage of stocks within one class 5 years later
10 (highest betas)	32.2	69.3
9	18.4	53.7
8	16.4	45.3
7	13.3	40.9
6	13.9	39.3
5	13.6	41.7
4	13.2	40.2
3	15.9	44.6
2	21.5	60.9
1 (lowest betas)	40.5	62.3

Source: W. F. Sharpe and G. M. Cooper, "Risk-Return Classes of New York Stock Exchange Common Stocks, 1931–1967," *Financial Analysts Journal* (March/April 1972).

percentage of the stocks that were in the same risk class 5 years later; the second column indicates the percentage of the stocks that were within one risk class 5 years later. For example, 32.2% of the stocks in risk class 10 (highest betas) continued to be in risk class 10 five years later. This was true for 40.5% of the lowest-risk class stocks. If no relationship existed between past and future betas, we would expect only 10% of the stocks in one time period to be in the same risk class in the next time period. Notice further that between 39% and almost 70% of the stocks were within one risk class of their original ranking 5 years later. Thus, there is obviously some predictive power in historical betas.

On the other hand, risk characteristics must also be subject to change over time, since the relationship between past and future betas was not perfect. Why do betas change over time? The answers are many. Part of the reason is simply measurement (statistical) errors in estimating historical betas from a sample of return observations. Probably more importantly, fundamental changes in the firm's operations affect the risk of its securities. For example, the change in Time's beta illustrated in the preceding section might have been at least partly the result of a major acquisition. And part of the reason is the tendency of betas to "regress toward the mean"—that is, the tendency for high and low betas to revert toward the average beta of 1.0 over time.

12-5-1 Regression toward the Mean   In a series of papers,[24] Blume observed that, over time, betas have a tendency to regress toward 1.0, the mean of all betas. That is, over time high betas tend to decrease toward 1.0 and low betas tend to increase toward the mean. Table 12-5 summarizes some of Blume's results. Betas were estimated over the 7-year time horizon of July 1947–June 1954 and eight portfolios were

[24]For a complete review of the literature on this topic see: M. E. Blume, "On the Assessment of Risk," *Journal of Finance* (March 1971); M. E. Blume, "Betas and Their Regression Tendencies," *Journal of Finance* (June 1975); M. E. Blume, "Betas and Their Regression Tendencies: Some Further Evidence," *Journal of Finance* (March 1979); and P. T. Elgers, J. R. Haltiner, and W. H. Hawthorne, "Beta Regression Tendencies: Statistical and Real Causes," *Journal of Finance* (March 1979).

formed, with portfolio 1 containing the lowest-beta stocks and portfolio 8 containing the highest-beta stocks. The betas for these same portfolios were then reestimated over the next two 7-year time periods, 1954–1961 and 1961–1968. Notice that the beta for portfolio 1 for the first time horizon was .36, whereas during the next two time horizons it increased to .57 and .72, respectively. The beta for portfolio 8 during the first time horizon was 1.47, which subsequently decreased to 1.32 and 1.15 over the next two time horizons.

In general, Blume found that over time high betas tend to decrease and low betas tend to increase toward 1.0. We can only speculate why this "regression toward the mean" occurs. Presumably positions of extreme risk moderate over time, either because of conscious choices made by management or because of economic conditions. It may be that managers, once they observe that their firm's securities are at an extreme-risk level (either high or low) make conscious choices to redeploy the firm's capital into assets which have more moderate risk characteristics. Or it may be that economic conditions moderate the characteristics of extreme-risk assets over time. For example, the risk characteristics of small, emerging industries probably moderate as the industry becomes larger and more mature.

For whatever reasons, it does appear that betas regress over time toward 1.0. Therefore, if historical betas are used as a starting point in estimating future betas, some allowances must be made for this tendency. Blume suggested using an equation similar to the following:

$$\beta_{t+1} = .35 + .65\beta_t \tag{12-6}$$

where β_{t+1} = beta to be predicted for next time horizon

β_t = historical beta measured over most recent time horizon

To illustrate, consider portfolio 1 in Table 12-5. At the end of the first time horizon (1947–1954), we would estimate the beta for the next time horizon (1954–1961) as follows:

$$\beta_{54-61} = .35 + .65\beta_{47-54} = .35 + .65(.36) = .58$$

TABLE 12-5   THE TENDENCY OF BETAS TO REGRESS TOWARD 1.0

Portfolio	Portfolio betas for different time horizons		
	July 1947–June 1954	July 1954–June 1961	July 1961–June 1968
1	.36	.57	.72
2	.61	.71	.79
3	.78	.88	.88
4	.91	.96	.92
5	1.01	1.03	1.04
6	1.13	1.13	1.02
7	1.26	1.24	1.08
8	1.47	1.32	1.15

Source: M. E. Blume, "Betas and Their Regression Tendencies," *Journal of Finance* (June 1975).

Note that the predicted beta of .58 is remarkably close to the actual beta of .57. Similarly, for portfolio 8 we would estimate the 1954–1961 beta to be 1.32 (.35 + .65 × 1.47), which turns out to be the same as the actual beta.

Of course, it is unreasonable to expect historical betas, adjusted for their regression tendency in the manner illustrated above, to predict future betas as well as these two examples. This is particularly true when estimating the betas of individual securities, as opposed to portfolios of securities. Nevertheless, the evidence suggests that this type of adjustment will definitely improve predictions of betas.

12-5-2 Betas and Company Fundamentals   While adjusting historical betas for their tendency to revert toward 1.0 improves predictions of future betas, even better predictions can be obtained if fundamental characteristics of the firm are considered. For example, Hamada[25] has shown theoretically that betas should be a positive function of leverage. This positive relationship between financial leverage and systematic risk has been well established empirically.[26] That is, the more debt in the firm's capital structure, the higher the stock's beta, *ceteris paribus*. Conversely, if a firm issued new stock and used the proceeds to retire debt, thus reducing its financial leverage, we might reasonably expect that its future beta will be lower than its historical beta— again, assuming everything else remains constant.

A study by Rosenberg and Marathe[27] explored the issue of how much beta prediction can be improved by utilizing the fundamental characteristics of the firm. While their study was relatively complex, some of the important features can be summarized as follows: First, they determined the historical relationship between betas and a large number of company characteristics. Then, based on these relationships, they estimated future betas in two ways—using only the company's fundamental characteristics and second using the company's fundamental characteristics in conjunction with the stock's historical beta. Finally, the results of these two beta prediction techniques were compared with a benchmark prediction. The benchmark was based solely on the company's historical beta (after adjusting for the tendency to regress toward 1.0). Interestingly, the beta predictions based solely on fundamental characteristics represented a 45% improvement over the benchmark predictions based on historical betas. The use of fundamental characteristics in conjunction with historical betas resulted in an 85% improvement over the benchmark predictions.

These results strongly suggest that predictions of betas can be improved substantially by considering fundamental characteristics of the firm as well as the historical betas. Therefore, let's take a closer look at some of the Rosenberg-Marathe results. Table 12-6 lists the adjustments made to historical betas for six different fundamental firm char-

---

[25]R. Hamada, "The Effect of the Firm's Capital Structure on the Systematic Risk of Common Stocks," *Journal of Finance* (May 1972).

[26]Hamada, op. cit., empirically verified the positive relationship between financial leverage and beta, as did J. Thompson, "Sources of Systematic Risk in Common Stocks," *Journal of Business* (April 1976). Thompson's article reviews a number of earlier papers on this subject.

[27]B. Rosenberg and V. Marathe, "The Prediction of Investment Risk: Systematic and Residual Risk," *Proceedings of the Seminar on the Analysis of Security Prices*, Graduate School of Business, University of Chicago, 1975. Some of the results of this study are summarized in B. Rosenberg and J. Guy, "Prediction of Beta from Investment Fundamentals, Parts One and Two," *Financial Analysts Journal* (May–June and July–August 1976).

TABLE 12-6   BETAS AND COMPANY FUNDAMENTALS

Fundamental characteristic	Adjustment to beta for a difference of one standard deviation from the mean of all firms
Variance of cash flow	0.022
Variance of earnings	0.023
Growth in earnings per share	− 0.004
Market capitalization	− 0.043
Current dividend yield	− 0.044
Total debt to assets	0.041

All adjustments factors were statistically significant at the 95% level.

Source: The results shown above are for 6 out of 36 variables presented in Table 4 of B. Rosenberg and V. Marathe, "The Prediction of Investment Risk: Systematic and Residual Risk," *Proceedings of the Seminar on the Analysis of Security Prices*, Graduate School of Business, University of Chicago, 1975. The results for only these six variables were also reproduced in Table 3 of B. Rosenberg and J. Guy, "Prediction of Beta from Investment Fundamentals, Part Two," *Financial Analysts Journal* (July–August 1976).

acteristics. First notice that in each case the sign of the adjustment factors is consistent with what one might intuitively expect. For example, we would expect a positive relationship between the variance of the firm's cash flow and risk—that is, the more variable the cash flow, the higher the beta. Similarly, we would expect a positive relationship between beta and the variance of earnings, as well as beta and the ratio of total debt to assets. The negative relationship between beta and growth in EPS suggests that the stronger the earnings trend over time, the less risky the stock, *ceteris paribus*. The negative relationship between beta and dividend yield can be explained several ways. A larger part of the price of high-yield stocks derived from near-term dividends, and perhaps investors associate less risk with these larger, near-term dividends. A more likely explanation is based on the *duration* of stocks. Duration is discussed in detail in Chapter 15, but for now you can think of duration as a measure of the length of time over which investors receive interest, principal payments, and in the case of stocks, dividends. Because of their large current dividends, high-yield stocks have shorter durations than low-yield stocks, and as shown in Section 16-4, beta is positively related to duration.

To illustrate how the adjustment factors in Table 12-6 were used, suppose that the mean dividend yield for all firms at the time of their study was 4% and that the standard deviation was 2%. Then for a stock whose yield was 6% (one standard deviation above the mean), the estimate of beta would be *decreased* by 0.044. Similarly, suppose that the mean total debt to assets ratio was .9 and that the standard deviation was .3, and that this ratio was 1.5 for the same stock (two standard deviation above the mean). In this case the prediction of beta would be increased by 0.082, i.e., 2 × .041. All these adjustments factors would be summed and then added to 1.0, the average beta for all stocks. If the two factors mentioned above were the only factors considered, the predicted beta would be 1.038, i.e., 1.0 − .044 + .082 = 1.038.

These calculations are only meant to be illustrative of the approach used by Rosenberg and Marathe. They actually considered over 50 characteristics of the firm. In addition, the size of the adjustment factors presented in Table 12-6 represented the "best fit" *at the time of their study*, and the actual size of the adjustment will vary over time. However, this should provide the interested reader with some appreciation of how fundamental characteristics might be incorporated into the prediction of systematic risk or beta. This should be of interest as the additional work involved in making beta predictions based on company fundamentals appears to be worth the effort. A recent study indicated that a model using betas adjusted for company fundamentals provided 67% more predictive power of future betas than did a model based solely on historical betas adjusted for the tendency to regress toward the mean.[28]

12-5-3 Betas and Industry Factors   In addition to fundamental characteristics *unique* to each firm, Rosenberg and Marathe also found that the industry the firm is in affects its beta. The first column of Table 12-7 lists the average beta for a number of industries. As one might expect, there are substantial differences in the systematic risk between industries. The betas range from a high of 1.80 for the air transport industry to a low of .36 for the gold stocks.

Perhaps of more interest, however, is the second column labeled "Adjustment factor." The industry adjustment represents the amount that the beta for a stock in a particular industry should be adjusted *after all adjustments have been made for its fundamental characteristics*, as described in the preceding section. For example, if a company had a below-average debt ratio, its beta would have been adjusted downward, etc. Then, after all the adjustments based on the company's fundamental characteristics had been made, if the company was in the nonferrous metals industry its beta would have been further adjusted downward by .142.

Apparently, company characteristics such as variability of earnings, debt ratios, and dividend yield do not fully capture the risk associated with each industry. One example of this might be the utilities industry. A fundamental company characteristic such as earnings variability does not capture the fact that, while a utility's earnings may fluctuate over time, it is extremely unlikely that a utility will go into bankruptcy, even in today's era of large cost overruns associated with the construction of new power plants. Probably largely because of this, Rosenberg and Marathe found that the betas for energy utility stocks had to be adjusted downward by .237 after making all the adjustments based on the individual utility's fundamental characteristics.

Similar downward adjustments were made to tobacco stocks, bank stocks, telephone stocks, and gold stocks. Relatively large upward adjustments were made to the stocks of companies in the electronics, air transport, miscellaneous finance, and travel and outdoor recreation industries. While the results reported in Table 12-7 are very likely sensitive to the time period of the study, they do illustrate the fact that it is unlikely that individual company characteristics will completely capture all the aspects of systematic risk. Consequently, the analyst needs to be alert to the industries in which the company operates.

---

[28]B. Rosenberg, "Prediction of Common Stock Betas," *Journal of Portfolio Management* (winter 1985). For a different approach to adjusting historical betas in order to obtain better predictions of future betas, see S. Carvell and P. Strebel, "A New Beta Incorporating Analysts' Forecasts," *Journal of Portfolio Management* (fall 1984).

TABLE 12-7 BETAS AND INDUSTRY FACTORS

Industry	Values of beta	Adjustment factor
Nonferrous metals	.99	−.142*
Energy raw materials	1.22	−.030
Construction	1.27	.062
Agriculture, food	.99	−.140*
Liquor	.89	−.165*
Tobacco	.80	−.279*
Apparel	1.27	.019
Forest products, paper	1.16	−.016
Containers	1.01	−.140*
Media	1.39	.124*
Chemicals	1.22	.011
Drugs, medicine	1.14	−.099*
Soaps, cosmetics	1.09	−.067*
Domestic oil	1.12	−.103*
International oil	.85	−.143*
Tires, rubber goods	1.21	.050
Steel	1.02	−.086*
Producer goods	1.30	.043
Business machines	1.43	.065
Consumer durables	1.44	.132*
Motor vehicles	1.27	.045
Aerospace	1.30	.020
Electronics	1.60	.155*
Photographic, optical	1.24	.026
Nondurables, entertainment	1.47	.042
Trucking, freight	1.31	.098
Railroads, shipping	1.19	.030
Air transport	1.80	.348*
Telephone	.75	−.288*
Energy, utilities	.60	−.237*
Retail, general	1.43	.073
Banks	.81	−.242*
Miscellaneous finance	1.60	.210*
Insurance	1.34	.103
Real property	1.70	.339*
Business services	1.28	.029
Travel, outdoor recreation	1.66	.186*
Gold	.36	−.827*
Miscellaneous, conglomerate	1.14	.089*

*Statistically significant at the 95% level or higher.
Source: Table 3 of B. Rosenberg and V. Marathe, "The Prediction of Investment Risk: Systematic and Residual Risk," *Proceedings of the Seminar on the Analysis of Security Prices*, Graduate School of Business, University of Chicago, 1975. These results were also reproduced in Table 2 of B. Rosenberg and J. Guy, "Prediction of Beta from Investment Fundamentals, Part Two," *Financial Analysts Journal* (July–August 1976).

12-6 TRADITIONAL RISK MEASURES

Long before the concept of systematic risk was developed, the investment community had been interested in other measures of risk, which we will loosely classify as traditional risk measures. As a general rule, these traditional risk measures have

TABLE 12-8   COMPONENTS OF TRADITIONAL RISK MEASURES

Standard & Poor's Quality Rating

The S&P Quality Rating for earnings and dividends of common stocks is divided into the following eight categories:

A+	Highest	B+	Average	C	Lowest
A	High	B	Below average	D	In reorganization
A−	Above average				

Growth and stability of earnings over the past 10 years are the key elements in the S&P Quality Ratings. The ratings will be adjusted, depending upon the size of the firm. In general, larger firms will be assigned a higher rating for a given earnings and dividend record, while smaller firms will be assigned a lower rating

---

Value Line Safety Rank

The Value Line Safety Ranks range from 1 to 5, with a rank of 1 indicating the lowest risk and a rank of 5 indicating the greatest risk. The Safety Rank is computed by averaging two other Value Line indexes: the Price Stability Index and the Financial Strength Index.

The Price Stability Index is a ranking based on the standard deviation of weekly stock price changes over the most recent 5 years. The top 5% (lowest standard deviations) carry a Price Stability Index of 100; the next 5% receive a ranking of 95; and so on down to a ranking of 5 for the highest standard deviations.

The Financial Strength Ratings range from A+ + for those firms deemed to have the best relative financial strength to a low of C. The primary variables used to determine this rating are equity coverage of debt, equity coverage of intangibles, quick ratio, accounting methods, variability of return, fixed charge coverage, stock price stability, and company size.

Sources: Standard & Poor's Stock Guide, New York; and A. Bernhard, *How to Use the Value Line Investment Survey, A Subscriber's Guide*, Value Line, Inc., New York.

concentrated on the variability of earning and dividends, or financial leverage, or a combination of both. Illustrative of these traditional risk measures are the Standard & Poor's Quality Rating for Earnings and Dividends and the Value Line Safety Rank. Table 12-8 provides a general description of how these risk measures are computed. Notice that many of the variables used to compute these traditional risk measures are the same as or similar to those used by Rosenberg and Marathe to improve predictions of beta. Standard & Poor's concentrates largely on the stability (or variability) of earnings and dividends, as well as the size of the firm. Value Line also considers variability of return (which is just the variability of earnings scaled by capital or equity) and firm size. In addition, Value Line considers a number of leverage ratios. Thus, it appears that many of the traditional risk measures at least partially proxy for systematic risk.

12-7 SUMMARY

In this chapter we provided an overview of how investment professionals analyze and quantify risk. Since risk directly affects the discount rate used in determining security prices, this is an important topic.

Risk, when defined as the variance of return, can be decomposed into several parts. One part is determined by an overall market factor; another part is due to industry factors; still other parts may be due to additional extramarket common factors such as dividend yield and firm size. Finally, a large part of the total risk associated with individual securities is due to factors unique to the firm itself. This unsystematic risk, of course, can be eliminated by diversification.

Estimating the systematic risk, or beta, of individual securities is not as straight-forward as it might appear at first glance. Before running regressions to estimate historical betas, questions concerning the appropriate return interval, time horizon, and index for market returns must be answered. In addition, more subtle problems concerning nonsynchronous trading must be addressed if the securities under consideration do not trade during every return interval, as is the case for stocks of many smaller firms.

To predict future betas we suggest using the historical beta as a starting point. However, historical betas should be adjusted for the tendency of betas to regress over time toward 1.0. In addition, if there have been recent changes in the fundamental characteristics of the firm, or if such changes are anticipated in the future, appropriate adjustments should be made to the historical beta.

Finally, some traditional risk measures were examined. Interestingly, these risk measures are typically based on fundamental firm characteristics which have also been shown to be factors in determining betas. Thus, it appears that the traditional analysis of risk has been consistent, or at least complementary, to the approaches suggested by modern capital market theory.

SUGGESTED READINGS

Before starting to use regression to estimate betas, it might be wise to review Section 8-4, which deals with regression. If further review is needed, the following textbooks are good references:

J. Neter, W. Wasserman, and M. Kutner, *Applied Linear Regression Models*, Irwin, Homewood, Ill., 1983.

R. Folger and S. Ganapathy, *Financial Econometrics*, Prentice-Hall, Englewood Cliffs, N.J., 1982.

The whole issue concerning the choice of index was started by the paper frequently referred to as "Roll's Critique."

R. Roll, "A Critique of the Asset Pricing Theory's Tests," *Journal of Financial Economics* (March 1977).

As its title suggests, this paper is primarily concerned with testing asset pricing theories. Its principal conclusion is that asset pricing theories which utilize the "market portfolio" are essentially untestable because we cannot observe the true "market portfolio." In addition, several side issues are developed in this paper, one of which is that betas and, consequently, measures of alpha depend upon the index choice. The following are papers which deal with the choice of index issue:

R. Roll, "Ambiguity When Performance Is Measured by the Securities Market Line," *Journal of Finance* (September 1978).

D. Peterson and M. L. Rice, "A Note on Ambiguity in Portfolio Performance Measures," *Journal of Finance* (December 1980).

R. J. Fuller, *Capital Asset Pricing Theories—Evolution and New Frontiers*, Chapter 3, Financial Analysts Research Foundation, Charlottesville, Va., 1981.

A recent article has argued that adjusting historical betas in a fashion similar to Blume and others does not produce better estimates of future betas. See:

G. A. Hawawini and A. Vora, "Is Adjusting Beta Estimates an Illusion?" *Journal of Portfolio Management* (fall 1983).

An excellent starting point for studying how ex ante estimates of both systematic risk (beta) and total risk (variance) are made is:

B. Rosenberg and J. Guy, "Prediction of Beta from Investment Fundamentals," Parts One and Two, *Financial Analysts Journal* (May–June and July–August 1976).

For a more detailed discussion of these issues, see:

B. Rosenberg and V. Marathe, "The Prediction of Investment Risk: Systematic and Residual Risk," *Proceedings of the Seminar on the Analysis of Security Prices*, Graduate School of Business, University of Chicago (November 1975).

B. Rosenberg and V. Marathe, "Common Factors in Security Returns: Microeconomic Determinants and Macroeconomic Correlates," *Proceedings of the Seminar on the Analysis of Security Prices*, Graduate School of Business, University of Chicago (May 1976).

D. J. Thompson, "Source of Systematic Risk in Common Stocks," *Journal of Business* (April 1976).

QUESTIONS

1 How would you estimate the risk-free real rate?
2 Of the three traditional aspects of risk (business risk, financial risk, and liquidity risk), which do you think might be most closely associated with systematic risk?
3 How might you go about estimating liquidity risk?
4 Besides industry factors, name some possible sources of extramarket covariation. How would you eliminate the variation of return associated with these extramarket factors?
5 Is beta phlogiston? Develop your answer in terms of short-time horizons vs. long-time horizons. Hint: see Figure 12-4.
6 Discuss some of the issues that must be resolved before performing regressions to estimate historical betas.
7 What problem is particularly severe when estimating betas for small-firm stocks?
8 Under what circumstances might you be interested in ex post betas? in ex ante betas?
9 Firm A had a beta of 1.15 and acquires firm B which also had a beta of 1.15. If the earnings and cash flow of A and B are uncorrelated, what do you think will be the future beta of the combined firms, everything else held constant?
10 If firm A issues debt to finance the acquisition of firm B, what effect will this have on the future beta of the combined firms?
11 Why do you suppose gold stocks have such low betas? Why is the adjustment factor in Table 12-7 such a large, negative number?

PROBLEMS

1 Given no other information than firm Z's historical beta of 1.40, what is your estimate of its future beta?

2 Given your estimate of firm Z's future beta in Problem 1, and the fact that the firm has recently increased its total debt ratio from the mean debt ratio for all firms to two standard deviations above the mean, what is your estimate of its future beta? Hint: Use Table 12-6.

3 Given the information below: (a) compute the beta for XYZ, first using the DJIA as the market index and then recompute XYZ's beta using the S&P 500 as the market index; (b) compute the correlation coefficient for the DJIA and the S&P 500; (c) discuss your findings.

XYZ, %	DJIA, %	S&P 500, %
9	10	11
2	-4	1
8	6	6
19	14	13
-12	-5	-6
14	8	12

4 Suppose you had computed the beta for First Honest Bank Co. to be .95 based on its historical beta and a large number of fundamental characteristics of the company such as the growth and variability of its earnings and cash flow, the size of the firm, its debt ratio, and its current dividend yield. Are there any other adjustments you might want to make to this beta estimate?

CHAPTER 13

COMMON STOCK VALUATION MODELS

After reading this chapter, you should:

1 Understand the valuation principles underlying dividend discount models
2 Know how to use the three-phase dividend discount model and the *H* model
3 Understand the rationale and the key variables associated with *P/E* valuation models
4 Understand how cross-sectional regression models are used to evaluate common stock prices
5 Know how the Value Line ranking system is constructed
6 Be aware of the selection criteria proposed by Benjamin Graham

The investment process requires that a series of decisions be made. First, a decision has to be reached as to the risk level one is willing to tolerate. Then the investor has to decide what type or types of assets to purchase, such as stocks, bonds, or real estate. Once these decisions have been made, the investor must decide upon which specific assets are to be purchased. If common stocks are the chosen investment medium, does one invest in IBM, or General Motors, or any of the other several thousand available stocks? In order to make decisions as to which specific assets should be selected, valuation models are needed.

One solution to the common stock selection problem would be to assume that the securities markets are perfectly efficient. If this is the case, one can simply select at random a group of stocks within the desired risk class and expect to earn a normal return. However, this "passive" approach has typically not been followed by investors. Why? Perhaps investors persist in trying to identify undervalued securities because they are not aware of the efficient markets literature discussed in Chapter 5; perhaps investors have known all along that the securities markets are not perfectly efficient, as is also discussed in Chapter 5; or perhaps investors simply have an inflated view of their ability to consistently identify undervalued securities. For whatever reasons, most investors do attempt to "pick winners"; that is, they attempt to select undervalued securities. The purpose of this chapter is to present a number of valuation models which have been used in the past for selecting individual common stocks.

13-1 AN EXAMPLE OF A STOCK VALUATION MODEL

For investment purposes (and most other purposes), a good model is one that predicts well. In order to make good forecasts, the model should account for the principal relationships between the variable to be predicted and those factors which will cause the predicted variable to change in the future. Models which do not account for these *cause-effect relationships* most likely will not provide good forecasts, even if they "explained" well the behavior of the predicted variable in the past.[1] For example, it is well known that church attendance and beer sales are highly correlated. Yet these two variables (probably) do not have any cause-effect relationship. Rather they both have increased proportionately with the increase in population over time. If a model had been constructed to forecast beer sales based on church attendance, such a model would have produced substantial forecast errors during years the legal drinking age was changed in various states and certainly during the prohibition years! This is because such a model would fail to account for the critical cause-effect relationships between beer sales and such key variables as the age of the population and the legal environment.

Likewise, to construct a good stock valuation model we need to identify the key determinants of stock prices. In the preceding chapters we argued that stock prices should equal the present value of all future dividends paid to the owners of the stock, discounted at an appropriate rate. Thus, *if one can forecast future dividends accurately and if one can determine the appropriate discount rate*, a model for determining under- and overvalued stocks can be constructed which may provide good forecasts. The implicit forecast of such a model is that undervalued stocks will produce positive abnormal returns over some future time period and that overvalued stocks will generate below-normal returns in the future.

One example of a stock valuation model based on the present value of dividends is that which has been used by Kidder Peabody & Co., a large investment banking firm. The results from their model's analysis of Boise Cascade's stock price as of September 15, 1980, are presented in Table 13-1. The top part of Table 13-1 presents a summary of the analysis, while the bottom part presents year-by-year projections of a number of key variables, including dividends. The first items in the summary are Kidder Peabody's estimate of the risk-free rate (9.2%) and their expected return for the market (17.0%). Therefore, the equity risk premium, or the market price of risk, is equal to 17.0% − 9.2%, or 7.8%. Based on a linear market model similar to those described in Chapter 4, the following market line is utilized to estimate required returns:

$$R(r_i) = 9.2\% + 7.8\% \text{ FRE} \tag{13-1}$$

where FRE stands for Kidder Peabody's "fundamental risk estimate"—an ex ante estimate of market-related risk, based on historical betas with adjustments made when the firm changes its capital structure or operating characteristics. Given the expected return for Boise Cascade of 18.9% (which is determined from the information in the year-by-year projections) and the FRE of 1.09, Kidder Peabody then computed for Boise Cascade a required return of 17.7% and an associated alpha of 1.2%.

---

[1] F. Black points this out well in "The Trouble with Econometric Models," *Financial Analysts Journal* (March/April 1982).

$$R(r_i) = r_f + [E(r_m) - r_f] \, FRE$$
$$= 9.2\% + 7.8\% \, (1.09) = 17.7\%$$

$$\alpha_i = E(r_i) - R(r_i) \qquad\qquad (13\text{-}2)$$
$$= 18.9\% - 17.7\% = 1.2\%$$

Thus, this approach used by Kidder Peabody is very similar to that suggested in Chapter 4. A security market line (SML) was constructed, then the expected return for securities was compared with the required returns implied by the SML, and finally, alphas were calculated. In this case, the positive alpha of 1.2% for Boise Cascade implies that the stock was undervalued and should have been considered as a possible buy candidate.

Other information is also supplied in the top part of Table 13-1. For example, the "zero-alpha price" of $46.95 is the present value of Boise Cascade stock if the required return of 17.7% is used to discount the expected dividends. This zero-alpha price is 21.2% above the current market price of $38.75. In addition, the top part of Table 13-1 lists historical growth rates for earnings (14.9%), the payout ratio (1.5%), and dividends (16.6%).

The year-by-year projections listed in the bottom part of Table 13-1 illustrate the common stock valuation model used by Kidder Peabody to determine the expected return for individual stocks. These projections are divided into four phases. For phase 1, which covers the first 9 years, earnings are estimated for each year, as is a payout ratio. Multiplying the estimated earnings by the estimated payout ratio will, of course, provide an estimate of dividends for each year during phase 1. For phase 2 the growth rate of earnings is expected to plateau at 13.5% and the payout ratio is also forecast to be a constant—in this case 38.0%. Given these estimates, the dividends during phase 2 can also be estimated. Phase 3 in the Kidder Peabody model represents a 25-year transition period during which the earnings growth rate is expected to systematically decline to a perpetual (steady-state) average of 9% and the payout ratio is expected to increase systematically to a perpetual, steady-state average of 48%. Once again, given the earnings growth rate and the expected payout ratio, the expected dividends during phase 3 can be estimated. For phase 4 the assumptions of the constant growth dividend discount model[2] are evoked, with earnings and dividends expected to grow at a constant 9.0% in perpetuity for Boise Cascade.

In this way, an estimate of a perpetual stream of dividends for Boise Cascade is generated. The expected return $E(r)$ is the rate which discounts this dividend stream to the current price of the stock. Mathematically,

$$P_0 = \sum_{t=1}^{\infty} \left(\frac{E(D_t)}{[1 + E(r)]^t} \right) \qquad\qquad (13\text{-}3)$$

[2] Recall from Chapter 10 that the constant growth dividend discounts model is expressed as

$$P_t = \frac{D_t(1 + g)}{r - g}$$

TABLE 13-1 KIDDER PEABODY & CO., INC., SECURITIES VALUATION SYSTEM (SALUS)

Boise Cascade Corp. (BCC)   Data as of 7/31/80   Report Date 9/15/80

— Summary Information —

(1) Current Market Environment:
- Risk-Free Rate of Return — 9.2%
- Average Expected Return of the Market — 17.0%
- Equity Risk Premium — 7.8%

(2) Security-Related Information:
- Price — 38.75
- Estimated Yield — 4.5%
- Fundamental Risk Estimate (FRE) — 1.09

(3) Valuation Information:
- Expected Return — 18.9%
- Required Return — 17.7%
- Alpha — 1.2%

(4) Implied Price Change:
- Zero-Alpha Price — $46.95
- Alpha-Implied Price Change — 21.2%
- Rank in Universe — 30/330

(5) Estimated Five-Year Least-Squares Growth Rates:
- Earnings — 14.9%
- Payout — 1.5%
- Dividends — 16.6%

— Year-by-Year Projections —

(1) Fiscal Years	(2) Earnings Growth Rate(%)	(3) Earns. Per Share	(4) Div Payout(%)	(5) Incrm. Div.	(6) Div. Growth Rate(%)	(7) Dividends Per Share	(8) Present Value Factor	(9) PV Of Div.	(10) Sum Of PV Of Div.	(11) % Term. Value	(12) Steady-State ROE
Last		6.52	22.1			1.44	1.000000				
1 — 1980	−33.3	4.35	40.2	0.31	21.5	1.75	0.841194	1.472	1.472	3.8	
2 — 1981	20.7	5.25	35.2	0.10	5.7	1.85	0.707608	1.309	2.781	7.2	
3 — 1982	33.3	7.00	31.4	0.35	18.9	2.20	0.595236	1.310	4.091	10.6	
4 — 1983	28.6	9.00	30.6	0.55	25.0	2.75	0.500709	1.377	5.468	14.1	
5 — 1984	16.7	10.50	29.5	0.35	12.7	3.10	0.421193	1.306	6.773	17.5	
6 — 1985	16.2	12.20	31.1	0.70	22.6	3.80	0.354306	1.346	8.120	21.0	
7 — 1986	15.8	14.10	32.6	0.80	21.1	4.60	0.298040	1.371	9.491	24.5	
8 — 1987	14.9	16.20	34.6	1.00	21.7	5.60	0.250709	1.404	10.895	28.1	
9 — 1988	14.2	18.50	36.2	1.10	19.6	6.70	0.210895	1.413	12.308	31.8	

PHASE 1—Near Term:

Minimum 5 Years —
Maximum 10 Years

PHASE 2—Plateau:

#		Year	Earnings Benchmark [13.5]	10.0%,	Earnings Relative [38.0]	1.35;	Payout Benchmark	40.0%,	Payout Relative	0.95
10	—	1989	13.5	21.00	38.0	19.1	7.98	0.177404	13.723	35.4
11	—	1990	13.5	23.83	38.0	13.5	9.06	0.149231	15.075*	38.9
12	—	1991	13.5	27.05	38.0	13.5	10.28	0.125532	16.365	42.2
13	—	1992	13.5	30.70	38.0	13.5	11.67	0.105597	17.597	45.4
14	—	1993	13.5	34.85	38.0	13.5	13.24	0.088828	18.773	48.4

[6 Years]

| 15 | — | 1994 | 13.5 | 39.55 | 38.0 | 13.5 | 15.03 | 0.074721 | 19.896 | 51.3 |

PHASE 3—Transition:

#		Year	Earnings Benchmark	10.0%,	Earnings Relative	1.35;	Payout Benchmark	40.0%,	Payout Relative	0.95
16	—	1995	13.5	44.88	38.0	13.6	17.07	0.062855	20.969	54.1
17	—	1996	13.4	50.91	38.2	13.8	19.43	0.052873	21.996	56.8
18	—	1997	13.3	57.70	38.4	13.9	22.13	0.044477	22.981	59.3
19	—	1998	13.2	65.33	38.6	14.0	25.23	0.037414	23.925	61.7
20	—	1999	13.1	73.87	39.0	14.1	28.78	0.031472	24.830	64.1
21	—	2000	12.9	83.39	39.4	14.1	32.82	0.026474	25.899	66.3
22	—	2001	12.7	93.97	39.8	14.0	37.41	0.022270	26.532	68.5
23	—	2002	12.5	105.67	40.3	13.9	42.61	0.018733	27.330	70.5
24	—	2003	12.2	118.58	40.9	13.7	48.46	0.015758	28.094	72.5
25	—	2004	11.9	132.74	41.5	13.5	55.03	0.013256	28.824	74.4
26	—	2005	11.7	148.23	42.1	13.3	62.35	0.011151	29.519	76.2
27	—	2006	11.4	165.12	42.7	13.0	70.48	0.009380	30.180	77.9
28	—	2007	11.1	183.46	43.3	12.7	79.46	0.007890	30.807	79.5
29	—	2008	10.8	203.33	43.9	12.4	89.34	0.006637	31.400	81.0
30	—	2009	10.6	224.79	44.5	12.1	100.13	0.005583	31.959	82.5
31	—	2010	10.3	247.92	45.1	11.7	111.88	0.004697	32.484	83.8
32	—	2011	10.0	272.82	45.7	11.4	124.62	0.003951	32.977	85.1
33	—	2012	9.8	299.60	46.2	11.0	138.38	0.003323	33.437	86.3
34	—	2013	9.6	328.39	46.6	10.7	153.18	0.002796	33.865	87.4
35	—	2014	9.4	359.36	47.0	10.4	169.06	0.002352	34.262	88.4
36	—	2015	9.3	392.70	47.4	10.1	186.07	0.001978	34.631	89.4
37	—	2016	9.2	428.67	47.6	9.8	204.26	0.001664	34.970	90.2
38	—	2017	9.1	467.55	47.8	9.5	223.69	0.001400	35.284	91.1
39	—	2018	9.0	509.71	48.0	9.3	244.46	0.001177	35.571	91.8
40 (25 Years)	—	2019	9.0	555.59	48.0	9.1	266.68	0.000990	35.836	92.5

PHASE 4—Steady State:

#		Year	Earnings Benchmark [9.0]	10.0%,	Earnings Relative [48.0]	0.90;	Payout Benchmark	40.0%,	Payout Relative	1.20	
41	—	2020	9.0	605.59	48.0	24.00	290.68	0.000833	36.078	93.1	17.3
51	—	2030	9.0	1433.65	48.0	56.82	688.15	0.000148	37.628	97.1	17.3
61	—	2040	9.0	3393.98	48.0	134.51	1629.11	0.000026	38.279	98.8	17.3
71	—	2050	9.0	8034.78	48.0	318.44	3856.70	0.000005	38.552	99.5	17.3
81	—	2060	9.0	19021.30	48.0	753.87	9130.20	0.000001	38.667	99.8	17.3
91	—	2070	9.0	45030.30	48.0	1784.68	21614.50	0.000000	38.715	99.9	17.3
101	—	2080	9.0	106603.00	48.0	4225.00	51169.40	0.000000	38.735	100.0	17.3

PHASE 4—Steady State: Earnings Benchmark | Earnings Relative | Payout Benchmark 40.0%; | Payout Relative 1.20

Source: "Quantitative Research," No. 3 (September 1980), Kidder, Peabody & Co., New York.

where $E(D_t)$ is the expected dividend for time period t. Thus, for Boise Cascade,

$$\$38.75 = \frac{\$1.75}{[1 + E(r)]^1} + \frac{\$1.85}{[1 + E(r)]^2}$$
$$+ \cdots + \frac{266.68}{[1 + E(r)]^{40}} + \frac{P_{40}}{[1 + E(r)]^{40}} \quad (13\text{-}4)$$

Because the assumptions of the constant growth dividend discount model are applied beginning in the forty-first year, the price of the stock in year 40 can be written as

$$P_{40} = \frac{E(D_{41})}{E(r) - g} = \frac{290.68}{E(r) - .09} \quad (13\text{-}5)$$

substituting this value for P_{40} into Equation (13-4) yields

$$\$38.75 = \frac{\$1.75}{[1 + E(r)]^1} + \frac{\$1.85}{[1 + E(r)]^2} + \cdots$$
$$+ \frac{\$266.68}{[1 + E(r)]^{40}} + \frac{\$290.68}{[1 + E(r)]^{40}[E(r) - .09]} \quad (13\text{-}6)$$

One can now solve for $E(r)$ in a fashion similar to that used in Section 14-3 to estimate the yield to maturity. A guess is made at the correct discount rate, the dividends are discounted at this rate, and the present value is compared with the current stock price. Once discount rates are chosen that result in present values which "bracket" the current price of $38.75, one can estimate the expected return for Boise Cascade by interpolation. In this example an expected return of 18.9% will discount the estimated dividends to the current price.

Thus, Kidder Peabody uses a *dividend discount model* to determine the expected return for individual securities. These expected returns are then compared with the required return suggested by a security market line, and alphas for individual stocks are computed. One should bear in mind that this valuation model is only as good as the estimates upon which it is based. If the forecasts for earnings, payout ratios, and dividends are not very good, one would have little confidence in the resultant alphas. Similar statements can be made with respect to the estimated security market line and the estimates of risk for each of the individual stocks. Nevertheless, this type of valuation model *is quite consistent with the notion that stock prices represent the present-value future dividends*. Thus, if the estimates of dividends, risk, and the security market line are reasonably accurate, the model may make reasonably good predictions.

On the other hand, this model is also fairly complex. It requires specific estimates of earnings and dividends for the first 5 to 10 years, and divides the future into four separate phases. A valuation model which is less complex than the Kidder Peabody model but more realistic than the constant growth dividend discount model might prove to be a useful tool for the security analyst. The simplified dividend discount models presented in the next section represent a middle ground between the complex and tedious task of estimating dividends for each year and the oversimplified constant growth dividend discount model.

13-2 SIMPLIFIED DIVIDEND DISCOUNT MODELS

Let's examine the last three phases in the Kidder Peabody model as shown in Table 13-1. These three phases are labeled the plateau, transition, and steady-state phases, respectively. Notice that during the plateau phase, earnings (and dividends, with the exception of the first year of this phase) grow at a constant rate of 13.5%. Then, during the transition phase the growth rate for earnings and dividends decreases in a systematic fashion until the growth rate levels off at 9.0% in the final, steady-state phase. As noted earlier, during this last phase, earnings and dividends are assumed to grow at a constant rate forever. This allows one to use the constant growth model to determine a value for the dividends beyond year 40, thus eliminating the need to estimate a perpetual stream of dividends.

The Kidder Peabody model is an adaptation of what we call the three-phrase dividend discount model. This model was initially developed by Molodovsky,[3] and later refined by Bauman[4] and Fuller[5] and has proved to be quite popular. Today, various versions of the three-phase model are used by many investment management organizations.

13-2-1 The Three-Phase Model Rather than assuming that dividends grow at a constant rate forever, as the constant growth model does, the three-phase dividend discount model assumes that there are three different phases to the growth pattern of dividends. In the beginning phase (phase 1), dividends are assumed to grow at a constant rate g_a for a period of A years. After phase 1 there is a transition period which accounts for the years $A + 1$ through B. During this transition period the growth rate of dividends declines in a linear fashion[6] from the beginning growth rate to an assumed constant and perpetual growth rate of g_n. (If g_a is less than g_n, the growth rate would increase during the transition period to g_n.) This constant, perpetual rate g_n is frequently referred to as the firm's long-run, "normal" growth rate.

Figure 13-1 illustrates the growth rate pattern for dividends during the three different phases, assuming the beginning growth rate is higher than the long-run, normal growth rate. Note that the growth rate for any particular time period during the transition phase can be expressed as

---

[3]N. Molodovsky, "Common Stock Valuation—Principles, Tables, and Applications," *Financial Analysts Journal* (March–April 1965).

[4]W. S. Bauman, "Investment Returns and Present Values," *Financial Analysts Journal* (November/December 1969).

[5]R. J. Fuller, "Programming the Three-Phase Dividend Discount Model," *Journal of Portfolio Management* (summer 1979).

[6]A number of variations of the three-phase model are being used by practitioners today. For example, some analysts allow for the possibility that dividends may decline during the transition stage in a nonlinear fashion. However, given the inherent imprecision in estimating future dividends, it is unlikely that such refinements will improve the basic three-phase model very much.

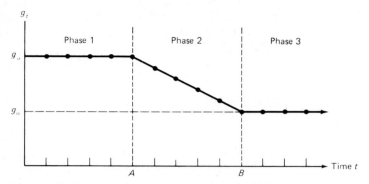

FIGURE 13-1   The dividend growth rate pattern for the three-phase dividend discount model.

$$g_t = g_a - (g_a - g_n) \frac{t - A}{B - A} \tag{13-7}$$

When t is equal to B we are at the end of the transition phase and one can easily see that the growth rate becomes the long-run constant growth rate of g_n. Thus, given estimates of g_a, A, B, and g_n, and the dividend for the most recent 12 months D_0, the dividends for all future time periods can be calculated. Then, given an appropriate discount rate one can compute the present value of the expected dividends and compare this value with the current stock price.

An example will help illustrate the three-phase dividend discount model. Assume you estimate, after careful analysis, that a particular stock's dividend will increase at a rate of 6% for the next 2 years, that the growth rate will then decline over the next 3 years to a 3% rate which will continue indefinitely thereafter. Also, you estimate that the appropriate discount rate is 8%. Thus, $g_a = 6\%$, $A = 2$, $g_n = 3\%$, $B = 5$, and $r = 8\%$. Given that this stock's dividend for the previous year was $1.00, your estimate of the growth rate and dividend for each year would be as follows:

	Year	Growth rate, %	Dividend
Phase 1	1	6	$1.000(1.06) = $1.06
	2	6	$1.060(1.06) = $1.124
Phase 2	3	5	$1.124(1.05) = $1.180
	4	4	$1.180(1.04) = $1.227
	5	3	$1.227(1.03) = $1.264
Phase 3	6	3	$1.264(1.03) = $1.302

To illustrate how the growth rate is calculated for each year in phase 2, consider year 3, which is the first year of the transition period. Using Equation (13-7),

$$g_t = g_a - (g_a - g_n)\frac{t - A}{B - A}$$

$$g_3 = 6\% - (6\% - 3\%)\frac{3 - 2}{5 - 2} = 6\% - (3\%)1/3 = 5\%$$

Given this set of estimated dividends and a discount rate of 8%, the present value of the expected dividends would be $22.36, calculated as follows:

$$P_0 = \frac{1.06}{(1.08)^1} + \cdots + \frac{1.264}{(1.08)^5} + \frac{1.302}{(1.08)^5 (.08 - .03)} = \$22.36 \quad (13\text{-}8)$$

This value of $22.36 would then be compared with the current stock price to determine whether the stock was under- or overpriced.

The advantage of the three-phase dividend discount model is that the analyst only has to make four estimates (g_a, A, g_n, B) in order to calculate the firm's entire stream of dividends. In addition, given the discount rate r, the stock price can be estimated using the following equation:

$$P_0 = D_0 \sum_{t=1}^{A} \left(\frac{1 + g_a}{1 + r}\right)^t + \sum_{t=A+1}^{B} \left(\frac{D_{t-1}(1 + g_t)}{(1 + r)^t}\right) + \frac{D_B(1 + g_n)}{(1 + r)^B(r - g_n)} \quad (13\text{-}9)$$

Phase 1   Phase 2   Phase 3

where D_B is the dividend in year B and g_t is previously defined in Equation (13-7).

Unfortunately, Equation (13-9) becomes quite tedious to solve by hand if there are more than 2 or 3 years in phase 2, the transition stage.[7] Another drawback to the three-phase model is that one cannot directly solve for the discount rate r, given the current stock price and the estimates concerning the dividend growth rates. Rather, an iterative process must be used, which is a tedious process to do by hand.

Recently Fuller and Hsia[8] have developed a simplified dividend discount model which overcomes the computational drawbacks of the three-phase model, while retaining its attributes. We will call this model the H model.

13-2-2 The H Model   Although the derivation of the H model is rather complex, the model itself is very simple. The H model is based upon an implicit growth rate pattern such as that shown in Figure 13-2. The dividend growth rate starts at a level of g_a. If g_a is greater than g_n, the growth rate immediately begins to decline to the long-run normal growth rate of g_n. At H years the growth rate is exactly halfway between g_a and g_n, and at $2H$ years the growth rate levels off at the expected long-run normal growth rate for the firm.

---

[7]However, computers and programmable calculators, once programmed, can solve this equation quickly and easily. Algorithms for programming the three-phase model are presented in R. J. Fuller, op. cit.

[8]R. J. Fuller and C. C Hsia, "A Simplified Model for Estimating Stock Prices of Growth Firms," *Financial Analysts Journal* (May–June 1984).

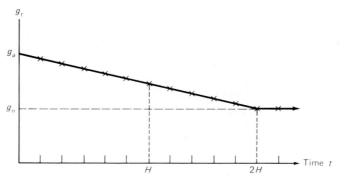

FIGURE 13-2   The dividend growth rate patttern for the *H* model.

The equation for the *H* model is quite simple and is expressed as

$$P_0 = \frac{D_0}{r - g_n} [(1 + g_n) + H(g_a - g_n)] \qquad (13\text{-}10)$$

Notice that while the *H* model allows for changing dividend growth rates over time (as does the three-phase model), to solve Equation (13-10), one needs to use only basic arithmetic.

There is also a simple and intuitive interpretation of the *H* model. First notice that if g_a is equal to g_n, Equation (13-10) reduces to the equation for the constant growth model. Second, if we rewrite Equation (13-10) as

$$P_0 = \frac{D_0 (1 + g_n)}{r - g_n} + \frac{D_0 H(g_a - g_n)}{r - g_n}$$

Value based on   premium or discount due to
normal growth rate   +   abnormal growth rate

we can see that the price of a stock is equal to the capitalized value of its dividends based on a long-run normal growth rate g_n *plus* a premium due to the above-normal growth g_a, and this premium is proportional to *H*. (If g_a is less than g_n, the stock sells at a discount to the capitalized value of the dividends, assuming normal growth, because of the initial period of below-normal growth.)

Another attribute of the *H* model is that one can solve directly for the discount rate *r*, given the current stock price, by simply rearranging the terms in Equation (13-10):

$$r = \frac{D_0}{P_0} [(1 + g_n) + H(g_a - g_n)] + g_n \qquad (13\text{-}11)$$

Notice that solving for *r* in the *H* model also only requires basic arithmetic—again, a much simpler process than the iterative procedure necessary to solve for *r* in the three-phase model.

Finally, the H model will generate results which are very similar to those of the more complicated three-phase model if one assumes that H is halfway through the transition phase of the three-phase model—that is, H is halfway between A and B, as shown in Figure 13-3. Under this assumption, H can be interpreted in either of two ways: (1) H is half the amount of time required for the growth rate to change from g_a to g_n; or (2) in the context of the three-phase model, H is halfway through phase 2, the transition phase.

To illustrate the H model, consider the previous example for which the three-phase estimates were:

$$D_0 = \$1 \qquad g_a = 6\% \qquad A = 2 \text{ years}$$
$$B = 5 \text{ years (ie., phase 2 lasts for 3 years)}$$
$$g_n = 3\% \qquad \text{and} \qquad r = 8\%$$

Assuming that H is halfway through the transition phase results in H being 3½ years. Using these estimates as inputs, the H model generates a price of $22.70, calculated as follows:

$$P_0 = \frac{\$1}{.08 - .03} \left[(1.03) + 3\frac{1}{2}(.06 - .03) \right] = \$22.70$$

This compares with the price of $22.36 generated by the three-phase model. This is typical—under most conditions, the H model and the three-phase model generate answers which are quite similar. Since the H model is substantially easier to solve mathematically and also allows one to solve directly for the discount rate, we suspect that as more investors become aware of it, the H model will become as popular as the three-phase model.

13-2-3 An Example To illustrate how the H model and the three-phase model might be used to identify under- or overpriced stocks, consider the case of American Home Products. In February 1985, AHP was selling for $59 per share. At that time

FIGURE 13-3 Comparison of the dividend growth rate pattern for the three-phase model vs. the H model.

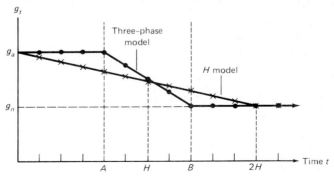

Value Line was forecasting a dividend growth rate of 11% for the next 4 years. Since Value Line does not publish any estimates of long-run, normal growth rates or transition periods, we will assume that AHP's long-run, normal dividend growth rate will eventually be 5%, or approximately the average historical growth rate for industrial stocks.[9] We will assume that AHP's growth rate will decline from 11% to 5% over a period of 16 years—thus, the halfway point, H, is 8 years. (This is the same as assuming, for example, that $A = 4$ and $B = 12$ in the framework of the three-phase model.) Thus, we will set $g_a = 11\%$, $g_n = 5\%$, and $H = 8$. To determine the discount rate, let's suppose that the following security market line is appropriate for determining required returns:[10]

$$R(r) = 10\% + 5\% \ \beta \tag{13-12}$$

Since AHP's beta was estimated at .85 by Value Line, this would suggest a discount rate (required return) of 14.25%.

$$R(r) = 10\% + 5\%(.85) = 14.25\%$$

Given these forecasts and the fact that AHP's 1984 dividend was $4.26, the price of AHP would be estimated by the H model to be $70.46, calculated as follows using Equation (13-10):[11]

$$P_0 = \frac{D_0}{r - g_n} [(1 + g_n) + H(g_a - g_n)]$$

$$= \frac{4.26}{.1425 - .05} [1.05 + 8(.11 - .05)] = \$70.46$$

Comparing this price estimated by the model with the market price of $59, one would conclude that AHP was underpriced. Of course, if we used different estimates of the dividend growth rates and the discount rate, a different conclusion might be reached. Thus, the H model is like every other model in the sense that *the answers it generates are no better than the estimates used as inputs for the model.*

To illustrate how the H model might be used to estimate the return expected by investors, given the current stock price and estimates of dividend growth rates, again consider the case of American Home Products. Using Equation (13-11), the expected return would be calculated as follows:

[9]Most studies of historical stock returns have found the average dividend growth rate to be in the 4 to 5% range over the period 1926 to the late 1970s. See, for example, R. G. Ibbotson and R. A. Sinquefield, *Stocks, Bonds, Bills and Inflation: The Past and the Future*, The Financial Analysts Research Foundation, 2d ed., Charlottesville, Va., 1982. This study is discussed in Chapter 3.

[10]Historically, the security market line has averaged approximately a 4% intercept (roughly the risk-free rate) and a 5% risk premium, where risk is measured in terms of beta. Thus, the typical stock has averaged approximately a 9% return in the past. (Again, see Ibbotson and Sinquefield, op cit.) To adjust for current (February 1985) market conditions, we increased the intercept (risk-free rate) to 10%.

[11]The three-phase model yields a price of $66.86 under these assumptions.

$$E(r) = \frac{D_0}{P_0} [(1 + g_n) + H(g_a - g_n)] + g_n$$

$$= \frac{\$4.26}{\$59} [1.05 + 8(.11 - .05)] + .05 = 16.05\%$$

Finally, let's consider how alphas might be calculated. As indicated by Equation (13-2), alpha is defined as the difference between the expected return (given the stock's current price and the expected growth rate of dividends) and the required return (typically based on a security market line analysis). Using the H model, the expected return for AHP was estimated at 16.05%. The required return, based on the security market line of Equation (13-12) and AHP's beta of .85, was calculated to be 14.25%. Thus, the alpha for AHP would be estimated at +1.80%:

Expected return	16.05%
Required return	(14.25%)
Alpha	+1.80%

Recall that positive alphas are associated with stocks believed to be underpriced. This, of course, was the case with respect to AHP, based on the H model and our assumptions concerning the dividend growth rates.

> Before continuing, you should:
> 1 Understand, in general, how dividend discount models work
> 2 Recognize the advantages and disadvantages of a model such as that used by Kidder Peabody compared with a model such as the H model or the three-phase model
> 3 Be able to calculate the price or expected return, using the H model
> 4 Know how to solve for the expected return for a stock given an estimated stream of dividends and the current stock price using the three-phase model. To prove to yourself that you understand the procedure, solve problem 1 at the end of this chapter

13-3 DETERMINANTS OF *P/E* RATIOS

Traditionally, investors have utilized price/earnings ratio (*P/E*) models more than dividend discount models, although the latter have been gaining more and more popularity in recent years. The *P/E* ratio is simply the price per share divided by the earnings per share. While not as theoretically rigorous as dividend discount models, *P/E* ratio models have a number of attractive attributes. First, the *P/E* ratio provides a convenient standard for comparing the prices of shares of stock which have different levels of earnings per share, since the *P/E* ratio indicates the *price per dollar of earnings*. Second, for stocks which do not currently pay dividends, a *P/E* ratio model may be easier to use than a dividend discount model. (However, *P/E* ratio models are difficult to use in analyzing companies which report deficit earnings.) Third, the estimates used as inputs in *P/E* ratio models *may* be easier to make than the estimates necessary for dividend discount models.

On the other hand, one drawback to some *P/E* ratio models is that their conceptual framework is not as theoretically sound as that of the dividend discount model. Another drawback is that some *P/E* ratio models indicate only the *relative* level of *P/E* ratio that is appropriate for a particular stock, rather than indicating *explicitly* what the *P/E* should be. For example, a model might indicate that the *P/E* ratio for XYZ Corp. should be ''higher'' than the S&P 400 *P/E* but does not indicate how much higher.

As a starting point for developing a conceptual framework for *P/E* ratio models, consider first the constant growth dividend discount model developed in Chapter 10:

$$P_0 = \frac{D_1}{r - g} \tag{13-13}$$

By noting that the dividend can be written as earnings *E* multiplied by the payout ratio *b*, and dropping the time subscript to simplify the notation, the constant growth model can be written as

$$P = \frac{Eb}{r - g}$$

Rearranging terms to solve for the *P/E* ratio, we have the general relationship

$$P/E = \frac{b}{r - g} \tag{13-14}$$

Thus, *P/E* ratios can be viewed as a function of three variables—the payout ratio, the discount rate, and the growth rate.

Based on Equation (13-14), the higher the payout ratio, the higher the *P/E* ratio, everything else held constant. The same positive relationship holds for *P/E* ratios and growth rates. However, there is a negative relationship between *P/E* ratios and discount rates—that is, the higher the discount rate, the lower the *P/E* ratio and vice versa.

In order to see how one might use these relationships to analyze a *P/E* ratio for a particular stock, consider the data in Table 13-2. This table lists payout ratios, growth rates, return on equity (which will be discussed later), and *P/E* ratios over the time period 1970–1979 for IBM, Hart, Schaffner & Marx, and the S&P 400.[12] Note that over the 10-year period, the average *P/E* ratio was 22.1 for IBM, 12.8 for the S&P 400, and 11.0 for Hart, Schaffner & Marx (HSM). For the most recent year (1979), the *P/E* ratios ranged from 13.9 (IBM) to 4.9 (HSM).

---

[12]In this analysis, rather than using the S&P 500 as a benchmark, we use the S&P 400, which is composed of only industrial stocks because IBM and HSM are also industrial stocks. The S&P 500 consists of 400 industrial stocks, 40 utility stocks, 40 financial stocks, and 20 transportation stocks.

TABLE 13-2 *P/E* RATIO ANALYSIS FOR IBM AND HART, SCHAFFNER & MARX (1970–1979)

	IBM				S&P 400				Hart, Schaffner & Marx			
Year	b	g, %	ROE, %	P/E	b	g, %	ROE, %	P/E	b	g, %	ROE, %	P/E
1970	.539	33.3	19.2	33.0	.597	−0.9	10.5	16.2	.615	0.0	8.2	18.2
1971	.553	8.3	18.1	34.4	.528	−1.9	11.4	19.3	.672	0.0	7.3	23.6
1972	.489	3.8	19.2	35.5	.471	1.3	12.4	19.2	.497	0.0	9.6	17.3
1973	.415	3.7	20.8	28.5	.393	8.1	15.2	14.8	.467	7.5	10.4	10.1
1974	.446	24.1	20.8	16.5	.384	6.9	15.4	9.2	.647	2.3	7.3	7.4
1975	.488	17.3	19.6	15.3	.442	1.6	12.6	11.4	.619	−25.0	5.0	8.3
1976	.501	22.7	20.9	16.6	.398	12.4	14.0	11.7	.391	5.0	8.2	7.2
1977	.546	25.0	21.7	14.5	.429	16.7	15.2	9.6	.400	14.3	8.7	7.0
1978	.541	15.2	24.9	12.7	.441	7.9	14.7	8.7	.383	11.1	9.6	5.9
1979	.667	19.4	22.3	13.9	.376	12.9	17.9	7.7	.359	10.0	10.6	4.9
Average	.518	17.3	20.8	22.1	.446	6.5	13.9	12.8	.505	2.5	8.5	11.0

b = payout ratio
g = growth rate of dividends per share
ROE = return on equity = earnings per share divided by beginning book value per share
P/E = average annual *P/E* ratio
Sources: = Computed from data obtained from Standard & Poor's Corporation and Value Line.

To analyze the *P/E* ratios in terms of payout ratio *b*, growth rate of dividends *g*, and discount rate *r*, first consider the case of IBM. The payout ratio for IBM averaged .518, which is greater than the average payout ratio for the S&P 400 index of .446. By itself, a higher payout ratio would suggest that IBM should sell at a higher *P/E* than the S&P 400. IBM's average growth rate of dividends (17.3%) is also substantially higher than the growth rate for the index (6.5%). Again, this would suggest that IBM should sell at a higher price/earnings ratio than the S&P 400 index.

Finally, assume that the discount rate is proportional to the security's beta, as suggested by the single-factor market model and the CAPM. During this period, IBM's historical beta varied from slightly above 1 to slightly below 1. Thus, its systematic risk was very similar to that of the S&P 400, which of course, would have a beta close to 1. Therefore, with respect to the discount rate *r*, one would expect IBM and the index to sell at approximately the same *P/E* ratio. When one considers all three factors together, the payout ratio *b*, the growth rate *g*, and the discount rate *r*, it is obvious that IBM should have sold at a higher *P/E* ratio than the S&P 400 index, and it did.[13]

When one considers the case of Hart, Schaffner & Marx, the opposite conclusion is drawn, although the results are not as clear-cut. While HSM's average payout ratio of .505 was slightly higher than that of the S&P 400, its average dividend growth rate

---

[13]This analysis, for the sake of simplicity, ignores the ex post, ex ante distinction. *P/E* ratios should be based on expectations concerning future growth rates, discount rates, and payout ratios. The data in Table 13-2 are historical (ex post) data. However, it is likely that investors' expectations regarding the growth prospects, future payout ratios, and future risk of IBM, the S&P 400, and HSM were qualitatively similar to the respective historical data. Thus, the general conclusions of this analysis probably would not be significantly different if ex ante data had been available and used in lieu of the ex post data.

was *substantially* lower (2.5% vs. 6.5%). HSM's beta during this time period was generally slightly below 1.0, averaging approximately .95. When all three factors influencing *P/E* ratios are considered, the below-average dividend growth rate must have dominated, resulting in HSM selling at a *P/E* ratio below that of the S&P 400 index.

One should bear in mind that the above analysis is based on a *ceteris paribus* argument—that is, when the effect of one of the three variables (*b*, *g*, or *r*) is considered, *everything else is held constant*. Of course, "everything else" can rarely be held constant. For example, if the firm increases the payout ratio, fewer funds may be available to invest in profitable projects—this will have the effect of reducing the firm's growth rate. This relationship was formally demonstrated in Section 7-5, where we show that the growth rate (under the assumptions of a constant return on equity and no external financing) is equal to the return on equity (ROE) times the quantity 1 minus the payout ratio. That is,

$$g = ROE(1 - b) \qquad (13\text{-}15)$$

Of course, in practice, firms do use external financing and ROE does change over time. Nevertheless, Equation (13-15) represents a reasonable "first approximation" for the growth rate of firms. Therefore, substituting Equation (13-15) into (13-14), we find

$$P/E = \frac{b}{r - ROE(1 - b)} \qquad (13\text{-}16)$$

Thus, *P/E* ratios can be expressed as a function of payout ratios, discount rates, and either growth rates or return on equity. Notice in Equation (13-16) that the larger the payout ratio *b*, the larger the numerator and the larger the *P/E*; but the larger *b* is in the denominator, the lower the *P/E* ratio. This is because increasing the payout ratio increases the current dividend but, at the same time, decreases the potential growth rate. Consequently, the relationship between payout ratios and *P/E* ratios is ambiguous.

We can proceed one step further in analyzing *P/E* ratios by utilizing the DuPont formula (which is also discussed in Chapter 7). According to the DuPont formula, the return on equity can be written as

$$ROE = ROA \cdot L \qquad (13\text{-}17)$$

That is, the return on equity is equal to the firm's return on total assets (ROA) multiplied by its leverage ratio L.[14] Substituting Equation (13-17) into Equation (13-16), we have

$$P/E = \frac{b}{r - ROA(L)(1 - b)} \qquad (13\text{-}18)$$

[14]Algebraically

$$ROE = EAT/EQ$$

TABLE 13-3   THE DETERMINANTS OF *P/E* RATIOS

$P/E = f$	Payout ratio $(+)b$	Discount rate $(-)r$				Growth rate $(+)g$		
		$(-)r_f$	$(-)r_m$	$(-)\beta$		$(+)$ROE		$(-)b$
				$(-)L$	$(\pm)\delta$	$(+)$ROA		$(\pm)L$
						$(+)$PM	$(+)$ATO	

b = payout ratio
r = required discount rate
g = growth rate of dividends per share
r_f = nominal risk-free rate
r_m = expected return on the market index
β = measure of systematic risk
ROE = return on equity
ROA = return on total assets

L = total assets divided by equity
PM = after-tax profit margin
ATO = total asset turnover ratio
δ = operating characteristics which affect systematic risk, such as stability of sales and operating earnings or correlation of sales and earnings with GNP or total corporate profits
    The "+" or "−" sign in front of each variable indicates that *P/E* ratios are a positive or negative function of the variable.

ROE can be further broken down by noting that the return on assets is equal to profit margin (PM) times asset turnover (ATO). That is, ROA = PM × ATO. Table 13-3 summarizes the functional relationships between *P/E* ratios and all the variables discussed so far. The three primary determinants of *P/E* ratios (b, r, and g) make up the first row of variables. Below the discount rate r are the risk-free rate r_f, the return on the market index r_m, and beta (β)—the three variables which determine the discount rate in the framework of the CAPM. Below beta are the leverage ratio L, and δ, a general symbol which represents all the operating characteristics of the firm which affect the stock's systematic risk. In a similar fashion, the variables ROE and b, which primarily determine the growth rate, are listed below g. Finally, the variables which determine the return on equity are listed below ROE.

In Table 13-3, the plus or minus sign indicates whether *P/E* ratios are a positive or negative function of the variable. One can see from this table that the relationship between the payout ratio and the *P/E* ratio is ambiguous, as noted earlier. When considered in isolation of the other variables, there is a positive relationship between

---

where EAT = earnings after taxes and EQ = stockholders' equity. The leverage ratio L is defined as total assets A divided by stockholders' equity. That is,

$$L = A/EQ$$

Return on assets (ROA) is defined as

$$ROA = EAT/A$$

Thus, return on equity can be expressed as

$$ROE = \frac{EAT}{A} \times \frac{A}{EQ} = ROA \cdot L$$

which is the DuPont formula See Section 7-5 for further discussion of these relationships.

b and *P/E* ratios. However, when the effect of the payout ratio on growth is considered, there is a negative relationship between *b* and *P/E*'s.

A similar ambiguity exists between leverage ratios and *P/E* ratios. Assuming the firms's earning power exceeds the interest rate on debt, there is a *positive* relationship between *L* and ROE, which in turn suggests a positive relationship between leverage and *P/E* ratios. On the other hand, the use of debt increases the financial leverage of the firm and consequently increases the risk associated with the common stock. Thus, the stock's beta increases. The higher the beta, the higher the discount rate and the lower the *P/E* ratio. This translates into a *negative* relationship between *L* and *P/E*'s. Consequently, the relationship between *P/E* ratios and leverage is complex.

Thus, the general approach utilized in this section helps to identify the functional relationships between *P/E* ratios and the variables in Table 13-3, although there is some ambiguity concerning the payout ratio and the debt ratio. In addition, while this conceptual type of analysis might indicate the *relative* level of *P/E* ratio (compared with the *P/E* for some appropriate index such as the S&P 400), it does not indicate the specific level of *P/E* ratio that is appropriate for a certain stock. For example, the previous analysis of IBM clearly indicated that IBM's stock should command a *P/E* greater than that of the S&P 400. Unfortunately, it did not tell us how much greater. The cross-sectional regression models discussed in the next section are designed to answer this question.

13-4 CROSS-SECTIONAL REGRESSION MODELS

One method of constructing a model which will give explicit quantitative estimates of *P/E* ratios is to assume that *P/E*'s are linear and additive functions of some, or all, of the variables listed in Table 13-3. Given this assumption, multiple regression can be used to estimate the "average" relationship *at one point in time* between *P/E*'s and payout ratios, growth, etc. To do this, one first collects the relevant data on *P/E* ratios and the variables assumed to be the determinants of *P/E*'s for a *cross section* of companies for a particular time period.

For example, we might calculate the *P/E* ratios for 200 different stocks as of December 31, 1987. The *P/E* ratio is called the dependent variable because it depends upon a number of attributes (called the independent variables). In this example, we will assume that the independent variables are the stock's payout ratio and growth rate of dividends per share. Thus, estimates of *b* and *g* would also be collected as of December 31, 1987, for each of the 200 companies in the example. Then, using the procedure of multiple regression (which is available in most computer statistical packages), the average relationship between *P/E* ratios and the two variables *b* and *g* would be estimated. Once this average relationship is determined for all stocks, we can estimate the *P/E* for each individual stock and compare this estimated value with the actual *P/E*. If the actual *P/E* for a particular stock is greater than its estimated *P/E*, we might conclude that the stock is overpriced, and vice versa.

One of the first studies to employ this methodology was performed by Whitbeck and Kisor.[15] Using data generated by the research department of the Bank of New

---

[15]V. S. Whitbeck and M. Kisor, Jr., "A New Tool in Investment Decision Making," *Financial Analysts Journal* (May/June 1963); reprinted in J. Lorie and R. Brealey, *Modern Developments in Investment Management*, 2d ed., Praeger Publishers, New York, 1978.

York as of June 1962 for 135 stocks, they computed the following average relationship between P/E's and three independent variables—payout ratio, growth, and risk, as defined below:

$$P/E = 8.2 + 1.5g + 6.7b - .2\delta \qquad (13\text{-}19)$$

where P/E = current price divided by "normalized" earnings per share[16]
        g = estimated annual percentage growth rate for "normalized" earnings per share
        b = estimated dividend payout ratio expressed in decimal form
        δ = expected standard deviation of earnings per share changes (expressed as a percentage) around estimated growth rate

Notice that the inputs into the model are reasonably consistent with the conceptual framework for P/E ratio models developed in the previous section, and that the inputs are ex ante in nature. While this study utilizes the expected growth rate for earnings, this will be the same as the growth rate for dividends if the payout ratio is constant. The expected dividend payout ratio is a second variable. Thus, the first two independent variables are perfectly consistent with the determinants of P/E ratios, as suggested earlier by Equation (13-14).

$$P/E = \frac{b}{r - g}$$

And, if discount rates are proportional to risk, the third variable (δ) is also reasonably consistent with Equation (13-14). While one might quarrel with the variable chosen to proxy for risk, bear in mind that this study was performed in 1962, well before papers developing the CAPM and betas had been published.

Of course, Equation (13-14) does *not* indicate that P/E ratios are a linear and additive function of these three variables as does the multiple regression model used in Equation (13-19). But recall that (13-14) was derived from the Gordon model, which is based on the strong and probably unrealistic assumption of constant growth. Thus, the exact functional relationship between P/E's and g, b, and δ is not known and the assumptions underlying the multiple regression model may be reasonable. As a minimum, the linear and additive relationship expressed in Whitbeck and Kisor's equation (13-19) has the attribute of being the easiest relationship with which to work.

Whitbeck and Kisor illustrate how their model works by using IBM and General Motors (GM) as examples. For IBM, they estimated a growth rate of 17%, a payout ratio of .25, and a standard deviation of earnings of 5%. Plugging these numbers into Equation (13-19) results in an estimated P/E of 34.4 for IBM.

$$P/E = 8.2 + 1.5(17) + 6.7(.25) - .2(5) = 34.4$$

---

[16]Normal earnings were defined as the earnings per share a company would generate at the midpoint of a business cycle.

At the time of this study (June 1962), IBM's actual *P/E* was 35.3—thus, the estimated *P/E* was within 3% of the actual *P/E*.

For General Motors, they estimated a growth rate of 3%, a payout ratio of .75, and a standard deviation of earnings of 20%. Using these numbers as inputs for Equation (13-19) results in an estimated *P/E* of 13.7 for GM. The actual *P/E* for GM at that time was 15.4, or 12% more than the *P/E* estimated by the model. This analysis would suggest that GM was overpriced.

A trading strategy based on this model was developed as follows: (1) Each calendar quarter perform a cross-sectional regression on a large group of stocks and develop a model similar to Equation (13-19) for estimating *P/E* ratios. (2) Using the model, estimate the *P/E* ratio for each stock and compare it with the actual *P/E* ratio. (3) Then, form an "undervalued" portfolio at the beginning of the quarter arbitrarily consisting of all stocks whose actual *P/E* ratio is equal to or less than 85% of the estimated *P/E* ratio and form an "overvalued" portfolio consisting of stocks whose actual *P/E* ratio is equal to or more than 115% of the estimated *P/E*. (4) Compute the return for each portfolio over the quarter and compare this return with the return for the S&P 500 index over the same time period.

A limited test of this procedure was performed for the four quarters beginning with the fourth quarter of 1960 and ending with the third quarter of 1961. The results are reported in Table 13-4, and they appear to be promising. In each quarter the portfolio of "undervalued" stocks provided higher returns than the S&P 500, while the portfolio of "overvalued" stocks provided lower returns than the index.

However, before drawing the conclusion that this is a method for "beating the market," one should be aware of a number of caveats. First, the sample of stocks was relatively small and the number of time periods (four quarters) was quite small. Thus, their results could be due simply to luck. Further, each of the four quarters of this study represented a period of rising stock prices. If the risk factor was proxying for beta, the model may have tended to identify high-beta stocks as undervalued and low-beta stocks as overvalued. In an efficient and rising market, high-beta stocks

TABLE 13-4   PERFORMANCE OF THE WHITBECK & KISOR MODEL

Quarter	Change in price, %		
	Undervalued portfolio*	S&P 500	Overvalued portfolio*
1960—IV	11.9	6.6	5.7
1961—I	16.8	12.3	8.3
1961—II	3.0	1.0	−1.4
1961—III	3.2	2.4	2.1

* The undervalued portfolio consisted of those stocks for which the actual *P/E* was equal to or less than 85% of the model's estimated *P/E*; the overvalued portfolio consisted of those stocks for which the actual *P/E* was equal to or greater than 115% of the model's estimated *P/E*.

Source: V. S. Whitbeck and M. Kisor, Jr., "A New Tool in Investment Decision Making," *Financial Analysts Journal* (May/June 1963); reprinted in J. Lorie and R. Brealey, *Modern Developments in Investment Management*, 2d ed., Praeger, New York, 1978.

TABLE 13-5 MALKIEL AND CRAGG REGRESSION EQUATION

Year	Equation	R^2
1961	$P/E = 4.73 + 3.28g + 2.05b - .85\beta$	.70
1962	$P/E = 11.06 + 1.75g + .78b - 1.61\beta$	.70
1963	$P/E = 2.94 + 2.55g + 7.62b - .27\beta$	.75
1964	$P/E = 6.71 + 2.05g + 5.23b - .89\beta$	.75
1965	$P/E = .96 + 2.74g + 5.01b - .35\beta$	.85

Source: B. G. Malkiel and J. G. Cragg, "Expectations and the Structure of Share Prices," American Economic Review (September 1970).

should increase in price more than low-beta stocks. Also, the performance was based only on price changes and did not account for dividend payments. If the model tended to identify low dividend yield stocks as underpriced and high dividend yield stocks as overpriced, basing the "performance" on price change alone would tend to benefit the low dividend yield stock and penalize the high dividend yield stock. Finally, as discussed in Chapter 5, there may be other variables besides systematic risk, such as firm size, which determine common stock returns. Perhaps the Whitbeck and Kisor model was simply identifying small firms as underpriced.

A subsequent study by Malkiel and Cragg[17] did not find that cross-sectional regression models could be used to consistently earn abnormal profits. Cross-sectional regressions were performed on a group of 178 stocks at the beginning of each of the years 1961–1965. The dependent variable was again a P/E ratio based on "normalized" earnings. The three independent variables were expected earnings growth g and expected payout ratio b, and for this study, the risk measurement was the stock's beta (β). The regression equations for each of the 5 years are listed in Table 13-5, along with the R^2. Note that each of the regression coefficients is of the expected sign for each year. That is, for each year the regression coefficient for growth was positive; for each year the regression coefficient for the payout ratio was also positive; and for each year the regression coefficient for beta was negative. Note also that the R^2's ranged from .70 to .85. (Recall that R^2 measures the amount of variation in P/E ratios that is explained by the three independent variables.) Thus, this evidence suggests that the cross-sectional regression models explain a good deal of the cross-sectional variation in P/E ratios at a particular point in time.

However, the more interesting question is whether such models can be used to *predict future stock returns*. To test this, Malkiel and Cragg designated stocks as "undervalued" or "overvalued" (in a fashion similar to Whitbeck and Kisor) with mixed and generally poor results. (These results are not reported in Table 13-5.) In 1964, actual returns were slightly related to the predictions of the regression model. However for the other 4 years, the predictions of the models were of little or no value, and in one year the "overvalued" stocks actually outperformed the supposedly "undervalued" stocks.

[17]B. G. Malkiel and J. G. Cragg, "Expectations and the Structure of Share Prices," *American Economic Review* (September 1970).

On the other hand, before one gives up on this approach to identifying undervalued stocks, bear in mind that a model is no better than the estimates used as inputs for the model. Malkiel and Cragg were not security analysts. The expectational data they used were essentially consensus estimates, which one might expect to be reflected in security prices already. And it is entirely possible that their model did not account for all the variables which determine P/E ratios. As we shall see in the next section, the Value Line ranking system is similar (although more complex) to the cross-sectional regression approach. And the Value Line ranking system appears to be able to consistently identify mispriced securities.

Before continuing, you should:
1 Know the three primary determinants of P/E ratios
2 Understand how one can expand the relationship between P/E ratios and these three variables to include such variables as ROE and beta
3 Understand the general methodology of cross-sectional regression analysis and how such models might be used to identify mispriced securities
4 Be aware of some of the weaknesses in previous studies using cross-sectional regression models

13-5 THE VALUE LINE RANKING SYSTEM

Value Line is the largest investment advisory organization in the United States and probably in the world. The *Value Line Investment Survey* provides a wealth of data on 1700 publicly traded companies. In addition, Value Line ranks each of the stocks it follows according to anticipated performance over the next 12 months. Stocks ranked as group 1 are expected to perform best, while those ranked group 5 are expected to provide the lowest returns. The number of stocks in each group are as follows:

Group 1 Top 100
Group 2 Next 300
Group 3 Middle 900
Group 4 Next 300
Group 5 Bottom 100

These rankings are termed the "timeliness" rank by Value Line.

Recall from Section 5-5-2 that the Value Line ranking system has been carefully examined by academic researchers and appears to provide positive abnormal returns. Figure 13-4 lists the performance of the Value Line ranking system, as reported by Value Line in its *Selection & Opinion*. The reported returns are based on a strategy of forming portfolios at the beginning of each year based on the rank of each stock at that time and then holding the portfolios constant for the entire year. The next year new portfolios are formed based on the ranks of the stocks at the start of the second year, and so on.[18]

---

[18]This does not allow the composition of the portfolios to change during the year even though the ranks of the individual stocks may change. If one allows the composition of the portfolios to change each week

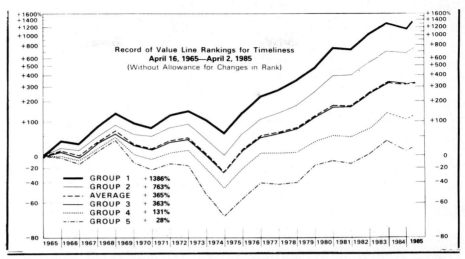

Record of Value Line Rankings For Timeliness   (Without Allowance for Changes In Rank)
April 16, 1965—April 2, 1985

Group	1965*	1966	1967	1968	1969	1970	1971	1972	1973	1974	1975
1	+ 33.6%	− 3.1%	+ 39.2%	+ 31.2%	− 17.7%	− 8.9%	+ 26.5%	+ 10.1%	− 17.1%	− 23.1%	+ 51.6%
2	+ 18.9	− 6.0	+ 31.9	+ 26.3	− 16.3	− 4.0	+ 17.4	+ 7.5	− 26.2	− 27.8	+ 53.0
3	+ 8.9	− 9.7	+ 30.1	+ 21.4	− 20.7	− 5.5	+ 12.2	+ 6.2	− 27.0	− 28.5	+ 52.9
4	+ 0.8	− 7.2	+ 25.1	+ 25.1	− 26.8	− 11.7	+ 14.2	+ 3.2	− 29.1	− 33.6	+ 48.4
5	− 1.2	− 12.4	+ 28.4	+ 25.9	− 35.7	− 13.1	+ 10.5	+ 2.9	− 43.1	− 36.8	+ 42.1
Avg	+ 10.1	− 7.9	+ 29.9	+ 24.6	− 22.1	− 7.5	+ 14.9	+ 5.5	− 27.7	− 29.6	+ 51.2

Group	1976	1977	1978	1979	1980	1981	1982	1983	1984	Apr. 16, 1965 to Apr. 2, 1985
1	+ 35.3%	+ 15.8%	+ 19.8%	+ 25.6%	+ 50.2%	− 1.9%	+ 33.7%	+ 25.2%	− 8.6%	+ 1386%
2	+ 36.3	+ 12.7	+ 16.1	+ 30.8	+ 37.4	+ 0.7	+ 29.0	+ 22.2	− 0.1	+ 763%
3	+ 33.8	+ 5.2	+ 9.2	+ 27.6	+ 20.8	+ 2.7	+ 25.5	+ 26.7	− 1.6	+ 363%
4	+ 36.1	− 0.2	+ 2.4	+ 23.1	+ 13.2	− 0.9	+ 18.5	+ 35.2	− 12.3	+ 131%
5	+ 38.2	− 2.8	+ 4.0	+ 39.9	+ 8.4	− 4.2	+ 19.9	+ 30.0	− 17.1	+ 28%
Avg	+ 35.1	+ 5.8	+ 9.6	+ 28.0	+ 23.4	+ 0.9	+ 25.0	+ 27.5	− 4.7	+ 365%

*April through December

Dow Jones Industrials   + 39%
N.Y. Stock Exchange Composite   + 120%

FIGURE 13-4   The Value Line record. [*Source:* Value Line, *"The Value Line Ranking System: A 20th Anniversary Retrospective,"* Selection and Opinion *(Apr. 19, 1985).*]

The results are very impressive. Over the total time period (April 16, 1965, through April 2, 1985) the various groups performed exactly as the rankings would suggest— the group 1 stocks outperformed the group 2 stocks which outperformed the group 3 stocks, etc. The difference in price appreciation between the groups was very signif-

as the ranks of some of the stocks are changed, the performance of the ranking system is even better than those reported in Figure 13-4. However, the performance results are not adjusted for commissions, which would obviously be higher under a system allowing for changes in rank during the year. Thus, the results in Figure 13-4 are probably a fairer representation of the performance an investor might achieve using the Value Line ranking system than are the results based on allowing for changes in ranks during the year.

icant. The total price appreciation of 1386% for the group 1 stocks represents a compound annual rate of price change of 14.4%. For the group 5 stocks, the price change was an insignificant 28%, or 1.2% compounded annually, over the 20 years. (While dividends were not included in these calculations, their inclusion would not qualitatively change the results.) Perhaps just as impressive as the overall results is the consistency of the ranking system year by year. In every year except 1976, 1979, and 1983 group 1 stocks outperformed the group 5 stocks. And in many years the performance of the five groups was exactly in line with their rankings.

Since the Value Line ranking system apparently has worked well in the past, it is worth studying. Fortunately, Value Line is willing to divulge how their rankings are determined.[19] The ranking procedure is a complicated process which is based on three components: (1) a relative valuation based on "earnings momentum," (2) an "earnings surprise factor," and (3) a value index. Points are given for each of these three components, with the total points determining the stock's ranking. The 100 stocks with the most total points are ranked as group 1, the next 300 as group 2, and so forth.

The "relative earnings momentum" is determined as follows: Each company's year-to-year change in quarterly earnings is computed (for example, fourth-quarter 1986 EPS compared with fourth-quarter 1985 EPS), and this percentage change is then divided by the average year-to-year quarterly earnings change for all stocks. (Analysts make some subjective adjustments for quarters affected by unusual factors such as labor strikes or changes in accounting procedures.) The stocks which rank in the top third of all companies based on relative earnings momentum are given a score of 1200 points, the middle third are given 800 points, and those in the bottom third are given 400 points.

The "earnings surprise" factor was added to the ranking system after a number of studies demonstrated that abnormal returns were associated with the stocks of companies which reported unusually large changes in quarterly earnings. (See Section 5-5-1 for a discussion of these studies.) The earnings surprise factor is based on the difference between actual reported quarterly earnings and Value Line's estimate of the quarterly earnings. The number of points assigned to each stock are as follows:

Difference between reported earnings and estimated earnings	Points assigned
−30% or more	−400
−15% to −29%	−200
−14% to +14%	0
+15% to 29%	+200
+30% or more	+400

[19]A. Bernhard, *Value Line Methods of Evaluating Common Stocks*, Arnold Bernhard & Co., New York, 1979.

The most complex of the three components which determine the Value Line timeliness rankings is what Value Line calls the "nonparametric value position." This value position (V) is calculated from the following equation:

$$V = a + b_1X_1 + b_2X_2 + b_3X_3 \qquad (13\text{-}20)$$

where X_1 = a score of from 1 to 10, depending on how the current year's earnings divided by the average earnings of all 1700 companies ranks, compared with the company's same ratio for the last 10 years

X_2 = a score from 1 to 10 based on the stock's relative price, where the ratios are calaculated as above with stock prices substituted for earnings

X_3 = a price momentum index which is the ratio of the stock's latest 10-week average relative price divided by its 52-week average relative price, where relative price is the stock price divided by the average price for all 1700 stocks

$a, b_1, b_2, b_3,$ = coefficients from a multiple regression based on over 12 years of stock market data

All companies are then given a rank from 1 to 1700 based upon their V value.

Finally, the points for each of the three major components (relative earnings momentum, earnings surprise factor, and V value) are added and the stocks are classified into group 1, group 2, etc., based upon their total points. Thus, the Value Line ranking system is a complex procedure. It is heavily weighted toward relative P/E ratios, earnings momentum, and "earnings surprises." Interestingly, it also includes a component (X_3 in the above equation) which would fall under the purely "technical" category. This variable is based strictly on historical price data, which has been shown to be of little value in predicting future prices. Nevertheless, in spite of its complexity and its partial reliance on historical price data, the Value Line ranking system appears to have worked in the past. Since this is public information, the interesting question is whether investors will begin to utilize Value Line's ranking system to such an extent that the Value Line timeliness ranks will be quickly reflected in stock prices and, as a result, will no longer be of value. This will be a classic test of market efficiency.

13-6 INVESTING WITH BENJAMIN GRAHAM

While the Value Line ranking system is quite complex, it may be that superior results can also be achieved using relatively simple selection criteria. In his classic book, *The Intelligent Investor*,[20] Benjamin Graham suggested simple selection rules that could be easily understood and utilized by the nonprofessional investor. (The 1973 edition is still in print, and while the examples may be dated, the book is worth reading.) Table 13-6 lists the selection criteria which appeared in each of the five editions of this book.

[20]B. Graham, *The Intelligent Investor*, 5th ed., Harper & Row, New York, 1973.

TABLE 13-6 CRITERIA FOR SELECTION (AND RETENTION) OF COMMON STOCKS BY THE DEFENSIVE INVESTOR IN EACH OF THE COPYRIGHT YEARS OF *THE INTELLIGENT INVESTOR*

Criteria	Copyright Year				
	1949	1954	1959	1965	1973
Some dividend paid since	1936	1940	1940	1940	1950
Size of firm	$50 million in assets or annual sales and be in upper 1/4 or 1/3 of its industry in size	$50 million in assets or annual sales and be in upper 1/4 or 1/3 of its industry in size	$50 million in assets or annual sales and be in upper 1/4 or 1/3 of its industry in size	$50 million in assets or annual sales and be in upper 1/4 or 1/3 of its industry in size	$50 million in assets or annual sales and be in upper 1/4 or 1/3 of its industry in size
Capitalization	Equity (at book value) at least 50% of total capitalization for industrial companies; at least 30% of total capitalization for utilities	Equity (at book value) at least 50% of total capitalization for industrial companies; at least 30% of total capitalization for utilities	Equity (at book value) at least 50% of total capitalization for industrial companies; at least 30% of total capitalization for utilities	Equity (at book value) at least 50% of total capitalization for industrial companies; at least 30% of total capitalization for utilities	Equity (at book value) at least 50% of total capitalization for industrial companies; at least 30% of total capitalization for utilities
Price-earnings ratio	Price not to exceed 20 times past 5 years' average earnings (or until five post World War II years have occurred, 25 times average earnings of 1936–1940)	Price not to exceed 20 times average earnings of past 6 years	Price not to exceed 25 times average earnings of past 5 years	Price not to exceed 25 times average earnings of past 7 years and not to exceed 20 times earnings of latest 12-month period	Price not to exceed 25 times average earnings of past 7 years and not to exceed 20 times earnings of latest 12-month period

Source: H. Oppenheimer and G. Schlarbaum, "Investing with Ben Graham: An Ex Ante Test of the Efficient Market Hypothesis," *Journal of Financial and Quantitative Analysis* (September 1981).

Although the criteria varied slightly from edition to edition, there were always four basic selection standards. First, the company had to have paid dividends for a certain minimum number of years. For example, in the 1949 edition, the company had to have paid dividends in every year since 1936. Second, there was a minimum size requirement which was the same in each edition—the company had to have reported at least $50 million in either sales or assets and be in the *upper* 1/4 (for industrials) or 1/3 (for utilities) of its industry in size. A third standard dealt with capitalization. For industrial companies at least 50% of total capital, based on book values, had to be equity; for utilities, at least 30% of total capital had to be equity. The fourth criterion dealt with *P/E* ratios. Although the standard varies slightly from edition to edition, in general the price should not exceed 25 times the average earnings of the past 5 years, nor should the price exceed 20 times the latest 12 months' earnings.

These are quite simple standards. Basically, to qualify for selection, stocks had to have a consistent dividend payment record, be reasonably large, be conservatively capitalized, and not sell above 20 times the latest 12 months' earnings. A recent study[21] tested these selection criteria to see if, indeed, investors would have been well advised by Benjamin Graham. The results of this study suggest that if investors had followed these selection rules, they would have earned positive abnormal returns of approximately 0.2% per month, or 2 1/2% per year, after adjusting for commissions and for changes in the market and the systematic risk of the stocks that met the selection criteria. These results are particularly impressive considering the fact that the selection criteria are *based entirely on historical data*. No estimates of future earnings or dividends are required.

It also appears that these results are *not* due to a size effect. Graham's size criteria would suggest that large company stocks would tend to be selected, and on average, this was the case. Thus, there is no easy explanation for the positive abnormal returns associated with the Benjamin Graham selection criteria.

Perhaps the explanation lies in a theory proposed by Miller[22] that, because of the restrictions on short selling, some high *P/E* ratio stocks can become overpriced and Graham's *P/E* criteria would eliminate high *P/E* stocks from one's portfolio.[23] Whatever the explanation, it is clear that investors should not ignore the stock selection criteria proposed by Benjamin Graham in the many editions of *The Intelligent Investor*.

13-7 SUMMARY

To be reliable, stock valuation models should account for the critical cause-effect relationships between stock prices and the variables which determine stock prices. In

---

[21]H. Oppenheimer and G. Schlarbaum, "Investing with Ben Graham: An Ex Ante Test of the Efficient Market Hypothesis," *Journal of Financial and Quantitative Analysis* (September 1981). Also, see H. Oppenheimer, "A Test of Ben Graham's Stock Selection Criteria," *Financial Analysts Journal* (September/October 1984).

[22]E. M. Miller, "Risk, Uncertainty and Divergence of Opinion," *Journal of Finance* (September 1977).

[23]There are a number of constraints on short selling. Short sellers do not receive the proceeds of the short sale on the day of the sale; many institutional investors are arbitrarily prevented from engaging in short selling; etc. Miller argues that constraints on short selling in the presence of heterogeneous expectations can lead to situations where the market price differs from the consensus price because some investors, who may feel a stock is overpriced, are prevented from short-selling the stock.

general, dividend discount models are based on the principle that stock prices are equal to the present value of the stock's future dividends. Specific dividend discount models, however, vary widely. The Kidder Peabody model presented in Section 13-1 is a fairly elaborate model which requires many estimates. On the other hand, the H model requires only four estimates but sacrifices some flexibility.

Regardless of which dividend discount model is used, an expected return for a stock can be determined, given the current stock price and forecast of future dividends. This expected return can then be compared with a required return based on a security market line and alphas computed for individual stocks. Or a required return can be used as an input to the model and a price estimated. This estimated price can then be compared with the current market price, allowing one to judge whether the stock is over- or underpriced.

P/E ratio models are also frequently used by analysts. It was shown that, conceptually, P/E ratios are functions of three primary variables—the dividend payout ratio, the growth rate of dividends, and the discount rate. In addition, these three variables can be broken down into a number of other variables, such as return on equity, debt ratio, return on assets, and profit margin.

One method of determining explicit estimates of the "appropriate" P/E ratio for an individual stock is the cross-sectional regression approach. By regressing the P/E ratios of a number of stocks against the variables which should influence P/E ratios (such as payout ratios and growth rates), one can determine an average relationship between P/E's and these variables. Given this average relationship, a P/E ratio can be calculated for each stock based on the regression model and compared with the stock's actual P/E ratio. If the model P/E is higher than the stock's actual P/E, the stock would be deemed to be underpriced, and vice versa. Unfortunately, the results are mixed as to whether or not such methods actually help forecast future stock returns.

On the other hand, the results for the Value Line ranking system clearly suggest that Value Line is able to discriminate among stocks and identify those which will provide positive, abnormal returns in the future. In addition, the selection criteria proposed by Benjamin Graham, which are very easy to use, also correctly identified stocks which subsequently provided superior returns. Thus, while one should not underestimate the efficiency of the securities markets, it appears that the careful and consistent use of stock valuation models may result in abnormal profits.

SUGGESTED READINGS

Before attempting to construct a stock valuation model (or, for that matter, any model) read:
F. Black, "The Trouble with Econometric Models," *Financial Analysts Journal* (March/April 1982).

A book that has stood the test of time and is still worth reading is:
B. Graham, *The Intelligent Investor*, 5th ed., Harper & Row, New York, 1973.

QUESTIONS

1 Using the constant growth dividend discount model, explain how inflation might affect the prices of common stocks.

2 Why do most, if not all, dividend discount models invoke at some point the assumptions of the constant growth dividend discount model?

3 Why do you suppose Whitbeck and Kisor used "normalized" earnings in the P/E model? In general, what do you think might be the relationship between P/E ratios based on reported earnings and the business cycle?

4 If you were to do a study similar to the Whitbeck and Kisor study, what variables would you choose as your independent variables for "explaining" differences in P/E ratios, and why would you choose these variables?

5 If you were to change any of the four selection criteria of Benjamin Graham, given the current market environment, which criteria would you change and why?

6 Assume, for the purposes of this question, that by using Value Line's ranking system, you can earn a 2% positive abnormal return per year. If the Value Line service costs $400 per year, what should be the minimum size of your portfolio in order to justify purchasing the service? What other factors might enter into your decision?

PROBLEMS

1 Tasty Foods' stock sells for $20 per share, and the most recent dividend was $1.00. An analyst, using the three-phase dividend discount model, estimates that the beginning growth rate of dividends g_a will be 10%, but this will last for only the first two years ($A = 2$). The growth will then decline to a constant, long-run normal growth rate of 7% ($g_n = 7\%$) over a 3-year transition period ($B = 5; B - A = 3$).

    a What is the expected growth rate in year 3, the first year of phase 2, the transition period?

    b What are the expected dividends in years 5 and 6?

    c If the analyst feels that 12% is an appropriate discount rate, given the risk characteristics of the stock, what is the present value of all expected future dividends?

    d What is the expected return associated with this stock, given the current market price of $20 and the analyst's estimates of future dividends?

    e What is the alpha for Tasty Foods' stock?

$P_0 = 23.56$
$E(r) = 12.88\%$
$\alpha = .88\%$

2 Using the H model,

    a What is the present value of the expected dividends for Tasty Foods in Problem 1?

    b What is the expected return?

    c What is the alpha?

$P/E = 24.82$

3 Using Equation (13-17), the Whitbeck-Kisor model as of June 1962, what P/E ratio would you estimate for KLM stock, given the following data:

> Estimated growth rate = 12%
> Estimated payout ratio = .45
> Standard deviation of earnings = 22%

4 Determine whether the following events will cause a stock's rank in the Value Line ranking system to change (up or down), *ceteris paribus*.

Down   **a** The stock reports a lower percentage increase in year-to-year quarterly earnings than the percentage change for the average stock.

up   **b** The percentage change in earnings in **a** is still much higher than Value Line estimated.

Down   **c** The ratio of the company's stock price to the average price for all 1700 stocks has been decreasing.

5 The following is adapted from the 1983 C.F.A. exam: Shown below are financial data on three corporations. Assume that payout ratios and P/E ratios will remain constant. Also assume that the growth rate of EPS from 1977 through 1982 will continue indefinitely. Which stock would you prefer to buy?

	Aaa Co.		Bee Co.		Sea Co.	
	1977	**1982**	**1977**	**1982**	**1977**	**1982**
EPS	$2.00	$2.94	$2.30	$3.70	$1.20	$2.10
P_0		40.00		60.00		40.00
D_0		1.60		1.80		1.00
Risk-adjusted required return, %		10		12		14

6 XYZ Corp. recently reported $6 earnings per share and a return on equity of 12%; it paid a $2 dividend. Using a discount rate of 10%, the Gordon model, and any additional assumptions you need, calculate the price of XYZ stock.

7 Dynamo Inc. is expected to pay out 30% of its earnings, earn 20% on its retained earnings, and not need any outside financing. An appropriate discount rate for Dynamo is 15%.

   a   What is the long-term expected growth rate of dividends and earnings for Dynamo?

   b   What is an appropriate P/E ratio for Dynamo?

   c   What portion of the total return investors earn from holding Dynamo stock is likely to come from capital gains?

   d   Which of the expectations listed above (payout ratio, return on equity, outside financing, discount rate) do you feel is the least realistic for a constant growth model and why?

PART FOUR

ANALYZING FIXED-INCOME SECURITIES

Fixed-income securities represent another large part of the U.S. capital markets. Despite the fixed nature of the payments associated with these securities, the analysis of fixed-income securities can be deceptively challenging.

Before beginning an analysis of any security, it is essential to be familiar with the basic characteristics of the security and the markets in which it is traded. Chapter 14 provides a description of the different types of fixed-income securities and their unique characteristics. In addition, the analytics of computing yields on fixed-income securities is presented. While simply an extension of the time value of money principles demonstrated in Chapter 9, there are some subtle issues concerning yields which the fixed-income investor needs to master.

Chapter 15 discusses the determinants of bond yields. Many concepts essential to understanding the pricing of bonds are presented in this chapter, such as the term structure of interest rates, default risk, and duration.

The final chapter in Part Four deals with bond trading strategies. However, before beginning to trade fixed-income securities, it is essential to understand the competitive nature of the marketplace. Consequently, this chapter first presents evidence regarding the degree of efficiency in the bond markets. Then specific trading strategies are discussed. The reader can decide whether or not such active trading strategies are superior to passive approaches for investing in fixed-income securities.

Finally, an acknowledgment. The material in these three chapters dealing with fixed-income securities is drawn largely from the work of Professor Robert Rogowski of Washington State University. His help is greatly appreciated.

CHAPTER 14

FUNDAMENTALS OF FIXED-INCOME SECURITIES

After reading this chapter, you should:

1 Know the characteristics of the different types of money market securities, bonds, and notes
2 Have some feel for the historical returns generated by various fixed-income securities
3 Understand the difference between promised yields and realized yields
4 Know how to calculate the promised yield to maturity and yield to first call
5 Understand the importance of coupon reinvestment rates

Fixed-income securities are another investment vehicle from which investors can choose. Although the term "fixed income" suggests that returns from these securities are certain, realized returns may differ (in some cases, dramatically) from expected returns. This misconception that returns are certain and the vast array of unique fixed-income securities confuse many investors. Therefore, this chapter presents a description of some fixed-income securities, an introduction to the different features of bond contracts, and a closer look at bond valuation. This discussion is then followed by Chapters 15 and 16, which cover bond yield determinants and fixed-income trading strategies, respectively.

An understanding of fixed-income securities is essential to sound investment management for several reasons. First, the addition of fixed-income securities to the universe of investment alternatives provides new diversification opportunities. Second, while fixed-income securities *usually* possess lower risks and returns than equities, periods of increased uncertainty concerning inflation may substantially increase the risk associated with fixed-income securities. Third, fixed-income securities have become an integral part of most investors' portfolios because of the growth of money market funds, and fixed-income securities may dominate the composition of pension funds in the future. Each of these reasons will be discussed in this and the following two chapters. But, before beginning, a description of the various classes of fixed-income securities is necessary.

14-1 CLASSES OF FIXED-INCOME SECURITIES

A fixed-income security is a debt instrument which promises to pay the holder a stipulated stream of future cash flows. This stream of cash flows usually includes periodic interest or coupon payments (computed as a percentage of the bond's face value or par value) and a lump-sum payment (the principal) equal to the face value. For example, the face (par) value of most corporate bonds is $1000, and coupons are paid on a semiannual basis. The issuer of the fixed-income security promises to pay the cash flow stream as scheduled; any delay may prompt the holder of the security to initiate bankruptcy proceedings. In the event of liquidation, the firm usually distributes the proceeds from the sale of assets first to the holders of fixed-income securities—any residual cash is then paid to the equity shareholders. On the other hand, if the firm is successful, the claims on interest and principal payments remain fixed while the equity shareholders may prosper through higher dividend payments.

Given the pattern of the cash flow stream, one would expect lower returns and less risk from fixed-income securities compared with equities. Table 14-1 shows that over the time period 1926–1984 long-term corporate bonds, long-term government bonds, and U.S. Treasury bills generated lower geometric and arithmetic mean returns than common stocks. Moreover, common stocks exhibit greater risk as measured by a higher standard deviation of returns.[1]

A vast menu of fixed-income securities exists. We will separate fixed-income securities into two groups according to *maturity*, where maturity is defined as the length of time between the date of issue and the date when the issuer will pay the principal. *Money market securities* are securities with maturities of 1 year or less. *Bonds or notes* are issued for periods greater than 1 year.

14-1-1 Money Market Securities Table 14-2 shows the mean rates for four different money market securities for 3- and 6-month maturities. As expected, the higher-risk securities exhibit higher returns. For example, negotiable certificates of deposit and commercial paper had mean returns of 6.92% and 6.61%, respectively, for the 6-month maturity, while on the lower-risk side, U.S. Treasury bills had a mean return of 6.06%. Let us examine these money market securities more closely.

---

[1]However, a recent study found that during periods of uncertain inflation, the expected return on bonds actually exceeded the expected returns on stocks owing to the increased volatility of interest rates. See B. L. Copeland, Jr., "Inflation, Interest Rates, and Equity Risk Premia," *Financial Analysts Journal* (May/June 1982).

TABLE 14-1   ANNUAL RETURNS 1926–1984

Series	Geometric mean, %	Arithmetic mean, %	Standard deviation, %
Common stocks	9.8	12.0	21.2
Corporate bonds, long-term	4.8	5.1	8.3
Government bonds, long term	4.1	4.4	8.2
U.S. Treasury bills	3.4	3.5	3.4
Consumer price index, (inflation)	3.1	3.2	4.9

Source: R. G. Ibbotson and R. A. Sinquefield, *Stocks, Bonds, Bills, and Inflation: 1986 Yearbook*, Ibbotson Associates, Chicago, 1986.

TABLE 14-2   MONEY MARKET SECURITIES: RATES FOR DIFFERENT MATURITIES (1971–1978)

	Mean, %	Std. dev., %	Coeff. of var.	Min.	(date), %*	Max.	(date), %
3-month maturity:							
Treasury bills	5.78	1.45	0.25	3.35	(2/72)	9.00	(12/78)
Commercial paper	6.60	2.01	0.30	3.75	(3/72)	12.00	(7/74)
Bankers' acceptances	6.52	2.01	0.31	3.75	(3/71)	11.50	(7/74)
Negotiable certificates of deposit	6.71	2.11	0.31	3.75	(2/72)	12.15	(9/74)
6-month maturity:							
Treasury bills	6.06	1.44	0.24	3.56	(3/71)	9.42	(9/74)
Commercial paper	6.61	1.71	0.26	4.25	(3/71)	11.50	(7/74)
Bankers' acceptance	6.61	1.84	0.28	3.75	(3/71)	11.00	(8/74)
Certificates of deposit	6.92	1.94	0.28	4.15	(3/71)	12.00	(8/74)

*Some minima occurred at several times; date shown is earliest time.
Source: M. G. Ferri and J. P. Gaines, "A Study of Yield Spreads in the Money Market: 1971 to 1978," *Financial Management* (autumn 1980), pp. 52–59.

U.S. Treasury bills (T-bills) are 91- to 360-day instruments with denominations of $10,000 to $1 million sold by the federal government. Usually on every Monday, the U.S. Treasury sells T-bills through a competitive bidding process.[2] T-bills are sold at a discount, which means that the return on a T-bill is the difference between the purchase price and the face value. For example, if the price of a 182-day T-bill is 93½, the annual rate of return is 12.86%, traditionally calculated (based on a 360-day year) as follows:

$$\frac{100 - 93\frac{1}{2}}{100} \times \frac{360}{182} = 12.86\%$$

This method of computing yields is called the *bank discount method* and is also used to determine the yields of bankers' acceptances and commercial paper. Note that the use of 360 days, rather than 365 days, and the use of the par value (100) in the denominator, rather than the purchase price, understates the true yield of T-bills.[3]

Safety and liquidity characterize T-bills. An active secondary market exists for T-bills so investors can easily sell them to obtain cash. With the federal government backing T-bills, the likelihood of late or zero payments on T-bills is nil. The 3-month

[2]Investors can bid on a competitive or noncompetitive basis. After all the bids are received, the Treasury accepts those competitive bids with the highest prices down to the point where the amount offered is reached. The Treasury allocates usually 10% or less of the offering to noncompetitive bids.

[3]For a discussion of how much the bank discount method understates the true yield, see P. W. Glasgo, W. J. Landes, and A. F. Thompson, "Bank Discount, Coupon Equivalent, and Coupon Yields," *Financial Management* (autumn 1982).

T-bill is, in fact, often referred to as the ''risk-free rate.'' Major T-bill investors include commercial banks, corporations, and money market mutual funds.

Commercial paper is a short-term, unsecured promissory note issued by a large corporation. Commercial paper sells at a discount, in denominations of $1000 to over $5 million, and maturities up to 270 days. Since commercial paper is unsecured, only those corporations with the highest credit ratings can sell these instruments. The commercial paper market has grown rapidly since the 1960s as corporate treasurers have gravitated to commercial paper because of its ready availability and low cost relative to bank loans. From the investor's viewpoint, the rate of return on commercial paper generally is slightly higher than that on T-bills, since commercial paper has a greater chance of default and lacks a good secondary market.

Bankers' acceptances are drafts (similar to checks) between individuals, corporations, and commercial banks which are used to finance international trade. However, they are also negotiable and therefore can be bought and sold in the money market. To illustrate how they work, suppose a U.S. firm imports goods from a French firm. The U.S. firm pays for the goods with a draft; the French firm is unsure of the value of the draft, so it requests that the U.S. firm have its draft accepted by a U.S. bank. The U.S. bank acccepts or guarantees the draft for a fee. The French firm can now either hold the acceptance until maturity or can discount the accceptance with a bank (either the bank guaranteeing the draft or a different bank) to receive the cash immediately. The discounting bank transfers the acceptance to the U.S. bank, which can then sell it in the money market. Since they are guaranteed by large commercial banks, bankers' acceptances are almost as safe as T-bills. They have maturities spanning 30 to 180 days, varying denominations, and a small secondary market.

Negotiable certificates of deposit (CDs) are marketable receipts for large deposits held by a bank for a specified time period and interest rate. For example, ABC Bank sells a $100,000 CD for 6 months at 8.5%. The holder can resell the CD any time prior to 6 months. Banks use CDs to gather funds from corporations and other institutions to finance their operations. CDs have denominations of $25,000 to $10 million, pay both interest and principal at maturity, and usually have maturities of 6 months or less.

The return on CDs (see Table 14-2) suggests that CDs are riskier than T-bills. While there is an organized and active secondary market for the CDs of larger banks, the holders of CDs recognize that deposits over $100,000 are uninsured by the Federal Deposit Insurance Corporation (FDIC). Thus, the risk of default exists for CDs, although the probability of such a default is small.

Federal agency securities include short-term instruments sold by federal, or federally sponsored, agencies. These agencies sell notes at a discount as well as long-term securities to finance their operations. The Federal Land Bank, the Export-Import Bank, and the Federal National Mortgage Association are just several of the agencies which were formed to provide financing for a particular industry by selling federal agency securities. The rates of return on agency securities tend to be slightly higher than those on T-bills. Investors perceive these securities as having greater risk because of the relatively small secondary market and the fact that they are only indirect obligations of the federal government.

Eurodollars are dollar-denominated deposits at foreign banks or U.S. foreign branches. Similar to CDs, these deposits are bought and sold in foreign money markets and tend to link interest rates throughout the world. Confidence in the U.S. dollar and its economic system and interest rate regulations in the United States led to the growth of the Eurodollar market. (Ironically, some observers place the birth of Eurodollars in eastern Europe where bankers in the early 1950s preferred holding U.S. dollar deposits in western European banks rather than U.S. banks.) Eurodollar deposits have higher rates of return than T-bills because of the risk of foreign and U.S. bank failure. Like CDs, Eurodollar deposits tend to involve large amounts with maturities of less than 6 months.

14-1-2 Bonds and Notes   Investors with holding periods greater than 1 year may choose among bonds or notes from a variety of issuers. Although recent bouts of high, volatile interest rates have reduced the trading volume of bonds and notes, the bond market remains substantial. Table 14-3 illustrates recent rates of return. Let us consider some of these securities individually.

U.S. Treasury notes and bonds are coupon issues with broad appeal. Notes have maturities of 1 to 7 years while bond maturities exceed 5 years. Both are available in *bearer form* where the interest is paid to whoever presents the coupon to the treasury on each coupon date, or in *registered form* where the owner of record (as recorded at the treasury) receives the coupon interest. The minimum purchase for most notes and bonds is $1000, but denominations may be as large as $1 million.

TABLE 14-3   NOTES AND BONDS RATES OF RETURN

	1984 interest rates, %
U.S. Treasury notes and bonds:	
1 year	10.89
2 year	11.65
3 year	11.89
5 year	12.24
7 year	12.40
10 year	12.44
20 year	12.48
GNMA securities	13.13
State and local government:	
Aaa	9.61
Baa	10.38
Corporate bonds:	
Seasoned issue	13.49
New issue (utility, Aaa)	13.81
Preferred stock	11.59

Source: Federal Reserve Bulletin (November 1985), pp. A-24 and A-38.

The Treasury generally offers new issues in exchange for maturing securities. This method of exchange refunding allows the investor to either exchange the maturing bonds for new bonds or receive the principal and final coupon payment. If the investor chooses to receive cash, he or she will sell the subscription rights for the new issue in the open market.[4]

Securities dealers make an active secondary market for Treasury notes and bonds. The price of an outstanding note or bond is expressed in percentages of $1000 par value and prices change by one thirty-second (1/32) of a point, where a point is equal to 1% of par value, or $10. To illustrate, Table 14-4 lists quotations for U.S. government bonds, notes, and bills, as reported in the November 29, 1985, *Wall Street Journal*. The first three symbols represent the coupon rate, the year of maturity, and the month of maturity. An ''n'' after the month indicates that the issue is a treasury note, as opposed to a bond. The next two numbers are the dealers' bid and offer quotations. To illustrate, consider the 11 3/4% treasury note due April 1986. Dealers will buy this note at 101.21, i.e., at 101 21/32% of par, or $1016.56. They will sell this note at 101.25, or $1017.81. The price changed −.1 (1/32 of 1% or $.3125) from the previous day. Finally, the last column of numbers indicates that the yield to maturity is 7.22%, based on the bid price of 101.21.

If an investor buys or sells notes or bonds on dates other than the seminannual coupon dates, the *accrued interest* is part of the seller's return. For example, an investor who sells a bond 1 month prior to the coupon date receives 5 months of accrued interest from the buyer. In this way the seller receives interest for the number of months he or she actually held the security, whether or not the sale date falls on a coupon date. The Appendix at the end of this chapter describes in detail how accrued interest is calculated.

Federal agency bonds and participation certificates are those longer-term securities offered by more than 40 agencies of the federal government. Agency securities sell at rates of return slightly higher than long-term treasury securities. For example, Table 14-3 shows that in 1984, Government National Mortgage Association (GNMA) securities provided rates of 13.13%, which exceeded 20-year U.S. Treasury bond rates of 12.48% by .65% or 65 *basis points* (a basis point is .01 of 1%). Agency securities provide financing for a variety of industries that the U.S. government has deemed beneficial to the public interest. For example, the Federal Home Loan Bank and the Federal National Mortgage Association provide funds to support the housing industry. These agency securities offer investors a potpourri of bonds with varying degrees of government backing and safety. All federally operated agencies, except the Tennessee Valley Authority, are fully backed by the government, whereas most government-sponsored agencies are backed only by the issuing agency.

Participation certificates are certificates which represent a claim on a pool of agency loans or mortgages. These loans and mortgages provide credit for international trade or for home mortgages. For example, the Government National Mortgage Association offers *Ginnie Mae pass-throughs*, which are a pool of mortgages. Ginnie Mae pass-throughs pay the holder monthly sums which include both interest and principal until

---

[4]Other forms of new issue offerings which the Treasury uses less frequently are advance and cash refunding. In these cases, the Treasury exchanges new securities or cash for outstanding notes or bonds. For more information, see D. Darst, *The Complete Bond Book*, McGraw-Hill, New York, 1975.

TABLE 14-4 A PARTIAL LISTING OF QUOTATIONS FOR U.S. GOVERNMENT BONDS, NOTES, AND BILLS

TREASURY BONDS, NOTES & BILLS

Wednesday, November 27, 1985

Representative mid-afternoon Over-the-Counter quotations supplied by the Federal Reserve Bank of New York City, based on transactions of $1 million or more.

Decimals in bid-and-asked and bid changes represent 32nds; 101.1 means 101 1/32. a-Plus 1/64. b-Yield to call date. d-Minus 1/64. k-Nonresident U.S. citizens exempt from withholding taxes. n-Treasury notes. p-Treasury note; nonresident U.S. citizens exempt from withholding taxes.

Treasury Bonds and Notes

Rate	Mat. Date		Bid	Asked	Bid Chg.	Yld.
10 1/2s,	1985	Nov n	99.31	100.3	.....	0.00
10 7/8s,	1985	Dec n	100.8	100.12	.....	5.83
14 1/8s,	1985	Dec n	100.18	100.22	.....	5.06
10 5/8s,	1986	Jan n	100.15	100.19	.....	6.70
10 7/8s,	1986	Feb n	100.25	100.29	.....	6.89
13 1/2s,	1986	Feb n	101.6	101.10	.....	6.70
9 7/8s,	1986	Feb n	100.14	100.18	.....	6.88
14s,	1986	Mar n	102.7	102.11	.....	6.52
11 1/2s,	1986	Mar n	101.8	101.12	.....	7.06
11 3/4s,	1986	Apr n	101.21	101.25	− .1	7.22
7 7/8s,	1986	May n	100.2	100.6	− .1	7.42
9 3/8s,	1986	May n	100.23	100.27	.....	7.42
12 5/8s,	1986	May n	102.10	102.14	+ .1	7.51
13 3/4s,	1986	May n	102.24	102.28	− .1	7.15
13s,	1986	Jun n	103	103.4	.....	7.40
14 7/8s,	1986	Jun n	104.2	104.6	.....	7.37
12 5/8s,	1986	Jul p	103.1	103.5	.....	7.67
8s,	1986	Aug n	100.3	100.7	.....	7.68
11 3/8s,	1986	Aug n	102.11	102.15	+ .1	7.72
12 3/8s,	1986	Aug p	103.4	103.8	.....	7.80
11 7/8s,	1986	Sep p	103.2	103.6	− .2	7.83
12 1/4s,	1986	Sep n	103.12	103.16	− .1	7.81
11 5/8s,	1986	Oct p	103.5	103.9	− .1	7.83
6 1/8s,	1986	Nov	99.8	100.8	− .1	5.85
•						
•						
•						
10 3/4s,	2005	Aug k	105.12	105.14	+ .15	10.11
7 5/8s,	2002-07	Feb	79.21	80.5	+ .4	9.88
7 7/8s,	2002-07	Nov	82.5	82.21	+ .3	9.81
8 3/8s,	2003-08	Aug	86.22	87.6	+ .13	9.79
8 3/4s,	2003-08	Nov	89.9	89.17	+ .16	9.91
9 1/8s,	2004-09	May	92.4	92.12	+ .9	9.97
10 3/8s,	2004-09	Nov	101.27	102.3	+ .6	10.12
11 3/4s,	2005-10	Feb	112.25	113.1	+ .3	10.19
10s,	2005-10	May	99.25	100.1	+ .3	10.00
12 3/4s,	2005-10	Nov	121.8	121.16	+ .18	10.21
13 7/8s,	2006-11	May	130.26	131.2	+ .6	10.22
14s,	2006-11	Nov	131.29	132.5	+ .2	10.24
10 3/8s,	2007-12	Nov	101.25	102.1	+ .9	10.14
12s,	2008-13	Aug	115.7	115.11	+ .8	10.25
13 1/4s,	2009-14	May	126.19	126.27	+ .14	10.21
12 1/2s,	2009-14	Aug k	120.3	120.7	+ .13	10.22
11 3/4s,	2009-14	Nov k	113.27	113.31	+ .14	10.18
11 1/4s,	2015	Feb k	111.17	111.21	+ .16	10.01
10 5/8s,	2015	Aug k	106.11	106.19	+ .14	9.93
9 7/8s,	2015	Nov	99.21	99.23	.....	9.90

U.S. Treas. Bills

Mat. date	Bid	Asked	Yield	Mat. date	Bid	Asked	Yield
	Discount			-1986-	Discount		
-1985-				3-20	7.14	7.10	7.36
12- 5	6.55	6.41	6.49	3-27	7.22	7.18	7.45
12-12	5.34	5.22	5.30	4- 3	7.26	7.22	7.50
12-19	5.82	5.78	5.88	4-10	7.28	7.24	7.54
12-26	6.86	6.80	6.93	4-17	7.28	7.24	7.55
-1986-				4-86	7.28	7.24	7.56
1- 2	6.85	6.79	6.92	5- 1	7.28	7.24	7.57
1- 9	6.94	6.88	7.03	5- 8	7.29	7.25	7.59
1-16	7.04	6.98	7.14	5-15	7.28	7.24	7.59
1-23	7.11	7.07	7.24	5-22	7.28	7.24	7.60
1-30	7.11	7.07	7.25	5-29	7.27	7.25	7.62
2- 6	7.18	7.14	7.34	6-12	7.24	7.20	7.58
2-13	7.21	7.17	7.39	7-10	7.30	7.26	7.65
2-20	7.21	7.17	7.39	8- 7	7.34	7.30	7.71
2-27	7.18	7.14	7.37	9- 4	7.34	7.30	7.74
3- 6	7.18	7.14	7.38	10- 2	7.34	7.30	7.77
3-13	7.17	7.13	7.38	10-30	7.34	7.30	7.80

Source: Wall Street Journal, Nov. 29, 1985.

maturity. Investor purchases of participation certificates provide the funds for the mortgages. The Federal National Mortgage Association (*Fannie Mae*) offers a similar certificate.

Municipal bonds and notes are securities that are issued by state and local governments and whose interest payments are exempt from federal taxes. While many U.S. government and agency securities are exempt from state and local taxes, only municipal securities offer investors coupons which are exempt from federal taxes. The rate of return on municipal securities reflects this tax treatment. Table 14-3 indicates that Aaa-rated municipal bonds provided a return of 9.61% in 1984. For an investor in a 35% tax bracket, a tax-free return of 9.61% on a municipal bond is equivalent to a 14.78% return on a fully taxable bond, such as corporate or U.S. government bonds. Recall that to convert after-tax returns to pretax returns, the after-tax return is divided by the quantity 1 minus the tax rate. In this case,

$$\frac{9.61\%}{1 - .35} = 14.78\%$$

Individuals in the higher income tax brackets, commercial banks, and casualty insurance companies are the largest investors in municipal bonds.

A wide variety of entities issue municipal securities. States, municipalities, school districts, townships, and organizations such as park districts and educational authorities tap the primary municipal market to (1) raise working capital until the expected receipt of funds or to (2) finance long-term capital projects. *Tax, revenue, or bond anticipation notes* are shorter-term securities designed to supply funds until taxes, revenues, or proceeds from a bond issue are received. Virtually all municipal notes sell in bearer form at a discount in denominations starting at $5000.

The majority of municipal securities are issued to finance long-term projects which benefit citizens within the municipality's jurisdiction. Table 14-5 shows the various purposes of municipal securities issued in 1981 and 1984. Clearly, municipal bonds finance a large number of different projects.

TABLE 14-5 MUNICIPAL BOND PURPOSE, 1981 AND 1984

	Amount ($ billions)	
Purpose of bonds	**1981**	**1984**
Education	$ 4,572	$ 7,553
Transportation	2,621	7,552
Utilities and conservation	8,149	17,844
Social welfare	19,958	29,928
Industrial aid	3,974	15,415
Other	5,536	15,758
Total	$44,810	$94,050

Source: Federal Reserve Bulletin (November 1985), p. A34.

TABLE 14-6   TYPES OF MUNICIPAL BONDS ISSUED

Bond type	Amount (in millions)			
	1978	1979	1980	1984
General obligation	$17,854	$12,109	$14,100	$ 26,485
Revenue	30,658	31,256	34,267	80,156
Total new issues	48,512	43,365	48,367	106,641

Source: Federal Reserve Bulletin (November 1985), p. A34.

Two general bond classes exist in the municipal bond market: *general obligation (GO) bonds* and *revenue bonds*. They differ by the source of funds for repayment. GO bonds are repaid from the general taxes collected by the issuer, whereas revenues generated by the project and/or special taxes repay the holders of revenue bonds. Thus, a municipality can raise taxes to pay coupons and principal for GO bonds while the revenue bond depends on the success of the facility which was financed. In recent years, state and local governments have, with some controversy, issued a type of revenue bonds called *industrial development bonds* where, for example, a town attracts a business firm by financing the construction of a plant at tax-exempt rates. Although revenue bonds are more risky than GO bonds, their use has increased. Table 14-6 shows that revenue bonds now comprise the majority of municipal issues.

One should not assume because GO bonds have the taxing power of the municipality as security that they are risk-free. There have been occasional instances of GO bonds defaulting, one of the better-known cases being the New York City bonds during the 1970s.

Municipal bond issues generally sell in *serial form*, with several different maturities for separate amounts of the total issue. The issue is offered to investors by underwriters who attach different coupons to the different maturities. The serial form of municipal issues exists to enable the state and local government to repay the issue over a series of years rather than in one lump sum at one time.

Corporate bonds are, obviously, the debt obligations of corporations and generally have a single maturity date. They sell in $1000 denominations and are priced as a percentage of par. Corporations utilize bonds to raise large amounts of capital at costs usually lower than other sources of debt capital.

Corporate bonds offer investors an often bewildering array of choices because of the amount and variety of bonds in the market. Table 14-7 shows that a total of $110 billion were issued in 1984. Rates of return on corporate bonds exceed that on U.S. Treasury bonds because of their relative lack of liquidity and greater likelihood of default. A secondary market exists for only those corporate bonds with large total issue sizes, typically for issues of $100 million or more. If one looks at bond trading activity on the New York Stock Exchange as reported in most newspapers, one would find a price quotation similar to the sample shown at the top of the next page from the November 29, 1985, issue of the *Wall Street Journal*.

Bond	Current yield	Sales in $1000s	High	Low	Last	Net change
Amoco 6s 98	8.5	10	70 5/8	70 5/8	70 5/8	− 7/8

This price quotation tells us that Amoco 6% coupon bonds due in 1998 traded 10 bonds, all at 70 5/8 (or $706.25 per $1000 bond). The current yield is 8.5% and the bond price decreased by 7/8 point ($8.75) from the previous day's price.

Secondary market dealers generally trade bonds in $100,000 round lots. Consequently, small investors will typically earn a substantially lower yield because of higher transaction costs associated with odd-lot trades.

Table 14-7 shows the major issuers of corporate bonds. Real estate and financial firms were the largest issuers of bonds in 1984, followed by manufacturers. Utility issues include gas, water, electrical, and telephone company bonds. The telephone bonds (securities of AT&T and the regional telephone companies) are generally viewed as the most liquid because of the large issue sizes and high credit ratings. Industrial bonds tend to have greater overall default risk than utilities but generally sell at lower yields because of the shorter average maturities. Transportation (railroad and airline) bonds have fairly high default risk and sell at yields higher than those of utility bonds.

Bonds are frequently classified as discount bonds, current coupon bonds, or premium bonds. *Discount bonds* refer to bonds which have coupon rates below current market interest rates—thus the bonds sell at a discount to par value. *Current coupon bonds* have coupon rates very close to their current yield to maturity and therefore the bonds sell at, or near, par value. *Premium bonds* are bonds with coupon rates that are higher than current market rates and consequently sell for more than par value.

Preferred stocks are corporate fixed-income securities that carry a specified fixed dividend, rather than coupons, and have no specified maturity date. Preferred stocks sell at a variety of market prices and usually carry dividends stated in dollar terms or as a fixed percentage of the issue price. Most preferred stock issues are listed on the New York Stock Exchange. Preferred means that the firm must pay the preferred stock dividend in its entirety before paying any common stock dividends, and in the event of liquidation, holders of preferred shares will receive preferential treatment vis-à-vis holders of common shares. *Cumulative* preferred refers to the practice that any unpaid

TABLE 14-7 AMOUNT OF CORPORATE BONDS BY ISSUER, 1984

Issuer	Amount (in millions)	Percent of total
Manufacturing	$ 24,607	22
Commercial and miscellaneous	13,726	13
Transportation	4,694	4
Public utility	10,679	10
Communication	2,997	3
Real estate and financial	52,980	48
	$109,683	100

Source: Federal Reserve Bulletin (November 1985), p. A38.

dividends in one year carry over to the following year until fully paid. Preferred dividends are paid on a quarterly basis, and unlike bonds, preferred stocks do not trade on an accrued interest basis.

Convertible bonds and convertible preferred stock are securities that an investor may convert at a stipulated ratio into common stock. Investors find convertible securities attractive because of (1) the benefits of receiving interest or dividend payments and (2) the potential for capital gains due to the conversion feature.

> Before continuing, you should:
> 1 Know the criteria for classifying fixed-income securities into either of two groups—money market securities or bonds and notes
> 2 Be aware of the characteristics of the different types of money market securities
> 3 Be aware of the characteristics of the different types of bonds and notes

14-2 BOND FEATURES

Bonds often confuse investors because of the bewildering set of special provisions attached to individual bond issues. The financial contract between the issuer of the bonds and the purchaser of the bonds is called the *bond indenture*. Thus, the unique characteristics of each bond will be identified in the bond indenture. To better understand these unique characteristics, a review of the terms collateral, call provision, sinking fund, and protective covenant is in order.

14-2-1 Collateral If you have ever noticed that the names of banks are often painted on the sides of railroad cars, you can appreciate the value of collateral. Collateral represents a pledge of real assets as insurance against the nonpayment of a loan or security. The railroad car represents collateral to the bank which financed it and whose name may appear on the side of the car. In your personal financial affairs, the collateral of your car or house is insurance to the lender in the event that you are unable to meet your financial obligations. Similarly, corporations often provide collateral protection to bondholders. The market value of real property held by state and local governments is the collateral for municipal bonds.[5] The holder of any financial contract clearly prefers the interest and principal in the form of cash since the conversion of real assets into cash is often costly. Nevertheless, collateral represents a good faith promise that the borrower will honor the financial contract and increases investor confidence since real assets are pledged as security.

Long-term corporate debt runs the gamut from having zero collateral to having substantial real assets pledged as collateral. *Debentures* are bonds secured only by the general credit of the corporation. The investor expects that the firm will generate enough earnings to make the scheduled payments since the firm has not pledged any assets as collateral. The bond indenture often includes covenants restricting the amount

---

[5]J. L. Treynor, "On the Quality of Municipal Bonds," *Financial Analysts Journal* (May/June 1982).

of secured and unsecured debt the firm can issue to protect the claims of the debenture holders.

Subordination specifies the order of payment if the firm must liquidiate its assets. *Subordinated debentures* are debentures which rank behind other unsubordinated debentures in the event of bankruptcy. Consequently, subordinated debentures are generally the riskiest fixed-income security issued by a firm, with the exception of income bonds.

Income bonds are unsecured bonds which do not promise to pay interest every annual or semiannual period. Income bonds pay interest *only if* earnings are sufficient to do so, and do not require the firm to pay missed interest from previous years, if any. Obviously, income bonds are very high risk instruments which are used primarily by corporations in the throes of reorganization.

Mortgage bonds are bonds backed by the pledge of some specified property of the issuer. For example, a firm may sell bonds secured by a mortgage on an office building. If the firm defaults on interest or principal payments, the bond trustee can foreclose on the mortgage and sell the office building to satisfy the claims on the bondholders. Many railroad and utility issues are mortgage bonds. The bond indenture will often specify that any new assets are immediately pledged to mortgage bonds and that new bonds backed by these same assets rank behind the original mortgage bondholder if bankruptcy occurs.

Equipment trust certificates are bonds usually sold by railroads or airlines to finance the purchase of a specific asset—typically, the locomotives or cars of the railroad or the planes of the airline. The assets tend to be highly marketable and easily delivered to the bondholders in the event of bankruptcy. Because the assets are an integral part of the operations of transportation firms, these equipment trust certificates are a rather secure investment.

Collateral trust bonds are securities backed by other securities. If the firm defaults, the bond trustee has the right to sell these specified securities to meet the payments to the bondholders. The bond trustee normally holds these pledged securities.

Before continuing, you should be aware that regardless of the type of collateral pledged as security for bonds, the true security behind long-term debt issues is the long-run earning power of the firm. (In the case of government issues, the true underlying security is the long-run taxing power of the government agency.) Subordinated debentures of profitable firms may, in fact, be more secure than first mortgage bonds of failing firms. Generally, the fact that a firm is failing is an indication that the market value of its real assets has declined. Thus, in analyzing the security of bonds, one has to estimate the long-run earning power of the firm. In this way, the analysis of bonds is similar to the analysis of common stocks.

14-2-2 Call Provisions Call provisions give the bond issuer the right to pay off (call in) a bond issue prior to maturity. The issuing firm enjoys the flexibility of being able to call the bonds if interest rates fall significantly, and it can issue new bonds at a lower interest cost. This practice of calling bonds and immediately reissuing new bonds at lower interest rates is termed *refunding*. Investors recognize that the existence of a call provision introduces more uncertainty. Consequently, investors require higher yields on callable bonds as compensation for this additional risk.

Call provisions may take several distinct forms, depending on when the bonds are callable. A bond that is callable right after the issue date exposes investors immediately to call risk. Most bonds, however, have deferred call provisions where the investor has a grace period during which the issuer may not call in the bonds. The typical deferment period is 5 or 10 years.

When an issuer brings bonds with a call provision to market, the issuer specifies a *call price*, the price at which the issuer will buy back the bonds. For example, the call price on a 10-year, immediately callable bond may be 114 for the first 4 years ($1140 per $1000 face value), 110 for the next 4 years, and 103 for the 2 years prior to maturity. The difference between the call price and par value is the *call premium*. Per our example, the call premium is $1140 − $1000 = $140 for the first 4 years, $100 for the next 4 years, and $30 for the final 2 years. The call premium varies widely, but the conventional practice is to set the initial call premium equal to 1 year's interest. For example, a bond with a 14% coupon rate might have an initial call price of 114.

The value of the call provision to the issuer and the degree of call risk to the bondholders varies inversely with interest rate expectations. If everyone expects interest rates to rise from current levels, the value of the call provision and call risk decrease because the issuer will not redeem the bonds only to reissue bonds at higher coupons than before. Conversely, expectations of lower interest rates signal greater value to the call provision and greater call risk. In this case, a difference in yields between bonds with and without call protection will emerge to reflect greater call risk.[6]

Issues of corporate, municipal, and U.S. Treasury bonds, as well as preferred stock, utilize call provisions. While most corporate bond and preferred stock issues have call provisions, the U.S. treasury usually attaches call provisions only to long-term bonds. Issuers of municipal GO bonds tend to use call provisions infrequently, whereas revenue bonds usually carry call provisions.[7]

14-2-3 Sinking Fund Provisions A sinking fund provision requires the issuing firm to retire a certain percentage of the corporate bond issue at stipulated points in time. It is similar to an installment loan. The bond trustee or the issuer operates the sinking fund and repurchases bonds either by calling in a certain number of bonds by lot or by buying bonds in the open market. Most sinking fund provisions have a deferment period and thereafter require retirement of part of the issue on a yearly basis.

Investors consider sinking funds as having two distinct components: a call provision and a form of risk reduction. The option of calling bonds by lot enables the issuer to refinance when interest rates fall below the issue's coupon rate. The issuer pays the holders of the called bonds an exercise price, usually par value, which is lower than the bonds' current market value. If interest rates are higher than the bonds' coupon rate, sinking fund requirements will be met by simply buying bonds in the market at

---

[6]F. Jen and J. Wert, ''The Effect of Call Risk on Corporate Bond Yields,'' *Journal of Finance* (December 1967).

[7]D. Kidwell, ''The Inclusion and Exercise of Call Provisions by State and Local Governments,'' *Journal of Money, Credit and Banking* (August 1976).

prices below par value. (Recall that if market rates are above the coupon rate, the bond will sell below par value, and vice versa.)

On the other hand, sinking fund provisions offer risk reduction in three ways. First, the early retirement of bonds tends to better protect investors from default. Since the value of the firm's assets secures the bonds and real assets may depreciate over time, the periodic retirement of bonds reduces bondholders' claims on depreciating real assets.[8] Second, when the market interest rate is above the coupon rate, the activity of the issuer purchasing bonds in the open market to meet sinking fund requirements tends to provide greater liquidity and supports the market price. Third, the possible existence of accumulation strategies by sophisticated investors may inject greater liquidity in the secondary market. When bonds sell at discounts, these investors may accumulate a sufficient number of bonds to force the issuer to call the bonds by lot. By refusing to sell in the market, the accumulator would earn the difference between the discount purchase prices and the call price.[9]

14-2-4 Protective Covenants The bond indenture usually contains several *protective covenants*. These protective covenants force the management of the firm to live within certain financial constraints and give bondholders greater confidence that the firm will pay the interest and principal as scheduled. Examples of covenants are limits on the amount of debt outstanding, and on the dividends paid to holders of common shares. For example, dividend payments may not be allowed if working capital falls below a specified amount or if a fixed charge coverage ratio falls below a certain level. Other restrictions may be placed on the amount of salary and bonus which can be paid to key management personnel.

14-3 YIELD TO MATURITY

In Chapter 10 we introduced the basic bond valuation model which is based on the notion that current prices represent the present value of the expected future cash payments to be received by the owner of the bond. For the typical bond with $1000 par value, the price P_0 can be written

$$P_0 = \frac{C_1}{(1 + r/2)^1} + \frac{C_2}{(1 + r/2)^2} + \cdots + \frac{C_{2n}}{(1 + r/2)^{2n}} + \frac{\$1000}{(1 + r/2)^{2n}} \qquad (14\text{-}1)$$

where C = semiannual coupon
  n = number of years to maturity
  r = appropriate rate, discounted semiannually

Since the coupon stream represents an annuity, the bond price formula can also be written as

$$P_0 = C \cdot \text{PVAF}_{r/2,2n} + \$1000\text{PVDF}_{r/2,2n} \qquad (14\text{-}1a)$$

[8]S. Myers, "Determinants of Corporate Borrowing," *Journal of Financial Economics* (November 1977).
[9]A. Kalotay, "On the Management of Sinking Funds," *Financial Management* (summer 1981).

where PVAF represents the present-value annuity factor and PVDF represents the present-value discount factor, as discussed in Chapter 9.

Given the price of a bond, its coupon rate, and the number of years to maturity, one can solve for the average rate[10] used to discount the bond's coupon and principal payments to its present price. This average discount rate is referred to as the bond's *yield to maturity* (YTM). To illustrate the simplest case, consider a 2-year *zero-coupon* bond priced at $857.63. A zero-coupon bond is one that pays only the principal amount at the end of its term to maturity and does not make any interim coupon payments. Since there is only a single payment of $1000 and the current price is known, we can solve for the yield to maturity by using Equation (9-3).

$$C_0 = \frac{C_n}{(1 + r)^n}$$

$$\$857.63 = \frac{\$1000}{(1 + r)^2}$$

$$r = \left(\frac{1000}{857.63}\right)^{1/2} - 1 = .0798 = 7.98\%$$

Thus, the YTM, or "average" discount rate, for these 2 years is slightly less than 8%. The YTM is the same as the *geometric mean return*, or what is also frequently referred to as the *internal rate of return* in many financial management textbooks.

So far our example has dealt with only a single cash flow received at the end of 2 years for the 2-year zero-coupon bond. Of course, most bonds provide a number of coupon payments as well as the final principal payment, and this complicates the procedure for calculating the yield to maturity. Essentially, we need to solve for r in Equation (14-1) where the current price P_0, coupon C, and years to maturity n are known. There are two methods we will use to estimate the yield to maturity: (1) solve for the approximate yield to maturity (AYTM) and (2) estimate the true YTM by interpolating.

14-3-1 The Approximate Yield to Maturity Method The AYTM method approximates a bond's yield to maturity by dividing the "average cash payments" to the bondholders by the "average investment" in the bonds. Equation (14-2) presents the calculations involved:

$$\text{AYTM} = \frac{2C + [(\$1000 - P_0)/n]}{(\$1000 + P_0)/2} \tag{14-2}$$

---

[10]The yield to maturity represents the geometric mean (average) of the "forward rate structure" over the life of the bond. For example, it might be that the 1-year forward rate for the first year of the bond's life is 10% and that the 1-year forward rate for the second year of the bond's life is approximately 6%. The geometric mean of these two 1-year forward rates would be 7.98%, which is also the yield to maturity. Forward rates are discussed in more detail in Section 15-1. The geometric mean is discussed in more detail in Section 8-1.

Notice that the numerator contains two coupon payments (i.e., the *annual* interest) plus the difference between the bond's value at maturity ($1000) and the current bond price, divided by the number of years to maturity. Thus, the numerator represents an attempt to measure the average annual cash flow to the bondholders. The denominator represents the average of the current price and the value of the bond at maturity— again, this is a crude approximation of the bondholders' average investment in the bond, assuming the bond is held until maturity. While the AYTM represents only a rough approximation of the true YTM, it does have the advantage of being relatively easy to calculate. For example, suppose we are interested in estimating the YTM for a 10% bond due in 20 years and priced at $900. Using Equation (14-2), the approximate yield to maturity is

$$\text{AYTM} = \frac{\$100 + [(\$1000 - 900)/20]}{(\$1000 + 900)/2} = \frac{\$105}{\$950} = .111 = 11.1\%$$

Notice that the $105 in the numerator includes the $100 annual interest, plus $5 which represents the change in the current bond price to the maturity value of $1000 averaged over the life of the bond. The $950 in the denominator approximates the average investment bondholders will have in the bond if they buy the bond at its current price of $900 and hold it until maturity when the $1000 principal amount will be paid.

While the AYTM has the advantage of being easy to calculate, it should be obvious that it represents only an approximation of the true YTM. The longer the life of the bond and the larger the difference between the current price and the $1000 maturity value, the greater will be the difference between the AYTM and the true yield to maturity.

14-3-2 Estimating YTM by Interpolation　Solving for the actual YTM for bonds is the same process as solving for the internal rate of return, which is a standard problem in most beginning finance textbooks. In words, one needs to identify the semiannual rate of return $r/2$, which will discount all the bond's future cash flows to its current price. To do this, one simply guesses at the rate of return, discounts the bond's cash flows, and compares this value with the current price. If this value is higher than the current price, a higher discount rate must be used; if the value is lower than the current price, a lower discount rate must be used. Once values both higher and lower than the current price are found, one knows that the YTM must fall some- where between the two discount rates and one can interpolate to get a close approx- imation of the true YTM.

To illustrate, consider the previous example of the 10%, 20-year bond selling at $900. As a starting point, what should we guess for a discount rate? Fortunately, with respect to bonds, we can make some intelligent guesses. We *know* that if a 10% semiannual discount rate (i.e., $r/2 = 5\%$) is used to discount a 10% coupon bond, the value of the bond's future cash flows will be $1000, or par value. (If this isn't clear, go back and review the very first example in Chapter 10.) We also know that since the bond is selling below par, the YTM must be greater than the coupon rate of

10% in our example. Further, since we calculated the AYTM to be 11.1%, there is a good chance that 12% will be higher than the true YTM. Thus, the true YTM will probably lie somewhere between 10% and 12%, and we can solve for it by interpolating, as follows: First, calculate the value of the bond using a 12% semiannual discount rate in Equation (14-1a).

$$P_0 = C \cdot \text{PVAF}_{r/2,2n} + \$1000\text{PVDF}_{r/2,2n}$$
$$= \$50\text{PVAF}_{.06,40} + \$1000\text{PVDF}_{.06,40}$$
$$= \$50(15.046) + \$1000(.097) = \$849.54$$

Second, interpolate for the YTM (r) as follows:

$$2\% \begin{bmatrix} \text{at } r = 10\% & P_0 = \$1000 \\ \text{at } r = \text{YTM} & P_0 = \$\ 900 \\ \text{at } r = 12\% & P_0 = \$\ 849.54 \end{bmatrix} 100 \end{bmatrix} 150.46$$

$$\text{YTM} = 10\% + \frac{100}{150.46}(2\%) = 11.33\%$$

Thus, we would estimate the YTM as 11.33% discounted semiannually. As always with interpolation, the narrower the brackets, the closer your answer will be to the true YTM. In this example the true YTM is 11.268%.[11] If the interpolation had been performed between brackets of 11% and 11.5%, the YTM would have been calculated to be 11.273%. However, for most purposes interpolating between brackets separated by 1 or 2% will provide an estimate of the YTM that is close enough.

Before continuing, you should:
1 Understand the term collateral and the various types of fixed-income securities which have collateral provisions
2 Understand how call provisions and sinking fund provisions work
3 Be aware of various types of restrictive covenants
4 Know how to estimate a bond's yield to maturity by using the AYTM method and by using interpolation
5 To prove to yourself that you understand the mathematics of bond pricing and YTM, show that a 12% coupon bond with 5 years to maturity and priced at par provides a 12% YTM using both the AYTM method and interpolation

---

[11]The true YTM is found by an iterative process of using successively smaller and smaller brackets. Fortunately, modern computers and some hand-held calculators are very good at this iterative process, and the exact YTM can be determined fairly easily now. In addition, bond tables also provide a very close estimate of the true YTM.

14-4 BOND YIELDS

Having discussed the different classes of bonds and some of their unique characteristics, we can now proceed to the interesting topic of how investors determine bond yields. Remember that the discount rates or yields to maturity in Equations (14-1) and (14-2) represent ex ante returns rather than ex post or actual, realized yields. The distinction between promised and realized yields and the role of coupon reinvestment is crucial to understanding bond returns. (In the language of bonds, the term *promised yield* is frequently used in lieu of *yield to maturity*.)

When an investor computes the yield to maturity on a bond, several simplifying assumptions are implicitly made. These are:

1 All coupon and principal payments are made on schedule.
2 The bond is held to maturity.
3 The coupon payments are fully and immediately reinvested at *precisely* the same interest rate as the promised yield to maturity.

Any violation of these assumptions will cause the yield to maturity that is eventually realized (hereafter realized yield) to differ from the promised yield.

14-4-1 Payment Assumption
The first assumption, that *coupon and principal payments will be made on schedule*, deals with the issue of default. The specter of default casts a long shadow on the first assumption underlying the bond formulas. If the bond issuer delays paying or fails to pay coupon interest and principal as scheduled, the realized yield will fall short of the promised yield. We shall examine default risk at some length in Chapter 15.

14-4-2 Holding-Period Assumption
The second assumption, concerning *holding the bond to maturity*, may be violated by either the issuer or the investor. The issuer may call the bond if interest rates fall substantially or the investor may choose to hold the bond for a period shorter than the time to maturity. First, consider a bond with a call provision. Given that the issuer may call the bond prior to maturity, the investor should be interested in both the promised yield to maturity and the promised yield to the first date at which the bond is eligible for call. In a fashion similar to the approximate yield to maturity, the *approximate yield to first call* (AYFC) is calculated as follows:

$$\text{AYFC} = \frac{2C + [(P_c - P_0)/N_c]}{(P_c + P_0)/2} \tag{14-3}$$

where the semiannual coupon C, call price P_c, current price P_0, and number of years to first call N_c are known. The AYFC is a rough approximation of the true promised yield to first call, which can be calculated using the process of interpolation and the bond price formula. For a callable bond with semiannual coupons, the bond price formula (assuming the bond will be called) is

$$P_0 = \sum_{t=1}^{2N_c} \frac{C}{(1 + r/2)^t} + \frac{P_c}{(1 + r/2)^{2N_c}} \tag{14-4}$$

where t represents each 6-month period and r is the appropriate discount rate.

To illustrate, suppose an investor wants to find the promised yield to first call of a 14% debenture, callable in 5 years at 114 with a current price of 101. Using Equation (14-3), the approximate yield to first call is

$$\text{AYFC} = \frac{\$140 + [(1140 - 1010)/5]}{(1140 + 1010)/2} = \frac{116}{1075} = 15.4\%$$

If the investor chooses the more precise route of interpolation, the promised yield to call is computed in three steps. First, since the approximate yield to first call was 15.4%, compute the bond price for, say, 16%.

$$P_0 = C \cdot \text{PVAF}_{r/2,2N_c} + \$1140\text{PVDF}_{r/2,2N_c}$$
$$= \$70\text{PVAF}_{.08,10} + \$1140\text{PVDF}_{.08,10}$$
$$= \$70(6.710) + 1140(.463) = \$997.75$$

Second, use a lower discount rate, say 14%, to determine a price which is higher than the current market price of $1010. At 14% the price would be $1071.17—the reader should verify this.[12] Third, having bracketed the market price, interpolate for the promised yield to first call (YFC) as follows:

$$2\% \begin{bmatrix} \text{at } r = 14\% & P_0 = \$1071.17 \\ \text{at } r = \text{YFC} & P_0 = \$1010 \\ \text{at } r = 16\% & P_0 = \$997.75 \end{bmatrix} 61.17 \Bigg] 73.42$$

$$\text{YFC} = 14\% + \frac{61.17}{73.42}(2\%) = 15.67\%$$

The fact that the yield to first call (15.67%) is greater than the bond's coupon rate of 14% does not necessarily mean investors will be better off if the bonds are called. The issuer will not call the bonds unless interest rates have fallen enough below the original 14% coupon rate to justify paying the call price of 114. Thus, the holder of the bonds will be faced with the problem of reinvesting the proceeds of the called bonds at lower interest rates. Whether or not the bondholder will be better off depends upon how low current interest rates are and the length of time the bondholder needs to reinvest the proceeds.

---

[12]Recall from the preceding section that when estimating the yield to maturity, using a discount rate equal to the coupon rate will always result in a price equal to par value, or $1000. However, when estimating the yield to call, the price will always be greater than par, as can be seen by this example; i.e., at 14% (the coupon rate) the price is equal to $1071. This is because when bonds are called, the investor receives the call price ($1140 in this example), which is greater than the par value that the investor receives if the bond is held to maturity.

Now consider the case where the investor purchases a bond at par on the date of issue, or on a coupon date (thus eliminating the problem of *accrued interest*[13]), and *plans to sell the bond before maturity*. Since bond prices vary with changes in interest rates, the market value of the bond when the investor sells is usually different from par value. Thus, if a bond is sold before maturity, the return from holding the bond is both the coupon interest and the change in price. The price change component of bond return may cause promised and realized yields to differ. If investors expect interest rates to change, they may utilize the expected sales price to compute a promised yield.

If an investor has a holding period which is less than maturity, the bond price and yield formulas become

$$APY = \frac{2C + [(P_s - P_0)/N_s]}{(P_s + P_0)/2} \tag{14-5}$$

$$P_0 = \sum_{t=1}^{2N_s} \frac{C}{(1 + r/2)^t} + \frac{P_s}{(1 + r/2)^{2N_s}} \tag{14-6}$$

where P_s = expected price at end of holding period of N_s years
APY = approximated promised yield

For example, suppose an investor decides to hold a 10-year, 14% debenture for 5 years and expects a price of 120 in 5 years, and the debenture was purchased at par. Using Equation (14-5), the approximate promised yield is

$$APY = \frac{\$140 + [\$(1200 - 1000)/5]}{(\$1200 + \$1000)/2} = \frac{\$180}{\$1100} = 16.4\%$$

If, instead, interest rates rise over the 5-year period and the bond's price is $980 at the end of year 5, the approximate *realized yield* (ARY) is

$$ARY = \frac{\$140 + [(\$980 - \$1000)/5]}{(\$980 + \$1000)/2} = \frac{\$136}{\$990} = 13.7\%$$

If, on the other hand, interest rates fell over the holding period so that the selling price is $1300, the ARY is

$$ARY = \frac{\$140 + [(\$1300 - \$1000)/5]}{(\$1300 + \$1000)/2} = \frac{\$200}{\$1150} = 17.4\%$$

From these examples, it should be readily apparent that interest rate movements will dramatically affect realized yields. Indeed, bond investments bear *price risk*

---

[13]See the Appendix at the end of this chapter for a discussion of accrued interest and how to calculate bond prices on noncoupon dates.

TABLE 14-8   AN ILLUSTRATION OF COUPON REINVESTMENT

Assumptions: 20-year 8% bond bought at par on issue date and held to maturity

Reinvest-ment rate, %	Coupon payments	Interest on interest	F.V. of coupon payments	(3) ÷ (4), %	F.V. of coupon payments + principal	Realized yield, %
(1)	(2)	(3)	(4)	(5)	(6)	(7)
0	$1600	$0	$1600	0	$2600	4.84
5	$1600	$1096	$2696	41	$3696	6.64
6	$1600	$1416	$3016	47	$4016	7.07
7	$1600	$1782	$3382	53	$4382	7.53
8	$1600	$2201	$3801	58	$4801	8.00
9	$1600	$2681	$4281	63	$5281	8.50
10	$1600	$3232	$4832	67	$5832	9.01

F.V. = future value.

The reinvestment rate and the realized yield are expressed as a stated annual rate. For example, a reinvestment rate of 5% implies that each of the 40 coupons is reinvested at 2½% compounded semiannually; a realized yield of 4.84% implies a semiannual return of 2.42%.

Source: Adapted from S. Homer and M. L. Leibowitz, *Inside the Yield Book*, Prentice-Hall, Englewood Cliffs, N.J., 1972, table 1.

whenever the investor chooses not to hold the bond until maturity. And the more volatile interest rates are, the greater the uncertainty that future market prices will not match expected prices.

14-4-3 Coupon Reinvestment   Coupon reinvestment refers to the third assumption required in order for promised yields to equal realized yields; namely, *coupons are immediately and fully reinvested and at interest rates equal to those prevailing when the bond was issued.* This assumption may be violated for several reasons. First, complete reinvestment of coupons is simply impossible to attain in most cases owing to commission costs and taxes. Coupon payments, with the exception of government and municipal bonds, are subject to federal and local income taxes.[14] The search for a bond with similar characteristics and the commission costs of buying a new bond also cause promised yields to exceed realized yields. The only bond which has almost complete coupon reinvestment is the zero-coupon bond.[15]

Second, and more importantly, since interest rates are not stable from week to week, the assumption that coupons are reinvested at a stable rate over the life of the bond is consistently violated. For example, suppose a 9% bond is purchased at a 9.5% promised yield to maturity. To earn a 9.5% realized yield over the life of the bond, investors must reinvest the $45 semiannual coupons at 9.5%. Table 14-8 illustrates

[14]Coupons on U.S. government bonds are exempt from state and local taxes, and municipal coupons are exempt from federal, state, and often local taxes.

[15]Unfortunately, even zero-coupon bonds do not provide complete protection from the reinvestment problem. For tax purposes, each year investors must amortize part of the discount and treat this amortization as taxable income.

the impact the reinvestment rate can have on realized yields. In this example, an investor is assumed to have purchased a 20-year 8% bond at par.

If the investor reinvests the coupons at a zero rate of return, the realized yield based on his total return is only 4.84% compounded semiannually, well below the coupon rate of 8% on the bonds he bought at par.[16] Conversely, the realized yield is 9.01% if the investor is able to reinvest the coupons at 10%. Only when the coupons are reinvested at exactly the promised yield to maturity (in this case 8%, since the bond was purchased at par) will the realized yield actually equal the promised yield. Also, note the relative importance of interest earned on the reinvested coupons. Column 5 lists the percentage of the total future value of the coupons represented by the "interest on interest." For example, at a 10% reinvestment rate, interest earned on the reinvested coupons represents 67% of the total future value of the coupons.

Thus, bond returns have three distinct components: coupon payments, the interest from coupon reinvestment, and the change in price. The coupon reinvestment income varies directly with interest rates. An unexpected rise in interest rates will increase the income from coupon reinvestment. Thus, coupon reinvestment risk represents the uncertainty of the levels of interest rates at which the coupons are reinvested. Notice that price risk and coupon reinvestment have opposite effects on total bond return as interest rates change—for example, an increase in interest rates will increase the interest earned on reinvestment coupons but will decrease the price of the bond. These relationships are particularly important to *immunization* strategies, which are discussed in Chapter 16.

Investors and bond issuers in recent years have recognized that volatile interest rates increase coupon reinvestment risk. The use of zero-coupon bonds (called zeros) and other discount bonds has come into vogue to reduce coupon reinvestment risk. Table 14-9 illustrates how smaller coupons result in higher realized yields if interest rates decline because discount bonds in effect automatically reinvest the amount of the discount at a rate equal to the original promised yield. Of course, the opposite would hold true if interest rates rose. Zeros offer investors a situation where promised and realized yields are identical (assuming the bonds are held to maturity and don't default) and also reduce call risk. However, the prices of zeros and other discount bonds are extremely volatile, since a greater part of the total return of these bonds rests on the principal payment due at maturity, the present value of which is affected more by interest rate changes than is the present value of coupon payments due in the near future.

---

[16]To calculate the realized yield, simply solve for the rate which discounts the future value of all the coupons and the principal to the price paid, which is $1000 in this example. For the 0% reinvestment rate example, set

$$1000 = \frac{1600 + 1000}{(1 + r/2)^{40}}$$

and solve for r. Recall that for a bond, coupons are paid semiannually; thus we use $r/2$, and the number of semiannual time periods is equal to twice the number of years to maturity.

TABLE 14-9 REALIZED YIELDS TO MATURITY FOR 20-YEAR
BONDS WITH VARIOUS COUPONS
Assuming the reinvestment rates drop from 16 to 12%
after 10 years

Coupon rate, %	Realized yield to maturity, %
16	14.248
15	14.254
14	14.261
13	14.270
12	14.279
11	14.290
10	14.303
9	14.319
8	14.338
7	14.362
6	14.392
5	14.435
4	14.495
3	14.581
2	14.728
1	15.029
0	16.000

Source: A. Silver, "Original Issue Deep Discount Bonds,"
Federal Reserve Bank of New York Quarterly Review (winter
1981–1982).

14-5 SUMMARY

The large number of different money market securities, bonds, and notes, and their associated risk and return characteristics provide investors with a great variety of investment possibilities. In order to take advantage of the opportunities for investing in fixed-income securities, one must first become acquainted with their unique features. Thus, the first part of this chapter provided a brief description of the more important types of fixed-income securities.

Intuitively, one might expect that fixed-income securities are less risky than common stocks and therefore have generated lower returns in the past. In fact, the historical record bears out this intuition. However, in more recent years interest rates have been unusually high and volatile. This market environment has substantially increased the challenge to the manager of bond portfolios.

We discussed the mathematics for computing the promised yield to maturity, or what is generally referred to as *the* yield to maturity. However, for the actual return realized by the bond investor to equal the promised yield to maturity, several things must happen. The most important requirements are that the investor must hold the bond to maturity and interest rates must remain constant over the remaining life of the bond. Of course, bonds may be called away or the investor may simply sell the bond before it matures. Either action will violate the first requirement for promised yields to equal realized yields.

In addition, interest rates obviously change over time. When such changes occur, coupons will be reinvested at rates other than the promised yield to maturity which existed at the time the bond was purchased. This will result in realized yields differing from promised yields.

This chapter presented an introduction to some of the basic knowledge needed to study fixed-income securities. The next chapter presents additional topics which should be understood by the fixed-income analyst. These topics include the term structure of interest rates and the risk structure of bonds, as well as issues such as marketability and taxes. The final chapter in this part of the book dealing with fixed-income securities will present a number of specific bond trading strategies.

SUGGESTED READINGS

The following are good, practical treatments of bonds and how they are used in constructing portfolios:

D. Darst, *The Complete Bond Book*, McGraw-Hill, New York, 1975.

H. G. Fong, ''Portfolio Construction: Fixed Income,'' Chapter 9 in J. Magin and D. Tuttle, *Managing Investment Portfolios, A Dynamic Process*, Warren, Gorham & Lamong, Boston, 1983.

An excellent description of most money market securities is:

T. Q. Cook and B. J. Summers, *Instruments of the Money Market*, Federal Reserve Bank of Richmond, 1981.

A thought-provoking article on the risk associated with municipal bonds is:

J. L. Treynor, ''On the Quality of Municipal Bonds,'' *Financial Analysts Journal* (May/June 1982).

QUESTIONS

1 If common stocks have provided, on average, higher returns than fixed-income securities, why should investors understand fixed-income securities?

2 Fixed-income securities always have lower returns than common stock. Comment.

3 Why do money market securities have different rates of return?

4 What are participation certificates and why are they important?

5 If the yield on a U.S. Treasury bond is 13.50%, what yield would an investor in the 40% tax bracket require as a minimum to invest in municipal bonds?

6 Compare and contrast corporate bonds and preferred stock.

7 Go to today's newspaper and compute the current yield to maturity for a bond of your choice using the AYTM method.

8 Why do investors gain confidence in the credit-worthiness of an issue of mortgage bonds even though the property which is mortgaged is illiquid?

9 If interest rates are low and are expected to rise, what is the value of a call provision to a bond issuer?

10 How does a sinking fund reduce the risk borne by investors? How does it increase risk?

11 Why is it highly unlikely that promised and realized yields will be equal?

PROBLEMS

1 A 6% coupon bond with 20 years to maturity is currently selling for $900. Estimate the yield to maturity (*a*) using the AYTM method and (*b*) by interpolation.

2 A 12%, 20-year debenture has a 10-year call deferment after which the bonds are callable at 110. If the current price is 96, compute the approximate yield to first call and the approximate yield to maturity.

3 From the information in Question 2, determine the exact promised yield.

4 What is the realized yield to maturity for a 10%, 5-year debenture bought at par if the bondholder fails to reinvest the coupons?

5 What is the realized yield to maturity of a 10%, 10-year bond bought at par if the reinvestment rate is 8% for the life of the bond?

6 What is the accrued interest on May 10, 1983, for an 8% coupon bond which pays interest on June 30 and December 31? Hint: See the Appendix.

7 What is the price of the bond in Question 6 if it matures on December 31, 1990, and its yield to maturity is 10%?

APPENDIX: Accrued Interest

The owner of a bond on the coupon payment date is entitled to receive the coupon, whether or not she has owned the bond for the entire previous 6-month period. Obviously many bond transactions in the secondary markets will occur on noncoupon payment dates. As the transaction date extends beyond the coupon date, the seller of the bond gives up an increasingly large fraction of the next coupon payment. In order to compensate the seller for the accrued fraction of the next coupon due her, bonds sell with *accrued interest*.

By convention, accrued interest is calculated as the coupon payment multiplied by the fraction of a semiannual period represented by the time of the transaction date beyond the most recent coupon date. To illustrate, let M equal the number of *complete* months until the next coupon payment date and D equal the number of days remaining in the current month. By convention, complete months are assumed to equal 30 days and a semiannual time period is assumed to equal 180 days.[17] Thus, the number of days remaining in any semiannual time period is equal to $30M + D$ and the number of days for which interest is accrued is equal to $180 - (30M + D)$. If C is equal to the dollar amount of a coupon payment, the accrued interest (AI) is computed as follows:

$$AI = C\frac{180 - (30M + D)}{180} \qquad (14A\text{-}1)$$

For example, suppose a 12% bond which pays interest on June 30 and December 31 of each year was purchased on January 15. In this case, $C = \$60$, $M = 5$, and $D = 16$. The accrued interest would be $4.67, calculated as follows:

$$AI = \$60\frac{180 - [(30)(5) + 16]}{180} = \$60\frac{14}{180} = \$4.67$$

[17] Accrued interest for corporate bonds, municipal bonds, and many federal agency bonds is calculated on the basis of a 30-day month, 180-day semiannual period. However, accrued interest for U.S. Treasury notes and bonds is calculated according to the exact number of days between coupon payments.

When bonds sell with accrued interest, the method of computing bond prices becomes more complicated. To determine the bond price based on the promised yield to maturity, perform the following steps:

1 Calculate the bond price using Equation (14-1) *as of the next coupon payment date*.
2 Add the coupon payment received on the next payment date.
3 Discount this sum back to the current date.
4 Finally, subtract from the above total the accrued interest which the buyer will have to pay the seller.

This process can be expressed mathematically in the following manner:

$$P_0 = \frac{\displaystyle\sum_{t=1}^{2N} \frac{C_t}{1 + r/2)^t} + \frac{1000}{(1 + r/2)^{2N}} + C}{(1 + r/2)^{(30M + D)/180}} - C\frac{180 - (30M + D)}{180} \tag{14A-2}$$

where N = number of years to maturity *after* the next coupon date
r = promised yield to maturity compounded semiannually

Notice that the first two terms in the numerator represent the price of the bond as of the next coupon date, which added to the coupon received on that date represents the total present value on the next coupon date. This amount is then discounted back to the present date, and the accrued interest is subtracted from this value. To illustrate, suppose the bond mentioned earlier was purchased on January 15, 1980 and matured on December 31, 1999, and that the expected yield to maturity was 10%. In this case, $N = 19\frac{1}{2}$ years, and the current price would be \$1171.38, calculated as follows:

$$\begin{aligned}
P_0 &= \frac{\displaystyle\sum_{t=1}^{39} \frac{60}{(1.05)^t} + \frac{1000}{(1.05)^{39}} + 60}{(1.05)^{166/180}} - 60\left(\frac{14}{180}\right) \\
&= \frac{1021.02 + 149.15 + 60}{(1.05)^{166/180}} - 4.67 = 1171.38
\end{aligned}$$

If the current market price is known, one can solve for the promised yield to maturity r using Equation (14A-2) and interpolation.

CHAPTER 15

DETERMINANTS
OF BOND YIELDS

After reading this chapter, you should:

1 Understand the primary determinants of bond yields
2 Be aware of the three theories concerning the term structure of interest rates
3 Know how to calculate a bond's duration
4 Understand the relationship between duration and bond price volatility

Four factors largely determine bond yields: (1) term to maturity, (2) default risk, (3) marketability, and (4) tax treatment. If we hold three factors constant, the impact of the remaining factor on yields becomes apparent. For example, if two bonds are identical except for default risk and sell at different yields, the difference in yields is attributable to the risk structure difference. To isolate the impact of each factor, we shall consider each factor separately with the assumption that the other three factors are held constant.

In addition, this chapter will examine the concept of duration, which is an alternative measure of the "length" of a bond. Since duration is also a measure of bond volatility, it is a concept that every bond investor should understand.

15-1 THE TERM STRUCTURE OF INTEREST RATES

The phrase "term structure of interest rates" refers to the yields of bonds which are identical except for maturity dates; i.e., their terms to maturity differ.

Investors sometimes evaluate yields of bonds with differing maturities by drawing what is called a *yield curve*. This is typically done by plotting yield and maturity for fixed-income U.S. government securities. Figure 15-1 shows the yield curve as of August 30, 1985, for U.S. Treasury notes and bonds. The shape of the curve is upward-sloping. An upward-sloping yield curve, which tends to exist during recessions or periods of early economic recovery, indicates that long-term interest rates exceed short-term rates. Occasionally, during periods of economic prosperity, yield curves slope downward, reflecting the fact that long-term interest rates are less than short-term rates.

Using the expectations theory we can infer implicit future short-term rates from the yield curve. But, to see this, one needs to first understand the difference between forward rates and spot rates.

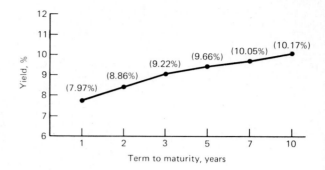

FIGURE 15-1 Yield curve for U.S. Treasury notes and bonds for the week ending Aug. 30, 1985. *(Source: Federal Reserve Bulletin, November 1985, p. A27.)*

15-1-1 Forward and Spot Rates   Recall that in Chapter 1 we argued that the rate of return investors require to invest is a function of three factors:

1 The time preference for consumption as measured by the real, risk-free rate of return
2 The expected rate of inflation
3 The risk associated with the investment

Thus, the required rate of return, which is the discount rate used in determining security prices, can be written as

$$r_t = \left(\begin{array}{c}\text{risk-free}\\\text{real rate}\end{array}\right)_t + \left(\begin{array}{c}\text{expected}\\\text{inflation}\end{array}\right)_t + \left(\begin{array}{c}\text{risk}\\\text{premium}\end{array}\right)_t$$

where the subscript t denotes a specific time period. A *spot rate* is the discount rate or required return quoted for the *current period*. For example, a 6-month T-bill has a current spot rate which indicates that a certain rate of return will be received by the holder of the T-bill over the next 6 months.

The discount rate for a future time period r_t is called a *forward rate*. For example, suppose a corporate treasurer knew that 1 year from now her firm would have excess cash to invest for a period of 3 months. Consequently, she might be interested in the forward rate for 90 day T-bills 1 year from now. Using the expectations theory (which is discussed in the next section) she could solve for the *implicit* forward rate. Or, based on the prices of *futures contracts* for T-bills, she could *explicitly* determine forward rates. Table 15-1 lists the prices and yields associated with futures contracts for T-bills as of November 27, 1985. The seller of a T-bill futures contract promises the buyer that at some future date she will be able to buy T-bills at a specified price and consequently a specified yield. For example, in Table 15-1 the futures contract price for 90-day T-bills maturing in March 1986 was $92.98. This price would provide the buyer a 7.02% (annualized) rate of return. In other words, on November 27, 1985, it was possible to "lock in" a forward rate of return for the first 3 months of 1986. Thus, by examining futures contracts for T-bills and other financial instruments, one can explicitly determine forward rates.

TABLE 15-1   FUTURES CONTRACT PRICES FOR 90-DAY T-BILLS (AS OF NOVEMBER 27, 1985)
[Treasury Bills (IMM)—$1 Million; Pts of 100%]

	Open	High	Low	Settle	Chg.	Discount Settle	Discount Chg.	Open interest
Dec.	92.94	93.00	92.92	92.96	+.01	7.04	−.01	17,080
Mar. 86	92.95	93.01	92.93	92.98	+.02	7.02	−.02	17,624
June	92.74	92.81	92.74	92.80	+.04	7.20	−.04	3,527
Sept.	92.50	92.52	92.50	92.52	+.04	7.48	−.04	1,076
Dec.	92.19	92.23	92.19	92.23	+.04	7.77	−.04	362
Mar. 87	—	—	—	91.68	+.05	8.32	−.05	214

Source: Wall Street Journal, November 29, 1985.

When calculating yields to maturity, we have previously assumed that forward rates are constant for each future time period. For example, for an 8% bond priced at par, each semiannual cash flow was assumed to be discounted at 4%. However, there is no reason, other than convenience, to assume that discount rates are the same for each time period.

To illustrate, consider the case of U.S. Treasury bonds for which there is no significant default risk and consequently we will assume no risk premium is involved in the required rate of return r_t. To further simplify the problem, assume that the expected real rate is constant. Given these assumptions, the forward rate for any particular time period is equal to the constant real rate plus the expected inflation rate for the time period in question. Since inflation rates have, in the past, varied substantially from period to period, investors will most likely have different inflation expectations for different future time periods. For example, assume that investors anticipate a constant real rate of 3% and that for the upcoming year (year 1) they anticipate an 8% inflation rate, but expect the inflation rate to drop to 6% in the second year. If this were the case, the forward rates investors would use in discounting risk-free government bonds would be

$$r_1 = 3\% + 8\% = 11\%$$
$$r_2 = 3\% + 6\% = 9\%$$

This is not just a theoretical exercise. As can be seen from Table 15-1, forward rates do, in fact, vary. On November 27, 1985, the forward rates for 90-day T-bills ranged from 7.02% for the March 1986 T-bill to 8.32% for the March 1987 T-bill.

Now, as a prelude to the expectations theory, we will examine how implicit forward rates might be estimated. The implicit forward rates associated with bonds of different maturities can be easily determined from current bond prices. Assume that two zero-coupon U.S. Treasury bonds sell today at the following prices:

1-year bond: $909.09
2-year bond: $857.63

Since both bonds are zero-coupon bonds, both promise only to pay $1000 at the end of their respective term to maturity.

The forward rate r_1 for the first year can be calculated in the same manner as any one-period rate of return using the 1-year bond:

$$\$909.09 = \frac{\$1000}{1 + r_1}$$

$$r_1 = \frac{\$1000}{\$909.09} - 1 = .10 = 10\%$$

Thus, the nominal rate of return for the first year required by investors purchasing U.S. Treasury bonds is 10%. Using r_1 and the 2-year bond price, we can determine the forward rate for the second year r_2 as follows:

$$\$857.63 = \frac{\$1000}{(1 + r_1)(1 + r_2)}$$

$$1 + r_2 = \frac{\$1000}{(1 + r_1)\$857.63} = \frac{\$1000}{(1.10)\$857.63}$$

$$r_2 = \frac{\$909.09}{\$857.63} - 1 = .06 = 6\%$$

The prices of these two bonds imply that investors require 10% to postpone consumption in the first year and 6% to postpone consumption in the second year. Given our assumption that the real rate is constant, investors must expect a lower inflation rate for the second year in this example. If the real rate fluctuates, the combination of the real rate and inflation is expected to be 4% less in the second year than in the first year.

15-1-2 The Expectations Theory   One of three major explanations of term structure of interest rates is the expectations theory. When investing in fixed-income securities, one option available to an investor with, say, a 3-year time horizon is to simply buy a bond with a 3-year maturity. However, several other options exist. The investor could buy a 1-year bond, reinvest the proceeds after the first year in a second 1-year bond, and reinvest the proceeds at the end of the second year into a third 1-year bond.[1] The *expectations theory* argues that the investor should expect to receive the same return from either strategy. Mathematically, the expectations theory states that

$$(1 + r_{1,n})^n = (1 + r_1)(1 + r_2) \cdots (1 + r_n) \qquad (15\text{-}1)$$

where the notation $r_{1,n}$ represents the yield to maturity for a bond beginning in the current time period and maturing in time period n. Note that the left-hand side of

---

[1]A third option would be to initially invest in a 2-year bond and reinvest at the end of the second year in a 1-year bond; a fourth option would be to initially invest in a 1-year bond and at the end of the first year reinvest in a 2-year bond. The expectations theory argues that each of these four options should produce the same return over the total time period.

TABLE 15-2   FORWARD RATES BASED UPON THE
EXPECTATIONS THEORY

Bond maturity	Yield to maturity* $r_{1,n}$, %	Implicit forward rates r_t, %	
1 year	7.97	r_1	= 7.97
2 years	8.86	r_2	= 9.76
3 years	9.22	r_3	= 9.94
5 years	9.66	$r_{4,5}$	= 10.32
7 years	10.05	$r_{6,7}$	= 11.03
10 years	10.17	$r_{8,10}$	= 10.45

*Yields for the week ending Aug. 30, 1985.
Source: Federal Reserve Bulletin, November 1985, p. A24.

Equation (15-1) represents the future value of $1 invested in an *n*-year bond, while the right-hand side represents the future value of $1 invested in a series of 1-year bonds over a period of *n* years.

To illustrate the expectations theory, consider the treasury bonds used to construct the yield curve in Figure 15-1. Table 15-2 lists these bonds and their yields to maturity. In addition, Table 15-2 lists the implicit forward rates r_t based upon this set of bonds. For example, the forward rate in year 2 is calculated as follows:

$$(1 + r_{1,2})^2 = (1 + r_1)(1 + r_2)$$

$$r_2 = \frac{(1 + r_{1,2})^2}{1 + r_1} - 1 = \frac{(1.0886)^2}{1.0797} - 1 = 9.76\%$$

Thus, based on the expectations theory, the forward rates are 7.97% in year 1, 9.76% in year 2, and 9.94% in year 3. Since the data do not include a 4-year bond, we cannot calculate the forward rate for year 4. However, by using the 5-year bond, we can calculate the *average* rate for the two years 4 and 5, which we will denote $r_{4,5}$. This turns out to be 10.32%, calculated as follows:

$$r_{4,5} = \left[\frac{(1.0966)^5}{(1.0922)^3} \right]^{1/2} - 1 = 10.32\%$$

In a similar fashion, the average forward rate for years 6 and 7 is calculated to be 11.03%, and the average rate for years 8, 9, and 10 is calculated to be 10.45%.[2]

---

[2]The average rate in years 8, 9, and 10 is solved for as follows:

$$(1 + r_{1,7})^7(1 + r_{8,10})^3 = (1 + r_{1,10})^{10}$$

$$r_{8,10} = \left(\frac{(1.1017)^{10}}{(1.1005)^7} \right)^{1/3} - 1 = 10.45\%$$

Based on this analysis, the implicit forward rates progressively increase for at least the next 7 years. Assuming that the real rate is constant and that these bonds are riskless, it would appear that investors in August 1985 expected progressively higher rates of inflation for the next several years.

Note that the expectations theory suggests that implicit forward rates reflect the market's consensus of expected future spot rates. In other words, implicit forward rates reflect investor expectations. Figure 15-2 depicts three possible yield curves. Based on the previous analysis, and assuming the expectations theory is correct, an upward-sloping yield curve implies that investors expect interest rates to rise in the future; a flat yield curve suggests investors expect no significant change in interest rates; and a downward-sloping curve implies that investors expect future spot rates to fall.

15-1-3 The Liquidity Premium Theory   A second explanation of the term structure of interest rates is the liquidity premium theory. History has shown that upward-sloping yield curves tend to occur more frequently. Under the expectations theory, this would imply that, on average, investors expect interest rates to rise. However, this is inconsistent with the fact that over the long run, spot rates have not exhibited any trend. Perhaps something else is contained in the implicit forward rates. To explain this historical pattern of generally rising yield curves but trendless spot rates, the liquidity premium theory was advanced. The liquidity premium theory states that investors demand a yield premium as compensation for investing longer-term. This is because investors are risk-averse and presumably believe that short-term securities carry less risk than long-term securities. Thus, a higher rate of return on long-term securities is necessary to attract investors.

Figure 15-3 shows this tendency. The expected spot rate is the rate investors expect to prevail when a particular time period becomes the current time period. Figure 15-3 depicts three possibilities: Investors expect spot rates to rise over time, to remain constant ("flat") over time, or to fall over time. Note that in each case, the implicit forward rates exceed the expected spot rates by the amount of the liquidity premium. Therefore, under the liquidity premium theory, forward rates include both investor

FIGURE 15-2   Expectations theory of term structure.

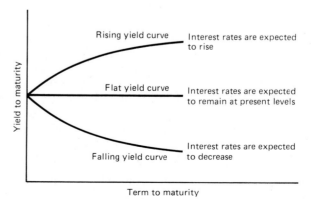

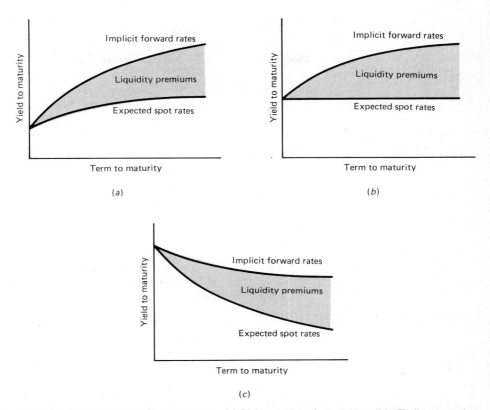

FIGURE 15-3   Liquidity premium theory of term structure. (*a*) Rising expected spot rates. (*b*) "Flat" expected
spot rates. (*c*) Falling expected spot rates.

expectations of future spot rates and liquidity premiums. Typically, this theory argues
that investors demand larger liquidity premiums as the term to maturity lengthens,
presumably because greater risk is associated with longer-term bonds.

Since the yield curve is constructed using government bonds, it is difficult to argue
that longer-term bonds contain greater default risk. The Treasury will always be able
to pay the nominal promised principal and interest (barring a collapse in our political
system) because of Congress's power to create money. However, a case can be made
that longer-term bonds do bear more risk associated with changes in interest rates. As
demonstrated in Chapter 14, the rate at which coupons are reinvested has a substantial
effect on the realized return, and the longer-term the bond, the greater the impact of
interest on interest. And, as we will show in Sections 15-5 and 15-6, longer-term
bonds have longer durations and consequently greater price variations for a given
change in interest rates. Thus, while long-term government bonds may not have any
more default risk than short-term bonds, they do have greater interest rate risk. This
would justify the existence of a liquidity premium for long-term bonds and help explain
why we generally observe upward-sloping yield curves.

15-1-4 The Segmentation Theory The segmentation theory explains term structure as a series of habitats or preference zones which certain investors select depending on term to maturity. For example, an investor with funds which are not needed for 5 years would choose securities with a 5-year maturity. Another investor might prefer a longer-term segment of the bond market. The demand and supply conditions for bonds within the distinct segments determine yields, and investors will switch habitats only if the lure of significantly higher expected risk-adjusted returns exists. Thus, the segmentation theory suggests that the yield curve reflects both the market's expectation of future short-term rates and the risk premiums necessary to cause habitat shifting.

The empirical evidence regarding which of these three theories best explains the term structure of interest rates is mixed. The most recent Ibbotson Sinquefield data suggests that there has not been any significant *realized* liquidity premium since long-term government bonds averaged 4.1% and T-bills averaged 3.4% over the 1926–1985 period (see Table 14-1). However, the ex ante yield curve is, on average, upward-sloping. Other studies suggest that preferred habitats exist.[3] A noncommitted conclusion is that expectations, liquidity premiums, and segmentation all may play a role in determining the term structure of interest rates.

15-2 DEFAULT RISK AND BOND YIELDS

Bonds identical except for the risk of default exhibit a pattern of yields that are called the *risk structure of bond yields*. In general, the greater the likelihood of default, the higher a bond's yield. For example, on August 13, 1982, the yield on long-term treasury bonds was 13.07% while long-term corporate bonds averaged 15.46%. The difference between the default-risk-free rate of 13.07% and the average corporate rate of 15.46% reflects investor beliefs concerning the chances that the average corporation will default on the coupon or principal payments.

15-2-1 Default Risk Measurement Investors typically utilize two approaches to measure default risk: (1) judge the financial characteristics of the security and its issuer, and (2) use credit ratings. To judge default risk from the security's and its issuer's financial characteristics, investors generally use a set of ratios compiled from the firm's financial statements. These financial ratios typically focus on such aspects as debt support, profitability, operating efficiency, growth potential, and funds flow. More sophisticated investors derive ranking systems from statistical models.

However, most investors prefer to use credit ratings to assess default risk. Credit rating agencies such as Moody's, Standard & Poor's, and Duff and Phelps offer rating services to bond issuers. The bond issuers pay the rating agency to evaluate the quality of the bond issue in order to increase the information flow to investors and, hopefully, increase the demand for their bonds. The rating agency determines the appropriate bond rating by assessing various factors. For example, Standard & Poor's judges the credit quality of corporate bonds largely by looking at the bond indenture, asset

---

[3]S. Dobson, R. Sutch, and D. Vanderford, "An Evaluation of Alternative Empirical Models for the Term Structure of Interest Rates," *Journal of Finance* (September 1976).

TABLE 15-3   RATING CATEGORIES OF CREDIT AGENCY FIRMS

Moody's	Explanation
Aaa	Best quality
Aa	High quality
A	Higher medium grade
Baa	Medium grade
Ba	Possess speculative elements
B	Generally lack characteristics of desirable investment
Caa	Poor standing; may be in default
Ca	Speculative in a high degree; often in default
C	Lowest grade

Standard & Poor's	Explanation
AAA	Highest grade
AA	High grade
A	Upper medium grade
BBB	Medium grade
BB	Lower medium grade
B	Speculative
CCC–CC	Outright speculation
C	Reserved for income bonds
DDD–DD	In default, with rating indicating relative salvage value

protection, financial resources, future earning power, and management.[4] More specifically, Standard & Poor's focuses on cash flow to judge a firm's financial viability.[5] The various rating categories are shown in Table 15-3. Moody's ratings range from Aaa, the highest credit quality, to C, the lowest credit quality or highest default risk. Standard & Poor's highest category is AAA while DDD-DD is their lowest rank.

The rating assigned to a bond issue directly affects its yield. The higher the rating, the lower is the bond's yield. Table 15-4 depicts this relationship during 1985 for municipal and corporate bonds. For example, Aaa-rated corporate bonds sold at an average yield of 11.02% in October 1985, which was 43 basis points lower than the average yield of 11.45% on Aa-rated corporates. This difference in yields is termed the *yield spread*. The yield spread between two rating categories provides us with a measure of the default risk premium. While yield spreads related to default risk are not constant over time, they do remain in the appropriate relative pattern. That is, Aaa-rated bonds always sell at lower yields than Aa bonds, which in turn sell at lower yields than A-rated bonds, and so forth. Investors often use the highest rating category

[4]H. Sherwood, *How Corporate and Municipal Debt Is Rated: An Inside Look at Standard and Poor's Rating System*, Wiley, New York, 1976.
[5]J. Clark, ''Some Recent Trends in Municipal and Corporate Securities Markets: An Interview with Brenton W. Harries, President of Standard and Poor's Corporation,'' *Financial Management* (spring 1976).

TABLE 15-4 BOND YIELDS (%) BY RATING

1985	Municipal				Corporate			
	Aaa	Aa	A	Baa	Aaa	Aa	A	Baa
May	8.52	8.88	9.14	9.54	11.72	12.30	12.70	13.15
June	8.24	8.39	8.60	9.02	10.94	11.46	11.78	12.40
July	8.34	8.55	8.76	9.18	10.97	11.42	11.92	12.43
August	8.49	8.81	9.11	9.50	11.05	11.47	12.00	12.50
September	8.70	9.03	9.33	9.63	11.07	11.46	11.99	12.48
October	8.65	9.00	9.25	9.59	11.02	11.45	11.94	12.36

Source: Moody's Bond Record, November 1985.

as a benchmark yield and compute yield spreads for lower-rated bonds. Thus, in October 1982 the yield spreads for corporate bonds were:

Aa	43 basis points
A	92 basis points
Baa	134 basis points

A number of research studies suggest that the determinants of credit ratings and yield spreads for corporate bonds include (1) debt ratios, (2) earnings levels, (3) earnings variability, (4) interest coverage, and (5) pension obligations.[6] Since about 75% of yield spread and ratings variability are explained with these variables, other subjective factors may play an important role. The yield spread pattern also changes in magnitude over the business cycle; yield spreads widen (narrow) during recessions (prosperous periods). A reasonable explanation of expanding and contracting yield spreads is that during recessions default risk rises more than proportionally for lower-quality firms because of reduced cash flows. Also, investors may become more risk-averse as their wealth decreases during recessions.[7]

It is important to recognize the limitations of credit ratings. First, credit ratings change infrequently. The rating agencies are physically unable to constantly monitor all the firms in the market. Second, the use of credit ratings imposes discrete categories on default risk when, in reality, default risk is a continuous phenomenon. Moody's recognized this in 1982 by adding numbers to the letter system, thereby increasing its number of rating categories from 9 to 19. Nevertheless, this limitation still pertains. Third, owing to time and cost constraints, credit ratings are unable to capture all the characteristics for an issuer and issue.

---

[6]L. Fisher, "Determinants of Risk Premiums on Corporate Bonds," *Journal of Political Economy* (June 1959); J. Ang and K. Patel, "Bond Rating Methods: Comparison and Validation," *Journal of Finance* (May 1975); R. S. Kaplan and G. Urwitz, "Statistical Models of Bond Ratings: A Methodological Inquiry," *Journal of Business* (March 1979); L. J. Martin and G. V. Henderson, "On Bond Ratings and Pension Obligations: A Note," *Journal of Financial and Quantitative Analysis* (December 1983).

[7]D. Jaffee, "Cyclical Variations in the Risk Structure of Interest Rates," *Journal of Monetary Economics* (July 1975).

15-2-2 Bankruptcy Prediction   Investors would like to be able to predict bankruptcies in order to avoid defaults on bonds (and sudden stock price declines). Thus, they look for techniques which forecast imminent corporate failures. These techniques generally fall into two categories: ratio analysis and market risk analysis.

The use of ratio analysis to predict bankruptcy has led sophisticated investors to a set of ratios with predictive ability. While these ratios vary from study to study, the ratios are similar types: profitability, leverage, and liquidity ratios. Management effectiveness is signaled by the profitability ratios. The leverage and liquidity ratios indicate the extent of long- and short-term borrowing. Examples of specific ratios are shown in Table 15-5. By using ratio analysis, these studies found that investors can predict bankruptcy up to 5 years before its occurrence. Of course, the closer to the actual bankruptcy, the greater is the predictive accuracy of the ratio set.

Analyzing market risk is another prediction technique. Rather than using accounting data, market risk analysis utilizes market-derived data to predict corporate failures. The crux of this technique is that increased likelihood of bankruptcy is disclosed by changes in market risk measures such as the variance of the rate of return of a certain stock and its beta. While beyond the scope of this text, the methodology used in one

TABLE 15-5   RATIOS AND BANKRUPTCY PREDICTION

Ratios with predictive ability:

  Moyer study:*
    Working capital/total assets
    Retained earnings/total assets
    Earnings before interest and taxes/total assets

  Altman, Haldeman, and Narayanan study:†
    Equity/total capital
    Current assets/current liabilities
    Retained earnings/total assets
    Earnings before interest and taxes/total interest payments
    Earnings before interest and taxes/total assets
    Total assets
    Stability of earnings (10-year trend)

  Dambolena and Khoury study:‡
    Net profits/sales
    Net profits/total assets
    Fixed assets/net worth and its standard deviation
    Funded debt/net working capital
    Total debt/total assets
    Standard deviation of inventory/net working capital

*R. Moyer, "Forecasting Financial Failure: Reexamination," *Financial Management* (spring 1977).
†E. Altman, R. Haldeman, and P. Narayanan, "Zeta Analysis: A New Model to Identify Bankruptcy Risk of Corporations," *Journal of Banking and Finance* (spring 1977).
‡I. Dambolena and S. Khoury, "Ratio Stability and Corporate Failure," *Journal of Finance* (September 1980).

study[8] to predict bankruptcy was based on observing the variance of stock returns for individual companies. For those firms that eventually went into bankruptcy, the variance of returns increased substantially long before the bankruptcy occurred. Although investors appeared to adjust gradually over a 4-year period to the declining solvency position of bankrupt firms, distinct signals of bankruptcy occurred up to 2 years prior to the event.

15-3 MARKETABILITY

Marketability also influences bond yields, but its effect is more varied and complex than maturity and default risk. In general, the greater the marketability of a bond, the lower is its yield, all other things being equal. We can define marketability, or liquidity, as the ability to buy or sell a bond without significant price concessions. As a general rule, *the larger the size of the bond issue, the greater its marketability*. However, two other factors, market conditions and the degree of substitutability, also affect the marketability of bonds.

Market conditions refer to the general state of the bond or capital markets at a particular time. Market size and transaction rates vary with different market conditions. For example, if interest rates are high, transaction volume may be relatively low owing to issuer reluctance to pay high borrowing costs. While the psychological side of investment is largely unexplored, casual observation suggests that market psychology does influence investor decisions. Investors may exaggerate their pessimism or optimism in their decision processes. Expectations of future inflation rates may vary widely over time, and uncertainty regarding interest rate levels will definitely influence investor psychology. Thus, the ability to buy or sell a bond without price concessions rests, in part, on the general condition of the capital markets.

The *degree of substitutability* is the extent to which investors will shift from security to security because of supply factors. Since both demand and supply factors simultaneously determine bond yields, the willingness of investors to substitute one security for another affects yields. For example, the bonds of the various regional telephone companies might be considered good substitutes. On the other hand, the bonds of a hospital management firm probably would not be considered a good substitute for the bonds of an automobile manufacturer.

Two opposing views of substitution exist: perfect substitution and market segmentation. Perfect substitution refers to the ability of investors to shift quickly among securities to take advantage of supply differences. Conversely, market segmentation is where risk preferences and tax, government, or behavioral constraints cause investors to form distinct clienteles for particular securities. Investors do not shift to other securities because of these constraints. Reality probably lies somewhere in the middle of these two views. Studies of U.S. Treasury, agency, and corporate bonds indicate that relative security supplies have little impact on bond yields.[9] On the other hand,

---

[8]J. Aharony, C. P. Jones, and I. Swary, "An Analysis of Risk and Return Characteristics of Corporate Bankruptcy Using Capital Market Data," *Journal of Finance* (September 1980).

[9]T. Cook and P. Hendershott, "The Impact of Taxes, Risk, and Relative Security Supplies on Interest Rate Differentials," *Journal of Finance* (September 1978); and J. Bildersee, "U.S. Government and Agency Securities: An Analysis of Yield Spreads and Performance," *Journal of Business* (July 1978).

the evidence in the municipal bond market suggests that relative security supplies and investor regulations do affect yield spreads.[10]

15-4 TAXES

A fourth factor which affects bond yields is taxes. Presumably, investors determine rates of return on an after-tax basis. In other words, the evaluation of various investment opportunities depends, in part, on the income tax bracket of the individual investor. We can consider taxes to be similar to commission costs; astute investors seek to minimize both.

Various debt instruments are subject to different forms of taxation. The obvious example is municipal bonds where the coupons are exempt from federal taxes, and also state taxes if the bonds are issued within the state or the state has a reciprocal agreement with adjoining states. To illustrate, assume that an investor has a choice between a corporate bond and a municipal bond. To properly compare yields on an after-tax basis, the investor must convert the corporate yield to an after-tax yield, as follows:

$$r_m = r_c(1 - T) \tag{15-2}$$

where r_m = yield on municipal bond
r_c = corporate bond yield
T = investor's marginal tax rate

If the investor is subject to a 35% marginal tax rate and can purchase a municipal bond yielding 10.25% and a corporate bond yielding 16%, the corporate bond is preferable since its after-tax yield is 10.4%. On the other hand, if the investor faces a 50% marginal tax rate, the corporate after-tax yield of 8% looks paltry compared with the municipal yield of 10.25%. Historically, municipal bond yields have been higher than corporate yields on an after-tax basis for marginal tax rates exceeding 35%.

The differential tax treatment of interest income and capital gains also affects bond yields. In particular, the favorable tax treatment of capital gains makes discount bonds attractive to investors.[11] The higher the discount, the greater is the capital gains' attraction and the lower the bond's yield. Figure 15-4 depicts the relationship between a seasoned 4¼% bond with a capital gains return component and a new bond selling at par. This figure assumes that the investor faces a 20% capital gains rate and a 40% ordinary tax rate. Note that the after-tax return for the seasoned bond with 20 years remaining to maturity is greater than that for a new bond with the same maturity and

---

[10]P. Hendershott and D. Kidwell, "The Impact of Relative Security Supplies," *Journal of Money, Credit and Banking* (August 1978); and D. Kidwell and T. Koch, "The Behavior of the Interest Rate Differential between Tax-Exempt Revenue and General Obligation Bonds: A Test of Risk Preferences and Market Segmentation," *Journal of Finance* (March 1982).

[11]Exceptions are T-bills, other money market instruments, and zero-coupon bonds, all of which sell on a discount basis, but the discount is taxed at ordinary tax rates.

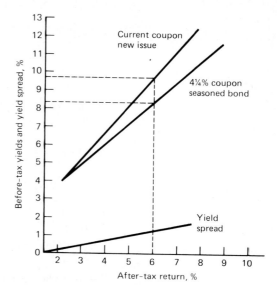

FIGURE 15-4   A comparison between before-
and after-tax yields for a
seasoned and new bond.
Adapted from J. Van Horne,
Financial Market Rates and
Flows, *Prentice-Hall, Englewood
Cliffs, N.J., 1978.*

coupons equal to the current market yield to maturity. The yield spread on the figure points out this difference, which is due solely to the seasoned bond's capital gains. The two bonds have identical before- and after-tax returns at a 4¼% pretax yield to maturity, since the seasoned bond would sell at par and thereby not provide any capital gain. At rates above 4¼%, the seasoned bond sells at a discount and therefore a lower before-tax yield because of the favorable capital gains tax rate on the discount. For example, the seasoned 4¼% coupon bond provides a 6% after-tax return when it is priced to yield slightly more than 8% pretax. To provide the same after-tax return of 6%, the current coupon bond must yield more than 9½% pretax.

Since it is clear that the tax features of different bonds and the tax rates facing investors influence bond yields and investment decisions, recognition of the changing nature of the tax laws is essential. Changes in capital gains and ordinary tax rates and in the tax treatment of certain types of bonds will alter the yield relationships discussed above.

Before continuing, you should:
1 Be able to identify the four primary determinants of bond yields
2 Understand the difference between spot rates and forward rates
3 Know how to estimate implicit forward rates based on the expectations theory
4 Be familiar with the three theories of the term structure of interest rates
5 Be aware of the major rating services for bonds
6 Understand the concept of yield spreads.

15-5 DURATION

When bond investors speak of the "length" of a bond, they are typically referring to the number of years to maturity. The term "short bonds" generally refers to bonds with less than 5 years to maturity, while the term "long bonds" generally refers to bonds with 10 or more years to maturity.

However, there is an alternative measure of the length of a bond called duration.[12] Based on discrete semiannual discounting, duration traditionally has been formulated as

$$D = \frac{\sum_{t=1}^{2n} tC(1 + r/2)^{-t} + 2nF(1 + r/2)^{-2n}}{P}$$

$$= \frac{1}{P}\left[\frac{1C}{(1 + r/2)^1} + \frac{2C}{(1 + r/2)^2} + \frac{3C}{(1 + r/2)^3} + \cdots + \frac{2n(C + F)}{(1 + r/2)^{2n}}\right] \quad (15\text{-}3)$$

where P = current price of bond
C = periodic coupon
r = current yield to maturity
n = number of years to maturity
F = face value (generally $1000)

In words, duration represents a weighted average of the time periods to maturity. The weights for each time period t are equal to the present values of the cash flows in each time period (coupons or principal payment multiplied by their respective discount factors) divided by the total present value (price) of the bond. It should be easy to see that *for a zero coupon bond, duration (measured in years) is equal to the bond's term to maturity n*, since the principal payment F multiplied by its discount factor represents 100% of the present value of the bond.

However, for a coupon bond at least part of the bond's present value is derived from the coupon stream, which results in the bond's duration being less than its term to maturity. An example will help illustrate. Consider an 8% bond with 4 years to maturity priced to provide a yield to maturity of 10%. Table 15-6 illustrates the calculation of the bond's duration, based on discrete discounting. To simplify the presentation, we will assume the coupons are received annually. Notice that the bond's

---

[12]For a more complete discussion of duration and bond volatility, see R. J. Fuller and J. W. Settle, "Determinants of Duration and Bond Volatility," *Journal of Portfolio Management* (summer 1984); and G. Bierwag, G. Kaufman, and A. Toevs, "Duration, Its Development and Use in Bond Portfolio Management," *Financial Analysts Journal* (July/August 1983). The seminal papers on this topic are: F. R. Macaulay, "Some Theoretical Problems Suggested by the Movements of Interest Rates, Bond Yields, and Stock Prices in the United States Since 1856," NBER, Columbia University Press, New York, 1938; B. G. Malkial, "Expectations, Bond Prices and the Term Structure of Interest Rates," *Quarterly Journal of Economics* (May 1962); M. Hopewell and G. Kaufman, "Bond Price Volatility and Term to Maturity: A Generalized Respecification," *American Economic Review* (September 1973); L. Fisher and R. Weil, "Coping with the Risk of Interest Rate Fluctuations: Returns to Bondholders from Naive and Optimal Strategies," *Journal of Business* (October 1971); and C. C. Hsia and J. F. Weston, "Price Behavior of Deep Discount Bonds," *Journal of Banking and Finance* (May 1981).

TABLE 15-6 ILLUSTRATION OF CALCULATING DURATION (DISCRETE DISCOUNTING)

Time period	Cash flow	×	Discount factor $(1 + r)^{-t}$	=	Present value
1	$80		.909		72.73
2	$80		.826		66.12
3	$80		.751		60.11
4	$80		.683		56.64
	$1000		.683		683.01
				$P =$	$936.60

Bond characteristics: Coupon = 8%
Yield to maturity = 10%
Years to maturity = 4

$$D = \frac{1(72.73) + 2(66.12) + 3(60.11) + 4(56.64 + 683.01)}{936.60}$$
$$= 3.57$$

This assumes the coupons are received annually. If the coupons are received semiannually, $D = 3.48$.

duration of 3.57 years is less than its term to maturity of 4 years. This is because part of the cash flows (the coupons) are received prior to the bond's maturity date. If the coupons are received semiannually, $2n = 8$ semiannual time periods, $C = \$40$, $r/2 = 5\%$, and duration would be 6.96 semiannual time periods, or 3.48 years. (The reader should verify this result as a check to see if you understand how duration is calculated based on discrete discounting.)

From this simple example, it should be obvious that as the number of time periods increases, the calculation of duration can become quite tedious. Fortunately, the equation for duration can be substantially simplified when the problem is formulated in terms of continuous discounting. In this case, duration can be expressed as[13]

$$D = \frac{1}{r} + \frac{n(r - c) - 1}{ce^{rn} + (r - c)} \tag{15-4}$$

where c = annual coupon rate
e = natural logarithm ($e \cong 2.718$)

Using this expression, duration for the bond illustrated in Table 15-6 would be 3.40 years, calculated as follows:

$$D = \frac{1}{.10} + \frac{4(.10 - .08) - 1}{(.08)(2.718)^{.4} + (.10 - .08)} = 3.40$$

[13] See Fuller and Settle, op. cit., for the derivation of Equation (15-4).

Because it is based on continuous discounting, Equation (15-4) will always produce estimates of duration that are slightly less than those produced by Equation (15-3), which is based on discrete discounting.

The concept of duration is important for a number of reasons. First, it is an alternative and perhaps more meaningful measure of the "length" of a bond. Second, duration is an important factor in some of the bond immunization strategies discussed in the next chapter. And third, duration is a direct measure of the sensitivity of bond prices to changes in interest rates, which is our next subject.

15-6 BOND VOLATILITY

We will define the sensitivity of bond prices to changes in interest rates, or what we term *bond volatility*, as follows:

> Bond volatility is the absolute value of the percentage change in bond price for a given change in yield to maturity.

Mathematically,

$$\text{Bond volatility} \equiv \left| \frac{\Delta P/P}{\Delta r} \right| \tag{15-5}$$

where $\Delta P/P$ = percentage change in price
Δr = change in yield to maturity

For example, if a bond's yield to maturity increases from 10% to 10½%, Δr would be ½%. If the bond's percentage change in price $\Delta P/P$, given this change in r, was 8%, this definition of bond volatility would measure the bond's volatility as 16, i.e., 8% divided by ½%. As another example, if the bond's volatility was measured at 16 and its yield to maturity *decreased* by 1%, we would expect a 16% *increase* in the bond price. (Remember that bond prices always move in the opposite direction of interest rates.)

There are other possible definitions of bond volatility. However, we prefer this definition for several reasons. First, by measuring volatility in terms of percentage price changes, we are able to compare the volatility of bonds which have substantially different prices. Second, most investors tend to think in terms of simple changes in yields Δr rather than percentage changes in yields $\Delta r/r$.[14] A third reason is that this definition of bond volatility can be shown to be equal to the duration of the bond.

---

[14]Bond volatility measured in terms of the percentage change in yield to maturity, i.e., $(\Delta P/P)/(\Delta r/r)$, is generally referred to as bond price elasticity.

TABLE 15-7 ILLUSTRATION OF $\Delta P/P \cong D(\Delta r)$

	Bond 1			Bond 2	
Before interest rate change	$c = .00$ $r = .10$ $D = 10.0$	$n = 10$ $P = \$367.88$		$c = .10$ $r = .10$ $D = 6.3$	$n = 10$ $P = \$1000.00$
After interest rate change	$r = .11$ $\Delta r = .01$	$P = \$332.88$		$r = .11$ $\Delta r = .01$	$P = \$939.35$
Estimated percentage price change	$\Delta P/P \cong 10.0(1\%) = 10.0\%$			$\Delta P/P \cong 6.3(1\%) = 6.3\%$	
Actual percentage price change	$\dfrac{332.88 - 367.88}{367.88} = 9.5\%$			$\dfrac{939.35 - 1000.00}{1000.00} = 6.1\%$	

D is calculated using Equation (16-5). Bond prices P are calculated using the following continuous discounting model:

$$P = F\left[\frac{c(1 - e^{-rn})}{r} + e^{-rn}\right]$$

Source: Adapted from R. J. Fuller and J. W. Settle, "Determinants of Duration and Bond Volatility," *Journal of Portfolio Management* (summer 1984).

15-6-1 Duration as a Measure of Bond Volatility For extremely small changes in yields, it can be shown that duration is identical to our definition of bond volatility.[15] For larger changes in yields, say Δr greater than ½%, this relationship is only approximately true. That is,

$$D \cong \frac{\Delta P/P}{\Delta r} \qquad \text{or} \qquad \Delta P/P \cong D(\Delta r) \qquad (15\text{-}6)$$

Thus, duration is not only a measure of how "long" a bond is, duration is also a measure of the bond's volatility. *The longer the bond's duration, the more volatile the bond.* That is, for a given change in yield to maturity, the longer the bond's duration, the greater will be its percentage change in price.

To illustrate this, consider the two bonds in Table 15-7. Both bonds have a term to maturity of 10 and a yield to maturity of 10%. Bond 1 is a zero-coupon bond, which results in a price of $367.88 and a duration of 10.0. (Recall that for zero-coupon bonds, duration is equal to term to maturity.) Bond 2 has a coupon rate of 10%, which results in a price of $1000.00 and a duration of 6.3. (Recall that if a bond's coupon rate and yield to maturity are the same, the bond's price will always equal $1000.) Now assume that interest rates suddenly increase by 1%, resulting in $r = 11\%$ for these bonds. Based on Equation (15-6), one can estimate the percentage price change due to the change in interest rates for bond 1 as follows:

$$\Delta P/P \cong D(\Delta r) \cong 10.0(1\%) \cong 10.0\%$$

[15]Hopewell and Kaufman, op. cit., were the first to show this.

Similarly, we would estimate the percentage price change for bond 2 to be 6.3%. The bottom part of Table 15-6 shows the actual results. Bond 1's price would drop to $332.88, a decrease of 9.5%, while Bond 2's price would drop to $939.35, a decrease of 6.1%.

The percentage price changes were not exactly equal to $D(\Delta r)$ because D is based on the derivative of P with respect to r, and derivatives are predicated on infinitely small changes in the variables. However, the percentage price changes of bonds with different durations will always be correctly ordered for a given change in yield to maturity. That is, longer-duration bonds will exhibit larger percentage price changes than shorter duration bonds for a given Δr, regardless of the size of Δr. And, for smaller changes in yields to maturity, $D(\Delta r)$ will provide very accurate estimates of the actual percentage price changes.[16]

Now, having examined the relationship between duration and bond volatility, let's take a close look at the factors which determine duration.

15-6-2 Determinants of Duration and Bond Volatility From Equation (15-5) one can see that there are only three factors which determine a bond's duration and volatility. These are (1) the coupon rate c, (2) the term to maturity n, and (3) the yield to maturity r. We will examine each of these factors and their relationship to duration individually.[17]

Coupon Rate Duration and the size of the coupon rate are inversely related. *That is, the larger the coupon rate, the lower duration and the less volatile the bond price.* This is because the owner of a high-coupon bond receives relatively more of the bond's cash flows during the early years of the bond's life. Table 15-8 illustrates this inverse relationship. In this table yield to maturity is held constant at 10% and duration is reported for three different coupon rates: 6%, 10%, and 14%. Notice that for any

---

[16]For example, suppose instead that r changed to 10.3% ($\Delta r = .3\%$). Bond 1's price would be $357.01 and the actual percentage change would be 2.96%. Using $\Delta P/P \cong D(\Delta r)$, the estimated percentage change would be 3.00%.

[17]For a more complete analysis of these relationships, see Fuller and Settle, op. cit.

TABLE 15-8 ILLUSTRATION OF THE COUPON EFFECT
Duration (for $r = 10\%$)

	Coupon		
n	6%	10%	14%
1	.97	.95	.94
5	4.24	3.93	3.71
10	7.05	6.32	5.89
20	9.59	8.65	8.19
30	10.16	9.50	9.21
∞	10.00	10.00	10.00

Source: R. J. Fuller and J. W. Settle, "Determinants of Duration and Bond Volatility," *Journal of Portfolio Management* (summer 1984).

choice of n, the larger the coupon rate, the lower the duration. For example, letting $n = 20$, the 6% coupon bond's duration is 9.59, vs. 8.65 for the 10% coupon bond, vs. 8.19 for the 14% coupon bond.

Term to Maturity The relationship between term to maturity and duration is more complex than one might suspect. However, *as a general rule, the longer the term to maturity, the longer the duration and the more volatile the bond*. This relationship makes intuitive sense because the longer the term to maturity, the longer one has to wait to receive at least part of the bond's cash flows. By examining Table 15-8, one can see that this relationship is generally true. For example, looking down the 10% coupon column, note that duration consistently increases as the term to maturity increases. The same holds for the 14% column. However, exceptions may arise in the case of discount bonds. (Discount bonds occur when the coupon rate is less than the yield to maturity, resulting in the bond selling below par.) For example, in looking down the 6% coupon column we see that duration appears to peak at 10.16 for a 30-year bond and then subsequently declines to 10.00 for a perpetual bond. However, unless the bond is selling at a very large discount, the point at which duration peaks and subsequently declines as n continues to increase represents such a long-term bond that it is of little practical importance—in most cases n has to be greater than 30 years, which is a longer term to maturity than that of practically all bonds in the marketplace.

Table 15-8 illustrates another interesting point concerning duration and bond volatility. Notice that for perpetual bonds, i.e., when n equals infinity, duration is the same (in this case, 10.00), regardless of the coupon size. This will always be true. *For perpetual bonds, duration will always equal the reciprocal of the bond's yield to maturity, regardless of the bond's coupon rate*. That is, for perpetuals, $D = 1/r$. A ready application of this principle would be to preferred stocks, as they are generally considered to be perpetuals. Thus, for preferred stocks, duration is simply equal to the reciprocal of the stock's yield to maturity, which is also its current yield. For example, a preferred stock which yields 8% has a duration of 12½ years.

Yield to Maturity The last of the three factors which affect duration and bond volatility is r, the bond's yield to maturity. There is an inverse relationship between duration (bond volatility) and the level of yield to maturity. That is, *the higher the yield to maturity, the lower duration and bond volatility, and vice versa*. There is an intuitive explanation for this relationship. Yield to maturity r is the discount rate used in determining the present value of the bond. As the discount rate increases, the present values of cash flows farther into the future become less, both in absolute terms and relative to the present values of earlier cash flows. Thus, the relative "weights" of more distant cash flows become less in the equation for duration, and by definition, duration decreases. By the same token, bond volatility decreases as r increases because more distant cash flows (the present values of which are more sensitive to changes in r) represent a smaller fraction of the price of the bond when the level of r is high. Thus, the sensitivity of the bond price to changes in r is less when r is high.

Figure 15-5 illustrates the inverse relationship between duration (bond volatility) and the level of yield to maturity. In this figure there are four pairs of curves—each pair consists of a solid line representing a coupon rate of 6% and a dashed line representing a coupon rate of 12%. Each pair of curves represents duration as n

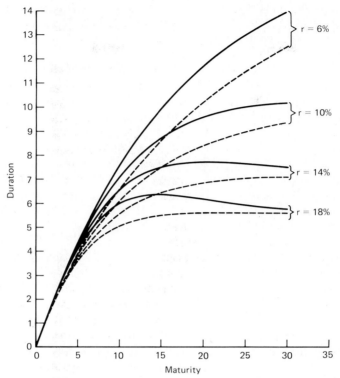

FIGURE 15-5   Duration vs. maturity for various yields; coupon rate = 6% (solid curves) and 12% (dashed curves). [*Adapted from R. J. Fuller and J. W. Settle, "Determinants of Duration and Bond Volatility,"* Journal of Portfolio Management *(summer 1984).*]

increases for a specific level of yield to maturity r. The uppermost pair of curves represents duration, as n increases, assuming that the yield to maturity is 6%. As r is increased to 10%, 14%, and 18%, notice that the pairs of curves systematically decrease. Thus, for any given coupon rate and term to maturity, duration and bond volatility decrease as the yield to maturity increases.

There are two other points worth observing in this figure. First, note that regardless of the level of yield to maturity, when n is between 0 and, say, 5 the duration curves are almost identical. Thus, for short-term bonds, term to maturity is by far the most important of the three factors which determine duration. Second, notice that each of the three pairs of curves for r = 10%, 14%, and 18% tends to flatten out after some critical level of n. That is, beyond some point, term to maturity does not affect duration very much.[18] Thus, for longer-term bonds, the most important factor affecting duration and bond volatility is the level of yield to maturity.

---

[18]For discount bonds ($r > c$), this point is $n = 1/(r - c)$. For premium bonds, the duration curve gradually approaches its asymptote of $1/r$, as n continues to increase. See Fuller and Settle, op. cit., and Hsia and Weston, op. cit.

Before leaving this topic, one might ask why we have observed relatively more variability in bond prices in years when interest rates (yields to maturity) have been high, since the higher r, the lower duration and bond volatility. The answer is that changes in bond prices are equal to duration times the change in the interest rate and periods of high interest rates tend to be associated with larger changes in interest rates. Thus, the relatively lower durations of bonds during periods of high interest rates have been more than offset by the larger changes (greater variability) of interest rates, resulting in greater variability in bond prices.

Before continuing, you should understand the following relationships:

1 Duration is a direct measure of bond price volatility

2 The higher the coupon rate c, the lower the duration and the less volatile the bond

3 As a general rule, the longer the term to maturity n, the longer duration and the more volatile the bond

4 The higher the level of interest rates r, the lower duration and the less volatile the bond

15-7 SUMMARY

This chapter discussed bond yield determinants. Knowledge of the factors which determine yield spreads is essential to the proper pricing of bonds. Term structure was first discussed. The relationship between spot and forward rates was highlighted to illustrate the effect of investor expectations on interest rates.

Investors frequently utilize the yield curve to depict the relationship between term to maturity and yield. Three theories have been advanced to explain the shape of the yield curve. The expectations theory holds that expected future spot rates and forward rates are similar and that expectations of future interest rates are the sole determinants of the yield curve's shape. The liquidity premium theory expands on the expectation theory by adding a liquidity premium as an inducement for risk-averse investors to invest in long-term bonds. The segmentation theory states that distinct preference zones (habitats) exist, in which supply and demand determine yields.

The risk structure of bond yields revolves around the assessment of default risk. Investors judge a bond's credit quality by looking at its credit rating or by computing various financial ratios and using other information. As one would expect, bond yields and credit ratings exhibit an inverse relationship. In order to effectively utilize credit ratings, one should know how the ratings are devised and their limitations. The prediction of bankruptcy also concerns investors; the use of financial ratios or market risk analysis enables investors to screen firms for bankruptcy potential.

Marketability and tax considerations are additional factors which influence investor decisions. Market conditions, market psychology, individual tax brackets, and the tax treatment of a specific debt instrument all affect bond investments.

We also examined the concept of duration as an alternative measure of the length of a bond. Duration accounts for both the size of the bond's cash flows and the time period in which they are paid. Thus, in many respects duration is a better measure of the length of a bond than is term to maturity. In addition, duration is a direct measure of the sensitivity of a bond's price to changes in interest rates, or what we term bond volatility. Finally, duration is an important variable in many of the bond trading strategies discussed in the next chapter.

SUGGESTED READINGS

An important, but unfortunately difficult to read, article on the term structure of interest rates is:

J. Cox, J. Ingersoll, and S. Ross, "A Re-examination of Traditional Hypotheses about the Term Structure of Interest Rates," *Journal of Finance* (September 1981).

The following are all readable articles on duration and its many uses in analyzing bonds:

G. O. Bierwag, G. Kaufman, and A. Toevs, "Duration, Its Development and Use in Bond Portfolio Management," *Financial Analysts Journal* (July/August 1983).

R. Fuller and J. Settle, "Determinants of Duration and Bond Price Volatility," *Journal of Portfolio Management* (winter 1985).

R. W. McEnally, "Duration as a Practical Tool for Bond Management," *Journal of Portfolio Management* (summer 1977).

F. Reilly and S. Rupinder, "The Many Uses of Bond Duration," *Financial Analysts Journal* (July/August 1980).

QUESTIONS

1 Go to the most recent *Federal Reserve Bulletin* and construct a yield curve.

2 Why are forward rates important in bond investment decisions?

3 What is the expectations theory of term structure and how is it related to market efficiency?

4 According to the liquidity premium theory, implicit forward rates are biased upward. Why?

5 In general, why might a liquidity premium exist for longer bonds?

6 What is a yield spread and how do investors utilize yield spreads to assess default risk?

7 A credit rating is a precise measurement of a bond's default risk. Comment.

8 Debt ratios, earnings levels, earnings variability, and interest coverage partially explain why bonds are located in a certain rating category. What other factors are important?

9 How do investors predict bankruptcy? What are the key variables used to make such predictions?

10 What is the relationship between marketability and bond yields? Why is this a less distinct, or more fuzzy, relationship?

11 How do tax considerations influence a bond investment decision?

12 Why does $D(\Delta r)$ not provide the exact percentage change in bond price for a given change in yield to maturity?

PROBLEMS

1 If zero-coupon U.S. Treasury bonds sell today at $955 for the 1-year maturity and $910 for the 2-year maturity, what are the 1-year forward rates for years 1 and 2?

2 If the annualized rates for treasury obligations are

3-month	13.78%
6-month	14.28%
9-month	14.41%
12-month	14.20%,

determine the market's forecast of 90-day interest rates over the next year using the expectations theory.

3 Prove that the higher the coupon, the lower a bond's price volatility.

4 Calculate the duration of a 12% bond with a 3-year maturity and annual coupons, using both Equations (15-3) and (15-4), and a discount rate of 14%.

5 Using Table 15-4, what marginal tax rates make investors indifferent between municipal and corporate bonds for May 1985 for all four rating classes?

6 Consider a 6% coupon bond with a yield to maturity of 9% and 15 years remaining to maturity. (*a*) What is the bond's current price, assuming a coupon was just paid, i.e., no accrued interest? (*b*) What is the bond's duration? (*c*) What percentage price change might you expect if the yield to maturity suddenly increased to 9½%? (*d*) What would be the exact percentage price change?

7 Assume that the following yields exist on government bonds:

1-year bond	8%
2-year bond	10%
4-year bond	9%.

a Based on the expectations theory, what is the implicit forward rate in year 2?
b Based on the expectations theory, what can you say about the forward rate in year 3?

8 An 8%, 10-year bond is currently priced at $767 to yield 12% to maturity.
a What is the bond's duration?
b Given a change in interest rates of ½%, what percentage change would you expect in the bond's price?

9 On May 20, 1983, the following yields to maturity existed for long-term bonds:

U.S. government	10.38%
Aaa corporate	10.69%
Aa corporate	10.99%
A corporate	11.48%
Baa corporate	11.74%

a What were the yield spreads for Aaa, Aa, A, and Baa corporate bonds on this date based on the U.S. government rate?
b If economic conditions subsequently improved, would you expect any change in these yield spreads, and if so, why?

CHAPTER 16

STRATEGIES FOR FIXED-INCOME PORTFOLIOS

After reading this chapter, you should:

1 Be aware of the evidence regarding bond market efficiency
2 Understand the general types of bond portfolio objectives and several strategies, both active and passive, which might be used to achieve these objectives
3 Know that duration is a key element in passive immunization strategies
4 Recognize the problems associated with using the market model to measure the risk of bonds
5 Know how some bond swaps are executed
6 Be aware of the potential value of having portfolios which contain both stocks and bonds
7 Be aware that for pension funds the best strategy may be to hold only bonds

Bond investors, like any other group of investors, seek to maximize their returns, subject to an acceptable level of risk. This chapter describes various fixed-income trading strategies that can be used to achieve this objective. The question is, which investment strategies are rational and worth the effort in today's bond market?

To answer this question, an understanding of the degree of *efficiency* in the bond market is important. As noted in Chapter 5, market efficiency refers to the speed and accuracy with which current market prices reflect investor expectations. In an efficient market investors will, on average, earn a normal return for a given level of risk because mispriced securities are rare. Competition among investors for abnormal returns will eliminate any obvious mispricing opportunities and, on average, cause current prices to mirror the fair values of securities. The bond market, like the stock market, appears to be reasonably efficient—the empirical evidence suggests that mispriced bonds are the exception, rather than the rule.

16-1 BOND MARKET EFFICIENCY

Recall that the efficient market hypothesis (EMH) is generally divided into three categories—the weak, semistrong, and strong forms. Briefly, the weak-form EMH indicates that current prices fully reflect historical price information, the semistrong form suggests that prices reflect all publicly available information, and the strong form holds that prices reflect all public and private information.

The empirical evidence regarding these three forms of market efficiency for bonds is sparse relative to the numerous studies on stock market efficiency. Researchers do not have easy access to price and volume data on a daily basis for bonds owing to the small number of secondary market trades. Indeed, many bond quotations are merely dealer judgments rather than actual trades. For these reasons, the empirical tests regarding bond market efficiency are less numerous and more subject to error than the tests regarding stock market efficiency.

16-1-1 Government Bond Market Efficiency One study of the weak-form EMH avoids these data problems by investigating the independence of T-bill prices, since there is a very active secondary market in T-bills. Roll tested T-bill price behavior over the 1949–1964 period and found that prices were serially independent.[1] Thus, charting past T-bill price patterns should not be any more profitable than charting stock prices.

Semistrong-form tests have also tended to use T-bill or government bond data to avoid data problems. The efficiency of the T-bill market sector was investigated by Fama, and by Hamburger and Platt.[2] Fama jointly tested whether inflation forecasts are reflected in T-bill prices and the speed of such information processing. He found that for 1- to 6-month T-bills, prices reflect inflation information so that investors cannot earn excess returns trading on this information. Hamburger and Platt examined various monetary and income variables and found that interest rate expectations reflect these variables quickly. A study of Canadian government bonds also found that public information is quickly reflected in bond prices.[3]

One can summarize the semistrong-form tests involving other sectors of the bond market either as tests of the accuracy of market timing or as tests for the existence of mispriced bonds. Market timing tests focus on interest rate forecasting; consistent identification of interest rate turning points would earn investors abnormal profits. Likewise, consistent identification of mispriced bonds would provide excess profits. Let us first consider interest rate forecasting skill and then the issue of mispriced bonds due to rating changes.

16-1-2 Interest Rate Forecasts A plethora of studies exist which address the question of whether or not experts can accurately forecast changes in interest rates.[4] Since experts utilize historical interest rates and other publicly available information, these tests are evidence concerning both the weak and semistrong forms of the EMH.

---

[1]R. Roll, *The Behavior of Interest Rates: An Application of the Efficient Market Model to U.S. Treasury Bills*, Basic Books, New York, 1970.

[2]E. Fama, "Short-Term Interest Rates as Predictors of Inflation," *American Economic Review* (June 1975); and M. Hamburger and E. Platt, "The Expectations Hypothesis and the Efficiency of the Treasury Bill Market," *Review of Economics and Statistics* (May 1975).

[3]J. Pesando, "On the Efficiency of the Bond Market: Some Canadian Evidence," *Journal of Political Economy* (December 1978).

[4]For example, see M. Prell, "How Well Do the Experts Forecast Interest Rates?" Federal Reserve Bank of Kansas City *Monthly Review* (September–October 1973); D. Fraser, "On the Accuracy and Usefulness of Interest Rate Forecasts," *Business Economics* (September 1977); and J. W. Elliott and J. Baier, "Econometric Models and Current Interest Rates: How Well Do They Predict Future Rates?" *Journal of Finance* (September 1979).

In general, these studies find that the experts *cannot* outperform naive forecasts. This suggests that historical interest rate patterns provide no clues to the future and that interest rates quickly reflect publicly available information. Indeed, one study suggests that the most accurate forecast is that there will be no change in interest rates.[5]

The expert forecasts are either (1) surveys of executives and economists of major corporations and financial institutions or (2) econometric models using past price data, money and income data, and/or data from a number of different sectors of the financial markets. The lack of forecasting ability on the part of such experts is not unreasonable, given the number of sophisticated investors competing to predict changes in interest rates and consequently turning points in the bond market. Such competition would suggest that market efficiency is a reasonable outcome. Consequently, the ability of investors to earn abnormal profits by forecasting interest rates is questionable.

16-1-3 Bond Rating Changes   If investors could trade on the day or week following a bond rating change and earn abnormal profits owing to a systematic mispricing of bonds, the bond market would be semistrong *inefficient*. Bond rating agencies will change a firm's bond rating based on (1) a specific event, such as the announcement of new debt financing (where a rating had to be assigned), new equity financing, or a merger; or (2) a gradual change in the firm's financial condition which the agency observes during their periodic review process. If investors anticipate bond rating changes, no abnormal price movement should occur when the agency alters the rating. If investors do not anticipate rating changes and markets are efficient, any abnormal price changes should occur *immediately* after the announcements of the rating changes—thus eliminating any chance of achieving abnormal profits by trading on the announcements of rating changes. On the other hand, markets would be considered inefficient if abnormal price changes occurred over a period of time after announcements, since one could implement a successful trading strategy of simply buying bonds whose ratings had been increased and selling bonds whose ratings had been lowered.

The evidence regarding market efficiency with respect to bond rating changes is mixed. Katz found no market inefficiencies concerning bond rating changes for public utility bonds.[6] As a result, investors could not earn abnormal profits on the basis of public reports of rating changes. Grier and Katz examined public utility and industrial bond prices.[7] They also found the market to be efficient with respect to rating changes for public utility bonds. However, they did find that the market was inefficient with respect to bond rating decreases for industrial bonds. Another study of public utility bond prices by Hettenhouse and Sartoris found the market efficient with respect to rating decreases, but not rating increases.[8] These three studies suggest that semistrong-form efficiency may not exist for public utility and industrial bonds, at least with respect to public announcements concerning rating changes.

---

[5]Elliott and Baier, op. cit.

[6]S. Katz, "The Price Adjustment Process of Bonds to Rating Reclassification: A Test of Bond Market Efficiency," *Journal of Finance* (May 1974).

[7]P. Grier and S. Katz, "The Differential Effects of Bond Rating Changes among Industrial and Public Utility Bonds by Maturity," *Journal of Business* (April 1976).

[8]G. Hettenhouse and W. Sartoris, "An Analysis of the Informational Value of Bond Rating Changes," *Quarterly Review of Economics and Business* (summer 1976).

On the other hand, there is evidence supporting semistrong-form efficiency which suggests that investors do anticipate rating changes, and by 7 to 18 months. Weinstein[9] found no evidence of any price reaction 6 months prior to and after a rating change for public utility and industrial bonds, which suggests that investors anticipated rating changes more than 6 months in advance. Pinches and Singleton,[10] using stock returns to reflect the impact of rating changes, also found results consistent with semistrong-form efficiency. Their study revealed that stock prices anticipate rating changes resulting from changing financial conditions of the firm by 15 to 18 months, and by more than 6 months for rating changes resulting from specific events. Since bond ratings are determined, in part, by publicly available information, it would not be unreasonable to find that bond rating changes are anticipated by investors.

Although some of the earlier studies supported the existence of abnormal profit opportunities, these results may have been caused by the lack of continuous bond trading data and a domination of the bond market by large institutions who usually trade in relatively large blocks. Thus, one may infer from this review of studies on bond rating changes that the bond market is *reasonably* semistrong-form efficient. That is, mispriced bonds and abnormal profit opportunities due to anticipation of rating changes are rare.

16-2 PORTFOLIO OBJECTIVES AND STRATEGIES

Before investors construct a bond portfolio, they must answer two critical questions: (1) what is the portfolio's objective? and (2) what strategy is appropriate to meet this objective, given current market conditions? The portfolio objective depends upon the investor's future cash requirements and the investor's tolerance for risk. For example, a 30-year-old woman who is in the early stages of her career may choose to live dangerously with her bond investments and pursue the objective of maximizing capital gains. On the other hand, a 60-year-old man nearing retirement may choose an objective of maximizing current income. Let us consider some possible strategies for bond portfolios.

16-2-1 Passive Strategies and Immunization
It appears that forecasting interest rates on the basis of historical or publicly available information is a questionable exercise since even experts have not been successful at this task. The evidence on bond market efficiency also suggests that the government bond markets are reasonably efficient and that only astute investors may be able to identify and trade mispriced bonds in other sectors. Thus, *passive portfolio management* may be appropriate for a sizable number of bond investors. With passive management, investors forgo the search for mispriced bonds and the task of forecasting interest rates. Rather, investors seek to earn normal rates of return for a certain risk level and to minimize transaction costs. One method of achieving this objective is to adopt an immunization strategy.

[9]M. Weinstein, "The Effect of a Rating Change Announcement on Bond Price," *Journal of Financial Economics* (December 1977).

[10]G. Pinches and J. C. Singleton, "The Adjustment of Stock Prices to Bond Rating Changes," *Journal of Finance* (March 1978).

Immunization is the process of constructing a bond portfolio so that the realized return will always at least equal the promised return, because of the relationship between the portfolio's duration and its holding period. By structuring the portfolio so that its *duration is equal to the holding period of the investor*, the portfolio manager offsets price risk and coupon reinvestment risk. This results in the bond portfolio providing a return very close to the portfolio's promised yield which existed at the start of the holding period, *regardless of any changes in interest rates which occur during the holding period*.

To illustrate, recall that an unexpected rise in interest rates decreases bond prices and increases the income from coupon reinvestment. The net impact on total bond portfolio return depends on the relative magnitude of these two effects. Table 16-1 illustrates these relationships. For a flat yield curve, bonds with 10-, 15-, and 20-year maturities all yield 7.50%.

However, if rates rose to 9% and remained at that level for the 10-year planning period, then only the 15-year maturity has a realized yield (7.52%) approximately

TABLE 16-1   EFFECTS OF AN UNEXPECTED INCREASE IN INTEREST RATE ON THREE BOND STRATEGIES PER $100

	Time to maturity		
	10 years	**15 years**	**20 years**
Duration, years	7.8	10.1	11.6
Beginning bond price	$82.63	$77.71	$74.31
Promised annual return, %	7.50	7.50	7.50
No change in interest rates			
Bond price after 10 years	$100.00	$ 89.73	$ 82.63
Coupons paid	50.00	50.00	50.00
Reinvestment of coupons semiannually @ 7½%	22.54	22.54	22.54
Total future value of investment	172.54	162.27	155.17
Realized annual return, %	7.50	7.50	7.50
Immediate increase to 9%			
Bond price after 10 years	$100.00	$ 84.17	$ 73.98
Coupons paid	50.00	50.00	50.00
Reinvestment of coupons semiannually @ 9%	28.43	28.43	28.43
Total future value of investment	178.43	162.60	152.41
Realized annual return, %	7.84	7.52	7.32
Loss in bond price	0.00	−5.56	−8.65
Gain in reinvestment income	5.89	5.89	5.89
Net change	+5.89	+0.33	−2.76

Given: Flat yield curve = 7½%
 Coupon bond rate = 5%
 Planning period = 10 years
Source: G. O. Bierwag, G. Kaufman, R. Schweitzer, and A. Toevs, "The Art of Risk Management in Bond Portfolios," *Journal of Portfolio Management* (spring 1981).

equal to the promised yield. The reason is that the duration (10.1 years) is almost equal to the planning period of 10 years. The 10-year maturity bond has a higher realized yield (7.84%) because of the increase in income from coupon reinvestment. For the 20-year bond the effect of a lower bond price more than offsets the higher income on the reinvested coupons, resulting in a lower realized yield of 7.32%. But for the 15-year bond with a duration of 10.1 years the gain in reinvestment income of 5.89 is almost entirely offset by the loss in bond price of 5.56. If a bond with a duration exactly equal to 10 had been available, the change in interest rates would exactly offset the change in reinvestment income. Thus, *immunization reduces and potentially can completely eliminate interest rate risk for portfolios by equating the duration and intended holding period of the portfolio.*

The historical evidence suggests that an immunization strategy produces the desired result of equality of promised and realized yields for default-free bond portfolios over time.[11] Table 16-2 indicates that even though promised yields exceeded realized yields for an immunization strategy by .078%, this strategy did generate realized yields that were most frequently within 5 basis points of promised yields. Table 16-2 compares four strategies. The "immunization strategy" assumes a flat yield curve and equal interest rate changes for all maturities.[12] The "maturity strategy" is a portfolio with a maturity equal to the 10-year holding period. The "rollover strategy" consists of 1-year bonds that are successively rolled over each year. The "long bond" strategy is a 20-year bond which is sold after the 10-year holding period. As the last two columns show, the immunization strategy has the greatest consistency in equating promised and realized yields. For example, 86% of the time the immunization strategy generated realized returns that were closer to the promised return than did the maturity strategy. Note also that 48% of the time, the duration strategy generated realized returns that were within 5 basis points of the promised return.

The immunization strategy suggests that the determinants of interest rate risk are the individual investor's holding period and the duration of the portfolio. Thus, if an investor chooses a passive strategy, the choice of the appropriate bond portfolio depends on the investor's optimal holding period and the corresponding immmunizing duration.

16-2-2 Active Bond Portfolio Management　Active bond portfolio managers try to achieve abnormal profits by trading bonds on the basis of either interest rate forecasts or opinions regarding individual bond prices. The search for these profits revolves around two fundamental aspects of investment: timing and selection. Timing in the bond market refers to interest rate forecasting. Selection concerns the individual bonds to be included in the portfolio. The evidence presented previously concerning interest rate forecasting suggests that market timing based on publicly available information is probably a fruitless activity. However, bond selection may have abnormal profit potential—at least the existence of numerous bond traders who execute "swaps"

[11]G. O. Bierwag, G. Kaufman, R. Schweitzer, and A. Toevs, "The Art of Risk Management in Bond Portfolios," *Journal of Portfolio Management* (spring 1981).

[12]Different assumptions about the shape of the yield curve, and the direction and magnitude of unexpected interest rate changes lead to different immunizing durations. But Bierwag et al. found that the portfolio with an immunizing duration based on the simplest assumptions immunizes almost as well as more complex strategies and appears to be the most cost-effective.

TABLE 16-2 PROMISED AND REALIZED YIELDS FOR ALTERNATIVE PORTFOLIO STRATEGIES
(10-Year Planning Period 1925–1978)

Strategy	Promised (annual average), %	Realized (annual average), %	Realized minus promised, %	Closer to promised than maturity strategy, %	Within 5 basis points of promised, %
			1925–1978		
Immunization	3.364	3.286	− .078	86	48
Maturity	3.364	3.329	− .035	—	16
Rollover	3.364	2.927	− .437	2	7
Long bond	3.364	3.194	− .170	9	7
			1925–1949		
Immunization	3.697	3.552	− .145	93	13
Maturity	3.697	3.465	− .232	—	0
Rollover	3.697	1.801	− 1.896	0	0
Long bond	3.697	4.749	+ 1.052	7	0
			1940–1963		
Immunization	2.257	2.214	− .043	79	50
Maturity	2.257	2.214	− .043	—	36
Rollover	2.257	2.074	− .183	7	14
Long bond	2.257	1.987	− .270	21	21
			1954–1978		
Immunization	4.064	4.026	− .038	87	80
Maturity	4.064	4.234	+ .170	—	13
Rollover	4.064	4.848	+ .784	0	7
Long bond	4.064	2.767	− 1.297	0	0

Source: G. O. Bierwag, G. Kaufman, R. Schweitzer, and A. Toevs, "The Art of Risk Management in Bond Portfolios," *Journal of Portfolio Management* (spring 1981).

suggests that some bond market participants believe that abnormal profits may exist. *Bond swaps* are the simultaneous purchase and sale of two or more bonds with similar characteristics to earn a yield differential. We shall consider specific bond swaps in the next section of this chapter.

The active bond portfolio manager must make decisions with respect to three major factors: an interest rate forecast (if any), maturity structure, and individual bond selection. Since total portfolio return reflects the combination of these three decisions, it is useful for understanding active bond portfolio management (and for measuring performance) to decompose total return. Figure 16-1 illustrates this decomposition of total portfolio return. The known aspect of total returns is the promised yields of the bonds in the portfolio which would be earned if no changes occurred in other factors. That is, the portfolio would earn X percent if interest rates stayed constant over, say, the next quarter. The unknown aspect of return involves the judgment of the portfolio manager. Specifically, the interest rate effect shows how well the manager forecasts interest rate changes on the maturity composition of the portfolio. Any change in interest rates and the maturity structure of the bond portfolio clearly influence the

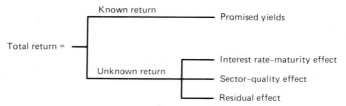

FIGURE 16-1   Decomposition of bond portfolio returns. [*Source: P. Dietz, R. Fogler, and D. Hardy, "The Challenge of Analyzing Bond Portfolio Returns,"* Journal of Portfolio Management *(spring 1980).*]

unknown return component. The sector-quality effect refers to the major bond sectors such as corporates, utilities, and agencies, and to the credit ratings of the bonds in the portfolio. The residual effect is due to any remaining factors influencing return such as call provisions or sinking funds. These last two effects (sector-quality and residual effects) are the result of the bond portfolio manager's individual bond selection decisions and are considered in more detail in the next section, which discusses bond swaps. For now, let's examine the first of these effects, the interest rate effect, on the unknown portion of a bond portfolio's return.

The maturity structure of a portfolio influences return due to its interaction with interest rate expectations. Three general maturity structures exist: *maturity concentrated, laddered*, and *barbell portfolios*. Maturity concentrated portfolios are utilized when the manager has a definite interest rate opinion. For example, a manager who expects interest rates to fall would concentrate on long-term maturities (or durations) since the prices of these bonds will increase the most.

Laddered and barbell portfolios are illustrated in Table 16-3. The 15- and 10-year laddered portfolios have maturities evenly spaced so that the same amount matures and is reinvested each year. This maturity structure provides average returns over an interest rate cycle and implies no interest rate forecast on the part of the portfolio manager. The barbell structure includes both short- and long-term bonds with no funds invested in intermediate-term bonds. Table 16-3 shows two types of barbell configurations. A barbell structured portfolio purportedly has greater liquidity than laddered portfolios because of the heavier concentration of short-term bonds, and higher returns (assuming the yield curve is upward-sloping) because more funds are invested in long-term bonds. Similar to the maturity concentrated portfolio, the barbell structure exposes the investor to price and reinvestment risk which implies an interest rate opinion.

Before continuing, you should:

1   Be aware of the results of several studies concerning the ability of investors to forecast interest rates
2   Be aware of the results of several studies concerning the efficiency of government bond markets and bond rating changes
3   Understand the difference between active and passive strategies for managing bond portfolios
4   Know how the concept of duration is used in immunizing bond portfolios

TABLE 16-3 EXAMPLES OF LADDERED AND BARBELL STRUCTURES FOR A
$20 MILLION PORTFOLIO

Years to maturity	15-year laddered	10-year laddered	50–50 barbell	70–30 barbell
1	$ 1,333,333	$ 2,000,000	$ 2,000,000	$ 2,800,000
2	1,333,333	2,000,000	2,000,000	2,800,000
3	1,333,333	2,000,000	2,000,000	2,800,000
4	1,333,333	2,000,000	2,000,000	2,800,000
5	1,333,333	2,000,000	2,000,000	2,800,000
6	1,333,333	2,000,000	0	0
7	1,333,333	2,000,000	0	0
8	1,333,333	2,000,000	0	0
9	1,333,333	2,000,000	0	0
10	1,333,333	2,000,000	0	0
11	1,333,333		2,000,000	1,200,000
12	1,333,333		2,000,000	1,200,000
13	1,333,333		2,000,000	1,200,000
14	1,333,333		2,000,000	1,200,000
15	1,333,333		2,000,000	1,200,000
	$20,000,000	$20,000,000	$20,000,000	$20,000,000

16-3 BOND SWAPS

A bond swap is the simultaneous purchase and sale of two or more bonds with similar characteristics in order to earn a yield differential. Differences among bonds in coupons, default risk, interest rates, maturity (duration), marketability, tax treatment, call provisions, sinking funds, and other factors determine the potential profitability of the swap. For example, suppose an investor monitors the yield spread between Aaa- and Aa-rated bonds and finds that this spread has widened to 75 basis points from its historic average of 50 basis points. Believing this wider than normal yield spread is a temporary aberration, the investor will buy Aa-rated bonds and sell Aaa-rated bonds until, hopefully, the yield spread returns to the historic average of 50 basis points. Investors utilize swaps for a variety of purposes, but the overriding objective is to generate incremental capital gains or income from switching bonds.

Regardless of the reason for the swap, bond swapping presupposes that the investor has a *superior* ability to identify a short-lived anomaly, or mispricing, in the bond markets. Of course, in a truly efficient market, even the superior analyst won't be able to engage in profitable swaps on a *consistent* basis. Thus, before engaging in a bond swap strategy, the investor should first assess the relative efficiency of the markets in which he or she competes.

When evaluating bonds, investors who do engage in bond swaps search for two factors, large yield differentials and short workout periods. The workout period is the period of time in which a realignment of bond values takes place. In general, the larger the yield differential between bonds and the shorter the workout period, the greater is the return from the bond swap. Investors face the risks that the yield differentials may not change as anticipated and that the workout period will be longer than expected. Because of these risks, some investors close out their swap positions quickly if the market moves in an unexpected direction.

The evaluation of swaps is a difficult task even with computer programs. A simple approach to this evaluation is *horizon analysis*.[13] Horizon analysis is a logical framework which decomposes the various aspects of swap returns into four components with different levels of risk. The certain return components are those aspects of yield changes which are attributable to (1) the passage of time (time component) and (2) the coupon interest. Uncertainty surrounds (3) the realization of any capital gains due to changes in the yield to maturity (Δ yield component) and (4) the interest on reinvested coupons, a return component of increasing importance as the holding period increases. Thus,

$$
\begin{array}{ccccc}
& \text{time} & \text{coupon} & \Delta \text{ yield} & \text{interest on} \\
\text{Total return} = & \text{component} + & \text{interest} + & \text{component} + & \text{reinvested coupons} \\
& \text{(certain)} & \text{(certain)} & \text{(uncertain)} & \text{(uncertain)}
\end{array}
$$

To illustrate horizon analysis, consider Table 16-4, which lists various prices for a 14½% coupon bond. Let's examine the bondholder's total return, assuming the bond is purchased with 10 years to maturity and a 13% yield to maturity, and sold 1 year later at an 11% yield to maturity. The initial purchase price would be $1081.22, which can be found in the 10-year column and the 13% row in Table 16-4. One year later, and with a yield to maturity of 11%, the bond would be priced at $1195.90, resulting in a capital gain of $114.68. This capital gain can be broken down into two components—the certain time component, which assumes no change in yield to maturity, and the uncertain component due to changes in yield to maturity. Notice that if the yield had not changed, the bond price with 9 years to maturity would be $1077.17, resulting in a decrease of $4.05 in price due simply to the passage of time (the time component).[14] However, because of the change 1 year later in yield to maturity from 13% to 11%, the bond price would increase from $1077.17 to $1195.90—thus, the uncertain gain due to the change in yield would be $118.73. To complete the example, we must recognize the coupon interest and the interest on the reinvested coupon interest. The total coupon interest for 1 year is $145, and interest on the first coupon reinvested at 13% for the final 6 months is $4.71 ($145/2 × 13% × 1/2). By placing these return components over the purchase price of $1081.22, we compute the total return of 24.5%:

$$
\begin{aligned}
\text{Total return} &= \frac{-4.05 + 118.73 + 145.00 + 4.71}{1081.22} \\
&= \frac{264.39}{1081.22} = 24.5\%
\end{aligned}
$$

If the workout period is shorter, say 6 months, the yield and coupon components will comprise a greater and lesser proportion, respectively, of total return. If interest

[13]M. Leibowitz, "Horizon Analysis for Managed Portfolios," *Journal of Portfolio Management* (spring 1975).

[14]This systematic decrease in price over time for a premium bond (increase in price for a discount bond) is obvious once one notes that the bond will be redeemed at par on the maturity date.

TABLE 16-4   AN ILLUSTRATION OF HORIZON ANALYSIS

Prices for a 14½% coupon bond, for various yields to maturity and time to maturity

Yield to maturity, %	Time to maturity		
	10 years	9½ years	9 years
10	1280.35	1272.52	1262.52
11	1209.37	1203.72	1195.90 ↑
12	1141.85	1139.10	1135.17 ↑
13	1081.22 →	1079.82 →	1077.17
14	1026.06	1025.78	1025.07

Example of horizon analysis: Purchase bond at 13% YTM with 10 years to maturity and sell 1 year later, at which time YTM changes to 11%.

Certain components
- price change due to passage of time $\dfrac{1077.17 - 1081.22}{1081.22} = -0.4\%$
- coupon interest $\dfrac{145.00}{1081.22} = 13.4\%$

Uncertain components
- price change due to Δ yield $\dfrac{1195.90 - 1077.17}{1081.22} = 11.0\%$
- interest on reinvested coupons $\dfrac{(75.50)(.13)(\frac{1}{2})}{1081.22} = 0.4\%$

Total return $\dfrac{-4.05 + 145.00 + 118.73 + 4.71}{1081.22} = \underline{24.5\%}$

Source: Adapted from M. Leibowitz, "Horizon Analysis for Managed Portfolios," *Journal of Portfolio Management* (spring 1975).

rates were to fall from 13% to 11% in 6 months, the total return is 18.0% for the 6-month period (39.2% on an annualized basis).

$$\text{Total return} = \frac{1079.82 - 1081.22}{1081.22} + \frac{1203.73 - 1079.82}{1081.22} + \frac{72.50}{1081.22} + \frac{0}{1081.22}$$

$$= -.00129 + .11459 + .06705 = .180 = 18.0\%$$

Thus, horizon analysis provides a mechanism for evaluating the returns generated by bonds. Now, let us consider two categories of bond swaps to illustrate how investors attempt to earn abnormal profits by trading bonds.

TABLE 16-5 SUBSTITUTION SWAP

Bond currently held: 30-year, 7% government bond priced at $1000 to yield 7%

Bond offered for swap: 30-year, 7% government bond priced at $987.70 to yield 7.10%

Assumed workout period: 1 year

Reinvestment rate: 7%

	Current bond	New bond
Dollar investment per bond	$1000.00	$987.70
Total coupons received	70.00	70.00
Interest on one coupon @ 7% for 6 months	1.23	1.23
Principal value at year-end @ 7% YTM	1000.00	1000.00
Total dollars accrued	$1071.23	$1071.23
Total dollar gain	71.23	83.53
Gain per invested dollar	.07123	.08458
Realized semiannual compound yield	7.00%	8.29%
Value of swap	129 basis points in 1 year	

Source: Sidney Homes and Martin Leibowitz, *Inside the Yield Book*, Prentice-Hall, Englewood Cliffs, N.J., 1972, p. 84.

16-3-1 Substitution Swap   A substitution swap is an exchange of one bond for a perfect substitute bond to earn several basis points due to a transitory mispricing.[15] For example, an investor might hold a 30-year, 7% government bond yielding 7% and be offered an identical bond yielding 7.10%. The expectation is that the 7.10% yield on the offered bond will fall to the level of the bond currently held. The investor makes a substitution swap by selling the bond yielding 7% and purchasing the bond yielding 7.10%. Table 16-5 describes this swap. The realized yield for the bond with the promised yield of 7.10% will be 8.29%, assuming the bond is priced to yield 7.00% at the end of 1 year. For the bond currently held, 7.00% is both the promised and the realized yield. Thus, the investor will earn an additional 129 basis points in 1 year by selling the bond currently held and buying the bond offered. Of course, this swap is not riskless. There is risk from a slower workout period than anticipated, from adverse interim yield differentials, from adverse changes in overall interest rates, and from the possibility that the bond offered is not a perfect substitute for the bond held. For example, if the workout time is the total 30 years to maturity, the investor will earn only a slight improvement in yield (less than 10 basis points per year due to the assumed constant reinvestment rate).

16-3-2 Intermarket Spread Swap   The intermarket spread swap refers to the switching of bonds from different market sectors. The motive behind this swap is the investor's belief that yield differentials, or yield spreads, between two market sectors are out of their proper alignment. In contrast with the substitution swap, the two bonds

[15]The classification of various swaps into substitution swaps and other categories was first described in S. Homer and M. Leibowitz, *Inside the Yield Book*, Prentice-Hall, Englewood Cliffs, N.J., 1972.

in the intermarket spread swap are entirely different bonds—for example, an industrial bond is swapped for a utility bond.

Investors execute intermarket spread swaps in two directions. One direction is to buy a new bond offered at a higher yield and sell the bond currently held. The expectation is that the intermarket spread will *narrow* with the yield of the new bond decreasing (relative to the bond held) and its price rising. The higher price will produce a capital gain. The second direction is where the new bond has a lower yield than the bond currently held. In this case the investor expects the yield spread to *widen*, which would lower the yield of the newly acquired bond (relative to the bond held) and raise its price sufficiently to offset the yield decline.

An example of an intermarket spread swap in the direction of narrowing yield spreads is shown in Table 16-6. The rationale of the swap is that the normal spread of 50 basis points will narrow to 40 basis points. By switching to the corporate bond yielding 7.00% with the expectation that its yield will fall to 6.90%, the bond's price will rise from $1000 to $1012.46, *if the swap works out as expected*. This price plus the coupon interest and the interest on the reinvested coupon results in total value of $1083.69 at the end of the year. Thus, the investor will earn 8.20% for the year, which represents a gain of 170 basis points in 1 year over the alternative of continuing to hold the government bond.

An investor who makes intermarket spread swaps faces several risks. The market may move in an adverse direction, the workout period may elongate, and adverse interim price movements may occur. Or the rationale for the swap may be swamped

TABLE 16-6 INTERMARKET SPREAD SWAP IN THE DIRECTION OF NARROWING SPREADS

Bond currently held: 30-year, 4% government bond priced at $671.82 to yield 6.50%

New bond offered for swap: 30-year, 7% Aaa corporate bond priced at $1000 to yield 7%

Assumed workout period: 1 year

Reinvestment rate: 7%

Swap rationale: Spread of 50 basis points will narrow to 40 basis points with corporate bond yielding 6.90% and government bond continuing to yield 6.50%

	Current bond	New bond
Dollar investment per bond	$671.82	$1000.00
Coupons	40.00	70.00
Interest on one coupon @ 7% for 6 months	.70	1.23
Principal value at year-end	675.55	1012.46
Total dollars accrued	$716.25	$1083.69
Total dollar gain	44.23	83.69
Gain per invested dollar	.0661	.0837
Realized semiannual compound yield	6.50%	8.20%
Value of swap	170 basis points in 1 year	

Source: Sidney Homer and Martin Leibowitz, *Inside the Yield Book*, Prentice-Hall, Englewood Cliffs, N.J., 1972, p. 90.

by other differences between the two bonds. Clearly, swaps are not for the faint-hearted and involve a considerable amount of market knowledge.

There are many other types of swaps we could discuss—tax swaps, for example. One type of tax swap might involve substituting nontaxable municipal bonds for taxable corporate bonds of the same risk to increase the investor's after-tax return. Similarly, high-coupon bonds selling near par might be swapped for low-coupon bonds selling at a large discount in order to increase the after-tax return because of the differential tax rate on capital gains vs. interest income. The serious bond investor will want to examine bond swaps in more detail, and the starting point is *Inside the Yield Book* by Homer and Leibowitz, one of the references at the end of this chapter.

16-4 BONDS AND THE MARKET MODEL

As discussed in Chapter 4, systematic risk, or beta, provides a measure of risk for individual stocks and equity portfolios. The market model indicates that the return on a stock is a function of its systematic risk. However, the usual perception of bond risk is to consider separately interest rate risk and default risk without any mention of systematic risk in a portfolio framework. A natural question then becomes, does the market model have any relevancy for bond risk analysis, and if not, why not?

Underlying portfolio theory and the market model is the fact that diversification reduces portfolio risk without sacrificing any return. However, if bonds have risk composed entirely of systematic or market risk, diversification will not reduce total portfolio risk.

Default and interest rate risk are largely systematic in nature according to several recent studies.[16] Bonds tend to default at low points in the business cycle—thus, the probability of default for individual bonds should vary systematically as business conditions vary. However, the empirical evidence regarding the link between beta and default risk or agency ratings is mixed. While one study found no relationship between beta and rating,[17] another did find a direct relationship.[18] The difference between these two studies may rest on the use of investment-grade (Baa and higher rated) bonds in the former study and all rated bonds (Aaa through C) in the latter study. Since bond ratings are determined largely by the financial characteristics of the issues, default risk probably is both unsystematic and systematic in nature. That is, firm-specific, or unsystematic, factors are likely determinants of default risk, in addition to systematic, or economywide, factors. If this is the case, at least part of the risk associated with bonds is diversifiable.

Interest rate risk is also systematic in nature. For default-free bonds, bond prices and beta are related through the concept of duration:[19]

---

[16]F. Reilly and M. Joehnk, "The Association between Market Determined Risk Measures for Bonds and Bond Ratings," *Journal of Finance* (December 1976); J. Boquist, G. Racette, and G. Schlarbaum, "Duration and Risk Assessment for Bonds and Common Stock," *Journal of Finance* (December 1975); G. Alexander, "Applying the Market Model to Long-Term Corporate Bonds," *Journal of Financial and Quantitative Analysis* (December 1980); and M. Weinstein, "The Systematic Risk of Corporate Bonds," *Journal of Financial and Quantitative Analysis* (September 1981).

[17]Reilly and Joehnk, op. cit.

[18]Weinstein, op. cit.

[19]See Alexander, op. cit., and R. A. Jarrow, "The Relationship between Yield, Risk, and Return of Corporate Bonds," *Journal of Finance* (September 1978).

$$\beta_t = -D_t \frac{\text{Cov}(dr_t, R_{mt})}{\sigma^2(R_{mt})} \tag{16-1}$$

where β_t = beta of bond at time t

dr_t = change in yield to maturity

R_{mt} = rate of return on market portfolio

D_t = duration of bond at time t

Note that the covariance of changes in yields to maturity with the return on the market portfolio will be *negative* because increases in R_{mt} will be associated with increases in security prices, which in turn will be associated with decreases in the discount rate (yield to maturity) for bonds. Thus, Equation (16-1) indicates that *bonds with longer durations will have larger betas*. However, there are several problems with this relationship. The most important problem is that a bond's interest rate risk, as measured by duration, continually changes as the bond matures, thereby making the bond's beta unstable over time. In other words, the covariance of returns between any two bonds or a bond and the market portfolio are likely to be unstable over time.[20] Empirical evidence bears out the latter statement; tests of monthly price changes for corporate bonds and of quarterly price changes for government bonds indicate that the bond return–duration relationship is nonlinear.[21]

So it appears that even though beta or systematic risk is related to interest rate and default risk, these relationships are unstable over time and nonlinear. This suggests that the use of beta, duration, or any other *single* factor to measure bond risk is unwise. Consequently, the analyst will want to consider each bond's interest rate risk (as measured by duration) and default risk, as well as the unique characteristics of the bond such as call and sinking fund provisions.

16-5 PORTFOLIOS OF STOCKS AND BONDS

Although the benefits of diversification may be limited for bond portfolios, diversification across stocks and bonds may provide superior risk and return characteristics. That is, a portfolio with a combination of bonds and stocks may provide superior risk-adjusted returns compared with portfolios comprised solely of bonds or solely of stocks. A recent study supports this point with its finding that gains from diversification among major asset categories are substantial.[22]

This study was designed to test whether an active, market-timing strategy of changing the proportions of the portfolio's assets invested in treasury bills, treasury bonds, corporate bonds, and common stocks could produce superior returns. The actual strat-

[20]Boquist, Racette, and Schlarbaum, op. cit.; and G. O. Bierwag, G. Kaufman, and A. Toevs, "Single Factor Duration Models in a Discrete General Equilibrium Framework," *Journal of Finance* (May 1982).

[21]Alexander, op. cit.; and P. Dietz, R. Fogler, and A. Rivers, "Duration, Nonlinearity, and Bond Portfolio Performance," *Journal of Portfolio Management* (spring 1981).

[22]R. Grauer and N. Hakansson, "Higher Return, Lower Risk: Historical Returns on Long-Run, Actively Managed Portfolios of Stocks, Bonds, and Bills," *Financial Analyst Journal* (March–April 1982). More recently, R. Grauer and N. Hakansson, "Returns on Levered, Actively Managed Long-Run Portfolios of Stocks, Bonds and Bills, 1934–1983," *Financial Analysts Journal* (September–October, 1985).

egy used was relatively complex and beyond the scope of this text. In addition, the results purporting to show that the timing strategy achieved abnormal profits are debatable. However, the study did highlight the advantages of diversifying across various asset classes, such as bonds and stock.

Figure 16-2 illustrates the results for the 1936–1978 period, where RL stands for a portfolio consisting entirely of treasury bills, GB stands for an all-treasury bond portfolio, CB stands for an all corporate bond portfolio, and CS stands for an all common stock portfolio. If an investor had simply rolled over T-bills (that is, bought T-bills, held them until maturity, and reinvested the proceeds in new T-bills), he would have earned a geometric mean return of approximately 3.0% per year with an associated standard deviation of 2.5%. At the other end of the risk-return spectrum, an all common stock, buy-and-hold strategy would have produced a geometric mean return of 9.6% and a standard deviation of 18.1%.

There are several worthwhile points to be made concerning Figure 16-2. First, note that the T-bill rate, which is frequently thought of as the risk-free rate, varies over time. Thus, in a multi-time-period environment, even a default-free investment still bears risk because of changing reinvestment rates. Second, unless the returns on T-

FIGURE 16-2   Geometric means and standard deviations of returns, 1936 to 1978 (annual portfolio revision, no leverage). RL = all T-bills; GB = all government bonds; CB = all corporate bonds; CS = all common stocks; 1 = risk neutrality; −75 = very high risk aversion. [*Source: R. Grauer and N. Hakannson, "Higher Return, Lower Risk: Historical Returns on Long-Run, Actively Managed Portfolios of Stocks, Bonds, and Bills,"* Financial Analysts Journal *(March–April 1982).*]

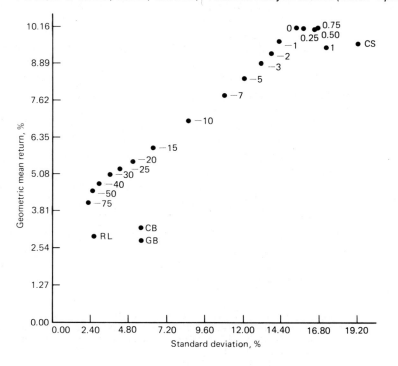

bills, T-bonds, corporate bonds, and common stocks are *perfectly* correlated, we would expect some reduction in risk by diversifying across each of these classes of assets. Indeed, this was the case. The point denoted '' − 75'' represents the outcomes for the most risk-averse strategy in this study. Note that the standard deviation of this portfolio (which was 2.2%) was *less* than the standard deviation associated with an all T-bill strategy—yet the portfolio for this very risk-averse strategy generally contained all four asset classes, including common stocks. This should not be particularly surprising. Recall from Chapter 3 that combinations of assets with returns that are not perfectly correlated will tend to push the ''efficient frontier'' to the left on the risk-return graph. Now, consider the portfolio denoted ''0.75,'' which represents the results of a relatively aggressive strategy. Notice that the return for this portfolio is higher than the return for the all common stock portfolio. This is due, in part, to the lower variability of return of this portfolio, which contained fixed-income securities as well as stocks. The lower variability resulted in the geometric return of the diversified portfolio being higher than the return of the more variable all common stock portfolio.

These intriguing results imply that investors can enhance portfolio return by diversifying across both fixed-income securities and common stocks. The assumptions that extremely risk-averse investors should always invest in bills or bonds, or that very aggressive investors should invest only in stocks, are questionable. Clearly, a judicious mix of bills, bonds, and stocks over time shows promise as a way to potentially enhance portfolio return while also reducing risk.

16-6 PENSION FUNDS AND BOND PORTFOLIOS

Many portfolio managers of pension funds tend to avoid bonds and invest their funds mainly in common stocks because of the greater returns associated with stocks. Their rationale is: A pension fund is a long-term portfolio and common stocks will likely provide higher returns than bonds over long time periods. Also, common stocks are potentially an inflation hedge. This line of reasoning suggests that bonds have a minor role in pension fund management. However, if one considers the tax environment of the pension fund and the corporation involved, bonds may play a leading role in pension fund management.

The tax treatment of pension funds has two salient features: (1) all corporate contributions to the pension fund are tax-deductible and (2) the interest and dividends earned on pension fund assets are not taxed as long as they remain in the fund or are used to pay pension benefits. These tax features provide an incentive for the pension fund manager to invest *all* the pension fund in bonds. Contrary to accepted practice, *an all-bond pension fund may maximize both shareholders' and pensioners' welfare because of tax arbitrage.*[23]

Table 16-7 provides a hypothetical illustration of the potential advantages obtainable by switching a pension fund's assets from common stocks to bonds. Suppose that

---

[23]I. Tepper, ''Taxation and Corporate Pension Policy,'' *Journal of Finance* (March 1981); F. Black, ''The Tax Consequences of Long-Run Pension Policy,'' *Financial Analysts Journal* (July/August 1980); and F. Black and M. Dewhurst, ''A New Investment Strategy for Pension Funds,'' *Journal of Portfolio Management* (summer 1981).

TABLE 16-7 A HYPOTHETICAL ILLUSTRATION OF SUBSTITUTING BONDS FOR COMMON STOCKS IN A PENSION FUND

	Before switch		After switch	
	Bonds	**Equity**	**Bonds**	**Equity**
Balance sheet				
Firm liabilities	–0–	$4000	$1000	$3000
Less: Fund assets	–0–	(1000)	(1000)	–0–
Consolidated	–0–	$3000	–0–	$3000
Income statement				
EBIT		$1000		$1000
I at 15%		(–0–)		(150)
EBT		1000		850
Taxes at 40%		(400)		(340)
EAT		600		510
Less fund's pro rata share		(150)		–0–
EAT available for nonfund shareholders		450		510
Fund's annual income:				
Pro rata share of EAT		150		–0–
Interest		–0–		150
		150		150

initially the firm had issued common stock with a market value of $4000, and that the firm's pension fund owned $1000 of the firm's own common stock and no other asset. Also, assume that the pension fund needs to earn $150 per year in order to meet the future pension benefits that will be owed to the employees. Since the firm must ultimately make up any future shortfall of the pension fund (if any should occur), the fund is, in fact, a liability of the firm. Viewing the pension fund as a part of the firm, we can consolidate the two entities by simply subtracting the assets of the fund from the liabilities of the firm. Thus, on a consolidated basis the stock owned by the fund is similar to treasury stock, leaving $3000 of the firm's stock outstanding in this example.

Now, suppose that the firm issues $1000 of 15% bonds and that the fund buys the bonds from the firm. At the same time, the firm uses the proceeds from the bonds to buy back the $1000 of its stock owned by the fund. The firm would continue to have $3000 of stock outstanding. In addition, on a consolidated basis the bonds owned by the fund would offset the bonds issued by the firm, resulting in no debt outstanding.

Thus, on a consolidated basis, the balance sheet remains unchanged after the switch. However, the income statement is changed and, because interest payments are tax-deductible, both the shareholders and the beneficiaries of the pension fund will be better off. Earnings before interest and taxes, of course are unaffected by this switch and remain the same—in this example, EBIT is equal to $1000. Before the switch the firm did not have any interest expense and therefore earnings before taxes are also $1000, and assuming a 40% tax rate earnings after taxes are $600. However, one-fourth of this, or $150, in effect belongs to the future beneficiaries of the pension fund, since before the switch the fund owns 25% of the stock. Thus, before the switch $450 of earnings is available for the nonfund shareholders.

After the fund's switch from stocks to bonds, the firm pays $150 dollars of interest, reducing earnings before taxes to $850 but also reducing taxes by $60, from $400 to $340. This leaves earnings after taxes of $510, all of which now belongs to the nonfund shareholders. Thus, the earnings available to the shareholders has been increased by $60. Since the pension fund's earnings are tax-free, the beneficiaries of the pension fund have the same income, $150. And the beneficiaries' future pensions are more secure because the more profitable the firm, the more likely the firm will be able to meet its future pension obligations. The loser in this switch is the government, since it will collect $60 less in taxes.

While this is a rather contrived example, it does illustrate the tax advantage of holding bonds in the pension fund, as opposed to common stock. In a more realistic example, the pension fund would probably not own the stock of the parent firm, but rather it would own a diversified portfolio of stocks. However, this does not present a serious problem, at least conceptually. The firm should still issue bonds, the proceeds from which would now be used to buy a portfolio of stocks similar to that held by the fund. The fund should sell its portfolio of stocks and buy bonds with characteristics similar to those issued by the firm. Thus, the bonds held by the fund would offset those sold by the firm, and on a consolidated basis the balance sheet would remain roughly unchanged. But the amount of taxes paid by the firm would be reduced because of the interest expense deduction. Thus, as long as the deductibility of interest expense by the firm and the tax-free status of pension fund earnings are not repealed by Congress, a strong case can be made for making bonds the major component of pension fund assets.

16-7 SUMMARY

This chapter discussed a number of bond investment strategies. The ground rules were first set by considering the extent of market efficiency in the bond market. The use of historical price patterns was shown to have little predictive value for the government bond sector and for interest rate forecasts. Even the experts have a difficult time forecasting interest rates from publicly available information. However, the evidence concerning individual bonds is mixed. Some studies suggest individual bonds may be mispriced and that transitory abnormal profit opportunities may exist in some sectors of the bond market. Other studies indicate that the bond markets are semistrong-form efficient with respect to individual bond selection. Thus, more work needs to be done in this area before we can draw firm conclusions.

Investors vary according to their objectives and strategies toward bond portfolios. While some investors prefer current income, others seek to maximize capital gains. We examined the continuum of bond portfolio objectives and then compared active and passive management strategies. Passive strategists avoid interest rate forecasting and may adopt an immunization strategy to offset price risk and coupon reinvestment rate risk. An immunization strategy will most often result in realized yields equaling promised yields.

Although active management defies market efficiency, numerous investors engage in active strategies. Two types of bond swaps were examined—substitution and intermarket spread swaps. The investor trades identical bonds with a substitution swap and bonds from entirely different sectors of the bond market with an intermarket spread swap. Bond swaps require extensive bond market expertise to identify transitory price misalignments, and the increasing number of sophisticated investors and improving technology makes bond swapping a difficult task.

Although the market model is an important approach to quantifying risk and return for common stock portfolios, its applicability to bond portfolios is open to question. While interest rate risk and default risk may be related to systematic risk, bond betas are inherently unstable over time.

The chapter closed with two additional thoughts. First, a portfolio which is diversified across T-bills, bonds, and stocks may provide higher returns and lower risk than portfolios consisting entirely of any one type of asset. In fact, it may be possible to construct a diversified portfolio which includes common stocks and still has less risk than a portfolio completely invested in T-bills. The other new concept is that owing to the tax laws, pension funds should hold only bonds. On an after-tax basis, both shareholders and beneficiaries of the pension fund may be better off.

SUGGESTED READINGS

The starting point for studying in more detail bond trading strategies, particularly bond swaps, is:

S. Homer and M. Leibowitz, *Inside the Yield Book*, Prentice-Hall, Englewood Cliffs, N.J., 1972.

The following are recent articles which should be useful to the serious bond investor:

M. Adler, "Global Fixed Income Portfolio Management," *Financial Analysts Journal* (September/October 1983).

C. Billingham, "Strategies for Enhancing Bond Portfolio Returns," *Financial Analysts Journal* (May/June 1983).

G. Fong and O. Vasicek, "The Tradeoff between Return and Risk in Immunized Portfolios," *Financial Analysts Journal* (September/October 1983).

G. Fong, C. Pearson, and O. Vasicek, "Bond Performance: Analyzing Sources of Returns," *Journal of Portfolio Management* (spring 1983).

M. L. Leibowitz, "The Dedicated Bond Portfolio in Pension Funds—Parts I and II," *Financial Analysts Journal* (January/February and March/April 1986).

M. L. Leibowitz and A. Weinberger, "Contingent Immunization—Parts I and II," *Financial Analysts Journal* (November/December 1982 and January/February 1983).

F. H. Trainer, "The Uses of Treasury Bond Futures in Fixed-Income Portfolio Management," *Financial Analysts Journal* (January/February 1983).

QUESTIONS

1 Bond market efficiency is empirically unproved. Comment.

2 Why might a bond rating change not be anticipated by investors?

3 What advice would you give an individual investor seeking to speculate in the bond market?

4 What is a bond swap and what are its implications for current and future market efficiency?

5 If you expect interest rates to fall, what maturity structure would you impose on your bond portfolio?

6 Immunization strategies may not always cause equality between realized and promised yields. Why?

7 How would an individual investor assess risk from a passive management vantage point?

8 How is the systematic risk of bonds related to interest rate risk and yet virtually unusable for practical purposes?

9 What is horizon analysis and why is it useful?

10 How are the substitution and intermarket spread swaps similar?

11 An all-bond portfolio is the best portfolio for certain market periods. Comment.

12 Can an argument be made that pension funds invested in common stocks may become extinct. Why?

13 Drawing on the efficient markets literature, do you believe intermarket spread swaps are a viable strategy?

PART FIVE

ASSET PRICING
THEORIES

This section provides background for Asset Pricing Theories. The models that are developed from these theories are known as equilibrium models and as such provide an understanding of how prices are formed in the market place.

Chapter 17 describes the assumptions and analytical framework underlying the Capital Asset Pricing Model (CAPM) as well as the Arbitrage Pricing Theory (APT). The CAPM is the earliest developed model of equilibrium and is perhaps the most widely used model. The key notion underlying the CAPM is that systematic risk and not total risk is the relevant component of risk for securities and portfolios. Furthermore, the CAPM asserts that return should be proportional to systematic risk. Under certain conditions, the risk measure and risk-return relationship derived from the APT is the same as the CAPM. The APT however derives an equilibrium relationship using fewer and perhaps somewhat more plausible underlying assumptions. On the other hand, testing the model is substantially more difficult.

Chapter 18 describes empirical tests of the asset pricing models. Having been developed earlier than the APT, the CAPM has a more extensive history of testing. Results of the tests are promising in broadly verifying the implications of the CAPM. At the same time, the tests also indicate that empirical data do not correspond exactly with the implications of the CAPM; there are notable divergences. Tests of the APT are much more limited and the conclusions considerably more tentative than is the case of the CAPM.

Chapter 19 describes option pricing theory. The models that derive from this theory can be broadly classified as models for pricing derivative securities. For example, an option is a derivative security that has value that is contingent on an underlying security; stock or bond. The Black-Scholes option valuation model is the classic model of option valuation and is the one we describe in this chapter.

CHAPTER 17

CAPITAL MARKET THEORY

After reading this chapter, you should:

1 Have a better understanding of the CAPM—its underlying assumptions, and its implications for risk and return

2 Be aware of some of the different versions of the CAPM, such as the zero-beta CAPM

3 Understand the implications of the tax-adjusted CAPM, such as the strategy known as *yield tilt*

4 Have a basic understanding of the relatively new capital market theory known as APT—arbitrage pricing theory

Capital market theory deals with the relationship between risk and return. In Chapters 3 and 4 we introduced some of the basic concepts. Chapter 3 largely dealt with how to quantify risk and return both for individual securities and for portfolios. In the process, the risk-reducing nature of diversification was illustrated. Chapter 4 introduced the market model, and to a lesser extent, the capital asset pricing model (CAPM). These models argue that the measure of *individual* security risk is its beta and that there is a linear relationship between return and beta. However, in Chapters 3 and 4, the reader was asked to accept these risk and return concepts based on simple, intuitive explanations. The purpose of this chapter is to explore in more detail some of the theories of capital market equilibrium. In addition to examining the underlying assumptions of these theories, we will consider their implications for investors.

17-1 PORTFOLIO THEORY

Capital market theory deals with how asset prices are determined in the marketplace. As we have noted many times before, a price reflects the *expected* return and risk associated with an asset. Thus, capital market theories are ex ante theories. The starting point for developing theories concerning risk and return is Markowitz's portfolio theory.[1] Before beginning, however, we need to review how risk and return are quantified.

17-1-1 A Quick Review of Portfolio Mathematics Recall from Section 3-4 that the expected return for a portfolio $E(r_p)$ can be expressed as

[1] Harry M. Markowitz, "Portfolio Selection," *Journal of Finance*, vol. 7, no. 1 (March 1952), pp. 77–91.

$$E(r_p) = \sum_{i=1}^{n} E(r_i) \, W_i \tag{17-1}$$

where $E(r_i)$ represents the expected return for the ith asset and W_i represents the weight of the asset in the portfolio, i.e., the value of the asset held in the portfolio divided by the total value of the portfolio.

In Chapter 3 we argued that standard deviation of return is an appropriate measure of risk. Our argument was based on the intuitive notion that the more variable an asset's returns the riskier the asset, as future returns will be more uncertain or harder to predict. Since standard deviation σ is the most commonly accepted measure of variability, it was also chosen as the measure of risk for portfolios. Recall from Chapter 3 that variance σ_p^2 of portfolio returns is expressed as

$$\sigma_p^2 = \sum_{i=1}^{n} \sum_{j=1}^{n} \mathrm{Cov}_{ij} \, W_i \, W_j = \sum_{i=1}^{n} \sigma_i^2 \, W_i^2 + 2 \sum^{*} \mathrm{Cov}_{ij} \, W_i W_j \tag{17-2}$$

where Cov_{ij} represents the covariance between the returns of the ith and jth assets, and $* = (n^2 - n)/2$, the number of unique covariance terms. The standard deviation σ_p, of course, is simply the square root of the variance.

Finally, recall that the correlation coefficient ρ_{ij} is a standardized measure of covariance.

$$\rho_{ij} = \frac{\mathrm{Cov}_{ij}}{\sigma_i \, \sigma_j} \quad \text{or} \quad \mathrm{Cov}_{ij} = \rho_{ij} \, \sigma_i \, \sigma_j \tag{17-3}$$

These are the basic equations necessary to understand the development of Markowitz's portfolio theory. If you do not feel comfortable with these constructs, a review of Chapter 3, particularly Sections 3-3 to 3-5, will be helpful before proceeding.

17-1-2 Markowitz's Assumptions   The capital-asset pricing model builds on the Markowitz model, and because of that it automatically makes the assumptions listed in the top part of Table 17-1 that are necessary for that model of portfolio theory. In particular, it assumes (1) that investors are risk-averse expected utility maximizers, (2) that they choose their portfolios on the basis of the mean and variance of return, and (3) that they have a one-period time horizon that is the same for all investors. The implications of these assumptions are that investors will diversify and will want to select portfolios from somewhere on the efficient frontier.

17-1-3 The Efficient Frontier   The notion of efficiency can be best illustrated by means of Figure 17-1. (The underlying fundamentals for this notion were developed in Section 3-3, and the reader may wish to refer to that section as background to this concept.) The vertical axis refers to expected return, the horizontal axis refers to risk as measured by the standard deviation of return, and the shaded area represents the set of all the possible portfolios that could be obtained from a given group of securities

TABLE 17-1 ASSUMPTIONS FOR THE CAPM

Common to both the Markowitz model and the CAPM:
1 Investors are risk-averse expected utility maximizers
2 Investors choose portfolios on the basis of their expected mean and variance of return
3 Single holding period that is the same for all investors

Additional assumptions:
4 Unrestricted borrowing and lending at the risk-free rate
5 Investors have homogeneous expectations regarding the means, variances, and covariances of security returns
6 No taxes and no market imperfections such as transactions costs

by varying the porportionate holdings of each security. A certain level of return and a certain risk will be associated with each possible portfolio. Thus, each portfolio is represented by a single point in the shaded area of the figure.

Note that the efficient set is represented by the upper left-hand boundary of the shaded area between points A and B. Portfolios along this efficient frontier dominate those below the line. Specifically, they offer higher return than those at an equivalent level of risk or, alternatively, entail less risk at an equivalent level of return. For example, note that portfolio C, which does not lie on the efficient boundary, is dominated by portfolios D and E, which do lie on the efficient boundary. Portfolio D offers greater return than portfolio C at the same level of risk, while portfolio E entails less risk than portfolio C at the same level of return.

Rational investors will thus prefer to hold efficient portfolios—that is, ones on the line and not those below it. The particular portfolio that an individual investor selects from the efficient frontier depends on the investor's degree of aversion to risk. An investor who is highly averse to risk will hold one on the lower left-hand segment of the frontier, while an investor who is not too risk-averse will hold one on the upper portion. In more technical terms, the selection depends on the investor's risk aversion,

FIGURE 17-1 The portfolio possibility set.

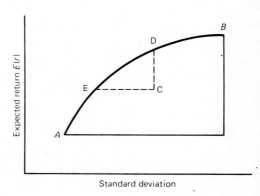

which might be characterized by the nature and shape of the investor's risk-return utility function.

17-2 THE CAPITAL ASSET PRICING MODEL

As noted, the capital asset pricing model was developed by building on the portfolio theory pioneered by Markowitz. William Sharpe[2] in 1964, John Lintner in 1965,[3] and Jan Mossin[4] in 1967 laid the basis for the capital asset pricing model (CAPM). As a model of general equilibrium in the market, the CAPM provides explicit implications with respect to (1) the behavior of security prices, (2) the sort of risk-return relationship that one would expect, and (3) the appropriate measure of risk for securities. The CAPM has had, in turn, a wide-ranging impact on such areas of the investment profession as security valuation, risk analysis, and performance measurement.

17-2-1 Additional Assumptions In order to develop a model that goes beyond the implications of portfolio theory, there was need for researchers to make stronger assumptions than those used to develop the Markowitz model. The bottom part of Table 17-1 lists these additional assumptions. Note that one of these is that a risk-free asset exists and that borrowing and lending at the risk-free rate is unrestricted. While treasury bills are risk-free in nominal terms and are usually taken as a proxy for a risk-free asset, there is question whether in an inflationary environment there is such a thing as a risk-free asset; i.e., there will be uncertainty of real return. After developing the model assuming the existence of a risk-free asset, we'll examine the effect on the model of relaxing this particular assumption.

Another assumption of the CAPM is that investors have homogeneous expectations regarding the means, variances, and covariances of security returns. This assumption suggests that every investor has an identical view of the prospects for each security. This, in turn, allows us to derive the model in a relatively straightforward fashion as well as to develop implications that are relatively unambiguous. Actually, the model can be derived assuming only that there is a "considerable consensus"[5] by investors regarding future prospects. However, the derivation becomes more complex and the implications less clear than when homogeneous expectations are assumed.

The model's additional assumptions of no taxes and other market imperfections, such as transactions costs, are needed to make possible the arbitraging of "mispriced" securities, thus forcing an equilibrium price. When the assumption of no taxes is relaxed, the question arises as to whether high-dividend stocks offer higher pretax returns than do low-dividend stocks of equivalent risk. This is currently a subject of considerable theoretical debate and much empirical testing. We'll develop an alternative form of the CAPM assuming a tax effect in this chapter and discuss the empirical

[2] William F. Sharpe, "Capital Asset Prices: A Theory of Market Equilibrium under Conditions of Risk," *Journal of Finace*, vol. 19, no. 3 (September 1964), pp. 425–442.

[3] John Lintner, "Security Prices, Risk, and Maximal Gains from Diversification," *Journal of Finance*, vol. 20, no. 12 (December 1965), pp. 587–615.

[4] Jan Mossin, "Equilibrium in a Capital Asset Market," *Econometrica*, vol. 34, no. 4 (October 1966).

[5] John Lintner, "The Aggregation of Investors' Judgments and Preferences in Purely Competitive Security Markets," *Journal of Financial and Quantitative Analysis* (December 1968), pp. 347–400.

evidence regarding this issue in detail in the next chapter. Correspondingly, the existence of transactions costs means that securities can be potentially mispriced by an amount equal to transactions costs. This effect will vary depending on the type and size of the transaction.

Given these assumptions, the implications are that there is a capital asset pricing model consisting of a capital market line (CML) and a security market line (SML). The capital market line provides the framework for determining the relationship between expected return and risk for portfolios of securities. Correspondingly, it indicates the appropriate measure of risk for a portfolio. The security market line provides the framework for determining the relationship between expected return and risk for individual securities as well as for portfolios. The security market line also indicates the appropriate measure of risk for securities. It is useful to first cover the CML as it provides a foundation for a better understanding of the SML that, in turn, has broader application in understanding the risk-return trade-off in the marketplace.

17-2-2 Lending and Borrowing   The capital market line (CML) is usually derived under the assumption that there exists a riskless asset available for investment. It is further assumed that investors can borrow or lend as much as desired at the risk-free rate r_f. Given this opportunity, investors can then mix risk-free assets with a portfolio of risky assets M to obtain the desired risk-return combination. Letting W_f represent the proportion invested in the risk-free assets and $1 - W_f$ represent the proportion invested in the risky asset, we can use Equation (17-4) to calculate the expected return on the combination or portfolio.

$$E(r_p) = r_f W_f + r_m (1 - W_f) \qquad (17\text{-}4)$$

The top part of Table 17-2 uses this formula to calculate expected returns associated with three investor options: (1) mixing lending with risky assets, (2) investing only in the risky asset, and (3) mixing borrowing with risky assets.

The lending example assumes that the investor apportions one-half of his funds to the risk-free asset ($W_f = .5$) and the other half to the risky asset. The leverage example assumes that the investor borrows (negative lending or $W_f = -.5$) at the risk-free rate and invests one-half again as much in the risky assets. The intermediate example assumes exclusive investment ($W_f = 0$) in risky assets.

Note that lending provides the lowest return of 7.5%, borrowing the highest at 12.5%, and exclusive investment in the risky asset an intermediate return of 10%. While borrowing increases expected return and lending reduces expected return, there is a trade-off in terms of increased and decreased risk. Intuitively, when one invests in risk-free *and* risky assets, the total risk of the portfolio is less than that of the risky asset alone. Contrariwise, when one borrows to buy additional risky assets, the total risk of the portfolio increases over that of the risky asset alone. The latter case is commonly known as financial leverage.

To calculate the variance of the portfolio we can use Equation (17-5):

$$\sigma_p^2 = \sigma_f^2 W_f^2 + \sigma_m^2 (1 - W_f)^2 + 2\text{Cov}_{fm} W_f (1 - W_f) \qquad (17\text{-}5)$$

TABLE 17-2   RISK-RETURN FOR DIFFERING COMBINATIONS OF BORROWING AND LENDING

		Return		
Proportion in risk-free W_f	Risk-free return $r_f,\%$	Proportion in risky asset $1 - W_f$	Risky return $r_m,\%$	Portfolio return $r_p,\%$
.5	5	.5	10	7.5
0	5	1.0	10	10.0
−.5	5	1.5	10	12.5

Risk
$\sigma_p = \sigma_m(1 - W_f)$ where $\sigma_m = 20\%$

Proportion in risky asset $1 - W_f$	Portfolio risk $\sigma_p,\%$
.5	10
1.0	20
1.5	30

Risk-return trade-off				
Portfolio return $r_p,\%$	Risk-free return $r_f,\%$	Risk premium $r_p - r_f,\%$	Portfolio risk $\sigma_p,\%$	Factor of proportionality $(r_p - r_f)/(\sigma_p)$
7.5	5.0	2.5	10	.25
10.0	5.0	5.0	20	.25
12.5	5.0	7.5	30	.25

Note that the value of the first term is zero because the return on the riskless asset has zero variance by definition; that is, $\sigma_f = 0$. The third term has a value of zero. This can be seen by rewriting Cov_{fm} as $\rho_{fm}\,\sigma_f\sigma_m$. Thus the variance of the portfolio depends entirely on the proportion which is invested in the risky asset or, equivalently, the proportion invested in the risk-free asset. The variance and standard deviation of a combined portfolio of risky and risk-free assets can be expressed as follows:

$$\sigma_p^2 = \sigma_m^2 (1 - W_f)^2$$
$$\sigma_p = \sigma_m(1 - W_f)$$

We have calculated, in the middle part of Table 17-2, the risk values associated with the three alternative versions of investing in the previous example. In particular, it shows the risk associated with (1) investing .5 of funds in a risk-free asset, (2) investing exclusively in risky assets, and (3) borrowing and investing .5 again as much in the risky portfolio. Note that the risk is greatest for the borrowing alternative ($\sigma_p = 30\%$) that had the greatest return and is lowest for the lending alternatives ($\sigma_p = 10\%$) that had the lowest return. Investing exclusively in risky assets provided intermediate risk as it did return.

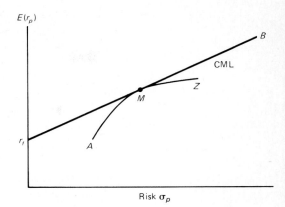

$E(r_p)$

B

CML

Z

M

r_f

A

Risk σ_p

FIGURE 17-2   The capital market line.

As a matter of fact, the *risk premiums* are proportional to risk, where the risk premium for a portfolio is defined as the quantity $r_p - r_f$. In the lower half of Table 17-2 the ratio of the risk premium to σ_p is calculated. Note that this ratio is a *constant* .25, indicating that one unit of risk premium is accompanied by four units of risk.

17-2-3 The CML   The possibility of lending and borrowing changes the original efficient frontier to appear as the straight line r_fMB shown in Figure 17-2. This line, which rises from the interest rate r_f on the vertical axis and is tangent to the efficient frontier at point M, sets out all the alternative combinations of the risky portfolio M with riskless borrowing and lending.[6] The segment from point r_f to point M includes the mixed portfolios of risky securities and bonds. Levered portfolios (combinations of M with riskless loans) are represented by points along the line beyond point M.

Since according to the CAPM all investors have identical (homogeneous) expectations, they will all observe a risk-return diagram as illustrated in Figure 17-2. Every investor will then desire to construct a portfolio consisting of the risk-free asset and portfolio M. Because all investors hold the same risky portfolio, then, in equilibrium, it will include all securities in proportion to their market value. If this were not true, prices would adjust until the value of the security was consistent with its proportion in portfolio M. This portfolio of all risky assets is referred to as the market portfolio.[7]

The investor can now attain any point along the line r_fMB by combining the portfolio of risky assets M with the riskless asset r_f or by levering the portfolio M by borrowing and investing the funds in M. Portfolios on r_fMB are preferred to portfolios on the curved line between A, M, and Z, since they offer greater return for a given level of risk. Portfolios on r_fMB dominate those made up exclusively of risky assets. Thus,

[6] Note that the portfolio of risky assets represented by point M has the property of maximizing the angle formed when a straight line is drawn from point r_f to any point on the curve. The portfolio M is therefore the one that provides the maximum return per unit of risk (standard deviation).

[7] The market portfolio is a critical notion underlying the capital asset pricing model. Recent work by Roll (see Chapter 18) casts doubt on the ability to identify such a portfolio and to conduct valid tests of the explanatory power of the model as well as to apply the principles of the CAPM in practice. One of the merits of arbitrage pricing theory, an alternative theory of asset pricing discussed later in the chapter, is that it does not depend on the existence or identifiability of a market portfolio.

the ability to borrow and lend at the risk-free rate changes the efficient frontier from the curve AMZ to the straight line $r_f MB$.

The line $r_f MB$ which is formed by the action of all investors mixing the market portfolio and the risk-free asset is called the *capital market line (CML)*. Mathematically, the CML can be described in terms of the risk-free rate and the return on the market portfolio.

$$E(r_p) - r_f = \frac{E(r_m) - r_f}{\sigma_m} \sigma_p \tag{17-6}$$

In words, the equation says that for a portfolio on the capital market line, the expected rate of return in excess of the risk-free rate is proportional to the standard deviation of that portfolio.[8] The slope of the capital market line has been called the "price of risk." As Equation (17-6) shows, this slope equals the risk premium for the market portfolio $E(r_m) - r_f$ divided by the risk of the market portfolio σ_m. Thus, the price of the risk is the additional expected return for each additional unit of risk or, alternatively, the reward per unit of risk.

We can refer to Ibbotson and Sinquefield for the period 1926 through 1982, described in Chapter 3, to develop a crude benchmark for what the price of risk might have been over that 56-year period. In particular, the return on the S&P 500 over that period was 9.1%, while the standard deviation of the market was approximately 22%. Using the 3.0% return on treasury bills as a proxy for the risk-free rate and plugging these values into Equation (17-6) would have indicated a slope of .28. Investing in the market portfolio provided a reward of 6.1% (9.1 − 3.0) for bearing a risk corresponding to a standard deviation of 22%, making the slope of the CML equal to .28 (6.1/22). Thus for each additional 1% of risk σ, investors earned an additional .28 return over the period 1926–1982.

Note that the capital market line provides a risk-return relationship and measure of risk for *efficient portfolios* (those that plot on the CML). In particular, it indicates that the appropriate measure of risk for an efficient portfolio is the standard deviation of return of the portfolio σ_p. It also indicates that there will be a linear relationship between risk as measured by the standard deviation and expected return for these efficient portfolios.

---

[8] This formula can be derived by first rearranging the equation for the standard deviation of portfolio return from

$$\sigma_p = \sigma_m(1 - W_f)$$

to obtain $(1 - W_f) = \sigma_p/\sigma_m$ and $W_f = 1 - \sigma_p/\sigma_m$ and then substituting these expressions in the formula for expected return

$$E(r_p) = r_f W_f + r_m(1 - W_f)$$

Simplifying, we obtain Equation (17-6).

Before continuing, you should:

1 Know how the capital asset pricing model relates to the basic portfolio theory of Markowitz
2 Know how to derive the capital market line using the assumption of riskless borrowing and lending
3 Understand how the capital market line provides the risk-return relationship and measure of risk for efficient portfolios
4 Understand the critical nature of a market portfolio

17-3 THE SECURITY MARKET LINE

While the capital market line (CML) shows the appropriate measure of risk and the risk-return relationship for *efficient portfolios*, it doesn't indicate the risk-return trade-off for *other portfolios and individual securities*. This is because these portfolios and securities are inefficient as illustrated by the fact that they plot below the CML (refer to Figure 17-2 to see this). Correspondingly, the standard deviation of return is not an appropriate measure of the risk of inefficient portfolios and individual securities. There is a component of risk in the total (as measured by the standard deviation) that is unnecessary: it can be diversified away and thus will not be rewarded in the market.

Fortunately, Sharpe[9] extended the analysis to identify the component of risk that will be compensated by the market. It is known as systematic risk and is commonly measured by the familiar beta concept. It is a measure of risk that applies to all assets and portfolios whether efficient or inefficient. In addition, Sharpe developed the security market line (SML) that specifies the relationship between expected return and risk, again for all assets and portfolios whether efficient or inefficient.[10] His deviation is, however, fairly complex; so we'll merely provide a more direct and intuitive derivation of the SML.

We can best begin illustrating this by considering that the only risky portfolio that investors want to own is the market portfolio—given the assumptions of the CAPM and the analysis of prior sections. Thus, for an individual security, the measure of risk that is of interest is the additional risk that the security adds to the risk of the market portfolio. Recall from the analysis in Chapter 3 that the variance of a portfolio is equal to the weighted sum of the covariances of the individual securities in the portfolio. If we isolate an individual security from the market portfolio, its marginal contribution to the variance of the market portfolio can, for all practical purposes, be expressed as the covariance of the security's returns with the market portfolio's return. That is, for the ith security, the relevant measure of risk is Cov_{im}. To standardize this measure, we can divide by the standard deviation of the market portfolio to obtain

---

[9] Sharpe, op. cit.

[10] In Sharpe's original September 1964 *Journal of Finance* article, the SML is formally derived in footnote 22, page 438. Also, in *Investment* (2d ed., Prentice-Hall, Englewood Cliffs, N.J., 1983, Appendix 7-a, pp. 169–170) Sharpe provides a proof that beta is the measure of risk.

Cov_{im}/σ_m, which is the *systematic risk* of the security. Using this as the measure of risk, we show that the expected rate of return $E(r_i)$ for security i must fulfill the equation

$$E(r_i) - r_f = \frac{E(r_m) - r_f}{\sigma_m} \text{Cov}_{im}/\sigma_m \qquad (17\text{-}7)$$

Note that Equation (17-7) is similar to the CML equation (17-6) in that expected return in excess of the risk-free rate is proportional to the market price of risk but differs with respect to risk measures. For efficient and perfectly diversified portfolios that plot on the CML, Equation (17-6) indicates that total risk as measured by the standard deviation will be rewarded. In comparison, Equation (17-7) shows that for inefficient portfolios below the capital market line, the market price of risk rewards only the systematic component of total risk. The other component of risk for inefficient portfolios, which is known as specific risk, is independent of fluctuations in market return and hence can be diversified away. Since investors can easily eliminate this component of risk and still maintain return constant as we saw in Chapter 3, the market will not reward it. As a consequence, in the world of the CAPM, higher return will be associated only with higher nondiversifiable (systematic) risk.

Equation (17-7) can be rewritten in a perhaps more familiar form:

$$E(r_i) - r_f = \frac{\text{Cov}_{im}}{\sigma_m^2} [E(r_m) - r_f] \qquad (17\text{-}8)$$

Note that the first term on the right-hand side of the equation is the same as the beta of the stock so that we can then restate the equation in its more familiar format as follows:

$$E(r_i) = r_f + B_i [E(r_m) - r_f] \qquad (17\text{-}9)$$

It's useful to note at this point that for all practical purposes, the beta coefficient in the equation of the SML is the same as the beta of the market (single-index) model. As a result, for application and testing of the relationship, researchers and practitioners ordinarily use the market model. Recall that we illustrated the way that the market model can be used to calculate betas in Chapter 4.

Before proceeding, it is important to note that the existence of a market portfolio is a critical notion underlying the CAPM. We'll see in the next chapter that some researchers have questioned the testability and practicality of the CAPM because of the problems of properly identifying an "ex ante efficient market portfolio." Arbitrage pricing theory (APT) is an alternative model that derives equilibrium without assuming a market portfolio; so it will be useful to cover this model at the end of the chapter for the added perspective it provides in understanding equilibrium in the capital markets.

17-3-1 Risk-Return Relationship   When the equation of the security market line is plotted in expected return beta coordinates, it yields a straight line as shown in Figure 17-3. Note that the vertical axis refers to expected return while the horizontal axis uses beta rather than standard deviation as the measure of risk. The line is determined by the return on the risk-free asset which, by definition, has a beta of zero and the expected return on the market which has a beta of 1.00, also by definition. In equilibrium, all securities and portfolios—efficient and inefficient—will plot along the security market line.

Since all securities are expected to plot along the SML, the line provides a direct and convenient way of determining the expected return on a security. In particular, each beta level might be considered to represent a risk class and all securities that fall in that risk class would be expected to earn a return appropriate for that class. Presuming that we know the beta of the security, we could directly use the SML formula to solve for the expected return or, alternatively, use the security market line graph to generate an expected return for the security.

To illustrate, Table 17-3 shows some market data along with data for two hypothetical securities, A and D. Note that the risk-free rate is assumed to be 5% and the expected market return 12% to provide an expected market risk premium of 7%. Security A has a beta of 1.20, while security D has a beta of .80. Given market data and the beta for a security, the expected return can be calculated by means of the security market line equation as illustrated in the body of the table. Security A has an expected return of 13.4%, while security D has an expected return of 10.6%.

Alternatively, one can derive an expected return for the security graphically, as illustrated in Figure 17-4. This chart locates the security market line according to the market data shown in Table 17-3. Once this and the beta values are known for the security, one can plot the securities and read off the expected return from the vertical axis. For example, stock A having a beta of 1.20 has an expected return of 13.4%, while stock D having a beta of .80 has an expected return of 10.6%. The expected returns are, of course, the same as those derived in Table 17-3 by use of the security market line formulation.

As a matter of interest, we might use the security market line graph as a means of classifying securities. Those with betas greater than 1 and plotting on the upper part

FIGURE 17-3   The security market line.

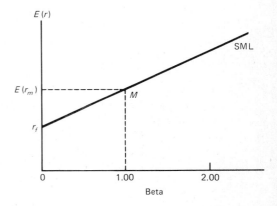

TABLE 17-3   SECURITY MARKET LINE DATA

	Expected return E(r),%	Risk-free rate r_f,%	Beta B_I	Market risk premium $E(r_m) - r_f$,%
Market	12.0	5	1.00	7
Security A	13.4	5	1.20	7
Security D	10.6	5	.80	7

of the line, for example, security A, will be classified as aggressive, while those with betas less than 1 and plotting on the lower part of the line, for example, security D, will be classified as defensive. Aggressive securities would be expected to earn above-average returns, while defensive securities would be expected to earn below-average returns, as can be seen from the security market line graph.

17-3-2 Under- and Overvalued Securities   The security market line also provides a framework for evaluating the relative attractiveness of securities. In particular, high-risk stocks are expected to offer high returns by virtue of their risk level. The question is whether they are offering returns more or less than proportional to their risk. Conversely, low-risk stocks are expected to offer lower returns by virtue of a lower risk level. Again, the question is whether they are offering returns more or less than proportional to their risk.

Figure 17-5 illustrates how the security market line provides an explicit framework for making this appraisal. This figure shows a hypothetical market line with nine securities plotted relative to the line. Note that securities A, B, and C plot above the line while securities X, Y, and Z plot below the line. Securities M, N, and O plot on the line. At the same time, securities A, M, X plot at a beta level of .80, B, N, and Y plot at a beta of 1.00, and C, O, and Z plot at a beta of 1.20. Each of the three sets of securities is in the same risk class, and there are three classes representing high, low, and average risk.

FIGURE 17-4   Security market line.

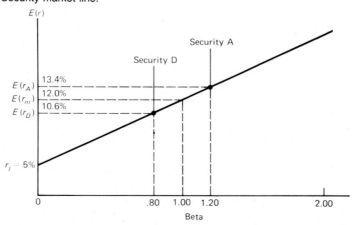

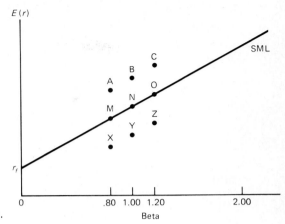

FIGURE 17-5   The market line and security valuation.

In the market line context, stocks that plot above the line presumably are undervalued (attractive) because they offer a higher expected return than stocks of similar risk. Stocks A, B, and C that plot above the line are undervalued relative to their beta class. The prices of these stocks are too low, and we can see from the simple rate of return formulation that they would have to rise—leading to above-average performance—to raise the denominator and lower the required return of the stock:

$$E(R_i) = \frac{E(P_i) - P_0 + \text{Div.}}{P_0}$$

On the other hand, a stock is presumably overvalued (unattractive) when it is expected to produce a lower return than issues of comparable risk. Stocks X, Y, and Z that plot below the line are overvalued relative to their beta class. The prices of these stocks are too high, and in this case we can see from the return formulation that they would have to fall—leading to below-average performance—to lower the denominator and thereby raise the return of the stocks.

Stocks M, N, and O that plot on the line are appropriately valued in the context of the market line. These stocks are offering returns in line with their riskiness. The prices of these stocks are "right," and one would expect average stock performance since these are neither under- nor overvalued. Stocks plotting off the market line would thus be evidence of mispricing in the marketplace.

There are, in turn, three major reasons why there would be mispricing in the securities market. The first is transactions costs that may reduce investors' incentive to correct minor deviations from the SML; the cost of adjustment may be greater than or at least equal to the potential opportunity presented by the mispricing. Second, investors subject to taxes might be reluctant to sell an overvalued security with a capital gain and incur the tax. Finally, imperfect information can affect the valuation of a security. Some investors are less well informed than others and may not observe mispricing and hence not act on these opportunities.

Figure 17-6 is an idealized illustration of how the SML would look when actual market conditions are as we just described. In this case, all securities would not be

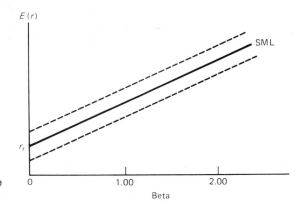

FIGURE 17-6   Security market line in the presence
of market imperfections.

expected to lie exactly on the SML. Therefore, in practice, the SML is a band instead of a thin line. The width of this band varies directly with the imperfections in the market.

Before continuing, you should:

1 Understand why total risk is not the appropriate measure for inefficient portfolios and individual securities
2 Understand why systematic risk is the relevant component of risk for securities and portfolios
3 Know the risk-return relationship provided by the security market line and the measure of risk represented by beta
4 Understand how the SML can be used as a framework for appraising security valuation

---

17-4 ZERO-BETA CAPM MODEL

We'll see in the next chapter that empirical evidence is broadly consistent with the sort of risk-return relationship suggested by the CAPM. At the same time, this evidence also suggests that the model may be deficient with respect to one or more of its underlying assumptions. Specifically, the evidence implies that the assumption of the existence of a risk-free asset and ability of investors to borrow and lend freely at this rate may not be a valid representation of the workings of the marketplace. Furthermore, it seems reasonable on the basis of casual observation that this might be one of the more questionable assumptions used in deriving the model.

To begin with, the fact is that investors generally cannot borrow and lend at the same rate. Financial intermediaries charge a higher rate on their loans than the rate at which they borrow to provide a spread that incorporates a profit margin and premium to compensate for the credit risks of the borrower. Investors thus pay a higher rate on borrowed funds than they would receive for lending funds.

In addition, in an inflationary environment, there is no such thing as a risk-free investment. Treasury bills have normally been cited as a reasonable proxy for a risk-free asset. These instruments are free of credit risk and by virtue of their short-term nature virtually free of interest rate risk. Treasury bills are, in fact, essentially riskless in nominal terms, but not in real terms. They are subject to purchasing power risk that becomes more severe as the rate of inflation becomes more intense.

Black,[11] realizing this problem and observing the empirical evidence, amended the CAPM to accommodate these violations of the risk-free asset assumption. His analysis indicated that it was possible to substitute for the risk-free asset an asset that he referred to as a *zero-beta asset or portfolio*. This is a portfolio which has a return that is designed so as to have no correlation with the market. The zero-beta version of the CAPM has a structure similar to the original Sharpe-Lintner CAPM, but now has the zero-beta factor r_z rather than the risk-free rate r_f in the equation.

$$E(r_i) = E(r_z) + B_i[E(r_m) - E(r_z)] \qquad (17\text{-}10)$$

Figure 17-7 illustrates the modified security market line. Note that the intercept of the line (designated r_z) would be at a higher level than the risk-free rate (designated r_f).[12] The fact that the intercept is higher in the amended model also means that the slope of the line will be less than in the presence of a risk-free asset. We would also expect that the slope of the line would vary over time as the return on the zero-beta factor fluctuated. All this is, of course, more in line with empirical results to be described in the next chapter, implying that the Black zero-beta model is a better explanation of the risk-return relationship than the pure version of the security market line (SML).

[11] Fischer Black, "Capital Market Equilibrium with Restricted Borrowing," *Journal of Business*, vol. 45, no. 3 (July 1972), pp. 444–455.

[12] The zero-beta factor, while not correlated with the market, would be expected to have some variance associated with it, unlike a risk-free asset, which would have no variance.

FIGURE 17-7 Security market line: original CAPM (solid line) vs. zero-beta CAPM (dashed line).

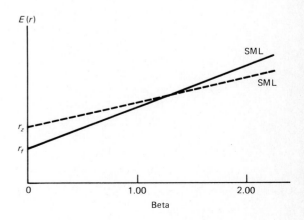

17-5 ADJUSTING FOR TAXES

As noted at the outset, the simple form of the CAPM is derived ignoring the presence of taxes. The implication of this assumption is that investors are indifferent about receiving income in the form of capital gains or dividends and that all investors hold the same portfolio of risky assets. Taxes, however, are a fact of life, and more importantly for the pricing of securities, capital gains are taxed, in general, at a lower rate than dividends. We might then expect that investors with different tax status would hold different portfolios of risky assets even when expectations about pretax returns for those portfolios were the same. Correspondingly, we would expect equilibrium prices for those assets to differ from a circumstance where taxes did not matter.

17-5-1 A Tax-Adjusted CAPM Michael Brennan[13] was the first researcher to consider formally the impact on capital asset prices of differential tax rates on capital gains and dividend income. In developing a tax-adjusted model, Brennan made the usual assumptions used in deriving the simplified form of the CAPM but also assumed that dividend yields are certain. Allowing for the impact of differential taxes, the return on any asset or portfolio is given by the following tax-adjusted CAPM:

$$E(r_i) = r_f(1 - T) + B_i[E(r_m) - r_f - T(D_m - r_f)] + TD_i \qquad (17\text{-}11)$$

where $T = \dfrac{T_d - T_g}{1 - T_g}$

T_d = economywide average tax rate on dividends

T_g = economywide average tax rate on capital gains

D_m = dividend yield on market portfolio

D_i = dividend yield on ith stock

Note in Brennan's model that if the tax rate on dividend income equals the tax rate on capital gains, the tax-adjustment parameter $T = 0$, and this model reduces to the simple form of the CAPM. If there are differential taxes, expected return depends linearly on beta as in the simple form of the CAPM, but there is need to adjust the market return for the impact of taxes on the dividend yield of the market portfolio. In addition, expected pretax return of the security or portfolio becomes a function of a second factor: the dividend yield of the security or portfolio adjusted by the tax-factor-effect parameter T.

When dividend income is on average taxed at a higher rate than capital gains (as in the U.S. economy), the tax-adjustment parameter T is positive and expected pretax return is an increasing function of dividend yield. High-yield stocks would be expected to offer higher pretax returns than low-yield stocks of the same systematic risk. Correspondingly, the expected return will be higher as the differential tax rate between

---

[13] Michael Brennan, "Taxes, Market Valuation, and Corporate Financial Policy," *National Tax Journal*, vol. 25 (1970), pp. 417–427.

dividend income and capital gains is higher: the T parameter becomes larger as the tax differential increases. The fact that expected pretax return increases as dividend yield rises is intuitively appealing, since the larger the fraction of return paid in the form of dividends the more taxes the investor will have to pay and the larger the pretax return required.

17-5-2 Yield Tilt   If securities are priced according to the tax-augmented expression (17-11), it has implications for investor behavior. It implies that investors should weight their portfolio holdings toward or away from dividend yield according to their tax bracket. That is, investors should still hold widely diversified portfolios that resemble the market portfolio, except that they will now be tilted in favor of those stocks in which the investor has a comparative advantage. For example, investors in high income tax brackets should hold a lesser percentage of high-yield stocks in their portfolio than the percentage of the market portfolio these stocks constitute, while they should hold more low-yield–high-capital-gains stocks in order to maximize their after-tax return. Correspondingly, investors in low tax brackets would be advised to tilt their portfolios toward high-yield stocks, since the tax disadvantage of these stocks is less to them than it is to the average stockholder.

While a yield tilt strategy may have some potential for increasing after-tax returns, there is a cost in terms of additional nonmarket risk introduced by following such a strategy. That is, a tilted portfolio will most likely have more nonmarket (residual) risk than a portfolio well diversified across all yield levels. For example, many high-yield stocks are those of regulated public utilities, and their prices tend to move together over and above common movements with the level of the overall stock market. Similarly, low-yield ''growth'' stocks also tend to move together. The investor thus needs to determine whether the potential additional return from following the yield tilt strategy is worth incurring the added nonmarket risk.

Furthermore, there is debate as to the magnitude or even the presence of a tax effect in the pricing of securities. The special tax status of certain institutional investors and counterbalancing tax strategies available to investors tend to offset the impact of taxes on the return to investors, thus reducing the tax effect on the pricing of securities. The following are factors that reduce the significance of a tax effect and hence the efficacy of a yield tilt strategy.

1 Corporations can exclude from taxable income 85% of the dividends received from another corporation, and in fact have a tax incentive to receive dividends.

2 Many institutions, such as pension funds and foundations, are basically tax-exempt. If high-yield stocks offered higher pretax returns, these investors would have an incentive to tilt their portfolios to high-yield stocks. Such a process would tend to drive up the price of the high-yield stocks, thus potentially reducing their returns to the same level provided by similar-risk, low-yield stocks.

3 Institutional restrictions such as ''legal lists'' have tended to favor stocks that pay at least some dividend. If these restrictions have any effect on pricing, it would probably be to raise the price and lower the return of high-yield stocks, and to lower the price and raise the return of low-yield stocks.

4 To an investor who needs cash regularly, it might be cheaper (even after taxes) to receive dividends than to raise cash by periodically selling stock and incurring transaction costs.

5 Finally, Miller and Scholes[14] and others have argued that investors, by using various tax shelter strategies, do not pay taxes at high enough rates to be concerned about the distinction between dividends and capital gains.

Whether these countervailing forces are powerful enough to eliminate a tax effect is essentially an empirical question. The empirical evidence that we evaluate in the next chapter with respect to this issue seems mixed as to whether there is in fact a tax effect. Some studies by competent researchers indicate the existence of this effect, while other studies by equally competent researchers indicate no significant tax impact in the pricing of capital assets. Furthermore, even those studies verifying the existence of a tax effect also show that the magnitude of the effect is rather limited in the pricing of stocks, perhaps on the order of 30 basis points per annum. Executing a yield tilt strategy would thus seem to depend primarily on the strength of the investor's personal conviction as to the presence of a tax factor.

17-6 ARBITRAGE PRICING THEORY

Ross[15] has developed an alternative model of equilibrium in the securities markets. It is known as arbitrage pricing theory (APT) and does not depend critically on the notion of an underlying market portfolio. Instead, it is a model that derives returns from the properties of the process generating stock returns and employs arbitrage pricing theory to define equilibrium. Under certain circumstances, it derives a risk-return relationship identical to the security market line of the CAPM. We'll thus conclude this chapter by covering the APT, both for the additional perspective it offers in studying the equilibrium process as well as for the reinforcement it provides to the existence of a risk-return relationship in the marketplace.

17-6-1 The APT Model It's useful to begin describing arbitrage pricing theory by indicating the assumptions on which it is based and comparing these with the assumptions used in developing the capital asset pricing model. As with the CAPM, the APT assumes (1) that investors have homogeneous beliefs, (2) that investors are risk-averse utility maximizers, and (3) that markets are perfect so that factors like transaction costs are not relevant. In contrast to the CAPM, APT does not assume (1) a single-period investment horizon, (2) that there are no taxes, (3) that investors can freely borrow and lend at the risk-free rate, and (4) that investors select portfolios on the basis of the mean and variance of return.

The additional assumption that the APT makes is with regard to the process generating security returns. In particular, APT assumes that *security returns are generated*

---

[14] Merton Miller and Myron Scholes, "Dividends and Taxes," *Journal of Financial Economics* (December 1978), pp. 333–364.

[15] S. Ross, "Return, Risk and Arbitrage," in Friend and Bicklser, eds., *Risk and Return in Finance*, (Ballinger, Cambridge, 1976).

according to what is known as a factor model. This model takes the view that there are underlying factors that give rise to returns on stocks. Examples of these factors might include such economic variables as real economic growth and inflation, or such financial variables as dividend yield and capital structure.

Assuming that the factor model is descriptive of the return generating process as well as making the three previously stated assumptions, Ross uses an arbitrage argument to develop a model of equilibrium pricing. Since illustration of this derivation would be excessively complex and would not serve our purposes, we'll omit it (those interested may refer to the Ross articles referenced in the footnote). Instead, we'll only show the final form of the risk-return relationship derived from the APT:

$$E(r_i) = r_z + b_{i1}[E(r_1) - r_z] + b_{i2}[E(r_2) - r_z] + \ldots \qquad (17\text{-}12)$$

Note that the APT risk-return relationship is linear. Since the APT does not assume an ability to borrow and lend freely at the risk-free rate, the r_z that is directly derived from this model could represent either a risk-free return (if available) or the zero-beta return that was derived by Black for the amended version of the CAPM. The term $[E(r_i) - r_z]$ represents the risk premium that is associated with the factor, and is alternatively represented by the symbol λ. The b coefficient measures the responsiveness of the stock to changes in the factor. If we assume that there is only a single factor determining security returns, the basic APT return equation is similar in form to the SML:

$$E(r_i) = r_z + b_i \lambda \qquad (17\text{-}13)$$

We should also note that if the market portfolio was the only factor that influenced security returns, the equation would be identical to the security market line of the CAPM. However, it should be emphasized that the market portfolio plays no special role in the APT—the market portfolio may or may not be one of the factors influencing security returns. Consequently, the problems of identifying the market portfolio when testing the CAPM (see Chapter 18) are not an issue in testing the APT.

Presuming that there is only a single factor, the APT pricing relationship is a straight line on a graph of expected return $E(R_i)$, and systematic risk with respect to factor 1 as illustrated in Figure 17-8. Note that there are three plots: A, D, and U representing three portfolios with no diversifiable risk. Portfolio A has above-average risk ($b = 1.20$), while D has below-average risk ($b = .80$) and U has average risk ($b = 1.00$). Portfolios A and D are offering returns proportional to their risk: 13.4% and 10.6%, respectively, and are thus fairly priced. Portfolio U is offering more return (15.0%) than would be warranted by its risk and is thus undervalued.

Portfolio U thus presents a profit opportunity, and we can illustrate how this can be converted into a riskless arbitrage as follows. For example, to construct a portfolio with the same risk as portfolio U, an investor could apportion half his investment to portfolio A and the other half to portfolio D. Since the risk of the resulting combination is simply a weighted average of the risks of the individual components ($1/2 \times .80 + 1/2 \times 1.20$), the risk of the combination would be 1.00. Correspondingly, the return

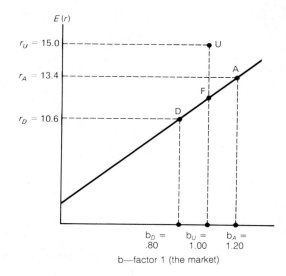

FIGURE 17-8   Arbitrage pricing model with a single factor, the market.

of the combination would be a weighted average of the returns of the components (1/2 × 10.6% + 1/2 × 13.4%) and would be 12% for the combination. This return would be in line with the portfolio's riskiness as illustrated on the graph but would be less than the 15% offered by portfolio U.

The data in Table 17-4 illustrate how we can convert the return differential between two portfolios of equal risk into a riskless arbitrage. For example, an investor could sell $1000 of portfolio F short, obtain the proceeds, and invest the $1000 long in portfolio U.[16] Note that this transaction involves no net cash outlay by the investor as shown by the zero net investment in the arbitrage portfolio. Correspondingly, there would no risk assumed as the two portfolios have identical risk and the process of buying and short selling equal amounts nets to a zero-risk position; i.e., the arbitrage portfolio beta is zero. There would, however, be a positive return to the investor of $30.

Since an investor could obtain a return with no investment and no risk, the investor (or investors) would continue to engage in this arbitrage. This activity of selling portfolio F short (and hence portfolios A and D) would drive down the price of portfolios

[16] As a practical matter investors do not have use of the full amount of the proceeds of a short sale. As a result, there may be some slight impediment to the arbitraging mechanism.

TABLE 17-4   UNDERTAKING A RISKLESS ARBITRAGE

	Investment	Return	Risk (*b*)
Portfolio U	+ $1000	+ $150	1.0
Portfolio F	− 1000	− 120	− 1.0
Arbitrage portfolio	0	$ 30	0

A and D, raising their expected returns, while the activity of buying portfolio U would drive up its price and lower its expected return.

This activity will continue until the return on portfolio U is equal to that of portfolio F. All three portfolios, A, D, and U, will then lie on the line, thus illustrating how the arbitrage process keeps the risk-return relationship linear. Note that this process of arbitrage might just as well be considered in the context of the security market line as the process preventing securities from diverging from that line. As before, however, we would expect that the presence of imperfections, like transactions costs, taxes, and imperfect information, would mean that securities plot only within a band around the line rather than on it.

17-6-2 What Are the Factors?   While the APT is a theoretically appealing model of capital market equilibrium, a major impediment to implementing the model is determining what are the underlying factors that are priced in the market. The APT model per se does not provide any perspective in identifying these factors, nor for that matter does it indicate the number that should be significant in asset pricing. One might conjecture that such economic variables as real economic growth or inflation would be important or that such financial variables as corporate creditworthiness or dividend-paying characteristics would be fundamentally important in determining the prices of securities. Correspondingly, we might assert that at least one factor—the market effect—is important in pricing stocks, and conjecture that the total number is likely to be limited to, say, less than 10 significant factors.

Identifying the number and nature of the arbitrage factors is thus a matter of empirical research. Unfortunately, this line of investigation is only now beginning, and we'll see in the next chapter that the results to date provide only a limited perspective on the question. Because of the speculative nature of the investigation, it's also likely that the research process will be a long one and that forthcoming results may be ambiguous rather than definitive in resolving the issue.

17-7 SUMMARY

This chapter describes the capital asset pricing model and its two main components: the capital market line and the security market line. Describing the capital market line provides perspective for the security market line that has broad use in establishing a risk-return relationship as well as the relevant measure of risk for securities and portfolios of securities. The capital asset pricing model provides the insight that the relevant risk for securities and portfolios is systematic risk and provides a measure of that risk which is beta. Since the other component of risk for inefficient portfolios and individual securities is diversifiable, it will not be rewarded and hence does not enter into the risk-return relationship provided by the security market line.

The CAPM is, however, dependent on the notion of an underlying market portfolio and has been criticized because of the difficulty of identifying an ex-ante efficient market portfolio. Arbitrage pricing theory is an alternative model of market equilibrium that does not depend on the need for an underlying market portfolio. In addition, APT has a nice advantage of requiring less restrictive assumptions than the CAPM. Finally, the APT can incorporate more complex types of equilibrium than where there is merely a single factor—the market—and is thus more general than the CAPM. On the other hand, APT does not indicate what the underlying factors are that generate security returns. To date there have been few empirical studies aimed at identifying these factors, and even these few have had only limited success in researching the question.

SUGGESTED READINGS

In addition to those readings suggested at the end of Chapter 4 and relating to capital market theory, the following would be helpful:

William F. Sharpe, "Capital Asset Prices: A Theory of Market Equilibrium under Conditions of Risk," *Journal of Finance* (September 1964), pp. 425–442. A classic article in the subject yet readable and worthwhile in providing perspective on the subject.

M. C. Jensen, "Capital Markets: Theory and Evidence," *Bell Journal of Economics and Management Science* (autumn 1972), pp. 357–398. A comprehensive yet readable survey of the theoretical development of the CAPM along with empirical evidence bearing on the model.

Stephen Ross, "Return, Risk and Arbitrage," in Friend and Bicklser, eds., *Risk and Return in Finance*, (Ballinger, Cambridge, 1976). Derives the arbitrage pricing theory and discusses its relevance.

Richard Roll and Steven Ross discuss the relevance of the APT to investment practice in the May–June 1984 issue of the *Financial Analysis Journal*.

James L. Farrell, *Guide to Portfolio Management*, illustrates with practical applications how capital market theory can be helpful to investors in the areas of security valuation, risk analysis, and performance measurement.

QUESTIONS

1 Compare the assumptions needed for Markowitz's portfolio theory with those necessary for capital market theory.

2 Explain the concept of an efficient portfolio.

3 Explain how the existence of unlimited borrowing and lending opportunities allows one to change the form of the efficient frontier.

4 Why is the existence of a market portfolio a critical notion underlying the capital asset pricing model?

5 Why doesn't the standard deviation of return provide a suitable measure of risk for individual securities and inefficient portfolios?

6 Why is systematic risk the relevant component for individual securities and inefficient portfolios?

7 When is systematic risk equivalent to total risk?

8 If a security plots above the security market line, is it under- or overvalued?

9 If a security plots below the security market line, does its price need to rise or fall in order to plot back on the line?

10 What are some reasons why securities might plot off the security market line?

11 Explain why riskless borrowing and lending may not be a practically valid assumption, and how that potential deficiency changes the risk-return relationship indicated by the security market line.

12 Explain how the existence of differential taxes would change the risk-return relationship of the capital asset pricing model.

13 Outline a strategy that investors might follow if taxes do in fact have an effect on the pricing of stocks.
14 List some arguments why taxes may not in fact impact the pricing of stocks.
15 Compare the underlying assumptions of the arbitrage pricing theory with those of the capital asset pricing model.
16 When would the risk-return relationship of the APT be equivalent to that of the security market line?
17 Compare the advantages and disadvantages of the APT and CAPM.

PROBLEMS

1 Refer to Table 17-2. Compute the returns to the three investors assuming that the market return is 5% and then 2%.
2 Assume that the market price of risk is one-third, that the risk-free rate is 9%, and that the standard deviation of market return is 21%; then determine the expected return on the market.
3 Assume that the risk-free rate is 9% and the expected return of the market is 15%. Graph the security market line and indicate where securities that are aggressive would plot and where those that are defensive would plot.
4 Security J has a beta of .70, while security K has a beta of 1.30. Calculate the expected return for these securities, using security market line data from the preceding problem.
5 Refer to the data in Figure 17-8. Assume that there is another portfolio, O, that has a beta of .9, and is offering a return of 10%. Illustrate the process of arbitrage that equilibrates the return of this portfolio.
6 Portfolio K pays a dividend of $2, sells at a current price of $50, and is expected to sell at $52 at the end of the year. It has a beta of 1.10. Refer to the data in Table 17-3 and determine at what price the portfolio should sell to be in equilibrium with portfolios A and D.
7 Presuming that the tax rate on dividend income is 40%, while the tax rate on capital gains is 20%, calculate the tax factor T in the tax-adjusted CAPM.
8 Assume that differential taxes matter and using the same tax rates on dividend income and capital gains as in the preceding problem, determine the expected return for a stock with a beta of 1.20 and a dividend yield of 6%. Assume the expected market return is 15% and the dividend yield is 4%, while the risk-free rate is 8%.
9 Determine the expected return for a stock with a beta of .90 and a yield of 2% where differential taxes matter. Assume the same data as in the preceding problem.

CHAPTER 18

EMPIRICAL TESTS
OF ASSET PRICING MODELS

After reading this chapter, you should:

1 Be able to describe the general methodology for empirically testing the CAPM

2 Be able to describe the problems encountered in empirically testing the CAPM

3 Be able to describe the test methodology and results of researchers such as Black, Jensen, and Scholes and Fama and McBeth

4 Understand the test procedures and results of tests of the tax-augmented CAPM

5 Understand the problems and techniques for testing the APT model

The capital asset pricing model is a rigorously derived equilibrium model that has certain intuitive appeal. At the same time, the model is a simplification of reality and as such may be sufficiently abstract to be inappropriate for practical application. It's thus important to test the CAPM and any competing asset pricing model, or any model for that matter, to assess how well they describe the actual behavior of security market prices as well as to determine how well the underlying assumptions of each model conform to reality.

The purpose of this chapter is to discuss empirical tests of the capital asset pricing model (CAPM) and the arbitrage pricing model (APM). We begin by describing the standard methodology for conducting such tests as well as the rationale for using ex post data as a proxy for investor expectations. We then describe the early tests of the CAPM model that primarily focused on the ability of the model to explain a risk-return relationship in the marketplace. After discussing this, we describe two studies that characterize the more recent empirical evaluations that focus on evaluating more aspects of the CAPM. This more elaborate analysis, in turn, allows us to assess how well the underlying assumptions of the CAPM conform to observed price behavior in the market. In this regard, we'll specifically test to see whether the zero-beta and tax-adjusted versions of the CAPM provide added perspective beyond that offered by the simplified form of the CAPM. We conclude by generally discussing work by Richard Roll that calls into question whether the CAPM is at all amenable to empirical testing. Finally, we will discuss some recent empirical tests of the APM.

18-1 CAPM EMPIRICAL TEST METHODOLOGY

The CAPM risk-return relationship described by the security market line (SML) equation is an expected or ex ante relationship. The returns that the model refers to are expected returns, while the beta that it refers to is derived from expected covariances and variances of returns. That is, the relationship is forward- rather than backward-looking and should embody investors' expectations. Ideally then, in testing the CAPM one would like to have data on expected returns and expected beta values for individual securities or portfolios of securities. Expectations, however, are difficult to observe, especially with respect to the risk attributes of securities.

Consequently, in testing the CAPM risk-return relationship researchers have relied on realized or historic data as inputs. The critical assumption here is that if enough historical observations are available in a test, ex post returns and ex post betas will, on average, approximate investors' expectations regarding risk and return. For example, researchers might derive returns over, say, the most recent 10-year period and assume that these realized values were representative of expectations during that period.

For specific purposes of testing the simple form of the CAPM, researchers have frequently utilized the single-index market model that has the following form:[1]

$$r_i = r_f + \beta_i (r_m - r_f) + e_i \tag{18-1}$$

In this case, the risk-free rate r_f becomes analogous to the intercept term, while the market model beta β_i proxies for the CAPM beta. The return on the market is expressed in risk-premium form $(r_m - r_f)$, while the error term e_i has the same meaning as for the market model. While use of this model is convenient for testing, we should also note that any test of the CAPM now becomes a test not only of the validity of that model but also of the appropriateness of the underlying market model relationship. Assuming the validity of the single-index relationship and that realized returns are proxies for expectations, researchers estimate betas by regressing the returns of individual securities or groups of securities r_i against the returns of some market index r_m utilizing the following time-series equation for each security:

$$r_{it} = a_i + \beta_i (r_{mt} - r_{ft}) + e_{it} \tag{18-2}$$

The number of observations in each regression is equal to the number of return intervals during the period of study—for example, if monthly data are used for a 5-year period, there will be 60 return observations for each regression. The time-series regressions utilized to estimate betas for each security are referred to as the "first-pass regressions."

Once betas have been calculated, they can be plotted against the returns of individual securities or portfolios of securities. For this purpose, the average ex post return of the security or portfolio realized over the period of the study is taken as representative for the beta return relationship.

Figure 18-1 is a risk-return diagram illustrating this for a hypothetical set of, say, 100 securities. Note that the figure shows the plots of the beta-return values for each of the securities as well as a line fitted to the plotted points. The equation for fitting the line to the plots is a cross-sectional regression equation and has the following form:

---

[1]See Chapter 4 for a discussion of the market model.

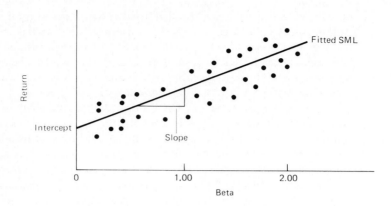

FIGURE 18-1 Empirical security market line.

$$r_i = \gamma_0 + \gamma_1 \beta_i + u_i \qquad (18\text{-}3)$$

Note that there is only one cross-sectional regression of average return against beta. For this cross-sectional regression, the number of observations is equal to the number of securities (or portfolios), and this regression is frequently referred to as the "second-pass regression."

In testing the risk-return relationship, researchers are concerned with assessing how well this fitted line conforms to the theoretical security market line. If the fitted line conformed perfectly with the theoretical, it should show the following characteristics. First, it would be expected that the line would be upward-sloping, thereby verifying that securities or portfolios with higher systematic risk earned higher returns than those with lower risk, at least over longer periods of time.[2] On average, there should be a linear relationship between beta and return, verifying that other "nonsystematic" factors are not important in determining returns. Finally, it would be expected that the constant term, or intercept, in the equation γ_0 would be equal to the risk-free rate r_f. Correspondingly, the slope of the line γ_1 would be expected to be equal to the average market risk premium $r_m - r_f$ during the period used.

There have been numerous tests of the security market line relationship. Complete reporting of these analyses and results would, however, require considerable space and would not be appropriate to the intention of this book. We'll instead focus on a few of the most representative types of studies to illustrate methods of testing, some of the problems encountered in testing, as well as the degree of conformance of the tested relationships to the theoretical CAPM. For a more comprehensive review of

[2]On average, over a long period of time, we would expect the market return to be greater than the risk-free rate—otherwise risk would not be rewarded in the marketplace. However, if the time horizon of an empirical study happened to include only a bear market, that is, $r_m < r_f$, then the ex post SML should be downward-sloping.

these tests (to be discussed) and others, see Jensen,[3] Modigiliani and Pogue,[4] and Rogalski and Tinic,[5] and for a more technical review, see Roll.[6]

18-1-1 Test of Risk-Return Relationship It's useful to begin by reviewing three studies that are representative of those tests that focused on the power of the CAPM model to explain a risk-return relationship between securities. Two of these tests by Sharpe[7] and Jensen[8] are characteristic of those in the early stage of the development of the CAPM. Specifically, those early tests of the model were concerned with determining how closely the return of large portfolios, in particular mutual funds, were explained by the risk levels of those portfolios. Since these studies dealt with explaining portfolios rather than individual stocks, we could think of these tests as being more directly a test of the risk-return relationship for the capital market line, i.e., the relationship between the return of well-diversified portfolios and the standard deviation of the portfolios. In fact, some researchers used standard deviation rather than beta as the measure of risk. For large portfolios—and ones that are presumably highly efficient—the two measures are of course closely similar.

The first of these early tests by Sharpe himself was a follow-up empirical study to test the CAPM framework that he had described in a prior year's article. In this study, Sharpe selected a sample of 34 mutual funds that were large and representative of differing fund investment objectives. He then computed average annual rates of return and standard deviations of those returns for the 34 mutual funds for the years 1954–1963.

Sharpe's inquiry indicated that higher-risk funds earned higher returns over the period than lower-risk funds. This was in line with what the CAPM model would imply for a period where stock prices were in a generally rising trend: the return on the market was in excess of the risk-free return over the 1954–1963 period. Furthermore, the correlation between average return and standard deviation exceeded .80 over the period. Sharpe's study also showed that the risk-return relationship of the funds was approximately linear.

A subsequent study by Michael Jensen was also noteworthy in testing the risk-return explanatory power of the CAPM. Jensen's study differed somewhat from Sharpe's in that he used beta coefficients rather than the standard deviation as a measure of

[3]M. C. Jensen, "Capital Markets: Theory and Evidence," *Bell Journal of Economics and Management Science* (autumn 1972), pp. 357–398. M. C. Jensen, "The Foundations and Current State of Capital Market Theory," in M. C. Jensen, ed., *Studies in the Theory of Capital Markets,* Praeger, New York, 1972, pp. 1–46.

[4]F. Modigliani and G. A. Pogue, "An Introduction to Risk and Return," *Financial Analysts Journal* (March–April, May–June 1974), pp. 68–86, respectively.

[5]R. J. Rogalski and S. M. Tinic, "Risk Premium Curve vs. Capital Market Line: A Re-Examination," *Financial Management* (spring 1978), pp. 73–83.

[6]R. Roll, "A Critique of the Asset Pricing Theory's Tests," *Journal of Financial Economics* (March 1977), pp. 129–176.

[7]William F. Sharpe, "Risk Aversion in the Stock Market: Some Empirical Evidence," *Journal of Finance* (September 1965), pp. 416–422.

[8]Michael C. Jensen, "Risk, the Pricing of Capital Assets and the Evaluation of Investment Portfolios," *Journal of Business* (April 1969), pp. 167–247.

risk. On the basis of returns on 115 open-end mutual funds for the period 1955–1964, he concluded that high returns are associated with high volatility or systematic risk. He also found evidence that beta coefficients are valid measures of risk.

These two studies tested for the presence of a predicted CAPM-like risk-return relationship using managed portfolios—mutual funds—as a basis for analysis. In contrast, the Sharpe and Cooper study[9] is a test of the risk-return relationship predicted by the CAPM using all NYSE common stocks over the 1931–1967 period. It is thus a quite comprehensive test in terms of both the stock universe as well as the time period covered, and a good example of studies of this sort. Since the Sharpe and Cooper study was reviewed in some detail in Chapter 14, we'll merely summarize the results of that test. Readers interested in the test methodology used by these researchers should refer to Section 14-3.

Table 18-1 shows the results of following the 10 different risk strategies tested by Sharpe and Cooper over the period from 1931 to 1967. Note that on average, strategy 10, which is the high-risk strategy, provided a return of over 22% per year, while strategy 1, which is the low-risk strategy, provided less than 12%. While the values did not decrease uniformly, the general relationship is in line with the expected: portfolios composed of securities in lower risk-return classes tend to provide lower average returns. At the same time, note that the realized beta of decile 10 in fact turned out to be the highest at 1.42 while the beta of decile 1 was the lowest at .58, with the intervening decile beta values generally, albeit not perfectly, in line with the forecast risk ranking.

Figure 18-2 is a risk-return diagram that plots the average returns and beta values from Table 18-1. Note that the plots closely cluster around the fitted line; the fitted relationship is highly significant, with over 95% of the variation in expected return explained by the differences in beta. Furthermore, the line is upward-sloping, indicating

---

[9]W. F. Sharpe and G. M. Cooper, "Risk-Return Classes of New York Stock Exchange Common Stocks, 1931–1967," *Financial Analysts Journal* (March–April 1972), pp. 46–52.

TABLE 18-1 AVERAGE RETURN AND BETA—10 INVESTMENT STRATEGIES (1931–1967)

Strategy	Average return	Beta
10	22.67	1.42
9	20.45	1.18
8	20.26	1.14
7	21.77	1.24
6	18.49	1.06
5	19.13	.98
4	18.88	1.00
3	14.99	.76
2	14.63	.65
1	11.58	.58

Source: W. F. Sharpe and G. M. Cooper, "Risk-Return Classes of New York Stock Exchange Common Stocks, 1931–1967," *Financial Analysts Journal* (March–April 1972), pp. 46–52.

FIGURE 18-2 Average returns vs. beta, 1931–1967. Average return = 5.53651 + 12.74855(beta value). [*Source: W. F. Sharpe and G. M. Cooper, "Risk-Return Classes of New York Stock Exchange Common Stocks, 1931–1967," Financial Analysts Journal (March–April 1972), pp. 46–52.*]

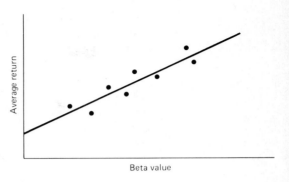

that there was a positive relationship between return and beta (during this period the market rose on the average). Finally, an examination of the figure provides confidence that the relationship is both strong and linear.

> Before continuing, you should:
> 1 Know the major specifications for testing the empirical to the theoretical security market line
> 2 Understand the general procedure for testing the CAPM
> 3 Understand the sort of risk-return relationship that is implied by the CAPM and know the results of studies of that relationship
> 4 Understand the problems encountered in empirically testing the CAPM

18-2 TESTING CAPM SPECIFICATIONS

As noted before, more recent tests have been concerned more with evaluating specifications of the CAPM than with merely assessing the form of the risk-return relationship. Specifically, these later studies were concerned with determining to what extent the intercept from the testing equation was aligned with the risk-free rate of return, and whether the slope of the second-pass regression was equal to the risk premium $r_m - r_f$ earned over the period. Furthermore, these studies wished to assess whether there were other risk factors being priced in addition to market or systematic risk. Specifically, these studies focused on assessing whether residual risk was being priced in the market.

Unfortunately, the initial studies[10] testing these additional specifications of the CAPM did not use techniques that were appropriately powerful. As a consequence, the test results contained biases and the empirical estimates of the CAPM specifications were misleading.

---

[10] An early empirical study of the CAPM performed by John Lintner and reproduced in George Douglas, *Risk in the Equity Market: An Empirical Appraisal of Market Efficiency* (University of Microfilms, Inc., Ann Arbor, Mich., 1968) is a good example of the deficiencies encountered in those initial tests of the broader specification of the CAPM.

Miller and Scholes[11] in a classic article provide an analysis of the statistical problems inherent in all empirical tests of the CAPM. The major problem that they noted in tests was the error that can arise in measuring the true beta of a security. This creates a bias in the estimated coefficients (intercept and slope) from the estimated second-pass regression of return against beta. As a result there will be a downward-biased estimate of the risk premium and upward-biased estimate of the risk-free rate. Correspondingly, the measurement error may result in the residual variance from the regression serving as a proxy for the true beta. This, in turn, can create a spurious correlation between realized return and residual variance in the second-pass regression when, in fact, no relationship exists between return and unsystematic risk.

18-2-1 Time-Series CAPM Test   Black, Jensen, and Scholes (BJS)[12] conducted a test of the CAPM that has set the standard for subsequent empirical testing of the model. BJS built on the research of Miller and Scholes to design a test that directly dealt with the problem of adequately measuring the betas of securities. They also pioneered a portfolio testing technique that helped reduce measurement errors as well as the problems of residual variance. In testing the CAPM, BJS used the following time-series model:

$$r_{pt} - r_{ft} = a_p + \beta_p(r_{mt} - r_{ft}) + e_{pt} \qquad (18\text{-}4)$$

When this equation is estimated on time-series data, the regression coefficient a_p should be equal to zero if the simple CAPM describes returns. Because the errors in the regression equation will be correlated across individual securities, it will be inappropriate to test the CAPM by estimating this equation across a sample of individual securities.[13] To alleviate this problem, BJS devised the aforementioned testing procedure (18-4) that involved running time-series regressions on portfolios rather than on individual securities. The returns and betas evaluated in this case would be portfolio rather than individual measures, but the errors would be relatively free of cross-sectional interdependencies. As a result, the standard error of the intercept could be used to test the difference of the a_p parameter estimate from zero.

In forming portfolios, it's desirable to have a wide range of betas so as to assess more easily the effect of systematic risk on return. One can ensure this most easily by simply ranking securities on the basis of beta and then assigning securities according to the beta value. Just as described in the Sharpe and Cooper study, one would simply take the 10% of securities in the sample with highest betas and form an equally weighted portfolio that would be designated decile 10. Correspondingly, we would take another 10% of securities with the next highest beta and form a second portfolio, and proceed

[11]M. H. Miller and M. Scholes, ''Rates of Return in Relation to Risk: A Re-Examination of Some Recent Findings,'' in Jensen, ed., *Studies in the Theory of Capital Markets,* Praeger, New York, 1972.

[12]F. Black, M. C. Jensen and M. Scholes, ''The Capital Asset Pricing Model: Some Empirical Tests,'' in Jensen, ed., *Studies in the Theory of Capital Markets,* Praeger, New York, 1972.

[13]Securities will show correlation beyond a general market effect due to factors such as industry and sector movements, thereby creating a bias in estimates of the standard error. As a result, the standard error cannot be used to reliably test the level of significance of an alpha value from the regression.

accordingly until we had formed a final portfolio designated decile 1 consisting of the lowest-beta securities.

However, in forming these portfolios, we cannot simply use a directly calculated beta because of the potential bias that will be introduced. For example, stocks in the highest portfolio deciles would be more likely to have overestimated betas; that is, high-beta portfolios would have positive measurement error. This error would in turn introduce a negative bias into the estimate of the intercept parameter a_p from the regression. To avoid this problem, one can use what is known in econometrics as an *instrumental variable*. This is a variable that is highly correlated with the true beta but can be observed independently. For this purpose, BJS used the beta calculated from the previous 5 years of monthly data. As a matter of interest, this technique has become standard practice in many CAPM tests.

BJS used this approach to rank securities by beta and form 10 portfolios, using a universe of all securities listed on the NYSE. They did this for each year over the 1931 to 1965 study period and calculated yearly returns in order to derive a series of 35 returns for each of 10 portfolios. For example, the yearly returns on decile 10 represented the return for the highest-risk portfolio over the period, while the yearly return for decile 1 represented the return for the lowest-risk portfolio, and similarly for the other deciles. Using these returns, BJS then regressed these on a market index over the full 1931 to 1965 study period and four subperiods within that 35-year period to derive return, beta, and intercept parameter estimates for each of 10 portfolios.

Table 18-2 shows beta, excess return $r_p - r_f$, and intercept values from the BJS regression over the full study period. Note that the rank ordering of the realized betas is exactly in line with the deciles, indicating that the procedure for assigning securities to risk deciles had good forecasting power. Correspondingly, the excess return, defined as average portfolio return less the risk-free rate, ranked in perfect order and in line

TABLE 18-2   TIME-SERIES RISK-RETURN STATISTICS (1931–1965)

Portfolio	Realized beta (β_p)	Average excess return $r_p - r_f$	Alpha (α_p)	$t(\alpha_p)$*
10	1.56	2.13	−.08	−.43
9	1.38	1.77	−.19	−1.99
8	1.25	1.71	−.06	−.76
7	1.16	1.63	−.02	−.24
6	1.06	1.45	−.05	−.89
5	.92	1.37	.06	.79
4	.85	1.26	.05	.70
3	.75	1.15	.08	1.18
2	.63	1.09	.20	2.31
1	.50	.91	.20	1.86
Market	1.00	1.42	0.00	0.00

* t statistic for the alpha parameter estimate.
Source: F. Black, M. C. Jensen and M. Scholes, "The Capital Asset Pricing Model: Some Empirical Tests," in Jensen, ed., *Studies in the Theory of Capital Markets,* Praeger, New York, 1972.

with what would be expected given the riskiness of the portfolio. That is, the high-risk decile 10 portfolio showed the highest average excess return, and the low-risk decile 1 portfolio showed the lowest average excess return, with the other portfolio excess returns ranking accordingly.

Note, however, that the intercept from the regression is relatively large at the extremes of the deciles, and for portfolios 1, 2, and 9 the $t(a_p)$ (t statistics for the alpha parameter estimates) are significantly different from zero. Finally, note that the intercept for portfolios with above-average betas (greater than 1) is consistently negative, while the intercepts of portfolios with below-average betas (less than 1) are consistently positive. This is a phenomenon that is consistent with the zero-beta version of the CAPM that would have the following form in an empirical test:[14]

$$r_i = a_i + r_f (1 - \beta_i) + \beta_i r_m \tag{18-5}$$

If the zero-beta version of the CAPM explains security prices, the intercept parameter should have the following value:

$$a_i = (r_z - r_f)(1 - \beta_i) \tag{18-6}$$

Recall that we noted in the preceding chapter that r_z should be greater than r_f. Thus, the term $r_z - r_f$ should be positive. As a result, the parameter a_i should be negative when the beta of the portfolio security is greater than 1 and should be positive when the beta of the portfolio or security is less than 1. The empirical results in Table 18-2 are in line with this expectation, indicating that the zero-beta version of the CAPM provided a better explanation of the risk-return relationship in the market over the study period than the simple form of the CAPM.

Figure 18-3 shows a plot of the average return of the 10 portfolios against the beta of those portfolios, using data for the full period of the study. Note that the plots are close to the fitted line, indicating a high correlation between beta and return; the R^2 for the cross-sectional relationship was .98, which is highly significant. Also, the line was upward-sloping, showing a positive relationship between beta and return. This is consistent with what would be expected for a period when the risk premium in the market was positive.

On the other hand, the intercept of .00359 from the regression was significantly positive, whereas the expected value according to the simple form of the CAPM would be zero.[15] Correspondingly, the slope of the regression line of .01080 was less than the realized risk premium of .01420, which would be the expected value if the simple form of the CAPM held. The subperiod graphs of the relationship shown in Figure 18-4 display the same sort of pattern: higher than expected intercept and lower slope. Because BJS specifically designed a test procedure to control for measurement errors,

---

[14]The implications of the zero-beta version of the CAPM are that

$$r_i = r_z (1 - \beta_1) + \beta_i r_m$$

The model tested is Equation (18-5).

[15]The intercept value of .00358 is a monthly return which is approximately 4% when annualized.

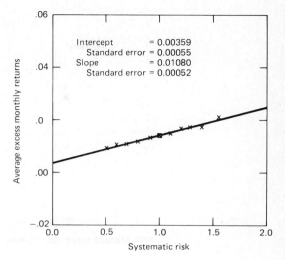

FIGURE 18-3 Average excess monthly returns vs. systematic risk for the 35-year period 1931–1965 for each of 10 portfolios (denoted by X) and the market portfolio (denoted by ☐).

it is unlikely that these results merely demonstrate the same sort of biases as reflected in prior studies. Again, the zero-beta version of the CAPM appears to provide a better explanation of the risk-return relationship over the study period.

18-2-2 Cross-Sectional CAPM Test   A second landmark test of the CAPM that is interesting to review is a study by Fama and MacBeth (FM).[16] In comparison with the BJS study, FM used a cross-sectional rather than time-series methodology. Unlike earlier tests, however, this methodology does not suffer from the sort of biases that characterized those earlier studies. Furthermore, this methodology allowed FM to test more aspects of the CAPM than had been possible previously. Like the BJS study, the FM test set a standard for subsequent tests of models of equilibrium pricing in the capital markets.

In testing the CAPM, FM used the following procedures. They first calculated betas for a universe of listed securities using the prior 5 years of monthly returns. They then ranked securities according to the calculated beta and formed them into 20 rather than only 10 portfolios. Following this procedure, they developed a series of 402 monthly returns for each of the 20 portfolios over the 1935–1968 study period. In contrast to BJS, they ran a cross-sectional regression for each month of the study period using the 20 portfolios. This cross-sectional regression had the following form:

$$r_p = \gamma_0 + \gamma_1 \beta_p + \gamma_2 \beta_p^2 + \gamma_3 \sigma_p + u_p \qquad (18\text{-}7)$$

Note that this is a multiple regression of the monthly return of the portfolio against three variables: (1) beta (β_p), (2) beta squared (β_p^2), and (3) residual risk (σ_p). If the CAPM is the appropriate model of security returns, we would expect, on average, the

---

[16]Eugene Fama and J. MacBeth, "Risk, Return, and Equilibrium: Empirical Tests," *Journal of Political Economy* (May–June 1973), pp. 607–636.

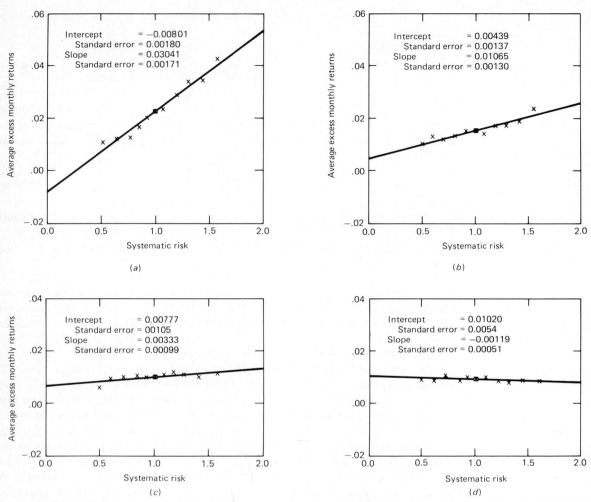

FIGURE 18-4   Average excess monthly returns vs. systematic risk for the 105-month periods (*a*) January 1931–September 1939, (*b*) October 1939–June 1948, (*c*) July 1948–March 1957, and (*d*) April 1957–December 1965 for each of 10 portfolios (denoted by X) and the market portfolio (denoted by ⊡).

coefficient on the beta variable γ_1 to be positive, indicating the usual positive trade-off between risk and return. At the same time, we would expect the coefficient on the residual-risk variable γ_3 to be zero, indicating that other factors are not significant in explaining return, and that the coefficient on the beta-squared term γ_2 would be zero as well to verify the linearity of the relationship. (If the risk-return relationship is nonlinear, a quadratic expression might provide a better explanation of the portfolio returns, in which case γ_2 would be significantly different from zero.) Finally, we could examine the size of the intercept and coefficient on the beta variable to assess whether the simplified form of the CAPM or zero-beta version is a better explanation of the risk relationship across securities.

Table 18-3 shows the values of the parameters from estimating Equation (18-7) over the full 1935–1968 study period. The values of the coefficients are averages of these values for 402 individual months over the period. For example, the coefficient of the beta variable is simply the sum of the individual month values divided by the 402-month study period. Correspondingly, the *t* statistics are derived as a function of the standard deviation of the value of the monthly coefficients over the period. As usual, a high average value and low standard deviation would lead to a high *t* statistic and high level of significance, while a low average value and high standard deviation would result in a low *t* statistic and level of significance.

Note that the coefficient on the beta term is positive and significant at the .05 level, verifying the expected positive relation between beta and return. At the same time, the coefficients on the beta-squared and residual-risk terms were not significantly different from zero. This result suggests that other nonsystematic factors were not significant in explaining returns and that the relationship was linear over the study period.

Since both theory and empirical evidence indicated that variables other than systematic risk had no influence on returns, better estimates of the form of the risk-return relationship can be made by excluding these variables. As a result, FM reestimated the cross-sectional relationship over the full study period using only beta as the explanatory variable for the return of the 20 portfolios. Table 18-4 shows the coefficient and *t* statistics for the reestimated equation for the 1935–1968 period.

Note that the coefficient on the beta variable is positive and highly significant for the full study period, again verifying the positive risk-return relationship in the market. The table also shows that the intercept parameter is positive and significantly different from zero. More importantly for distinguishing between the simplified and zero-beta version of the CAPM, the results show that there was a significant difference between the value of the intercept and the actual risk-free rate of return $a - r_f$ over the 1935–1968 study period. Correspondingly, the coefficient on the beta term γ_2 is generally less than the realized risk premium $r_m - r_f$ over the period. An intercept value in excess of the risk-free rate and a beta coefficient term less than the realized risk

TABLE 18-3 CROSS-SECTIONAL MULTIPLE
REGRESSION RESULTS (1935–1968)

Variable	Coefficient	*t* statistic
Intercept	.0020	.55
Beta	.0114	1.85
Beta squared	− .0026	− .86
Residual risk	.0516	1.11

Source: Eugene F. Fama and James D. MacBeth. "Risk, Return and Equilibrium: Empirical Tests," *Journal of Political Economy* (May–June 1973), pp. 622–623.

TABLE 18-4   RISK-RETURN RELATIONSHIP (1935–1968)

Variable	Coefficient	t statistic
Beta	.0085	2.57
Intercept	.0061	3.24
Intercept minus risk-free rate	.0048	2.55

Source: Eugene F. Fama and James D. MacBeth, "Risk Return and Equilibrium: Empirical Tests," *Journal of Political Economy* (May–June 1973), pp. 622–623.

premium is again more consistent with the zero-beta version of the CAPM than with the simplified form.

Before continuing you should:

1 Understand the procedure used by BJS and how that overcame previously encountered problems of empirical testing
2 Be able to describe the BJS test results and understand how those are in conformity with the zero-beta version of the CAPM
3 Be able to contrast the Fama-MacBeth test methodology to the BJS test methodology
4 Compare the results of Fama-MacBeth's study with that of the BJS study

18-3 TEST OF THE TAX-ADJUSTED CAPM

Recall we noted in the preceding chapter that the CAPM was developed under the assumption that taxes do not have an effect on the pricing of securities. We know, of course, that taxes exist and, more importantly, for capital asset pricing, that capital gains are taxed at a lower rate than ordinary income. Because of this tax differential, one might presume that stocks would be priced differentially to compensate for a tax effect. Specifically, one might presume that high-yield stocks would be priced to provide a higher pretax return than high-growth low-yield stocks to compensate for an adverse tax status.

However, we also noted in the preceding chapter several countervailing arguments that would offset the adverse tax status of high-yield vs. high-growth–high-capital-gain stocks. Whether these factors are powerful enough to offset the tax effect is essentially an empirical question. We'll devote the remainder of this section to reviewing a few of the more important studies on the subject and conclude with an overall assessment of the likely impact of taxes on capital asset pricing.

Table 18-5 lists some of the salient empirical studies that relate to the impact of taxes on the pricing of capital assets. Note that the studies are arrayed in chronological order. In general, the latter-stage studies were concerned with directly testing the impact of taxes on the CAPM whereas the early tests were primarily concerned with

TABLE 18-5   EMPIRICAL STUDIES ON DIVIDEND TAX EFFECT

Study	Date	Study result
Durand and May	1960	No investor preference
Elton and Gruber	1970	Capital gain preference
Black and Scholes	1974	Insignificant effect
Miller and Scholes	1978	No investor preference
Litzenberger and Ramaswamy	1979	Dividend tax effect
Blume	1979	Mixed result
Long	1979	Dividend preference

studying the differential price action of high-yield over low-yield stocks. Note also that the studies are classed as to whether the results indicated a tax impact in the pricing of securities or whether no effect manifested itself.

Two early studies of the differential price behavior of high-yield and low-yield stocks that are useful to review are those by Durand and May[17] and Elton and Gruber.[18] Both studies evaluated the price action of stocks around the period when the stock was going ex-dividend. If investors do not have a preference for capital gains vs. dividends—there is no tax effect—then the price drop of the stock should be equal to the amount of the dividend paid out at the time. For example, if a dividend of $1.00 was paid, we would expect a corresponding drop of $1.00 in the price of the stock if taxes were not a factor in pricing the stock. On the other hand, if taxes were a factor, we would expect the price to drop by less than the amount of the dividend. In the case of the example stock, we would expect investor preference for capital gains over dividend income to result in a less than $1.00 drop in stock price.

In pursuing this line of research, Durand and May focused on the price behavior of AT&T as a widely held stock that would be representative of investor preferences. Durand and May computed the price drop of AT&T stock at each quarterly ex-dividend date from the first quarter of 1948 to the first quarter of 1959 for a total of 45 observations. On average, AT&T stock showed a price drop almost exactly (or at least insignificantly different from) the amount of the dividend, thus implying virtually no impact of taxes in the pricing of stocks.

Rather than focus on an individual stock, Elton and Gruber evaluated the price action of all NYSE listed stocks at ex-dividend dates over the 12-month period April 1, 1966, to March 31, 1967. They chose this study period because there was virtually no movement in the general level of stock prices, and as a result little need to adjust for the impact of a general stock price trend on the analysis. Elton and Gruber's study showed that stock prices on average dropped 22% less than the amount of the dividend at ex-dividend dates. These results indicated a preference for capital gains over div-

---

[17]D. Durand and F. May, "The Ex-Dividend Behavior of American Telephone and Telegraph Stock," *Journal of Finance* (March 1960), pp. 19–31.

[18]Edwin J. Elton and Martin J. Gruber, "Marginal Stockholder Tax Rates and the Clientele Effect," *Review of Economics and Statistics* (1970), pp. 68–74.

TABLE 18-6   EX-DIVIDEND PRICE CHANGES vs. DIVIDEND YIELD

Decile	Dividend yield	Ratio of price change to dividend yield
1	.0124	.6690
2	.0216	.4873
3	.0276	.5447
4	.0328	.6246
5	.0376	.7953
6	.0416	.8679
7	.0452	.9209
8	.0496	.9054
9	.0552	1.0123
10	.0708	1.1755

Source: Edwin Elton and Martin Gruber, "Marginal Stockholder Tax Rates and the Clientele Effect," *Review of Economics and Statistics* (February 1970), pp. 68–74.

idends as well as implying that the marginal rate of taxation of dividends was on the order of 36.4%.[19]

In addition, Elton and Gruber grouped securities into 10 differing yield categories to determine whether investors in different tax brackets would tend to hold securities in different yield categories. For example, they tested to determine whether high-tax-bracket individuals would tend to hold low-yield securities while low-tax-bracket individuals would hold high-yield securities. The data in Table 18-6 show the average drop in price at ex-dividend dates for each of 10 yield categories and is generally consistent with the "clientele hypothesis." Investors attracted to stocks in the highest-yield group appear to be unwilling to give up a dollar of dividends unless they receive at least a dollar in expected capital gain, while those attracted to stocks in the lowest-yield groups appear to be willing to forgo a dollar of dividend in return for considerably less than a dollar in capital gain.

As noted before, more recent tests of the effect of taxes on security pricing have been within the context of the capital asset pricing model. The most direct way to test for this impact has been simply to test whether a tax-adjusted model of the sort that we covered in the preceding chapter provides a superior description of the risk-return relationship across securities. To empirically test the tax-adjusted CAPM in turn is merely a matter of augmenting the usual cross-sectional regression equation with a dividend yield factor D:

$$r_i = \gamma_0 + \gamma_1\beta_i + \gamma_2 D_i \qquad \text{18-8}$$

where r_i = pretax rate of return

---

[19]Elton and Gruber use the formula

$$\frac{P_b - P_a}{D} = \frac{1 - t_o}{1 - t_c}$$

Assume that t_c is one-half t_o or 25% to calculate the implied tax rate. When the empirically derived left-hand side of the equation is .7767, the implied calculated tax rate is 36.4%.

If investors have a preference for capital gains over dividends, we would expect the coefficient γ_2 on the dividend term to be significantly positive. This would indicate the pretax return on the security increases with yield: high-yield securities provide higher return than low-yield securities. Correspondingly, we could deduce from the size of the dividend coefficient γ_2 the marginal tax rate for dividend income, using the fact that this coefficient is equivalent to the T parameter in the Brennan tax-adjusted CAPM. Since the parameter

$$T = \frac{T_d - T_g}{1 - T_g}$$

we can then solve for the tax rate on dividends assuming a tax rate on capital gains T_g. For example, we could simply assume that T_g is $\frac{1}{2} T_d$.

Black and Scholes (BS)[20] tested a model of this sort for a universe of all NYSE listed securities over the 1926–1966 period. While their test results indicated that the coefficient on the dividend term was positive, it was not significantly positive in a statistical sense. Black and Scholes concluded that, within reasonable statistical boundaries, the trade-off between dividends and capital gains could easily be any amount between $1.00 for $1.00 and $1.00 for $0.50.

In a subsequent study, Litzenberger and Ramaswamy (LR)[21] also tested the dividend-augmented CAPM along lines similar to the BS study. They, however, used a more elaborate test methodology and also made a more precise determination of when dividends were received for the stock. As with BS, Litzenberger and Ramaswamy found the coefficient on the dividend term to be positive, but unlike BS, found it to be highly significant statistically. In addition, their results showing investors requiring 23.6% in extra return for every dollar of dividend and an implied marginal tax rate of between .236 and .382 for dividends are remarkably in line with those of Elton and Gruber, who used a completely different test methodology. Their results provide rather strong and positive support for dividends affecting equilibrium prices.

Despite the fact that the Litzenberger-Ramaswamy study is a highly regarded study that provides positive evidence in favor of a tax effect, subsequent research continues to cast doubt on the strength of that conclusion. In particular, Blume[22] in a 1979 study found that non-dividend-paying stocks provided significantly higher than normal returns over the study period similar to that of the LR research. One would have expected a below-average risk-adjusted return from this type of stock if investors had paid premium prices for the presumed tax advantage of capital appreciation. As a unique way of controlling for risk and other factors, Long[23] focused on analyzing a public

[20]F. Black and M. Scholes, "The Effects of Dividend Yield and Dividend Policy on Common Stock Prices and Returns," *Journal of Financial Economics* (March 1974), pp. 1–22.

[21]R. H. Litzenberger and K. Ramaswamy, "The Effect of Personal Taxes and Dividends on Capital Asset Prices: Theory and Empirical Evidence," *Journal of Financial Economics* (June 1979), pp. 163–195.

[22]Marshall Blume, "Stock Returns and Dividend Yields: Some More Evidence," Working Paper 1–79, Rodney L. White Center for Financial Research, University of Pennsylvania.

[23]J. B. Long, "The Market Valuation of Cash Dividends: A Case to Consider," *Journal of Financial Economics* (June–September 1978), pp. 235–264.

utility with two classes of stock, differing in that one class paid dividends while the other class provided returns only in the form of capital gains. Long found a clear and significant *preference* of investors for the dividend-paying class, in contrast to an expected preference for the capital gains class if a tax effect were important in the pricing of securities.

The studies reviewed in this section thus provide mixed conclusions with respect to the impact of taxes on the pricing of capital assets.

18-4 ROLE OF THE MARKET PORTFOLIO

Before concluding this chapter on empirical tests, we should review Richard Roll's[24] fundamental criticism of the relevance of these tests in affirming the CAPM as the appropriate model for describing a risk-return trade-off in the market. This criticism is aimed at one of the fundamental concepts underlying the CAPM—the concept of a market portfolio. Recall that the market portfolio contains all the securities in the universe and the weights of these securities are in proportion to their market values. This portfolio should, in turn, be an ex ante efficient portfolio, i.e., one that is offering the highest expected return at the expected risk level.

While the necessity of the market portfolio to be an efficient portfolio has been generally taken for granted by researchers, it becomes the crux of Roll's analysis. To begin with, Roll demonstrates that choice of the incorrect portfolio or index to proxy for the market portfolio can lead to misestimates of the systematic risk of individual securities and portfolios and hence can result in an inappropriate estimate of the security market line. Roll notes that this misestimation error is not of the usual statistical sort but is a basic bias that cannot be corrected by the use of more powerful statistical tools. It can only be avoided by properly identifying what is the ex ante efficient market portfolio.

Roll, however, indicates that identifying this portfolio is a highly difficult if not in fact impossible task, as it requires some mechanism or ability to capture investor expectations concerning all capital assets. As a result, Roll contends that empirical tests that have been conducted are not, in fact, tests of the security market line. Furthermore, because of the virtual impossibility of identifying the ex ante efficient market portfolio, Roll contends that it is unlikely that the capital asset pricing model can, in fact, be tested empirically.

While Roll's observation that no unambiguous test can be accomplished because of the difficulty of identifying the market portfolio exactly is technically correct, it is not so clear that the criticism is of practical significance. To begin with, the fact is that there have been many empirical studies of the relationship over differing time frames that have virtually all affirmed the CAPM risk-return relationship. Furthermore, even those studies that have used substantially different methodologies have also affirmed the relationship.

In view of this particular criticism, there have recently been studies that have

---

[24]Richard Roll, ''A Critique of the Asset Pricing Theory as Tests. Part I: On Past and Potential Testability of the Theory,'' *Journal of Financial Economics* (March 1977), pp. 129–176.

attempted to assess the sensitivity of the relationship to the use of differing market indexes. An example of such a study is one by Stambaugh[25] which constructed market proxies using diverse asset classes such as stocks, bonds, real estate, and durable goods, and combined these classes in varying proportions to construct differing indexes. We might note that these indexes, as is typically the case with virtually any kind of broad index, are highly correlated. Results of these tests using the various market proxies were virtually the same regardless of the market index and were in line with previous empirical studies that affirmed the risk-return relationship. From these initial tests, it appears that misestimation of the market proxy may have limited practical significance.

18-5 EMPIRICAL TESTS OF APT

In contrast to the CAPM, the arbitrage pricing model does not require identification of a market portfolio. As a result, it does not present the kinds of problems of testing that were pointed out by Richard Roll. The APM, however, presents other kinds of problems of testing that are perhaps as difficult if not more so than the one of identifying an ex ante efficient market portfolio. In particular, the APM requires identification of the number and types of underlying factors that drive the stock-generating process. As noted in the preceding chapter, the APT model per se does not provide any perspective in identifying these factors, nor for that matter does it indicate the number that should be significant in asset pricing. Assessing this more definitely is a matter of empirical testing that is perhaps even more speculative than testing the CAPM.

At the same time, there has been only limited and preliminary testing of the APT model, whereas the CAPM, as we have seen, has been tested rather extensively. We shall review three of the most representative of the empirical studies on the APT model: the original study by Roll and Ross[26] a follow-up study by Chen,[27] and the most recent study by Chen, Roll, and Ross.[28] These studies are indicative of the type of methodology used, problems encountered in the testing, and the sort of results that emerged from the tests.

Testing the APT requires a two-step process similar to the "first-pass" and "second-pass" regressions used in testing the CAPM. In the first step, factor analysis determines how many factors systematically influence the returns of the sample stocks. At the same time, factor analysis determines the factor loadings (b_j's) of each security on the factors. This step is analogous to estimating betas in the "first-pass" regression of the CAPM test. Once the b_j's are estimated, a cross-sectional multiple regression of the securities' average return against their b_j's is run to determine if the risk premiums (X_j's) are statistically significant and to determine how well they explain returns.

---

[25]R. F. Stambaugh, "Missing Assets, Measuring the Market Portfolio and Testing the Capital Asset Pricing Model," Ph.D. proposal, University of Chicago, 1980.

[26]Richard Roll and S. Ross, "An Empirical Investigation of the Arbitrage Pricing Theory," *Journal of Finance,* vol. 35 (1980), pp. 1073–1103.

[27]N. Chen, "Some Empirical Tests of the Theory of Arbitrage Pricing," *Journal of Finance* (December 1983), pp. 1393–1414.

[28]N. Chen, R. Roll, and S. Ross, "Economic Forces and the Stock Market," Working Paper 119, UCLA, (December 1983).

Roll and Ross used such an approach in their 1980 study. They began by factor analyzing a sample of all listed stocks over the 1962–1972 study period. Because of the difficulty of applying factor analysis across the whole stock sample, Roll and Ross subdivided the universe into 42 groups of 30 stocks and applied the analysis to these subgroupings. After determining each stock's factor loadings, they ran a cross-sectional regression for each of the 42 groups. This regression equation had the following form:

$$R_i = \lambda_0 + \lambda_1 b_1 + \cdots + \lambda_j b_j \qquad \text{18-9}$$

The independent variable is the stock's factor loading b_j. The regression coefficient λ for the jth factor loading represents the risk premium for that factor. If the arbitrage pricing theory is correct, one or more of the $\lambda_{j's}$ should be statistically significant. The λ_0 factor represents the risk-free rate or alternatively the zero-beta rate. Roll and Ross estimated the equation first imposing a risk-free rate of 6% and then without imposing a risk-free rate.

The top part of Table 18-7 lists the results for the cross-sectional regressions when 6% was assumed to be the risk-free rate. For 37 of the 42 groups (88.1%), at least one factor was statistically significant at the 95% level; for 24 of the groups (57.1%), at least two factors were significant; for a third of the groups, at least three factors were significant; and for approximately one-sixth of the groups, at least four factors were significant. The last column in the table lists the percentage of groups for which statistically significant factors would be found simply owing to chance if in fact no factors are actually significant. Note that the percentage of groups for which the factors were observed to be significant is much larger than what would occur by chance.

TABLE 18-7 TEST OF THE ARBITRAGE PRICING THEORY (1962–1972)

Number of factors	Number of groups with at least X factors significant at 95% level	Percentage of groups	Expected % due to chance
Imposed risk-free rate of 6%			
1	37	88.1	22.6
2	24	57.1	2.3
3	14	33.3	.1
4	7	16.7	.003
5	2	4.8	.00003
Risk-free rate not imposed			
1	29	69.0	22.6
2	20	47.6	2.3
3	3	7.1	.1
4	2	4.8	.003
5	0	0	.00003

Source: Roll and Ross, "Empirical Test of the Arbitrage Pricing Theory," *Journal of Finance* (June 1980).

In the bottom part of the table, results are reported for cross-sectional regressions in which the risk-free rate is estimated from the sample data, as opposed to assuming a 6% rate. In this case it appears that there may be only two significant factors. This result suggests that the three significant factors obtained when a 6% risk-free rate was assumed may be an overestimate due to an incorrect choice of the risk-free return.

While the Roll and Ross study provides some support for the presence of more than one factor and perhaps as many as four factors that are important in asset pricing, the study is not without flaws. To begin with, we saw that the number of factors that emerged from the study was dependent on the choice of a risk-free rate; an instability that casts doubt on the strength of the results. Second, the necessity of using subgroups rather than the total universe for the factor analysis calls into question whether the observed factors were the same across all 42 groups. Third, the time period of this study was relatively short—10 years—whereas most studies of the CAPM evaluated that model over spans of 40 and 50 years. Finally, some investigations view factor analysis as a less rigorous statistical procedure than regression analysis, which has been the prime test procedure for the CAPM model.

Chen followed up on the Roll and Ross study also using factor analysis to evaluate a universe of all listed securities over four equal subperiods within the 1963–1978 overall study period. As in the Roll and Ross study Chen was also compelled to subdivide the sample data into subgroups of 180 stocks each. Chen extracted the first five factors from the sample on the basis of the Roll and Ross study and other research that indicated the number of factors might be as many as five but would quite likely be no more than that number. Once these factors had been extracted, Chen ran a multiple regression of stock returns against these factors. This regression had the same form as in the Roll and Ross study.

Table 18-8 shows the results of the multiple regression of stock returns and the five factors over the four subperiods of the 1963–1978 study. Note that each of the factors is significant in at least one of the subperiods of the test period, thus providing support for the existence of the five factors in the pricing of securities. At the same time, the coefficient of determination for two of the subperiods was quite low, indicating that the relationship was not consistently powerful in explaining stock returns.

In comparison with Roll and Ross, Chen carried the analysis further to directly compare the explanatory power of the APT model with that of the CAPM. Chen first compared the coefficient of determination from the five-factor model with that of the simple beta model of the CAPM to show a somewhat greater level of explanatory

TABLE 18-8   CROSS-SECTIONAL REGRESSION OF RETURNS (1963–1978)

Period	λ_0	λ_1	λ_2	λ_3	λ_4	λ_5	R^2
1963–1966	.003	−.60*	−.27	.30*	.16*	−.29*	.28
1967–1970	.014	−.06	.29*	.04	.02	−.20*	.03
1971–1974	−.012	−.01	.13*	−.23	.07	−.03	.04
1975–1978	.034	−.43*	−.23*	.07	.05	.03	.14

*Indicates statistical significance.
Source: N. Chen, "Some Empirical Tests of the Theory of Arbitrage Pricing," *Journal of Finance* (December 1983), pp. 1393–1414.

power of the APT. In addition, Chen compared the capacity of the five-factor model to explain such market anomalies as the small-firm effect.[29] Chen showed that the five-factor model was seemingly able to capture this effect in contrast to the CAPM model, where a small-firm effect was significant in addition to a market effect in explaining returns.

While Chen's results provide some added support for a multiple-factor model in the pricing assets, Chen's study, as well as the Roll and Ross study, provide no perspective on the more interesting question of what are the factors. Chen, Roll, and Ross attempt to address this issue by testing for the economic or fundamental determinants of these pricing factors. The authors use the framework of the classic security-valuation model to conjecture that the critical underlying variables to evaluate are those systematic forces that change the discount rate (denominator of the valuation model) and expected cash flows (numerator of the valuation model).

In this regard, Chen, Roll, and Ross propose that such variables as industrial production, changes in the risk premium as measured by the yield spread between AAA and BAA bonds, excess returns on long bonds, and measures of unanticipated inflation are critical indicators of the forces impacting the valuation of securities. They then relate these economic variables to those systematic effects extracted from a universe of all listed securities over the 1953 to 1977 study period. The authors use the same sort of factor analytical approach for extracting the systematic forces (factors) as was used in the two previously described tests of APT model.

Chen, Roll, and Ross' test results show a relationship between these economic variables and the extracted stock return factors. Most interestingly, the economic variables seem to add more explanatory power beyond a stock market index when that effect is added to the equation. In other words, these economic variables appear to be helpful in explaining residual returns—returns after removal of the market. While the relationships emanating from the test are not overwhelmingly significant, they again provide support for a multiple-factor model of security returns. Although correlation is not necessarily causality, it would not seem unreasonable that the economic variables chosen would be related to stock returns. As noted in the preceding chapter, definitively identifying the true underlying economic variables that drive stock prices is likely to be a long and arduous endeavor.

18-6 SUMMARY

We have reviewed the evidence with respect to a trade-off between risk and return, and it appears that there is some systematic relationship between beta and return, and that beta is a useful measure of risk. We further examined the several specifications of the CAPM and found the evidence to be consistent with them, except that the intercept was consistently greater than its expected value: the risk-free rate. It appears

---

[29]Banz and Reinganum demonstrated that portfolios of small firms consistently earned returns notably higher than implied by the CAPM. See R. W. Banz, "The Relationship between Returns and Market Value of Common Stocks," *Journal of Financial Economics* (March 1981), pp. 3–18 and M. R. Reiganum, "Misspecification of Capital Asset Pricing: Empirical Anomalies Based on Earnings' Yields and Market Values," *Journal of Financial Economics* (March 1981), pp. 43–45.

that a zero-beta version of the CAPM may be a better description of the risk-return relationship in the marketplace. The evidence with regard to a tax-adjusted version of the CAPM is much more mixed, and we await further research before making a judgment on this issue. Correspondingly, we evaluated the empirical evidence with respect to the APT model, and while the results appear to be promising, they're also much too preliminary and limited to be conclusive as to the superiority of this model for explaining security returns. All in all, there appears to be a process of equilibrium at work in the marketplace, and the CAPM offers a promising description of how that process is taking place.

SUGGESTED READINGS

Studies by Michael Jensen, ''Capital Markets: Theory and Evidence,'' *Bell Journal of Economics and Management Science* (autumn 1972), pp. 357–398; ''The Foundations and Current State of Capital Market Theory'' in M. C. Jensen, ed., *Studies in the Theory of Capital Markets,* Praeger, New York, 1972, pp. 1–46, provide a comprehensive review of the methods of testing, problems encountered, and the results of tests of the capital asset pricing model.

F. Modigliani and G. A. Pogue, ''An Introduction to Risk and Return,'' *Financial Analysts Journal* (March–April, May–June 1974) provide a more concise yet more readable review of the tests of the CAPM than the Jensen reviews.

Richard Roll, ''A Critique of the Asset Pricing Theory's Tests,'' *Journal of Financial Economics* (March 1977), pp. 129–176, is an illuminating albeit technical analysis of the problems inherent in testing the CAPM.

F. Black, and M. C. Jensen, and M. Scholes, ''The Capital Asset Pricing Model: Some Empirical Tests,'' in Jensen, ed., *Studies in the Theory of Capital Markets,* Praeger, New York, 1972, is the pioneering empirical study of the risk-return relationship of the CAPM.

Eugene Fama and J. MacBeth, ''Risk, Return, and Equilibrium: Empirical Tests,'' *Journal of Political Economy* (May–June 1973), pp. 607–636, pioneered a cross-sectional test methodology that not only was useful in assessing the specifications of the CAPM but also has potential application in testing arbitrage pricing theory.

Edwin J. Elton and Martin J. Gruber, ''Marginal Stockholder Tax Rates and the Clientele Effect,'' *Review of Economics and Statistics* (1970), pp. 68–74, describe a straightforward and influential test for the possibility of tax effects in the pricing of common stocks.

QUESTIONS

1 Justify the use of historic data in empirical tests.

2 Describe how data are developed to generate an empirical proxy for the theoretical security market line.

3 List the specifications that the empirically derived security market line should conform to in order to be in conformity with the theoretical security market line.

4 What is the expected risk-return relationship for securities according to the CAPM, and what did the original researchers find in that regard?

5 Compare the risk-return relationship that would be observed when the market returns exceed the risk-free rate with that when the market return is below the risk-free rate.

6 What other specifications beyond the risk-return relationship are needed to be evaluated to fully appraise the CAPM?

7 Describe the statistical problems encountered in the early stage testing of these added specifications of the CAPM.

8 How did Black, Jensen, and Scholes cope with these statistical problems in their study?

9 Describe the portfolio building techniques that BJS used to build portfolios for a test of the CAPM.

10 Why couldn't BJS use directly calculated betas as a means of ranking securities for inclusion in artificially constructed portfolios?

11 What is an instrumental variable?

12 Describe the risk-return characteristics of the portfolios developed by BJS and assessed over the 1931–1965 study period.

13 What is the expected value of the intercept from the empirically derived security market line?

14 How did the intercept value generated by BJS differ from its expected value, and how is it consistent with the zero-beta version of the CAPM?

15 What is the expected value of the intercept if the zero-beta version of the CAPM is correct?

16 What is the sign of the intercept for high-beta securities compared with low-beta securities when the zero-beta version of the CAPM explains returns?

17 Contrast the Fama-MacBeth test methodology to the BJS test methodology.

18 What factors did Fama-MacBeth test for besides beta in their cross-sectional regression, and what results did they derive in their test?

19 How did Fama-MacBeth test for statistical significance of the parameters from their cross-sectional regressions?

20 How did Fama-MacBeth's test results compare with those of BJS?

21 Describe how Durand and May and Elton and Gruber tested for the presence of a tax effect in security pricing.

22 Compare the results of Durand and May with those of Elton and Gruber.

23 Describe how the CAPM model can be augmented to test for a tax effect.

24 Compare and contrast the results of the several studies that used the tax-augmented CAPM to test for a tax effect.

25 Describe Roll's criticism of the empirical tests of the CAPM and how the identification of a market portfolio is a key element of this criticism.

26 What are the inherent empirical problems encountered in testing the APT model?

27 Describe the general testing procedure used by researchers to assess the APT model and compare that with the procedures used to test the CAPM.

28 Describe Roll and Ross' results in testing the APT model.

29 What additional insights did the Chen study add beyond that of Roll and Ross' study?

30 What underlying economic variables did Chen, Roll, and Ross relate to the extracted stock return factors, and why might these seem to be reasonably appropriate underlying variables?

CHAPTER 19

OPTIONS

After reading this chapter you should:

1 Understand how option strategies provide risk-reducing techniques different from portfolio diversification and the use of borrowing and lending
2 Be able to derive the gross and net return on the option at expiration
3 Know the differing patterns of returns offered by bonds, stocks, calls, and puts
4 Understand how stock price variance, time, and interest rates influence the value of an option
5 Understand the importance of the hedge ratio as an underlying concept for option valuation
6 Be able to derive option values using the Black-Scholes option valuation formula

There are essentially three methods for managing the risk of a portfolio: (1) diversification, (2) changing the leverage in the portfolio, and (3) hedging strategies or insurance. Diversification is the process of mixing risky securities together in a portfolio to reduce risk to its lowest level while holding the level of return constant. We described the notion underlying this process in Chapter 3, where we discussed portfolio theory and "the magic of diversification." Changing the leverage in the portfolio can be accomplished by increasing or reducing the proportion of riskless fixed-income securities held in the portfolio. This process was described in Chapter 17 as a part of the analysis of the capital market line and its relevance to capital market theory. Insurance differs from these other two risk-management procedures and can be accomplished by the employment of options. The prime purpose of this chapter is to discuss this third method of risk management—i.e., insurance via the use of options.

Options have been used for centuries in a variety of business dealings, such as real estate, commodity purchases, and securities. In the United States, securities options have a tainted past as there were a number of abuses in the years that preceded the 1929 crash. Since formation of the Chicago Board Options Exchange (CBOE) in 1973, options trading has expanded rapidly as the instruments have gained respectability and various types of investors have learned of their varied uses. Basically, options have several unique properties that set them apart from other securities.

1 *Limited loss*   Losses are limited to the amount paid for the option while enjoying much of the profit potential of the underlying security position.

2 *High leverage potential*   Only a relatively small amount of money may be needed to obtain high profits.

3 *Limited life*   The option ceases to exist after the expiration date. Long positions are considered to be wasting assets.

The chapter begins by defining an option and describing the two basic types of options: calls and puts. We shall then describe the differing patterns of returns provided by options and compare these with the patterns that are achievable when dealing with conventional securities, i.e., stocks and fixed-income securities. After describing this, we shall indicate several ways that options can be used to provide an insurance function in managing the risk of the portfolio. We shall conclude by discussing the basic factors that give value to options, and we'll describe one formal option pricing model based on these factors.

19-1 SECURITY OPTIONS

It is useful to begin this discussion of options by defining some terms. In general, we can define an option as an agreement between two parties exchanging the right to buy or sell an asset at a later date for an agreed price. This agreed price is called the exercise price, or more commonly the "striking" price. For the right to buy or sell common stock, the buyer of the option in effect pays the writer (seller) a price for selling the option. The price of an option is commonly referred to as the "premium." The premium is a dollar amount which generally ranges between 5 and 30% of the market value of the underlying common stock. We'll discuss in a later section of the chapter methods of valuation for establishing this price or premium.

The most common forms of security options are puts and calls. A call gives the buyer the right to buy from the writer a specified number of shares, generally 100, of a certain stock at any time on or before the expiration date of the option.[1] The buyer of a call profits, and the writer loses, if the market value of the stock rises above the striking price by an amount exceeding the premium. For example, if the price of the call is $5 and the exercise price is $60, the buyer would gain if the price of the stock were above $65 at expiration. A put provides the buyer with the opposite opportunity, the right to sell shares at any time within the option period at the striking price. The buyer of a put profits if the market value of the stock when the put is exercised is below the striking price by more than the premium.[2] For example, if the price of the put is $5 and the exercise price is $60, the put buyer would gain if the price of the stock were below $55 at expiration.

---

[1] Options can be written to provide for exercise: (1) at any time prior to expiration or (2) only at expiration. Those options that allow exercise at any time over the life of the option are known as American calls or puts. Options that allow exercise only at the date of expiration are known as European calls or puts. The added flexibility that American options provide gives them more value than European options. The American option, as the name would imply, is the predominant type that is traded on the U.S. markets.

[2] There are four other kinds of options which are a combination of puts and calls. A straddle is a combination of a put and call, giving the buyer the right to either buy or sell stock at the exercise price. If the price of the stock fluctuates sufficiently, the buyer may exercise both the put and call portions of the straddle. A strip is two puts and one call at the same exercise price for the same period. A spread consists of a put and a call option on the same security for the same time period at different exercise prices. A strap is two calls and one put at the same contracted exercise price and for the same period. Evaluation of these more complex options is better left to a more specialized book.

OPTION TERMINOLOGY

Premium: price paid for the option
Striking price: exercise price
Writer: seller of the option
Call option: gives the right to buy stock
Put option: gives the right to sell stock

Table 19-1 illustrates the way that the option process works with respect to a put and a call for a single hypothetical stock. The table shows the current price of the stock, which is $60 per share, as well as the exercise price of the put and call, which is also $60 for both options. The expiration date for the two options is January 1986 while the current date is July 1985, so that each has a term to expiration of 6 months. This means in the case of the call that the holder can buy the stock at $60 per share at any time over the 6-month term to expiration, while in the case of the put, it means that the holder can sell the stock for $60 per share at any time between July 1985 and January 1986.

For example, assume that we held the call to expiration and the price of the stock at that time was $70 per share. We could exercise the call option at that time and buy the stock for $60 per share and then sell it at the market price of $70. This would yield an expiration value of $10 per call and a $5 profit after subtracting the $5 cost of the option as shown in the first column of Table 19-1 by the row labeled "profit."

With respect to the put, the option is of value as long as there is some chance that the stock price will move below the exercise price. For example, assume that we held the put to expiration and the price of the stock at that time was $53 per share. We could buy the stock at $53 per share and then exercise the option so that a sale price of $60 is realized. At the expiration date the value of the put would be $7, resulting in a profit of $3, which is shown in the second column of the table.

The value of a call option on the expiration date is relatively simple to compute.

TABLE 19-1   PUT AND CALL VALUATION

	Call	Put
Current market price of stock	$60	$60
Exercise price of option	$60	$60
Current date	July 1985	July 1985
Expiration date	Jan. 1986	Jan. 1986
Term to expiration	6 months	6 months
Price of stock at expiration	$70	$53
Option value at expiration*	$10	$7
Current market price of option	$5	$4
Profit*	$5	$3

*These returns disregard commissions and the costs of tying up the dollar cost of the options. Adjustment for these costs would lower the returns to the option strategies.

Let C = value of call
S = price of stock
E = exercise price

Thus, on the expiration date:

$$C = S - E \quad \text{for } S > E \tag{19-1}$$
$$= 0 \quad \text{for } S \leqslant E$$

Figure 19-1 also graphs this formulation and indicates that the higher the stock price is above the strike price ($60), the higher the value of the call. At the same time, when the stock price is below the strike price ($60), the call price is zero at all stock price levels. Note that the downside risk of the call is limited to the price paid for the call.

The general formula for computing the value of a put P at expiration is

$$P = E - S \quad \text{for } S < E \tag{19-2}$$
$$= 0 \quad \text{for } S \geqslant E$$

This formula again says that the value of the put is simply the difference between the price of the stock at expiration and the striking price, which for purposes of this illustration is $60 per share. Figure 19-2 graphs the formulation for the value of a put at expiration and indicates that the lower the stock price is below the exercise price of $60, the higher the value of the put. At the same time, when the stock price is at or above the strike price ($60), there is a constant zero price for the put. As in the case of calls, the risk on puts is limited.

The previous calculations and graphs illustrate values of puts and calls at expiration. In order to compute the profit on the option, we would simply subtract the price or

FIGURE 19-1 Value of a call at expiration.

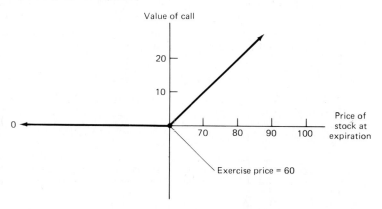

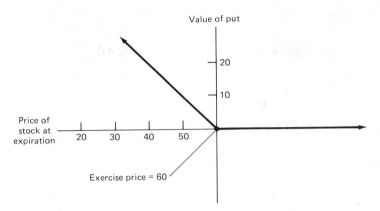

FIGURE 19-2   Value of a put at expiration.

cost of the option from the expiration value.[3] When a call option expires and the stock is below the striking price, the result is a net loss equal to the price paid for the call while expiration of a put with the stock price above the strike price would also result in a net loss equal to the price for the put. Adjustments for the cost of the option also result in a lowering of profitability at all levels of return. They effectively raise the break-even price for the buyer of the call and lower the break-even price for the buyer of the put.

19-2 THE LISTED OPTIONS MARKET

We should note that previous discussion provides an overly simplified example of the mechanics of options trading. In practice, trading in options generally takes place through one of the organized exchanges: Chicago Board of Options Exchange (CBOE), the American Stock Exchange, the Philadelphia, Baltimore, Washington Exchange, or the Pacific Stock Exchange. These exchanges offer several significant advantages to investors. First, option contracts listed on these exchanges are standardized and at the same time simple. For example, each option has a fixed striking price. Also, options listed on an exchange come due at specific times throughout the year, such as January, April, July, and October. Options expire on the Saturday after the third Friday within each of the 4 months; investors can sell options through that Friday and can exercise them by that Saturday. In addition, the exchange guarantees performance of the contract in the event of failure on the part of the original writer. Finally, the exchange promotes a more efficient market by providing information quickly and making it widely available on prices, volume, and other attributes of an option.

As a result of these factors, the listed options market has a liquidity that an unlisted or over-the-counter market would not, and trading in options can generally take place

---

[3]To calculate the relative return on the option, we would divide the net return by the investment base, which in this case would be the price or cost of the option. As noted before, we'll discuss the factors giving value to options and describe a model for determining their value based on these factors in the final part of this chapter.

continuously over the life of most listed options. Availability of an actively traded options market thus allows an option holder the choice of either exercising his option at expiration or selling it in the market prior to expiration. Correspondingly, the writer of an option on a stock that is now selling above its exercise price may wish to close out this position by going into the open market and purchasing the same option contract. The purchase of the option then cancels the position.

19-3 PROFIT PATTERNS

As indicated before, the primary attraction of options is that they allow investors to obtain a pattern of returns that would be unattainable when dealing exclusively with more conventional sorts of securities.[4] In order to illustrate this, we shall compare the return on options—calls and puts—with that attainable by investing in stocks and bonds. We shall illustrate these patterns for both long and short positions in the different securities. We'll rely heavily on the same sort of graphs that we have just discussed—Figures 19-1 and 19-2—to compare the patterns of return. These graphs are useful in illustrating an individual strategy as well as in making comparisons between strategies.[5] For example, any two strategies can be compared at any stock price by transferring the profit-loss line from one graph to the other or by preparing a new graph and imposing both strategies on that graph.

Table 19-2 provides data for four securities: a short-term bond, a common stock, a put option, and a call option. Note that the assumptions about the hypothetical stock are the same as we used in the previous section. Also, the characteristics of the put and call that are written against the stock are the same with respect to the striking price and term to expiration.

We have ignored in the analysis other factors such as dividends, commission costs, taxes, interest, or opportunity costs that can affect the profit and loss to the different strategies. These can be important in the actual execution of an option strategy and should be understood and evaluated in this regard. For our purposes, however, at-

---

[4]There are other securities that are options or have optionlike features. For example, a warrant is a call option issued by the firm whose stock serves as the underlying security. A major difference between warrants and options is the limitation on the amount of the former outstanding. A specific number of warrants of a particular type will be issued; the total cannot easily be increased and typically will be reduced as the warrants are exercised. An option, however, can be created whenever two parties wish to create one; thus the number outstanding is not fixed. Consequently, options are more suitable for providing the function of risk transfer or insurance that we are primarily concerned with in this book.

[5]Their disadvantage lies in the fact that they describe the profit or loss only at expiration, and not at intermediate times, i.e., prior to expiration.

TABLE 19-2   STOCK, BOND, AND OPTION DATA

	Stock	**Bond**	**Call**	**Put**
Current price	$60	$95	$ 5	$ 5
Exercise price	—	—	$60	$60
Term to expiration	—	6 months	6 months	6 months
Price at termination	Variable	$100	Variable	Variable

tempting to fully consider these factors would unnecessarily complicate the analysis. Several excellent books and articles that are listed in the reference section to this chapter provide perspective on the impact of these other factors in managing options programs.

Figure 19-3 shows the profit and loss associated with the different strategies—both conventional and option-related. They all indicate the return that would be earned on the particular security at differing price levels of the hypothetical stock at the end of the 6-month assumed holding period for the security. The lines showing the pattern of returns essentially give a notion of the way that the security's return responds to changes in the price of the hypothetical stock.

Figure 19-3a shows the profits associated with investing in the short-term fixed-income instrument. Note that the return pattern here is a horizontal straight line. Variations in the price of the stock have no effect on the return of this security, as the profit of $5 is certain at least in nominal terms over the 6-month holding period. Fixed-income securities would generally show this sort of pattern, but with divergence from this pattern increasing with the length of maturity of the obligation; i.e., long-term bonds show greater fluctuation in price and hence return then short-term bonds.

Figure 19-3b shows the pattern of returns associated with purchasing and holding the stock long, while Figure 9-13c shows the pattern associated with selling the stock short.[6] Note that when the stock is held long profits increase directly in line with increases in the stock price, while losses increase directly with decreases in the stock price. For example, a buyer of stock at $60 would realize a $10 profit if the stock went to $70, and a $10 loss if it dropped to $50. Conversely, when the stock is sold short profit increases with decreases in the stock price and losses accrue when the price increases. For example, a short seller of stock at $60 would realize a profit of $10 if the stock dropped to $50 and a loss of $10 if it increased to $70. The lines in the two charts (b and c) show similar patterns except that the long position for the stock is upward-sloping while the short position is downward-sloping. The long buyer's gain is the short seller's loss and vice versa.

Figure 19-3d shows the pattern associated with purchasing a call. The position here can be most usefully compared with the position of a long holder of the stock. Note first that the buyer of the call derives a greater percentage gain on her investment when the stock price rises than the long holder of the stock. For example, when the stock rises to $70, the call buyer derives a net profit of $5 (the expiration call value of $10 less $5 cost of the call) for a 100% gain vs. a 17% gain for the long holder of the stock. The call buyer has greater leverage than the long holder of the stock. At the same time, the potential loss to the call buyer is limited to the $5 price of the call, whereas the potential loss to the stock buyer is $60. The call buyer will suffer a total loss even if the stock price remains even (at $60) over the period, whereas the stockholder will break even.

Figure 19-3e shows the pattern associated with purchasing a put. The position here can be most usefully compared with the position of a short seller of the stock. Note first that the buyer of the put derives a greater percentage gain on his investment when

---

[6]For a description of short selling, refer to Chapter 2.

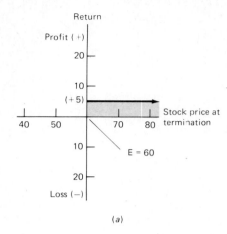

(a)

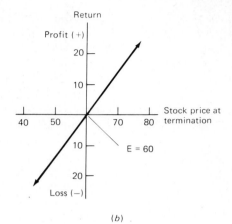

(b)

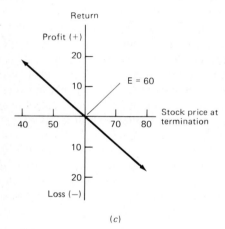

(c)

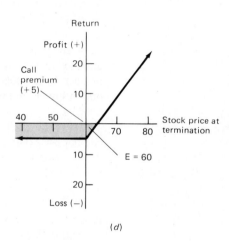

(d)

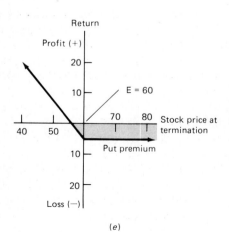

(e)

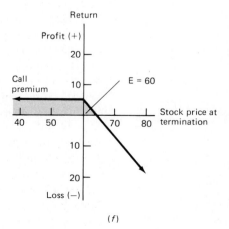

(f)

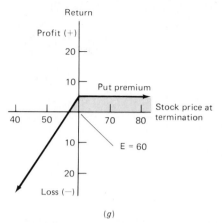

(g)

FIGURE 19-3 Profit and loss from various strategies. (a) Buy a short-term bond; (b) purchase the stock; (c) sell the stock short; (d) buy a call; (e) purchase a put; (f) sell a call; and (g) sell a put.

the stock price declines than the short seller of the stock. For example, when the stock declines to $50, the put buyer derives a net profit of $5 ($10 gross gain less $5 cost of put) for a 100% gain vs. a 17% gain for the short seller of the stock. Again, the option buyer, in this case the buyer of a put, has greater leverage than the short seller of the stock. At the same time, the loss to the put buyer is limited to the price of the put, whereas the loss to the short seller is unlimited, since stock prices can only go to zero on the downside but are theoretically unlimited on the upside. The put buyer will, as in the case of a call buyer, suffer a total loss even if the stock price remains even (at $60) over the period, whereas the short seller will essentially break even.

Figure 19-3f shows the pattern associated with selling a call, while Figure 19-3g shows the pattern associated with selling a put. Note that the call seller derives a fixed profit (the call premium) as long as the stock price remains below the exercise price but can suffer unlimited losses when the price rises above the exercise price. In this case, the profit is the $5 premium for the call and loss accrues when the price rises above $65. Conversely, the put seller earns a fixed profit as long as the stock price remains above the striking price but can suffer losses to the extent that the price of the stock declines below the exercise price. In this case, the profit is the $5 premium for the put and loss accrues when the price declines below $55. Note that in the case of the call seller the risk position is similar to that of a short seller of stock, while for the put seller the risk position is similar to a purchaser of stock. In both cases, the reward is the option premium or the price of the call or put as the case may be.

As noted before, options allow the investor to attain patterns of return that are not available from the more conventional ways of investing. It should be fairly evident that the return patterns attainable from conventional stock and bond strategies shown in Figure 19-3a, b, and c contrast sharply with those attainable from the option strategies shown in Figure 19-3d, e, f, and g. These differing patterns associated with option strategies can in turn be combined with conventional strategies to obtain more desirable risk-return combinations for the portfolio than would be available when only conven-

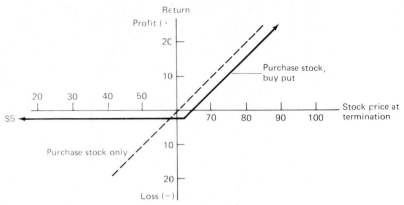

FIGURE 19-4 Protective put strategy. Dashed line: purchase stock only; solid line: purchase stock, purchase put.

tional approaches are considered. Furthermore, strategies like selling puts or calls that would seemingly appear unattractive when used alone become attractive for certain purposes when used in combination.

Given the differing patterns of returns available from conventional and option-related strategies and the many ways of combining these patterns, there are innumerable types of portfolio strategies that might be discussed. We'll focus, however, on only a few of those portfolio strategies. First, discussing all or even many of the available combinations would be beyond the scope of this book. More importantly, we'll focus on those that have been accepted as being prudent in a fiduciary sense and are either being implemented currently or will be in the near future. In this regard, there are three that are particularly relevant for discussion: (1) protective—buy the stock and buy a put; (2) covered-call writing—own the stock and sell a call; and (3) artificial convertible bond—buy bonds and buy calls.

19-3-1 Protective Put Strategy   Figure 19-4 shows graphically the protective put strategy. It illustrates that the investor in this case holds the stock long, and at the same time purchases a put on the stock. The resulting graph is in effect a combination of the chart (Figure 19-3*b*) showing the results of purchasing a stock and the chart (Figure 19-3*e*) showing the results of purchasing a put. The graph illustrates that the long holder of the stock participates fully in the upward movement of the stock. For example, the investor earns a $5 net profit (gross gain less cost of the put) on the stock when it goes to $70, a $15 net profit when it goes to $80, and so on. The investor's return opportunity is unaltered. However, the investor has limited the downside risk on the stock to the exercise price of the put, which in this case is $60. The net loss in this case, even in the event of a decline below $60, would be the $5 cost of the put. The use of the put has in effect truncated the return distribution.[7]

---

[7]Note that this combination of being long stock and long put results in a position that is equivalent to outright purchase of a call, as can be seen by comparing this chart with Figure 19-3. This ability to obtain equivalent positions indirectly in turn implies that within limits the put price should be linked to the corresponding call price. In particular, puts and calls should be priced equivalently, or there should be what is known more popularly as put and call parity.

The strategy would be especially desirable to those investors particularly concerned with protecting against downside fluctuations in stocks. This could be especially important for, say, a fire and casualty insurance company that needs to maintain a certain level of policyholder surplus available to sustain its underwriting effort. Reductions in the value of the investment portfolio—particularly the stock portion—would directly translate into a reduction in the surplus account and lead to an impairment of the ability of the company to operate effectively. Use of the protective put in this instance would help the company insure against having to sell stocks at an inopportune time to avoid impairing the surplus account.

This protection, of course, has a cost, which in this case is the price or cost of the put. Over time, this cost of insurance will penalize the return on the portfolio, reducing it by this cost from what it otherwise would be. The investor needs to assess whether the insurance is worth the cost. In the case of a fire and casualty insurance company it would seem beneficial. Whatever the decision, it is clear that the availability of the put gives any potential investor greater latitude in tailoring her portfolio strategy.

There are alternative ways of purchasing protective puts for a portfolio. One is to directly buy a put on the portfolio. This will provide downside protection just as we have illustrated in Figure 19-4 but will naturally have a cost. An alternative way is to use trading rules to move portfolio assets between equities and cash and thereby construct an artificial or synthetic put. The notion of such a put, originally developed by Leland and Rubinstein,[8] is now being offered commercially as a means of developing insurance for an equity portfolio. This synthetic put provides downside protection and has a cost just as a conventional put. Appendix A describes the underlying theory and mechanics for constructing a synthetic put, and along with that illustrates an analytical method for evaluating the cost of hedging strategies like the protective put.

19-3-2 Covered-Call Writing   Figure 19-5 shows graphically the strategy of covered-call writing. It illustrates that the investor in this case holds the stock long, and

[8]Hayne Leland and Mark Rubinstein, "Replicating Options with Positions in Stock and Cash," *Financial Analysts Journal* (July–August 1981), pp. 63–72.

FIGURE 19-5   Covered-call writing strategy. Dashed line: purchase stock only; solid line: purchase stock, sell call.

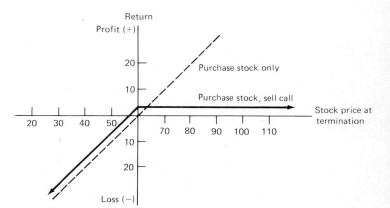

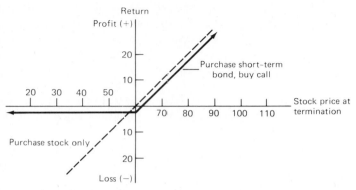

FIGURE 19-6   Artificial convertible bond strategy. Dashed line: purchase stock only; solid line: purchase short-term bond, buy call.

at the same time sells (or writes) a call on the stock. The resulting graph is in effect a combination of the chart (Figure 19-3b) showing the results of purchasing a stock and the chart (Figure 19-3f) showing the results of selling a call. The use of the call again truncates the return distribution but in this case puts a ceiling on the upside potential of the stock. The seller of the call in this instance is exposed to the downside movements of the stock but is not subject to the unlimited risk associated with selling the call outright where the risk position is similar to a short seller of the stock.

This sort of strategy might appeal to an investor who had a negative outlook on the market at a particular time. Outright sale of the stock might incur transactions costs that are unacceptable or could perhaps be prohibited entirely for legal or institutional reasons. Selling covered calls provides a partial hedge against a negative market scenario. The investor at least earns the premium income from selling the option that could be, say, 5% to 10% of the value of the portfolio on average. This incremental return provides some offset against downside risk.

Again, this insurance has a cost. In this case, it is the forgone opportunity to capitalize on strong upward movements in the stock or the market in general. When the stock moves above the striking price it will be called away from the writer and the incremental return above the call premium would go to the buyer of the call. Persistent selling of call options over time would almost certainly result in a loss (opportunity cost) of this portion of the return distribution. Risk has been reduced, but again, so has return.

19-3-3 Artificial Convertibles   Figure 19-6 shows graphically the strategy that we have termed one of creating an artificial convertible bond.[9] It illustrates that the

---

[9]Convertible bonds are hybrid securities. They are similar to other bonds in the sense of a promised stream of interest payments, maturity or par value, and other features typical of those fixed-income securities. But they differ in one very important respect: convertible securities can be exchanged for common stock, at a predetermined exchange ratio, at the option of the investor. The conversion feature thus provides an opportunity to share in any appreciation in the price of the underlying common stock.

investor in this case buys a short-term, fixed-income security such as treasury bills or commercial paper, and at the same time buys a call on the stock. The resulting graph is in effect a combination of the chart (Figure 19-3*a*) showing the results of purchasing a short-term, fixed-income security, and the chart (Figure 19-3*d*) showing the results of buying a call. The call allows the investor to participate in the favorable fortunes of the stock (price movements above the $60 exercise price), while the fixed-income security provides some certain income. This income in turn offsets the cost of the call or alternatively can be viewed as providing protection against downside risk which would be a complete loss when the stock remains below the exercise price.

This strategy would be appealing to those who wish to participate in the equity market but are concerned with controlling their exposure to the risk associated with stocks. Hybrid securities like convertibles provide this opportunity as they can be viewed as a bond with options or warrants attached that provide a call on the equity of the company. Investors can manufacture the same opportunity, albeit one with a generally shorter time horizon, combining call buying with fixed-income investment as we've just illustrated. Here the investor gets the downside protection of a less risky instrument—the bond—and at the same time reaps some of the benefits of stock ownership through the call.

Again, this downside protection or insurance has its costs. In this case, it is the forgone opportunity to fully participate in the favorable fortunes of the company. The fixed-income portion of the package is by definition fixed and will not appreciate when the stock price moves up. The only opportunity to participate is through the call, and typically investors executing this strategy would commit a minor portion of funds to calls compared with the commitment to fixed-income securities. Proponents of this strategy in fact suggest something like a commitment of 90% of the total to fixed-income securities and 10% to calls.

The three examples of combining option strategies with conventional methods of investing all illustrate the added latitude that options provide in allowing an investor to tailor a particular strategy to his needs or risk-return preferences. Note also that the insurance provided by the option strategies has had a cost in terms of either reducing return or at least altering the return distribution. Options and combined strategies do not offer the proverbial "free lunch." The only way that investors can use options to earn above-average risk-adjusted returns is by identifying mispriced options. The following section is thus devoted to developing insights into the valuation of options. This is both to help in perhaps identifying undervalued options and to help avoid incurring too great an option cost that would dissipate the benefits of the strategy.

A convertible bond is, for practical purposes, a bond with nondetachable warrants plus the restriction that only the bond is usable to pay the exercise price. If the bond were not callable, the value of this package of one bond and several latent warrants would equal the value of a straight noncallable bond plus that of the warrants. However, most convertible bonds are callable and thus involve a double option: the holder has an option to convert the bond to stock, and the issuing corporation has an option to buy the bond. To further complicate the situation, the value of a risky bond is greater, the smaller the risk of default, and other things equal, the greater a corporation's stock price, the lower the risk that it will default on outstanding bonds.

Before continuing, you should:

1 Know how the pattern of returns compares across stocks, bonds, puts, and calls
2 Understand how the positions of buyers and sellers of calls and puts are analogous to long and short positions in common stocks
3 Be able to compare and contrast the protective put, covered-call writing, and artificial convertible bond strategies
4 Understand how to derive the value of an option at expiration

19-4 OPTION VALUATION MODELS

As we noted, we shall conclude this chapter by discussing more formal models for valuing options. The one that we shall particularly focus on is the Black-Scholes option valuation model.[10] It is one that formally considers the kind of factors that are important in determining the level of option prices. It is theoretically well developed and has been subjected to extensive empirical testing. It is also widely used.

In the analysis so far, we have assumed that the current price of the stock is the same as the exercise price of the stock and that any evaluation of the option is with respect only to the expiration date. We shall now discuss valuation in a more general context where we can consider the appropriate value of the option at any time before expiration as well as at expiration. Also, we shall consider how the value of the option varies as the price of the stock varies around the exercise price, both above and below the exercise price prior to expiration. Analyzing this in a more general context, in turn, means that we need a slightly different option valuation diagram than the one we have been discussing so far.

Figure 19-7 shows a diagram that is suitable for appraising the value of an option both before and at expiration. The horizontal axis is much the same as shown in previous diagrams except that the stock prices are broken into three separate zones: (1) "out of the money" where the stock price is below the exercise price; (2) "at the money," or close to the exercise price; and (3) "in the money," where the stock price is above the exercise price. The vertical axis refers to the value of the call rather than the profit and loss associated with the strategy, as was the case with the previous diagrams.

Note that the lower solid line that runs along the horizontal axis below the exercise price and bisects the angle above the exercise price is identical to the line used in previous diagrams to portray value at expiration of a call option. This line might alternatively be thought of as a lower bound establishing a minimum economic value for an option. At stock prices above the exercise price, the option would have a minimum value (expiration value) of $S - E$, represented in the diagrams as the height of the 45° line. Below the exercise price, the option would have zero value at expiration.

---

[10]Fischer Black and Myron Scholes, "The Pricing of Options and Corporate Liabilities," *The Journal of Political Economy* (May–June 1973), pp. 637–654.

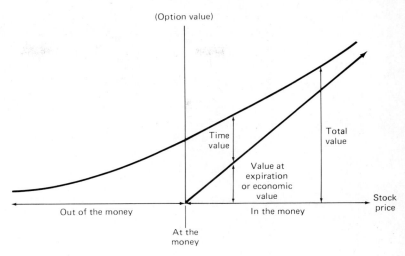

FIGURE 19-7   Value of the option.

Prior to expiration, however, the option will have value in excess of this baseline economic value that we will refer to as the time value of the option. The way that this value varies around the exercise price of the option is illustrated by the curved line on the diagram. Note that the time value of the option is at the maximum when the price of the stock is at the exercise price. This excess or time value decreases' when the price of the stock moves away from the exercise price in either direction.

Table 19-3 illustrates this notion of the time value of the option by showing the economic value of the option; the time value of the option; and the total value of the option, which is the sum of the time value and economic value of the option. It shows these values again using a 6-month option on a hypothetical stock with an exercise price and current price of $60. These values were calculated at prices above, below, and at the exercise price using the Black-Scholes option valuation formula, which we shall describe and illustrate later in the chapter.

Note from the table that the value of the option increases as the price of the stock is higher and reaches its highest value of $23.80 at the $80 high price of the stock. When the stock price is at or below the exercise price of $60, the option has no economic value. It, however, has some value—time value—to reflect the probability

TABLE 19-3   OPTION VALUES

Stock price	Economic value	Time value	Total value ϕ
$40	$ 0	$0.22	$ .22
50	0	1.97	1.97
60	0	6.86	6.86
70	10	4.58	14.58
80	20	3.80	23.80

that the stock might move above the exercise price before expiration. For example, when the stock is at $50, the option has a time value of $1.97 that represents its total value; i.e., it has no economic value. When the stock is above the exercise price of $60, the option has value that consists of both economic value and time value. As the stock price increases, economic value becomes the predominant component of total value. For example, at the $80 high price, economic value is $20 ($80 current price less $60 exercise price), and time value is $3.80.

The table also indicates, as we have noted before, that the time value of the option is at a maximum when the stock is at the exercise price but is lower when the stock is above or below the exercise price. For example, at the $80 high price, the time value of $3.80 is only about one-half the value at the exercise price of $60, while at a price of $50 the time value of $1.97 is less than one-third of the value at the exercise price. The reason that the time value is smaller at lower prices is that there is less chance of a profit on the call, i.e., greater chance of total loss. At higher prices, the option becomes more like the stock in terms of its variance, beta, and capital investment. As a result, there is less reason to pay a premium over its economic value.[11]

19-4-1 Factors Affecting Option Values   There are three prime factors that influence the value of an option, i.e., the level of the time value curve on the diagram. These are (1) the expected variance in price or return of the underlying stock, (2) the time remaining to expiration of the option contract, and (3) the level of interest rates. Dividends on the underlying stock[12] can also influence the value of the option, but since this factor is generally of only secondary importance, we shall mainly focus on discussing the influence of the three primary factors of valuation.

We can begin analyzing how the variance in price of the underlying stock influences the value of the option by reference to the two diagrams in Figure 19-8. The diagrams compare the payoffs at expiration of two options with the same exercise price and the same stock price and where the exercise price and stock price are equal. The only difference is that the price of stock B at its option's expiration date is harder to predict than the price of stock A at its option's expiration date. The probability distributions superimposed on the diagrams illustrate the greater uncertainty associated with stock B than with stock A; i.e., stock B has a wider distribution or variance than stock A.[13]

Note that in both cases there is a 50% probability that the stock price will decline below the exercise price and thereby make the option worthless. However, when the stock price rises above the exercise price, there is a greater probability that stock B will have a greater value than stock A. The option on stock A correspondingly has a greater probability of a higher final payoff than stock B. Since the probability of a

---

[11]It should be noted that stock itself might be considered as an option on the stock value: the exercise price is zero and the expiration date is infinite. This option would, of course, not maintain any premium over the stock itself. This might be attributed to the fact that the "option" is "deep-in-the-money."

[12]Listed options do not receive the dividends accruing to the stock over the holding period. This makes the stock more attractive relative to the options, at least in this sense. To take advantage of this, the investor may want to execute or sell the option prior tto the ex-dividend date.

[13]Actually, the lognormal distribution is more commonly used to portray the distribution of stock price changes. For clarity of exposition, we have simply used the normal distribution.

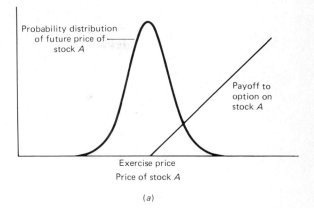

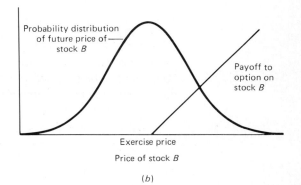

FIGURE 19-8 Stock price distribution and option payoff.

zero payoff is the same for the two stocks, the option on stock B should be worth more than that on stock A.

Figure 19-9a illustrates how the greater underlying variability of the stock affects the time value line of the option. Note that the value line of an option on a stock with greater variability will be at a higher level than an option on a stock with lower variability. The upper line might be considered as illustrative of the value of the option on stock B while the lower line is illustrative of the value of the option on stock A. Note that in the limit when the variance of the stock is zero, as it would be at expiration, the value of the option should correspond to the baseline economic value; i.e., the time value will be zero.

The principle illustrated here is that the greater the expected variance of price changes for a stock the higher should be the option value from that stock. For example, comparing two companies with current stock prices approximately the same and with 6-month options with the same exercise price showed that the option of the more risky oil and gas exploration company—Mesa Petroleum—sold at $3.75, whereas the option on the more mature and stable company, Morgan Guaranty, sold at $2.00. This is

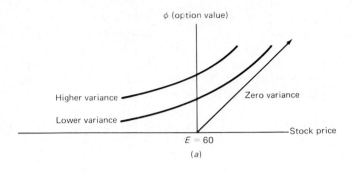

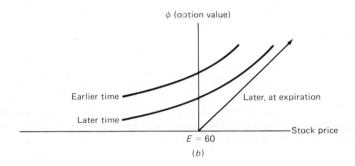

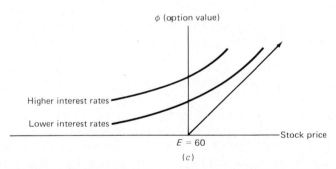

FIGURE 19-9 Factors affection time value of option: (*a*) variance, (*b*) time, and (*c*) interest rates.

because investors would expect Mesa Petroleum to trade over a wider range (have higher variance) than Morgan Guaranty. Observation of the values of options over time bears this out that options on higher-risk stocks persistently tend to have greater value than those on lower-risk stocks. This again derives from the fact that the variance of return of the stock is a prime determinant of the value of the option.[14]

[14]We shall see later in the chapter that estimating the variability of the underlying security is perhaps the most critical input to determining the appropriate value of an option. For the moment, assume that the standard deviation estimate is a given. We shall discuss ways of developing this estimate in the final section of this chapter.

The second factor that is important in determining the value of an option is the time remaining to expiration of the option. It seems reasonable that the longer the life of the option the greater the opportunity for the price of the stock to move into the favorable region of the distribution, i.e., the greater the chance to move into the area above the exercise price. More analytically, we know that the variance of the distribution of returns or price changes will increase with time. In fact, the standard deviation increases with the square root of time so that a stock with a standard deviation of return over a 3-month period of 5% would be expected to have a standard deviation of 10% over the full-year or four-quarter period (i.e., standard deviation of 5% times the square root of four quarters). In effect this increased variance due to the lengthening of the time horizon gives added value to the option. Conversely, the maturing of the option (reduction in term to maturity) automatically reduces the value of the option. Figure 19-9*b* illustrates that over time the curve shifts down as the variance becomes smaller until at expiration it lies on the baseline, as we previously noted it should.

The third major factor determining the value of an option is the level of interest rates. Higher interest rates lead to greater value, while lower interest rates lead to lower values for options. We can justify this in two ways. First, investors can obtain leverage in stock investing by borrowing (establishing a margin account) or by purchasing calls, and in this sense the two techniques can be considered as competitive investment strategies. When interest rates rise, the cost of the margin account increases and makes this technique relatively less attractive than the call strategy. Investors would presumably be attracted to the use of calls, thereby driving their prices up. Second, we noted that a strategy of buying fixed-income securities (treasury bills) and calls is equivalent to creating an artificial convertible security. This quasi-equity security can, in turn, be considered as an alternative or a competitor instrument to the stock. At higher interest rates, more can be earned on the treasury bill portion of the "convertible" package. This makes the overall approach relatively more attractive and should lead to greater demand for calls with the attendant upward pressure on call prices. Figure 19-9*c* illustrates the effect on the option value curve by showing that the curve will be at a high level at higher interest rates and lower at lower rates of interest.

> Before continuing, you should:
> 1 Understand that valuation of an option differs at expiration from valuation prior to expiration and be able to describe how the diagrams differ between valuation at and prior to expiration
> 2 Be able to define the terms "in-out of-at" the money
> 3 Be able to contrast economic value and time value of an option and know how the time value of the option varies as the price of the underlying common stock varies
> 4 Understand how the three factors of variance, time, and interest rates influence the value of an option

19-4-2 Hedge Ratio The data shown in Table 19-4 help to illustrate the significance of the shape of the option value curve. It illustrates this using our hypothetical

TABLE 19-4 OPTION CURVE DATA

Stock price (1)	Option value φ (2)	Slope or hedge ratio (3)	Calls to neutralize stock (4)
$40	$ 0.22	.06	16.67
50	1.97	.32	3.12
60	6.86	.65	1.54
70	14.58	.87	1.15
80	23.80	.96	1.04

stock again as it ranges in price from $40 to $80 per share. Column 1 shows the stock price, while column 2 shows the value of the option at that price and is the same as we showed in Table 19-3. Column 3 shows the slope of the curve at the particular price level; this slope is also known as the hedge ratio. The slope will in turn change with the price level. As the price of the stock increases more and more above the exercise price, the slope will approach 1 (a 45° angle). As the price of the stock declines below the exercise price, the slope of the curve approaches zero (a horizontal line). Note that in this case, the slope is .65 at the exercise price of $60 and .96 at the highest price of $80.

For ease of interpretation, column 4 shows the reciprocal of the slope. It tells the number of short call options that will neutralize a long position in the stock. Correspondingly, it represents the number of long call options that will neutralize a short position in the stock. Note that when the stock price is $50 it would take 3.12 short calls to neutralize a position in the stock. Also note that the ratio decreases as the stock price increases, so that at $80 per share it takes only 1.04 calls to neutralize a position in the stock.

Using these hedge ratios, one can then ensure that gains (losses) on long positions are offset exactly by losses (gains) on short positions, so that the investor's beginning and ending wealth positions are identical. Figure 19-10 illustrates more specifically the way this process of hedging eliminates investment risk. The diagram is a plotting of the option values against the stock price as it ranges from $40 to $80. It shows the value of the option at the exercise price of $60 and allows us to assess how the value of the option changes as the stock price varies around the exercise price.

Note that the value of the call option rises or falls by $0.65 when the stock price changes by $1.00. Recall from Table 19-4 that the reciprocal of the hedge ratio at the exercise price of $60 is 1.54 to 1, indicating that the investor can protect against the stock price change by selling 1.54 call options for $6.86 each. In this instance, when the stock price declines by $1.00 to $59, the investor gains $1.00 on the short position in the options. The reason that the investor gains is that it is now possible to repurchase the 1.54 call options for $1.00 less than they were sold, as each option has declined by $0.65 with the fall in the stock price. Correspondingly, when the stock rises by $1.00 to $61, the investor gains $1.00 on the stock position but loses $1.00 on the short position in the options. In this case, the cost of repurchasing the two options is $1.00 more than they were sold, as each has risen by $0.65.

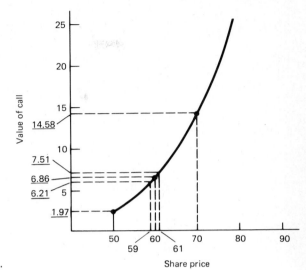

FIGURE 19-10   Stock price and value of call option.

For any sufficiently small change in the stock price, the relationship between the stock and option price change is effectively linear. However, for larger changes the relationship is curved so that gains and losses will not be perfectly offsetting. For example, when the stock price rises to $70 the figure shows that there will be a gain of $10 on the long position in the stock, but a loss of $11.89 [1.54 × ($14.58 − $6.86)] on the short position in the options. Similarly, if the price falls to $50, there will be a loss of $10 on the long position in the stock but a gain of only $7.53[1.54 × ($6.86 − $1.97)] on the short position in the options. The hedge ratio is thus a valid indicator only for small changes in price and over short intervals of time.[15]

19-4-3 The Black-Scholes Formula   The operation of hedging and the hedge ratio are critical notions underlying the Black-Scholes option valuation model. In particular, the model is based on the fact that it is possible, subject to a number of assumptions, to set up a perfectly hedged position consisting of a long position in an underlying stock and a short position in options on that stock, or a long position in the option and a short position in the stock. By perfectly hedged, they mean that over a stock price interval close to the current price, any profit resulting from an instantaneous increase in the price of the stock would be exactly offset by an instantaneous loss on the option position, or vice versa.[16]

The Black-Scholes formula, then, is developed from the principle that options can completely eliminate market risk from a stock portfolio. Black and Scholes postulate

---

[15]It should be noted that it would be difficult to maintain a completely neutral position over time in that all factors, including time, are changing.

[16]The Black-Scholes assumption that one can instantly and continuously rebalance the position means that the relationship between the stock price and option value is effectively linear so that gains and losses are exactly offsetting.

that the ratio of options to stock in this hedged position is constantly modified at no commission cost to offset gains or losses on the stock by losses or gains on the options. Because the position is theoretically riskless, we would expect the hedge to earn the risk-free rate somewhat analogously to the assumption invoked in deriving the capital asset pricing model. Given that the risk-free hedge should earn the risk-free rate, this implies that the option premium at which the hedge yields a return equal to the risk-free, short-term interest rate is the fair value of the option. If the price of the option is greater or less than fair value, the return from a risk-free hedged position could be different from the risk-free interest rate. This is inconsistent with equilibrium, and we would expect the option price to adjust toward fair value.

Using this notion, Black-Scholes then go on to derive an explicit formula for determining the price of the option:

$$C = S[N(d_1)] - E(e^{-rt})[N(d_2)] \tag{19-3}$$

where

C = market value of option
S = current market price of underlying stock
$N(d_1)$ = cumulative density function of d_1 as defined below
E = exercise price of call option
r = ''risk-free'' interest rate
t = time remaining before expiration (in years, e.g., 180 days = .5)
$N(d_2)$ = cumulative density function of d_2 as defined below:

$$d_1 = \frac{\ln(S/E) + (r + .5\sigma^2)t}{\sigma\sqrt{t}}$$

$$d_2 = \frac{\ln(S/E) + (r - .5\,\sigma^2)t}{\sigma\sqrt{t}}$$

$\ln(S/E)$ = natural logarithm of S/E
σ = standard deviation of annual rate of return on underlying stock

Although the formula appears quite forbidding, using it is fairly direct. The major inputs are (a) current stock price S, (2) exercise price E, (3) the time to maturity t, (4) the market interest rate r; and (5) the standard deviation of annual price changes σ. The first three inputs are readily observable from current market quotes or known items of data. The market interest rate must be estimated but can be established fairly easily. One obvious source is the rate on prime commercial paper that is quoted daily in the *Wall Street Journal* for different maturities ranging from 30, 60, and 90 to 240 days. One should use the rate for the maturity that corresponds to the term of the option. The other input that must be estimated, the standard deviation of the stock price change, is a more difficult estimate and one where errors of estimate can have a significant impact on the established option value.

There are several techniques for estimating the variability of the stock price. One might use historically derived values of the standard deviation of price changes of the stock as an estimate of the standard deviation to be generated in the future. The time period over which measurements are made becomes important in this regard; too long a period may result in the inclusion of irrelevant observations and too short a period may exclude valuable information, i.e., not be representative. In this regard, some recommend use of the most recent 6 months' or year's daily trading data as the best measurement interval.

An alternative way to estimate the variability of a stock is to use the option valuation formula itself. Rather than using the valuation formula to assess the proper price of an option, one can observe the current price of an option and deduce what the standard deviation of the stock price is implied from the option valuation formula. Calculation of the implied deviation over a series of past periods and an averaging of these may provide a more accurate assessment of the basic variability of the stock than computing the standard deviation based on ex post stock values.

In either case, there may be a need to adjust these historically derived estimates for possible future changes in the variability of the stock price. Here one would want to examine those underlying factors that are basic determinants of the riskiness of securities: (1) interest rate risk, (2) purchasing power risk, (3) business risk, and (4) financial risk. If the exposure of the stock to these factors was changing, the historically derived variability estimate should be adjusted to reflect this. For example, if the company was now financing more heavily with debt, its exposure to financial risk would be greater than historically and future variability would be expected to be greater than in the past.

To illustrate use of the Black-Scholes option pricing formula,[17] we can use the following inputs for a hypothetical option: (1) $S = 60$, (2) $E = 60$, (3) $r = .12$ (the rate on 180-day prime commercial paper), (4) $t = 6$ months—.50 year, and (5) $\sigma = .30$. Given these inputs, we can begin by calculating values for d_1 and d_2:

$$d_1 = \frac{\ln(60/60) + [.12 + 1/2(.09)](.5)}{.3 \quad \sqrt{.5}} = .389$$

$$d_2 = \frac{\ln(60/60) + [.12 - 1/2(.09)](.5)}{.3 \quad \sqrt{.5}} = .177$$

Using a table for the cumulative normal distribution, we then compute

$$N(d_1) = N(.389) = .651$$
$$N(d_2) = N(.177) = .563$$

The value of the call is then computed as

$$C = 60(.651) - 60 [e^{-.12(.5)}](.563) = 6.86$$

To assess whether the call option was undervalued or overvalued, we could compare this calculated value with the market price of the call. For example, an actual market

---

[17]Some calculators, such as the TI-59, have prepackaged programs for calculating option values. Naturally, availability of these programs speeds up the calculation of option values considerably.

TABLE 19-5 OPTION VALUES AS A FUNCTION OF INTEREST RATES AND STANDARD DEVIATION

Interest rate	Standard deviation		
	.20	.30	.40
.10	4.97	6.54	8.15
.12	5.32	6.86	8.44
.14	5.69	7.19	8.45

price of, say, $5.00 for the call would indicate that the call is undervalued, and an investor might take advantage of this by directly buying the call. Alternatively, the investor could be protected against adverse stock price changes by buying the call and selling the stock short. Recall from a previous section that this action can provide us with a riskless hedge. According to the Black-Scholes valuation model, the *appropriate hedge ratio to use for this purpose is given by N(d₁)*, or in this case .651. This means that for every call option purchased, .651 shares of stock should be sold short, or alternatively, for every share of stock sold short, we should purchase 1.54 calls.

While the Black-Scholes model is a theoretically elegant one, we should note before concluding that there are some concerns with respect to practical application of the model. To begin with, we should be concerned with the realism of the basic assumption of being able to set up a riskless hedge by rebalancing continuously and instantaneously. In actual practice, there are transaction costs that would impede the continuous process of buying and selling securities; i.e., these costs could eventually dissipate any investment return. In addition, while price changes are generally small over a short interval, there are occasions where the price change can be quite sizable. Finally, the assumption of a risk-free rate is one that we commented on previously as being unrealistic.

With respect to the actual estimate of option values, we should emphasize the importance of developing appropriate inputs to the model. This is because differences in the estimates—interest rate and standard deviation—can affect the calculated value of the option significantly. Table 19-5 illustrates this by showing calculated values for options using different values for the interest rate input: 10%, 12%, and 14%, and the standard deviation input: .20, .30, and .40 to the Black-Scholes formulation.

Note, for example, that use of a 10% interest rate rather than a 12% rate, as in the example shown in this section, would provide an option value of $6.54, or 5% lower than in the prior calculation. Alternatively, use of a .40 estimate of the standard deviation or one that is 33% greater than the original estimate of .30 would provide an option value of $8.44, or 23% greater than calculated in Table 19-5. The sensitivity of option values to variations in these inputs, especially with respect to the standard deviation, should emphasize that the avoidance of input error should be a prime consideration in the use of the model.

19-5 SUMMARY

Most options activity is linked to other investment decisions or positions. This is because the use of options allows one to alter the return distribution of the underlying position(s); different strategies may be used to reduce risk or to boost leverage and returns. Of particular interest are those strategies that provide the portfolio manager with the insurance capability that was mentioned in the introduction to this chapter. The purest insurance play is the protective put where the minimum value of the underlying stock is guaranteed over the life of the option. In comparison, covered-call writing provides limited insurance through the proceeds of selling the upside potential of the underlying stock.

Given the right market price of the option, these strategies would be desirable for anyone (free puts would be coveted by all investors). Thus, the big question always is: "Does the option price plus transactions costs warrant the use of these or other strategies?" Some insight might be provided by appealing to theoretical valuation models, such as the Black-Scholes formula. However, one must be wary of the model limitations as well as the need to provide suitable inputs, particularly with regard to estimates of the variance of the underlying stock. In the final analysis, one must decide whether the market price of the option justifies a given strategy—given the risk preference of the portfolio manager.

SUGGESTED READINGS

The classic article showing option evaluation in an equilibrium context is by Fischer Black and Myron Scholes, "The Pricing of Options and Corporate Liabilities," *Journal of Political Economy* (May–June 1973), pp. 637–654. An article by John Cox, Stephen Ross, and Mark Rubinstein, "Option Pricing: A Simplified Approach," *Journal of Financial Economics* (September 1979) shows an alternative and perhaps more intuitively appealing derivation of an option pricing relationship that is equivalent to the Black-Scholes model.

Clifford Smith, "Option Pricing," *Journal of Financial Economics* (January–March 1976), pp. 3–51, provides a good review of the development, empirical testing, and deficiencies of options pricing models. William Sharpe has a chapter in his book *Investments*, Prentice-Hall, Englewood Cliffs, N.J., 1978, that offers a clear and intuitively appealing explanation of option pricing theory.

A book by Gary Gastineau, *The Stock Options Manual*, McGraw-Hill, New York, 1979, clearly describes the chracteristics of options and the types of strategies investors might employ using options. Fischer Black in "Fact and Fantasy in the Use of Options," *Financial Analysts Journal* (July–August 1975), pp. 36–72, well describes the usefulness and pitfalls in application of options in investing.

QUESTIONS

1 Define exercise price, expiration date, and premium for an option.
2 Compare and contrast a call option and a put option.
3 Describe the advantages provided to options trading by the existence of an organized options exchange.
4 How does the return to a bond, stock, call, and put change as the price of the underlying stock rises in price?
5 Conversely, how does the return to a bond, stock, call, and put change as the price of the underlying stock declines in price?
6 How is the position of a call buyer analogous to a holder of a common stock, and how do their positions differ?

7 How is the position of a put buyer analogous to a short seller of a common stock, and how do their positions differ?

8 How is the position of a call seller analogous to the short seller of a common stock?

9 How is the position of a put seller analogous to the holder of a common stock?

10 Explain how one might execute a protective put strategy.

11 What are the advantages of a protective put strategy, and what are the costs of undertaking such a strategy?

12 Explain how one might execute a strategy of covered-call writing.

13 What are the advantages of a covered-call strategy, and what are the costs of undertaking such a strategy?

14 Explain how one might artificially construct a convertible bond.

15 In what way would the artificial convertible bond strategy be appealing to investors?

16 What is meant by an option being (a) in the money, (b) out of the money, and (c) at the money?

17 What is meant by the time value of an option? Compare that with the economic value of the option.

18 How does the time value of an option change as the price of a stock varies, and when is this value at a maximum?

19 Why does an option have value even when the stock is selling well below the exercise price?

20 Explain why the time value of an option decreases both when the stock price declines below the exercise price as well as when it increases above the exercise price.

21 Explain why lengthening the time to expiration will increase the value of an option.

22 Discuss how interest rates impact the value of an option.

23 Discuss why valuation of an option at expiration differs from valuation prior to expiration.

24 Explain what is the hedge ratio and discuss how it is relevant to the valuation of options.

25 Explain why the hedge ratio is relevant for option evaluation only over relatively small price changes and time intervals.

26 Discuss the notions underlying the Black-Scholes option valuation model.

27 Discuss techniques one might use to estimate the price variability of the underlying common stock.

28 Why might observed option values differ from those calculated according to the Black-Scholes option valuation model?

PROBLEMS

1 A call option has a striking price of $40. Calculate the expiration value on the option when the stock price is $50 at expiration and when it is $40 at expiration.

2 Calculate the net return to the option at expiration if the premium had been $3.

3 A put option has a striking price of $40 and sells at a premium of $3. Calculate the expiration value on the option when the stock price is $50 at expiration and when it is $30 at expiration.

4 Assume that an investor has purchased a call option and a put option each at a price of $3 and with an exercise price of $27. Determine the value and net profit of each assuming that the stock sells at (a) $35, (b) $27, and (c) $22 at expiration. Also, determine the net profit on the combined position under each terminal stock price assumption.

5 Assume that a bond yields 10%, a stock sells at $20, and a call and put on the stock each sell at $3 and have an exercise price of $20. Graph the profit and loss from the following categories:

a Buy the bond
b Sell the bond short, i.e., borrow
c Buy the stock
d Sell the stock short
e Buy the call
f Sell the call
g Buy the put
h Sell the put

6 An investor holding 100 shares of stock sells a call for $5 with a striking price of $50. What is the return to the seller if the stock goes to $70?

7 What would be the return to the call seller if the stock price declined to $40?

8 An investor holds 100 shares of a stock and buys a put for $5 with a striking price of $50. What is the return to the put buyer if the stock goes to $70?

9 What would be the return to the put buyer if the stock price declined to $40?

10 Discuss and show graphically how one would undertake a protective put strategy.

11 Show graphically the effect on the value of an option of:

    a An increase in the variability of the underlying stock

    b A reduction in the maturity of the option from 6 months to 3 months

    c An increase in interest rates from 10% to 12%

12 The hedge ratio for a particular stock is .333. Evaluation shows that the option is overvalued. Indicate what action should be taken to earn a "risk-free" profit.

13 Assume that a stock is selling at $30, has an exercise price of $40, a maturity of 3 months, and a standard deviation of .50 for the underlying stock, and that the current interest rate is 15%. Calculate the value of the option using the Black-Scholes model, and indicate the hedge ratio.

APPENDIX: Synthetic Protective Puts

This appendix describes the theory and mechanics for the synthetic put.[18] The analysis is based on the binomial probability model that is most easily illustrated for a single period. When considered in a multiple-period context that can be extended to a continuous sequence of periods that are infinitesimally small, we shall see that the model is equivalent to the Black-Scholes option pricing model that is derived under the assumption of instantaneous adjustment to changing prices.

We cover five major issues with respect to the synthetic protective put in this appendix. First, we illustrate the underlying mechanism for constructing synthetic options: calls and puts. We next show the equivalence between hedging with listed puts and creating synthetic puts. Third, we show the risk-return trade-off for hedging with puts and compare that to outright purchase of stock and investment in a risk-free bond. Fourth, we evaluate the cost of hedging, both for listed and synthetic puts. Finally, we illustrate how the structure of a synthetic option compares to the Black-Scholes option valuation model. This comparison, in turn, provides added intuition into the option valuation process.

19-A1 SYNTHETIC OPTIONS

A call option is the equivalent of a levered position in the underlying stock. Consider a stock currently selling for $50 per share. (Although all our examples of synthetic options are framed in terms of single stocks, they apply equally to portfolios; we use single stocks only for simplicity and to allow a direct comparison between listed and synthetic options.) Assume that next period the stock will sell for either $25 or $100 and that a call option on each share is available with a striking price of $50. Transaction costs are zero and the risk-free rate of interest is 25%.

To construct a riskless hedge, we need to first determine the appropriate hedge ratio. To do this, let:

---

[18]This appendix follows closely the excellent article by J. Clay Singleton and Robin Grieves, "Synthetic Puts and Portfolio Insurance Strategies," *Journal of Portfolio Management* (spring 1984), pp. 63–69.

$$r = \text{risk-free rate} = 25\% \text{ per year}$$
$$S_t = \text{current price of stock} = \$50$$
$$E = \text{exercise price} = \$50$$
$$C_t = \text{current price of call}$$
$$B = \text{amount invested in risk-free asset}$$
$$N = \text{hedge ratio, i.e., number of calls purchased}$$
$$\text{vs. number of shares of stock purchased}$$

If the hedge is perfect, the cash flows will be identical for both the strategy of purchasing calls and the leveraged stock purchase strategy. The initial cash outlay for the call strategy is simply $L_t N$, whereas the initial cash outlay for the leveraged stock purchase strategy is $S_t - B$. (For clarity of exposition we express the hedge ratio with respect to the call rather than the stock). Since these must be equal in a perfect hedge, we can write our hedging equation as follows:

$$L_t N = S_t - B \qquad (19A\text{-}1)$$
$$= 50 - B$$

The future cash flows will depend upon the future stock price, which we assumed will be either $25 or $100. If the future stock price is $25, the value of the option will be zero since the stock price is below the exercise price. Given this outcome, the value of the call strategy, assuming a perfect hedge, will be

$$0 = S_{t+1} - B(1 + r) \qquad (19A\text{-}2)$$
$$1.25B = 25$$

If the future stock price turns out to be $100, the value of a single call at expiration will be $50 ($100 − $50) and the value of the call strategy will be

$$C_{t+1}N = S_{t+1} - B(1 + r) \qquad (19A\text{-}3)$$
$$50N = 100 - (1.25)B$$

Solving for B in Equation (19A-2), we can see that we need to borrow $20 at the risk-free rate. Substituting $20 for B into Equation (19A-3), we can solve for N, the hedge ratio:

$$50N = 100 - (1.25)20$$
$$N = 1.5$$

The hedge ratio of 1.5 indicates that in a perfect hedge, the purchase of 1.5 calls is equivalent to borrowing $20 at the risk-free rate for every share of stock purchased.

The only thing that remains to be determined is the current price of the call option. Since we now know the hedge ratio and the amount to be invested in the risk-free asset for each share of stock, we can solve for the call price using Equation (19A-1):

$$1.5C_t = 50 - 20$$
$$C_t = 20$$

We can now see that if a hedge ratio of 1.5 is used and $20 is borrowed at the risk-free rate for each share of stock, a call price of $20 will result in a perfect hedge; i.e., the cash flows for both strategies will be identical. This is illustrated in Example 1, where the cash flows for a strategy involving two shares of stock are presented. (For two shares of stock, $40 would be borrowed at the risk-free rate, and three call options would be utilized.)

Example 1

Strategy	Initial cash outlay	Ending cash flow $S_{t+1} = 25$	Ending cash flow $S_{t+1} = 100$
1. Buy 3 calls @ $20	3 × $20 = $ 60	3 × $ 0 = $0	3 × $ 50 = $150
2. Buy 2 shares of stock	2 × $50 = $100	2 × $ 25 = 50	2 × $100 = $200
@ $50; borrow $40 @ 25%	$ (40) $ 60	40 × $1.25 = 50 0	40 × $1.25 = $ (50) $150

Since the leveraged stock purchase strategy (number 2) illustrated in example 1 can replicate a listed call, we refer to it as a *synthetic call*. Furthermore, the availability of this synthetic call strategy provides an arbitrage mechanism for ensuring that calls sell at their appropriate value. In this case, the calls must be priced at $20 to preclude the opportunity for riskless arbitrage profits. The impossibility of such profits is at the heart of option pricing.

Using the same numerical example and no arbitrage condition, Example 2 shows that a put is a short position in the stock with the proceeds (and additional money) lent at the market rate of interest.[19]

That is:

$$P_t N = -S_t + B \tag{19A-4}$$
$$= -50 + B$$

Example 2

Strategy	Initial cash outlay	Ending cash flow $S_{t+1} = 25$	Ending cash flow $S_{t+1} = 100$
1. Buy 3 puts @ $10	3 × $10 = $30	$ 75	$ 0
2. Sell 1 share short ($50/share)	$ 50	$ -25	$ -100
Lend (25% interest)	-80	100	100
Net	$ -30	$ 75	$ 0

[19]With large portfolios, the short sale discussed here is simply selling some shares already held. We shall drop the short sale requirement in the next example.

$$P_t N = -S_{t+1} + B(1 + r) \tag{19A-5}$$
$$25N = -25 + B(1.25)$$

To preclude arbitrage profits, the puts must be priced at $10 each.

The replicating strategy (number 2) in example 2 is referred to as a *synthetic put*. We now see that the protective put strategy can take alternative forms. One form is to invest and buy listed puts. Another form is to invest and develop synthetic puts using short sales. Or, as we shall see in the next section, one can create synthetic puts by using the portfolio cash position.

19A-2 HEDGING STRATEGIES

Because we can mimic the returns to listed puts without buying them, we can hedge portfolios with synthetic puts. Example 3 demonstrates how we can construct the hedge. A portfolio of three shares can be hedged by purchasing puts, by selling short and investing the proceeds, or by keeping some assets in cash. Example 3 also demonstrates that identical ending cash flows are possible with and without short sales by buying only two shares (or selling one of three if they are already held) and buying bonds.

Example 3

Strategy	Beginning cash flow	Ending cash-flow stock price	
		$25	$100
1. Buy 3 shares ($50/share)	−$150	$ 75	$300
Buy 3 puts ($50 striking price)	− 30	75	0
Net	−$180	$150	$300
2. Buy 3 shares ($50/share)	−$150	$ 75	$300
Sell 1 share short ($50/share)	50	−25	−100
Lend (25% interest)	− 80	100	100
Net	−$180	$150	$300
3. Buy 2 shares ($50/share)	−$100	$ 50	$200
Lend (25% interest)	− 80	100	100
Net	−$180	$150	$300

19A-3 HEDGING AND THE RISK-REWARD TRADE-OFF

The protective put is a hedging strategy and as such it's useful to compare the risk-return characteristics of hedging to other investments. To analyze the risks and rewards of hedging with puts, we proceed as follows. First, we assume that investors are risk-averse and that they demand a risk premium of 10% to invest in the risky stock. Given this and using the same risk-free rate of 25% as before, we can calculate the probabilities of increases and decreases in the stock price using the following:

$$S(1 + r + k) = Up + Dq \qquad \text{(19A-6)}$$
$$1 = p + q$$

where S = price of stock ($50)
   r = risk-free rate (25%)
   k = risk premium
   U = price the stock moves up to ($100)
   p = probability of an upward movement
   D = price the stock moves down to ($25)
   q = probability of a downward movement

$$50(1 + .25 + .10) = 100p + 25q$$
$$1 = p + q$$

In this case, $p = .5667$ and $q = .4333$.

Using this data, example 4 illustrates the cash flows and derives the returns from $180 invested according to the following strategies: (1) outright purchase of stock; (2) hedging the stock purchase with listed puts; (3) hedging with synthetic puts; and (4) purchase of a risk-free security (bond).

Example 4

Strategy	Beginning cash flow	Ending cash flow stock price	
		$25	$100
1. Buy 3.6 shares	−$180	$ 90	$360
	Expected return = $243		
2. Buy 3 shares ($50/share)	−$150	$ 75	$300
Buy 3 puts ($50 striking price)	− 30	75	0
Net	−$180	$150	$300
	Expected return = $235		
3. Buy 2 shares ($50/share)	−$100	$ 50	$200
Lend (25% interest)	− 80	100	100
Net	−$180	$150	$300
	Expected return = $235		
4. Lend (25% interest)	−$180	$225	$225
	Expected return = $225		

The expected return to an unhedged portfolio (with 3.6 shares = $180 invested) is ($25 × 3.6 × .4333 + $100 × 3.6 × .5667)/$180 = 243/180 = 1.35, or 35%, with a standard deviation of 133.79. The return to the hedged portfolio (using either listed or synthetic puts) is ($150 × .4333 + $300 × .5667)/$180 = 235/180 = 1.3056, or 30.56%, with a standard deviation of 74.33. Therefore, the puts reduce expected returns by $8 ($243 − $235).

TABLE 19A-1   RISK-RETURN FOR DIFFERING STRATEGIES

Strategy	Expected ending cash	Percent return	Std. deviation of expected ending cash
Buy puts (18 at $10, $50 striking price)	$195	8.33	223
Buy bonds ($180 each)	225	25.00	0
Buy shares and hedge with listed puts ($50 striking price)	235	30.56	74
Buy shares and hedge with synthetic puts ($50 striking price)	235	30.56	74
Buy stock (3.6 shares/$50)	243	35.00	134
Buy calls (9 at $20, $50 striking price)	255	41.87	223

The return to a bond portfolio is ($225 × 1.0)/$180 = 225/180 = 1.25, or 25%, with a standard deviation of 0. (These and other strategies are summarized in Table 19A-1.)

Hedging reduces the portfolio risk, *but it does so only at a cost in the form of lower expected returns.* We have also included the returns to the bond portfolio, to avoid leaving the impression that hedging is a bargain because it can cut risk almost in half (portfolio standard deviation of 74.33 vs. 133.79) for an $8 reduction in expected return ($243 − $235). For $10 less in expected returns, in this example, risk can be cut to zero by lending or buying bonds.

19A-4 COSTS OF HEDGING

For synthetic puts, where does the $8 hedging cost come from? Example 4 shows that the cost is the opportunity lost by investing $80 in bonds instead of stocks, because money invested in stocks earns 10% more than bonds on average. Hedging with synthetic puts moves some capital from risky equities into safe bonds. The opportunity cost of hedging in stocks and bonds vs. investing only in stocks is exactly the amount of money invested in bonds times the rate of return forgone—the difference between the stock's expected return and the bond rate ($80 × .10 = $8).

For listed puts, where does the $8 hedging cost come from? Because the expected value of three puts is $32.50 ($75 × .4333), the implied interest rate in buying puts is 8.33% ($30 × 1.0833 = $32.50). Thus, hedging with listed puts moves $30 out of equities and into puts. The opportunity cost is the difference between the 35% expected rate of return on stocks and the 8.33% expected return on the puts times the amount of money invested in puts (.35 − .0833 = .2667 × $30 = $8).

The expected rate of return on puts is lower than the risk-free rate. Because puts are negatively correlated with stocks, investors will accept a lower return in exchange for the ability to hedge.

19A-5 HEDGING OVER MULTIPLE TIME PERIODS

When more than one time period or event is considered, synthetic options become trading rules for moving portfolio assets between equities and cash (or cash instruments). Consider a two-event hedge. We might think of the prior examples as 1-year hedges, where the stock price had one possible sudden change at year-end. Now we are considering a 1-year hedge where the stock can take one sudden change at midyear and a second sudden change at year-end. If we were to cut the time periods shorter and shorter (more possible changes per year) in the limit we would examine a continuous distribution of stock prices.

As a matter of fact, the simple binomial model we have been using can be extended to the Black-Scholes model by allowing the time interval to approach zero and continuously rebalancing the hedge. We can see the relationship between the two option pricing approaches more clearly by first expressing the basic hedging equation (19A-1) so that the hedge ratio N is with respect to the stock rather than the call:

$$C = SN - B \tag{19A-1}$$

We can then compare this equation with the Black-Scholes option pricing formula:

$$C = S[N(d_1)] - E(e^{-rt})[N(d_2)] \tag{19-3}$$

Note that the arithmetic form of each equation is the same. The first term $S[N(d_1)]$ is the amount of money invested in stock, with the hedge ratio $N(d_1)$ being the fraction of a share that must be purchased. The second term, $-E(e^{-rt})[N(d_2)]$, is the amount invested in the risk-free asset. The negative sign means that the amount is borrowed. We might thus interpret the Black-Scholes formula as the instantaneous value of the hedging equation.

PART SIX

PORTFOLIO MANAGEMENT

The three chapters in this part provide perspective on the portfolio management process. Underlying the material in these chapters is the basic notion of diversification as developed by Markowitz and elements of the asset pricing theory as described in the prior three chapters.

Chapter 20 begins by describing portfolio construction with respect to broad asset classes: stocks, bonds, and money market instruments. We describe several alternative ways of developing return and risk inputs and then illustrate how the basic Markowitz portfolio construction algorithm provides an asset mix that represents an optional risk-return combination. This process is known in the trade as asset allocation. We then go on to describe a framework for understanding how investors can balance risk and return in developing strategies for managing securities within particular asset classes such as, for example, securities within the equity class. Finally, we show what characteristics managers should monitor in assessing the basic structure of the portfolio.

Chapter 21 describes mutual funds both for their importance as institutional investors as well as their use in illustrating techniques of portfolio evaluation. In this regard, we illustrate several techniques for calculating risk-adjusted performance along with the rationale for why it is important to consider risk as well as return when calculating performance. We then go on to describe techniques for breaking down aggregate performance into components of market timing and stock selection. This sort of breakdown is helpful in developing better perspective in understanding how performance comes about and whether or not it is sustainable into the future.

Chapter 22 describes international investing. The rationale for investing internationally is again based on the underlying notion of diversification developed by Markowitz. Broadening the universal of eligible securities to an international set improves the opportunities for diversification and thereby increases the prospect of developing an improved risk-return portfolio combination. Offsetting this prospect is the exposure to an additional risk: currency risk.

CHAPTER 20

PORTFOLIO CONSTRUCTION AND ANALYSIS

After reading this chapter you should:

1 Know the necessary steps in developing a proper asset allocation
2 Be aware of the ways that one develops risk and return inputs in the asset-allocation process
3 Know the prime components of risk and return for equities and how these interrelate in developing active/passive strategies of investment
4 Have a basic understanding of how portfolio diagnostics based on portfolio theory can be helpful in targeting and controlling portfolio strategies over time

This chapter is concerned with portfolio construction and analysis. It begins by discussing asset allocation, which is the process of blending together broad asset classes such as stocks, bonds, and money market instruments, to obtain a portfolio that has optimal risk-return characteristics. We then go on to describe active/passive strategies for managing a portfolio over time. The focus here is on identifying those areas where there is potential for adding value in the process. Correspondingly, we indicate methods of hedging risk where the investor skills are not competitive in the marketplace: investors with below-average predictive capability should hedge risk by use of passive strategies. Finally, we describe ways of evaluating the characteristics of a portfolio both in terms of modern investment theory as well as along more traditional fundamental diagnostics. The next chapter on performance evaluation describes methods of assessing how well the process has worked in assembling a portfolio as well as executing active/passive techniques of investment management.

The asset-allocation process involves four key elements. First, the investor needs to determine the assets that are eligible for the portfolio. Second, it is necessary to determine expected return for these eligible assets over a holding period or planning horizon. Third, once returns have been estimated and risk assessed, techniques of optimization can be used to find portfolio mixes providing the highest return for each level of risk. The final step is to choose the portfolio (from the efficient frontier) that provides the maximum return at a tolerable risk level. The following sections describe this process in more detail.

20-1 ELIGIBLE ASSETS

As noted, the first step in the asset-allocation process is to determine the list of assets that are eligible for inclusion in the portfolio. The types of marketable assets that are generally considered by most investors fall into three major categories. First, there are cash equivalents or money market securities, which are characterized by very short maturities. Second, there is the fixed-income class. This type is further subdivided into bonds and preferred stocks because the legal obligation of the corporation on bonds and on preferred stocks is substantially different. Nevertheless, both offer essentially the same investment opportunity—a fixed income. Third, there is the equity, or common stock security, which does not provide for any specific income in the investment contract.

Table 20-1 compares the characteristics of the different major asset classes. Short-term securities such as treasury bills and commercial paper are representative of the class of cash equivalents. Note that the fixed-income category includes three types of bonds—U.S. government, municipals, and corporate—as well as preferred stock. Common stocks are, of course, shown as sole representative of that class. The columns show the major characteristics that are useful in distinguishing the different securities. These include maturity, form of return, certainty of return, and tax status. If the reader needs to review the characteristics of these different securities, see Chapters 2 and 14.

20-1-1 Market Values   Figure 20-1 shows the aggregate size and composition by asset class of a ''world market'' portfolio. The portfolio comprises cash equivalents, fixed-income securities, and common stocks. It is a world portfolio since it includes foreign as well as domestic (U.S.) securities. With the exception of real estate, the assets represented include the major classes generally available for investment.

The world portfolio aggregated $9271 billion as of the end of 1984. Note that cash equivalents represented a relatively minor portion of the portfolio. Fixed-income securities represented 54% of the portfolio, with foreign securities representing a somewhat greater portion than domestic securities. Common stocks comprised 35% of the total, with U.S. stocks representing a somewhat greater portion than foreign stocks.

TABLE 20-1   ASSET CLASS CHARACTERISTICS

Security class	Maturity of security	Form of return	Certainty of return	Tax status
Cash equivalents	Short	Discount	High	Fully taxable
Fixed-income: Bonds				
U.S. government	Long	Coupon	Certain	Fully taxable
Municipal	Long	Coupon	High	Not taxable
Corporate	Long	Coupon	High	Fully taxable
Preferred stock	Perpetual	Dividend	Moderately high	Partial exclusion
Common stock	Perpetual	Dividend and capital gain	Least certain	Some tax exclusion

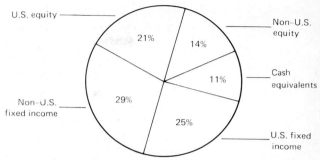

FIGURE 20-1   A world market portfolio of $9271 billion, Dec. 31, 1984. (*Source: G. Brinson and J. Diermeier, "A World Market Index," presentation to the Investment Technology Association, New York, Feb. 11, 1985.*)

Foreign securities—both fixed-income and common stock—represented 43% of the world portfolio, indicating that foreign investing should be an important consideration when undertaking an asset allocation.

Table 20-2 shows common stocks classified by trading markets: New York Stock Exchange (NYSE), American Stock Exchange (AMEX), and over-the-counter (OTC), which includes trading in all stocks not listed on one of the exchanges.[1] Note that NYSE securities represent 84.7% of the total, while OTC securities account for a larger proportion than the other listed market, AMEX. The table also shows the number of different stocks traded in each market. Note that a total of 5184 stocks make up the universe of regularly traded stocks; the OTC has the largest number of different stocks, but the NYSE handles the stocks with the highest average value.

20-1-2 Risk-Return Characteristics of Asset Classes   It is also useful to calculate returns for asset classses over various past intervals. First, this helps evaluate the

---

[1]We have included only those OTC stocks that are quoted on the NASDAQ system that serves the OTC (NASDAQ stands for National Association of Securities Dealers Automatic Quotations). Inclusion in this system requires a certain minimum size and at least two active market makers in the stock. As noted in Table 20-2, there are 2983 companies that qualify for inclusion. There are, in addition, perhaps another 3000 to 4000 stocks actively traded on the OTC that are not quoted on the NASDAQ system. There may be another 10,000-plus issues on the OTC, but they are either quite small or inactively traded.

TABLE 20-2   COMMON STOCK CLASSIFIED BY STOCK EXCHANGE
(December 31, 1981)

Exchange	Market value, billions	% of total	Number of stocks	Average value, millions
NYSE	$1077.0	84.7	1435	$750
AMEX	59.7	4.7	766	78
OTC	134.5	10.6	2983	45
Total	$1271.2	100.0	5184	

Source: Wilshire Associates, Santa Monica, Calif.

behavior of the asset class over different economic episodes such as the business cycle. Second, returns measured over sufficiently long periods may be taken as representative of the returns that investors may have expected to have earned over the period. This may in turn be useful in establishing some benchmarks as to what investors might be expecting to earn in returns in the future. Finally, availability of returns can be used to compare the relative performance behavior across asset classes.

The research by Ibbotson and Sinquefeld that was described previously is particularly useful for this purpose.[2] Their data showed what kinds of returns have been available on asset classes of common stocks, corporate and government bonds, and treasury bills and the risk incurred over longer periods of time. In addition, this data allows us to see how risk and return compared across these asset classes. Finally, it allows one to determine the real return earned on classes of common stocks, bonds, and treasury bills over historic periods.[3] The reader may wish to refer back to Chapters 3 and 14 to review this research.

20-2 ESTIMATING RISK AND RETURN FOR ASSET CLASSES

Once the universe has been defined, it is necessary to develop risk and return estimates for the assets of interest. There are essentially two methods of estimating the risk-return relationship among securities. The first is to assume that the future will be like the past and to extrapolate this past experience into the future. At the other extreme is the scenarios approach, which involves establishing appropriate economic scenarios and then assessing the returns and risks associated with these scenarios. Generally, forecasts using this approach have a 3- to 5-year planning horizon. Forecasting by extrapolating the past into the future implicitly presumes an infinite planning or forecasting horizon. We shall begin by describing this approach and then cover the more complex scenario approach to forecasting risk-return relationships.

20-2-1 Using the Past to Forecast the Future   Since we'll first describe forecasting by the analysis of past data, we've reproduced the returns and risks associated

---

[2]Roger G. Ibbotson and Rex A. Sinquefeld, "Stocks, Bonds, Bills and Inflation: The Past (1926–1976) and the Future (1977–2000)," *Financial Analysts Research Foundation*, Charlottesville, Va., 1979.

[3]The nominal return R on a security, conceived as real return R_r, and compensating for inflation I, can be related as follows:

$$1 + R = (1 + R_r)(1 + I)$$

The real return can then be derived as

$$1 + R_r = \frac{1 + R}{1 + I}$$

By cross-multiplying this equation, we obtain

$$R_r = R - I - R_r I$$

which reduces to the following analytically useful approximation when

$$R_r = R - I$$

with asset classes in Table 20-3. Note that we're considering only three asset classes: common stocks, long-term bonds, and short-term treasury bills. This will simplify the analysis and improve the illustration. The returns and risks associated with the assets were developed over the 1926–1984 period. The returns are realized returns and include income and capital gains, while the risks are the standard deviation of return and correlation among the asset classes.

Note that stocks showed the highest return and treasury bills the lowest return, with bonds showing intermediate return. The risk of the assets as measured by the standard deviation of return was in line with the realized return where stock returns were the most variable and treasury bills the least variable. Finally stocks showed negative correlation over the period with treasury bills and slightly positive correlation with bonds, while treasury bills showed virtually no correlation with bonds.

In forecasting, investors will ordinarily assume that the standard deviations and correlations among assets realized over the past will persist in the future. They will, however, adjust projected returns for current levels of inflation, as theory and empirical research indicate investors are primarily concerned with real rather than nominal returns. Projections then assume that the real return earned in the future will be the same as that earned in the past. Nominal returns projected into the future will differ from past returns by the differences in the assumed future level of inflation and the rates realized in the past.

Table 20-4 shows the inflation rate for the 1926–1984 period, the realized real return for the three asset classes, and projected nominal returns incorporating current levels of inflation. Over the 1926–1984 period inflation was 3.0%, so that the real return on stocks was 6.5%, on bonds 1.4%, and on treasury bills close to zero. According to 1984 estimates, inflation was to proceed at a rate of 6.5%, or 3.5 percentage points more than in the past. Adding the current inflation rate to the real returns of the past period provides projected nominal returns, higher than in the past, of 13.0% for stocks, 7.0% for bonds, and 6.8% for treasury bills.

20-2-2 Subdividing Historical Data   We can develop further insights into projecting data into the future by subdividing the past 55 years into six natural periods. The first, 1929–1933, was a period of extreme deflation without recovery in the economy. The second period, 1934–1938, was a period of deflation with recovery. The third period, 1939–1945, was an extreme case of a controlled economy with both

TABLE 20-3   RISK AND RETURN CHARACTERISTICS OF MAJOR ASSET CLASSES (1926–1984)

Asset class	Return, %	Standard deviation	Correlation		
			Stocks	Bonds	Treasury bills
Stocks	9.5	22.5	1.0		
Bonds	4.4	7.6	0.1	1.0	
Treasury bills	3.3	3.3	0.2	0.0	1.0

Source: Ibbotson Associates, Capital Market Research Center, Chicago, Ill., 1985.

TABLE 20-4 NOMINAL RETURNS, INFLATION, REAL RETURNS, AND PROJECTED RETURNS FOR MAJOR ASSET CLASSES, %

Asset class	Nominal return (1926–1984)	Inflation rate (1926–1984)	Real returns (1926–1984)	Expected inflation (1984)	Projected return
Stocks	9.5	3.0	6.5	6.5	13.0
Bonds	4.4	3.0	1.4	6.5	7.9
Treasury bills	3.3	3.0	.3	6.5	6.8

Source: James L. Farrell, Jr., "The Dividend Discount Model: A Primer," *Financial Analysts Journal* (November–December 1985).

prices and interest rates set by regulatory agencies. The fourth, 1946–1965, was an extended period of stable prosperity. In the fifth period, 1966–1980, inflation began to accelerate and real growth slowed. The final period, 1981–1984, was one of disinflation, that is, decelerating inflation.

Table 20-5 shows the performance of stocks, bonds, and treasury bills over these six periods. The six historical capital market environments with their frequency of occurrence are shown across the top of the table. The frequency of occurrence was determined simply as the percentage of the total 55-year period encompassed by a particular market environment; for example, the market was in an environment of deflation with no hope of recovery for the 5-year period 1929–1933, or 9% of the 1929–1984 period. The returns realized by the asset classes and the inflation rates over each of the six periods are also shown.

Note that stocks did poorly during the initial period of deflation with no recovery and during the recent period of inflation. On the other hand, stocks did quite well during the period of deflation with recovery as well as during the 1946–1965 period, when real economic growth was favorable and inflation moderate. Stocks performed moderately well during the period of controls. Real economic growth and low inflation appear to be favorable environments for stocks, while high inflation and low or declining real growth are unfavorable for stocks.

TABLE 20-5 HISTORICAL CAPITAL MARKET EXPERIENCE (1929–1984), %

Capital market environments	Deflation Without recovery	Deflation With recovery	Controls	Good times	Inflation	Disinflation
Years	1929–1933	1934–1938	1939–1945	1946–1965	1966–1980	1981–1984
Frequency of occurrence	.09	.09	.12	.36	.27	.07
Stocks	−6.70	15.30	11.50	15.00	5.60	16.50
Bonds	6.20	7.80	3.50	2.30	4.60	17.70
Treasury bills	1.90	0.20	0.20	1.90	5.70	9.70
Inflation rate	−5.00	1.30	3.90	2.90	6.90	5.10

Source: James L. Farrell, Jr., *Guide to Portfolio Management,* McGraw-Hill, New York, 1983.

Bonds performed well during the two deflationary periods and showed relatively poor performance during the three periods subsequent to 1938. Bonds again performed well in the recent period of disinflation. In a sense, bonds provide a hedge against slow economic growth and deflation but suffer in a relative sense in other periods. Treasury bills, on the other hand, appear to provide some hedge against inflation, as indicated by their performance in line with the rate of inflation in the recent period, 1966–1980. During other periods treasury bills were less attractive relative to both stocks and bonds.

The data here well illustrate that the performance of broad asset classes can diverge considerably from the longer-term average over shorter time intervals. Economic conditions change, and some of the factors that gave rise to the longer-term average performance may not be relevant at all in the future or may again cause quite wide performance divergences by individual asset classes over shorter intervals. Subdividing historic data can give the analyst perspective in identifying that component of history that is most relevant for the future. Correspondingly, looking at subdivided history in this way may be helpful in identifying likely future economic episodes (scenarios) and the way that these might impact on asset class behavior. Identifying relevant economic scenarios is a key element of the scenario forecasting approach to be discussed in the next section.

20-2-3 Scenario Forecasting   The other major approach to developing returns and assessing risk for securities is the scenario approach. The scenario approach differs from the historical approach with respect to both the analytical difficulty in developing the forecast and the appropriate time horizon for the forecast. To begin with, the scenario approach requires greater analytical effort and forecasting skill than the approach of extrapolating history into the future. The trade-off is, of course, the greater flexibility in dealing with changing environments and hence deriving more effective forecasts of future returns.

While forecasting with the historical approach implies an infinite forecasting horizon, the scenario approach requires a more explicit statement of the forecast period. Generally, forecasters will choose an intermediate-term forecasting horizon of, say, 3 to 5 years. This time horizon forces planners to look beyond seasonal and cyclical prices and interest rates. At the same time, this planning horizon is not so remote as to be beyond the capability of developing some objective and useful forecasts of value.

In addition, this time horizon provides the appropriate perspective for shorter-term portfolio decision making. Once longer-term benchmark yields and price levels for security classes have been established, tactical portfolio decisions flow naturally from the interaction of (1) short-term fluctuations around these benchmark yields and price levels and (2) a predetermined long-term investment plan. It is in this latter respect that we can differentiate market timing, which is a shorter-term tactical approach, from asset allocation, which is a longer-term strategic approach to determining and changing the composition of the portfolio.

Figure 20-2 illustrates the necessary steps to implement the forecast. The diagram shows that the first step is to identify the possible range of economic environments that could exist. Five scenarios are listed, and the task here is to describe the real growth-inflation paths that could occur in each. We should note that the number of

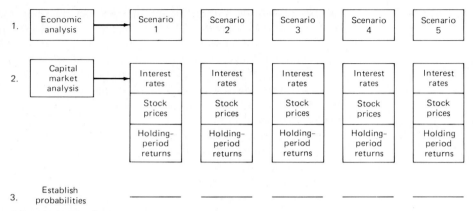

FIGURE 20-2 Scenario forecasting process.

scenarios considered will vary as economic conditions change as well as according to the disposition of the individual forecaster; so that five scenarios listed in the figure should be considered as only illustrative of the process. The next step is to develop for each scenario the implications for interest rates, stock prices, and holding-period returns for each asset class. The third step is to determine the probability associated with the occurrences of each scenario.

20-3 DETERMINING THE OPTIMUM MIX

The next step in the process is to develop the appropriate mix and weighting of individual asset classes in an overall portfolio context. For this purpose, we can use the classical optimization techniques developed by Markowitz (see Chapter 3 for a description of the Markowitz theory of portfolio analysis). Recall that the portfolio optimization algorithm developed by Markowitz traces out a frontier of portfolios that indicates the mix and weighting of individual securities within the portfolio. These portfolios are, in turn, efficient in the sense that they provide highest return at a given level of risk.

In order to implement this process, one needs estimates of expected returns, variances, and covariances of returns for the individual assets to be considered for inclusion in the portfolio. For purposes of asset allocation, this is a matter of developing input estimates for individual asset classes such as, for example, classes of stocks, bonds, and money market instruments.[4] To illustrate this process, we in fact used asset class

---

[4]For purposes of asset allocation, the Markowitz method is perfectly appropriate. The necessary input estimates are limited by the nature of the problem; a relatively small number of asset classes will be considered, probably ranging from as few as three and not likely to exceed a dozen. For larger universes, the estimation problem, especially with respect to covariance estimates, becomes intractable. As a result, there is need to resort to use of index models that considerably reduce the burden of input estimation. For a more complete description of index model methods, refer to Chapter 2 in James L. Farrell, Jr., *Guide to Portfolio Management*, McGraw-Hill, New York, 1983.

returns, variances, and covariances developed by the techniques described in previous sections of this chapter.

Table 20-6 shows three of the efficient portfolios from the frontier generated by the algorithm: (1) a high-risk portfolio (*H*), (2) a medium-risk portfolio (*M*), and (3) a low-risk portfolio (*L*). The table shows the expected return associated with each portfolio and the risk of the portfolio as measured by the standard deviation. In addition, the table shows the composition of the portfolio—the percentage weighting of each asset class in the portfolio.

Note that the proportion of stock held in optimum portfolios is directly related to their risk. As risk-return increases, the optimum equity portion increases; the reverse is true with treasury bills, as large holdings are associated with lower-risk portfolios. Bonds have higher weights in medium-risk portfolios than in either high- or low-risk mixes.

The final step in the asset-allocation process is to choose the portfolio that meets the requirements of the investor. Those with a higher tolerance for risk would choose the higher-risk portfolio. Presumably these investors are willing to tolerate a higher probability of not achieving a certain minimum return in order to earn a higher return. On the other hand, those with a lower tolerance for risk would choose the lower-risk portfolio. They are presumably more interested in achieving a certain minimum return.

Before continuing, you should:

1 Be aware of the kinds of asset classes that are available for investment and the basic differentiating features of these classes
2 Understand the concept of a world portfolio
3 Be aware of how risk and return differed across asset classes over long historic periods as well as how returns varied as economic conditions changed
4 Understand how forecasting using historic returns and risk differs from the scenario approach to forecasting
5 Know the major steps to developing an asset allocation.

TABLE 20-6   OPTIMUM PORTFOLIOS, %

	Portfolio		
	H	*M*	*L*
Expected return	12.1	11.6	10.8
Standard deviation	10.9	8.2	4.8
Asset mix:			
Stocks	85	63	35
Bonds	5	25	10
Treasury bills	10	12	55
Total	100	100	100

Source: James L. Farrell, Jr., *Guide to Portfolio Management*, McGraw-Hill, New York, 1983.

20-4 MANAGING THE PORTFOLIO OVER TIME

Once the investor has established an asset allocation, there is need to determine how the portfolio is to be managed over time. One alternative is to maintain the percentage allocation of asset classes and to keep the security holdings within asset classes in place over the established holding period, which might, for example, be a 5-year planning period. This would constitute a passive strategy and would imply that the investor did not have skill in assessing relative attractiveness across asset clases or identifying under- and overvalued individual securities within those asset classes. Alternatively, the investor could determine to be active with respect to percentage allocation and security selection within asset classes. This would constitute an active approach to portfolio management and would imply that the investor assessed that he had skill in making these decisions. In the following sections, we describe a framework for thinking about active/passive strategies of portfolio management.

20-4-1 Components of Risk and Return   We can best illustrate the active/passive portfolio strategy condition by first describing the components of risk and return within the equity market. We can further illustrate this within the framework of index models for explaining equity returns. Recall from a prior chapter that the single index model is one that explains returns by assuming that the general market effect is the sole factor impacting across securities in a universe. Other effects are assumed to be unique to individual securities within this model framework.

Recall, however, that we reviewed research in Chapter 14 showing that there are factors that impact across subclasses of securities and create correlation additional to that of the general market, i.e., extra-market correlation.[5] For example, stocks that are expected to grow at above-average rates—growth stocks—tend to perform well or poorly as a group. Correspondingly, classes of cyclical, stable, and energy stocks tend to show similar group behavior. Finally, stocks classified into traditional industries, such as the steel or drug or food industry, tend to perform well or poorly as a group.

Table 20-7 shows the major sources of risk and the percentage that these factors explain of the total risk of a typical stock. Note that there are four sources of risk rather than two: general market effect and a unique factor that are assumed when using the single-index model. The additional two sources, (1) a broad market sector effect, and (2) an industry effect, combined, explain 25% of the total risk of a stock or almost as much as accounted for by the general market effect. There is, thus, a need for a multi-index model to accommodate these extra effects and the reader may wish to refer to the suggested readings at the end of this chapter for a description of this model.

20-4-2 Analyzing Portfolio Risk and Return   Index models provide particularly useful insights into analyzing the risk-return characteristics of a portfolio, as these

---

[5]Benjamin King, ''Market and Industry Factors in Stock Price Behavior,'' *Journal of Business* (January 1966), pp. 139–191, showed that an industry effect explained approximately 10% of the realized returns of stocks over the 1926–1960 period. James L. Farrell, Jr., ''Analyzing Covariation of Returns to Determine Homogeneous Stock Groupings,'' *Journal of Business* (April 1974), pp. 181–207, showed that a broader than industry effect explained an additional 15% of the realized returns of stocks over the 1961–1969 period.

TABLE 20-7   SOURCES OF EQUITY RISK

Source	% of risk
General market	30
Market sector: growth, cyclical, stable, energy	15
Industry affiliation	10
Specific	45
Total	100

Source: James L. Farrell, Jr., "Analyzing Covariation of Return to Determine Homogeneous Stock Groupings," *Journal of Business* (April 1974), pp. 186–207.

models allow one to categorize the sources of risk and return into individual identifiable components, as shown in Figure 20-3. The figure shows that the components of return can be considered as (1) market-related, (2) group-related, or (3) security-specific. Correspondingly, there are risks associated with each of these return components, and we've seen that (1) the beta coefficient β_m is a general measure of exposure to market risk, (2) the relative weighting of the groups with respect to the market indicates exposure to group risk or extra-market covariance,[6] and (3) residual risk Var(e) measures the uncertainty of earning the specific return.

Since the general market effect is a predominant source of return and risk for a portfolio, managers should be concerned with monitoring the exposure of the portfolio to this source to determine whether the portfolio positioning is consistent with longer-run policy targets or whether it is appropriate for current market conditions. For example, if the outlook for the market was judged to be especially favorable, the manager might well desire to take advantage of this forecast by raising the portfolio beta above its current level. Conversely, if the forecast were for a declining market, the appropriate strategy would be to lower the beta from its current level. Finally, if the manager is uncertain of the direction of the market and wishes to hedge against

[6]Barr Rosenberg, "Extra-Market Components of Covariance in Security Returns," *Journal of Financial and Quantitative Analysis* (March 1974), pp. 263–274.

FIGURE 20-3   Components of risk and return.

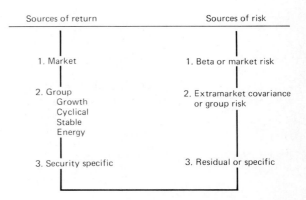

this uncertainty, the appropriate strategy would be to keep the portfolio beta in line with the market beta of 1.00, that is, maintain a neutral posture toward the market.

In addition, it's important that the manager evaluate the exposure of the portfolio to the group component to determine whether the positioning in growth, cyclical, stable, and energy stocks is appropriate for current market conditions. There may be periods when an individual group is judged to be particularly attractive, and the manager may desire to tilt the portfolio toward that grouping by weighting it more heavily in the portfolio. Conversely, a certain grouping may be deemed to be particularly unattractive, and the manager would then tilt away from the grouping by weighting it less heavily in the portfolio. When the manager has no opinion about the attractiveness of the groups, the strategy would be to hedge against the risk of adverse group moves by weighting the groupings in line with their position in the overall market.

Finally, index models indicate that the measure of security-specific return is the alpha value and that this is a desirable aspect when positive and undesirable when negative. Correspondingly, the measure of the uncertainty associated with earning the specific return is the variance of the residual, and this will be large as the portfolio is poorly diversified or small when the portfolio is well diversified. Portfolio managers should therefore endeavor to construct the portfolio in such a way that the resulting alpha is positive and large but should also be aware of the amount of residual risk that is incurred in constructing such a portfolio. The lower the nonmarket risk the greater will be the certainty of attaining the positive alpha, while the greater the nonmarket risk the lower will be the certainty of attaining the positive alpha.

20-4-3 Active/Passive Strategies   In addition to offering a way of analyzing the risk-return characteristics of a portfolio, Figure 20-3 provides a framework for thinking about investment strategies. In particular, organizations can, in endeavoring to achieve investment objectives, pursue an active or a passive strategy with respect to each or a combination of these risk-return components.

Organizations that pursue an active strategy with respect to the market component are known as "market timers." These organizations implement their strategy by varying the cash position or beta of the equity portion of the portfolio according to the forecast direction of the market. Correspondingly, organizations wishing to maintain a passive stance with respect to market timing would maintain the beta of their portfolios in line with the target for achieving longer-term portfolio objectives.

An active strategy with respect to industries or broad market sector has been termed a policy of "group rotation."[7] Pursuit of such a strategy would entail shifting the sector or industry weighting in the portfolio depending on the assessed outlook for the groups. For example, an organization that assessed the outlook for growth stocks to be unfavorable and cyclicals to be favorable in 1972 would have underweighted the growth component and overweighted the cyclical component of the market. Again, an organization that assessed it had no capability to forecast in this respect and desired to pursue a passive strategy with regard to this risk-return component would set portfolio

[7]James L. Farrell, Jr., "Homogeneous Stock Groupings: Implications for Portfolio Management," *Financial Analysts Journal* (May–June 1975), pp. 50–62.

weights in the broad market sectors and major industries in line with their weight in the market index.

An active strategy with respect to individual stocks (''stock selection'') is a strategy used extensively by investment organizations. Stocks that are identified as most attractive would be overweighted with respect to their weighting in the market index, while those considered to be unattractive would not be held or underweighted relative to their position in the index. Organizations typically hold many individual stocks to hedge against the fact that their knowledge of the outlook for the individual stocks is at best imperfect. In portfolio analysis, this is known as diversification. When an organization considers that it has no ability to assess the outlook for individual stocks, it would logically hold many stocks and weight them in line with the weighting in an index. The most efficient way to attain this objective is to create an index fund, which is the ultimate in totally passive strategies.

Given this kind of framework for thinking about individual components of the stock return generating process, we can begin to describe more specifically the kinds of investment products that an organization might offer based on combinations of active and passive strategies associated with each component. In this regard, we have chosen to analyze three types of strategies that would seem to be general enough that they would provide perspective on a multitude of variations. These strategies include (1) remain totally passive with respect to all three return components—stock, group, and market; (2) remain passive with respect to market and group components and active with respect to stock selection; and (3) determine to be active with respect to all three components.

Figure 20-4 is a diagram illustrating the risk-return characteristics of the three types of strategies to be discussed. These are labeled respectively as (1) totally passive or index fund, (2) stock selection, and (3) totally active. The horizontal line is a performance benchmark or return relative to the market. Anything above the market return line is an above-average return. Anything under the market return line is a below-average return. The dashed line represents the expected return relative to the market

FIGURE 20-4   Risk-return characteristics of investment strategies.

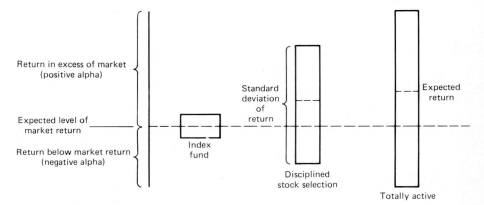

associated with each strategy. The height of the bar represents the expected return range or risk associated with that strategy.

Note that the index fund strategy is located at the lower end of the risk-return spectrum. It remains totally passive with respect to return opportunities. An index fund is expected to offer no incremental return relative to the index, but it is also expected to show relatively little divergence from that neutral performance. At the other extreme, the totally active strategy undertakes to take advantage of all three return opportunities: market timing, group rotation, and individual stock selection.[8] If an organization had predictive capability with respect to all three return opportunities, it would earn a return above that of the market or index fund. It would, at the same time, experience a greater expected return range or risk associated with that return. No one is always right with predictions.

The intermediate case actively capitalizes on stock selection capability. It is passive or neutral with respect to market and group influence. With predictive capability in stock selection, an organization would expect to earn an above-average return—not as much as the totally active strategy, but greater than the index fund. At the same time, the organization expects to experience return variablity greater than an index fund but less than the totally active strategy. The potential for error is not as great as with the totally active strategy because it is not exposed to the risks of the other two return opportunities.

Before continuing, you should:

1 Be aware of the major components of risk and return in the equity market
2 Understand the difference between active and passive portfolio strategies
3 Have an understanding of how analysis of the components of risk and return can be helpful in designing active/passive strategies
4 Understand the trade-off between risk and return as one becomes more active with respect to an investment strategy

---

[8] When an organization undertakes an active strategy using both market timing and group rotation, it is likely that the market risk of the portfolio will at times diverge from a beta of 1, a risk in line with the market. An organization that engages in an actual policy of "timing" the market will at times have betas that differ from that of the market. For example, an organization acting on a forecast of a falling market should have a beta of less than 1, while a forecast of a rising market would imply a beta greater than 1. The diagram in Figure 20-2 assumes that over a market cycle the positive beta divergences will be offset by negative beta divergences. As a result, this diagram presumes that over time the organization's market risk will average out to that of the market—that is, have a beta of 1 as measured against a broadly representative market index. For those organizations deliberately pursuing a long-run policy of keeping the market risk above or below the market level—that is, a beta above or below 1—this diagram would be inadequate, as it assumes that the realized return is at the same level as the market risk. When risk differs from the market, the returns earned in excess or below the market may or may not be representative of above- or below-average performance. These returns would have to be adjusted for the experienced risk level of the fund to determine whether the performance had in fact been inferior or superior. Chapter 21 discusses techniques for making this adjustment.

20-5 PORTFOLIO DIAGNOSTICS

Whatever strategy the investor pursues, whether it is a totally passive or totally active strategy or a combination active/passive strategy, there is need for portfolio diagnostics. These diagnostics are necessary to appraise whether the portfolio constructed by the manager is in keeping with the strategy determined as appropriate for the investor. The diagnostic tools that are quite useful in this regard evolve out of the Markowitz model of portfolio theory[9] and Sharpe's single-index model simplification.[10]

The critical aspects of the portfolio that derive from these models are the exposure of the portfolio to market risk and the degree of diversification of the portfolio. The beta of the portfolio provides a measure of exposure to market risk while the coefficient of determination (R^2) provides a measure of diversification. These can be used as measures of the market risk exposure and diversification of the portfolio over a past period.

20-5-1 Market Risk Performance measurement is, however, historically oriented while portfolio analysis is essentially forward-looking. There is need to assess at a given point in time what the current risk exposure of the portfolio is and how it is likely to behave in the future. This is because portfolio security holdings as well as the weightings of those holdings change over time. Correspondingly, the risk character of individual holdings can also change so that the current composition of the portfolio can differ significantly from its composition over a historic measurement period. For this reason, market risk and diversification assessments are made using cross-sectional measures. These cross-sectional measures are made using risk estimates for individual holdings that currently comprise the portfolio.

To obtain a market risk estimate for the portfolio, it is a matter of first developing a beta estimate for each of the securities in the portfolio as described in Chapter 12. Once individual security beta estimates are obtained, each beta is then weighted by the proportion that its stock represents in the portfolio, and the weighted values are summed to obtain the cross-sectional beta for the portfolio.

Table 20-8 illustrates the calculation of a cross-sectional beta for a hypothetical portfolio of five representative securities. The first column shows the weighting of each security in the portfolio while the second shows the beta of the stock. The third column shows the weighted values for each stock (beta times portfolio weight). The total of this column is the cross-sectional beta of the portfolio. Note that this hypothetical portfolio has a beta of 1.1 or a market sensitivity 10% greater than that of a portfolio constructed to be exactly like the S&P 500. If 1.1 were consistent with the risk (beta) objective of the fund, no change would be suggested in weighting the securities or types of securities in the portfolio.

On the other hand, if the calculated beta were too high, the appropriate course of action would be to reweight the portfolio holdings, i.e., to increase the weightings of

---

[9]Harry Markowitz, *Portfolio Selection: Efficient Diversification of Investment*, Wiley, New York, 1959.
[10]William F. Sharpe, ''A Simplified Model for Portfolio Analysis,'' *Management Science* (January 1963), pp. 277–293.

TABLE 20-8 COMPUTATION OF THE CROSS-SECTIONAL PORTFOLIO BETA

Company	Proportion of portfolio	Beta	Weighted values
Raychem	.11	1.65	.18
Great Lakes Chemical	.11	1.40	.15
Emery Air Freight	.17	1.25	.21
General Electric	.23	1.05	.24
Exxon	.38	.85	.32
	1.00		1.10

low-beta stocks and decrease the weights of high-beta stocks. Alternatively, high-beta stocks could be replaced with low-beta stocks. Conversely, if the calculated beta were lower than desirable for portfolio objectives, the suggested action would be to reweight toward higher-beta stocks or to remove low-beta stocks and add high-beta stocks. In either case, cash or short-term "risk-free" securities such as treasury bills or commercial paper could be added or subtracted to alter the beta of the portfolio. Since these instruments have betas of zero (by virtue of being risk-free), adding them would decrease the beta, while their subtraction would increase the beta of the portfolio.

Investors not only can use this method to calculate a cross-sectional beta for their portfolio but also can use the technique for calculating cross-sectional betas for purchase and sales programs. These betas are calculated in the same way as for the overall portfolio except that the securities and weightings in each program (purchase and sales) represent projected intentions rather than actual holdings. Some investment funds periodically (generally monthly) make such calculations as a means of monitoring the risk posture of the fund on a regular basis.

Table 20-9 shows the type of report that one such investment organization uses to monitor the risk exposure of the fund. The first row of the report shows the size of

TABLE 20-9 PORTFOLIO STRUCTURE
(June 30, 1985)

	S&P 500	Fund	Fund vs. S&P 500	Program Purchases	Program Sales	Fund projected
Market value, millions		$3088		$359	$48	$3399
Risk characteristics (beta):						
Equity portfolio	1.00	1.10		1.11	1.21	1.10
Risk sectors						
1. 0–0.93	52%	25%	−27%	27%	0%	25%
2. 0.94–1.08	20	20	0	14	19	19
3. 1.09–1.23	13	23	+10	14	48	22
4. 1.24–1.43	11	20	+9	43	8	23
5. 1.44 and over	4	12	+8	2	25	11
	100%	100%		100%	100%	100%
Cash and equivalents	—	2%				2%
Total portfolio	1.00	1.08				1.08

the portfolio as of June 30, 1985 (approximately $3 billion), as well as the projected size of the purchase and sales program. Note that the sales program is relatively insignificant when compared with the purchase program. The second row shows the cross-sectional beta of the equities in the portfolio. The fund's beta was 1.1, compared with a beta of 1.0 for the S&P 500.

The middle rows of the report show the weighting of the portfolio in five beta sectors (from the lowest-beta stocks to the highest) as well as the weighting of the S&P 500 in these same five sectors. This allows one to determine whether the fund has an unusual concentration (relative to the S&P 500) in any particular beta sector that might lead to unexpectedly adverse performance. It is noteworthy that the fund has a higher proportion of its portfolio in high-beta stocks and a lower proportion in low-beta stocks than the S&P 500. This is, of course, the sort of distribution that would be expected for a fund with an overall beta greater than 1.0.

The table also shows the weighted beta of the purchase and sales program. On June 30, 1985, the purchase program had a weighted beta of 1.11 while the sales program had a weighted beta of 1.21. Weighting the purchase and sales program with the current portfolio results in virtually no change in the cross-sectional beta of the equities in the portfolio.

It is useful at this point to emphasize that the importance of making this calculation is to determine whether the current purchase and sales program is consistent with the outlook for the general market. For example, a forecast of a rising market would suggest increasing the current portfolio beta level and require a purchase program heavily weighted with high-beta stocks and a sales program heavily weighted with low-beta stocks. On the other hand, a forecast of a declining market would suggest decreasing the current portfolio beta level. A projection of no change in the portfolio beta, as shown in Table 20-9, implies a neutral outlook for the market.

The next to last row of Table 20-9 shows the fund position in risk-free assets. This percentage can vary between 0 and 5%, with the lower limit due to legal restrictions against fund borrowing and the upper limit a policy constraint. This fund advertises itself as a virtually all-equity variable annuity, hence the low allowed limit on cash. Also recall that since cash and short-term securities have betas of zero, an increase in this category reduces the portfolio beta while a decrease increases the beta. The fund's 2% cash position on June 3, 1985, resulted in a total portfolio beta of 1.08, which is less than the 1.10 beta of the equities alone.

20-5-2 Diversification   Investors also need to evaluate the current diversification characteristics of the portfolio and again should do this by considering the current portfolio composition of securities and weightings. Here the procedure would be to calculate how the current composition of securities correlated with the S&P 500 over a prior 5-year period. The derived R^2 would provide a measure of the current and presumably prospective diversification character of the fund. A high R^2 would be indicative of a well-diversified portfolio while a low R^2 would be indicative of an underdiversified or concentrated portfolio. As a general benchmark, a portfolio with an R^2 in excess of .90 would be considered to be well diversified.

An alternative but complementary measure of diversification is the standard error of portfolio return. This measure is also derived from the regression of portfolio return against market return. Graphically, it is a measure of how closely or poorly the plotted data points fit around a regression line. Points that cluster closely to the line would indicate a well-defined relationship and a highly diversified portfolio, while a wide scatter around a regression line would indicate a poorly defined relationship and a relatively undiversified portfolio. The individual return points in Figure 20-5 showing the relationship between fund return and the S&P 500 are closely clustered around the line and indicate a fund that is well diversified.

Mathematically, the standard error provides a measure of the extent to which the fund return might vary from what would be expected given a certain level of market return. Assuming a normal distribution, plus and minus one standard error would indicate the bounds within which two-thirds of the fund's return should fall, while plus and minus two standard errors would indicate the bounds within which 95% of the fund's returns should fall. For example, a portfolio with a standard error of 5% and a market beta would be expected to show a return that was within 5% of the market two-thirds of the time and within 10% of the market 95% of the time. If the market return was 15%, we should be 67% confident that the fund's return was between 10% and 20% and should be 95% sure that the return was between 5% and 25%.

The standard error is in fact a more useful measure for targeting and controlling the diversification level of the portfolio over time than is the R^2. To begin with, the standard error is a measure that can be compared most directly with prospective return opportunities to more easily make a risk-return trade-off evaluation. For example, a

FIGURE 20-5   The relationship between the market rate of return and the rate of return on the fund.

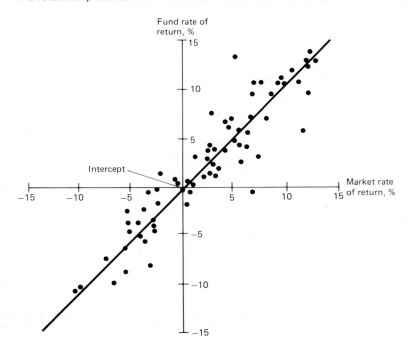

standard error of say 3% associated with a particular strategy can be most directly appraised against an incremental return (alpha value) of say 2% that is expected from the strategy. This risk-return combination can then be compared against other risk-return combinations that can be expressed in the same expected incremental return–standard error trade-off. The investor can, in turn, evaluate the extent to which added return has a cost in terms of added risk across a whole array of strategies. In effect, the standard error measure of risk fits well into the sort of framework that we illustrate in Figure 20-4 as a means of evaluating the risk-return trade-off associated with differing active/passive strategies.

Furthermore, the standard error provides a more precise gauge for controlling diversifiable risk of a portfolio to ensure that it meets the specified risk characteristics associated with the strategy. Given a targeted standard error associated with a strategy, the manager can observe over time, say month by month or quarter by quarter, the pattern of returns generated by the portfolio to determine whether the returns generated fall within the standard error bounds associated with the strategy. For example, a strategy with a standard error of say .5% that might well characterize the standard error associated with an index fund would be expected to have shown returns over a performance period that were virtually all (95% of the time) within plus and minus 1% of the market return. Return deviations outside this central bound would be indicative of an out-of-control investment process and suggest the need for corrective action.

Table 20-10 shows market risk and diversification parameters that might typically be associated with the three types of strategies illustrated in Figure 20-4. Note that the risk specifications for the index fund are quite restrictive. This is consistent with the objective of delivering a return virtually identical with that attributed to an index such as say the S&P 500. Investors are generally willing to tolerate only minor divergences from this objective; hence the narrow standard error tolerance of plus and minus 50 basis points. Even this minor deviation mainly reflects the necessity to deal with transactions costs and the difficulty of achieving "perfect" diversification in a practical sense.

On the other hand, the risk specifications associated with a totally active strategy are by nature much more flexible. While the target market risk for the totally active manager is 1.00 in this case (it could be higher or lower as the manager style varies), the range of .80 to 1.20 reflects the fact that this manager is expected to engage in market timing and vary the market risk exposure from its target level of 1.00 over time. Correspondingly, the standard error specification of 10% reflects the fact that

TABLE 20-10   ACTIVE/PASSIVE STRATEGIES, RISK-RETURN SPECIFICATIONS

	Index fund	Combination active/passive strategy	Totally active
Return relative to S&P 500, %	0	1	3
Market risk, beta	1.00	1.00	.80–1.20
Standard error tolerance, %	.50	3.50	10.00

the manager is expected to actively concentrate the portfolio in those sectors or industries deemed to be of greatest attraction at any particular time. For such a manager, a consistently low standard error over time would indicate that the manager is "overly diversified" and not making active group and industry rotation decisions consistent with a stated strategy objective. In this sense, high diversification as evidenced by a low standard error would be indicative of a failure to properly execute the strategy.

The combination active/passive strategy, as illustrated by our example of a stock selection strategy, exemplifies the attributes of the two extreme strategy types. As with the index fund strategy, the target beta of 1.00 is consistent with a forsaking of the market timing method of active management. Unlike the index fund strategy, however, the standard error specification of 3 to 4% reflects a tolerance for some variation from the market return in the quest for some added value from active stock selection. Correspondingly, the standard error specification of 3 to 4% is substantially less than a totally active strategy to reflect the desire to avoid the risk of overly heavy portfolio concentration in individual sectors or major industries.

20-5-3 Conventional Diversification Benchmarks

In evaluating the diversification characteristics of a portfolio along conventional lines, investors commonly use industry and sector classification schemes. These classifications have economic appeal but, as noted before, have been documented as meaningful classifications for the co-movement of prices of subgroups of stocks. Use of these classifications can serve as a more intuitive cross check on the statistical measures of diversification: the R^2 and standard error. For investors pursuing highly active group and industry rotation strategies, industry and sector classification will, in fact, be more useful in helping these investors implement strategies.

One generally available method of industry classification is the S&P 500 breakdown of companies into 96 different industries. Investors often use these, as they are generally consistent with the economic characteristics of the underlying companies and tend to be representative of the underlying co-movement of securities with many of the categories. For purposes of simplifying the analysis, some investors will further consolidate these 96 industries into a smaller group of major or master industries. Table 20-11 shows one such consolidation into some 35 industries that would seem to preserve the notion of differing industries and achieve simplification in the process. Other investors will consolidate companies or industries into economic sectors such as, say, consumer durables or transportation as a means of simplification and at the same time with a view to capturing some common underlying characteristic across the companies included. Finally, some investors use the observed price action of stocks to classify them into sectors that are homogeneous with respect to behavior in the market. We noted that this sort of analytical approach identified groupings of growth, cyclical, stable, and energy stocks as having such characteristics.

Using these methods of classification, the investor would do well to evaluate the weighting of the portfolio in these sectors and industries relative to the S&P 500 to determine whether the portfolio structuring was consistent with the goals of the strategy. At one extreme, investors executing an index fund strategy should find that the portfolio weighting in differing sectors and industries should closely approximate if not be

TABLE 20-11   S&P 500: MAJOR INDUSTRY CLASSIFICATIONS
AND WEIGHTINGS
(November 30, 1985)

Industry	Weighting, %
Chemicals	3.2
Metals and mining	1.1
Paper	1.3
Steel	.6
Building—forest products	.6
Building and construction	1.0
Electrical equipment	3.2
Machinery	1.3
Autos and trucks	2.7
Auto-related	1.2
Leisure-related	2.0
Photo and optical	.9
Printing and publishing	2.2
Retail—general	4.9
Beverages	2.2
Drugs	4.8
Foods	3.4
Hospital supply and services	2.1
Retail—food	1.0
Tobacco	1.4
Oil—domestic	4.9
Oil—international	6.4
Banks	2.3
Financial services	2.0
Insurance	3.1
Electronics	2.8
Office equipment—services	.3
Office equipment	8.4
Telecommunications	2.3
Utility—telephone	5.3
Utility gas, pipeline	.7
Utility—electric	4.8
Airlines	.5
Railroads	1.8
Diversified	3.0

identical to the weighting in the S&P 500 to ensure that the portfolio is close to perfectly diversified. On the other hand, investors pursuing active strategies, especially those oriented to group rotation, should find the portfolio weighting in major groupings and industries to be significantly different from that of the S&P 500.

Table 20-12 illustrates this analysis with respect to the weighting in economic sectors for a hypothetical fund. Note that the fund is overweighted in technology and financial sectors but underweighted in energy and consumer staples sectors. This weighting would imply that the fund has a favorable outlook for the technology and financial sectors but a pessimistic outlook for the energy and consumer staples sectors. The

TABLE 20-12   S&P 500: CLASSIFIED BY ECONOMIC SECTOR
(November 30, 1985)

Sector	S&P 500 weighting, %	Fund weighting, %	Divergence
Basic materials	6.2	6.2	
Capital goods/construction	9.2	9.2	
Consumer cyclical	16.1	16.1	
Consumer staples	17.2	10.0	−7.2
Energy	13.4	4.7	−8.7
Financial	7.3	15.0	+8.7
Technology	13.8	21.0	+7.2
Utilities	10.8	10.8	
Transportation and services	3.0	3.0	
Miscellaneous	3.0	3.0	
	100.0	100.0	

weighting would imply that the fund has a neutral outlook for these sectors and is thus taking a passive stance with respect to these groups.

20-6 SUMMARY

This chapter described the major steps needed to develop an asset allocation. In this regard we illustrated ways of developing return and risk inputs that are essential to the process. We next dealt with the components of risk and return that are important in described equity market behavior. We also described ways of characterizing investment strategies in the equity. The final part of the chapter was concerned with portfolio diagnostics. Here we presented techniques of analyzing the portfolio that are based on the Markowitz/Sharpe theory of portfolio analysis as well as more conventional measures.

SUGGESTED READINGS

James L. Farrell, Jr., *Guide to Portfolio Management*, McGraw-Hill, New York, 1983, offers an extensive and readable review of asset-allocation techniques and active/passive strategies along with practical examples of these investment methods.

Roger G. Ibbotson and Rex A. Sinquefield, *Stocks, Bonds, Bills, and Inflation: The Past (1926–1976) and the Future (1977–2000)*, Financial Analysts Research Foundation, Charlottesville, Va., 1979, provides extensive data on historical risk and returns for major asset classes and offers a good illustration of how to implement the historical approach in forecasting the risk-return relationship for these major asset classes.

Jack Treynor and Fischer Black, "How to Use Security Analysis to Improve Portfolio Selection," *Journal of Business* (January 1973), pp. 66–86, is the classic theoretical article on the active/passive approach to investment management.

Benjamin King, "Market and Industry Factors in Stock Price Behavior," *Journal of Business* (January 1966), pp. 139–190, is a classic article showing how factor models can be used to analyze stock price data. It documents the existence of an industry effect on stock price behavior.

James L. Farrell, Jr., ''Homogeneous Stock Groupings—Implications for Portfolio Management,'' *Financial Analysts Journal* (May–June 1975), documents the existence of broader than industry market subgroupings and illustrates how these can be used in an active/passive management mode.

QUESTIONS

1 List the four essential steps to obtaining an asset allocation.
2 Briefly describe the concept of a world market portfolio and indicate the general composition of such a portfolio.
3 Describe how return and risk varied over major asset classes over the long historic period from 1926.
4 Define real return on an asset.
5 What is the difference between realized return and expected return?
6 Give a general description of how one uses the historic approach to making a forecast.
7 How do forecasters accommodate differing inflation levels when making a forecast?
8 How can subdividing historical data be helpful in making a forecast?
9 Briefly describe the components to a scenario method of forecasting.
10 In what major respects does the scenario approach differ from the historical approach to forecasting?
11 Differentiate between an active and a passive investment strategy.
12 Explain the notion of extra-market correlation.
13 What are the major components of equity returns, and what risks correspond to each?
14 What is the measure of security-specific returns, and what risk is associated with it?
15 How does one ensure that the portfolio is hedged (neutralized) against the market timing risk?
16 What is the logical strategy for an investor to pursue if the investor judges she has no skill in evaluating the relative attractiveness of the market, groups, or individual stocks?
17 Briefly explain the kind of risk-return trade-off one would anticipate when moving from passive to more active strategies.
18 What purposes do portfolio diagnostics serve in managing a portfolio?
19 What is the difference between a time-series derived beta and a cross-sectional beta?
20 What are statistical measures of the diversification of a portfolio?
21 Explain how adding or subtracting cash can change the beta of a portfolio.

CHAPTER 21

MUTUAL FUNDS
AND PERFORMANCE
EVALUATION

After reading this chapter, you should:

1 Have an understanding of the basic characteristics of mutual funds
2 Know the proper way of computing portfolio returns for the purpose of evaluating performance
3 Be aware of several different approaches for evaluating performance on a risk-adjusted basis
4 Understand how the primary components of performance, stock selection and market timing, can be evaluated

Evaluating historical portfolio performance is important to the investor in several respects. First, it enables the investor to appraise how well the portfolio manager has done in achieving desired return targets and how well risk has been controlled in the process. Second, it enables the investor to assess how well the manager has achieved these targets in comparison with other managers or, alternatively, with some passive investment strategy, such as an S&P 500 index fund. Finally, it provides a mechanism for identifying weaknesses in the investment process and for improving these deficient areas. In this sense, performance evaluation can be viewed not only as a way of appraising the worth of portfolio management but also as a feedback mechanism for improving the portfolio management process.

This chapter is concerned with evaluating portfolio performance. In this evaluation we cover the method of calculating returns and discuss appropriate measures of risk. We not only discuss methods of comparing relative performance based only on rate of return but also consider measures—known as composite performance measures—that consider risk as well as return. We further discuss ways of analyzing the productivity of two major methods of generating above-average performance: market timing and stock selection.

We'll use investment companies as a vehicle to illustrate the methods of calculating these portfolio performance measures. The data for these funds are publicly available, standardized, and representative of the investment experience of professional portfolio managers. In addition to providing a representative example of the activities of professional portfolio managers, investment companies are interesting to study because of their ready availability as viable investment vehicles for individual as well as institutional investors. Because of this, we begin this chapter by describing the general characteristics of mutual funds.

21-1 INVESTMENT COMPANIES

Investment companies are financial intermediaries. They offer investors a vehicle for investing in such securities as money market instruments, corporate and government bonds, municipal bonds, and common stocks. Our focus in this chapter is on those investment companies that provide investors with a conduit for investing in common stocks. Two major fund categories are available for common stock investors: (1) closed-end funds, and (2) open-end funds. Open-end funds are commonly referred to as *mutual funds*.

21-1-1 Closed-End Funds   A closed-end investment company is so named because its basic capitalization is limited, or "closed." These firms sell shares much as a regular industrial company does, but instead of raising proceeds from the stock sale to purchase land, equipment, and inventory, the closed-end investment company uses the proceeds to purchase securities of other firms. After the initial offering, the closed-end companies' shares are traded on organized exchanges, like those of any other company. Thus, when an investor buys shares in a closed-end investment company, he must generally buy them from another person. Buyers and sellers pay normal commissions on such transactions.

Closed-end investment companies regularly publish the net asset value per share of the fund. This is calculated by first aggregating the market value of the individual securities held in the portfolio and then dividing by the number of shares outstanding. For example, a fund with securities aggregating $100 million in value and with 10 million shares outstanding would have a net asset value per share of $10. Naturally, the net asset value will change daily as the market prices of individual securities in the portfolio fluctuate. Over time, the value may change as the investment company issues more shares or retires shares.

There is no necessary relationship between the price of a closed-end share and its net asset value: the shares may sell for the current net asset value per share, for more— a premium—or for less—a discount. The financial press regularly reports the net asset value of closed-end funds based on end-of-week market values and calculates a premium or discount of current price of the closed-end fund from net asset value. Figure 21-1 illustrates these data as of June 15, 1984, and shows that some funds were selling at a discount from net asset value, and others at a premium to net asset value.

Table 21-1 shows year-by-year discounts and premiums to net asset value for nine closed-end funds and an average of the nine funds over the period 1972–1982. With the exception of three funds and for only a few years out of the period, the tendency was for funds to sell at a discount from net asset value. At the same time, note that there was significant variation over the years in the magnitude of the discount and the size of the premium to net asset value.

The fact that the price of a closed-end fund differs from its net asset value, with the magnitude of the difference varying from time to time, introduces an added source of risk and potential return. By purchasing shares at a discount, an investor may be able to increase her return. Even if the discount remains constant, the effective dividend yield will be greater than that of an otherwise similar no-load, open-end company. If the discount is substantial when the shares are purchased, it may subsequently narrow

PUBLICLY TRADED FUNDS

Friday, April 11, 1986

Following is a weekly listing of unaudited net asset values of publicly traded investment fund shares, reported by the companies as of Friday's close. Also shown is the closing listed market price or a dealer-to-dealer asked price of each fund's shares, with the percentage of difference.

	N.A. Value	Stk Price	% Diff		N.A. Value	Stk Price	% Diff
Diversified Common				CentSec	15.00	13½−	10
Stock Funds				Claremont	48.70	49	+ 0.6
AdmExp	21.46	19⅛−	10.9	CLAS	8.18	6¾	
BakerFen	56.29	48 −	14.7	CLAS Pfd	41.83		
Gem II Inc	14.31	13¾−	3.9	EmMedTch	16.02	14½−	9.5
Gem II Cap	9.42	12⅝+	34.0	Engex	20.62	16½−	19.9
GenAInv	22.17	19⅝−	11.5	EaStrat	b13.55	12½−	7.8
GSOTrust	9.40	10½+	11.7	Italy	11.63	13⅛+	12.9
Lehman	17.01	15⅛−	11.1	Japan	17.78	15 −	15.6
NiagaraSh	18.06	15¾−	12.8	Korea Fd	18.73	26	+38.8
Source	40.05	42⅞+	7.1	ML Cnv Cap	12.10	9 −	25.6
Tri-Contl	31.53	29¼−	7.2	ML Cnv Inc	a9.34	13½+	44.5
Specialized Equity				Mexico	b3.80	2¾−	27.6
and Convertible Funds				Pete&Res	25.24	25¾+	2.0
AmCapCv	32.13	32½+	1.2	PilReg	9.69	9⅞+	1.9
ASA	b51.09	36⅜−	28.8	Z-Seven	22.55	23	+ 2.0
BancrftCv	31.29	30¾−	1.7	a-Ex-dividend.		b-As	of
Castle	29.90	29⅝−	.9	Thursday's close. z-Not available.			
CenCanada	5.11	4⅝−	9.5				

FIGURE 21-1 Closed-end fund net asset value and price quotations. [*Source: Reprinted with permission of The Wall Street Journal, Dow Jones & Company, Inc. (June 18, 1984). All rights reserved.*]

and the return will be even greater. On the other hand, if the discount increases, overall return may be less than that of an otherwise comparable open-end fund. The latter possibility makes closed-end fund shares riskier than those of similar open-end funds.

21-1-2 Open-End Funds The open-end investment company, alternatively referred to as a mutual fund, is characterized by the continual selling and redeeming of its shares. In other words, the mutual fund does not have a fixed capitalization. It sells its shares to the investing public whenever it can at their net asset value per share, and it stands ready to repurchase these shares directly from the investment public for their net asset value per share. In the case of a "no-load" mutual fund, the

TABLE 21-1 YEAR-END DISCOUNTS AND PREMIUMS, CLOSED-END FUNDS, PERCENT

Diversified companies	1982	1981	1980	1979	1978	1977	1976	1975	1974	1973	1972
Adams Express Co.	−4	−15	−18	−21	−22	−12	−21	−23	−25	−14	−14
Baker, Fentress & Co.	−26	−30	−32	−37	−38	−34	−37	−46	−58	−54	−41
General American Investors	+7	+6	−3	−17	−27	−17	−18	−26	−13	−17	−4
Lehman Corp.	+4	−4	−15	−20	−29	−20	−18	−20	−22	−20	−13
Nautilus Fund	−5	−14	−13								
Niagara Share Corp.	−2	−0	+2	−19	−24	−15	−15	−4	+4	−4	−7
Source Capital	−9	−16	−14	−21	−20	−20	−24	−8	−45	−49	−53
Tri-Continental Corp.	−8	−20	−25	−23	−22	−12	−21	−22	−14	−13	−19
U.S. and Foreign Securities	−4	−20	−21	−25	−27	−22	−27	−25	−26	−21	−3
Diversified investment company average	−5	−12	−15	−22	−25	−19	−23	−23	−24	−25	−19

Source: Investment Companies, Wiesenberger's Financial Services, New York, 1983.

investment company sells its shares by mail to the investor. Since no salesperson is involved, there is no sales commission (load). In the case of a "load" fund, the shares are sold by a salesperson whose commission (load) is added to the net asset value. This process is called "front-end loading," thus the name "load fund." The load charge or commission is generally about 8% of the sale price.

Figure 21-2 shows a portion of the quotations for open-end mutual funds provided for each trading day in the financial press. The net asset value, based on closing prices for the fund's securities on the day in question, is shown first. This is followed by the "offer" price—the net asset value plus the load charge applicable to the smallest possible purchase. For no-load funds this column contains the letters "NL." The final column indicates the difference (in dollars) between the day's net asset value per share and that computed at the close of the previous trading day.

Mutual funds offer investors several advantages. First, because of their large size, they offer broad diversification across security types and industries not generally possible for small investors. Also, these institutions are able to obtain lower brokerage commissions than an individual small investor. Furthermore, these funds offer investors liquidity in the form of ready marketability or an ability to redeem shares with the fund itself. Finally, mutual funds provide full-time professional investment management that may result in performance superior to what might be generated by the individual investor.

For providing these services, funds charge a management fee based on the market value of the fund's assets. These fees generally range from less than .25% of the value of net assets to somewhat over 1% of net assets, with .5% the most typical management fee. In addition to the fee paid for investment management services, there are administrative and custodial expenses. Total annual expenses, including the management fee, average somewhat less than 1% of the value of all assets for large investment companies. Many funds require their management company to cover all costs over a specified amount, effectively limiting total expenses.

Information about mutual funds is available in the popular financial press as well as in specialized publications. One of the best sources of investment company information available to the investor is Wiesenberger's *Investment Companies*, issued annually. The publication provides summary information about individual companies that typically includes a history of the fund, statement of objectives, something about its portfolio composition, key statistical data, and the result of a hypothetical $10,000 investment in the fund over a 10-year period. The publication also provides such other information as comparative data on the universe of funds as well as subsets of that universe. More current performance data and other information are available from the Arthur Lipper Mutual Fund service as well as Computer Direction Advisors.

21-1-3 Mutual Fund Objectives   Mutual funds state specific investment objectives in their prospectuses. For example, the main types of objectives are growth, growth-income, balanced, income, and industry-specialized funds. *Growth funds* strive for large capital gains, while *growth-income funds* seek both dividend income and capital gains from common stocks. The *balanced fund* generally holds a portfolio of diversified common stocks, preferred stocks, and bonds with the hope of achieving capital gains

MUTUAL FUNDS

Friday, April 11, 1986

Price ranges for investment companies, as quoted by the National Association of Securities Dealers. NAV stands for net asset value per share; the offering includes net asset value plus maximum sales charge, if any.

Flex Fund	12.78	N.L.	...	Totl Ret	10.74	N.L.	...
44 Wall St	3.92	N.L.−	.12	Val Tr	30.51	N.L.+	.04
44 WS Eqt	5.76	5.82−	.04	**Lehman Group:**			......
Founders Group Funds:				Captl	19.38	N.L.+	.23
Growth	9.74	N.L.	...	Invst	19.87	N.L.−	.28
Income	15.35	N.L.−	.04	Opprt	27.34	N.L.+	.23
Mutual	11.10	N.L.−	.02	Leverage	8.68	N.L.+	.05
Special	32.25	N.L.+	.13	**Lexington Group:**			
FPA Funds:				CpLdr fr	14.98	16.05+	.09
Capital	13.34	14.50+	.06	Gold Fd	3.76	N.L.+	.08
New Inc	9.62	10.13	...	Gnma	8.10	N.L.−	.01
Paramt	13.93	15.22+	.03	Growth	11.28	N.L.−	.02
Perennl	18.81	20.56−	.02	Resrch	18.90	N.L.−	.01
Franklin Group:				**Liberty Family Fds:**			......
AGE Fd	3.81	3.97+	.02	Am Lead	13.56	N.L.−	.02
Cal TxFr	6.99	7.28	...	Tax Free	10.41	N.L.−	.06
Corp Csh	9.38	N.L.	...	US Gvt S	8.82	N.L.+	.01
D N T C	11.47	12.37+	.03	Ltd Term	12.76	13.12+	.01
Equity	6.75	7.28−	.01	Lndner Dv	24.53	N.L.	...
Fed TxF	11.63	12.11−	.04	Lindner Fd	20.69	N.L.+	.07
Gold Fnd	8.06	8.69+	.18	LMH Fund	28.17	N.L.−	.01
Growth	15.15	16.33−	.04	**Loomis Sayles Funds:**			
Income	2.27	2.45+	.01	Cap Dev	24.09	N.L.−	.05
Ins TxFr	11.63	12.11−	.04	Mutual	23.46	N.L.−	.15
MN Ins	11.67	12.16−	.03	**Lord Abbett:**			
N Y Tax	11.53	12.01−	.01	Affilatd	(z)	(z)	...
OHIn TF	11.35	11.82−	.03	Bnd Deb	x10.67	11.66−	.29
Optn Fd	6.28	6.77	...	Devl Gro	8.80	9.62+	.03
Mich TF	11.32	11.79−	.03	Govt S	3.35	3.59−	.01
US GvSc	7.51	7.82	...	TxF Natl	10.74	11.28−	.08
Utilities	7.89	8.51−	.01	TxFr NY	10.88	11.42−	.11
Freed Gold	16.38	17.24−	.01	Value Ap	12.79	13.98+	.06
Freed Reg	12.61	13.41+	.02	**Lutheran Brotherhood:**			
FundTrust:			....	Broth Fd	17.23	18.14−	.02
Aggr f	13.82	N.L.+	.11	Bro Inc	x9.00	9.47−	.07
Grow f	13.26	N.L.+	.09	Bro .MBd	8.17	8.60−	.03
GroInc	13.08	N.L.+	.07	**Mass Financial Services:**			
GT Pacific	21.44	N.L.+	.32	MIT	13.75	14.82−	.05
Gatewy Op	15.02	N.L.+	.06	MFD	14.10	15.20	...
Geico ARP	25.94	N.L.−	.02	MIG	12.84	13.84+	.02
GenAgg G	21.31	N.L.+	.09	MCD	13.41	14.46	...
Genl Elec Invest:				MSF	9.83	10.60+	.01
Elf TxE	11.41	N.L.−	.02	MEG	19.67	21.21+	.13
Elfn Inc	12.13	N.L.+	.01	MFG	10.39	10.91	...
Elfn Tr	29.82	N.L.−	.06	MFI B	12.23	13.19−	.05
S&S LT	12.56	N.L.	...	MGH	9.98	10.48	...
S&S Pro	40.79	N.L.+	.10	MST Md	10.48	11.00	...
Genl Secur	13.89	N.L.+	.01	MFB	15.00	16.17−	.03
Genl TxEx	14.40	N.L.−	.03	MFH	7.22	7.78−	.01
Gintel Group:			....	MMB	10.60	11.13−	.01
Cap App	11.32	N.L.−	.02	MMH	10.31	10.82−	.01
Erisa	41.75	N.L.−	.19	MST NC	11.17	11.73	...
Gintl Fd	91.96	N.L.−	.32	MST VA	10.73	11.27−	.01
Grad Emr	13.31	N.L.−	.03	MST Ma	10.63	11.16	...
Grad EstG	15.58	N.L.−	.08	MTR	10.99	11.85−	.03
GIT Incm	10.00	N.L.−	.01	Mathers	18.79	N.L.−	.06
GIT TxFr	11.71	N.L.−	.02	Meeschr C	28.50	N.L.+	.03
Grth IndSh	10.92	N.L.+	.02	**Merrill Lynch:**			
GrF Wash	11.83	12.45	...	Basc Val	17.54	18.76	...
Guardian Funds:				Cal TxE	11.42	N.L.−	.01
Bond	12.20	N.L.−	.02	Captl Fd	25.87	27.67−	.05
Park Av	22.80	24.92	...	Corp Dv	10.85	11.07	...
Stock	17.36	N.L.	...	EquiBd 1	14.18	14.77−	.03
Hamltn Fd	7.88	8.61	...	Fed Sec	10.27	10.95−	.01
Hartwll Gt	11.53	N.L.+	.05	FdF Tm	15.31	N.L.	...
Hartwll Lv	16.85	N.L.+	.06	Hi Incm	8.60	8.96	...
Hawaii TF	10.88	11.33−	.06	Hi QualP	11.90	12.40+	.01
Heartlnd	15.40	16.13	...	Intl Hldg	14.31	15.64+	.08
Hrtg Cap	10.97	11.31+	.02	Inter TP	11.74	11.98−	.01
HorcM Gr	25.59	N.L.+	.27	Muni Ins	7.98	8.31−	.01
Hutton EF Group:				Mun HY	10.48	10.92−	.01
Bond r	13.26	N.L.−	.04	NY Muni	10.96	N.L.−	.01
EmrgG r	15.27	N.L.+	.06	Ltd Mat	9.87	9.97	...
Growth r	15.64	N.L.−	.02	Nat Res	10.58	N.L.+	.04
Optn Inc	9.16	N.L.	...	Pacific	24.08	26.61+	.41
GOV Sec	10.69	N.L.−	.02	Phoenx	13.62	14.57−	.04
Basc Val	12.53	N.L.−	.01	Retire	11.21	N.L.−	.03
Cal Muni	10.92	11.38−	.01	Ret Inc	10.02	N.L.−	.01
Nat Mun	11.67	12.16−	.01	Sci Tech	12.17	13.30+	.12
NY Muni	11.15	11.61−	.01	Sp'l Valu	16.29	17.42+	.06
Prec Mtl	10.24	N.L.+	.19	Mid Amer	7.58	8.28−	.02

FIGURE 21-2   Mutual fund net asset value quotations. [*Source: Reprinted with permission of* The Wall Street Journal, *Dow Jones & Company, Inc. (June 18, 1984). All rights reserved.*]

TABLE 21-2 CLASSIFICATION OF MUTUAL FUNDS BY INVESTMENT OBJECTIVE
(As of December 31, 1982)

Type of fund	Number of funds	Combined assets, millions	% of total assets
Common stock:			
Maximum capital gain	92	11,068	15.6
Growth	157	22,794	32.1
Growth and income	108	20,382	28.7
Specialized	22	880	1.2
Balanced	24	3,070	4.3
Income	126	12,914	18.1
Total	529	71,108	100.0

Source: *Investment Companies*, Wiesenberger's Financial Services, New York, 1983.

and dividend and interest income, while at the same time conserving the principal. *Income funds* concentrate heavily on high-interest and high-dividend yielding securities. The *industry-specialized mutual fund* obviously specializes in investing in selected industries such as health care, airlines, or natural resources or energy stocks.

Table 21-2 provides an indication of the number of mutual funds of various types and the amount of assets under their control. The fund categories are also arrayed generally with respect to their return prospects and degree of price stability. For example, we would expect all common stock funds to provide higher returns over the long term but experience greater price variability than the balanced or income fund categories. Within the stock category, we would expect growth funds to offer higher returns but have greater price variability exposure than growth and income funds. Specialized common stock funds would not be as well diversified but would be appealing to investors who are optimistic about the prospects for these industries.

These differing fund objective categories also appear to be consistent with differing risk levels whether measured in terms of total risk (standard deviation) or in terms of systematic risk (beta). The data in Table 21-3 illustrate this for a universe of 38 large representative mutual funds classified into three broad categories: 12 growth funds, 15 income-growth funds; and 11 balanced funds.[1] The table shows beta as a measure of risk as well as average quarterly returns earned over two time periods; 1957–1968 and 1969–1974. The earlier time period represents a period of generally rising stock prices—a long-term bull market—while the latter period represents a period of generally declining stock prices—a long-term bear market. Using these two time periods allows us to evaluate the risk-return relationship over two widely differing stock market episodes as well as to appraise the consistency of the risk ranking measures over time.

Note that the average beta within each of the three fund categories was in line with what might be expected: growth funds showed the highest risk, balanced funds the lowest risk, and income-growth funds intermediate risk. Furthermore, the risk measures

[1]John McDonald, ''Objectives and Performance of Mutual Funds, 1960–1969,'' *Journal of Financial and Quantitative Analysis* (June 1974) generated results similar to these using a sample of 123 mutual funds.

TABLE 21-3   RISK-RETURN RELATIONSHIP FOR MUTUAL FUNDS

Fund objective	1957–1968 bull market			1969–1974 bear market		
	Range of betas	Average beta	Average quarterly return	Range of betas	Average beta	Average quarterly return
Growth (12)	.99–1.25	1.13	2.36	.97–1.25	1.12	(1.65)
Income-growth (15)	.80–1.07	.92	1.81	.80–1.10	.95	(.93)
Balanced (11)	.58–.91	.76	1.27	.70–.92	.78	(.56)
S&P 500		1.00	1.74			(.85)

Source: James L. Farrell, Jr., and Fischer Black, "Mutual Fund Performance," Unpublished studies, 1969, 1975.

for the categories displayed stability between time periods: note that the average betas of the three categories were relatively similar between time periods. Finally, the individual fund betas were generally close to the average for the category, as indicated by the range of betas within each category. The calculated beta values for the three fund groupings are in line with the riskiness that is implied by the investment objective of the fund category.

In addition, the data in Table 21-3 show the risk-return relationship for two time periods: 1957–1968 and 1969–1974. Note that in the earlier period of generally rising stock prices high-risk growth funds provided the highest average return while low-risk balanced funds offered the lowest. Conversely, during the latter period of generally declining stock prices, high-risk growth funds showed the greatest losses while low-risk balanced funds suffered the least losses. As expected, high risk was rewarded the most during the bull market but penalized the most during the bear market, while low risk was rewarded the least in the bull market but penalized the least during the bear market.

These data, in turn, have implications for evaluating the performance of funds with disparate investment objectives. For example, growth funds will be at a disadvantage during a bear market such as occurred during 1969–1974, but will be favored during a bull market period such as occurred between 1957 and 1968. Evaluating funds with such differing investment objectives on the basis of rate of return only comparisons can lead to an overestimate or underestimate of the real value of the performance of a fund. The return earned over a period of time by a fund will be heavily dependent on the risk profile of the fund and the market environment encountered over that period.

Thus, there is need to evaluate the return that the fund earned in the context of the risk that was undertaken. One approach to this evaluation is to first group funds in equivalent risk categories and then compare returns. When evaluating funds across differing risk levels, there is a need to specifically adjust return for the riskiness of the fund. Composite risk measures provide such a mechanism, and we'll be describing these and other aspects of the performance evaluation problem in the following sections.

21-2 CALCULATING FUND RETURNS

The first step in evaluating the performance of investment managers is to calculate the rate of return earned over the relevant comparison period. As before, return is defined to include changes in the value of the fund over the performance period plus any income earned over that period. Returns for investment portfolios, however, can be distorted by cash flows—in or out—of the fund during the interim between valuation. In particular, contributions to the fund during a period of rising markets will inflate the value of the fund and hence the calculated rate of return, while withdrawals will reduce the value and calculated return. Conversely, contributions to the fund during a period of falling prices will reduce the return, while withdrawals would inflate the return comparison. Thus, the method of calculating returns is the same as presented throughout this text, *except that adjustments must be made for contributions and withdrawals of cash.*

Panel A at the top of Table 21-4 illustrates this phenomenon for a hypothetical fund that experiences a cash flow at the middle of the year. Note that the fund has a value of $800,000 at the beginning of the year and that this increases to $880,000 by midyear. With a cash inflow of $220,000 at midyear and further appreciation to the end of the year, the fund value at the end of the year is $1,320,000. The percentage change in fund value over the year, including the cash flow, would be 65%, as compared with a change in value of 32% if there had been no interim cash flow.

Since the manager usually has no control over the timing of these flows, it is necessary to adjust for interim cash flows to properly evaluate the skill of the manager. One technique is to calculate a return at the time of each cash flow and then link (compound) these returns to derive what is known as a *time-weighted return* over the period of interest. Panel B of Table 21-4 illustrates that we adjust the return by separately calculating a return of 10% (880,000/800,000) for the first 6 months of the year, and a 20% return for the second 6 months after the receipt of the cash flow.

TABLE 21-4   CALCULATING THE RATE OF RETURN

	Period	
	1st half	**2nd half**
Panel A:		
Value before cash flow	$800,000	$ 880,000
Cash flow	0	$ 220,000
Amount invested	$800,000	$1,100,000
Ending value	$880,000	$1,320,000
Change in value, %	10	50
Change in value over full year, %		65
Panel B:		
Earned return per period, %	10	20
Time weighted return over periods 1 and 2, %		32
Panel C:		
Units outstanding	800 units	1,000 units
Beginning unit value	$ 1,000	$ 1,100
Ending unit value	$ 1,100	$ 1,320
Change in unit value	10 %	20 %
Change in value over full year		32 %

Linking, or compounding, these two 6-month returns provides a time-weighted return of 32% that is the appropriate measure of return for the manager. That is,

$$1.10 \times 1.20 = 1.32 - 1 = 32\%$$

A second way to adjust for cash inflows and outflows to the fund is to use the unit-value method. When cash inflows occur, new units are issued, and when cash outflows occur, units are retired. As a result, the number of units change when cash flows occur but the value per unit remains constant. Again using our hypothetical fund, and presuming 800 units outstanding at the begining of the year, the value per unit or net asset value would be $1000 at the beginning of the year and $1100 at June 30. With cash flow of $220,000 at July 1, 200 additional units would be issued so that the value per unit would remain $1100 at the beginning of the second half of the year. At the end of the year, the total value of the fund would be $1,320,000, but the net asset value (NAV) would be $1320 since 1000 units are outstanding rather than the 800 at the beginning. The NAV of $1320 at the end of the year compared with the NAV of $1000 at the beginning of the year obviously results in a return of 32% for the year.

Mutual funds use the unit-value method so that cash flows result in changes in units but not net asset value. As a result, evaluation of mutual fund performance can directly use beginning- and ending-period net asset values when calculating returns. The one-period rate of return r_p for a mutual fund is then simply defined as the change in net asset value NAV plus its cash disbursements D and capital gains disbursements C and is calculated as follows:

$$r_p = \frac{(\text{NAV}_t - \text{NAV}_{t-1}) + D_t + C_t}{\text{NAV}_{t-1}} \qquad (21\text{-}1)$$

This is the same as the holding-period formula that we've illustrated in prior chapters, the only difference being that explicit provision needs to be made for capital gains distributions.

Using this method, we calculated returns for a universe of mutual funds for the 3-year 1978–1980 period that are shown in Table 21-5. The funds shown in the table are the 17 largest all-stock mutual funds with a history of performance over the full 1978–1980 period. These funds should be representative of the investment performance of large, stock-oriented mutual funds. Also shown is the return by the S&P 500 over the same period to provide a benchmark of performance.

Note that the funds are ranked from highest to lowest with respect to return earned over the period. Twelve funds had a higher return than the S&P 500, while five funds had a lower return over the period. As noted before, however, a straight rate of return comparison in evaluating performance is incomplete. The differential return earned could have been due entirely to the differential risk exposure of the funds. The following sections describe some techniques for adjusting for risk and determining whether return earned is greater or less than expected for the fund given the risk incurred.

TABLE 21-5   MUTUAL FUND RATE OF RETURN (1978–1980)

Fund	Rate of return
Technology Fund	22.9
Massachusetts Investor Growth Stock	15.4
Putnam Investors Fund	14.8
Templeton Growth Fund	13.0
National Investors Corp.	12.9
Putnam Growth Fund	12.5
Pioneer	12.3
Dreyfus	11.6
Chemical	11.3
Fidelity Trend	9.7
Massachusetts Investors Trust	9.0
Fidelity Fund	7.8
S&P 500	7.8
Affiliated	7.7
Investment Company of America	7.4
Windsor Fund	6.9
Price Rowe Growth Fund	6.4
Investors Stock	4.5

Before continuing, you should:

1 Understand the term "net asset value" and how it is calculated
2 Know the difference between closed-end and open-end investment companies and which of these are typically referred to as mutual funds
3 Know the difference between no-load and load mutual funds
4 Be aware that different mutual funds have different objectives and consequently different risk characteristics
5 Understand how to compute time-weighted returns for funds

21-3 RISK-ADJUSTED PERFORMANCE

The comparisons in Table 21-5 provide a useful perspective on performance but are based only on rate of return. Since the differential return earned by a manager may be due to a difference in the exposure to risk from that of the index or typical manager, there would be merit in attempting to adjust the return for any differences in risk exposure. For this purpose, there are essentially three major methods of assessing risk-adjusted performance: (1) return per unit of risk, (2) differential return, and (3) components of performance. These methods are interrelated and evolve out of the sort of risk-return theory described in Chapters 3, 4, and 17 of this book.

21-3-1 Return per Unit of Risk   The first of the risk-adjusted performance measures is the type that assesses the performance of a fund in terms of return per unit of risk. The technique here is to relate the absolute level of return achieved to the level of risk incurred to develop a relative risk-adjusted measure for ranking fund performance. According to this method, funds that provide the highest return per unit of risk would be judged as having provided the best performance, while those providing the lowest return per unit of risk would be judged as the poorest performers.

Figure 21-3 is a risk-return diagram illustrating the reason that return per unit of risk is an appropriate standard for judging performance. The vertical axis represents return. The horizontal axis represents risk, which for our current purpose we interpret in a generalized sense to represent either standard deviation or beta. The diagram shows the plots for three funds, designated A, M, and Z, where the fund M represents the market fund (say the S&P 500) and funds A and Z are hypothetical funds.

Note that fund Z provides the highest absolute return, while fund A provides the lowest return and fund M an intermediate return. Fund A, however, ranks highest in terms of return per unit of risk, fund Z the lowest, and fund M at an intermediate level. As shown in Chapter 17[2] assuming that investors can borrow or lend freely at the risk-free rate r_f, it is possible to attain any point along the line from r_f through the plot of fund A. Investors should prefer this line (r_f) to the other two formed by borrowing and lending and investing in funds M and Z. This is because the line r_fA provides a higher return at all levels of risk than the line r_fM, which in turn dominates the line r_fZ.

There are two alternative, yet similar methods of measuring return per unit of risk: (1) the reward to variability ratio developed by William Sharpe, referred to as the Sharpe ratio;[3] and (2) the reward to volatility ratio developed by Jack Treynor, referred to as the Treynor ratio.[4] The Sharpe ratio is simply the ratio of the reward, defined

---

[2]This process is directly analogous to the borrowing and lending mechanism used to construct the capital market line and described in Chapter 17. In this case, the investor constructs his own market line by borrowing and lending in combination with the most desirable portfolio and then positions himself at the desired risk level to attain the highest return per unit of risk.

[3]William F. Sharpe, ''Mutual Fund Performance,'' *Journal of Business* (January 1966), pp. 119–138.

[4]Jack L. Treynor, ''How to Rate Management of Investment Funds,'' *Harvard Business Review* (January–February 1965), pp. 63–70.

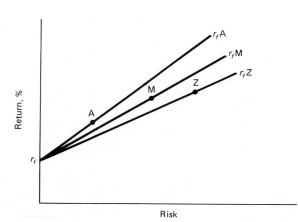

FIGURE 21-3 Risk-return relationship: market portfolio and two hypothetical portfolios.

as the realized portfolio return r_p in excess of the risk-free rate, to the variability of return as measured by the standard deviation of return (σ_p). The Treynor ratio is the ratio of the reward, also defined as the realized portfolio return r_p in excess of the risk-free rate r_f, to the volatility of return as measured instead by the portfolio beta (β_p).

$$\text{Sharpe ratio (SR)} = \frac{r_p - r_f}{\sigma_p} \qquad (21\text{-}2)$$

$$\text{Treynor ratio (TR)} = \frac{r_p - r_f}{\beta_p} \qquad (21\text{-}3)$$

The two performance ratios thus differ only in that one considers total risk as measured by standard deviation, while the other considers only market risk as measured by beta. Recall from the discussion in Chapter 3 that the standard deviation as a measure of total risk is appropriate when evaluating the risk-return relationship for well-diversified portfolios. On the other hand, when evaluating less than fully diversified portfolios or individual stocks, the relevant measure of risk is the beta coefficient, as discussed in previous chapters.

The appropriate return per unit of risk measure to use will therefore depend on one's view as to the relevant risk measure. For those investors where the portfolio being evaluated comprises the total or predominant representation in the particular asset class, the total variability of return as measured by standard deviation should be the relevant risk measure. On the other hand, for some investors the portfolio being evaluated is only one component of the investor's representation in the asset class. An example of this is where major pension plan sponsors use several different managers within an asset class. For those investors employing a multimanager strategy, the beta coefficient is the appropriate measure of risk.

Table 21-6 illustrates the calculation of the two return per unit of risk measures using the two hypothetical funds—A and Z—along with the market fund as a benchmark for comparison. Note that the market fund provided a .333 return per unit of standard deviation and exceeded the Sharpe ratio of .250 return provided for Z, but was below the Sharpe ratio of .400 provided for fund A. According to the reward to volatility ratio, the market fund provided a return per unit of beta of 7, which again exceeded the Treynor ratio of 6 for fund Z but was below the Treynor ratio of 9

TABLE 21-6   CALCULATION OF RISK PER UNIT OF RETURN RATIOS MARKET FUND AND TWO HYPOTHETICAL FUNDS

Fund	Return r_p, %	Risk-free rate r_f, %	Excess return $r_p - r_f$, %	Standard deviation S_p, %	Sharpe ratio $r_p - r_f/S_p$	Beta (β_p)	Treynor ratio $r_p - r_f/\beta_p$
A	8	2	6	15	.400	.67	9
M	9	2	7	21	.333	1.00	7
Z	10	2	8	32	.250	1.33	6

derived for fund A. Using either measure, the ranking of the funds was identical: fund A the best, fund Z the worst, and the market fund an intermediate performer.

As a matter of fact, the ranking according to both measures—reward to variability and reward to volatility—*will be identical when the funds under consideration are perfectly diversified*, or for all practical purposes, when the funds are highly diversified. The rankings of the two measures may, however, diverge as the funds being appraised are less highly diversified.[5] For example, a poorly diversified fund that ranks highly on the reward to volatility ratio compared with another fund that is highly diversified will rank less favorably and may, in fact, rank lower on the basis of the reward to variability ratio. This is because the less diversified fund will show relatively greater risk when using the standard deviation than the better diversified fund. As noted before, *the appropriate measure of risk-adjusted performance depends on whether the investor considers the fund as its total representation in the asset class or as only one of many funds.*

21-3-2 Differential Return (Alpha)   A second category of risk-adjusted performance measures is the type referred to as differential return measures and is directly related to the discussion in Section 4-4 concerning the calculation of ex post security market lines. (The reader may wish to review that section before proceeding.) The underlying objective of this technique is to calculate the return that should be expected for the fund given the realized risk of the fund and compare that with the return actually realized over the period. In making this comparison, it is assumed that the investor has a passive or naive alternative of merely buying the market portfolio and adjusting for the appropriate level of risk by borrowing or lending at the risk-free rate. Given this assumption, the most commonly used method of determining the return that should have been earned by the fund at a given level of risk is by way of the ex post alpha formulation:

$$N(\bar{r}_p) = r_f + \beta_p(r_m - r_f)$$
$$a_p = \bar{r}_p - N(\bar{r}_p)$$

Note that this formula is the same in form as the formula for the security market line (SML) that was described in Chapter 4. The difference is that the variables are expressed in terms of realized returns and risk rather than ex ante variables as would be appropriate for the SML. The equation is graphically represented as the line $r_f M$ in Figure 21-4. (Note the similarity to Figure 4-4.) Also shown are the two hypothetical funds—A and Z—from the preceding section that we can use to illustrate use of the equation for performance evaluation.

To evaluate the performance of fund A, we would insert the appropriate variables from Table 21-6 into the formula:

$$N(\bar{r}_p) = 2\% + \beta_p(9\% - 2\%) \qquad = 6.7\%$$
$$a_p = \bar{r}_p - N(\bar{r}_p) = 8.0\% - 6.7\% = 1.3\%$$

---

[5]Note that the hypothetical funds, though not perfectly diversified, are sufficiently highly diversified, so that the relative ranking does not change as the measurement standard differs.

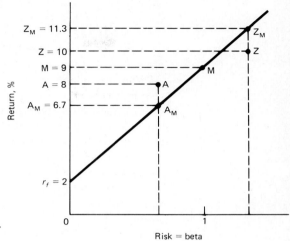

FIGURE 21-4 Differential returns for funds A and Z.

Given these data, fund A would have been expected to have earned 6.7% over the period. The fund actually earned 8.0%, as indicated in Table 21-6, and thus provided a differential return or risk-adjusted return of 1.3%. This difference is represented graphically as the distance $A - A_M$ in Figure 21-5.

Similarly, we can evaluate the performance of fund Z by also inserting the appropriate variables from Table 21-6 into the formula:

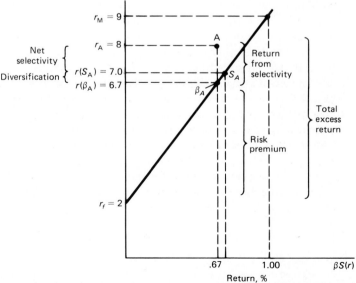

FIGURE 21-5 Decomposition of performance. [*Source: Eugene F. Fama, "Components of Investment Performance," Journal of Finance (June 1972), pp. 551–567.*]

$$r_p = 2\% + 1.33 (9\% - 2\%)$$
$$r_p = 11.3\%$$

Given these data, fund Z would have been expected to have earned 11.3% over the period. The fund actually earned 10%, as indicated in Table 21-6, and thus provided a differential return or risk-adjusted return of -1.3%. This difference is represented graphically as the distance $Z - Z_M$ in Figure 21-4.

This risk-adjusted return measure was developed by Michael Jensen and is sometimes referred to as the Jensen measure.[6] In addition to providing the method for calculating the differential return, Jensen also provided a way of determining whether the differential return could have occurred by chance or whether it is significantly different from zero in a statistical sense. This is possible because, in practice, the Jensen measure is ordinarily derived by running a regression of monthly or quarterly returns of the fund being evaluated against the return of a market index over the relevant performance period. The regression equation ordinarily takes the following form:

$$r_p - r_f = \alpha_p + \beta_p (r_m - r_f) + e$$

Note that the regression equation is in the same form as the previous equation except that we've added an intercept term (alpha) and an error term (e). The error term allows us to assess how well the regression equation fits the data, with a low error indicating a well-defined relationship and a high error indicating a poorly defined relationship. The intercept term measures the extent to which the fund under evaluation provided above- or below-average performance, with a negative value indicating below-average performance, and a positive value above-average performance.

In turn, the alpha value can be tested to see if it is significantly different from zero in a statistical sense using the t statistic for alpha. When the alpha value is high and the error in the regression is low, the t statistic will be high, while a low alpha value and high regression error results in a low t statistic. A t statistic in excess of 2 is strongly indicative that the performance—either positive or negative—is highly significant in a statistical sense; i.e., there is a small probability that the performance results came about as a result of chance. In terms of the two hypothetical funds, the t statistic of $+2.5$ for fund A indicated that the performance was above-average and significantly so in a statistical sense, while the t statistic of -1.0 for fund Z indicated that its below-average performance could have occurred by chance.

21-3-3 Comparison of Performance Measures Table 21-7 illustrates the calculation of the three risk-adjusted return measures for the 3-year period 1978 to 1980 for a sample of 17 mutual funds as well as the S&P 500 that provides a benchmark for comparison. The mutual funds include all those with assets over $50 million, with eight classified as having an investment objective of growth G and the other nine

---

[6]Michael C. Jensen, "The Performance of Mutual Funds in the Period 1945–1964," *Journal of Finance* (May 1968), pp. 389–416.

TABLE 21-7   COMPARISON OF RISK-ADJUSTED PERFORMANCE MEASURES (1978–1980)

	Excess return	Standard deviation	Beta	R^2	Sharpe ratio		Treynor ratio		Differential return (Alpha)	
1. Affiliated (IG)	7.7	16.9	1.02	95	.46	(12)	7.55	(12)	−0.2	(12)
2. Chemical (G)	11.3	16.6	.99	93	.68	(7)	11.41	(7)	3.4	(7)
3. Dreyfus (IG)	11.6	18.1	1.07	92	.64	(8)	10.84	(8)	2.6	(14)
4. Fidelity Fund (IG)	7.8	17.5	1.05	94	.45	(13)	7.43	(13)	−0.4	(14)
5. Fidelity Trend (G)	9.7	22.5	1.31	89	.43	(14)	7.40	(14)	−1.0	(16)
6. Invest. Co. of America (IG)	7.4	18.3	1.06	89	.40	(16)	6.98	(16)	−0.8	(15)
7. Investors Stock (IG)	4.5	16.1	.94	89	.28	(18)	7.79	(18)	−2.4	(18)
8. Mass. Inv. Growth Stk (G)	15.4	18.2	1.09	94	.85	(3)	14.13	(3)	5.7	(3)
9. Mass. Inv. Trust (IG)	9.0	17.9	1.09	97	.50	(10)	8.26	(10)	0.4	(10)
10. Natl. Inv. Corp. (G)	12.9	20.4	1.22	94	.64	(9)	10.57	(9)	2.4	(9)
11. Pioneer (IG)	12.3	17.6	1.04	92	.70	(6)	11.83	(6)	3.6	(6)
12. Price (Rowe) Growth Stk (G)	6.4	17.9	1.04	93	.36	(17)	6.15	(17)	−1.5	(17)
13. Putnam Growth Fund (G)	12.5	14.6	.89	96	.86	(4)	14.04	(4)	5.2	(4)
14. Putnam Investors Fund (IG)	14.8	17.6	1.04	92	.84	(2)	14.23	(2)	5.5	(2)
15. Technology Fund (G)	22.9	21.6	1.27	91	1.06	(1)	18.03	(1)	10.5	(1)
16. Templeton Growth Fund (G)	13.0	18.2	1.02	82	.73	(5)	12.94	(5)	4.4	(5)
17. Windsor Fund (IG)	6.9	16.9	.94	80	.41	(15)	7.34	(15)	−0.2	(13)
Averages for all funds	10.9	18.1	1.06	92	.61		10.41		2.2	
S&P 500	7.8	16.1	1.00	100	.48	(11)	7.80	(11)	0.0	(11)

Source: Computer Directions Advisor, Silver Spring, Md.

classified as having an investment objective of growth with income $G - I$. The data are thus generally representative of the investment behavior of large all-stock mutual funds over this performance period.

Note that the table shows excess returns earned by the fund along with the standard deviation and beta of the fund over the 3-year period. The table also shows the R^2 of the fund as a measure of the degree of diversification of the fund. (The higher the R^2, the more the fund is correlated with the market index and the less unsystematic risk in the fund, the better diversified the fund.) The last three columns show the reward to variability (Sharpe) ratio of the fund, the reward to volatility (Treynor) ratio of the fund, and the differential return (alpha) of the fund. The numbers in parentheses show the ranking of the individual funds according to each of the three risk-adjusted return measures.

Note that the realized excess return of the funds ranged betwen 6.4% and 22.9% with an average of 10.9% that was above that of the S&P 500 for the period. The betas of the funds ranged between .89 and 1.27 with an average of 1.06 or slightly greater than that of the market as represented by the S&P 500. Note that the R^2 of the funds averaged around .92, indicating that while the funds are less than *perfectly* diversified, nevertheless they are highly correlated with the market. As a result, the riskiness of the funds is relatively larger when measured by the standard deviation than when measured by the beta coefficient. Over this period, the average standard deviation of the funds was 18.1%, 1.12 times the 16.1% standard deviation of the market.

Note that the performance of the individual funds is consistent for alternative measures, as can be seen by the fact that the performance rankings of the funds are fairly similar with respect to all three measures. This is not surprising given the fact that we're evaluating large, relatively well-diversified funds; i.e., the riskiness of the funds differs little whether evaluated on the basis of standard deviation or of market risk. In comparison with the overall market, the funds did better than the market over the period. Using the reward to variability ratio, 10 of the 17 funds had a better ratio than the market, while the reward to volatility ratio showed 10 of 17 funds showing better risk-adjusted performance. On the basis of differential return, 10 funds showed a positive return with four funds having t values in exeess of two times, thereby indicating performance that was statistically significant according to this measure.[7]

Before continuing, you should:

1 Understand why it is necessary to consider risk as well as return when evaluating performance

2 Know the three methods of making risk adjusted performance comparisons

3 Understand how the goals of investors govern the appropriate use of either the Treynor or Sharpe performance measure

4 Know how the differential return measure (alpha) relates to the concept of a security market line

21-4 COMPONENTS OF INVESTMENT PERFORMANCE

The risk-adjusted performance measures previously discussed are primarily oriented to an analysis of the overall performance of a fund. For some purposes, it is useful to develop a more refined breakdown and assess the sources or components of performance. Eugene Fama has provided an analytical framework that elaborates on the three previously discussed risk-adjusted return methods to allow a more detailed breakdown of the performance of a fund.[8] We'll conclude this section on risk-adjusted performance analysis by discussing his approach.

Figure 21-5 is a risk-return diagram from the Fama study illustrating that framework of performance analysis. The vertical axis, as is usual, refers to return, while the horizontal axis shows risk measured in terms of beta. The diagonal line plotted on the diagram is the equation of the security market line (SML), using the same data from Table 21-6, i.e., market return r_m of 9% and a risk-free rate r_f of 2%. It again provides the benchmark for assessing whether the realized return is more or less than commensurate with the risk incurred.

For purposes of illustration, the data on the realized return ($r_A = 8\%$) and market risk ($\beta_A = .67$) of the hypothetical fund A, also shown in Table 21-6, are plotted on

---

[7]Mutual funds as a group obviously did quite well over this period; however, the period of evaluation is so short that it would not be appropriate to draw firm conclusions about the relative superiority or inferiority of the funds.

[8]Eugene Fama, "Components of Investment Performance," *Journal of Finance* (June 1972), pp. 551–567.

the diagram and designated as point A. The diagram shows that at the market risk level β_A of the fund it would have been expected to have earned the return $r(\beta_A)$ = 6.7%. This expected return is composed of a risk-free component of 2% shown as the distance from the baseline to r_f and a risk premium of 4.7% (.67 × 7%) shown as the distance r_f to $R(\beta_A)$. The fund actually earned a return of 1.3% greater than normal and is shown as the distance r_A to $r(\beta_A)$. We can designate this incremental return as the return to selectivity.

21-4-1 Stock Selection   Using the framework shown below, we can examine the overall performance of the fund in terms of superior or inferior stock selection and the normal return associated with a given level of risk:

$$
\begin{array}{rcll}
\text{Total excess return} &=& \text{selectivity} & + \text{ risk} \\
r_A - r_f &=& r_A - r(\beta_A) & + r(\beta_A) - r_f \\
8\% - 2\% &=& (8\% - 6.7\%) & + (6.7\% - 2\%) \\
6\% &=& 1.3\% & + 4.7\%
\end{array}
$$

In striving to achieve above-average returns, managers will generally have to forsake some diversification that will have its cost in terms of additional portfolio risk. We can use this framework to determine the added return that should be expected to compensate for this additional diversification risk. We do this by first using the capital market line equation (CML) to determine the return commensurate with the incurred risk as measured by the standard deviation of return. (The case is discussed in Chapter 17.) Again using data from Table 21-6 the standard deviation of the market σ_m is 21%, the standard deviation of fund A (σ_A) is 15%, and risk-free rate and market return are the same as before. We can determine the normal return for fund A, $r(\sigma_a)$ using total risk as follows:

$$
\begin{aligned}
r(\sigma_a) &= r_f \ \ + (r_m - r_f)\ \sigma_a/\sigma_m \\
&= 2\% + (9\% - 2\%)\ 15\%/21\% \\
&= 7\%
\end{aligned}
$$

The difference between this return of 7% and that expected when only considering market risk RB_A of 6.7% is the added return for diversification, $RS_A - RB_A$ or in this case 7% − 6.7% = .3%. In terms of the diagram, it is the distance $r(\beta_A)$ to $r(\sigma_A)$. The net selectivity of the fund then becomes the overall selectivity less whatever penalty or added return is needed to compensate for the diversification risk. The diagram shows that the net selectivity of the fund is the distance $r_A - r(\sigma_A)$. In terms of formulation, the net selectivity can be shown as follows:

$$
\begin{aligned}
\text{Net selectivity} &= [r_A - r(\beta_A)] - [r(\sigma_A) - r(\beta_A)] \\
&= (8\% - 6.7\%) - (7\% - 6.7\%) \\
&= 1.3\% - .3\% \\
&= 1.0\%
\end{aligned}
$$

Because the diversification measure is always nonnegative, net selectivity will always be equal to or less than selectivity.[9] The two will be equal only when the portfolio is completely diversified, as would be indicated by an R^2 with the market of 1.00. By comparing the R^2's of funds one can obtain a quick indication of the degree of diversification risk incurred by a fund. Funds with high R^2's, say, .95 and above, have relatively little diversification risk, while funds with relatively low R^2's, say, .90 and below, have relatively large diversification risk.

To conclude this section, we can use the Fama components of performance framework to evaluate the mutual funds shown in Table 21-8. These are the same funds that we used in previous comparisons of risk-adjusted performance. Note that the table breaks down each of the funds' overall performance into that due to selectivity and the component due to risk. It further shows the expected return due to diversification and from that derives the net selectivity of the fund.

Note that all the funds, as would be expected, are less than perfectly diversified— R^2's less than 1.00—and as a result require added return to compensate for diversification risk. The required return ranges from .2% to .9%, with an average of .4% for the sample of funds. After adjusting for diversification risk, the funds on average showed a net return to selectivity of 1.8% with a high of 9.9% and a low of −2.9%.

[9]The Fama framework of analysis allows further and more elaborate comparisons. For our purposes, the one dealing with stock selectivity is most pertinent.

TABLE 21-8 COMPONENTS OF PERFORMANCE—LARGE ALL-STOCK MUTUAL FUNDS (1978–1980)

	Total excess return	Risk premium	Return from selectivity	Diversification	Net selectivity
1. Affiliated (IG)	7.7	7.9	−.2	.2	−.4
2. Chemical (G)	11.3	7.9	3.4	.2	3.2
3. Dreyfus (IG)	11.6	9.0	2.6	.5	1.9
4. Fidelity Fund (IG)	7.8	8.2	−.4	.3	−.7
5. Fidelity Trend (G)	9.7	8.7	1.0	.7	.3
6. Invest. Co. of America (IG)	7.4	8.2	−.8	.6	−1.4
7. Investors Stock (IG)	4.5	6.9	−2.4	.5	−2.9
8. Mass. Inv. Growth Stk (G)	15.4	9.7	5.7	.3	5.4
9. Mass. Inv. Trust (IG)	9.0	8.6	.4	.2	.2
10. Natl. Inv. Corp. (G)	12.9	10.5	2.4	.4	2.0
11. Pioneer (IG)	12.3	8.7	3.6	.4	3.2
12. Price (Rowe) Growth Stk (G)	6.4	7.9	−1.5	.3	−1.8
13. Putnam Growth Fund (G)	12.5	7.3	5.2	.2	5.0
14. Putnam Investors Fund (IG)	14.8	9.9	5.5	.4	5.1
15. Technology Fund (G)	22.9	12.4	10.5	.6	9.9
16. Templeton Growth Fund (G)	13.2	8.8	4.4	.8	3.6
17. Windsor Fund (IG)	6.9	7.1	−.2	.9	−1.2
Averages of all funds	10.9	8.7	2.2	.4	1.8
S&P 500	7.8	7.8	0	0	0

Source: Computer Directions Advisor, Silver Spring, Md.

This compares with an average gross return to selectivity of 2.2% with a low of -2.4% and high of 10.5%. The appropriate yardstick of performance—gross or net selectivity—will, of course, depend on whether the investor evaluates the performance of the fund manager as a single or multiple manager.

21-4-2 Market Timing   The previous analysis focused on the capability of managers in generating superior performance by means of stock-selection techniques. Managers can also generate superior performance by timing the market correctly, that is, by assessing correctly the direction of the market, either bull or bear, and positioning the portfolio accordingly. Managers with a forecast of a declining market can position a portfolio properly by increasing the cash percentage of the portfolio or by decreasing the beta of the equity portion of the portfolio. Conversely, a forecast of a rising market would call for reduction in the cash position or an increase in the beta of the equity portion of the portfolio.

One method for diagnosing the success of managers in this endeavor is to simply look directly at the way fund return behaves relative to the return of the market. This method first involves calculating a series of returns for the fund and a market index over a relevant performance period, and plotting these on a scatter diagram. For example, one could calculate quarterly returns for a fund and for the S&P 500 over, say, the 10-year period ending in 1983 and plot them on a scatter diagram. Given these plots, we could then fit a characteristic line.

If the fund did not engage in market timing and concentrated only on stock selection, the average beta of the portfolio should be fairly constant and a plotting of fund return against market return would show a linear relationship as illustrated in Figure 21-6a. If the manager changed the beta or cash position of the portfolio over time, but was unsuccessful in properly assessing the direction of the market, the plotting would still show a linear relationship. The unsuccessful market timing activity would merely introduce an additional scatter to the plots around the fitted relationship.

On the other hand, if the manager was able to successfully assess the market direction and change the portfolio beta accordingly, we would observe the sort of relationship shown in Figure 21-6b. When the market increases substantially, the fund has a higher than normal beta and it tends to do better than otherwise. Correspondingly, when the market declines, the fund has a lower than normal beta and it declines less than it would otherwise. This causes the plotted points to be above the linear relationship at both high and low levels of market returns and would give a curvature to the scatter of points. To more properly describe this relationship, we can fit a curve to the plots by adding a quadratic term to the simple linear relationship:

$$r_p = a + br_m + cr_m^2$$

where r_p = return of the fund

r_m^2 = return on the market index, squared

a, b, c = values to be estimated by regression analysis

The curve fitted to the plots in Figure 21-6 indicates that the value of the c parameter of the quadratic term is positive. This indicates that the curve becomes steeper as one

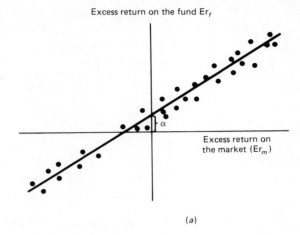

Excess return on the fund Er_f

Excess return on the market (Er_m)

(a)

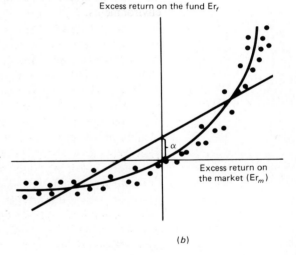

Excess return on the fund Er_f

Excess return on the market (Er_m)

FIGURE 21-6 Fund return vs. market return for (a) superior stock selection and (b) superior market timing. [*Source: J. L. Treynor and K. Mazuy, "Can Mutual Funds Outguess the Market?" Harvard Business Review (July–August 1966), pp. 131–136.*]

(b)

moves to the right of the diagram, and verifies that fund movements were amplified on the upside and dampened on the downside relative to the market. This verifies that the fund manager was anticipating market changes properly, and the superior performance of that fund can be attributed to skill in timing the market.

Treynor and Mazuy used this method to examine the performance of 37 mutual funds over the period from 1953 through 1962.[10] The fitted quadratic term for one of those funds was significantly different from zero, indicating skill on the part of that fund in anticipating changes in the market. The fitted relationships for the other funds,

[10]Jack L. Treynor and Kay Mazuy, "Can Mutual Funds Outguess the Market?" *Harvard Business Review* (July–August 1966), pp. 131–136.

however, evidenced no curvilinearity, and indicated that the funds in general did not demonstrate skill in timing the market.

This result, however, may have been a function of the kind of market conditions that prevailed over the study period. During that time, stock prices were generally rising and bear markets were limited in duration and not severely damaging on the downside. Opportunities to act on a forecast of a declining market would be limited during such a general market condition and managers would be well advised to generally engage in a buy and hold strategy.

In contrast, the market environment changed radically in the latter part of the 1960s. Bear markets became much more severe and longer in duration, a condition that persisted well into the 1970s. Conditions during such a period would be much more favorable for market timing strategies. Managers would have more operating time and greater incentive for engaging in this activity during such a period.

21-4-3 Cash Management Analysis   Farrell used the alternative but complementary method of directly analyzing the way mutual funds varied the cash percentage of the fund to assess the competence of funds in market timing in differing market environments.[11]

He compared fund results for the 1969–1975 period that was taken as representative of a market environment favorable to a strategy of market timing with the 1958–1968 period that was considered to be representative of a period favorable to a buy and hold policy. A total of 56 mutual funds were evaluated including (1) 15 growth funds, (2) 18 growth and income funds, (3) 13 balanced funds, and (4) 9 income funds. These funds were large and had an operating history over the full period of the appraisal.

The analysis proceeded as follows. First, cash as a percentage of assets at the end of the quarter was calculated for each fund over the full 1957–1975 period. This percentage was then averaged over all the quarters of the full period to obtain an estimate of the typical cash position of each fund. The actual percentage of cash at the end of each quarter can then be compared with this average to assess the extent to which the fund varied its cash position from its typical or average positioning. For example, funds as a group (in this sample) maintained an average cash position of 8% over the 1958–1975 period but varied this position by approximately plus or minus 10% around the average from a low of 0 to 1% to a high of 18 to 20%. This implies that funds are generally willing to commit 10% of their assets in acting on market forecasts.

To assess the degree to which variations in the cash percentage around the longer-term average have benefited or detracted from fund performance, two indexes were constructed for each fund. The first index is based on the average cash to other asset allocation experienced by the fund over the period of analysis. The second index is based on a quarter-to-quarter revision of the allocation percentages to match the actual quarter-to-quarter changes experienced by the fund over the period. In both cases, the return on the cash allocation is assumed to be that on treasury bills while the other asset allocation return is assumed to be the return on the S&P 500.

---

[11]James L. Farrell, Jr., "Is Market Timing Likely to Improve Performance?" paper presented at the spring 1976 seminar of the Institute for Quantitative Research in Finance, Scottsdale, Ariz.

Note that both indexes are made up of two "market" portfolios (T-bill portfolio and S&P 500 portfolio) and disregard specific security selection. The difference in performance between the two indexes depends entirely on quarter-to-quarter allocations by the fund which depart from long-term average allocations. The return of the actual allocation index minus the return of the average allocation index thus equals the gain or loss attributable to market timing. Table 21-9 uses hypothetical fund results to illustrate this method of market timing analysis.

The return on the S&P 500 was assumed to be 20% while the T-bill rate was set at 5% for the quarter. Note that the return on the actual allocation index (index 2) minus the return of the average allocation index (index 1) equals the gain or loss from market timing. In this case, there was a net loss from timing of 1.8% (17.0% − 18.8%). The fund was more heavily in cash than usual in a rising market.

The cash management activity of each fund in the sample was analyzed in similar fashion to assess the degree of success in market forecasting over the 1958–1968 and 1969–1975 periods. In addition, individual fund results were averaged over each of the four fund categories (growth, growth-income, balanced, and income) to provide a measure of market timing performance by broad fund classification. Finally, individual fund results were averaged over the total fund population to obtain a measure of the market timing performance of funds in the aggregate.

Table 21-10 shows increments of return (plus or minus) attributable to market timing over the 1958–1968 period and for each of the four fund categories—growth, growth-income, balanced, and income, as well as the average of all fund categories. Note from the bottom row of Table 21-10 that market timing added an average annual increment of .1% to fund performance in the 1969–1975 period in contrast to virtually no gain in the earlier 1958–1968 period. The increment was, however, so small that it is not significant in any statistical sense.

Note also that the income funds were the only funds that were able to contribute to the overall fund results in both periods. The other funds were essentially neutral in their impact. There were, however, six *individual* funds that achieved an incremental return that appeared to be significant, including Keystone K-2, Putnam Growth, Colonial, George Putnam, Keystone K-1, and Putnam Income. Table 21-11 compares the market timing impact on these funds.

Funds do not as a group make substantial shifts in asset positioning to take advantage of market swings. (Funds generally confine cash position changes within a range of ± 10%.) To the extent that funds did make shifts in portfolio structure over the 1958–

TABLE 21-9   HYPOTHETICAL MARKET TIMING RESULTS (ONE PERIOD)

	Index 1 (average)			Index 2 (actual)		
	Percent allocation	Return, %	Weighted return	Percent allocation	Return, %	Weighted return
Cash (T-bills)	8	5	.4	20	5	1.0
Equities (S&P 500)	92	20	18.4	80	20	16.0
Total	100		18.8	100		17.0

TABLE 21-10 MARKET TIMING IMPACT—FUND AVERAGES
(1958–1968 AND 1969–1975)

	1958–1960	1969–1975
Growth funds	.0	.2
Growth-income funds	−.1	.0
Balanced funds	.0	.1
Income funds	.2	.3
All funds	.0	.1

Source: James L. Farrell, Jr.: "Is Market Timing Likely to Improve Performance?" paper presented at the spring 1976 seminar of the Institute for Quantitative Research in Finance, Scottsdale, Ariz.

1968 period, the effort resulted in little or no incremental return (or realized loss for that matter). These results are consistent with those of Treynor, etc., for a similar period favorable to a buy and hold stock strategy. More surprisingly, the activity also added little significantly to overall fund results in the more favorable 1969–1975 period. There were, however, six funds that appeared to add significantly to performance by means of cash management, thereby providing some confirmation to the hypothesis that the market environment can have an impact on the potential for successful cash management.

21-5 SUMMARY

We began this chapter on performance evaluation by describing mutual funds. We showed that there are two major types of funds: closed-end and open-end. A prime difference between these two fund types is that the market price of the closed-end fund is likely to diverge from the net asset value (usually at a discount) whereas the open-end fund market price and net asset value should correspond. The divergence of market price from net asset value for closed-end funds may present investors with extraordinary opportunity for profit. Funds also differ with respect to investment objectives, and three major categories are growth, income-growth, and balanced. We saw that these three categories are also consistent with differences in the risk-return characteristics of the funds as measured by the beta characteristic of the funds. Since

TABLE 21-11 MARKET TIMING IMPACT—PERCENT PER
ANNUM, MOST SUCCESSFUL FUNDS

	Average 1958–1968	Average 1969–1975
Keystone K-1	.1	.8
Keystone K-2	.3	1.0
Putnam Growth	.2	.9
Colonial	.2	.8
Putnam Income	.3	1.0
George Putnam	.1	.6

there appears to be a positive trade-off between fund risk and return, there is a need to consider risk as well as return when evaluating fund performance.

In this chapter, we've also discussed the problems encountered in calculating a rate of return generated by an investment manager over a performance period, and the techniques that one can use to derive a "true" rate of return. Correspondingly, we illustrated the necessity for considering risk as well as return when evaluating performance, and described three techniques for making this comparison. Finally, we described techniques for evaluating the productivity of the two main components utilized by investment managers in seeking above-average returns: market timing and stock selection.

While evaluating past performance is useful, we should be cautious about drawing overly strong conclusions from the analysis. First, the risk-adjustment measures currently available have some biases and deficiencies that can lead to a less than completely comprehensive consideration of risk-adjusted performance. Second, the market environment is so highly competitive that the edge possessed by even the best of management organizations is likely to be slight. Currently available performance-measurement techniques are not likely to be powerful enough to clearly detect such a degree of superiority, at least over a relatively short time span. Finally, management organizations change over time: there is key personnel turnover, complacency can set in with success, the investment process can become stale, and the investment philosophy can change. All this means that past results are not necessarily indicative of future prospects. Nevertheless, historical performance evaluation can serve as the starting point for estimating future prospects and, perhaps more importantly, can serve as a feedback mechanism for improving the ongoing portfolio management process.

SUGGESTED READINGS

Eugene Fama in "Components of Investment Performance," *Journal of Finance* (June 1972), pp. 551–567, described the analytical approach to breaking performance into individual components: market timing and security selection. Fama developed this method within the risk-adjusted beta framework and applies it to the analysis of common stocks.

Peter Dietz, H. R. Fogler, and D. J. Hardy, "The Challenge of Analyzing Bond Portfolio Returns," *Journal of Portfolio Management* (spring 1980), pp. 53–58, also described a way of analyzing differing components of performance, but with an application to bonds. They indicate that the components of performance derive from three sources: (1) interest rate anticipation, (2) sector swapping, and (3) security selection. Interest rate anticipation is analogous to market timing in the equity arena, while sector swapping would be comparable with industry rotation in equities.

Michael C. Jensen, "The Performance of Mutual Funds in the Period 1945–1964," *Journal of Finance* (May 1968), pp. 389–416, pioneered a rigorous application of the capital asset pricing framework to the analysis of performance and developed the performance concept of differential return. He then applied that method to assessing the performance of mutual funds.

Jack L. Treynor, "How to Rate Management of Investment Funds," *Harvard Business Review* (January–February 1965), pp. 63–70, developed the characteristic line method of analysis as well as Treynor ratio as a benchmark of risk-adjusted performance. In a subsequent study Treynor along with Kay Mazuy, "Can Mutual Funds Outguess the Market?" *Harvard*

Business Review (July–August 1966), pp. 131–136, applied the characteristic line method to assessing market timing.

William F. Sharpe, "Mutual Fund Performance," *Journal of Business* (January 1966), pp. 119–138, developed the Sharpe ratio as a benchmark of performance and applied that to assessing mutual fund performance.

QUESTIONS

1 Compare and contrast closed-end and open-end mutual funds.
2 Define net asset value per share and discuss how the market price per share behaves relative to the net asset value per share for open-end and closed-end funds.
3 What advantages do mutual funds offer individual investors?
4 What are three major mutual fund categories, and how do they differ with respect to risk and return?
5 What adjustment needs to be made in calculating the return on mutual funds as opposed to, say, the return on a stock or a bond?
6 Explain the time-weighted return.
7 Explain why there is need to consider risk when evaluating performance.
8 Compare and contrast the two return per unit of risk performance measures. In what context is each best applied?
9 Explain the differential return performance measure as related to the capital asset pricing model.
10 Explain what is meant by net selectivity in the evaluation of stock performance.
11 Compare two methods of evaluating market timing capability.

PROBLEMS

1 The net asset value of the fund was $20 at the beginning of the year, increased to $30 by the end of the year, and then declined to $27 at the end of the second year. What was the return earned per annum, and what was the time-weighted return over the 2-year period?
2 The fund had a beginning of year asset value of $500,000 and end of year value of $600,000, at which time it suffered a cash outflow of $100,000. The value of the fund at the end of year 2 was $700,000. What was the time-weighted return over the 2-year period?
3 Refer to Table 21-6, and assume that all the data are the same except that fund A earned a return of 5% and fund Z earned 12%. Calculate the Sharpe ratio and Treynor ratio, and rank the performance of the three funds, including the market.
4 Assume again that fund A earned 5% and fund Z earned 12%. Calculate the differential return for the two funds, using the same risk data and market data as before.
5 Using the Fama framework of performance components, determine the selectivity, diversification return required, and net selectivity for fund Z.

CHAPTER 22

INTERNATIONAL INVESTING

After reading this chapter you should:

1 Understand that returns earned in local currencies can differ from returns earned in U.S. dollars for a U.S. investor investing internationally

2 Understand why international investing can be beneficial to portfolio diversification

3 Understand why the required return for international investing can be less than the required return for domestic investing

4 Know the fundamental determinants of exchange rates and how these interact to determine exchange rate levels

5 Understand how exchange rate variation creates an additional uncertainty (risk) in international investing

6 Be able to compare and contrast active and passive strategies of international investing

This chapter is devoted to discussing international equity investing. In particular, we will discuss how expanding the investment universe to include foreign equities should have a beneficial impact on performance. This is because foreign equities provide an expanded set of assets that generally show a low degree of correlation with domestic (U.S.) assets. Augmenting the universe of securities with these generally desirable (low-correlation) assets expands the efficient frontier and thereby increases the potential for constructing a portfolio that maximizes return at a given level of risk.

While foreign investing is likely to be beneficial to overall performance, it does differ from domestic investing in one major respect: security holdings will be denominated in several different currencies rather than one single currency, i.e., U.S. dollars. Since international investing means holding securities denominated in a variety of currencies whose relative values may fluctuate, it involves foreign exchange risk, i.e., the exposure to gain or loss on assets or liabilities denominated in some other currency. This additional risk aspect should thus be considered in determining the degree of commitment to international investing as well as the sort of strategy to be employed in executing the investment plan.

The chapter begins by describing the size and characteristics of the international equity market as well as the potential benefits to be derived from an international investment program. We'll then describe the importance of currency risk to international investing as well as a framework for analyzing the reasons for currency rate differentials and the fluctuations in these differentials over time. Finally, we will describe a passive strategy for investing in international markets as well as an active counterpart to the passive investment strategy.

22-1 THE INTERNATIONAL EQUITY MARKETS

Up to now this text has concentrated on U.S. securities, just as in the past American investors have tended to concentrate on domestic securities. However, as the data presented in the following sections indicate, the international security markets represent large, and potentially important, investment opportunities to U.S. investors. And, as the benefits of holding an internationally diversified portfolio have become understood, U.S. investors have begun to broaden their horizons to include foreign equity securities. Because of the size and importance of the international equity markets it is likely that this trend will continue.

22-1-1 Size and Character of International Equity Markets   Table 22-1 shows the market values of individual domestic and foreign equity markets as well as their proportional representation in the total international equity market. Note that the total

TABLE 22-1   NATIONAL EQUITY MARKETS

	Capitalization, July 1, 1985	
	In billions of U.S. dollars	As % of total
United Kingdom	$ 256.4	7.57
Germany	107.7	3.14
France	51.9	1.51
Spain	14.3	.42
Switzerland	53.3	1.55
Netherlands	37.8	1.10
Italy	38.9	1.13
Sweden	19.3	.56
Belgium/Luxembourg	12.6	.37
Denmark	10.0	.29
Norway	6.6	.19
Austria	2.9	.08
Total Europe	405.0	22.07
Japan	710.1	20.70
Hong Kong	34.1	.99
Singapore	25.4	.74
Australia	52.7	1.54
United States	1828.6	53.30
Canada	142.2	4.14
Mexico	2.7	.08
South Africa	23.3	.68
Total	3430.8	100.00

Source: Quantec Ltd., New York, N.Y. 1985.

international equity market was 3430 billion as of July 1, 1985. The U.S. (domestic) equity market represented 53%, or the largest proportion of the total, and reflects both the major size of the U.S. economy as well as the fact that the U.S. capital market is the most highly developed in the world. Japan ranked second, while several European markets (Great Britain, Germany, France, Switzerland, as well as Australia) represented meaningful proportions of the world total. Other markets were generally of less importance in terms of representation in the world market portfolio.

Figures 22-1 and 22-2 show the average annual realized rate of return and standard deviation of return for several of the major international equity markets over two time periods: 1960–1969 and 1970–1979. The first period represents one of relatively favorable economic activity worldwide, where currency exchange rates were fixed. The second period represents a more difficult environment where energy shortages and high inflation developed and where there was a change from fixed to flexible exchange rates. It's useful to separate the data into these two time periods both to analyze the way the risk and return changed over the period and to assess what might be a normal operating environment in the future.

Note that Figure 22-1a shows return (excluding dividends for lack of data) in terms of both local currency as well as dollars. Since foreign securities are denominated in local currency, returns are earned in terms of local currency but must be converted to dollars at the prevailing exchange rate in order to be realized by the domestic (U.S.) investor. For example, returns earned on German securities need to be converted into

FIGURE 22-1   (a) Rate of return (excluding dividends) and (b) standard deviation of return, 1960 to 1969. (*Source: Joel R. Swanson, "Investing Internationally to Reduce Risk and Enhance Return," Morgan Guaranty Trust Co., 1980.*)

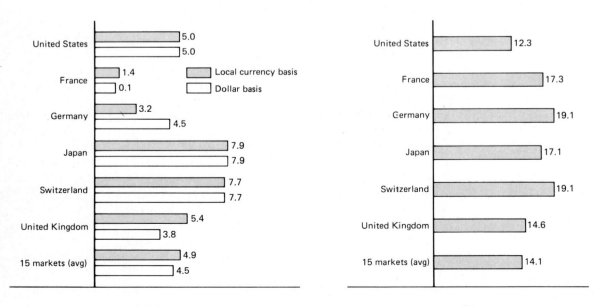

(a)   (b)

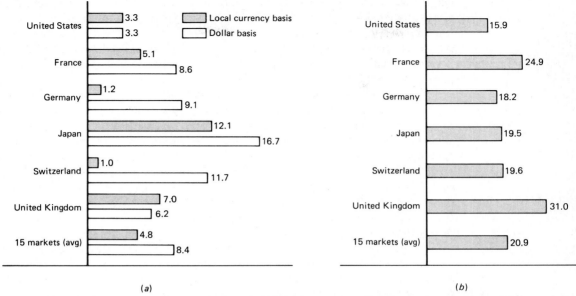

FIGURE 22-2 (a) Total rate of return at a compound annual rate, with dividends reinvested, and (b) standard deviation of return, 1970–1979. (*Source: Joel R. Swanson, "Investing Internationally to Reduce Risk and Enhance Return," Morgan Guaranty Trust Co., 1980.*)

dollars at the prevailing rate of exchange of marks for dollars, say at a rate of $0.50 for 1 mark, to be realized by the domestic (U.S.) investor.

Since exchange rates fluctuate over time, this conversion can result in an added gain or loss to the return earned in the foreign market. For example, assume that the rate of exchange for marks to dollars was .50 at the beginning of the year, but changed to .525 by the end of the year. This would mean that the mark would have appreciated (dollar depreciated) relative to the dollar over the year, resulting in a gain to a U.S. investor of 5% on currency over the year. This gain should be added to the return earned on the German market over the year, and if that had, for example, been 10%, then the net return would be 15.5%.[1] Naturally, if there had been a currency loss, this would reduce the investment return of 10% for the year.

Note in Figure 22-1a that returns stated in both local currency and dollar terms were virtually identical. This is a reflection of the relatively stable worldwide economic conditions and fixed exchange rates, with the only significant changes in the U.K. market, where devaluations over the period resulted in losses for foreign investors, and the German market, where upward revaluations resulted in currency gains. The U.S. market ranked somewhat above-average in terms of return performance over the period but showed the lowest variability as indicated by the standard deviation measures

---

[1] Denoting R_m as the market return and F_x as the currency change, we derive the return as follows:

$$(1 + R_m)(1 + F_x) - 1 = (1.10)(1.05) - 1 = 15.5\%$$

of Figure 22-1*b*. In terms of return per unit of risk (return divided by standard deviation) the United States would have ranked virtually at the top over the period.

In contrast to the earlier 1960–1969 period, Figure 22-2*a* shows significant differences between returns earned in local currencies and dollars across virtually all countries for the period 1970–1979. This reflects the unstable economic conditions of the latter period along with the switch from fixed to flexible exchange rates. The U.S. market performed somewhat below average when measured in terms of local currency. However, because of the generally declining value of the dollar (depreciating currency), U.S. investors in virtually all foreign markets would have made significant currency gains over the period. The net performance of the U.S. market relative to the foreign markets measured in dollars was virtually the poorest of all the markets. Figures 22-1*b* and 22-2*b* show the standard deviation of return of the countries over the two periods: 1960–1969 and 1970–1979.

The latter period variability was essentially similar to that of the earlier period, with the exception of the U.K. market, which showed a significant increase between periods. The U.S. standard deviation increased somewhat but still ranked as the least risky of the markets. We should note also that the standard deviation across markets was virtually identical whether measured in local currency or in dollars (data not shown). This reflects the fact that currency changes were generally independent of the return realized in the equity markets, thus neither adding to nor subtracting from variability in either this period or the earlier period.

22-1-2 Diversification Advantages of International Investments   While international investing would have obviously been of benefit to domestic (U.S.) investors in a period such as occurred between 1970 and 1979, a more fundamental reason for considering it is the favorable effects on portfolio diversification. This benefit derives from the opportunity that foreign markets offer in providing a wider array of (securities) with relatively low correlations. These can, in turn, be combined with domestic securities to generate a lower overall portfolio risk (standard deviation) than would be possible when investing exclusively in domestic assets.

This is, of course, the same principle from which the benefits of domestic diversification derive. Recall from chapter 12 that the typical security within the U.S. equity market would have a correlation with a U.S. market index of something on the order of .5. This means that there are some benefits to be derived from diversification as there is less than perfect correlation between securities, but that these benefits are limited because there is correlation that is significantly positive. We noted in Figures 3-3 to 3-5 that empirical studies show that diversification can reduce the standard deviation of a portfolio by 55% compared with the risk of a nondiversified portfolio, i.e., single security.

Table 22-2 shows the correlation between the returns of several major equity markets during the 1960–1969 and 1970–1979 periods. Note that the U.S. and Canadian markets showed a high degree of correlation, as might be expected from the high level of economic integration between the two countries. There was a significantly lower degree of correlation between the United States and the other countries during both periods. On average, the correlation across countries was on the order of .31 in the initial period and .37 in the latter period, indicating opportunities for diversification.

TABLE 22-2   CORRELATION: U.S. AND KEY FOREIGN
MARKETS 1960–1969 AND 1970–1979
(Return Excluding Dividends, Dollar Basis)

	Coefficient of correlation with U.S.	
	1960–1969	**1970–1979**
Canada	.81	.71
France	.27	.40
Germany	.36	.31
Japan	.08	.31
Switzerland	.49	.47
United Kingdom	.29	.46
15 markets (avg)	.31	.37

Source: Joel R. Swanson, "Investing Internationally to Reduce Risk and Enhance Return," Morgan Guaranty Trust Co., 1980.

Figure 22-3, which is similar to one used in Chapter 3 to illustrate the benefit of diversification, shows that it is possible to use this fact of imperfect correlation among international markets to reduce the risk of a portfolio below the level that is possible when dealing only with domestic securities. Note that the lower line, which represents portfolios consisting of both international securities and domestic securities, lies at a lower level over the full range of portfolio holdings than when diversification is limited exclusively to domestic investing. In the international case, portfolio risk is reduced to 33% of the risk of a typical stock (undiversified portfolio) or about one-third more than the reduction that is possible in the domestic diversification case.

FIGURE 22-3   Risk reduction through national and international diversification. [*Source: B. H. Solnik, "Why Not Diversify Internationally Rather Than Domestically?" Financial Analysts Journal (July–August 1974), pp. 48–54.*]

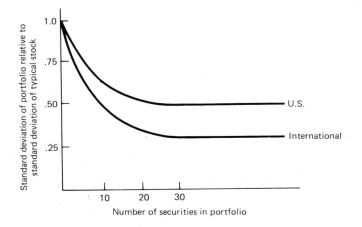

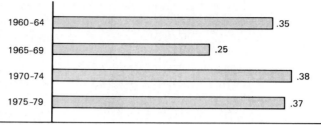

FIGURE 22-4   Correlation coefficients, U.S. market and average of 15 foreign markets. (*Source: Joel R. Swanson, "Investing Internationally to Reduce Risk and Enhance Return," Morgan Guaranty Trust Co., 1980.*)

The potential for international diversification is likely to persist into the future as the degree of correlation across international markets should remain relatively low. To begin with, many of the factors that affect stock values are peculiar to the individual domestic economy, such as tax laws, monetary policy, and general political climate. Furthermore, even factors that affect the world economy, such as a sudden change in oil prices, can impact individual economies differently. These differences, which are the basic source of a lack of synchronization among markets, should persist into the future.

In addition, the data in Figure 22-4 further confirm that the degree of correlation among international markets is likely to remain low. In particular, the table shows the correlations across markets broken down into several subperiods over the full 1960–1979 period. Note that correlations were high in the early 1960s, declined and were low in the mid- and late 1960s, but rose back to the early period levels in the latter part of the 1970s. While correlations have varied over time, there does not appear to be any widespread trend to greater correlation among the major equity markets. It would appear that the most recent correlation experience would be a realistic if not conservative expectation for the future.

22-1-3 Minimum Returns to Invest Internationally   Given that international investing provides added diversification that is unavailable from domestic sources alone, it would be useful to determine the minimum return that would have to be available to invest internationally. Presumably lower returns could be accepted from international investments than from domestic investments because of the favorable impact these securities would have on reducing portfolio risk. The minimum return, or hurdle rate in this context, could be considered that which would give us the same risk-return trade-off if we had invested exclusively in domestic securities:

$$\text{Risk/return (international)} = \text{risk/return (domestic)}$$

Recall from earlier analyses of the domestic equity market (Chapters 2 and 3) that the relevant risk of a security in a portfolio context is the contribution of that security to the portfolio risk. It is the systematic risk and not the total risk of the security that is relevant in the portfolio context. This analysis should, in turn, be applicable in an international context, and hence we can say that it is the systematic risk that is the relevant component to consider when structuring an internationally diversified port-folio.

Table 22-3 shows risk-return data for several foreign equity markets along with data for the U.S. (domestic) market. The first three columns show the following risk data: the standard deviation of return, the correlation with the U.S. market, and the beta of the foreign market with respect to the U.S. market. At any level of standard deviation or total risk, the beta will be high if the correlation between markets is high, and conversely it will be low if the correlation is low. Note that with respect to the standard deviation all the foreign markets have higher standard deviations than the U.S. market. However, the correlations with the U.S. market are relatively low, resulting in lower systematic risk as measured by beta values; i.e., the betas are less than 1.0.

Since the beta values are all lower than 1 (except the U.K.), this would imply a lower required return for investing in foreign equities than in U.S. equities. The fourth column in the table shows these required returns under the presumption that the required risk premium (return less risk-free rate) for investing in the U.S. market is 6%. Given that these betas are less than 1.0, the required risk premiums for the international equity markets are less than the required premium for investing in the U.S. market. It's thus possible to invest in international markets at the lower return derived in the table and still maintain the same risk-reward ratio. Even if international markets did not provide the same return as realized historically and didn't measure up to returns available in the domestic market, international investing could still be justifiable, because of the substantial risk-reducing potential of this activity.

TABLE 22-3 RISK AND REQUIRED RETURN MEASURES FOR FOREIGN MARKET PORTFOLIOS
(All Figures Estimated from Data for 1973–1977)

Country	Annualized standard deviation of returns (measured in U.S. dollars)	Correlation with U.S. market (S&P 500)	Market risk (beta) from U.S. perspective	Minimum risk premium from U.S. perspective
France	26.4	.50	.71	4.3
Germany	20.4	.43	.47	2.8
Japan	20.1	.40	.43	2.6
The Netherlands	21.9	.61	.72	4.6
Switzerland	22.7	.63	.77	4.7
United Kingdom	41.0	.51	1.13	6.8
United States	18.5	1.00	1.00	6.0

Source: D. R. Lessard, "An Update on Gains from International Diversification," unpublished, 1977.

Before continuing, you should:

1 Know the major international equity markets and their relative sizes
2 Understand the difference between returns earned in terms of local currency and those earned in U.S. dollars for a U.S. investor investing internationally
3 Understand why international investing can be beneficial to portfolio diversification
4 Understand why the required return from international investing can be less than the required return for domestic investing

22-2 CURRENCY RISK

While international investing would appear to be generally beneficial to portfolio performance, it does entail the additional risk of currency fluctuations. Given this additional risk, it then becomes a question of whether these exchange risks are so large as to offset the benefits of international diversification. A related question is what, if any, special strategies should be followed to reduce the impact of foreign exchange risk? We'll primarily deal with assessing the source and degree of exchange risk in this section and discuss the way that exchange risk is incorporated in active and passive strategies in later sections.

In assessing causes for exchange rate fluctuations we need to first differentiate between spot and forward exchange markets. The spot market is where currencies are exchanged immediately at the prevailing rate of exchange, e.g., $0.50 for 1 DM. The forward market is where traders buy and sell currency for delivery at a fixed future date but at a price that is set currently. Forward rates are typically quoted for delivery 1 month, 3 months, and 6 months hence; however, forward contracts generally can be arranged with most international banks for delivery at any specified date up to 1 year in the future. Contracts running beyond 1 year are also available but require special arrangements.

Table 22-4 illustrates by showing the spot and forward rates of exchange for the dollar and the German mark (DM) and British pound (£) as of December 31, 1979. Note that the forward DM was more expensive than the spot DM. In technical terms the forward DM was selling at a premium relative to the spot DM, and the longer the contract, the higher was the premium. In contrast, the forward pound was selling at a discount relative to the spot pound. Below the table is the formula for calculating the premium or discount on forward exchange. Note that the 6-month forward premium on DM was 6%, while there was a discount of .5% on the 6-month forward pound.

22-2-1 Fundamental Determinants of Exchange Rates Figure 22-5 provides a graphic framework for evaluating fundamental determinants of changing exchange rates.[2] The figure shows that there is a four-way interrelationship among expected

---

[2]Ian Giddy, "An Integrated Theory of Exchange Rate Equilibrium," *Journal of Financial and Quantitative Analysis* (December 1976), pp. 883–892, offers an excellent exposition of this analytical framework.

TABLE 22-4   SPOT AND FORWARD EXCHANGE RATES
(December 31, 1979)

	Exchange rate	
	$/£	$/DM
Spot	2.2320	.5799
1 month forward	2.2280	.5831
3 months	2.2211	.5886
6 months	2.2215	.5973

The percent premium or discount is calculated as follows:

Let S = spot rate
     F = forward rate
     n = number of months forward
     P = forward premium or discount, percent
          per annum

then $P = \dfrac{F - S}{S} \times \dfrac{12}{n} \times 100$

For example, the forward premium on the 6 months forward DM as of December 31, 1979, was

$$P = \frac{.5973 - .5799}{.5799} \times \frac{12}{6} \times 100$$
$$= 6.0\% \text{ per annum}$$

differences in inflation, differences in interest rates, expected changes in exchange rates, and forward exchange rates. These interrelationships are consistent, so that once any three are established, the fourth is then determined. Similarly, if any one of them is violated, at least one other must be violated.

In Figure 22-5 the corners A to B indicate that the expected change in spot rates should be related to the expected difference in inflation rates in the two countries. To

FIGURE 22-5   Inflation, interest rates, premiums, and exchange rates. (*Source: R. Brealey and S. C. Myers, Financial Planning and Strategy, McGraw-Hill, New York, 1980.*)

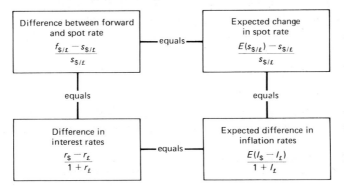

begin with, identical goods should trade at the same price even if they are traded in different markets. If there is a difference, those goods that can be bought more cheaply abroad will be imported, forcing down the price of the domestic product. Similarly, those goods that can be bought more cheaply in the United States will be exported, forcing down the price of the foreign product. In particular, the price of foreign goods when converted to dollars should be roughly the same as the price in the United States. For example, for U.S. and U.K. goods we would have sterling price of the goods times the exchange rate (dollars/pound) equals dollar price of the goods. Equivalently, the exchange rate (dollars/pound) should equal dollar price of the goods divided by sterling price of the goods. If the price of sterling is always equal to the ratio of domestic prices, any change in the ratio of domestic prices must be matched by a change in the price of sterling. For example, if inflation is 5% in the United States and 10% in the United Kingdom, then, in order to equalize the dollar price of goods in the two countries, the price of sterling must fall by (.05 − .10)/1.10, or about 5%.

This relationship is based on the purchasing power parity (PPP) theorem. The PPP has been tested empirically, and one should be aware that the evidence may be sensitive to the countries, time periods, and price indexes that are selected for testing. Despite these difficulties, it seems reasonably clear from the evidence that over long time periods and during periods of hyperinflation (when monetary factors swamp real changes), PPP offers a fairly good description of exchange rate behavior. However, over shorter time periods, say, 3 to 12 months, it has not been uncommon to observe substantial exchange rate changes, say, 10 to 20%, which are unrelated to commodity price changes.

Corners *B* to *C* in Figure 22-5 indicate that differences in interest rates should be also related to differences in inflation rates. This relationship derives from the Fisher effect, which indicates that investors are interested in real rather than nominal returns. If this is so, then prices of securities, or alternatively, interest rates should adjust to provide the expected real return. We would in turn expect this to occur across different countries, so that there would be a tendency toward an equalization of real returns or real interest rates between countries. Differences in inflation rates would then account for the difference in nominal interest rates across countries. Empirical evidence on this relationship is limited, and while we might expect that the real rate of interest would be equilibrated across countries over the longer term, we are also aware that there are impediments like exchange controls, government intervention in exchange markets, and taxes that can prevent this from occurring for extended periods.

The corners *C* to *D* in Figure 22-5 indicate that the difference in interest rates should be equal to the difference between forward and spot rates. This relationship is based on what is known as the interest rate parity theorem and is a very strong relationship, since it is based on arbitrage. It must match the difference in interest rates, or else investors will be able to profit without bearing any risk. They could do this by borrowing in the country with the relatively low interest rate (including the cost of forward cover), investing in the money market in the country with the high rate, and removing the exchange risk by covering in the forward market.

For example, if interest rates were 10% in the United States, investing $1 million would net $1.1 million at the end of the year. Presuming that the interest rate were 12% in the United Kingdom and the spot rate of exchange was $2/£1, the investor could convert the $1 million to £500,000 and invest at the higher interest rate for a return of £560,000 at the end of the year. Since the future rate of exchange is uncertain, the investor can avoid risk (potential loss) by selling sterling forward at the prevailing forward rate, which in equilibrium should be $1.964/£1. Converting the proceeds at this rate ($1.964 \times 560,000$) gives the same dollar proceeds of $1.1 million as investing directly in the United States. The gain on interest rates is offset by the loss on foreign exchange, as should be the case according to the analysis in Figure 22-5. Empirical tests in markets like Eurocurrency markets where such factors as exchange controls and tax considerations are not factors indicate that this relationship holds almost exactly. In other markets, the relationship will diverge as tax factors and potential exchange controls are more significant considerations.

Finally, from corners D and A at the top of the quadrilateral in the figure we expect the difference between forward and spot rates to be equal to the expected change in the spot rate. For example, a 1-year-forward rate of $2/£1 should mean that traders expect the spot rate in 1 year's time to be $2/£1. If they expected it to be higher than this, no one would be willing to sell pounds at the forward rate; if they expected it to be lower, no one would be willing to buy at the forward rate. Alternatively, if forward rates differed from anticipated exchange rates, market participants would be induced to speculate on the difference between them, tending to move the forward rate toward the expected future spot rate. Empirical tests indicate that the forward rate is an unbiased estimate of future spot rates; that is, it consistently neither underestimates nor overestimates future spot rates, and in this respect provides a good standard for assessing forecasting expertise.[3]

22-2-2 Managing Currency Risk If the relationships just described held exactly, we'd expect that interest rates and security prices would reflect expected changes in exchange rates and currency would not represent a separate risk in international investing. We noted, however, that there is only a long-run tendency toward equilibrium and that real-world factors like taxes, exchange controls—both actual and potential— and transactions costs can further distort equilibrium. As a result, we would expect that exchange rates would diverge in the short run and would exhibit substantial unexpected fluctuations that investment managers need to consider in designing and implementing active and passive strategies of international investing.

In order to protect against currency risk, investors may hedge by borrowing or entering into forward currency contracts. These hedging strategies of course have a cost that may well outweigh the incremental risk reduction.[4] Alternatively, the investor might protect against currency risk by simply investing across many foreign markets.

---

[3]While the forward premium is an unbiased prediction of future exchange rate changes, it is a poor predictor in the sense that it explains only about 10% of the fluctuations in the future spot rate. This suggests that the bulk of the short-run exchange rate changes are dominated by unanticipated events and that the forward premium sits roughly in the middle of a wide distribution of exchange rate expectations. Alternatively, it implies that there is ample opportunity to apply forecasting techniques to attempt to explain this unaccounted-for exchange rate variation.

[4]In order to protect against currency risk, investors may hedge by borrowing or entering into forward currency contracts. These hedging strategies, of course, have a cost that may well outweigh the incremental risk reduction. Estimates are that the cost of such hedging for most major currencies is on the order of .5 to .7% per annum.

In this way, losses on weak currencies would tend to be offset by gains on strong currencies. Presumably, passive strategies that entail holding a broadly diversified portfolio of international securities would benefit from this risk-reducing effect over the short term, while over the long term, as markets tend toward equilibrium, passive investors would find their exposure to currency risk to be minimal.

On the other hand, investors following an active strategy that involves overweighting in attractive countries or markets and underweighting in unattractive markets will by virtue of this activity become exposed to the currency risk, as the investor is taking a bet on the currency in addition to the market. This strategy in effect cancels the balancing-out effect of a passive, or world investing, strategy. Therefore, such investors should carefully consider the direction and magnitude of currency movements and incorporate these explicit forecasts into their assessment of the relative attractiveness of the different markets. This would enable them to avoid undue penalties from possible currency risks and to capitalize on potential opportunities from an especially well positioned currency.

22-3 A PASSIVE INTERNATIONAL INVESTMENT STRATEGY

As is the case with domestic investing, investors in the international market can pursue an active or passive strategy or combinations of these alternative approaches. One way of investing passively is to create an international index fund, just as domestic investors following a totally passive strategy would invest in an index fund designed to replicate, say, the S&P 500.

However, there are several major impediments to a direct application of the U.S. index approach in the international arena. First, there is no index that investors generally agree is representative of the world market portfolio, as is the case in the United States where indexes like the S&P 500, NYSE, and Wilshire 5000, though perhaps flawed nevertheless are deemed useful. Furthermore, many markets are dominated by only a handful of companies, and many other companies, though sizable, might be quite closely held and not readily marketable. Finally, there may be a greater degree of mispricing in foreign markets than in the United States with the attendant difficulties for passive strategies and indexing.

One passive approach that seems practical and at the same time provides a direct way of obtaining many of the benefits of international diversification is one that was devised by Batterymarch. This approach was to focus on the major world markets: Japan, United Kingdom, Germany, France, Switzerland, and Australia. They also included gold-mining stocks in the investment universe both because of their inflation hedging properties as well as the fact that they are a reasonably meaningful portion of the world market. These six countries and the gold-mining stocks represent 72.9% of the non-U.S.-Canadian world market, thus providing major representation in terms of capitalization in the world market while avoiding the difficulties inherent in operating across a multitude of smaller and perhaps less familiar markets. In addition, the strategy entailed investing only in the 10 largest companies that dominate the market, weighting within each of the six major equity markets.[5] This then provides a list that is both

[5]As of 1979, the top 10 companies on average constituted approximately one-third of the market weighting of the markets in six countries: Japan, United Kingdom, Germany, France, Switzerland, and

representative and manageable: it eliminates the necessity of monitoring a large array of unfamiliar and less marketable securities. These companies would presumably also be the least likely to be inefficiently priced and hence the most suitable for use in a passive mode.

Table 22-5 shows the weights of the 70 stocks in the portfolio grouped according to the seven major market categories. Each stock weighting represents its proportionate share of the total capitalization of the 70 companies in the universe. Note that the aggregate weighting of the companies within each major market is fairly similar to the weighting in a broader index of international equities. The strategy as intended appears to provide a reasonably representative proxy for a world portfolio.

Table 22-6 shows a simulation of the performance of this strategy over the 1971–1975 period compared with the performance of a broader market index, measured in both local and foreign currency. Note that the strategy tracks the performance of the market index reasonably well over the period and provides a total return that is close to that of the index. Furthermore, the returns of the strategy as well as the index are fairly similar whether measured in local or in foreign currency. This gives credence to the previous notion that passive international strategies (investing on a worldwide basis) should, on balance, provide a reasonably effective hedge against currency risk.

Before continuing, you should:
1 Be able to differentiate between spot and forward exchange rates and know how to calculate the premium or discount on forward exchange
2 Know the fundamental determinants of exchange rates and how these interact to determine exchange rate levels
3 Understand how exchange rate fluctuations create an additional uncertainty (risk) in international investing
4 Understand the general approach to executing a passive strategy of international investing

22-4 AN ACTIVE INTERNATIONAL INVESTMENT STRATEGY

An active strategy for investing internationally might be one that is oriented to identifying relatively attractive and unattractive national markets. A market that was identified as attractive would be overweighted in the portfolio, while one that was judged unattractive would be underweighted or perhaps even eliminated entirely from the portfolio. A decision to actively manage a portfolio in this fashion of course presupposes some predictive capability, just as a decision to manage passively would imply a lack of predictive capability.

Figure 22-6 shows the steps that an organization might follow in executing this sort of strategy. The first step is to develop explicit forecasts of the market return for each of the international markets of interest. Since active management means that an or-

---

Australia. The percentage ranged from a high of 63% in Switzerland to a low of 13% in Japan. This compares with the United States, where the top 10 companies represented 20% of the total capitalization of the market.

TABLE 22-5 INTERNATIONAL EQUITY DIVERSIFICATION (SAMPLE PORTFOLIO)
(October 31, 1976)

	Non-U.S. market, %	Batterymarch international portfolio, %
Japan:		
Toyota Motor		5.0
Nippon Steel		5.0
Matsushita El. Ind.		4.2
Nissan Motors		3.9
Sony		3.6
Hitachi		3.4
Tokyo Elect. Pwr		3.4
Sumitomo Bank		3.1
Sanwa Bank		2.8
Mitsubishi Bank		2.8
	31.2	42.8
United Kingdom:		
Shell T&T		4.1
British Petroleum		4.1
Imperial Chemical		3.4
Bat Industries		1.6
General Electric UK		1.4
Unilever		1.4
Marks and Spencer		1.2
Imperial Group		1.0
Beecham Group		.9
Barclays Bank		.9
	14.1	19.3
Germany:		
Siemens		2.4
Daimler Benz		2.2
BASF		1.5
Bayer		1.5
Deutsche Bank		1.5
Hoechst		1.4
RWE		1.2
VEBA		1.0
Dresdner Bank		1.0
Thyssen Huette		.8
	10.3	14.1
France:		
Michelin		1.7
Aquitaine SNPA		1.6
St. Gobain P-A-M		1.2
Air Liquide		.9
Pechiney-Ucine		.8
Dassault Breguet		.8
L'Oreal		.8
Correfour		.8
Française-Petroles		.8
Moulinex		.7
	6.0	9.0

TABLE 22-5 *(Continued)*

	Non-U.S. market, %	Batterymarch international portfolio, %
Australia:		
Broken Hill		1.6
Conzinco Rio Tinto		.8
MIM Holdings		.7
CSR		.6
Hamersley		.5
Myer Emporium		.4
Bougainville Copper		.4
Western Mining		.3
Bank New South Wales		.3
COMALCO		.3
	4.8	6.6
Switzerland:		
Nestle		.9
Schweiz Bankverin		.8
Schweiz Bankgessel		.7
Hoffman LaRoche		.7
Schweiz Kreditanstal		.5
Ciba-Geigy		.5
Sandoz		.3
Oerlikon-Buharle		.2
Aluminum Suisse		.2
Brown Boveri		.2
	4.3	5.8
Gold:		
West Driefontein		1.6
Western Holdings		1.2
President Brand		.8
Free State Geduld		.7
Western Deep Levels		.7
Blyvooruitzecht		.5
President Steyn		.5
	2.1	2.9
Total	72.9%	100.0%

Source: Batterymarch Financial Management Corporation International Index Fund, case study prepared by Robert Vandell, Colgate Darden School of Business Administration, 1977.

ganization is implicitly taking a position either ''long or short'' in currency, there is also a need to develop an explicit forecast of the change in currency over the planning period. The second step is to adjust these forecasts for the degree of predictive capability.[6] The third and final step is to consider risk along with expected returns and generate an optimal portfolio.

[6]James L. Farrell, Jr., *Guide to Portfolio Management*, McGraw-Hill, New York, 1983, illustrates how to adjust for predictive accuracy, and readers interested in the details of such adjustment would do well to refer to that publication.

TABLE 22-6 SIMULATED AND ACTUAL PERFORMANCE OF ANNUAL RETURNS
(Percentage Change)

	1971	1972	1973	1974	1975
Adjusted for currency fluctuation					
Foreign markets	29	27	−16	−24	33
Simulation	20	22	−13	−22	32
***Not* adjusted for currency fluctuation**					
Foreign markets	19	29	−21	−24	45
Simulation	9	23	−16	−26	45

Source: Batterymarch Financial Management Corporation International Index Fund, case study prepared by Robert Vandell, Colgate Darden School of Business Administration, 1977.

In making a forecast of the return of a foreign market, one could proceed along the lines outlined in Chapter 20, where we illustrated how forecasts are developed for the domestic equity market. Recall that we indicated that investors could rely heavily on historic data in making the forecast or could employ approaches like the scenario method, which relies more heavily on estimates of future trends in economic data and financial markets. In forecasting the exchange rate, one could use the currently available forward exchange rate as the best unbiased forecast of the future spot exchange rate.[7] Alternatively, the investor could rely on other means of developing nonconsensus forecasts of the future trend in exchange rates.

[7]We noted before that the forward rate provided an unbiased benchmark for evaluating forecasting capabilities. Using this benchmark, studies show that some commercially available forecasting services have the capability to improve on the forward rate forecast. This evidence indicates that active strategies incorporating exchange rate forecasts have opportunities for improving portfolio performance.

FIGURE 22-6 Executing an active international investment strategy.

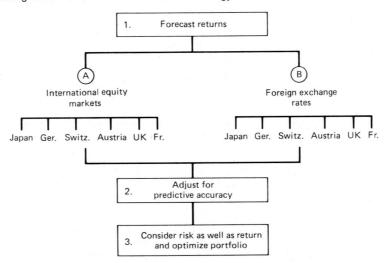

TABLE 22-7   RETURN FORECAST
CURRENCY, EQUITIES, AND TOTAL (1980)

	Currency forecast return, %	Equity market forecast return, %	Total return, %
United Kingdom	1.1	18.2	19.3
France	1.0	13.6	14.6
Germany	4.7	13.9	18.6
Switzerland	10.2	7.2	17.4
Hong Kong	0.0	19.4	19.4
Japan	6.1	10.8	16.9
Netherlands	1.8	11.6	13.4
Canada	1.3	15.8	17.1

Table 22-7 shows forecasts for eight major international markets developed by a leading international investment advisory organization for 1980. This organization uses an active approach to forecasting market returns and exchange rates, and the data in the table reflect adjustments for the organization's estimated degree of predictive capability. Note that the currency and market forecasts for each of the eight countries are shown separately. The last column combines the currency and market estimate to provide a projected total return for each country over the 1-year planning horizon.

Note that the Hong Kong, United Kingdom, and German markets ranked high in terms of total return forecast for the period. The German and Hong Kong equity markets were deemed to be of above-average attraction, while the German currency was forecast by the consensus to be relatively strong over the period. On the other hand, the French and Netherlands markets ranked at the bottom in terms of forecast return; the French equity market was rated as unattractive, while the Dutch currency outlook was rated as below-average. Other markets showed mixed patterns, with the equity market attractive but the currency unattractive, or vice versa. Hence these markets tended to rank in the middle with respect to total return over the forthcoming year.

22-5 FORMING OPTIMAL INTERNATIONAL PORTFOLIOS

In order to develop an optimal portfolio structure, we should consider risk as well as return, and the best way of doing this is within the framework of a portfolio optimization model such as those we discussed in Chapter 20. We would, of course, use the estimates developed in Table 22-7 as our projected return data inputs. For purposes of the illustration, we'll use the historic standard deviation and covariance relationships as risk inputs.

Figure 22-7 shows an efficient frontier of portfolios that was generated by the optimization routine using the risk and return inputs discussed.[8] It also shows the risk-

[8]Since the assets or, alternatively, countries to be considered for international diversification are unlikely to exceed 15 (in this case there are eight), return, variance, and covariance inputs can be readily developed. As in the case of asset allocation, the full-covariance Markowitz model can and is generally employed in generating an efficient frontier of internationally diversified portfolios.

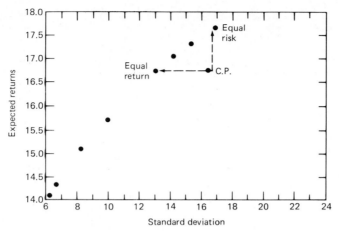

FIGURE 22-7   Efficient frontier and current portfolio.

return location of a current portfolio, designated C.P., that the organization held currently and was the object of the upgrading analysis. Note that the portfolio on the upper part of the efficient frontier offers a higher return at the same level of risk as the current alternative, while the portfolio in the lower part of the efficient frontier offers the same return at a lower level of risk. This dominance results both from the presumed capability to forecast and hence generate greater return than available to a passive investor, and from the more explicit consideration of risk (covariance relationships) than is possible without formal optimization procedures.

Table 22-8 shows the weightings of the individual countries in both portfolios (equal risk and equal return) from the efficient frontier compared with the weightings in the current portfolio. Note that the optimal portfolio carries relatively heavy weightings in the high-return countries: United Kingdom, Germany and Hong Kong, while indicating no weights in France and the Netherlands. The German market is, in a sense, acting as a substitute for the French and Dutch markets, which are highly correlated with the German market but have significantly lower forecast returns. The major divergence between the optimal and current portfolios is primarily due to these three countries. A shift from the French and Dutch markets to the German market would improve prospective return and/or reduce risk as indicated by the statistics on the expected return and standard deviation of the three portfolios.

22-6 SUMMARY

International investing expands the set of opportunities available to the investor and thereby offers the potential for generating a portfolio with a higher return per unit of risk. We have indicated that investors could attempt to capitalize on this potential through active or passive strategies of investing. If one chooses an active strategy of investing, there is a need to consider explicitly the risk of fluctuating exchange rates as well as deal with the problem of forecasting returns for the foreign markets of

TABLE 22-8 PORTFOLIO COMPOSITION

	Current portfolio, %	Optimal equal risk, %	Optimal equal return, %
Equities:			
United Kingdom	33	20	33
France	12	0	0
Germany	9	42	39
Switzerland	2	2	2
Hong Kong	5	5	5
Japan	19	23	19
Netherlands	5	0	0
Canada	2	2	2
	87	93	100
Cash equivalent	13	7	
Total	100	100	100
Expected return	16.75	17.65	16.71
Standard deviation	16.44	16.72	13.00

The optimal equal risk portfolio is one that has the same risk (approximates) as the current portfolio but as shown in Figure 22-7 has a higher return. Correspondingly, the equal return portfolio is one that has the same return as the current portfolio but as also shown on the figure has a lower risk. Both dominate the current portfolio.

interest. We illustrated a framework of analysis which explicitly considered forecasts of both foreign exchange rates and market returns.

While international investing appears to be generally beneficial, there are factors that represent potential obstacles, and these should be considered in implementing strategies of international investing. These factors include formal barriers to international transactions such as exchange controls, double taxation of portfolio income for certain investors in particular countries, and restrictions on ownership of securities according to the nationality of the investor. In addition, there are informal barriers such as the difficulty of obtaining information about a market, differences in reporting practices that make international comparisons difficult, transactions costs, and markets that are generally less liquid than the U.S. market. Finally, investors should be aware of the generally remote, yet extreme risk (in terms of consequences) of governmental confiscation or expropriation of foreign assets.

SUGGESTED READINGS

The following two articles provide a lucid and analytically sound justification, as well as motivation, for international diversification:

Donald F. Lessard, "World, Country and Industry Relationships in Equity Returns: Implications for Risk Reduction through International Diversification," *Financial Analysts Journal* (January–February 1976), pp. 31–38; and B. H. Solnik, "Why Not Diversify Internationally Rather than Domestically?" *Financial Analysts Journal* (July–August 1978), pp. 48–54.

Three articles that provide perspective on the relationship between the required return for international investing and the degree of integration of world capital markets are:

T. Agmon, "Country Risk: The Significance of the Country Factor for Share Price Movements in the United Kingdom, Germany and Japan," *Journal of Business* (January 1973), pp. 24–32.

F. Black, "International Capital Market Equilibrium with Investment Barriers," *Journal of Financial Economics* (December 1974), pp. 337–352.

M. Subrahamanyam, "On the Optimality of International Capital Market Integration," *Journal of Financial Economics* (March 1975), pp. 3–28.

An excellent analytical framework for understanding the relationship between the underlying fundamental determinants of the level of foreign exchange rates is: Ian Giddy, "An Integrated Theory of Exchange Rate Equilibrium," *Journal of Financial and Quantitative Analysis* (December 1976), pp. 883–892.

QUESTIONS

1 Identify the major international equity markets and compare the relative sizes of these markets.

2 Why might the return generated in local currency differ from the return earned in dollars for a U.S. investor investing internationally?

3 Why were returns stated in local currency and dollars virtually identical in the 1960–1969 period but significantly different in the 1970–1979 period?

4 Explain why international investing can be beneficial to portfolio diversification.

5 Why might the correlation across international equities continue to be low into the future?

6 Discuss why inclusion of foreign securities in a portfolio might be beneficial even if the expected return was less than that expected from domestic securities.

7 Differentiate between the spot and forward foreign exchange markets.

8 Define premium and discount on forward foreign exchange.

9 Explain why the difference between forward and spot rate should be equal to the expected change in the spot rate.

10 Explain how the expected change in spot rates for two countries should be related to the expected difference in inflation rates in the two countries.

11 Explain why differences in inflation rates between countries should be related to differences in interest rates.

12 Explain how the difference in interest rates between countries should be equal to the difference between forward and spot rates.

13 Explain how exchange rate variation creates an additional uncertainty (risk) in international investing.

14 Explain how one might go about executing a passive strategy of international investing.

15 Indicate the problems of conducting a totally passive international investment strategy, and suggest a workable way around these problems.

16 Indicate the essential elements of an active strategy of investing in international markets, and briefly describe the importance of each.

17 How might one use the forward rate as a benchmark in the forecasting of exchange rates?

18 Compare and contrast active and passive strategies of international investing.

PROBLEMS

1 Using the data in Figures 22-1 and 22-2, rank the countries according to return per unit of risk (standard deviation) for both the 1960–1969 and 1970–1979 periods.

2 Assume that the exchange rate of marks to dollars was $0.50 at the beginning of the year and $0.48 at the end of the year. Over the same period the return on German stocks had been 18%. What was the net return to the U.S. investor over the year?

3 Assume that the exchange rate of Swiss francs to dollars was $0.20 at the beginning of the year and $0.25 at the end of the year, while the Swiss market showed a return of -5%. What was the net return to the U.S. investor after the year?

4 The spot rate for the German mark is currently .4055 per dollar, while the 6-month forward rate is .4178 per dollar. Is the forward rate at a premium or discount? Calculate what it is.

5 The spot rate for the British pound is 2.230 per dollar, while the 6-month forward rate is 2.2215 per dollar. Calculate and indicate whether the pound is at a premium or discount.

6 Assume that the inflation rate in the United States is expected to be 8% over the next year, while in Britain it is expected to be 3%. What is the expected change in the currency spot rate over the next year?

7 The rate of inflation in the United States is expected to be 5% over the next year while in Britain it is expected to be 9%. The rate on 1-year bills in Britain is 12%. In equilibrium, what should be the rate on 1-year U.S. Treasury bills?

8 Assume that the rate of interest is 9% in the United States and 12% in the United Kingdom and that the spot rate of exchange is $2 per pound. Determine what the forward rate of exchange should be to ensure equilibrium.

9 Assume that the spot rate of exchange is $2.00 per pound, while the forward rate is $2.10 per pound. Determine the interest rate in the United States if the U.K. rate of interest is 7%.

FUTURE VALUE COMPOUND FACTORS FOR A SINGLE CASH FLOW

Appendix I FUTURE VALUE COMPOUND FACTORS FOR A SINGLE CASH FLOW
(Future value of $1 by the end of n years)

$$FVCF_{r,n} = (1 + r)^n$$

Interest rate per year

Number of years	1%	2%	3%	4%	5%	6%	7%	8%	9%	10%	11%	12%	13%	14%	15%
1	1.010	1.020	1.030	1.040	1.050	1.060	1.070	1.080	1.090	1.100	1.110	1.120	1.130	1.140	1.150
2	1.020	1.040	1.061	1.082	1.102	1.124	1.145	1.166	1.188	1.210	1.232	1.254	1.277	1.300	1.323
3	1.030	1.061	1.093	1.125	1.158	1.191	1.225	1.260	1.295	1.331	1.368	1.405	1.443	1.482	1.521
4	1.041	1.082	1.126	1.170	1.216	1.262	1.311	1.360	1.412	1.464	1.518	1.574	1.630	1.689	1.749
5	1.051	1.104	1.159	1.217	1.276	1.338	1.403	1.469	1.539	1.611	1.685	1.762	1.842	1.925	2.011
6	1.062	1.126	1.194	1.265	1.340	1.419	1.501	1.587	1.677	1.772	1.870	1.974	2.082	2.195	2.313
7	1.072	1.149	1.230	1.316	1.407	1.504	1.606	1.714	1.828	1.949	2.076	2.211	2.353	2.502	2.660
8	1.083	1.172	1.267	1.369	1.477	1.594	1.718	1.851	1.993	2.144	2.305	2.476	2.658	2.853	3.059
9	1.094	1.195	1.305	1.423	1.551	1.689	1.838	1.999	2.172	2.358	2.558	2.773	3.004	3.252	3.518
10	1.105	1.219	1.344	1.480	1.629	1.791	1.967	2.159	2.367	2.594	2.839	3.106	3.395	3.707	4.046
11	1.116	1.243	1.384	1.539	1.710	1.898	2.105	2.332	2.580	2.853	3.152	3.479	3.836	4.226	4.652
12	1.127	1.268	1.426	1.601	1.796	2.012	2.252	2.518	2.813	3.138	3.498	3.896	4.335	4.818	5.350
13	1.138	1.294	1.469	1.665	1.886	2.133	2.410	2.720	3.066	3.452	3.883	4.363	4.898	5.492	6.153
14	1.149	1.319	1.513	1.732	1.980	2.261	2.579	2.937	3.342	3.797	4.310	4.887	5.535	6.261	7.076
15	1.161	1.346	1.558	1.801	2.079	2.397	2.759	3.172	3.642	4.177	4.785	5.474	6.254	7.138	8.137
16	1.173	1.373	1.605	1.873	2.183	2.540	2.952	3.426	3.970	4.595	5.311	6.130	7.067	8.137	9.358
17	1.184	1.400	1.653	1.948	2.292	2.693	3.159	3.700	4.328	5.054	5.895	6.866	7.986	9.276	10.76
18	1.196	1.428	1.702	2.026	2.407	2.854	3.380	3.996	4.717	5.560	6.544	7.690	9.024	10.58	12.38
19	1.208	1.457	1.754	2.107	2.527	3.026	3.617	4.316	5.142	6.116	7.263	8.613	10.20	12.06	14.23
20	1.220	1.486	1.806	2.191	2.653	3.207	3.870	4.661	5.604	6.727	8.062	9.646	11.52	13.74	16.37
25	1.282	1.641	2.094	2.666	3.386	4.292	5.427	6.848	8.623	10.83	13.59	17.00	21.23	26.46	32.92
30	1.348	1.811	2.427	3.243	4.322	5.743	7.612	10.06	13.27	17.45	22.89	29.96	39.12	50.95	66.21

Appendix I (Continued)

Interest rate per year

Number of years	16%	17%	18%	19%	20%	21%	22%	23%	24%	25%	26%	27%	28%	29%	30%
1	1.160	1.170	1.180	1.190	1.200	1.210	1.220	1.230	1.240	1.250	1.260	1.270	1.280	1.290	1.300
2	1.346	1.369	1.392	1.416	1.440	1.464	1.488	1.513	1.538	1.563	1.588	1.613	1.638	1.664	1.690
3	1.561	1.602	1.643	1.685	1.728	1.772	1.816	1.861	1.907	1.953	2.000	2.048	2.097	2.147	2.197
4	1.811	1.874	1.939	2.005	2.074	2.144	2.215	2.289	2.364	2.441	2.520	2.601	2.684	2.769	2.856
5	2.100	2.192	2.288	2.386	2.488	2.594	2.703	2.815	2.932	3.052	3.176	3.304	3.436	3.572	3.713
6	2.436	2.565	2.700	2.840	2.986	3.138	3.297	3.463	3.635	3.815	4.002	4.196	4.398	4.608	4.827
7	2.826	3.001	3.185	3.379	3.583	3.797	4.023	4.259	4.508	4.768	5.042	5.329	5.629	5.945	6.275
8	3.278	3.511	3.759	4.021	4.300	4.595	4.908	5.239	5.590	5.960	6.353	6.768	7.206	7.669	8.157
9	3.803	4.108	4.435	4.785	5.160	5.560	5.987	6.444	6.931	7.451	8.005	8.595	9.223	9.893	10.60
10	4.411	4.807	5.234	5.695	6.192	6.728	7.305	7.926	8.594	9.313	10.09	10.92	11.81	12.76	13.79
11	5.117	5.624	6.176	6.777	7.430	8.140	8.912	9.749	10.66	11.64	12.71	13.86	15.11	16.46	17.92
12	5.936	6.580	7.288	8.064	8.916	9.850	10.87	11.99	13.21	14.55	16.01	17.61	19.34	21.24	23.30
13	6.886	7.699	8.599	9.596	10.70	11.92	13.26	14.75	16.39	18.19	20.18	22.36	24.76	27.39	30.29
14	7.988	9.007	10.15	11.42	12.84	14.42	16.18	18.14	20.32	22.74	25.42	28.40	31.69	35.34	39.37
15	9.266	10.54	11.97	13.59	15.41	17.45	19.74	22.31	25.20	28.42	32.03	36.06	40.56	45.59	51.19
16	10.75	12.33	14.13	16.17	18.49	21.11	24.09	27.45	31.24	35.53	40.36	45.80	51.92	58.81	66.54
17	12.47	14.43	16.67	19.24	22.19	25.55	29.38	33.76	38.74	44.41	50.85	58.17	66.46	75.86	86.50
18	14.46	16.88	19.67	22.90	26.62	30.91	35.85	41.52	48.04	55.51	64.07	73.87	85.07	97.86	112.5
19	16.78	19.75	23.21	27.25	31.95	37.40	43.74	51.07	59.57	69.39	80.73	93.81	108.9	126.2	146.2
20	19.46	23.11	27.39	32.43	38.34	45.26	53.36	62.82	73.86	86.74	101.7	119.1	139.4	162.9	190.0
25	40.87	50.66	62.67	77.39	95.40	117.4	144.2	176.9	216.5	264.7	323.0	393.6	478.9	581.8	705.6
30	85.85	111.1	143.4	184.7	237.4	304.5	389.8	497.9	634.8	807.8	1026	1301	1646	2078	2620

E.g.: If the interest rate is 10 percent per year, the investment of $1 today will be worth $1.611 at the end of year 5.

PRESENT VALUE DISCOUNT FACTORS FOR A SINGLE CASH FLOW

Appendix II   PRESENT VALUE DISCOUNT FACTORS FOR A SINGLE CASH FLOW
(Present value of $1 to be received at the end of n years)

$$PVDF_{r,n} = \frac{1}{(1+r)^n}$$

Interest rate per year

Number of years	1%	2%	3%	4%	5%	6%	7%	8%	9%	10%	11%	12%	13%	14%	15%
1	.990	.980	.971	.962	.952	.943	.935	.926	.917	.909	.901	.893	.885	.877	.870
2	.980	.961	.943	.925	.907	.890	.873	.857	.842	.826	.812	.797	.783	.769	.756
3	.971	.942	.915	.889	.864	.840	.816	.794	.772	.751	.731	.712	.693	.675	.658
4	.961	.924	.888	.855	.823	.792	.763	.735	.708	.683	.659	.636	.613	.592	.572
5	.951	.906	.863	.822	.784	.747	.713	.681	.650	.621	.593	.567	.543	.519	.497
6	.942	.888	.837	.790	.746	.705	.666	.630	.596	.564	.535	.507	.480	.456	.432
7	.933	.871	.813	.760	.711	.665	.623	.583	.547	.513	.482	.452	.425	.400	.376
8	.923	.853	.789	.731	.677	.627	.582	.540	.502	.467	.434	.404	.376	.351	.327
9	.914	.837	.766	.703	.645	.592	.544	.500	.460	.424	.391	.361	.333	.308	.284
10	.905	.820	.744	.676	.614	.558	.508	.463	.422	.386	.352	.322	.295	.270	.247
11	.896	.804	.722	.650	.585	.527	.475	.429	.388	.350	.317	.287	.261	.237	.215
12	.887	.788	.701	.625	.557	.497	.444	.397	.356	.319	.286	.257	.231	.208	.187
13	.879	.773	.681	.601	.530	.469	.415	.368	.326	.290	.258	.229	.204	.182	.163
14	.870	.758	.661	.577	.505	.442	.388	.340	.299	.263	.232	.205	.181	.160	.141
15	.861	.743	.642	.555	.481	.417	.362	.315	.275	.239	.209	.183	.160	.140	.123
16	.853	.728	.623	.534	.458	.394	.339	.292	.252	.218	.188	.163	.141	.123	.107
17	.844	.714	.605	.513	.436	.371	.317	.270	.231	.198	.170	.146	.125	.108	.093
18	.836	.700	.587	.494	.416	.350	.296	.250	.212	.180	.153	.130	.111	.095	.081
19	.828	.686	.570	.475	.396	.331	.277	.232	.194	.164	.138	.116	.098	.083	.070
20	.820	.673	.554	.456	.377	.312	.258	.215	.178	.149	.124	.104	.087	.073	.061
25	.780	.610	.478	.375	.295	.233	.184	.146	.116	.092	.074	.059	.047	.038	.030
30	.742	.552	.412	.308	.231	.174	.131	.099	.075	.057	.044	.033	.026	.020	.015

Appendix II (Continued)

Number of years	Interest rate per year														
	16%	17%	18%	19%	20%	21%	22%	23%	24%	25%	26%	27%	28%	29%	30%
1	.862	.855	.847	.840	.833	.826	.820	.813	.806	.800	.794	.787	.781	.775	.769
2	.743	.731	.718	.706	.694	.683	.672	.661	.650	.640	.630	.620	.610	.601	.592
3	.641	.624	.609	.593	.579	.564	.551	.537	.524	.512	.500	.488	.477	.466	.455
4	.552	.534	.516	.499	.482	.467	.451	.437	.423	.410	.397	.384	.373	.361	.350
5	.476	.456	.437	.419	.402	.386	.370	.355	.341	.328	.315	.303	.291	.280	.269
6	.410	.390	.370	.352	.335	.319	.303	.289	.275	.262	.250	.238	.227	.217	.207
7	.354	.333	.314	.296	.279	.263	.249	.235	.222	.210	.198	.188	.178	.168	.159
8	.305	.285	.266	.249	.233	.218	.204	.191	.179	.168	.157	.148	.139	.130	.123
9	.263	.243	.225	.209	.194	.180	.167	.155	.144	.134	.125	.116	.108	.101	.094
10	.227	.208	.191	.176	.162	.149	.137	.126	.116	.107	.099	.092	.085	.078	.073
11	.195	.178	.162	.148	.135	.123	.112	.103	.094	.086	.079	.072	.066	.061	.056
12	.168	.152	.137	.124	.112	.102	.092	.083	.076	.069	.062	.057	.052	.047	.043
13	.145	.130	.116	.104	.093	.084	.075	.068	.061	.055	.050	.045	.040	.037	.033
14	.125	.111	.099	.088	.078	.069	.062	.055	.049	.044	.039	.035	.032	.028	.025
15	.108	.095	.084	.074	.065	.057	.051	.045	.040	.035	.031	.028	.025	.022	.020
16	.093	.081	.071	.062	.054	.047	.042	.036	.032	.028	.025	.022	.019	.017	.015
17	.080	.069	.060	.052	.045	.039	.034	.030	.026	.023	.020	.017	.015	.013	.012
18	.069	.059	.051	.044	.038	.032	.028	.024	.021	.018	.016	.014	.012	.010	.009
19	.060	.051	.043	.037	.031	.027	.023	.020	.017	.014	.012	.011	.009	.008	.007
20	.051	.043	.037	.031	.026	.022	.019	.016	.014	.012	.010	.008	.007	.006	.005
25	.024	.020	.016	.013	.010	.009	.007	.006	.005	.004	.003	.003	.002	.002	.001
30	.012	.009	.007	.005	.004	.003	.003	.002	.002	.001	.001	.001	.001	.000	.000

E.g.: If the interest rate is 10 percent per year, the present value of $1 received at the end of year 5 is $0.621.

PRESENT VALUE
ANNUITY FACTORS

Appendix III PRESENT VALUE ANNUITY FACTORS
(Present value of $1 received at the end of each year)

$$PVAF_{r,n} = \frac{1 - \dfrac{1}{(1+r)^n}}{r}$$

Interest rate per year

Number of years	1%	2%	3%	4%	5%	6%	7%	8%	9%	10%	11%	12%	13%	14%	15%
1	.990	.980	.971	.962	.952	.943	.935	.926	.917	.909	.901	.893	.885	.877	.870
2	1.970	1.942	1.913	1.886	1.859	1.833	1.808	1.783	1.759	1.736	1.713	1.690	1.668	1.647	1.626
3	2.941	2.884	2.829	2.775	2.723	2.673	2.624	2.577	2.531	2.487	2.444	2.402	2.361	2.322	2.283
4	3.902	3.808	3.717	3.630	3.546	3.465	3.387	3.312	3.240	3.170	3.102	3.037	2.974	2.914	2.855
5	4.853	4.713	4.580	4.452	4.329	4.212	4.100	3.993	3.890	3.791	3.696	3.605	3.517	3.433	3.352
6	5.795	5.601	5.417	5.242	5.076	4.917	4.767	4.623	4.486	4.355	4.231	4.111	3.998	3.889	3.784
7	6.728	6.472	6.230	6.002	5.786	5.582	5.389	5.206	5.033	4.868	4.712	4.564	4.423	4.288	4.160
8	7.652	7.325	7.020	6.733	6.463	6.210	5.971	5.747	5.535	5.335	5.146	4.968	4.799	4.639	4.487
9	8.566	8.162	7.786	7.435	7.108	6.802	6.515	6.247	5.995	5.759	5.537	5.328	5.132	4.946	4.772
10	9.471	8.983	8.530	8.111	7.722	7.360	7.024	6.710	6.418	6.145	5.889	5.650	5.426	5.216	5.019
11	10.37	9.787	9.253	8.760	8.306	7.887	7.499	7.139	6.805	6.495	6.207	5.938	5.687	5.453	5.234
12	11.26	10.58	9.954	9.385	8.863	8.384	7.943	7.536	7.161	6.814	6.492	6.194	5.918	5.660	5.421
13	12.13	11.35	10.63	9.986	9.394	8.853	8.358	7.904	7.487	7.103	6.750	6.424	6.122	5.842	5.583
14	13.00	12.11	11.30	10.56	9.899	9.295	8.745	8.244	7.786	7.367	6.982	6.628	6.302	6.002	5.724
15	13.87	12.85	11.94	11.12	10.38	9.712	9.108	8.559	8.061	7.606	7.191	6.811	6.462	6.142	5.847
16	14.72	13.58	12.56	11.65	10.84	10.11	9.447	8.851	8.313	7.824	7.379	6.974	6.604	6.265	5.954
17	15.56	14.29	13.17	12.17	11.27	10.48	9.763	9.122	8.544	8.022	7.549	7.120	6.729	6.373	6.047
18	16.40	14.99	13.75	12.66	11.69	10.83	10.06	9.372	8.756	8.201	7.702	7.250	6.840	6.467	6.128
19	17.23	15.68	14.32	13.13	12.09	11.16	10.34	9.604	8.950	8.365	7.839	7.366	6.938	6.550	6.198
20	18.05	16.35	14.88	13.59	12.46	11.47	10.59	9.818	9.129	8.514	7.963	7.469	7.025	6.623	6.259
25	22.02	19.52	17.41	15.62	14.09	12.78	11.65	10.67	9.823	9.077	8.422	7.843	7.330	6.873	6.464
30	25.81	22.40	19.60	17.29	15.37	13.76	12.41	11.26	10.27	9.427	8.694	8.055	7.496	7.003	6.566

Appendix III (Continued)

Interest rate per year

Number of years	16%	17%	18%	19%	20%	21%	22%	23%	24%	25%	26%	27%	28%	29%	30%
1	.862	.855	.847	.840	.833	.826	.820	.813	.806	.800	.794	.787	.781	.775	.769
2	1.605	1.585	1.566	1.547	1.528	1.509	1.492	1.474	1.457	1.440	1.424	1.407	1.392	1.376	1.361
3	2.246	2.210	2.174	2.140	2.106	2.074	2.042	2.011	1.981	1.952	1.923	1.896	1.868	1.842	1.816
4	2.798	2.743	2.690	2.639	2.589	2.540	2.494	2.448	2.404	2.362	2.320	2.280	2.241	2.203	2.166
5	3.274	3.199	3.127	3.058	2.991	2.926	2.864	2.803	2.745	2.689	2.635	2.583	2.532	2.483	2.436
6	3.685	3.589	3.498	3.410	3.326	3.245	3.167	3.092	3.020	2.951	2.885	2.821	2.759	2.700	2.643
7	4.039	3.922	3.812	3.706	3.605	3.508	3.416	3.327	3.242	3.161	3.083	3.009	2.937	2.868	2.802
8	4.344	4.207	4.078	3.954	3.837	3.726	3.619	3.518	3.421	3.329	3.241	3.156	3.076	2.999	2.925
9	4.607	4.451	4.303	4.163	4.031	3.905	3.786	3.673	3.566	3.463	3.366	3.273	3.184	3.100	3.019
10	4.833	4.659	4.494	4.339	4.192	4.054	3.923	3.799	3.682	3.571	3.465	3.364	3.269	3.178	3.092
11	5.029	4.836	4.656	4.486	4.327	4.177	4.035	3.902	3.776	3.656	3.543	3.437	3.335	3.239	3.147
12	5.197	4.988	4.793	4.611	4.439	4.278	4.127	3.985	3.851	3.725	3.606	3.493	3.387	3.286	3.190
13	5.342	5.118	4.910	4.715	4.533	4.362	4.203	4.053	3.912	3.780	3.656	3.538	3.427	3.322	3.223
14	5.468	5.229	5.008	4.802	4.611	4.432	4.265	4.108	3.962	3.824	3.695	3.573	3.459	3.351	3.249
15	5.575	5.324	5.092	4.876	4.675	4.489	4.315	4.153	4.001	3.859	3.726	3.601	3.483	3.373	3.268
16	5.668	5.405	5.162	4.938	4.730	4.536	4.357	4.189	4.033	3.887	3.751	3.623	3.503	3.390	3.283
17	5.749	5.475	5.222	4.990	4.775	4.576	4.391	4.219	4.059	3.910	3.771	3.640	3.518	3.403	3.295
18	5.818	5.534	5.273	5.033	4.812	4.608	4.419	4.243	4.080	3.928	3.786	3.654	3.529	3.413	3.304
19	5.877	5.584	5.316	5.070	4.843	4.635	4.442	4.263	4.097	3.942	3.799	3.664	3.539	3.421	3.311
20	5.929	5.628	5.353	5.101	4.870	4.657	4.460	4.279	4.110	3.954	3.808	3.673	3.546	3.427	3.316
25	6.097	5.766	5.467	5.195	4.948	4.721	4.514	4.323	4.147	3.985	3.834	3.694	3.564	3.442	3.329
30	6.177	5.829	5.517	5.235	4.979	4.746	4.534	4.339	4.160	3.995	3.842	3.701	3.569	3.447	3.332

E.g.: If the interest rate is 10 percent per year, the present value of $1 received at the end of each of the next 5 years is $3.791.

FUTURE VALUE ANNUITY FACTOR

Appendix IV FUTURE VALUE ANNUITY FACTOR

(Future value of $1 invested at the beginning of each year for n years)

$$FVAF_{r,n} = \frac{(1+r)\,[(1+r)^n - 1]}{r}$$

rate per year

Number of years	1%	2%	3%	4%	5%	6%	7%	8%	9%	10%	11%	12%	13%	14%	15%
1	1.010	1.020	1.030	1.040	1.050	1.060	1.070	1.080	1.090	1.100	1.110	1.120	1.130	1.140	1.150
2	2.030	2.060	2.091	2.122	2.153	2.184	2.215	2.246	2.278	2.310	2.342	2.374	2.407	2.440	2.473
3	3.060	3.122	3.184	3.246	3.310	3.375	3.440	3.506	3.573	3.641	3.710	3.779	3.850	3.921	3.993
4	4.101	4.204	4.309	4.416	4.526	4.637	4.751	4.867	4.985	5.105	5.228	5.353	5.480	5.610	5.742
5	5.152	5.308	5.468	5.633	5.802	5.975	6.153	6.336	6.523	6.716	6.913	7.115	7.323	7.536	7.754
6	6.214	6.434	6.662	6.898	7.142	7.394	7.654	7.923	8.200	8.487	8.783	9.089	9.405	9.730	10.067
7	7.286	7.583	7.892	8.214	8.549	8.897	9.260	9.637	10.028	10.436	10.859	11.300	11.757	12.233	12.727
8	8.369	8.755	9.159	9.583	10.027	10.491	10.978	11.488	12.021	12.579	13.164	13.776	14.416	15.085	15.785
9	9.462	9.950	10.464	11.006	11.578	12.181	12.816	13.487	14.193	14.937	15.722	16.549	17.420	18.337	19.304
10	10.567	11.169	11.808	12.486	13.207	13.972	14.784	15.645	16.560	17.531	18.561	19.655	20.814	22.045	23.349
11	11.683	12.412	13.192	14.026	14.917	15.870	16.888	17.977	19.141	20.384	21.713	23.133	24.650	26.271	28.002
12	12.809	13.680	14.618	15.627	16.713	17.882	19.141	20.495	21.953	23.523	25.212	27.029	28.985	31.089	33.352
13	13.947	14.947	16.086	17.292	18.599	20.015	21.550	23.215	25.019	26.975	29.095	31.393	33.883	36.581	39.505
14	15.097	16.293	17.599	19.024	20.579	22.276	24.129	26.152	28.361	30.772	33.405	36.280	39.417	42.842	46.580
15	16.258	17.639	19.157	20.825	22.657	24.673	26.888	29.324	32.003	34.950	38.190	41.753	45.672	49.980	54.717
16	17.430	19.012	20.762	22.698	24.840	27.213	29.840	32.750	35.974	39.545	43.501	47.884	52.739	58.118	64.075
17	18.615	20.412	22.414	24.645	27.132	29.906	32.999	36.450	40.301	44.599	49.396	54.750	60.725	67.394	74.836
18	19.811	21.841	24.117	26.671	29.539	32.760	36.379	40.446	45.018	50.159	55.939	62.440	69.749	77.969	87.212
19	21.019	23.297	25.870	28.778	32.066	35.786	39.995	44.762	50.160	56.275	63.203	71.052	79.947	90.025	101.44
20	22.239	24.783	27.676	30.969	34.719	38.993	43.865	49.423	55.765	63.002	71.265	80.699	91.470	103.77	117.81
25	28.526	32.671	37.553	43.312	50.113	58.156	67.676	78.954	92.324	108.18	127.00	149.33	175.85	207.33	244.71
30	35.133	41.379	49.003	58.328	69.761	83.802	101.07	122.35	148.58	180.94	220.91	270.29	331.32	406.74	499.96

Appendix IV (Continued)

rate per year

Number of years	16%	17%	18%	19%	20%	21%	22%	23%	24%	25%	26%	27%	28%	29%	30%
1	1.160	1.170	1.180	1.190	1.200	1.210	1.220	1.230	1.240	1.250	1.260	1.270	1.280	1.290	1.300
2	2.506	2.539	2.572	2.606	2.640	2.674	2.708	2.743	2.778	2.813	2.848	2.883	2.918	2.954	2.990
3	4.066	4.414	4.215	4.291	4.368	4.446	4.524	4.604	4.684	4.766	4.848	4.931	5.016	5.101	5.187
4	5.877	6.014	6.154	6.297	6.442	6.589	6.740	6.893	7.048	7.207	7.368	7.533	7.700	7.870	8.043
5	7.977	8.207	8.442	8.683	8.930	9.183	9.442	9.708	9.980	10.259	10.544	10.837	11.136	11.442	11.756
6	10.414	10.772	11.142	11.523	11.916	12.321	12.740	13.171	13.615	14.073	14.546	15.032	15.534	16.051	16.583
7	13.240	13.773	14.327	14.902	15.499	16.119	16.762	17.430	18.123	18.842	19.588	20.361	21.163	21.995	22.858
8	16.519	17.285	18.086	18.923	19.799	20.714	21.670	22.669	23.712	24.802	25.940	27.129	28.369	29.664	31.015
9	20.321	21.393	22.521	23.709	24.959	26.274	27.657	29.113	30.643	32.253	33.945	35.723	37.593	39.556	41.619
10	24.733	26.200	27.755	29.404	31.150	33.001	34.962	37.039	39.238	41.566	44.031	46.639	49.398	52.318	55.405
11	29.850	31.824	33.931	36.180	38.581	41.142	43.874	46.788	49.895	53.208	56.739	60.501	64.510	68.780	73.327
12	35.786	38.404	41.219	44.244	47.497	50.991	54.746	58.779	63.110	67.760	72.751	78.107	83.853	90.016	96.625
13	42.672	46.103	49.818	53.841	58.196	62.909	68.010	73.528	79.496	85.949	92.926	100.47	108.61	117.41	126.91
14	50.660	55.110	59.965	65.261	71.035	77.330	84.192	91.669	99.815	108.69	118.35	128.86	140.30	152.75	166.29
15	59.925	65.649	71.939	78.850	86.442	94.780	103.93	113.98	125.01	137.11	150.38	164.92	180.87	198.34	217.47
16	70.673	77.979	86.068	95.022	104.93	115.89	128.02	141.43	156.25	172.64	190.73	210.72	232.79	257.15	284.01
17	83.141	92.406	102.74	114.27	127.12	141.44	157.40	175.19	194.99	217.04	241.59	268.89	299.25	333.01	370.52
18	97.603	109.28	122.41	137.17	153.74	172.35	193.25	216.71	243.03	272.56	305.66	342.76	384.32	430.87	482.97
19	114.38	129.03	145.63	164.42	185.69	209.76	236.99	267.79	302.60	341.94	386.39	436.57	493.21	557.11	629.17
20	133.84	152.14	173.02	196.85	224.03	255.02	290.35	330.61	376.46	428.68	488.11	555.72	632.59	719.96	819.22
25	289.09	341.76	404.27	478.43	566.38	670.13	794.17	940.46	1136.6	1318.6	1560.7	1846.8	2184.7	2583.4	3053.4
30	615.16	757.50	933.32	1150.4	1418.3	1748.6	2155.8	2657.4	3274.7	4034.0	4967.0	6112.5	7517.7	9240.0	11349.0

E.g.: If the interest rate is 10% per year, the future value of $1 invested at the beginning of each year for 5 years will be $6.716 at the end of the fifth year.

STANDARD AND POOR'S 500: ANNUAL DATA

Appendix V   STANDARD AND POOR'S 500: ANNUAL DATA

	Price						*Book	Annual
Year	High	Low	Avg.	Year end	EPS	Dividends	value	return
1926	13.66	10.93	12.59	13.49	1.24	0.69	n/a	0.1162
1927	17.71	13.18	15.34	17.66	1.11	0.77		0.3749
1928	24.35	16.95	19.95	24.35	1.38	0.85		0.4361
1929	31.92	17.66	26.02	21.45	1.61	0.97		(0.0842)
1930	25.92	14.44	21.03	15.34	0.97	0.98		(0.2490)
1931	18.17	7.72	13.66	8.12	0.61	0.82		(0.4334)
1932	9.31	4.40	6.93	6.89	0.41	0.50		(0.0819)
1933	12.20	5.53	8.96	10.10	0.44	0.44		0.5399
1934	11.82	8.36	9.84	9.50	0.49	0.45		(0.0144)
1935	13.46	8.06	10.60	13.43	0.76	0.47		0.4767
1936	17.69	13.40	15.47	17.18	1.02	0.72		0.3392
1937	18.68	10.17	15.41	10.55	1.13	0.80		(0.3503)
1938	13.79	8.50	11.49	13.21	0.64	0.51		0.3112
1939	13.23	10.18	12.06	12.49	0.90	0.62		(0.0041)
1940	12.77	8.99	11.02	10.58	1.05	0.67		(0.0978)
1941	10.86	8.37	9.82	8.69	1.16	0.71		(0.1159)
1942	9.77	7.47	8.67	9.77	1.03	0.59		0.2034
1943	12.64	9.84	11.50	11.67	0.94	0.61		0.2590
1944	13.29	11.56	12.47	13.28	0.93	0.64		0.1975
1945	17.68	13.21	15.16	17.36	0.96	0.66		0.3644
1946	19.25	14.12	17.08	15.30	1.06	0.71	11.19	(0.0807)
1947	16.20	13.71	15.17	15.30	1.61	0.84	12.49	0.0571
1948	17.06	13.84	15.53	15.20	2.29	0.93	14.53	0.0550
1949	16.79	13.55	15.23	16.76	2.32	1.14	15.17	0.1879
1950	20.43	16.65	18.40	20.41	2.84	1.47	16.77	0.3171
1951	23.85	20.69	22.34	23.77	2.44	1.41	18.66	0.2402
1952	26.59	23.09	24.50	26.57	2.40	1.41	20.15	0.1837
1953	26.66	22.71	24.73	24.81	2.51	1.45	20.76	(0.0099)
1954	35.98	24.80	29.69	35.98	2.77	1.54	22.09	0.5262
1955	46.41	34.58	40.49	45.48	3.62	1.64	25.09	0.3156
1956	49.74	43.11	46.62	46.67	3.41	1.74	26.35	0.0656
1957	49.13	38.98	44.38	39.99	3.37	1.79	29.44	(0.1078)
1958	55.21	40.33	46.24	55.21	2.89	1.75	30.66	0.4336
1959	60.71	53.58	57.38	59.89	3.39	1.83	32.26	0.1195
1960	60.39	52.30	55.85	58.11	3.27	1.95	33.74	0.0047
1961	72.64	57.57	66.27	71.55	3.19	2.02	34.85	0.2689
1962	71.13	52.32	62.38	63.10	3.67	2.13	36.37	(0.0873)
1963	75.02	62.69	69.87	75.02	4.02	2.28	38.17	0.2280
1964	86.28	75.43	81.37	84.75	4.55	2.50	40.23	0.1648
1965	92.63	81.60	88.17	92.43	5.19	2.72	43.50	0.1245
1966	94.06	73.20	85.26	80.33	5.55	2.87	45.59	(0.1006)
1967	97.59	80.38	91.93	96.47	5.33	2.92	47.78	0.2398
1968*	108.37	87.72	98.70	103.86	5.76	3.07	50.21	0.1106
1969	106.16	89.20	97.84	92.06	5.78	3.16	51.70	(0.0850)
1970	93.46	69.29	83.22	92.15	5.13	3.14	52.65	0.0401
1971	104.77	90.16	98.29	102.09	5.70	3.07	55.28	0.1431
1972	119.12	101.67	109.20	118.05	6.42	3.15	58.34	0.1898
1973	120.24	92.16	107.43	97.55	8.16	3.38	62.84	(0.1466)

Appendix V   (Continued)

Year	Price High	Price Low	Price Avg.	Price Year end	EPS	Dividends	*Book value	Annual return
1974	99.80	62.28	82.85	68.56	8.89	3.60	67.81	(0.2647)
1975	95.61	70.04	86.16	90.19	7.96	3.68	70.84	0.3720
1976	107.83	90.90	102.01	107.46	9.91	4.05	76.26	0.2384
1977	107.00	90.71	98.20	95.10	10.89	4.67	82.21	(0.0718)
1978	106.99	86.90	96.02	96.11	12.33	5.07	89.72	0.0656
1979	111.27	96.13	103.01	107.94	14.86	5.65	98.71	0.1844
1980	140.52	98.22	118.78	135.76	14.82	6.16	108.30	0.3242
1981	138.12	112.77	128.05	122.55	15.24	6.63	116.10	(0.0491)
1982	143.00	102.40	119.70	140.60	12.64	6.87	118.60	0.2141
1983	172.70	138.30	160.40	164.90	14.03	7.09	122.32	0.2251
1984	170.41	147.82	160.46	167.24	16.64	7.38	123.28	0.0627

*Book value pertains only to S&P 400.

STANDARD AND POOR'S
500: QUARTERLY DATA

Appendix VI   STANDARD AND POOR'S 500: QUARTERLY DATA

Qtr.	Price High	Low	Avg.	Qtr. end	EPS	Dividends	Qrtrly return
1936							
I	15.10	13.40	14.39	14.92	0.21	0.13	0.120
II	15.51	13.53	14.55	14.84	0.28	0.14	0.008
III	16.29	14.81	15.83	16.01	0.21	0.15	0.090
IV	17.69	16.04	17.10	17.18	0.32	0.18	0.089
1937							
I	18.68	16.93	17.93	17.92	0.30	0.19	0.051
II	17.71	15.12	16.30	15.40	0.34	0.21	−0.129
III	17.32	13.09	15.89	13.76	0.26	0.19	−0.096
IV	13.76	10.17	11.50	10.55	0.23	0.20	−0.214
1938							
I	11.95	8.50	10.89	8.50	0.14	0.20	−0.185
II	11.72	8.91	10.03	11.56	0.14	0.19	0.384
III	12.81	10.99	12.10	12.24	0.11	0.17	0.068
IV	13.79	12.32	12.94	13.21	0.25	0.13	0.090
1939							
I	13.23	10.98	12.43	10.98	0.21	0.13	−0.160
II	11.80	10.18	11.16	10.86	0.19	0.13	0.005
III	13.17	10.86	12.01	13.02	0.16	0.14	0.212
IV	13.21	12.19	12.65	12.49	0.34	0.16	−0.026
1940							
I	12.77	12.00	12.22	12.25	0.30	0.16	−0.008
II	12.59	8.99	10.84	9.98	0.24	0.16	−0.168
III	10.93	9.84	10.27	10.66	0.20	0.17	0.083
IV	11.40	10.38	10.75	10.58	0.31	0.17	0.010
1941							
I	10.86	9.53	10.13	9.96	0.31	0.17	−0.045
II	10.16	9.30	9.61	9.85	0.27	0.17	0.011
III	10.47	9.82	10.24	10.20	0.30	0.18	0.052
IV	10.17	8.37	9.32	8.69	0.28	0.18	−0.129
1942							
I	9.09	7.98	8.59	8.01	0.19	0.17	−0.065
II	8.53	7.47	8.03	8.30	0.21	0.17	0.059
III	8.90	8.23	8.64	8.85	0.26	0.16	0.081
IV	9.77	8.92	9.44	9.77	0.37	0.15	0.124
1943							
I	11.59	9.84	10.62	11.58	0.23	0.15	0.198
II	12.35	11.14	11.81	12.35	0.24	0.15	0.083
III	12.64	11.47	12.03	12.08	0.24	0.15	−0.011
IV	12.09	10.99	11.56	11.67	0.23	0.15	−0.018
1944							
I	12.31	11.56	11.91	12.02	0.22	0.16	0.041
II	13.02	11.67	12.22	12.98	0.23	0.16	0.096
III	13.27	12.35	12.80	12.78	0.22	0.16	−0.004
IV	13.29	12.67	12.94	13.28	0.26	0.16	0.051

Appendix VI   (Continued)

Qtr.	High	Low	Avg.	Qtr. end	EPS	Dividends	Qrtrly return
1945							
I	14.38	13.21	13.79	13.64	0.25	0.16	0.037
II	15.37	13.67	14.73	14.96	0.27	0.16	0.111
III	16.16	14.38	15.15	16.16	0.21	0.17	0.091
IV	17.68	16.30	16.96	17.36	0.23	0.17	0.086
1946							
I	18.71	16.81	17.87	18.08	0.19	0.17	0.051
II	19.25	18.03	18.65	18.43	0.21	0.17	0.030
III	18.54	14.33	16.95	14.96	0.26	0.17	−0.180
IV	15.54	14.12	14.86	15.30	0.40	0.18	0.037
1947							
I	16.20	14.77	15.39	15.17	0.40	0.18	0.002
II	15.24	14.09	14.59	15.21	0.38	0.19	0.019
III	16.12	14.85	15.43	15.11	0.37	0.20	0.006
IV	15.79	14.61	15.25	15.30	0.46	0.21	0.029
1948							
I	15.34	13.84	14.41	15.08	0.50	0.21	−0.001
II	17.06	15.12	16.12	16.74	0.53	0.21	0.126
III	16.92	15.19	16.04	15.49	0.58	0.22	−0.062
IV	16.70	14.75	15.56	15.20	0.68	0.23	0.002
1949							
I	15.62	14.38	15.01	15.06	0.59	0.25	0.006
II	15.07	13.55	14.55	14.16	0.55	0.26	−0.041
III	15.74	14.26	15.18	15.58	0.57	0.26	0.117
IV	16.79	15.52	16.18	16.76	0.61	0.29	0.103
1950							
I	17.61	16.65	17.15	17.29	0.64	0.29	0.047
II	19.40	17.34	18.34	17.69	0.72	0.30	0.042
III	19.45	16.68	18.30	19.45	0.75	0.33	0.119
IV	20.43	19.00	19.82	20.41	0.73	0.37	0.079
1951							
I	22.21	20.69	21.61	21.40	0.63	0.38	0.064
II	22.81	20.96	21.80	20.96	0.61	0.39	−0.003
III	23.71	21.10	22.77	23.26	0.54	0.38	0.124
IV	23.85	22.30	23.16	23.77	0.66	0.35	0.042
1952							
I	24.66	23.09	23.92	24.37	0.59	0.36	0.039
II	24.96	23.17	23.95	24.96	0.55	0.36	0.041
III	25.55	24.45	25.01	24.54	0.56	0.36	−0.005
IV	26.59	23.80	25.11	26.57	0.70	0.35	0.100
1953							
I	26.66	25.29	26.01	25.29	0.62	0.35	−0.036
II	25.25	23.54	24.50	24.14	0.63	0.36	−0.029
III	24.84	22.71	23.98	23.35	0.60	0.36	−0.020
IV	24.99	23.39	24.43	24.81	0.66	0.36	0.081

Appendix VI (Continued)

Qtr.	Price High	Low	Avg.	Qtr. end	EPS	Dividends	Qrtrly return
1954							
I	26.94	24.80	26.02	26.94	0.66	0.37	0.100
II	29.43	27.01	28.44	29.21	0.70	0.36	0.099
III	32.69	29.21	30.77	32.31	0.61	0.37	0.117
IV	35.98	31.68	33.53	35.98	0.80	0.39	0.130
1955							
I	37.52	34.58	36.30	36.58	0.85	0.39	0.027
II	41.03	36.83	38.38	41.03	0.96	0.39	0.133
III	45.63	41.19	43.15	43.67	0.83	0.41	0.073
IV	46.41	40.80	44.14	45.48	0.98	0.41	0.054
1956							
I	48.87	43.11	45.36	48.48	0.92	0.43	0.077
II	48.85	44.10	46.95	46.97	0.87	0.45	− 0.021
III	49.74	45.35	48.04	45.35	0.69	0.46	− 0.026
IV	47.60	44.38	46.15	46.67	0.93	0.44	0.039
1957							
I	46.66	42.39	44.31	44.11	0.91	0.43	− 0.045
II	48.24	44.14	46.46	47.37	0.89	0.43	0.085
III	49.13	42.42	46.11	42.42	0.74	0.44	− 0.095
IV	43.14	38.98	40.64	39.99	0.83	0.45	− 0.046
1958							
I	42.58	40.33	41.50	42.10	0.68	0.44	0.064
II	45.34	41.33	43.60	45.24	0.68	0.43	0.085
III	50.06	45.11	47.55	50.06	0.69	0.44	0.117
IV	55.21	49.98	52.31	55.21	0.84	0.44	0.113
1959							
I	56.67	53.58	55.51	55.44	0.90	0.44	0.012
II	58.68	55.69	57.51	58.47	0.97	0.45	0.063
III	60.71	55.14	58.73	56.88	0.72	0.45	− 0.019
IV	59.89	56.00	57.76	59.89	0.80	0.46	0.062
1960							
I	60.39	53.47	56.28	55.34	0.90	0.49	− 0.067
II	58.00	54.13	56.07	56.92	0.84	0.49	0.037
III	58.07	52.48	55.72	53.52	0.73	0.49	− 0.051
IV	58.11	52.30	55.33	58.11	0.80	0.49	0.096
1961							
I	65.06	57.57	62.00	65.06	0.72	0.49	0.128
II	67.39	64.40	65.98	64.64	0.78	0.49	0.001
III	68.46	64.41	66.83	66.73	0.75	0.49	0.040
IV	72.64	66.73	70.27	71.55	0.94	0.51	0.081
1962							
I	71.13	67.90	69.86	69.55	0.90	0.51	− 0.020
II	69.37	52.32	62.22	54.75	0.88	0.52	− 0.206
III	59.78	55.77	57.83	56.27	0.81	0.52	0.037
IV	63.10	53.49	59.62	63.10	1.08	0.53	0.133

Appendix VI   (Continued)

Qtr.	Price High	Price Low	Price Avg.	Qtr. end	EPS	Dividends	Qrtrly return
1963							
I	66.68	62.69	65.55	66.57	0.94	0.54	0.063
II	70.80	66.84	69.67	69.37	1.01	0.55	0.050
III	73.30	67.90	70.97	71.70	0.93	0.55	0.041
IV	75.02	69.61	73.27	75.02	1.14	0.57	0.056
1964							
I	79.38	75.43	77.55	78.98	1.10	0.58	0.061
II	81.69	78.64	80.30	81.69	1.16	0.60	0.042
III	84.28	81.32	82.88	84.18	1.07	0.61	0.038
IV	86.28	83.22	84.75	84.75	1.22	0.63	0.016
1965							
I	87.63	84.23	86.57	86.16	1.23	0.64	0.024
II	90.27	81.60	87.43	84.12	1.32	0.65	−0.016
III	90.65	83.85	86.93	89.96	1.21	0.67	0.077
IV	92.63	89.90	91.76	92.43	1.43	0.68	0.037
1966							
I	94.06	87.35	91.63	89.23	1.38	0.70	−0.027
II	92.42	83.63	88.15	84.74	1.44	0.71	−0.042
III	87.61	74.53	81.43	76.56	1.26	0.72	−0.088
IV	83.00	73.20	79.82	80.33	1.47	0.72	0.060
1967							
I	90.94	80.38	87.08	90.20	1.28	0.73	0.132
II	94.58	88.24	91.66	90.64	1.32	0.73	0.013
III	97.59	90.91	94.44	96.71	1.23	0.73	0.075
IV	97.51	91.14	94.54	96.47	1.50	0.73	0.006
1968							
I	96.72	87.72	91.63	90.20	1.39	0.74	−0.057
II	101.66	92.48	98.02	99.58	1.45	0.75	0.112
III	102.67	96.63	99.92	102.67	1.32	0.76	0.039
IV	108.37	102.86	105.23	103.86	1.60	0.77	0.020
1969							
I	103.99	97.98	100.93	101.51	1.45	0.78	−0.014
II	106.16	96.23	101.67	97.71	1.47	0.78	−0.003
III	99.61	89.48	94.47	93.12	1.37	0.79	−0.039
IV	98.33	89.20	94.28	92.06	1.49	0.79	−0.003
1970							
I	93.46	85.02	88.71	89.63	1.30	0.79	−0.017
II	90.07	69.29	79.20	72.72	1.36	0.80	−0.180
III	84.30	71.23	78.74	84.21	1.21	0.80	0.169
IV	92.27	82.79	86.23	92.15	1.26	0.79	0.104
1971							
I	101.21	91.15	96.73	100.31	1.39	0.78	0.097
II	104.77	97.59	101.47	99.70	1.46	0.78	0.002
III	101.34	93.53	98.55	98.34	1.32	0.77	−0.006
IV	102.21	90.16	96.41	102.09	1.53	0.77	0.047

Appendix VI   (Continued)

Qtr.	Price High	Low	Avg.	Qtr. end	EPS	Dividends	Qrtrly return
1972							
I	108.96	101.67	105.41	107.20	1.50	0.77	0.057
II	110.66	104.74	108.16	107.14	1.62	0.77	0.007
III	112.55	105.81	109.20	110.55	1.49	0.77	0.039
IV	119.12	106.77	114.04	118.05	1.81	0.79	0.076
1973							
I	120.24	108.84	115.00	111.52	1.88	0.79	−0.048
II	112.68	102.25	107.41	104.26	2.05	0.81	−0.057
III	109.85	100.53	105.08	108.43	1.95	0.82	0.048
IV	111.44	92.16	102.22	97.55	2.28	0.85	−0.091
1974							
I	99.80	90.66	95.67	93.98	2.08	0.86	−0.028
II	94.78	86.00	90.64	86.00	2.43	0.88	−0.075
III	86.02	63.54	75.66	63.54	2.32	0.90	−0.215
IV	75.21	62.28	69.42	68.56	2.06	0.90	0.094
1975							
I	86.01	70.04	78.81	83.36	1.64	0.92	0.229
II	95.19	80.35	89.07	95.19	1.94	0.93	0.154
III	95.61	82.09	87.62	83.87	2.12	0.93	−0.109
IV	91.46	82.93	89.11	90.19	2.26	0.92	0.086
1976							
I	103.42	90.90	99.53	102.77	2.34	0.92	0.150
II	104.28	98.63	101.62	104.28	2.53	0.94	0.025
III	107.83	101.27	104.31	105.24	2.42	0.96	0.019
IV	107.46	98.81	102.58	107.46	2.62	1.01	0.031
1977							
I	107.00	98.42	101.78	98.42	2.51	1.05	−0.074
II	101.19	96.12	99.03	100.48	2.87	1.09	0.033
III	101.79	95.04	98.05	96.53	2.71	1.13	−0.028
IV	96.74	90.71	93.95	95.10	2.80	1.17	−0.001
1978							
I	93.82	86.90	89.35	89.21	2.54	1.20	−0.049
II	100.32	88.46	95.93	95.53	3.18	1.23	0.085
III	106.99	94.27	101.66	102.54	3.05	1.26	0.087
IV	105.39	92.49	97.13	96.11	3.56	1.27	−0.049
1979							
I	102.48	96.13	99.35	101.59	3.51	1.30	0.071
II	103.34	98.06	101.18	102.91	3.86	1.34	0.027
III	110.51	101.59	106.22	109.32	3.70	1.38	0.075
IV	111.27	99.87	105.30	107.94	3.79	1.41	0.001
1980							
I	118.44	98.22	110.30	102.09	3.94	1.45	−0.040
II	116.72	99.20	108.40	114.24	3.51	1.49	0.134
III	130.40	114.93	123.28	125.46	3.40	1.52	0.112
IV	140.52	126.29	133.12	135.76	3.97	1.54	0.095

Appendix VI   (Continued)

Qtr.	Price				EPS	Dividends	Qrtrly return
	High	Low	Avg.	Qtr. end			
1981							
I	138.12	126.58	131.52	136.00	3.70	1.57	0.013
II	136.57	129.71	132.81	131.21	3.94	1.60	− 0.023
III	133.85	112.77	125.68	116.18	3.66	1.63	− 0.102
IV	126.35	117.08	122.17	122.55	4.06	1.66	0.070
1982							
I	122.70	107.30	114.20	112.00	3.15	1.68	− 0.072
II	119.50	107.20	114.13	109.60	3.30	1.70	− 0.006
III	124.90	102.40	113.83	120.40	3.05	1.71	0.1146
IV	143.00	121.50	136.73	140.60	3.14	1.72	0.1814
1983							
I	153.70	138.30	147.67	153.00	2.93	1.73	0.1005
II	171.00	151.00	162.73	168.10	3.47	1.74	0.1111
III	170.40	159.20	165.53	166.00	3.76	1.75	− 0.001
IV	172.70	161.70	165.77	164.90	3.87	1.77	0.0034
1984							
I	169.28	154.29	160.36	159.18	4.16	1.80	− 0.023
II	161.90	149.03	155.76	153.18	4.41	1.83	− 0.026
III	168.87	147.82	160.54	166.10	4.12	1.85	0.0968
IV	170.41	161.67	165.19	167.24	3.95	1.88	0.0176

STANDARD AND POOR'S 500: MONTHLY RETURNS

Appendix VII STANDARD AND POOR'S 500: MONTHLY RETURNS

Month	Year									
	1926	**1927**	**1928**	**1929**	**1930**	**1931**	**1932**	**1933**	**1934**	**1935**
Jan.	0.0000	−0.0193	−0.0040	0.0583	0.0639	0.0502	−0.0271	0.0087	0.1069	−0.0411
Feb.	−0.0385	0.0537	−0.0125	−0.0019	0.0259	0.1193	0.0570	−0.1772	−0.0322	−0.0341
Mar.	−0.0575	0.0087	0.1101	−0.0012	0.0812	−0.0675	−0.1158	0.0353	0.0000	−0.0286
April	0.0253	0.0201	0.0345	0.0176	−0.0080	−0.0935	−0.1997	0.4256	−0.0251	0.0980
May	0.0179	0.0607	0.0197	−0.0362	−0.0096	−0.1279	−0.2196	0.1683	−0.0736	0.0409
June	0.0457	−0.0067	−0.0385	0.1140	−0.1625	0.1421	−0.0022	0.1338	0.0229	0.0699
July	0.0479	0.0670	0.0141	0.0471	0.0386	−0.0722	0.3815	−0.0862	−0.1131	0.0850
Aug.	0.0248	0.0515	0.0803	0.1028	0.0141	0.0182	0.3869	0.1206	0.0611	0.0280
Sept.	0.0252	0.0450	0.0259	−0.0476	−0.1282	−0.2973	−0.0346	−0.1118	−0.0033	0.0256
Oct.	−0.0284	−0.0502	0.0168	−0.1973	−0.0855	0.0896	−0.1349	−0.0855	−0.0286	0.0777
Nov.	0.0347	0.0721	0.1292	−0.1246	−0.0089	−0.0798	−0.0417	0.1127	0.0942	0.0474
Dec.	0.0196	0.0279	0.0049	0.0282	−0.0706	−0.1400	0.0565	0.0253	−0.0010	0.0394

	1936	**1937**	**1938**	**1939**	**1940**	**1941**	**1942**	**1943**	**1944**	**1945**
Jan.	0.0670	0.0390	0.0152	−0.0674	−0.0336	−0.0463	0.0161	0.0737	0.0171	0.0158
Feb.	0.0224	0.0191	0.0674	0.0390	0.0133	−0.0060	−0.0159	0.0583	0.0042	0.0683
Mar.	0.0268	−0.0077	−0.2487	−0.1339	0.0124	0.0071	−0.0652	0.0545	0.0195	−0.0441
Apr.	−0.0751	−0.0809	0.1447	−0.0027	−0.0024	−0.0612	−0.0400	0.0035	−0.0100	0.0902
May	0.0545	−0.0024	−0.0330	0.0733	−0.2289	0.0183	0.0796	0.0552	0.0505	0.0195
June	0.0333	−0.0504	0.2503	−0.0612	0.0809	0.0578	0.0221	0.0223	0.0543	−0.0007
July	0.0701	0.1045	0.0744	0.1105	0.0341	0.0579	0.0337	−0.0526	−0.0193	−0.0180
Aug.	0.0151	−0.0483	−0.0226	−0.0648	0.0350	0.0010	0.0164	0.0171	0.0157	0.0641
Sept.	0.0031	−0.1483	0.0166	0.1673	0.0123	−0.0068	0.0290	0.0263	−0.0008	0.0438
Oct.	0.0775	−0.0981	0.0776	−0.0123	0.0422	−0.0657	0.0678	−0.0108	0.0023	0.0322
Nov.	0.0134	−0.0866	−0.0273	−0.0398	−0.0316	−0.0284	−0.0021	−0.0654	0.0133	0.0396
Dec.	−0.0029	−0.0459	0.0401	0.0270	0.0009	−0.0407	0.0549	0.0617	0.0347	0.0116

Month	**1946**	**1947**	**1948**	**1949**	**1950**	**1951**	**1952**	**1953**	**1954**	**1955**
Jan.	0.0714	0.0255	−0.0379	0.0039	0.0197	0.0637	0.0181	−0.0049	0.0536	0.0197
Feb.	−0.0641	−0.0077	−0.0388	−0.0296	0.0199	0.0157	−0.0282	−0.0106	0.0111	0.0098
Mar.	0.0480	−0.0149	0.0793	0.0328	0.0070	−0.0156	0.0503	−0.0212	0.0325	−0.0030
Apr.	0.0393	−0.0363	0.0292	−0.0179	0.0486	0.0509	−0.0402	−0.0237	0.0516	0.0396
May	0.0288	0.0014	0.0879	−0.0258	0.0509	−0.0299	0.0343	0.0077	0.0418	0.0055
June	−0.0370	0.0554	0.0054	0.0014	−0.0548	−0.0228	0.0490	−0.0134	0.0031	0.0841
July	−0.0239	0.0381	−0.0508	0.0650	0.0119	0.0711	0.0196	0.0273	0.0589	0.0621
Aug.	−0.0674	−0.0203	0.0158	0.0219	0.0443	0.0478	−0.0071	−0.0501	−0.0275	−0.0025
Sept.	−0.0997	−0.0111	−0.0276	0.0263	0.0592	0.0013	−0.0176	0.0034	0.0851	0.0130
Oct.	−0.0060	0.0238	0.0710	0.0340	0.0093	−0.0103	0.0020	0.0540	−0.0167	−0.0284
Nov.	−0.0027	−0.0175	−0.0961	0.0175	0.0169	0.0096	0.0571	0.0204	0.0909	0.0827
Dec.	0.0457	0.0233	0.0346	0.0486	0.0513	0.0424	0.0382	0.0053	0.0534	0.0015

Appendix VII (Continued)

	Year									
Month	**1956**	**1957**	**1958**	**1959**	**1960**	**1961**	**1962**	**1963**	**1964**	**1965**
Jan.	−0.0347	−0.0401	0.0445	0.0053	−0.0700	0.0645	−0.0366	0.0506	0.0283	0.0345
Feb.	0.0413	−0.0264	−0.0141	0.0049	0.0147	0.0319	0.0209	−0.0239	0.0147	0.0031
Mar.	0.0710	0.0215	0.0328	0.0020	−0.0123	0.0270	−0.0046	0.0370	0.0165	−0.0133
April	−0.0004	0.0388	0.0337	0.0402	−0.0161	0.0051	−0.0607	0.0500	0.0075	0.0356
May	−0.0593	0.0437	0.0212	0.0240	0.0326	0.0239	−0.0811	0.0193	0.0162	−0.0030
June	0.0409	0.0004	0.0279	−0.0022	0.0211	−0.0275	−0.0803	−0.0188	0.0178	−0.0473
July	0.0530	0.0131	0.0449	0.0363	−0.0234	0.0342	0.0652	−0.0022	0.0195	0.0147
Aug.	−0.0328	−0.0505	0.0176	−0.0102	0.0317	0.0243	0.0208	0.0535	−0.0118	0.0272
Sept.	−0.0440	−0.0602	0.0501	−0.0443	−0.0590	−0.0184	−0.0465	−0.0097	0.0301	0.0334
Oct.	0.0066	−0.0302	0.0270	0.0128	−0.0007	0.0298	0.0064	0.0339	0.0096	0.0289
Nov.	−0.0050	0.0231	0.0284	0.0186	0.0465	0.0447	0.1086	−0.0046	0.0005	−0.0031
Dec.	0.0370	−0.0395	0.0535	0.0292	0.0479	0.0046	0.0153	0.0262	0.0056	0.0106

Month	**1966**	**1967**	**1968**	**1969**	**1970**	**1971**	**1972**	**1973**	**1974**	**1975**
Jan.	0.0062	0.0798	−0.0425	−0.0068	−0.0743	0.0419	0.0194	−0.0159	−0.0085	0.1251
Feb.	−0.0131	0.0072	−0.0261	−0.0426	0.0586	0.0141	0.0299	−0.0333	0.0019	0.0674
Mar.	−0.0205	0.0409	0.0110	0.0359	0.0030	0.0382	0.0072	−0.0002	−0.0217	0.0237
April	0.0220	0.0437	0.0834	0.0229	−0.0889	0.0377	0.0057	−0.0395	−0.0373	0.0493
May	−0.0492	−0.0477	0.0161	0.0026	−0.0547	−0.0367	0.0219	−0.0139	−0.0272	0.0509
June	−0.0146	0.0190	0.0105	−0.0542	−0.0482	0.0021	−0.0205	−0.0051	−0.0129	0.0462
July	−0.0120	0.0468	−0.0172	−0.0587	0.0752	−0.0399	0.0036	0.0394	−0.0759	−0.0659
Aug.	−0.0725	−0.0070	0.0164	0.0454	0.0509	0.0412	0.0391	−0.0318	−0.0828	−0.0144
Sept.	−0.0053	0.0342	0.0400	−0.0236	0.0347	−0.0056	−0.0036	0.0415	−0.1170	−0.0328
Oct.	0.0494	−0.0276	0.0087	0.0459	−0.0097	−0.0404	0.0107	0.0003	0.1657	0.0637
Nov.	0.0095	0.0065	0.0531	−0.0297	0.0536	0.0027	0.0505	−0.1082	−0.0448	0.0313
Dec.	0.0002	0.0278	−0.0402	−0.0177	0.0584	0.0877	0.0131	0.0183	−0.0177	−0.0096

Month	**1976**	**1977**	**1978**	**1979**	**1980**	**1981**	**1982**	**1983**	**1984**	**1985**
Jan.	0.1199	−0.0489	−0.0596	0.0421	0.0610	−0.0438	−0.0163	0.0348	−0.0065	0.0768
Feb.	−0.0058	−0.0151	−0.0161	−0.0284	0.0031	0.0208	−0.0512	0.0260	−0.0328	0.0137
Mar.	0.0326	−0.0119	0.0276	0.0575	−0.0987	0.0380	−0.0060	0.0365	0.0171	0.0018
April	−0.0099	0.0014	0.0870	0.0036	0.0429	−0.0213	0.0414	0.0758	0.0069	−0.0032
May	−0.0073	−0.0150	0.0136	−0.0168	0.0562	0.0062	−0.0288	−0.0052	−0.0534	0.0615
June	0.0427	0.0475	−0.0152	0.0410	0.0296	−0.0080	−0.0174	0.0382	0.0221	0.0159
July	−0.0068	−0.0151	0.0560	0.0109	0.0676	0.0007	−0.0215	−0.0313	−0.0143	−0.0026
Aug.	0.0014	−0.0133	0.0340	0.0611	0.0131	−0.0554	0.1267	0.0170	0.1125	−0.0061
Sept.	0.0247	0.0000	−0.0048	0.0025	0.0281	−0.0502	0.0110	0.0136	0.0002	−0.0321
Oct.	−0.0206	−0.0415	−0.0891	−0.0656	0.0186	0.0528	0.1126	−0.0134	0.0026	0.0447
Nov.	−0.0009	0.0370	0.0260	0.0514	0.1095	0.0441	0.0438	0.0233	−0.0101	0.0716
Dec.	0.0540	0.0048	0.0172	0.0192	−0.0315	−0.0265	0.0173	−0.0061	0.0253	0.0467

STUDENT'S *t* CRITICAL POINTS

Appendix VIII   STUDENT'S *t* CRITICAL POINTS

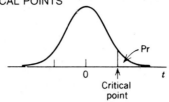

Pr d.f.	.25	.10	.05	.025	.010	.005	.001
1	1.000	3.078	6.314	12.706	31.821	63.657	318.31
2	.816	1.886	2.920	4.303	6.965	9.925	22.326
3	.765	1.638	2.353	3.182	4.541	5.841	10.213
4	.741	1.533	2.132	2.776	3.747	4.604	7.173
5	.727	1.476	2.015	2.571	3.365	4.032	5.893
6	.718	1.440	1.943	2.447	3.143	3.707	5.208
7	.711	1.415	1.895	2.365	2.998	3.499	4.785
8	.706	1.397	1.860	2.306	2.896	3.355	4.501
9	.703	1.383	1.833	2.262	2.821	3.250	4.297
10	.700	1.372	1.812	2.228	2.764	3.169	4.144
11	.697	1.363	1.796	2.201	2.718	3.106	4.025
12	.695	1.356	1.782	2.179	2.681	3.055	3.930
13	.694	1.350	1.771	2.160	2.650	3.012	3.852
14	.692	1.345	1.761	2.145	2.624	2.977	3.787
15	.691	1.341	1.753	2.131	2.602	2.947	3.733
16	.690	1.337	1.746	2.120	2.583	2.921	3.686
17	.689	1.333	1.740	2.110	2.567	2.898	3.646
18	.688	1.330	1.734	2.101	2.552	2.878	3.610
19	.688	1.328	1.729	2.093	2.539	2.861	3.579
20	.687	1.325	1.725	2.086	2.528	2.845	3.552
21	.686	1.323	1.721	2.080	2.518	2.831	3.527
22	.686	1.321	1.717	2.074	2.508	2.819	3.505
23	.685	1.319	1.714	2.069	2.500	2.807	3.485
24	.685	1.318	1.711	2.064	2.492	2.797	3.467
25	.684	1.316	1.708	2.060	2.485	2.787	3.450
26	.684	1.315	1.706	2.056	2.479	2.779	3.435
27	.684	1.314	1.703	2.052	2.473	2.771	3.421
28	.683	1.313	1.701	2.048	2.467	2.763	3.408
29	.683	1.311	1.699	2.045	2.462	2.756	3.396
30	.683	1.310	1.697	2.042	2.457	2.750	3.385
40	.681	1.303	1.684	2.021	2.423	2.704	3.307
60	.679	1.296	1.671	2.000	2.390	2.660	3.232
120	.677	1.289	1.658	1.980	2.358	2.617	3.160
∞	.674	1.282	1.645	1.960	2.326	2.576	3.090

BIBLIOGRAPHY

Adler, M.: "Global Fixed Income Portfolio Management," *Financial Analysts Journal*, September–October 1983.

Agmon, T.: "Country Risk: The Significance of the Country Factor for Share Price Movements in the United Kingdom, Germany and Japan," *Journal of Business*, January 1973.

Aharony, J., C. P. Jones, and I. Swary: "An Analysis of Risk and Return Characteristics of Corporate Bankruptcy Using Capital Market Data," *Journal of Finance*, September, 1980.

————— and I. Swary: "Quarterly Dividend and Earnings Announcements, and Stockholders' Returns: An Empirical Analysis," *Journal of Finance*, March 1980.

Alexander, G.: "Applying the Market Model to Long-Term Corporate Bonds," *Journal of Financial and Quantitative Analysis*, December 1980.

Alexander, S.: "Price Movements in Speculative Markets: Trends or Random Walks," *Industrial Management Review*, May 1961.

—————: "Price Movements in Speculative Markets: Trends or Random Walks, No. 2," *Industrial Management Review*, Spring 1964.

Ambachtsheer, K. P.: "Portfolio Theory and the Security Analyst," *Financial Analysts Journal*, November–December 1972.

—————: "Profit Potential in an 'Almost Efficient' Market," *Journal of Portfolio Management*, Fall 1974.

————— and J. L. Farrell, Jr.: "Can Active Management Add Value?", *Financial Analysts Journal*, November–December 1979.

Ang, J., and K. Patel: "Bond Rating Methods: Comparison and Validation," *Journal of Finance*, May 1975.

Archibald, T. R.: "The Return to Straight-Line Depreciation: An Analysis of a Change in Accounting Methods," *Empirical Research in Accounting: Selected Studies, 1967*, Supplement to *Journal of Accounting Research*, 1967.

—————: "Stock Market Reaction to the Depreciation Switch-Back." *The Accounting Review*, January 1972.

Bachelier, L.: "Theorie de la Speculation," Gauthier-Villars, Paris, 1900.

Ball, R.: "Anomalies in Relationships between Securities' Yields and Yield-Surrogates," *Journal of Financial Economics*, June–September, 1978.

————— and P. Brown: "An Empirical Evaluation of Accounting Income Numbers," *Journal of Accounting Research*, Autumn 1968.

————— and R. Watts: "Some Time Series Properties of Accounting Income," *Journal of Finance*, June 1972.

Banz, R. W.: "The Relationship between Return and Market Value of Common Stocks," *Journal of Financial Economics*, March 1981.

Bar-Yosef, S., and L. D. Brown: "A Reexamination of Stock Splits Using Moving Betas," *Journal of Finance*, September 1977.

Basu, S.: "Investment Performance of Common Stocks in Relation to Their Price-Earnings Ratios: A Test of the Efficient Market Hypothesis," *Journal of Finance*, June 1977.

—————: "The Relationship between Earnings' Yield, Market Value and Return for NYSE Common Stocks: Further Evidence," *Journal of Financial Economics*, June 1983.

Bauman, W. S.: "Investment Returns and Present Values," *Financial Analysts Journal*, November–December 1969.

Beaver, W. H.: "The Time Series Behavior of Earnings," *Empirical Research in Accounting: Selected Studies, 1970*, Supplement to *Journal of Accounting Research*, 1970.

———— and R. E. Dukes: "Interperiod Tax Allocation and Delta-Depreciation Methods: Some Empirical Results," *The Accounting Review*, July 1973.

Bernstein, L.: *Financial Statement Analysis: Theory, Application and Interpretation*, 3d ed., Irwin, Homewood, Ill., 1983.

Bierwag, G. O., G. Kaufman, R. Schweitzer, and A. Toevs: "The Art of Risk Management in Bond Portfolio," *Journal of Portfolio Management*, Spring 1981.

———— G. Kaufman, and A. Toevs: "Duration, Its Development and Use in Bond Portfolio Management," *Financial Analysts Journal*, July–August 1983.

———— and ————: "Single Factor Duration Models in a Discrete General Equilibrium Framework," *Journal of Finance*, May 1982.

Bildersee, J.: "U.S. Government and Agency Securities: An Analysis of Yield Spreads and Performance," *Journal of Business*, July 1978.

Billingham, C.: "Strategies for Enhancing Bond Portfolio Returns," *Financial Analysts Journal*, May–June 1983.

Bjerring, J., J. Lakonishok, and T. Vermaelen: "Stock Prices and Financial Analysts' Recommendations," *Journal of Finance*, March 1983.

Black, F.: "Capital Market Equilibrium with Restricted Borrowing," *Journal of Business*, Vol. 45, No. 3, July 1972.

————: "Fact and Fantasy in the Use of Options," *Financial Analysts Journal*, July–August 1975.

————: "International Capital Market Equilibrium with Investment Barriers," *Journal of Financial Economics*, December 1974.

————: "The Tax Consequences of Long-Run Pension Policy," *Financial Analysts Journal*, July–August 1980.

————: "The Trouble with Econometric Models," *Financial Analysts Journal*, March–April 1982.

————: "Yes, Virginia, There Is Hope: Tests of the Value Line Ranking System," *Financial Analysts Journal*, September–October 1973.

———— and M. Dewhurst: "A New Investment Strategy for Pension Funds," *Journal of Portfolio Management*, Summer 1981.

———— Jensen, M. C., and M. Scholes: "The Capital Asset Pricing Model: Some Empirical Tests," in M. C. Jensen (ed.), *Studies in the Theory of Capital Markets*, Praeger, N.Y., 1972.

———— and M. Scholes: "The Effects of Dividend Yield and Dividend Policy on Common Stock Prices and Returns," *Journal of Financial Economics*, March 1974.

———— and ————: "The Pricing of Options and Corporate Liabilities," *The Journal of Political Economy*, May–June 1973.

Blume, M.: "Betas and Their Regression Tendencies," *Journal of Finance*, June 1975.

————: "On the Assessment of Risk," *Journal of Finance*, March 1971.

————: "Stock Returns and Dividend Yields: Some More Evidence," Working Paper No. 1–79, Rodney L. White Center for Financial Research, University of Pennsylvania.

Boquist J., G. Racette, and G. Schlarbaum: "Duration and Risk Assessment for Bonds and Common Stock," *Journal of Finance*, December 1975.

Box, G., and G. Jenkins: *Time-Series Analysis: Forecasting and Control*, rev. ed., Holden-Day, San Francisco, 1976.

Brealey, R. A.: *An Introduction to Risk and Return from Common Stocks*, 2d ed., MIT Press, Cambridge, Mass., 1983.

Brennan, M.: "Taxes, Market Valuation, and Corporate Financial Policy," *National Tax Journal* Vol. 25, 1970.

Brown, L. D., and M. S. Rozeff: "The Superiority of Analyst Forecasts as Measures of Expectations," *Journal of Finance*, March 1978.

Brown, P., and R. Ball: "Some Preliminary Findings on the Association between the Earnings of a Firm, Its Industry, and the Economy," *Empirical Research in Accounting: Selected Studies, 1967*, supplement to *Journal of Accounting Research*, 1967.

Brown, R. M.: "Short-Range Market Reaction to Changes in LIFO Accounting Using Preliminary Earnings Announcement Dates," *Journal of Accounting Research*, Spring 1980.

Brown, S. J., and J. B. Warner: "Measuring Security Price Performance," *Journal of Financial Economics*, September 1980.

Chant, P.: "On the Predictability of Earnings per Share Behavior," *Journal of Finance*, March 1980.

Charest, G.: "Dividend Information, Stock Returns, and Market Efficiency—II," *Journal of Financial Economics*, June–September 1979.

Chen, N.: "Some Empirical Tests of the Theory of Arbitrage Pricing," *Journal of Finance*, December 1983.

———, R. Roll, and S. Ross: "Economic Forces and the Stock Market," Working Paper 119, UCLA, December 1983.

Chiras, D. P., and S. Manaster: "The Information Content of Option Prices and a Test of Market Efficiency," *Journal of Financial Economics*, June–September 1978.

Clark, J.: "Some Recent Trends in Municipal and Corporate Securities Markets: An Interview with Brenton W. Harries, President of Standard and Poor's Corporation," *Financial Management*, Spring 1976.

Clayton, G., and C. Spivey: *The Time Value of Money*, Sanders, Philadelphia, 1978.

Cook, T., and P. Hendershott: "The Impact of Taxes, Risk, and Relative Security Supplies on Interest Rate Differentials," *Journal of Finance*, September 1978.

Copeland, T., and D. Mayers: "The Value Line Enigma (1965–1978): A Case Study of Performance Evaluation Issues," *Journal of Financial Economics*, November 1982.

Cox, J., S. Ross, and M. Rubinstein: "Option Pricing: A Simplified Approach," *Journal of Financial Economics*, September 1979.

Dale, C., and R. Workman: "The Arc Sine Law and the Treasury Bill Futures Markets," *Financial Analysts Journal*, November–December 1980.

Darst, D.: *The Complete Bond Book*, McGraw-Hill, New York, 1975.

Davidson, S., S. F. Rasch, and R. Weil: "Behavior of the Deferred Tax Credit Account, 1973–1982," *Journal of Accountancy*, October 1984.

———, C. P. Stickney, and R. L. Weil: *Inflation Accounting: A Guide for the Accountant and Financial Analyst*, McGraw-Hill, New York, 1976.

Dietz, P., H. R. Fogler, and D. J. Hardy: "The Challenge of Analyzing Bond Portfolio Returns," *The Journal of Portfolio Management*, Spring 1980.

——— and ——— and A. Rivers: "Duration, Nonlinearity, and Bond Portfolio Performance," *Journal of Portfolio Management*, Spring 1981.

Dimson, E.: "Risk Measurement When Shares are Subject to Infrequent Trading," *Journal of Financial Economics*, June 1979.

Dobson, S., R. Sutch, and D. Vanderford: "An Evaluation of Alternative Empirical Models for the Term Structure of Interest Rates," *Journal of Finance*, September 1976.

Durand, D., and F. May: "The Ex-Dividend Behavior of American Telephone and Telegraph Stock," *Journal of Finance*, March 1960.

Eckel, N.: "An EPS Forecasting Model Utilizing Macroeconomic Performance Expectations," *Financial Analysts Journal*, May–June 1982.

Elgers, P. T., J. R. Haltiner, and W. H. Hawthorne: "Beta Regression Tendencies: Statistical and Real Causes," *Journal of Finance*, March 1979.

Elliott, J. W., and J. Baier: "Econometric Models and Current Interest Rates: How Well Do They Predict Future Rates?" *Journal of Finance*, September 1979.

Elton, E. J., and M. J. Gruber: "Marginal Stockholder Tax Rates and the Clientele Effect," *Review of Economics and Statistics*, 1970.

Fama, E. F.: "The Behavior of Stock Market Prices," *Journal of Business*, January 1965.

————: "Components of Investment Performance," *Journal of Finance*, June 1972.

————: "Efficient Capital Markets: A Review of Theory and Empirical Work," *Journal of Finance*, May 1970.

————: "The Empirical Relationship between the Dividend and Investment Decision," *American Economic Review*, June 1974.

————: "Risk, Return, and Equilibrium: Some Clarifying Comments," *Journal of Finance*, Vol. 23, No. 3, March 1968.

————: "Short-Term Interest Rates as Predictors of Inflation," *American Economic Review*, June 1975.

———— and H. Babiak: "Dividend Policy: An Empirical Analysis," *American Statistical Association Journal*, December 1968.

———— and M. Blume: "Filter Rules and Stock Market Trading Profits," *Journal of Business*, January 1966 Supplement.

————, L. Fisher, M. Jensen, and R. Roll: "The Adjustment of Stock Prices to New Information," *International Economic Review*, February 1969.

———— and J. MacBeth: "Risk, Return, and Equilibrium: Empirical Tests," *Journal of Political Economy*, May–June 1973.

Farrell, J. L., Jr.: "Analyzing Covariation of Returns to Determine Homogeneous Stock Groupings," *Journal of Business*, April 1974.

————: "A Disciplined Stock Selection Strategy," *Interfaces*, October 1982.

————: "The Dividend Discount Model: A Primer," *Financial Analysts Journal*, November–December 1985.

————: *Guide to Portfolio Management*, McGraw-Hill, New York, 1983.

————: "Homogenous Stock Groupings: Implications for Portfolio Management," *Financial Analysts Journal*, May–June 1975.

————: "The Multi-Index Model and Practical Portfolio Analysis," Occasional Paper No. 4, *Financial Analysts Research Foundation*, 1976.

Fisher, L.: "Determinants of Risk Premiums on Corporate Bonds," *Journal of Political Economy*, June 1959.

———— and R. Weil: "Coping with the Risk of Interest Rate Fluctuations: Returns to Bondholders from Naive and Optimal Strategies," *Journal of Business*, October 1971.

Fogler, R., and S. Ganapathy: *Financial Econometrics*, Prentice-Hall, Englewood Cliffs, N.J., 1982.

Fong, G., C. Pearson, and O. Vasicek: "Bond Performance: Analyzing Sources of Return," *Journal of Portfolio Management*, Spring 1983.

———— and O. Vasicek: "The Tradeoff between Return and Risk in Immunized Portfolios," *Financial Analysts Journal*, September–October 1983.

Foster, G.: *Financial Statement Analysis*, Prentice-Hall, Englewood Cliffs, N.J., 1978.

Foster, G.: "Quarterly Accounting Data: Time Series Properties and Predictive-Ability Results," *The Accounting Review*, January 1977.

Fraser, D.: "On the Accuracy and Usefulness of Interest Rate Forecasts, *Business Economics*, September 1977.

Fuller, R. J.: *Capital Asset Pricing Theories—Evolution and New Frontiers*, Financial Analyst Research Foundation, Charlottesville, Va., 1981.

————: "Programming the Three-Phase Dividend Discount Model," *Journal of Portfolio Management*, Summer 1979.

———— and C. C. Hsia: "A Simplified Model for Estimating Stock Prices of Growth Firms," *Financial Analysts Journal*, May–June 1984.

———— and J. W. Settle: "Determinants of Duration and Bond Volatility," *Journal of Portfolio Management*, Summer 1984.

Galai, D.: "Empirical Tests of Boundary Conditions for CBOE Options," *Journal of Financial Economics*, June–September 1978.

Gastineau, G.: *The Stock Options Manual*, McGraw-Hill, New York, 1979.

Giddy, Ian: "An Integrated Theory of Exchange Rate Equilibrium," *Journal of Financial and Quantitative Analysis*, December 1976.

Givoly, D., and J. Lakonishok: "The Information Content of Financial Analysts' Forecasts of Earnings: Some Evidence on Semi-Strong Inefficiency," *Journal of Accounting and Economics*, December 1979.

Gombola, M., and J. Ketz: "A Caveat on Measuring Cash Flow and Solvency," *Financial Analysts Journal*, September–October 1983.

Gonedes, N. J.: "Properties of Accounting Numbers: Models and Tests," *Journal of Accounting Research*, Autumn 1973.

Goodman, D. A., and J. W. Peavy: "Industry Relative Price-Earnings Ratios as Indicators of Investment Returns," *Financial Analysts Journal*, July–August 1983.

Gordon, M. J.: "Dividends, Earnings and Stock Prices," *Review of Economics and Statistics*, May 1959.

————: *The Investment, Financing, and Valuation of the Corporation*, Irwin, Homewood, Ill., 1962.

Graham, B.: *The Intelligent Investor*, 5th ed., Harper & Row, New York, 1973.

————, D. L. Dodd, and S. Cottle: *Security Analysis*, 4th ed., McGraw-Hill, New York, 1951.

Granof, M. H.: *Accounting for Managers and Investors*, Prentice-Hall, Englewood Cliffs, N.J., 1983.

Grauer, R., and N. Hakansson: "Higher Return, Lower Risk: Historical Returns on Long-Run, Actively Managed Portfolios of Stocks, Bonds, and Bills," *Financial Analyst Journal*, March–April 1982.

Grier, P., and S. Katz: "The Differential Effects of Bond Rating Changes among Industrial and Public Utility Bonds by Maturity," *Journal of Business*, April 1976.

Grossman, S., and R. Shiller: "The Determinants of the Variability of Stock Market Prices," *American Economic Review*, May 1981.

Groth, R., W. Lewellan, G. Schlarbaum, and R. Lease: "An Analysis of a Brokerage House Securities Recommendations," *Financial Analysts Journal*, February 1979.

Hagin, R. L.: *Modern Portfolio Theory*, Dow Jones-Irwin, Homewood, Ill., 1979.

Hamada, R.: "The Effect of the Firm's Capital Structure on the Systematic Risk of Common Stocks," *Journal of Finance*, May 1972.

Hamburger, M., and E. Platt: "The Expectations Hypothesis and the Efficiency of the Treasury Bill Market," *Review of Economics and Statistics*, May 1975.

Hendershott, P., and D. Kidwell: "The Impact of Relative Security Supplies," *Journal of Money, Credit and Banking*, August 1978.

Hettenhouse, G., and W. Sartoris: "An Analysis of the Informational Value of Bond Rating Changes," *Quarterly Review of Economics and Business*, Summer 1976.

Hodges, S. D., and R. A. Brealey: "Portfolio Selection in a Dynamic and Uncertain World," *Financial Analysts Journal*, March–April 1973.

Homer, S., and M. Leibowitz: *Inside the Yield Book*, Prentice-Hall, Englewood Cliffs, N.J., 1972.

Hopewell, M., and G. Kaufman: "Bond Price Volatility and Term to Maturity: A Generalized Respecification," *American Economic Review*, September 1973.

Hsia, C. C., and J. F. Weston: "Price Behavior of Deep Discount Bonds," *Journal of Banking and Finance*, May 1981.

Ibbotson, R. G.: "Price Performance of Common Stock New Issues," *Journal of Financial Economics*, September 1975.

———— and R. A. Sinquefeld: "Stocks, Bonds, Bills, and Inflation: The Past (1926–1976) and the Future (1977–2000)," *Financial Analysts Research Foundation*, Charlottesville, Va., 1982.

Jaffee, D.: "Cyclical Variations in the Risk Structure of Interest Rates," *Journal of Monetary Economics*, July 1975.

Jensen, M. C.: "Capital Markets: Theory and Evidence," *Bell Journal of Economics and Management Science*, Autumn 1972a.

————: "The Foundations and Current State of Capital Market Theory," in M. C. Jensen (ed.), *Studies in the Theory of Capital Markets*, Praeger, New York, 1972b.

————: "The Performance of Mutual Funds in the Period 1945–1964," *Journal of Finance*, May 1968.

————: "Risk, the Pricing of Capital Assets and the Evaluation of Investment Portfolios," *Journal of Business*, April 1969.

Jones, C. P., and R. H. Litzenberger: "Quarterly Earnings Reports and Intermediate Stock Price Trends," *Journal of Finance*, March 1970.

Joy, O. M., R. H. Litzenberger, and R. W. McEnally: "The Adjustment of Stock Prices to Announcements of Unanticipated Changes in Quarterly Earnings," *Journal of Accounting Research*, Autumn 1977.

Kaplan, R. S., and R. Roll: "Investor Evaluation of Accounting Information: Some Empirical Evidence," *Journal of Business*, April 1972.

———— and G. Urwitz: "Statistical Models of Bond Ratings: A Methodological Inquiry," *Journal of Business*, March 1979.

Katz, S.: "The Price Adjustment Process of Bonds to Rating Reclassification: A Test of Bond Market Efficiency," *Journal of Finance*, May 1974.

Kendall, M. G.: "The Analysis of Economic Time Series," *Journal of the Royal Statistical Society*, 1953.

Kidwell, D., and T. Koch: "The Behavior of the Interest Rate Differential between Tax-Exempt Revenue and General Obligation Bonds: A Test of Risk Preferences and Market Segmentation," *Journal of Finance*, March 1982.

Kieso, D. E., and J. J. Weygandt: *Intermediate Accounting*, 4th ed., Wiley, New York, 1983.

King, B. F.: "Market and Industry Factors in Stock Price Behavior," *Journal of Business*, January 1966.

Larcker, D. F., L. A. Gordon, and G. E. Pinches: "Testing for Market Efficiency: A Comparison of the Cumulative Average Residual Methodology and Intervention Analysis," *Journal of Financial Quantitative Analysis*, June 1980.

Largay, S., and C. Stickney: "Cash Flows, Ratio Analysis and the W. T. Grant Company Bankruptcy," *Financial Analysts Journal*, July–August 1980.

Latané, H. A., and C. P. Jones: "Standardized Unexpected Earnings—A Progress Report," *Journal of Finance*, December 1977.

————, O. M. Joy, and C. P. Jones: "Quarterly Data, Sort-Rank Routines, and Security Evaluation," *Journal of Business*, October 1970.

————, D. L. Tuttle, and C. P. Jones: "Quarterly Data: E/P Ratios vs. Changes in Earnings in Forecasting Future Price Changes," *Financial Analysts Journal*, January–February 1969.

Leibowitz, M.: "Horizon Analysis for Managed Portfolios," *Journal of Portfolio Management*, Spring 1975.

———— and A. Weinberger: "Contingent Immunization—Parts I and II," *Financial Analysts Journal*, November–December 1982, and January–February 1983.

Leland, H., and M. Rubinstein: "Replicating Options with Positions in Stock and Cash," *Financial Analysts Journal*, July–August 1981.

LeRoy, S., and C. LaCivita: "Risk Aversion and the Dispersion of Asset Prices," *Journal of Business*, October 1981.

Lessard, D. F.: "World, Country, and Industry Relationships in Equity Returns: Implications for Risk Reduction Through International Diversification," *Financial Analysts Journal*, January–February 1976.

Lev, B.: *Financial Statement Analysis: A New Approach*, Prentice-Hall, Englewood Cliffs, N.J., 1974.

———— and J. A. Ohlson: "Market-Based Empirical Research in Accounting: A Review, Interpretation, and Extension," *Journal of Accounting Research*, Vol. 20, Supplement 1982.

Levine, S. N. (ed.): *Financial Analyst's Handbook 2—Analysis by Industry*, Dow Jones-Irwin, Homewood, Ill., 1975.

Levy, R. A.: "The Predictive Significance of Five-Point Chart Patterns," *Journal of Business*, July 1971.

Lintner, J.: "The Aggregation of Investors' Judgments and Preferences in Purely Competitive Security Markets," *Journal of Financial and Quantitative Analysis*, December 1969.

————: *Risk in the Equity Market: An Empirical Appraisal of Market Efficiency*, University of Microfilms, Inc., Ann Arbor, Mich., 1968.

————: "Security Prices, Risk, and Maximal Gains from Diversification," *Journal of Finance*, Vol. 20, No. 12, December 1965.

Lintner, J.: "The Valuation of Risky Assets and the Selection of Risky Investments in Stock Portfolios and Capital Budgets," *Review of Economics and Statistics*, December 1965.

———— and R. Glauber: "Higgledy Piggledy Growth in America," reprinted in J. Lorie and R. A. Brealey, *Modern Developments in Investment Management*, Praeger, New York, 1972.

Little, I. M. D.: "Higgledy Piggledy Growth," *Bulletin of the Oxford Institute of Economics and Statistics*, November 1962.

———— and A. C. Rayner: *Higgledy Piggledy Growth Again*, Blackwell's, Oxford, 1966.

Litzenberger, R. H., and K. Ramaswamy: "The Effect of Personal Taxes and Dividends on Capital Asset Prices: Theory and Empirical Evidence," *Journal of Financial Economics*, June 1979.

Loeb, T. F.: "Trading Cost: The Critical Link between Investment Information and Results," *Financial Analysts Journal*, May–June 1983.

Long, J. B.: "The Market Valuation of Cash Dividends: A Case to Consider," *Journal of Financial Economics*, June–September 1978.

Lorie, J. H., and M. T. Hamilton: *The Stock Market, Theories and Evidence*, Irwin, Homewood, Ill., 1973.

Macaulay, F. R.: "Some Theoretical Problems Suggested by the Movements of Interest Rates, Bond Yields, and Stock Prices in the United States Since 1856," *NBER*, Columbia University Press, New York, 1938.

Magee, R. P.: "Industry-Wide Commonalities in Earnings," *Journal of Accounting Research*, Autumn 1974.

Makridakis, S., and S. Wheelwright: *Forecasting Methods and Applications*, Wiley, New York, 1978.

Malkial, B. G.: "Expectations, Bond Prices and the Term Structure of Interest Rates," *Quarterly Journal of Economics*, May 1962.

———— and J. G. Cragg: "Expectations and the Structure of Share Prices," *American Economic Review*, September 1970.

Mandelbrot, B.: "Forecasts of Future Prices, Unbiased Markets, and Martingale Models," *Journal of Business*, January 1960 Supplement.

Mao, J. C. T.: *Quantitative Analysis of Financial Decisions*, MacMillan, Toronto, 1969.

Markowitz, H. M.: "Portfolio Selection," *Journal of Finance*, Vol. 7, No. 1, March 1952.

————: *Portfolio Selection: Efficient Diversification of Investment*, Wiley, New York, 1959.

Martin, L. J., and G. V. Henderson: "On Bond Ratings and Pension Obligations: A Note," *Journal of Financial and Quantitative Analysis*, December 1983.

McDonald, J.: "Objectives and Performance of Mutual Funds, 1960–1969," *Journal of Financial and Quantitative Analysis*, June 1974.

Miller, M. H.: "Risk, Uncertainty, and Divergence of Opinion," *Journal of Finance*, September 1977.

———— and M. Scholes: "Dividends and Taxes," *Journal of Financial Economics*, December 1978.

———— and ————: "Rates of Return in Relation to Risk: A Re-Examination of Some Recent Findings," in Jensen (ed.), *Studies in the Theory of Capital Markets*, Praeger, New York, 1972.

Modigliani, F., and M. H. Miller: "The Cost of Capital, Corporation Finance, and the Theory of Investment," *American Economic Review*, June 1958.

Modigliani, F., and G. A. Pogue: "An Introduction to Risk and Return," *Financial Analysts Journal*, March–June 1974.

Molodovsky, N.: "Common Stock Valuation—Principles, Tables, and Applications," *Financial Analysts Journal*, March–April 1965.

Mossin, J.: "Equilibrium in a Capital Asset Market," *Econometrics*, Vol. 34, No. 4, October 1966.

Neiderhaffer, V., and P. Regan: "Earnings Changes, Analysts Forecasts, and Stock Prices," *Financial Analysts Journal*, May–June 1972.

Nelson, C. R.: *Applied Time Series Analysis for Managerial Forecasting*, Holden-Day, San Francisco, 1973.

Neter, J., W. Wasserman, and M. Kutner: *Applied Linear Regression Models*, Irwin, Homewood, Ill., 1983.

Oppenheimer, H., and G. Schlarbaum: "Investing with Ben Graham: An Ex Ante Test of the Efficient Market Hypothesis," *Journal of Financial and Quantitative Analysis*, September 1981.

Pesando, J.: "On the Efficiency of the Bond Market: Some Canadian Evidence," *Journal of Political Economy*, December 1978.

Petit, R. R.: "Dividend Announcements, Security Performance, and Capital Market Efficiency," *Journal of Fianance*, December 1972.

Pinches, G.: "The Random Walk Hypothesis and Technical Analysis," *Financial Analysts Journal*, March–April 1970.

———— and J. C. Singleton: "The Adjustment of Stock Prices to Bond Rating Changes," *Journal of Finance*, March 1978.

Reilly, R., and M. Joehnk: "The Association between Market-Determined Risk Measures for Bonds and Bond Ratings," *Journal of Finance*, December 1976.

Reinganum, M.: "A Direct Test of Roll's Conjecture on the Firm Size Effect," *Journal of Finance*, March 1982.

————: "Misspecification of Capital Asset Pricing: Empirical Anomalies Based on Earnings' Yields and Market Values," *Journal of Financial Economics*, March 1981.

Ricks, W.: "The Market's Response to the 1974 LIFO Adoptions," *Journal of Accounting Research*, Autumn 1982.

Rogalski, R. J., and S. M. Tinic: "Risk Premium Curve vs. Capital Market Line: A Re-Examination," *Financial Management*, Spring 1978.

Roll, R.: "A Critique of the Asset Pricing Theory's Tests," *Journal of Financial Economics*, March 1977.

————: "A Possible Explanation of the Small Firm Effect," *Journal of Finance*, September 1981.

————: "Ambiguity When Performance is Measured by the Securities Market Line," *Journal of Finance*, September 1978.

————: *The Behavior of Interest Rates: An Application of the Efficient Market Model to U.S. Treasury Bills*, Basic Books, New York, 1970.

———— and S. Ross: "The APT Model," *Financial Analysts Journal*,

———— and ————: "An Empirical Investigation of the Arbitrage Pricing Theory," *Journal of Finance*, Vol. 35, 1980.

Rosenberg, B.: "Extra-Market Components of Covariance in Security Returns," *Journal of Financial and Quantitative Analysis*, March 1974.

Rosenberg, B., and J. Guy: "Prediction of Beta from Investment Fundamentals," Parts One and Two, *Financial Analysts Journal*, May–June and July–August 1976.

Ross, S.: "Return, Risk and Arbitrage," in *Risk and Return in Finance*, Friend and Bicklser (eds.), Ballinger, Cambridge, 1976.

Samuelson, P. A.: "Proof that Properly Anticipated Prices Fluctuate Randomly," *Industrial Management Review*, Spring 1965.

Scholes, M. S.: "The Market for Securities: Substitution versus Price Pressure and the Effects of Information on Share Prices," *Journal of Business*, April 1972.

———— and J. Williams: "Estimating Betas From Nonsynchronous Data," *Journal of Financial Economics*, December 1977.

Sharpe, W. F.: "A Simplified Model for Portfolio Analysis," *Management Science*, January 1963.

————: "Capital Asset Prices: A Theory of Market Equilibrium under Conditions of Risk," *Journal of Finance*, Vol. 19, No. 3, September 1964.

————: *Investments*, 2d ed., Prentice-Hall, Englewood Cliffs, N.J., 1981.

————: "Likely Gains From Market Timing," *Financial Analysts Journal*, March–April 1975.

————: "Mutual Fund Performance," *Journal of Business*, January 1966.

————: "Risk Aversion in the Stock Market: Some Empirical Evidence," *Journal of Finance*, September 1965.

———— and G. M. Cooper: "Risk-Return Classes of New York Stock Exchange Common Stocks, 1931–1967," *Financial Analysts Journal*, March–April, 1972.

Shiller, R. J.: "Do Stock Prices Move too Much to Be Justified by Subsequent Changes in Dividends?", *American Economic Review*, June 1981.

————: "The Volatility of Long-Term Interest Rates and Expectation Models of the Term Structure," *Journal of Political Economy*, December 1979.

Shillinglaw, G., and P. E. Meyer: *Accounting: A Management Approach*, 7th ed., Irwin, Homewood, Ill., 1983.

Singleton, J. C., and R. Grieves: "Synthetic Puts and Portfolio Insurance Strategies," *Journal of Portfolio Management*, Winter 1983.

Skekel, R. and C. Fazzi: "The Deferred Tax Liability: Do Capital Intensive Companies Pay It?", *Journal of Accountancy*, October 1984.

Smith, C.: "Option Pricing," *Journal of Financial Economics*, January–March 1976.

Solnik, B. H.: "Why Not Diversify Internationally Rather Than Domestically?", *Financial Analysts Journal*, July–August 1978.

Stambaugh, R. F.: "On the Exclusion of Assets from Tests of the Two Parameter Model: A Sensitivity Analysis," *Journal of Financial Economics*, November 1982.

Subrahamanyam, M.: "On the Optimality of International Capital Market Integration," *Journal of Financial Economics*, March 1975.

Sunder, S.: "Relationship between Accounting Changes and Stock Prices: Problems of Measurement and Some Empirical Evidence," *Empirical Research in Accounting: 1973*, Supplement to *Journal of Accounting Research*, 1973.

———: "Stock Price and Risk Related to Accounting Changes in Inventory Valuation," *Accounting Review*, April 1975.

Tepper, I.: "Taxation and Corporate Pension Policy," *Journal of Finance*, March 1981.

Thompson, D. J.: "Source of Systematic Risk in Common Stocks," *Journal of Business*, April 1976.

Thompson, R.: "The Information Content of Discounts and Premiums on Closed-End Fund Shares," *Journal of Financial Economics*, June–September 1978.

Trainer, F. H.: "The Uses of Treasury Bond Futures in Fixed-Income Portfolio Management," *Financial Analysts Journal*, January–February 1983.

Treynor, J. L.: "How to Rate Management of Investment Funds," *Harvard Business Review*, January–February 1965.

———: "On the Quality of Municipal Bonds," *Financial Analysts Journal*, May–June 1982.

———: "Toward a Theory of the Market Value of Risky Assets," unpublished manuscript, 1961.

——— and F. Black: "How to Use Security Analysis to Improve Portfolio Selection," *Journal of Business*, January 1973.

——— and K. Mazuy: "Can Mutual Funds Outguess the Market?" *Harvard Business Review*, July–August 1966.

Valentine, J. L.: *Investment Analysis and Capital Market Theory*, Occasional Paper Number 1, The Financial Analysts Research Institution, Charlottesville, Va., 1975.

Wagner, W. H., and S. C. Lau: "The Effect of Diversification on Risk," *Financial Analysts Journal*, November–December 1971.

Watts, R. L.: "The Information Content of Dividends," *Journal of Business*, April 1973.

———: "Systematic 'Abnormal' Returns after Quarterly Earnings Announcements," *Journal of Financial Economics*, June–September 1978.

Waud, R. N.: "Public Interpretation of Discount Rates Changes: Evidence on the 'Announcement Effect'," *Econometrica*, Vol. 38, No. 2, 1974.

Weinstein, M.: "The Effect of a Rating Change Announcement on Bond Price," *Journal of Financial Economics*, December 1977.

———: "The Systematic Risk of Corporate Bonds," *Journal of Financial and Quantitative Analysis*, September 1981.

Whitbeck, V. S., and M. Kisor, Jr.: "A New Tool in Investment Decision Making," *Financial Analysts Journal*, May–June 1963.

Williams, J. B.: *The Theory of Investment Value*, Harvard University Press, Cambridge, Mass., 1938.

Woolridge, J. R.: "Ex-Date Stock Price Adjustment to Stock Dividends: A Note," *Journal of Finance*, March 1983.

INDEX

Supplement to
THE VALUE LINE INVESTMENT SURVEY

Published by VALUE LINE, INC.

DOW JONES INDUSTRIAL AVERAGE
1920-1983
(Quarterly Price Ranges)

Dividends per Share × 22.3

10%
5%
0
−5%

	1920	'21	'22	'23	'24	'25	'26	'27	'28	'29	1930	'31	'32	'33	'34	'35	'36	'37	'38	'39	1940	'41	'42	'43	'44	'45	'46	'47	'48	'49	1950	'51	'52	'53
	9.12	2.10	9.11	8.25	10.88	13.89	11.39	8.72	15.97	19.94	11.02	4.09	(0.51)	2.11	3.91	6.34	10.07	11.49	6.01	9.11	10.92	11.64	9.22	9.74	10.07	10.56	13.63	18.80	23.07	23.54	30.70	26.59	24.78	27.23
	5.79	3.89	3.95	4.51	5.16	5.53	5.54	6.04	9.76	12.75	11.13	8.40	4.62	3.40	3.66	4.55	7.05	8.78	6.11	7.06	7.59	6.40	6.30	6.57	6.69	7.50	9.21	11.50	12.79	16.34	16.13	15.43	16.11	
	48.2	46.4	51.6	55.3	61.0	69.4	75.2	77.9	84.1	91.3	91.2	86.9	81.8	80.5	80.7	82.5	85.5	88.3	87.1	95.6	98.7	103	107	113	118	122	131	149	160	170	194	203	213	244
	9.9	NMF	10.2	11.4	9.2	9.6	13.3	20.0	14.2	15.6	21.4	NMF	NMF	NMF	25.1	18.9	16.1	14.5	22.0	15.7	12.3	10.5	11.6	13.8	14.3	16.1	14.1	9.4	7.8	7.6	7.0	9.7	10.9	10.1
	15.6	18.7	23.5	20.9	19.4	24.2	27.4	28.9	23.2	24.4	21.2	16.5	14.0	24.6	26.8	26.4	23.0	18.9	26.6	23.3	19.1	16.0	16.7	21.4	21.9	25.4	25.6	19.3	15.6	14.0	13.4	15.8	17.5	17.1
	18.9	4.5	17.7	14.9	17.8	20.0	15.1	11.2	19.0	21.8	12.1	4.7	−0.6	2.1	4.8	7.7	11.8	13.0	6.9	9.5	11.1	11.3	8.6	8.6	8.5	8.6	10.4	12.6	14.4	13.8	15.8	13.1	11.6	11.1
	10.1	2.9	9.8	8.7	10.9	10.4	7.5	5.0	7.0	6.4	4.7	3.0	−0.8	2.5	4.0	5.3	6.2	6.9	4.5	6.4	8.1	9.6	8.6	7.2	7.0	6.2	7.1	10.6	12.8	13.1	14.2	10.3	9.1	9.9
	6.4	5.4	4.3	4.8	5.2	4.1	3.6	3.5	4.3	4.1	4.7	6.1	7.2	4.1	3.7	3.8	4.3	5.3	3.8	4.3	5.2	6.2	6.0	4.7	4.6	3.9	3.9	5.2	6.4	7.1	7.5	6.3	5.7	5.8
	—	−77.0	NMF	−9.4	31.9	27.7	−18.0	−23.4	83.1	24.9	−44.7	−62.9	−87.5	NMF	85.3	62.1	11.2	14.1	−47.7	51.6	19.9	6.6	−20.8	5.6	3.4	4.9	29.1	38.7	22.1	−2.0	30.4	−13.4	−6.8	9.9
	—	−32.8	1.5	14.2	14.4	7.2	0.2	9.0	61.6	30.6	−12.7	−24.5	−45.0	−26.4	7.6	24.3	54.9	24.5	−43.3	22.7	15.5	7.5	−15.7	−1.6	4.3	1.8	12.1	22.8	24.9	11.2	26.1	1.3	−5.6	4.4
	—	−3.7	11.2	7.2	10.3	13.8	8.4	3.6	8.0	8.6	−0.1	−4.7	−5.9	−1.6	0.2	2.2	3.6	3.3	−1.4	9.8	3.2	4.4	3.9	5.6	4.4	3.4	7.4	13.7	7.4	6.2	14.1	4.6	4.9	14.5
	—	−74.1	NMF	−0.7	42.8	38.1	−10.5	−18.4	90.1	31.3	−40.0	−59.9	−86.7	NMF	89.3	67.4	17.4	21.0	−43.2	58.0	28.0	16.2	−12.2	12.8	10.4	11.1	36.2	49.3	34.9	15.1	44.6	−3.1	2.3	19.8
	—	−27.4	5.8	19.0	19.6	11.3	3.8	12.5	65.9	34.7	−8.0	−18.4	−37.8	−22.3	11.3	28.1	59.2	29.8	−39.5	27.0	20.7	13.7	−9.7	3.1	8.9	5.7	16.0	28.0	31.3	18.3	33.6	7.6	0.1	10.2
	6.1	6.0	5.1	5.1	5.0	4.9	4.7	4.6	4.5	4.8	4.5	4.6	5.0	4.5	4.0	3.6	3.2	3.3	3.2	3.0	2.8	2.8	2.8	2.7	2.7	2.6	2.5	2.6	2.8	2.7	2.6	2.9	3.0	3.2
	15.8	−10.7	−6.3	1.8	0.2	2.5	1.0	−1.9	−1.3	0.0	−2.5	−8.8	−10.3	−5.1	3.4	2.5	1.0	3.6	−1.9	−1.4	0.0	5.0	10.7	6.1	1.7	2.3	8.5	14.4	7.8	−1.0	1.0	7.9	2.2	0.8
	−9.7	16.7	11.4	3.3	4.8	2.4	3.7	6.5	5.8	4.8	7.0	13.4	15.3	9.6	0.6	1.1	2.2	−0.3	5.1	4.4	1.8	−2.2	−7.9	−3.4	1.0	0.3	−6.0	−11.8	−5.0	3.7	1.6	−5.0	0.8	2.4
	109.9	81.5	103.4	105.4	120.5	159.4	166.6	202.4	300.0	381.2	294.1	194.4	88.8	108.7	110.7	148.4	184.9	194.4	158.4	155.9	152.8	133.6	119.7	145.8	152.5	195.8	212.5	186.9	193.2	200.5	235.5	276.4	292.0	293.8
	66.8	63.9	78.6	85.8	88.3	115.0	135.2	152.7	191.3	198.7	157.5	73.8	41.2	50.2	85.5	96.7	143.1	113.6	99.0	121.4	111.8	106.3	92.9	119.3	134.2	151.4	163.1	163.2	165.4	161.6	196.8	239.0	256.4	255.5
	90	73	93	94	100	134	152	175	227	311.2	236.3	138.6	64.6	83.7	98.3	120.0	162.2	166.4	132.4	142.7	134.7	121.8	107.2	134.8	143.3	169.8	191.6	177.6	179.9	179.5	216.3	257.6	270.8	276.0
	91.5	69.6	74.2	85.3	84.9	93.3	97.2	95.1	97.1	103.4	90.7	76.1	58.3	55.8	65.3	72.5	82.7	90.9	85.0	90.9	100.0	125.0	158.4	192.1	210.6	212.4	209.8	233.0	259.0	258.3	286.5	330.8	348.0	366.8
	1920	'21	'22	'23	'24	'25	'26	'27	'28	'29	1930	'31	'32	'33	'34	'35	'36	'37	'38	'39	1940	'41	'42	'43	'44	'45	'46	'47	'48	'49	1950	'51	'52	'53